SUGAR AND SLAVERY
An Economic History of the British West Indies
1623-1775

RICHARD B. SHERIDAN

with a Foreword by Hilary Beckles

Canoe Press
●Barbados ●Jamaica ●Trinidad and Tobago

Canoe Press
University of the West Indies
1A Aqueduct Flats Kingston Jamaica W I

© 1974, 1994 by Richard B. Sheridan. All rights reserved
Printed in Jamaica

ISBN 978-976-8125-13-2

First published in 1974 for the Department of History,
University of the West Indies, by Caribbean Universities Press

Reprinted 2007

The map of "The West Indies about 1750" (p. xx) is after Richard Pares, *War and Trade in the West Indies 1739-1763* (Clarendon Press, 1936). The four prints (pp.110, 116) from William Clark's *Ten Views of the Island of Antigua* (1823) are reproduced by courtesy of the West India Committee Library. Richard Ligon's map of Barbados (p.135) is reproduced by courtesy of the Trustees of the British Museum. The map of the "Sugar Planting Areas of Jamaica 1793" (p.209) is based on the map in P.P. Courtenay, *Plantation Agriculture* (G. Bell, 1965), which is generalized from Bryan Edwards, History of the British Colonies in the West Indies (1793). The plan of the Parnassus Plantation (p.226) is taken from the Dawkins Family Papers on loan to the West India Reference Library (Institute of Jamaica) from the Sugar Manufacturers' Association (of Jamaica) Ltd. Much of the material contained in chapter eleven originally appeared in the author's article "Africa and the Caribbean in the Atlantic Slave Trade" in *The American Historical Review*, vol.77, no.1 (Feb. 1972). Cover illustration is taken from Ingvar Zangenberg, *Dansk Vestindien for 250 år siden* (Copenhagen, 1981). Reproduced with the permission of Dorte Zangenberg.

CATALOGUING IN PUBLICATION DATA

Sheridan, Richard B.
Sugar and slavery: an economic history of
the British West Indies, 1623-1775 / Richard B. Sheridan;
with a foreword by Hilary Beckles.

p. cm.
Reprint. Originally published: Eagle Hall 15,
Barbados: Caribbean Universities Pr., 1974.
Includes bibliographical references.
Includes index.
ISBN 978-976-8125-13-2
1. Sugar trade – West Indies, British. 2. Slavery–
West Indies, British. 3. West Indies, British –
Economic conditions. 4. West Indies, British –
Social conditions. I. Beckles, Hilary, 1955-
II. Title.
HC155.5.S53 1994   330.9'729–dc–20

Cover design (pbk) Prodesign Ltd., Jamaica

PRINTED BY PHOENIX PRINTERY LTD.

To the memory of my Mother and Father
For Audrey, Richard and Margaret

Contents

	Key to Abbreviations	xi
	Foreword	xii
	Preface	xvi
One	The Tropic Empire	
	1 Historians and Histories of the West Indies	1
	2 The Colonial Debate	5
	3 Caribbean Island Economies	11
	4 Economic Growth and the Colonies	14
	5 Conclusion	16
Two	'Sugar, The Inseparable Companion of Tea'	
	1 The Impact of the New World	18
	2 Patterns of Sugar Consumption	20
	3 English Sugar Consumption	21
	4 British and French Sugar Consumption	24
	5 The Rich and the Poor	26
	6 Tea and Sugar	27
	7 Sugar Refining in Great Britain	29
	8 Consumption and Population Growth	30
	9 Scottish and Irish Markets	31
	10 London and the Outports	32
	11 British North American Markets	33
	12 Conclusion	33
Three	The Hated Navigation Acts, 1650–1700	
	1 Views on the Navigation System	36
	2 Ousting the Dutch	37
	3 The Mercantile Theory of Colonies	40
	4 The Navigation Acts	41
	5 The Planters' Discontent	44
	6 The Planters' Response	44
	7 The Export Duty	48
	8 Efforts to Close the Loopholes	49
	9 The Sugar Duties in England	50
	10 Conclusion	53

Four	Planter Politics, 1701–1775	
	1 The Changing Structure of the Sugar Market	54
	2 The Planters' Market Strategy	55
	3 Curbing the Inter-island Trade	57
	4 The Planter Interest in the House of Commons	58
	5 The Members of Parliament	60
	6 The Planters' Strategy in the House of Commons	66
	7 The Sugar Monopoly	71
	8 Conclusion	74
Five	The Settlement of the Sugar Colonies	
	1 England on the Eve of Colonization	75
	2 Guyana and the Carribbees	77
	3 Problems, Projects, and Projectors	80
	4 The Courteen Brothers and Barbados	81
	5 Sir Marmaduke Royden and Barbados	82
	6 Early Settlement of St Christopher	84
	7 The Nevis Settlement	86
	8 Montserrat and Antigua	87
	9 Maurice Thompson	88
	10 Sir Martin Noell and Thomas Povey	90
	11 Conquest and Early Settlement of Jamaica	92
	12 Conclusion	95
Six	Geographic and Economic Influences	
	1 Introduction	97
	2 Cane Sugar: Origin and Dispersal	98
	3 Sugar Production in the American Tropics	100
	4 Location Factors	102
	5 The Role of Livestock	105
	6 Growing the Canes	107
	7 The Art of Making Sugar	112
	8 Stages in the Growth of the Sugar Economy	118
	9 The Geographic Base of Production	122
Seven	Barbados, The Brightest Jewel in Our Crown of Trade	
	1 An Island of 'Firsts'	124
	2 The Physical Setting	125
	3 The Sugar Revolution	128
	4 The Drift Toward Monoculture	134
	5 Conserving the Soil of Barbados	140
	6 The Slave Economy	141
	7 Further Estate Consolidation	143
	8 The Turning Away from Intensive Monoculture	147

Contents

Eight		*His Majesty's Leeward Islands*	
		Part I. St Christopher, Nevis, Montserrat	
	1	*The Collective View*	148
	2	*St Christopher: Descriptive Account*	149
	3	*Christopher Jeaffreson, St Kitts Planter*	152
	4	*St Kitts in the French Wars*	154
	5	*The Settlement of the French Lands*	155
	6	*Further 18th Century Developments*	159
	7	*Nevis: Descriptive Account*	161
	8	*Nevis Merchants and the Sugar Industry*	162
	9	*The Stapleton Plantations in Nevis*	164
	10	*The Pinneys of Nevis and Bristol*	167
	11	*John Herbert and Admiral Lord Nelson*	169
	12	*Montserrat: Descriptive Account*	170
	13	*The Political Anatomy of Montserrat*	172
	14	*Career Profiles of Montserrat Planters*	177
	15	*The Small Planters of Montserrat*	181
	16	*Conclusion*	183
Nine		*His Majesty's Leeward Islands*	
		Part II. Antigua	
	1	*Introduction*	184
	2	*Samuel Winthrop, Early Planter and Governor*	186
	3	*The Slow Recovery from the French Invasion*	189
	4	*The Plantocracy*	191
	5	*Economic Structure and Trends, 1700–75*	194
	6	*Dr Walter Tullideph, Scottish Planter*	197
	7	*Colonel Samuel Martin of Greencastle Estate*	200
	8	*Descriptive Accounts by Two Scottish Visitors*	203
	9	*The Near-Monoculture Regime*	205
	10	*Conclusion*	205
Ten		*Jamaica, The Fairest Island*	
	1	*The Physical Environment*	208
	2	*The Early Sugar Industry*	210
	3	*The War Years, 1689–1713*	214
	4	*Laggard Growth, 1714–39*	216
	5	*Expansion and Growth, 1740–75*	222
	6	*Liguanea Parish, 1753*	222
	7	*The Dawkins' Estates*	224
	8	*William Beckford, Planter-Historian*	227
	9	*The Wealth of Jamaica*	229
	10	*Conclusion*	232

Sugar and Slavery

Eleven	Slavery and Sugar		
	1 Introduction	234	
	2 Indians and White Servants	235	
	3 Afro-Caribbean Economic History	238	
	4 Stages in Caribbean Plantation Slavery	241	
	5 The Dimensions of the Slave Trade	245	
	6 Britain's Leadership in the Slave Trade	249	
	7 Africa's Ability to Supply Manpower	253	
	8 Runaways and Rebels	254	
	9 Slavery on Roaring River Plantation	257	
	10 The Profitability of Slavery	259	
	11 Conclusion	260	
Twelve	The English Merchant as Banker		
	1 Introduction	262	
	2 Plantation Capital Requirements	264	
	3 The High Rate of Capital Depreciation	266	
	4 The Importance of Trade Credit	269	
	5 Debtor-Creditor Conflict	274	
	6 The West India Loan Market	278	
	7 Conclusion	281	
Thirteen	The Planter's Agent as Banker		
	1 Introduction	282	
	2 17th Century Commission Agents	285	
	3 The Credit Act of 1732	288	
	4 Changing Financial Methods	290	
	5 The Loan Market in the West Indies	294	
	6 Capital Drain or Capital Inflow?	295	
	7 The Agents Concerned with Jamaica	298	
	8 The Agents Concerned with the Lesser Antilles	300	
	9 Conclusion	305	
Fourteen	A Grand Marine Empire		
	1 The Plantation Base of Trade	306	
	2 Dimensions of Trade	308	
	3 Trade with the Mother Country and Ireland	311	
	4 Trade with North America	314	
	5 Trade with Africa and the Informal Empire	316	
	6 Trading Methods	319	
	7 The Merchant System	322	
	8 The London Commission System	328	
	9 Ships and Shipping	332	

	10 Commission System and Other Branches of Trade	335
	11 Conclusion	338
Fifteen	Rum and Molasses in British Imperial Trade	
	1 Technological and Economic Possibilities	339
	2 17th Century Market Limitations	340
	3 18th Century Markets	342
	4 Markets in the Mother Country	344
	5 The Irish Rum Market	350
	6 Illicit Trade and Markets in North America	352
	7 Contributory Factors	357
	8 Conclusion	358
Sixteen	Planters and Plantership	
	1 Introduction	360
	2 The Nonconformists	364
	3 The Sephardic Jews	366
	4 The Scotsmen and Irishmen	368
	5 The Professionals and Administrators	370
	6 The Merchants	374
	7 The Art of Plantership	377
	8 Profit and Loss	381
	9 Absenteeism	385
	10 Conclusion	387
Seventeen	Booms and Slumps in War and Peace, 1623–1713	
	1 Introduction	389
	2 Fluctuations in the Sugar Industry	390
	3 The Era of Minor Staples	393
	4 The Sugar Revolution	395
	5 The Impact of the Navigation Acts	396
	6 Barbados and the Recession of the 1680s	398
	7 The Leeward Islands and Jamaica	402
	8 Economic Fluctuations in Wartime	404
	9 King William's War, 1689–97	407
	10 Queen Anne's War, 1702–13	409
	11 Conclusion	411
Eighteen	The Drive to Monoculture, 1714–1755	
	1 Introduction	415
	2 Postwar Prosperity, 1714–20	419
	3 The Uneven 'Twenties	422

Sugar and Slavery

	4 *Recession and Recovery in the 'Thirties*	426
	5 *War and Trade, 1739–48*	433
	6 *Monoculture and Monopoly, 1749–55*	439
	7 *The New Informal Empire*	442
	8 *Conclusion*	445
Nineteen	*The Sugar Colonies and the Industrial Revolution, 1756-1775*	
	1 *Introduction*	447
	2 *The Seven Years' War*	448
	3 *The Ceded Islands*	452
	4 *The Free Port System*	459
	5 *The Credit Crisis of 1772*	463
	6 *The West India Balance of Payments*	467
	7 *Profits and Absenteeism*	470
	8 *The Industrial Revolution*	475
	9 *Slavery and its Critics*	479
	Appendices	487
	Select Bibiography	507
	Index	523

Key to Abbreviations

B.M. Add. MSS – Additonal Manuscripts, British Museum, London.

Cal. S.P. Col. – Calendar of State Papers, Colonial Series, America and West Indies, 43 vols., London.

C.O. – Colonial Office, Public Record Office, London.

D.N.B. – Dictionary of National Biography.

J.P.R.O. – Jamaica Public Record Office, Spanish Town.

Lascelles & Maxwell L.B. – Letter Book of Messrs Lascelles & Maxwell, London sugar factors.

Martin L.B. – Letter Books of Colonel Samuel Martin of Antigua and England.

P.R.O. – Public Records Office, London.

Treas. – Treasury series, Public Record Office, London.

Tullideph L.B. – Letter Books of Dr Walter Tullideph of Antigua and Scotland.

Note

All dates given before 1752 are Old Style except that the year is taken to begin on 1 January

Foreword

Professor Hilary Beckles
Dean, Faculty of Arts and General Studies
Head, Department of History
University of the West Indies, Cave Hill

When in 1974 the first edition of this book appeared, its author had already established a solid reputation on both sides of the Atlantic as a leading economic historian of England's West Indian slave plantations. In these islands, particularly among University historians and their students, it was received as a pioneer work by a reputable scholar who had found it necessary to prepare a teaching text and guide to further research in the area of economic history. For scholars of the wider North Atlantic system it represented a consolidation of ideas already articulated in seminal essays published between 1957 and 1972.

The text, then, represented the primary research highway on which Sheridan had travelled for the better part of his academic career. From his long sojourn in London's archives he emerged with the reputation as a leading source on manuscript data pertaining to early West Indian history. Students and colleagues alike sought his opinion on bibliographical matters, and all awaited the publication of this book. Few could claim during the 1960s possession of a detailed knowledge of the many challenges, crises and predicaments facing the 18th century West Indian sugar planters and mercantile associates. Sheridan's research, therefore, deepened the general understanding and indicated the way towards a West Indian perspective on the issues.

This academic journey had also taken Sheridan to the West Indies; importantly it took him into the intellectual circle of young West indian historians involved in the process of promoting an insider perspective on the region's historical narrative. His arrival was timely, and the time spent in the West Indies had much to do with the empirical shape and conceptual tenor of the book. At the University of the West Indies (UWI) he discussed his research, and engaged the views of Douglas Hall, Elsa Goveia, Woodville Marshall, Roy Augier, Philip Sherlock and many others involved in the definition and creation of an indigenous historiographic tradition. The UWI then was a forum described as boiling with research enthusiasm, and typically West Indian in that it welcomed from any quarter quality academic contributions.

Foreword

When the text appeared in the summer of 1974 it was greeted as a seminal contribution to an "insider" discourse, and Sheridan was received as a prominent member of the group of anti-colonial historians who had placed the mythic imperialist historiography in circumstances conducive to its retreat. It was, therefore, academically compelling in 1974, and indicative of Sheridan's professional and social standing within the UWI, that the book was published in the region by the then recently established, but shortlived, Caribbean Universities Press.

It was not understood in 1951, however, when the core ideas of what was to become this book were submitted as a doctoral dissertation at London University, that Sheridan's work would be closely linked to the seminal 1944 book by Eric Williams, the outstanding West Indian historian who later became Prime Minister of Trinidad and Tobago. The book in question is *Capitalism and Slavery* which, after two decades of quiet existence, burst out in the mid 1960s as the most contentious work produced on slavery in the Atlantic World — a reputation it continues to enjoy, or endure! By 1974, however, Sheridan was considered the principal defender of Williams' main thesis, holding forth against an avalanche of criticisms from Euro-American scholars determined to demonstrate the relative unimportance of Caribbean slavery to the process of wealth accumulation that produced Europe's grand take-off into self-sustained growth during the 18th century. By this time, Sheridan had explicitly proclaimed his admiration for Williams' work. In a number of published essays he indicated his belief in the essential correctness of Williams' view that the West Indian slave-based economy — in its productive, distributive, and financial dimensions — had emerged a net exporter of capital by the mid 17th century, and had made the critical contribution to metropolitan surplus which ensured the deepening of the industrialization process and its irretrievability.

The effect of Sheridan's essays was to bring systematic empirical rigour to Williams' general theory. For the first time a detailed analysis of the West Indian economic circumstance, though focused on Jamaica as the principal 18th century colony, was available as a means of testing Williams' capital transfer model. His 1968 essay, "The Wealth of Jamaica in the 18th Century", outlined an assessment of the model, and in 1969 he expanded the conceptual framework with the publication of "The Plantation Revolution and the Industrial Revolution". By 1974, then, when *Sugar and Slavery* (*SAS*) appeared, it constituted a major missile from the Caribbean in what was considered then the most aggressively contested transatlantic historical discourse.

Sugar and Slavery

As a measure of Sheridan's standing amongst scholars of Caribbean slavery, he was invited to present a summary bibliographical and historiographical essay on Williams' *Capitalism and Slavery* at a major conference on the subject held in 1984. This gathering of leading researchers, organized by the distinguished Barbara Solow and Stanley Engerman, was mandated to assess Williams' contribution to the scholarship on the origins of 18th century English industrialism within the context of the post 1944 historiography in which Sheridan had played a most productive role. Conference debate, and the subsequent publication of proceedings, indicated the extent to which research had progressed and proliferated since *SAS* was published but, at the same time, they magnified its reputation by illuminating the role it played as a generator of research and publications.

While it remains true that *SAS* is very much a fine product of traditional economic history, no scholar today can attract the attention of peers within this discipline by using the narrative style employed so effectively by Sheridan. Quantitative methods, particularly those of the econometricians and cliometricians, have assumed methodological hegemony in the search for new answers to the old questions asked by Sheridan in 1974. While in some areas new data have come to the fore, resulting in exciting revisions of opinions, in most cases these methodological departures have added little by way of a clearer understanding of the specific historical processes under investigation. Under this circumstance, *SAS* has maintained its place as indispensable reading for students and faculty.

A persistent criticism, however, has to do with the technical organization of the text rather than the methodological scaffold which holds it together. The view that its organization into some nineteen sections and 184 subsections results in a measure of repetition, less than efficient use of evidence, and an excessive leaning in the direction of narrative rather than analysis, has remained a reasonable one. Clearly, much of this has to do with the tensions that result from an attempt to interface and blend the grace of a narrative thematic style with the galloping rhythm of a sequential/chronological approach. The planter class of the 17th and 18th centuries lived in radically different worlds, and therefore required different tools and policies to manage their affairs. But, they were a social élite placed in the same relations to the ownership of resources, and considered their role as economic managers, political administrators, and social agents in much the same way. While organizational infelicities sometimes result from conceptual fuzziness and theoretical uncertainty, in this instance it has more to do with the matter of seeking an excessively comprehensive coverage.

Foreword

Hindsight has also indicated that the text was very much an analysis of history from above that paid little attention to the economic activities of groups other than the empowered planter-merchant élites. The commercial worlds of slaves, free blacks and coloureds, for example, are not explored as important and determining parts of the colonial economy. Yet, the evidence was available to indicate the extent to which the internal marketing systems of most colonies were fashioned and directed largely by those marginalized and criminalized elements whose commercial propensities could not be contained by restrictive legislation. By the mid 18th century, the market culture of these groups had matured and constituted an important link in the circuit of capital.

Conceptually, therefore, there was little that was radical about *SAS* outside of the departure from the Eurocentric imperialist tradition. The writing of history from below was not an established development, and *SAS* occupied what was then considered a methodological centre stage. By 1974, in addition, the teaching of Caribbean economic history at the UWI was well on the way, and *SAS*, and related essays, occupied the "highly recommended" section of reading lists. It is instructive to note, therefore, that the University of the West Indies has maintained a very serious interest in this text. As a sort of conceptual progeny of the defunct Caribbean Universities Press, The Press UWI, by issuing this reprint, is clearly demonstrating a recognition not only of its academic value within the teaching exercise, but also of its intellectual legacy. This 21st anniversary reprint will be welcomed by scholars and students now as it was in 1974.

Preface

The present study is an expansion of a University of London doctoral dissertation which was submitted in 1951. In this study, attention was focused on the West India sugar trade from 1660 to 1756, including its political regulation, markets, commercial and financial organization, and fluctuations. Rather limited attention was given to the production of sugar on West India plantations and the institution of slavery. Efforts to reconstruct the sugar trade led beyond the public records to the private papers of planters and merchants, including the valuable Tullideph letter-books.

Post-dissertation studies have extended both the topical and time dimensions of my history of Britain's Caribbean empire. Sabbatical leave from the University of Kansas enabled me to work in the London archives for the greater part of a year. Here I read widely on the early settlements in the West Indies, as well as the economic history of the years from 1756 to 1775. In the Manuscript Room of the British Museum I came across the papers of Colonel Samuel Martin, foremost sugar planter of Antigua and a contemporary of Dr Walter Tullideph. Besides much commercial and financial information, the Martin papers gave me insights into plantation layout and organization, the slave labour regime, and especially the agrarian aspects of plantation management, or what Martin termed the 'art of plantership'.

After my second stay in England my research emphasis shifted from problems of political regulation, trade, and finance, as viewed from Whitehall and the City of London, to those concerned with slave-plantations in the West Indies. A Fulbright research grant to the University of the West Indies in 1962–3 enabled me to continue my plantation studies. At the Island Record Office at Spanish Town, the old capital of Jamaica, I found deeds, wills, tax rolls, land patents, powers of attorney, personal property inventories, crop accounts, and other records. This rich store of manuscripts bears on many aspects of plantation history.

In this book I have tried to describe and assess the role of the West Indies in the emerging Atlantic economy, with special reference to the British Empire. Topics largely external, but intimately related, to the West Indies occupy the first four chapters. These include the markets for sugar products, mercantile thought and its translation

Sugar and Slavery

into policies and practices, the changing nature of the Acts of Trade and Navigation, and the rise of the planter interest in the House of Commons. Chapters Five to Eleven inclusive are concerned with the economic history of the British sugar colonies, both collectively and individually. The chapters on settlement and geographic and economic influences take up themes that were common to the islands and serve as an introduction to chapters dealing with the economic history of individual islands. The economic history of slavery and the slave trade completes this section of the book. External economic relationships are the keynote of Chapters Twelve to Fifteen inclusive, detailing the methods of trade, shipping, and finance, and including a discussion of the important by-products, molasses and rum. Chapter Sixteen seeks to discover the social origins of the sugar planters and to evaluate their performance as owner-managers of large-scale agro-industrial enterprises. Finally, three summary chapters are concerned with the sugar industry as it was affected by such things as peace and war, hurricanes and droughts, insect pests, market fluctuations, and fiscal burdens.

The sugar industry, with its slave labour force and monopoly market structure, was regarded by Adam Smith and his followers as a case study in the pathology of capitalism. However plausible this view may be, it must nevertheless be discarded by the economic historian who views capitalism as an institutional complex which has changed in time and place. Smith's utopian economics has little light to shed on the sugar industry and the mercantile phase of capitalism in which that industry played a major role. It is the contention of this study that, however inhumane, the sugar industry made a notable contribution to the wealth and maritime supremacy of Great Britain.

Many people have assisted me with this work. I am much indebted to Professor F. J. Fisher of The London School of Economics and Political Science under whose generous and skilful guidance I first set to work on this study. As a postgraduate student at L.S.E., I also profited by the kindness, learning, and wisdom of Professors Richard H. Tawney and T. S. Ashton. Although illness prevented the late Professor Richard Pares from serving on my examining board for the PhD degree, I have the highest respect for his scholarship and have benefited immensely from his writings on West India history. Professors K. G. Davies, W. A. Cole, Gary Walton, Richard S. Dunn and William I. Davisson kindly made available to me statistical data on sugar and slavery. The late Sir Herbert Ogilvy provided generous hospitality and let me use the letter-books of his ancestor, Dr Walter

Preface

Tullideph. I am indebted also to the partners in the firm of Messrs Wilkinson and Gaviler for permission to use the Lascelles and Maxwell letter-book, and to the heirs of Sir Francis J. Davies for permission to quote extracts from the Martin letter-books. Numerous individuals helped me at the Public Record Office, British Museum, and the libraries at L.S.E., Senate House, and the West India Committee in London. I am also indebted to the generosity of Mr Taylor Milne of the Institute of Historical Research and the directors of the Goldsmith's Library.

I owe much to the encouragement and advice of Professor Douglas G. Hall of the University of the West Indies. He is my long-time friend and counsellor. I also wish to thank the Fulbright authorities for making it possible to do research in Jamaica, and to the many people there who gave generously of their time, wisdom, and hospitality. Among others, I acknowledge the help of Professor W. G. Rimmer, Dr Woodville Marshall, Kenneth Ingram, Clinton V. Black, J. M. Sudu, W. E. Gocking, Shirley Gordon, and S. A. G. Taylor. I admire the works of Dr Eric Williams, Prime Minister of Trinidad and Tobago, and recall with pleasure a conversation with him on West India historiography. At the University of Puerto Rico I was given aid and advice by Professors Thomas G. Mathews and Harry Hoetink.

My obligation to the University of Kansas is especially heavy. My research and writing have been supported by two sabbatical leaves and two summer research grants. I am indebted to the advice and assistance of my Kansas University colleagues, especially Richard S. Howey, Edward G. Nelson, Leland J. Pritchard, Ronald R. Olsen, Duncan McDougall and John P. Augelli. I have also had assistance from the following graduate students: Richard Lobdell, Lynn Steele, Michael Brodhead, Jon Kepler, Walter Page, and Luis Mayor. Miss Edna Turner and Mrs John Clark helped me with typing and photo-duplication. I should also take this opportunity to thank the editors of the following journals for granting permission to refer to material and quote extracts from my articles: *The Journal of Economic History*, *The Economic History Review*, *Agricultural History*, *The Jamaican Historical Review*, and *The American Historical Review*.

In 1971, I was a visiting professor at the College of the Virgin Islands, where the editing of this work was completed.

My greatest debt is to my wife, Audrey, who has lived with this manuscript since the beginning. Without her counsel and encouragement, it would not have been written.

Richard B. Sheridan

Lawrence, Kansas
30 June, 1970

SUGAR AND SLAVERY
An Economic History of the British West Indies
1623-1775

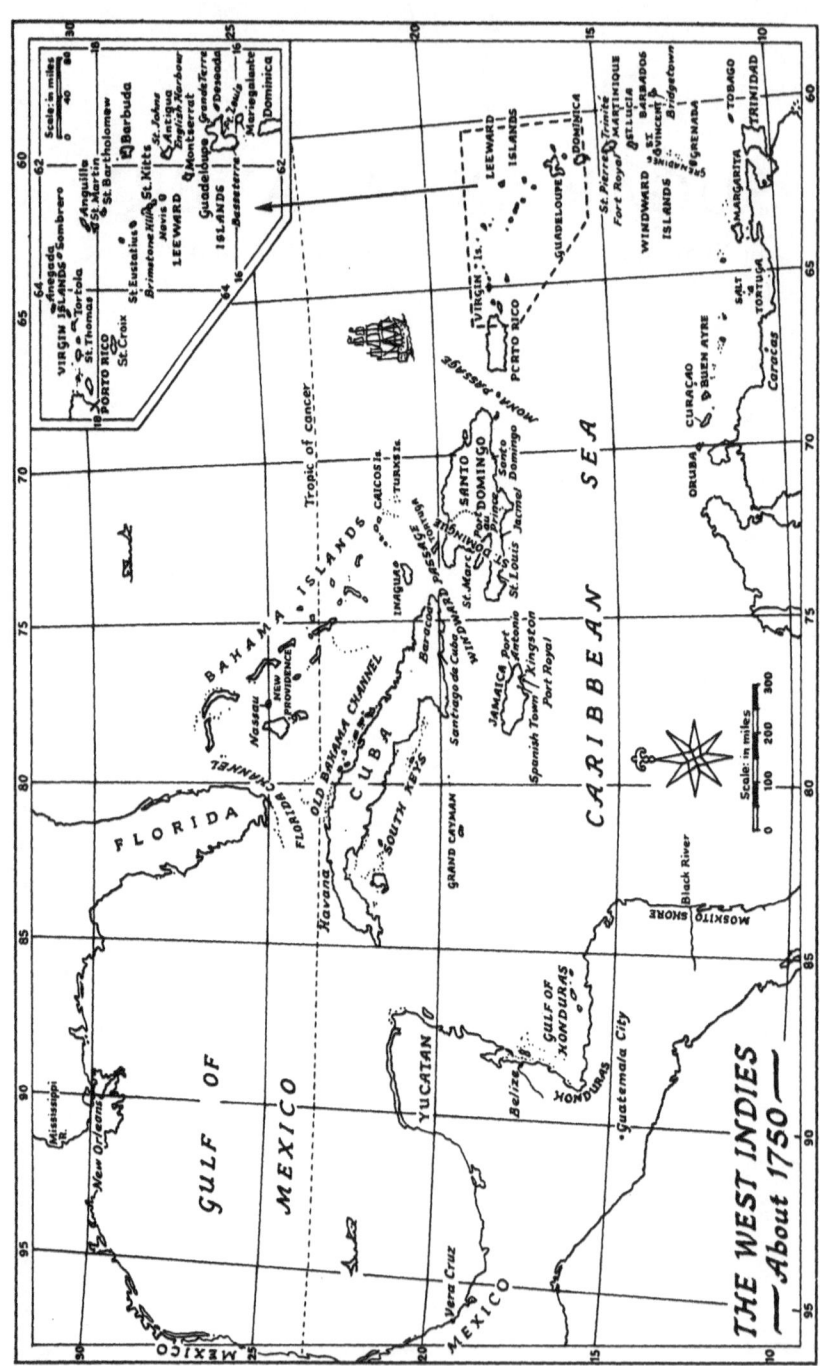

CHAPTER ONE

The Tropic Empire

> The amazing importance which has attended the culture of the sugar cane, is perhaps one of the most extraordinary instances of the effect of agriculture that the world has produced, and it shews clearer than any other circumstance wherein consists the true and beneficial nature of colonies: the profit which this nation reaps from her islands in the West Indies ought above all other things to make her attentive to every particular in the culture of the sugar cane.[1]
>
> Anon., *American Husbandry*, 1775

1 HISTORIANS AND HISTORIES OF THE WEST INDIES

To Europeans and North Americans the British West Indies are commonly regarded as tourist resorts, 'islands in the sun' where one may find palatial hotels fronting on sandy beaches of the Caribbean Sea and regaling their guests with rum punch and exotic foods to the accompaniment of steel bands and calypso artists. Below this foamy surface of affluence will be found densely populated islands, inhabited chiefly by the descendants of African slaves, together with the mulatto descendants of Europeans and Africans, East Indians, Amerindians, Chinese, Syrians, and Europeans. To the intricate ethnic and cultural mosaic are added contrasts in wealth and poverty, teeming slums and shanty towns in the enervating port cities, mansions and middle-class housing estates in suburban and rural areas of higher elevation. On all sides one is confronted with the old and the new. Decaying windmill towers, sugar works, and mansion houses evoke memories of a former age of lordly white planters and black slaves, while factories, bauxite mines, and petroleum refineries remind one that tropical islands have not escaped the spreading tentacles of the new industrialism.

Not only is the old and new written indelibly on the physical landscape. New nations and island colonies on the verge of political independence are also looking to the past and the future. Their leaders are searching for identity, a 'cultural garb' symbolic of their aims and ideals to clothe their bare political frame and give meaning

---

1 Anon., *American Husbandry*, ed. Harry J. Carman (New York, 1939), vol. 2, p. 408.

Sugar and Slavery

to their newly-achieved independence. Conscious of the interdependent relationship between the direction of past change and their aspirations for future development, they are turning to folklore, archaeology, anthropology, and, above all, to recorded history in their search for identity.[2]

There have been many histories of the British West Indies, each reflecting not only the individuality of its author but also the dominant cultural and social milieu of his time. Historical interpretation has thus varied in time and place. Late Elizabethan and early Stuart historians wrote of the great wealth of the Spanish Indies, of the exploits of Drake and Hawkins in diverting some of this wealth to the mother country. Explorers, privateersmen and buccaneers were the heroes of historians who regarded the West Indies as a plunder preserve.

Though international rivalry and wars on land and sea continued to be a dominant theme to the end of the Napoleonic Wars, a number of historians of the 17th and 18th centuries were drawn to the more prosaic themes of settlement, economic development, and trade. Besides the descriptive histories written by itinerant governors, clergymen, doctors, and merchants, there were published the more substantial works of the planter-historians, of whom Edward Long and Bryan Edwards are notable examples.[3]

In the period before 1776 the planter histories were concerned with ten 'sugar islands'. All but one are small islands in the long arc of the Lesser Antilles — Barbados, St Christopher, Nevis, Montserrat, Antigua, Dominica, Grenada, St Vincent and Tobago. Some one thousand miles to the west of the Lesser Antilles lies the much larger island of Jamaica, the leading sugar colony of the British Empire in the 18th century.

Other historical interpretations became dominant as the age of adventure and expansion of tropical agriculture gave way to decline and reform. Critics of mercantilism attacked the privileged commercial standing of the West Indies, missionaries and humanitarians the evils of slavery, political reformers the financial burden of colonial military and civil establishments. In brief, the political and social costs of empire became a dominant theme in the age of revolution and reform.

Subsequent historians have expanded on old themes and developed new themes as historical movements have ebbed and

2 Wendell Bell and Ivar Oxaal, *Decisions of Nationhood: Political and Social Development in the British Caribbean* (Denver, 1963–4), pp. 61–5.
3 Edward Long, *The History of Jamaica* (London, 1774); Bryan Edwards, *The History, Civil and Commercial, of the British Colonies in the West Indies* (London, 1793).

flowed and hitherto undiscovered source materials have called for reassessment of established views. Slave emancipation, missionary endeavour, and the decline of the plantocracy were dominant themes of 19th century writers, among whom were Anthony Trollope and James Anthony Froude.[4]

Revived interest in Caribbean history was a feature of the late 19th and early 20th centuries, at a time when Britain and the United States were engaged in a new phase of tropical imperialism. To single out one name in this cursory survey of West Indian historiography, Alfred Thayer Mahan, the American naval historian, was concerned with the source and deployment of seapower in the Caribbean and the need for American penetration of the region.[5]

Moving into the 20th century, other American historians rediscovered British Caribbean history in its intimate relationship to their own colonial past. Charles M. Andrews, the Yale University historian, not only published numerous volumes of colonial history but also delved deeply into British archives and inspired his students to do likewise. One of his students, Frank W. Pitman, published a comprehensive history of the British West Indies which sheds much light on the background of the American War of Independence.[6] Among the numerous Americans with a special interest in the West Indies are George L. Beer, the historian of British colonial policy; Elizabeth Donnan, compiler of documents on the slave trade; Frank J. Klingberg, founder of a school of humanitarian history of which J. Harry Bennett is a leading member; and Lowell J. Ragatz, whose historical and bibliographical works entitle him to front rank among historians of the Caribbean region in the 20th century.[7] Similarly, Canada's past links with the Caribbean colonies have been investigated by certain historians of the north country, of whom Harold A. Innis is a notable example.[8]

4 Anthony Trollope, *The West Indies and the Spanish Main* (London, 1859); James Anthony Froude, *The English in the West Indies or the Bow of Ulysses* (London, 1885).
5 A. T. Mahan, *The Influence of Sea Power upon History 1660–1783* (London, 1890).
6 Charles M. Andrews, *The Colonial Period of American History* (New Haven, 1938); Frank W. Pitman, *The Development of the British West Indies 1700–1763* (New Haven, 1917).
7 George L. Beer, *The Origins of the British Colonial System, 1578–1660* (New York, 1908);——, *The Old Colonial System, 1660–1754* (New York, 1912);——, *British Colonial Policy, 1754–1765* (New York, 1907); Elizabeth Donnan, *Documents Illustrative of the History of the Slave Trade* (Washington, D.C., 1930–2); Frank J. Klingberg, *The Anti-Slavery Movement in England* (New Haven, 1926); J. Harry Bennett, *Bondsmen and Bishops, Slavery and Apprenticeship on the Codrington Plantations of Barbados, 1710–1838* (Berkeley and Los Angeles, 1958); Lowell J. Ragatz, *The Fall of the Planter Class in the British Caribbean, 1763–1833* (New York, 1928);——, *A Guide for the Study of British Caribbean History, 1763–1834* (Washington, D.C., 1932).
8 Harold A. Innis, *The Cod Fisheries, The History of an International Economy* (New Haven, 1940).

Sugar and Slavery

Old and new themes have been developed by British historians of the 20th century. Arthur P. Newton has been concerned with international rivalry in the Caribbean area; Vincent T. Harlow with imperial policy and the history of Barbados; John H. Parry with the general history of the West Indies in collaboration with Sir Philip M. Sherlock; Archibald·P. Thornton with colonial policy; Kenneth G. Davies with the slave trade; William L. Burn with slave emancipation and apprenticeship; James A. Williamson with colonial policy and the pioneer settlements in the Lesser Antilles; Sir Lewis Namier with the planter interest in the House of Commons; Dame Lillian Penson with the colonial agents; and Sir Alan Burns with a general history of the British West Indies.[9] Foremost among the British Caribbean historians of this century was Richard Pares who pioneered new interpretations of economic and military history based on extensive research in the public records and the private papers of families and business firms.[10]

By far the most remarkable development of recent decades has been the writing and teaching of local history in the West India area itself. For some years now West Indians have been going to universities and historical archives in Great Britain and the United States to pursue local and imperial themes, and then returning to continue the writing and teaching of history. Prominent among them are Dr Eric Williams, Prime Minister of Trinidad and Tobago;[11] and Professors Douglas Hall and Elsa V. Goveia, Dr Roy Augier, and Dr Woodville Marshall — all of the University of the West Indies.[12]

---

9 A. P. Newton, *The European Nations in the West Indies 1493–1688* (London, 1933); V. T. Harlow, *History of Barbados 1625–85* (Oxford, 1926);——, and F. Madden (eds.), *British Colonial Developments 1774–1834: Select Documents* (Oxford, 1953); J. H. Parry and P. M. Sherlock, *A Short History of the West Indies* (London, 1957); A. P. Thornton, *West-India Policy under the Restoration* (Oxford, 1956); K. G. Davies, *The Royal African Company* (London, 1957); W. L. Burn, *Emancipation and Apprenticeship in the British West Indies* (London, 1937);——, *The British West Indies* (London, 1951); J. A. Williamson, *The Caribbee Islands under the Proprietary Patents* (Oxford, 1925); Sir Lewis Namier, *The Structure of Politics at the Accession of George III* (London, 1929);——, *England in the Age of the American Revolution* (London, 1930); Lillian M. Penson, *The Colonial Agents of the British West Indies* (London, 1924).
10 Richard Pares, *War and Trade in the West Indies 1739–1763* (Oxford, 1936);——, *A West-India Fortune*. (London, 1950);——, *Yankees and Creoles The trade between North America and the West Indies before the American Revolution* (Cambridge, Mass., 1956);——, *Merchants and Planters* (Cambridge, 1960); ——, *The Historian's Business and Other Essays*, ed. R. A. and Elisabeth Humphreys (Oxford, 1961).
11 Eric Williams, *Capitalism and Slavery* (Chapel Hill, 1944);——*The Negro in the Caribbean* (Manchester, 1942).
12 Douglas G. Hall, *Free Jamaica 1838–1865 An Economic History* (New Haven, 1959, London, 1969); Elsa V. Goveia, *A Study on the Historiography of the British West Indies to the End of the 19th Century* (Mexico, 1956); ——, *Slave Society in the British Leeward Islands at the End of the 18th Century* (New Haven and London, 1965); F. R. Augier, D. G. Hall, S. C. Gordon and M. Reckord, *The Making of The West Indies* (London, 1960).

Moreover, the study of West Indian history has been given new impetus by the establishment of the University of the West Indies, the participation of its history and education faculties in projects of research, writing, and instruction; and renewed interest in archival collections and the inclusion of West Indian history in the curriculum of the primary and secondary schools of the region. Similarly, local history societies and extra-mural tutors have done much to generate an interest in the history of the West Indies.

Many histories based on many themes, some illuminating certain facets of the West India story and others cast in the ambitious mould of general history, leave the conscientious student of the region in a state of bewilderment. But the sense of bewilderment may be reduced substantially if attention is focused on themes that have concerned historians of the present century.

Common to a substantial number of British, American, and West Indian historians of the present century has been an interest in the economic aspects of Caribbean society in the 17th and 18th centuries. Slavery and the slave trade, plantation life, changing relationships between Britain and her Caribbean colonies — these are themes which have received scholarly attention, although not in the form of a comprehensive economic history. On the other hand, widely divergent views have been expressed concerning the contribution of the colonies to the economic development of the mother country. The present study, by focusing on economic relationships between the sugar colonies and the mother country from the period of earliest colonial settlement to the outbreak of the American War of Independence, is intended to contribute to an understanding of imperial economic development.

2 THE COLONIAL DEBATE

In the final paragraph of his *Wealth of Nations*, Adam Smith reiterated his weighty argument that the mercantile system had been a snare and delusion, that it should either be completed by means of fiscal reform or be given up.

> The rulers of Great Britain have, for more than a century past, amused the people with the imagination that they possessed a great empire on the west side of the Atlantic. This empire, however, has hitherto existed in imagination only. It has hitherto been, not an empire, but the project of an empire: not a gold mine, but the project of a gold mine; a project which has cost, which continues to cost, and which, if pursued in the same way as it has been hitherto, is likely to cost, immense expence, without being

> likely to bring any profit; for the effects of the monopoly of the colony trade, it has been shewn, are, to the great body of people, mere loss instead of profit.[13]

To Edmund Burke, on the other hand, the preservation of the colonies was of infinite importance. After pointing out that the trade with North America and the West Indies was in 1775 'within less than £500,000 of being equal to what this great commercial nation, England, carried on at the beginning of this century with the whole world', he vehemently denied that this trade was 'an unnatural protuberance that has drawn the juices from the rest of the body'. Indeed, he argued the reverse:

> It is the very food that has nourished every other part into its present magnitude. Our general trade has been greatly augmented, and augmented more or less in every part to which it ever extended; but with this material difference, that of the six millions which in the beginning of the century constituted the whole mass of our export commerce, the colony trade was but one-twelfth part: it is now (as part of sixteen millions) considerably more than a third of the whole. This is the relative proportion of the importance of the colonies at these two periods; and all reasoning concerning our mode of treating them must have this proportion as its basis, or it is a reasoning weak, rotten, and sophistical.[14]

Smith and Burke thus stood at opposite poles in assessing the role of colonies in the economic growth of the mother country. Similarly, modern historians, who might be expected to take advantage of their 20/20 hindsight to achieve a resolution of this issue, are nonetheless divided. The neo-Smithians, while assigning a role to colonies and overseas trade, tend to focus upon such indigenous forces of change as science and technology, entrepreneurship, and capital formation, acting and reacting in such a manner as to lower the institutional barriers to economic growth.[15] On the other hand, the neo-Burkians would argue that the economic growth took place in a larger setting, that in the case of Great Britain the preconditions for the Industrial Revolution not only included the indigenous change but also the redirection of trade from Continental Europe to the American colonies. The Atlantic Empire, it is maintained, gave access to new sources of primary products, new markets, new fields of investment

---

13 Adam Smith, *An Enquiry into the Nature and Causes of the Wealth of Nations* (1776) (Modern Library, New York, 1937), pp. 899–900.
14 Edmund Burke, 'On Conciliation with the Colonies', 22 March, 1775, in *Speeches and Letters on American Affairs*, ed. Ernest Rhys (London, 1945), pp. 84–6.
15 T. S. Ashton, *An Economic History of England: The 18th Century* (London, 1955), pp. 124–9; Phyllis Deane and W. A. Cole, *British Economic Growth 1688–1959, Trends and Structure* (Cambridge, 1962), pp. 82–97.

— in sum, the innovations which were both cause and effect of the fundamental locational shift in the world's economy.[16]

The neo-Burkians claim that the sugar industry and the slave trade were important sources of wealth for the mother country. Not only did this wealth infuse the landed aristocracy, they maintain, but it also supported, and in some cases directly financed, the infant manufacturers who launched the Industrial Revolution. It is argued that slave-grown sugar yielded large profits to a substantial planter oligarchy who, upon repatriating their wealth, purchased landed estates, intermarried with the aristocracy, and formed a bloc of Parliamentarians who so influenced imperial policy in their own interest as to lay the foundation for dismemberment of the British Empire in North America.[17]

Countering these arguments are the neo-Smithians who assert that instead of being a source of wealth, the sugar colonies were a drain on the mother country, partly in terms of governmental and military expense, partly in private capital and credit to support the heavy debt structure of the sugar economy. They state categorically that sugar 'did not finance the industrialization of England ... nor did it finance the landed aristocracy of England, since only one peerage was based on a West India fortune!'[18]

While most mercantile writers regarded colonies as important sources of wealth and power, they were not uncritical of certain aspects of colonization. The two principal objections to colonies were that they made an unwelcome drain on the metropolitan population, and that some of the colonies failed to fulfil their function of producing raw materials non-competitive with those raised in the mother country.[19]

English mercantile writings point to a reversal in the attitude toward emigration to colonies in the 17th century. In the period before 1660 it was widely believed that England was suffering from over-population and that colonies provided a desirable outlet for the unemployed, destitute, and undesirable elements of society. After 1660, on the other hand, improved economic conditions and lessened political and social tension led to growing resistance to

16 Ralph Davis, 'English Foreign Trade, 1700–1774', *The Economic History Review*, 2nd ser., vol. XV, no. 2 (Dec. 1962), pp. 285–303; Kenneth Berrill, 'International Trade and the Rate of Economic Growth', *Econ. Hist. Rev.*, 2nd ser., vol. XII, no. 3 (April 1960), pp. 351–9.
17 Pitman, *Development of British West Indies*, pp. 334–60; Ragatz, *Fall of Planter Class*, pp. vii–x; Williams, *Capitalism and Slavery*, pp. 209–12.
18 Pares, *The Historian's Business*, p. 61; A. Farnie, 'The Commercial Empire of the Atlantic, 1607–1783', *Econ. Hist. Rev.*, 2nd ser., vol. XV, no. 2 (Dec. 1962), pp. 209–10.
19 Klaus E. Knorr, *British Colonial Theories 1570–1850* (Toronto, 1944), pp. 105–6.

emigration. However, perceptive mercantile writers who distinguished between colonies of exploitation and colonies of settlement, were unwilling to support a blanket injunction on emigration. Thus Sir Josiah Child, writing in 1668, observed that

> The People that evacuate from us to Barbadoes, and the other West India Plantations... do commonly work one Englishman to ten or eight Blacks; and if we keep the Trade of our said Plantations intirely to England, England would have no less Inhabitants, but rather an encrease of People by such Evacuation, because that one Englishman, with the Blacks that work with him, accounting what they eat, use and wear, would make employment for Four Men in England... whereas peradventure of ten men that issue from us to New England and Ireland, what we send to or receive from them, doth not employ one man in England.[20]

Child and other writers suggest that the expansion of England was in large measure motivated by a desire to achieve what might be termed a temperate-tropical balance, or a complementary economic relationship based on the products of different climatic zones. 'Concerning our Plantations in America,' wrote Carew Reynell in 1679, 'the Southern Plantations are the most advantageous to us; and it were well hereafter we planted no more behither Jamaica, but settled and removed, if possible, rather our Northern Colonies more forward...'.[21]

Probably the best developed argument for settling colonies in tropical latitudes was that of Arthur Young, the agricultural writer. He maintained that while the soils and productions of the colonies were 'as various as the climates in which they are situated, the value of them can only be estimated with a view to their usefulness in a commercial light'. Since the British Isles produced everything necessary for the life of man, 'the colonies were planted for superfluous commodities, which must be procured by trade of other nations, if not produced at home'. As with other mercantile writers, Young valued the tropical and subtropical colonies most highly.

> It appears upon the whole, that the staple productions of our colonies decrease in value in proportion to their distance from the sun. In the West Indies, which are the hottest of all, they make to the amount of 8 l. 12s. 1d. per head. In the southern continental ones, to the amount of 5 l. 10s. In the central ones, to the amount of 9s. 6½d. In the northern settlements, to that of 2s. 6d. This scale surely suggests a most important lesson — to avoid colonizing in northern latitudes![22]

---

20 Sir Josiah Child, *A New Discourse of Trade* (London, 1718), pp. 215–16.
21 Carew Reynell, *The True English Interest* (London, 1679), p. 90.
22 Arthur Young, *Political Essays Concerning the Present State of the British Empire* (London, 1772), pp. 2, 14, 326.

Young was thus convinced of the 'infinite importance' to Great Britain of staple colonies in the lower latitudes.

But not all Englishmen were happy with the influx of superfluities which in their opinion encouraged the poor to indulge in luxury consumption to the detriment of their own well-being as well as diverting consumption away from English manufacturers. Lord Sheffield noted that

> The Iron, &c. of Russia, the tobacco, rice, naval stores, &c. of the Southern Provinces, are returns more advantageous to us than bills of exchange, or specie; they are more beneficial than the products of the West Indies; because the latter are luxuries mostly consumed among ourselves, but the others are absolutely necessary to our navigation and manufactures.[23]

Sheffield neglected to emphasize the industrial raw materials from the West Indies, of which raw cotton was to supply England's leading industry in the Industrial Revolution. Moreover, he should have called attention to the production of a variety of manufactures which found a market in the plantations. Even the criticism of luxury consumption did not go unanswered. Edmund Burke, among others, maintained that such consumption excited industry, nourished emulation, and inspired some sense of personal value in all ranks of society.[24]

Other critics, of whom Adam Smith was undoubtedly the foremost, were of the opinion that the mercantile system diverted an undue amount of British capital to the colonies when the same capital might be employed to greater advantage in British agriculture and industry. 'All the different regulations of the mercantile system', he wrote, 'necessarily derange more or less this natural and most advantageous distribution of stock'.[25] In his long disquisition on the evils of the mercantile system, Smith seems to argue that the sugar colonies were chronically indebted to the mother country. Conceivably, repatriated profits might be larger than the service charge on debts owed by West Indians to British merchants. William Beckford, the planter-historian, was one of several writers who argued against the Smithian view. 'It should be considered, that the person who acquires a competence in another country, does not draw any wealth from his own, at the same time that what he makes, or at least the greater part of it, flows back again to enrich the parent

---

23 John Lord Sheffield, *Observations on the Commerce of the American States* (London, 1784), pp. 226–7.
24 Edmund Burke, *The Present State of the Nation* (1769), in *The Works of Edmund Burke*, ed. E. B. Willis (London, 1925), vol. 1, p. 357.
25 Smith, *Wealth of Nations*, p. 595.

Sugar and Slavery

stream'.[26] Even Adam Smith was willing to concede that the 'natural good effects of the colony trade' more than counterbalanced to Great Britain 'the bad effects of the monopoly'. The new produce and the new capital which had been created by the colony trade maintained in Great Britain 'a greater quantity of productive labour, than what can have been thrown out of employment by the revulsion of capital from other trades of which the returns are more frequent'.[27]

Another line of attack was that the monopoly of the colonial trade over-priced tropical staples in home markets. Again, Adam Smith led the chorus of criticism, observing that 'in the system of laws which has been established for the management of our American and West Indian colonies, the interest of the home-consumer has been sacrificed to that of the producer with a more extravagant profusion than in all our other commercial regulations'.[28] Smith and other critics of the mercantile system maintained that the Navigation Acts channelled British sugar products into a home market which was protected from the products of foreign colonies by prohibitive duties. Moreover, it was argued that productive capacity in the colonies failed to expand in relation to home demand, a condition which brought vigorous complaints from British sugar refiners and traders who asserted that rich planters were consciously restricting production in an effort to extract monopoly profits from consumers. Among the defenders of the colonial interest was Bryan Edwards, who, while denying that Englishmen might purchase sugar more cheaply in the foreign colonies, maintained that even if such price differentials had existed, Britain would still need sugar colonies of her own to absorb British manufactures which were denied entry into foreign dependencies. Furthermore, he called attention to the employment in the colonial trade of numerous ships and sailors, on which the maritime strength of the kingdom so greatly depended.[29]

Joining in the chorus of criticism were leaders in the North American colonies who charged that their economic interests were being sacrificed to those of the West Indians. From the North came appeals for free trade in Caribbean waters, at a time when the foreign sugar colonies offered a larger and more remunerative market for American foodstuffs and building materials, as well as supplying

26 William Beckford, *A Descriptive Account of the Island of Jamaica* (London, 1790), vol. 2, p. 319.
27 Smith, *Wealth of Nations*, pp. 574–5.
28 Ibid., p. 626.
29 Edwards, *History of British West Indies* (London, 1801), vol. 2, p. 476.

sugar products more cheaply than their British rivals.

Although the attack on the slave trade and the institution of slavery in the colonies did not gather momentum until the late decades of the 18th century, not a little criticism was voiced in the period of this study. Adam Smith condemned slavery on grounds of efficiency, holding that the labour of slaves was dearer to their masters than that of free men. Probably more prevalent were criticisms motivated by sentiments of religion and humanity. As early as 1671 George Fox, the founder of Quakerism, had admonished the planters of Barbados to treat their Negroes kindly and bring them up in the Christian faith. Other Quakers, including John Woolman and Anthony Benezet, were concerned about the evils of the peculiar institution, as were the Moravians who had established missions in the West Indies, by the mid-18th century period.[30]

3 CARIBBEAN ISLAND ECONOMIES

Despite these and other criticisms, the slave-plantation colonies to the south of the Mason-Dixon line, and particularly the Caribbean colonies, were widely regarded as the most precious jewels in the crown of trade. Situated in a tropical island world easily accessible to sea-going vessels, the sugar colonies supplied Europeans with a variety of exotics in growing demand, took off European manufactures, gave employment to ships and seamen, provided raw materials for processing and manufacturing industries, generated a variety of auxiliary trades ranging from African slaves to Newfoundland codfish, were favourably situated for a lucrative entropôt trade with Spanish America, provided a field for fortune hunters, yielded revenue to European governments, and gave rise to wealth and income which revived the image of the Indies as a source of fabulous riches after the precious metal mines of New Spain began to falter.

The world of 17th and 18th century mercantilism witnessed the rise of the Caribbean sugar industry as the chief source of new wealth. Indeed, cane sugar was probably the most valuable commodity in all the world's trade of the 18th century.[31] Arnold Heeren, the German historian, wrote of the ever increasing importance of colonies 'from the time that their productions,

---

30 See Chapter 19, pp. 480–3.
31 William Ashworth, *A Short History of the International Economy* (London, 1952). pp. 28–9.

especially coffee, sugar, and tea, began to come into more general use in Europe'.[32]

Europeans carried the sugar cane to the American tropics and developed slave-plantation economies in sparsely settled areas. Conceivably, such economies might have been located in West Africa. But tropical Africa had a reputation for being the white man's grave, and there was the further hazard of slaves escaping to their tribal homes. On the other hand, slaves might be more easily disciplined on small Caribbean islands, while Europeans were more prone to settle where the heat of the tropics was mitigated by the trade winds. Trade winds not only contributed to health and comfort, but they also determined the direction of sea lanes in an age of sailing ships as well as powering the sugar mills that crushed the canes. These and other factors, including the proximity of the West Indies to the cheap foodstuffs and building materials of North America and the fabled riches of the Spanish Indies, help to explain why European nations valued their sugar colonies so highly.

The impact of the tropics, while of primary concern to calculating writers on trade, did not go unobserved by men of letters. 'If we consider our own country in its natural prospect, without any of the benefits and advantages of commerce, what a barren uncomfortable spot of earth falls to our share,' wrote Joseph Addison, the English essayist. Fortunately, England had been successful in developing outlying dependencies and the sea power which enabled her to receive ships laden with the harvest of every climate. As Addison expressed it,

> Nature indeed furnishes us with the bare necessaries of life; but traffic gives us a great variety of what is useful, and at the same time supplies us with everything that is convenient and ornamental. Nor is it the least part of our happiness that whilst we enjoy the remotest products of the North and South, we are free from those extremities of weather which give them birth.[33]

Englishmen were thus able to refresh their eyes with the 'green fields of Britain' at the same time that their palates were feasted with the fruits 'that rise between the tropics'.[34]

The impact was not confined to tropical staples, for the metropolis was also the destination of a considerable number of wealthy planters. The West Indian who returned to Britain to live on the profits of his slave-manned plantation was a conspicuous figure in the

---

32 Arnold H. L. Heeren, *A Manual of the History of the Political System of Europe and its Colonies* (1809), trans. Henry G. Bohn (London, 1873), pp. 172, 199.
33 Joseph Addison, *The Spectator*, 19 May 1711.
34 Idem.

The Tropic Empire

18th century. He acquired a reputation for hospitality, conspicuous consumption, and slavish imitation of the landed aristocracy. Not infrequently he was the butt of ridicule. It should not be thought that profligacy was widespread, for it will be shown that numerous absentees became improving landlords, merchants, manufacturers, military officers, doctors, clergymen, lawyers and politicians. It is also an exaggeration to believe that the absentees who cut a fine figure in the metropolis made up a large proportion of the white inhabitants of the colonies. While the absentees may have numbered several thousand and their wealth and influence was disproportionate to their numbers, they were only a fraction of the Britishers who remained in the tropics. Furthermore, the white inhabitants of the colonies were far out-numbered by the Negro slaves who served as hewers of wood and drawers of water.

The migration of Englishmen to the tropics commenced in the 1620s, the same decade that witnessed the first settlements in New England. After a foothold was established on several islands on the eastern fringe of the Caribbean, the settlers turned to such activities as hide hunting, privateering, and the cultivation of subsistence crops and minor staples. Then about 1640 the introduction of sugar cane from the Portuguese colony of Brazil led to an economic transformation. In the vanguard was the island of Barbados which, already thickly populated, witnessed an exodus of smallholders whose lands were purchased or otherwise appropriated and consolidated into sugar plantations. Large numbers re-emigrated to Jamaica, the former Spanish colony, which was destined to become the leading British sugar colony in the 18th century. Despite the mother country's policy of making the West Indies a dumping ground for undesirables, the white population grew slowly after about 1660. On the other hand, Negro slaves were imported from Africa in such numbers that they eventually outnumbered the whites by as much as ten to one.

On the eve of the American War of Independence, ten British islands in the West Indies contained approximately 51,000 whites and 420,000 Negro slaves, of which Jamaica possessed 18,400 and 205,000, respectively. Moreover, between March 1774 and March 1775, 384 ships, carrying 131,778 casks of sugar arrived in the port of London.[35] In the latter year there are grounds for believing that the fixed and movable wealth of the British sugar colonies amounted to £30 million sterling, of which more than half was the immediate property of, or owing to, persons in Great Britain.[36]

35 Pitman, *Development of British West Indies*, pp. 369–90; Burn, *The British West Indies*, pp. 85–6.
36 See Chapter 19, pp. 470–2.

Sugar and Slavery

The combination of fertile soil and a tropical climate gave the Caribbean islands a comparative advantage in the production of cane sugar. Indeed, so much labour and capital was concentrated upon the cultivation and processing of the sweetening substance that the colonies became dependent on imported supplies of labour, manufactures, foodstuffs, draft animals, and building materials. Africa supplied the labour force, North America the foodstuffs, draft animals, and building materials, while Great Britain provided a wide assortment of goods, and most of the shipping, insurance, financial, and mercantile services.

4 ECONOMIC GROWTH AND THE COLONIES

Most impressive to Englishmen of the 17th century was the rise of the Dutch Republic to a position of European dominance in fishing, shipping, trade, manufacturing and finance. Sir William Petty had the Dutch experience in mind when he wrote:

> Those who predominate in Shipping, and Fishing, have more occasions than others to frequent all parts of the World, and to observe what is wanting or redundant every where, and what each People can do, and what they desire, and consequently to be the Factors, the Carriers for the whole World of Trade. Under which ground they bring all Native Commodities to be Manufactured at home, and carry the same back, even to that Country in which they grew, all which we see.[37]

The Dutch were said to have imported for manufacture and re-export the sugars of the West Indies, the timber and iron of the Baltic, the hemp of Russia, the lead, tin, and wool of England, the quicksilver and silk of Italy, and the yarns and dyestuffs of Turkey.

Petty apparently assumed that peoples with wants and redundancies already existed so that trade and manufacturing might be developed by merely searching out such peoples and their trade goods. European traders who went to the Orient not only found spices and other tropical staples, but also fabrics and metalwares which, both in quality and price, far surpassed the handicraft productions of their homelands. Partly for this reason, a balance of trade problem was encountered. Europeans had few things except precious metals to exchange for Eastern luxuries, thus obviating the development of a reciprocal and growth-generating trade in manufactures and primary products.

37 Sir William Petty, *Political Arithmetic*, in *The Economic Writings of Sir William Petty*, ed. Charles H. Hull (Cambridge, 1899), vol. 1, p. 301.

The Tropic Empire

In most parts of Africa and the New World the Europeans encountered preliterate peoples whose cultures were based on food gathering or shifting agriculture and whose wants and redundancies were limited. Great wealth, it is true, came from the precious metal mines of the New World, but the indigenous peoples who produced such wealth consumed only limited quantities of European manufactures. An alternative solution was for Europeans to impress tropical peoples into slavery, transport them to areas where environmental and locational factors were more favourable, and, in short, secure the benefits of combined and constant labour in slave-plantation economies. In this way abundant and regular supplies of tropical staples might be assured and compact markets for European wares might be created. Trade in the New World setting thus involved the prior creation of complementary export economies where wants and redundancies could be depended upon to ensure the reciprocal flow of manufactures and primary products. In the words of Edmund Burke, this colony trade was 'a new world of commerce in a manner created'.[38]

But strict regulation of the colonies and their trade was necessary if the benefits were to centre in the mother country. Accordingly, colonial trade was confined to English or colonial ships and sailors, English manufacturers were given preferential treatment in colonial markets, sugar and other staple commodities had to be shipped directly to England, and a preferential duty system checked the growth of colonial sugar refineries. In other words, the colonies should buy English goods and pay for them with products which England needed, while the trade should employ English merchants and vessels, thereby providing freights, profits, and interest. By means of the Navigation Acts, wrote John Cary, 'the Kingdom is become the centre of trade, and standing like the sun in the midst of its plantations, does not only refresh them, but draws profit from them, and so indeed is it a matter of exact justice that it should be so'.[39]

As artificial creations tied to the metropolis by the Acts of Trade, the export economies in the West Indies came to play a significant role in the economic development of Great Britain. Essentially the growth process involved the diversion of capital and labour from domestic agriculture and conspicuous consumption, activities subject to the law of decreasing returns, into Atlantic empire trade and manufacturing for export, activities which came to yield in-

38 Burke, *The State of the Nation*, in *The Works*, vol. 1, p. 344.
39 John Cary, *An Essay towards regulating the Trade, and Employing the Poor, of this Kingdom* (London, 1717), p. 50.

creasing returns.⁴⁰ By means of the Navigation Acts and absentee landlordism, the metropolis served as a magnet for the profits, interest, commissions, and shipping returns of colonial production, shipping and trade. The spending of this income generated investment in a variety of manufacturing and commercial enterprises; for example, shipbuilders and manufacturers of hardware and textiles supplied inputs for the sugar economy, while sugar refiners and textile mills processed the colonial raw materials. Instead of permitting the growth of these activities in the colonies, mercantile policy forced the development of the secondary and tertiary sectors of the export economies in the metropolis. According to the terminology of Professor Hirschman, income from the colonial export sector gave rise to backward linkages, forward linkages, and final demand linkages. On this basis it may be argued that the Industrial Revolution, rather than gowing out of elements indigenous to the domestic economy, was largely a response to the impact of Greater Britain, that is, a change in productive techniques and organization induced by the creation of colonial export economies.⁴¹

5 CONCLUSION

As the 17th century Englishman was a close student of Dutch ascendancy in the maritime world, so the 19th century European turned to the British model of industrial and commercial wealth and power. Friedrich List, the German political economist, drew up a blueprint for German ascendancy which was based on the experience of Britain's island empire. Instead of acquiring her empire 'in a fit of absence of mind', List maintained that conscious policy shaped the development of Britain into a great commercial, manufacturing, and maritime power. As the world's metropolis, she supplied all nations with manufactures and took in exchange raw materials and agricultural produce. England had thus become 'an example and a pattern to all nations ... especially in the acquisition of the natural riches of tropical countries, and in the civilization of barbarous races or of such as have retrograded into barbarism'. Indeed, List

---

40 Frederic C. Lane, 'National Wealth and Protection Costs', in *War as a Social Institution The Historian's Perspective*, ed. Jesse D. Clarkson and Thomas C. Cochran (New York, 1941), pp. 42–3.
41 Albert O. Hirschman, *The Strategy of Economic Development* (New Haven, 1960), pp. 98–119.

The Tropic Empire

maintained that 'the progress of industry in the manufacturing countries of the temperate zone' was caused chiefly by 'the interchange of manufactured goods for raw materials and natural products, and especially for the products of tropical countries'.[42]

---

42 Friedrich List, *The National System of Political Economy* (1841), trans. S. P. Lloyd (London, 1885), pp. 161–2, 263–70, 365–6.

CHAPTER TWO

'Sugar, The Inseparable Companion of Tea'

> With tea, sugar and tobacco finding their way into all homes (whether through the custom house or the smuggler's cave) and with timber mainly supplied from abroad, we are approaching the historical confines of modern England, a community that subsists as the centre of a great overseas Empire and a greater overseas trade providing articles of common consumption for all classes.[1]
>
> George Macauley Trevelyan, 1945

1 THE IMPACT OF THE NEW WORLD

In calling attention to the impact of the New World upon Europe, Adam Smith observed that the general advantages of the discovery and colonization of America were 'first, in the increase of its enjoyments; and secondly, in the augmentation of its industry'. From the New World came a variety of commodities which Europeans would not have otherwise possessed, 'some for conveniency and use, some for pleasure, and some for ornament, and thereby contributes to increase their enjoyments'.[2] Writing a few decades after the Scottish economist, Arnold Heeren noted the great influence which exotic commodities, especially coffee, sugar, and tea, had had on Europe. Not only had they influenced politics, he observed, but they had also reformed social life. 'In a word, without these productions, would the states in the west of Europe have acquired their present character?'[3]

It is a commonplace of economic history that after the Middle Ages, commodities which had formerly been used by the upper classes were adopted by other sections of society. Changes in dietary

---

1 G. M. Trevelyan, *English Social History, A Survey of Six Centuries, Chaucer to Queen Victoria* (London, 1945), pp. 387–8.
2 Adam Smith, *An Enquiry into the Nature and Causes of the Wealth of Nations* (1776) (Modern Library, New York, 1937), p. 557.
3 Arnold H. L. Heeren, *A Manual of the History of the Political System of Europe and its Colonies* (1809), trans. Henry G. Bohn (London, 1873), pp. 172–3.

and drinking habits were sufficiently great to be significant in any consideration of commerce. Penetration of tropical and semi-tropical regions yielded a rich harvest of foodstuffs to lend variety to the coarse fare of man in the northern latitudes. Both the East and West Indies made their special contribution to the daily repast of the European. Spices, which were a great aid in making rotting meat palatable, spread northward from the time of the Crusades. Venice, Portugal, and Holland waxed fat on the profits of the spice trade until the 18th century witnessed a decline occasioned by the European's demand for sweet in preference to spiced dishes, and the progress in animal husbandry which ensured a supply of fresh meat throughout the year.

Practically all of the economic plants of the Asian and African tropics had been introduced into the New World by the 18th century. But owing to such factors as comparative transport costs, the quality and supply of labour, and commercial policy, a crude division of labour developed between the Asiatic and American tropics. The latter enjoyed a comparative advantage in commodities of low value and high bulk — sugar and tobacco, for example, rather than spices and tea.

Numerous tropical productions entered Europe from the New World. Food crops not only included sugar, but also rice and certain tropical fruits. To cocoa and chocolate, which were first obtained on a considerable scale from Mexico, was later added coffee which the Dutch brought to Surinam early in the 18th century. Even spices were not precluded, for ginger and allspice were commercial crops of some importance. Then there were the highly prized raw materials of manufacture — indigo, dye woods, and cotton. In 1690, Sir Dalby Thomas enumerated the leading staples of the West Indies as sugar and its molasses and rum by-products, indigo, logwood, cotton, and ginger; 'not to speak of the many *Druggs, Woods, Cocoa, Piemento*, and *Spices*, besides *Raw-Hides*, etc. which comes from those parts, nor of the great quantity of *Gold* and *Silver* we have of the *Spaniards* for *Negroes*, and English Manufactory carryed by our sloops from our Collonies to them'.[4]

The importance of tropical and semi-tropical commodities in the import trade of England is borne out by the overseas trade statistics compiled by Elizabeth Boody Schumpeter. Heading the imports which are classified into nine groups are 'groceries', consisting of tea, coffee, sugar, rice, pepper, and a variety of other tropical, semi-tropical or oriental produce. In 1700 this group comprised 16.9 per

---

4 Sir Dalby Thomas, *An Historical Account of the Rise and Growth of the West India Collonies* (London, 1690), p. 9.

cent of all imports, by official value, as compared with 34.9 per cent in 1800. None of the other eight groups exceeded 6 per cent of total imports in 1800. Among the grocery items brown sugar and molasses were the most prominent. They made up, by official value, two-thirds of the group in 1700 and two-fifths in 1800. Tea came next, rising from a mere 167,000 lb in 1700 to over 23 million lb in 1800. Coffee imports were negligible until the late decades of the century when they moved upward so rapidly that their official value was nearly equal to that of brown sugar.[5]

2 PATTERNS OF SUGAR CONSUMPTION

Sugar had been classified with such luxuries as spices and silk. For many centuries it was regarded as a superfluity, a rare and costly addition to the ordinary diet and highly regarded for its medicinal properties. Except for the privileged few, honey was the only sweetening in use throughout Europe. Supplies of cane sugar entered northern Europe in greater quantities in the 16th and 17th centuries, first from the Coast of Barbary, then from such Atlantic islands as Madeira and St Thome, and finally from the New World. By the early 17th century Francis Bacon called attention to the fact that 'sugar hath put down the use of honey insomuch that we have lost those observations and preparations of honey which the ancients had when it was more in price'.[6]

Thomas Tryon, a late 17th century sugar merchant of London, commented on the growing importance of this sweetening substance. Enumerating the various uses to which sugar was put in his day, he noted

> how many Thousand Acres of Land are by the use of this noble Plant, made of five times the value or more, than otherwise they would have been as having brought a great number of Fruits, Grains and Seeds into use, that were... but little valued formerly, such as Apples, Pears, Plumbs, Apricocks, Gooseberries, Currants, and many more of the like nature.[7]

Tryon also mentions 'the many brave and exhilrating Drinks that are made of the Juices of our Fruits, by the assistance of Sugar, such as

---

5 E. B. Schumpeter, *English Overseas Trade Statistics 1697–1808. With an Introduction by T. S. Ashton* (Oxford, 1960), pp. 10–14.
6 *The Works of Francis Bacon*, ed. Basil Montagu (Philadelphia, 1848), vol. 2, pp. 82, 116.
7 Thomas Tryon, *Tryon's Letters, Domestick and Foreign, To Several Persons of Quality, Occasionally distributed in Subjects* (London, 1700), p. 219.

'Sugar, The Inseparable Companion of Tea'

Cherry Wine, Currant Wine, Gooseberry Wine, Rasberry Wine, Cowslip Wine, and many more . . .'. Sugar was said to have increased the King's customs by occasioning many foreign commodities to be imported which were unheard of in former days. Included among them were 'Cocoa, of which the most agreeable Pottage is made, which if it were not for Sugar, would be but of little use; and several other Foreign Fruits and Drugs, as Tea, Coffee, etc.'. 'Physicians and Apothecaries', he observed, 'cannot but think themselves highly befriended by this noble Juice, since more than half their Mediciens are mixed and compounded with Sugar'. Confectioners were said to have made 'about Two Hundred sorts of Sweet-Meats with Fruits of our own Growth'.[8]

From Tryon's account it is evident that sugar altered European life in a number of ways. By the middle of the 18th century it had become a staple article of diet among large sections of European society. Some of the factors that made for increased consumption were enumerated by Edward Long, the Jamaica planter-historian:

> The prodigious improvements made of late years in the general commerce of Europe, particularly inland navigation . . . so that, the inhabitants everywhere becoming richer, and more communicative with one another, the consumption of sugar has been extended among many thousand, perhaps millions, who before were equally unable either to procur or to pay for it.[9]

3 ENGLISH SUGAR CONSUMPTION

The extension of sugar consumption among millions of Englishmen may be illustrated by the statistics of imports, re-exports, and retained imports.

Table 2.1 shows that English sugar consumption probably increased about four-fold in the last four decades of the 17th century. It trebled in the first four decades of the next century and more than doubled again from 1741–5 to 1771–5. If it is assumed that one-half of the imports were retained in 1663, the consumption of England and Wales increased about twenty-fold in the period from 1663 to 1775. The fact that the population increased from 4½ million to only 7½ million in the same period is indicative of a marked increase in per capita consumption.

It is evident from Table 2.1 that a growing proportion of the imports were retained for home consumption. During the last four

---

8 Ibid., pp. 219–21.
9 Edward Long, *The History of Jamaica* (London, 1774), vol. 1, p. 524.

Sugar and Slavery

Table 2.1

*Colonial sugar imports, re-exports,
and retained imports, England and Wales, 1663–1775**
(annual averages in 000 cwt)

Years	Imports	Re-exports	Retained imports	Percentage retained
1663 –	148.0			
1669 –	190.5			
1690 –	257.0			
1698–1700	471.1	190.4	280.7	59.6
1701–05	357.9	95.5	262.4	73.3
1706–10	401.3	100.8	300.5	74.9
1711–15	484.6	142.1	342.5	70.7
1716–20	653.2	180.1	473.1	72.4
1721–25	671.2	99.3	571.9	85.2
1726–30	860.9	174.7	686.2	79.7
1731–35	848.5	106.8	741.7	87.4
1736–40	790.1	70.0	720.1	91.1
1741–45	778.5	100.1	678.4	87.1
1746–50	878.2	116.7	761.5	86.7
1751–55	965.4	72.5	892.9	92.4
1756–60	1,320.4	218.3	1,102.1	83.5
1761–65	1,476.6	413.0	1,063.6	72.0
1766–70	1,611.3	232.1	1,379.2	85.6
1771–75	1,811.8	268.9	1,542.9	85.2

**Statistics apply to Great Britain after 1755*

Source: British Museum Add. MSS 36,785; Public Record Office (P.R.O.), London, C.O. 318/1, f. 5; Customs 3/1–4; John MacGregor, *Commercial Statistics* (London, 1850), vol. 5, p. 382.

decades of the 17th century the estimated increase was from one-third to more than one-half.[10] If the war years are excluded, retained imports as a percentage of total imports increased from about 60 to between 85 and 90 per cent during the first three-quarters of

---

10 John Campbell, *Candid and Impartial Considerations on the Nature of the Sugar Trade* (London, 1768), p. 30; Public Record Office, London. C.O. 31/2, ff. 179–80.

the 18th century. The percentage was even higher if the colonial sugar re-exported from England to Ireland is included in retained imports. England thus retained a growing portion of her sugar imports until only negligible quantities remained to supply countries other than Ireland.

The decline of the re-export trade was of widespread concern to mercantile writers and spokesmen for the sugar industry. Various reasons were assigned for the failure to supply both home and foreign markets. Planters complained of high duties and extortionate middlemen's charges; refiners claimed that they were denied drawbacks of import duties on the export of their product; merchants and shippers charged the planters with land engrossment, 'seeking nothing farther, than to supply our Consumption at home...'.[11] All were agreed that British sugar was failing to meet the competition of the French and Dutch product in Continental markets.

The years following the Treaty of Utrecht witnessed a marked deterioration of the export of colonial produce. By the year 1724, sufficient concern had been expressed to cause the Board of Trade to make a thorough investigation of the sugar and tobacco trades. Testimony and reports were submitted by numerous merchants engaged in the export trade. All admitted to the weakened competitive position of British sugar products in Continental markets. In part, they attributed this to the great increase in home consumption; in part, to the competition of Dutch, French, and Portuguese on the Continent. According to one witness:

> No Nation runs down the European market so much as the French, for they are so impatient for quick return, that at Amsterdam I observed for many years, that when either Suriname Sugars arrived in the winter, or that English plantation Sugars were consigned to us in that season, we laid them up in warehouses to wait for an advantagious market & the Spring Consumption, whereas the French never housed their Sugars but sold them from the lighters in lotts by auction at any time.[12]

Other causes consisted of the 4½ per cent export duty, the enumeration dues, import duties in England, and the lack of complete drawbacks on re-exported sugar.[13]

In proposing remedies that might help British sugar interests regain the Continental market, several merchants argued for a direct trade between the colonies and foreign markets. However, the Board of

11 P.R.O. London. C.O. 388/95, I(17): Report of Merchant Adventurers at Hamburg, 12 Sept. 1764.
12 Ibid., C.O. 388/24, R 142: Memorial to the Board of Trade, 16 June 1724; C.O. 391/33: Board of Trade Journal, 24 June 1724.
13 Frank W. Pitman, *The Development of the British West Indies 1700–1763* (New Haven, 1917), pp. 170–1.

Sugar and Slavery

Trade was not receptive to this proposal and fifteen years were to elapse before the planters succeeded in pushing through the Direct Export Act.

The strong upward movement in retained imports should not obscure short-term movements in consumer demand. Besides tea and coffee, the demand for sugar was linked with the demand for fruit and alcoholic beverages. Edward Long wrote that 'a plentiful crop of apples greatly increases the Consumption of Sugar (Computed by some at eight thousand hogsheads) and this fruit particularly in the western counties, furnishes no inconsiderable part of both of the aliment and drink of the common people'.[14] Dr Tullideph wrote from London in April 1751: 'am in hopes that Sugars will answear tolerably well Provided Jamaica fails and you have a good Crop of Apples'. Several years later he wrote from London: 'Sugars are lately started here ... oweing ... to a demand from Ireland ... and the approach of the ensueing elections, and I really believe Sugars must keep up pretty high at home especially the latter ones'.[15] In years of poor grain harvests Parliament prohibited the distillation of malt spirits, thus forcing distillers to purchase quantities of molasses and low-grade sugar for the distillation of molasses spirits.

Patterns of trade were altered in wartime. Both in the War of 1739–48 and the Seven Years' War (1756–63), re-exports increased in consequence of the British blockade of Continental ports, captures of enemy sugar vessels and cargoes, and the conquest and occupation of enemy sugar islands.

4 BRITISH AND FRENCH SUGAR CONSUMPTION

British consumption was more than two and a half times greater than that of France in 1775, according to the figures shown in Table 2.2. The disparity was even greater in terms of per capita consumption, for it has been estimated that the population of France was about 25 million in 1750, as compared with some 6 million for England and Wales.

Contemporaries were of the opinion that French consumption lagged behind that of Britain owing to the disparate levels of wealth and affluence. 'If the wealth of *France* was as great or as generally diffused, that is, if the mass of their people were as thoroughly

14 Long, *History of Jamaica*, vol. 1, p. 524.
15 *Tullideph L. B.*, vol. 2: Lre. to Dr Walter Sydserfe in Antigua, 13 April 1751; Lre. to William Hare, Merchant in Bristol, 20 Sept. 1753.

'Sugar, The Inseparable Companion of Tea'

Table 2.2

The British and French sugar trades compared, 1775
(000 cwt)

	Imports	Re-exports	Retained imports	Percentage retained
Great Britain	2,002.2	414.8	1,587.4	79.3
France	1,601.2	1,002.0	599.2	37.4

Source: David MacPherson, *Annals of Commerce* (Edinburgh, 1805), vol. 3, p. 583; John MacGregor, *Commercial Statistics* (London, 1850), vol. 5, p. 382.

employed, and thereby as easy in their circumstances, as the bulk of the *British* nation actually are, they would then of course consume much more [sugar] and export far less', was the judgement of one Englishman.[16]

The drinking habits of the English and French people influenced sugar consumption both directly and indirectly. By the early years of the 18th century Englishmen were consuming quantities of sugar with tea. Moreover, rum punch was growing in popularity as malt and molasses spirits began to supplant wine and brandy. In France, on the other hand, tea and rum were relegated to a minimal role and wine continued to be the national drink.

Little is known of consumption patterns in other parts of Europe, but it appears that, like France, these countries tended to lag behind Britain. Thomas Tryon commented on the consumption of strong drink, meat, bread, butter, cheese, sugar, spices, fruit, and clothing: 'Tradesmen and other common people of England have spent and consumed greater quantities of such things than half Europe; the Tradesmen and poor of other Nations hardly knowing their names, and much less their natures'.[17] Very similar was Lord Sheffield's observation more than eight decades later that sugar 'is not commonly used in one half of Europe'.[18]

---

16 Campbell, *Nature of the Sugar Trade*, p. 31.
17 Thomas Tryon, *England's Grandeur, and Way to get Wealth* (London, 1699), p. 23.
18 John Lord Sheffield, *Observations on the Commerce of the American States* (London, 1784), pp. 162, 168.

5 THE RICH AND THE POOR

Until the late years of the 17th century English sugar consumption seems to have been confined rather closely to the wealthy sections of society. It was Sir Dalby Thomas's opinion that 'the greatest consumption of Sugars is made by themselves [our Legislators], and the rest of the Rich and Opulent People of the Nation'.[19] Lower income groups cannot be dismissed, however, because they were reported to have used quantities of molasses, treacle and low-quality sugar. Great quantities of treacle were used by the poorer sort of people 'to sweeten some of their Eatables, and to make drinkable Liquors'. The changing habits of the 'two or three thousand working Tradesmen' who lived 'in the several out parts of London' attracted the attention of Thomas Tryon, who observed that 'when they had full Employment ... most of [their] money was spent every Week in the Neighbourhood in Strong-Drink, several sorts of Flesh, Bread, Butter, Cheese, Sugar, Spice, Spanish Fruit and in Cloathing, which caused a quick Circulation in all Business'.[20]

During the 18th century the demand for sugar grew so rapidly among all sections of English society that few people considered it a luxury. Even the poorest Englishman was accused of imprudent indulgence. 'The 18th century pamphleteers', writes Dr Gilboy, 'were loud in their condemnation of the growth of luxury among the poor. The increasing use of wheat bread, tea, sugar, butter, as well as various other amenities of life was frowned upon'.[21] Edward Long went so far as to assert that 'sugar is so generally in use, by the assistance of tea, that even the poor wretches living in almshouses will not be without it'.[22]

Improvements in internal communication and transportation made sugar products accessible to working-class consumers in regions where transport costs had formerly limited the market to wealthy inhabitants. Where rivers had been dredged and made navigable to their headwaters, bulky commodities could be transported in growing quantities to inland regions. Defoe relates in his *Travels* that the merchants of Bristol drove on the river Avon 'a very great trade

---

19 Thomas, *Historical Account of West Indies*, p. 8; F. J. Fisher, 'The Development of London as a Centre of Conspicuous Consumption in the Sixteenth and Seventeenth Century', *Transactions of the Royal Historical Society*, 4th ser., vol. XXX (London, 1948), pp. 37–50.
20 Tryon, *England's Grandeur*, p. 17; Joseph Massie, *A State of the British Sugar-Colony Trade* (London, 1759), p. 24.
21 Elizabeth W. Gilboy, *Wages in Eighteenth Century England* (Cambridge, Mass., 1934), p. 229.
22 Long, *History of Jamaica*, vol. 1, p. 525.

'Sugar, The Inseparable Companion of Tea'

for sugar, oil, wine, tobacco, iron, lead and in a word, all heavy goods which are carried by water almost as far as Warwick'.[23]

Liverpool-West India merchants rivalled those of Bristol by the second quarter of the 18th century. Here the construction of the 'Old Dock' between 1699 and 1717 contributed materially to the expansion of overseas trade. The trade of Liverpool also benefited from improvements in river navigation and the construction of turnpikes. With the aid of improved transport Liverpool supplied sugar markets in the growing industrial centres of Yorkshire and Lancashire. It was not merely a coincidence, writes Dr Gilboy, that the manufacturing cities of Manchester and Birmingham 'were characterized by a laboring class with steadily increasing real wages and economic and social ambition'.[24]

Not only was the English market widened, but it was also deepened. Extremes of wealth and poverty persisted, it is true, but the tendency toward a wider diffusion of wealth and income was observed by contemporaries. This was particularly the case with the 'trading, middling sort of people', of whom Defoe wrote in 1727: 'they are infinitely richer than the same class of people in any other nation in the world. As they are richer, so they live better, fare better, wear better, and spend more money than they do in any other countries. They eat well, and they drink well'.[25]

Modern historians tend to support the views of Defoe. 'Economic circumstances made the first half of the Eighteenth Century an age of relative plenty for the working class', writes Professor Trevelyan.[26] Dr George, the historian of 18th-century London, maintains that the period between 1700 and 1757 or 1765 was 'one of the chief periods of working-class prosperity in this country'.[27]

6 TEA AND SUGAR

The rise in real wages meant that the average Englishman had more disposable income. After the early years of the 18th century there was a temptation to spend a larger proportion of this income on sugar because of the widespread consumption of tea. The relation-

23 Daniel Defoe, *A Tour Through England and Wales* (1724) (London, 1928), vol. 2, pp. 36–7, 42; W. E. Minchinton, 'Bristol – Metropolis of the West in the Eighteenth Century', *Trans. Royal Hist. Soc.*, 5th ser., vol. 4 (1954), pp. 69–89.
24 Gilboy, *Wages in England*, p. 242.
25 Daniel Defoe, *A Plan of English Commerce* (1728), in John R. McCulloch (ed.), *A Select Collection of Scarce and Valuable Tracts on Commerce* (London, 1859), pp. 138–9.
26 Trevelyan, *English Social History*, p. 410.
27 M. Dorothy George, *London Life in the Eighteenth Century* (London, 1925), p. 26.

Sugar and Slavery

ship between tea and the Englishman's temperament has often drawn comment. 'Tea, which refreshes and quietens', writes Professor Fay, 'is the natural beverage of a taciturn people, and, being easy to prepare, it came as a godsend to the world's worst cooks'.[28]

Contemporaries regarded tea and coffee drinking as an important reason for the increased consumption of sugar. A London merchant stated in 1724: 'The Consumption of Sugar in England, by the great use of Tea and Coffy is very much encreased, of late, especially by the cheapness of Tea which will alwise enlarge the Consumption'.[29] The *Barbados Gazette* printed a letter in 1735, which stated: 'The use of Sugar in this Kingdom has augmented very much in the last thirty Years, which is undoubtedly owing to the encreased Consumption of Tea and Coffee within that Period'.[30] The joint demand for tea and sugar was noted by another contemporary who observed that 'these two commodities were generally consumed together, and it being computed that there is from Twelve to Sixteen Pounds of Sugar us'd with every Pound of Tea'.[31] Writing in 1774, Edward Long attributed the 'prodigious augmentation' in the home consumption of sugar to 'the low prices of teas for some years past'.[32]

After tea was introduced into Scotland in 1682 by the Duke of York, the habit spread quite rapidly. 'Sugar, the inseparable Companion of Tea, came to be the Possession of the very *poorest* Housewife, where formerly it had been a great Rarity, — and thereby was *at hand*, to mix with Water and Brandy, or Rum'.[33]

The price of tea and sugar had to be easily within the reach of the ordinary Englishman before he could consume these commodities in any quantity. The fall in the price of tea was very rapid. The first tea that reached the London market in 1652 sold for the remarkable price of £3 10s per lb. Nine or ten years later it had fallen to about £2 0s. Though the price had declined to a little more than 20s per lb by the end of the century, tea did not become cheap enough to be a general drink until well into the next century. During the first half of the 18th century consumption rose as prices fell. Tea sold by the East India Company, writes Dr Krishna, 'came down from 16s. 2d.

---

28 C. R. Fay, *English Economic History mainly since 1700* (Cambridge, 1948), p. 147.
29 P.R.O. London. C.O. 388/24, R 142: Memorial to the Board of Trade, 16 June 1724.
30 Anon., *Caribbeana, Containing Letters and Dissertations on the British Sugar Colonies* (London, 1741), vol. 2, p. 64.
31 Anon., *Reasons against laying an Additional Duty on Muscovado Sugar* (London, 1743/4), single sheet.
32 Long, *History of Jamaica*, vol. 1, p. 519–21.
33 Duncan Forbes, *Some Considerations on the Present State of Scotland* (1744), quoted in J. C. Drummond and Anne Wilbraham, *The Englishman's Food, a History of Five Centuries of English Diet* (London, 1939), pp. 242–3.

'Sugar, The Inseparable Companion of Tea'

per lb. during 1708–12 to 4s. 10d. in 1745–47, and in the war years rose to only 5s. 5d., in spite of the new duty of five per cent imposed to defray the charges of the war'.[34] Tea entered for home consumption increased two and a half times from 1745 to 1775; in the latter year it amounted to over 6 million lb.[35]

Sugar prices, on the other hand, experienced a less than proportionate decline. From a retail price of about 1s 0d to 1s 6d per lb at the beginning of the 17th century, the level dropped to 6d per lb or less by the close of the century. During Queen Anne's War the retail price of ordinary sugar increased to about 1s per lb. After the war the price returned to the old level, remaining fairly steady at about 6d per lb from 1714 to 1756, after which it rose slightly. Throughout the period wholesale prices fluctuated more widely than retail prices. This was especially the case after the mid-1730s, when the wholesale level rose appreciably without much influence on retail prices. Since many more cups of tea were consumed at a relatively lower cost than the teaspoons of sugar which sweetened the brew, it seems reasonable to maintain that the demand for sugar was supported to a considerable extent by cheap and abundant tea.[36]

7 SUGAR REFINING IN GREAT BRITAIN

Besides tea drinking, Britain's sugar refining industry affords a measure of the rise in living standards and the refinement of taste. It is generally accepted that the first English sugar refinery was established in London about 1544. Slow and uneven growth characterized the industry during the 16th and most of the 17th centuries. After 1660, however, more refineries were needed to supply the home and overseas markets. In 1695, it was observed that the number of refining houses had grown from eight 'to near Thirty within this Twenty Years; and this chiefly by the Increase of Brown Sugar from our Plantations'. An estimated 5,000 tons of brown sugar were said to be refined annually at that time.[37]

More rapid expansion characterized the first three-quarters of the 18th century. Evidence relating to this expansion appears in a

---

34 Bal Krishna, *Commercial Relations between India and England 1601–1757* (London, 1927), pp. 195–6.
35 Phyllis Deane, and W. A. Cole, *British Economic Growth 1688–1959, Trends and Structure* (Cambridge, 1962), p. 355.
36 Schumpeter, *English Overseas Trade Statistics*, p. 60; John MacGregor, *Commercial Statistics* (London, 1850), vol. 5, p. 382; Appendix IV.
37 Anon., *The Case of the Refiners of Sugar in England, Stated* (London, 1695), single sheet

Sugar and Slavery

refiner's pamphlet of 1753. Approximately 120 refining houses were then operating in England and Scotland, of which eighty were situated in London and twenty in Bristol. People 'immediately concerned' in the industry were said to number 1,800. It was further 'proved that 3/4ths at least of the Muscovado Sugar imported from our Plantations are brought for refining here', and that '41,000 tons were imported last year'.[38] The upgrading of consumption patterns augmented the demand for raw sugar. Joseph Massie said that two pounds of muscovado sugar yielded one pound of the finest loaf sugar, 'and *Three* Pounds of *brown* [or muscovado] *Sugar* are to be reckoned for every *Two* Pounds of *Powder Sugar*, or of Sugar that is nearly white, the latter of which is called *Clayed Sugar*, because Clay is used in refining it'.[39]

8 CONSUMPTION AND POPULATION GROWTH

The demand thus increased because the average Englishman consumed larger quantities of a product that was improved by the refiner, but it also increased because there were more Englishmen. The population of England and Wales is estimated to have been 5,826,000 in 1701, 7,052,000 in 1771, and 9,156,000 in 1801. Stagnation during the first four decades of the century was followed by accelerated population growth from about 1740 to 1760 and again from 1780 onwards.[40]

Generally speaking, townsmen were heavier consumers of sugar than countrymen. London gained in relative population, but not very rapidly. Roughly one citizen out of every eleven in England and Wales was a Londoner at the time of the Plague and the Fire; the proportion was about one in ten in Defoe's day; and by the first census in 1801 it was one in nine. The growth was much more rapid in the seaport and industrial towns of Bristol, Manchester, Liverpool, Sheffield, Leeds, Halifax, Birmingham, and Coventry. Most of these towns were situated in Lancashire, the West Midlands, the West Riding, and Tyneside, where there was a marked population increase between 1714 and 1742. Daniel Defoe was impressed by the remarkable growth of Liverpool. He declared that on his first visit in 1680, it was 'a large, handsome, well built and encreasing or thriving

---

38 Anon., *An Account of the Late Application to Parliament, From the Sugar Refiners and Grocers of London, Westminster, Southwark, and Bristol* (London, 1753), pp. 42–5.
39 Joseph Massie, *A Computation of the Money that hath been exorbitantly Raised upon the People of Great Britain by the Sugar-Planters* (London, 1760), single sheet.
40 Deane and Cole, *British Economic Growth*, p. 6.

'Sugar, The Inseparable Companion of Tea'

town'; at his second visit in 1690, it was 'much bigger than at my first seeing it'; and at his third visit in 1726, it was 'more than double what it was at the second ... and it still visibly encreases both in wealth, people, business and buildings'.[41]

9 SCOTTISH AND IRISH MARKETS

At a time when the English market was expanding internally and absorbing greater quantities of sugar, a similar expansion was taking place in the British Isles market. After Scotland was joined to England and Wales by the Act of Union in 1707, substantial quantities of colonial sugar were channelled to that market. Annual imports averaged 68,154 cwt from 1771 to 1775.[42] The chief import centres were Port Glasgow and Greenock in the west, and Leith (the port of Edinburgh) and Dundee in the east. Within three years of the opening of Port Glasgow's trade with the West Indies in 1732, there were four vessels from that port trading to Jamaica, one to Barbados, one to Antigua, and two to St Christopher. To meet the growing demand, refineries were built along the Clyde. Glasgow boasted five such establishments by 1736.[43]

Edinburgh had become such an important market by 1751, that the Edinburgh Sugar-House Company was organized with an authorized capital stock of £10,000. The articles of co-partnership noted:

> that the Consumpt of SUGARS in the CITY of EDINBURGH, and the Neighbourhood thereof, is much increased; and that an Intercourse of Trade is now carried on between the Port of LEITH and the SUGAR-COLONIES in the BRITISH AMERICAN PLANTATIONS, whereby the Trade and MANUFACTURE of refining and baking SUGARS in EDINBURGH, or the Suburbs thereof, may be very beneficial....[44]

Other refineries were constructed at Port Glasgow, Aberdeen, and Dundee. By the eve of the American War of Independence at least ten such establishments were operating in Scotland.

The British Isles market was further augmented when British sugar planters gained a protected market for their commodities in Ireland. To a considerable extent the Molasses Act of 1733 diverted trade

---

41 Defoe, *Tour through England and Wales*, vol. 2, pp. 255–6; G. D. H. Cole, *Persons and Periods* (London, 1945), p. 64.
42 Henry Hamilton, *An Economic History of Scotland in the Eighteenth Century* (Oxford, 1963), p. 119, Appendix XI.
43 William F. MacArthur, *History of Port Glasgow* (Glasgow, 1932), pp. 69–71.
44 *Articles of the Sugar-Copartnery at Edinburgh* (Edinburgh, 1751), p. 1.

Table 2.3

Re-exports of British brown sugar to Ireland and to all other countries (annual averages in 000 cwt)

Years	To Ireland	To other countries	Total	Percentage to Ireland
1716–20	18.7	154.5	173.2	10.8
1728–32	34.1	116.9	151.0	22.6
1733–37	40.3	23.0	63.3	63.7
1748–52	58.9	27.4	86.3	68.3
1753–57	57.7	32.3	90.0	64.1
1773–74	156.2	48.7	204.9	76.2

Source: P.R.O., London. Treasury 64/273 (1); Treas. 276(B), (358), (359), (364), (365), (368), (385).

from France and her sugar colonies to Britain and her tropical dependencies. Table 2.3 shows that growing quantities of sugar were re-exported from Britain to Ireland. After observing that 'the Home Consumption of *Ireland* is greatly increased of late Years by the Increase of Refiners and Refining Houses', a mid-century pamphleteer concluded that 'the Consumption of Ireland may I think properly be called Home Consumption ....'.[45]

10 LONDON AND THE OUTPORTS

The tendency of Irish and Scottish markets to absorb sugar formerly re-exported to European markets helps to explain why London's import and re-export trade declined in relation to that of the outports. Bristol and Liverpool lost some of their coastal trade in sugar products when ports like Lancaster and Whitehaven began a direct trade with the West Indies. But this loss was probably counterbalanced by re-exports to Ireland and trade with such industrial towns as Manchester and Birmingham. London's share of all sugar imported into England and Wales declined from over four-fifths at

---

45 *Sugar Refiners and Grocers Application to Parliament*, p. 38; Sheffield, *Observations on Commerce*, p. 167.

the beginning of the 18th century to about two-thirds on the eve of the American Revolution.[46]

The Martin Papers point to other reasons for the shift from London to the outports, and especially to Liverpool. Samuel Martin, the Antigua planter, had begun to consign a growing proportion of his sugar to the Liverpool market by the early 1770s. On 5 February 1775, he informed his eldest son of his intention to consign one-half of his expected crop of 200 hogsheads to a merchant in Liverpool:

> The Liverpool Market is so much preferable to that of London, especially in regard to petty-charges, and the sale weights of Sugar, for there is no pilfering at Liverpool, the weight of the King's duty, and the Sale weights are the same, and the price generally better than London, as you will find evident by the Comparison of the Sales.[47]

In numerous letters Martin complained that his London consignments had been pilfered.

11 BRITISH NORTH AMERICAN MARKETS

Despite the widespread smuggling of foreign sugar products, not a little legally traded sugar entered the Thirteen Colonies from the British West Indies. Lacking continuous and comprehensive statistics, it is only possible to show the volume of trade for selected sugar colonies in selected years.

Tables 2.4 and 2.5 indicate that Barbados exported proportionately more sugar to North America than did Jamaica. Sugar exports went part way to pay for imported supplies of North American provisions, lumber, and horses, which were of relatively greater importance to tiny Barbados than to its capacious and less densely populated sister island.

12 CONCLUSION

The overwhelming importance of home consumption is evident from a summary view of the export markets of the British West Indies on the eve of the American Revolution. Great Britain and Ireland took about 94 per cent of total exports, while the remaining 6 per cent was almost evenly divided between the Thirteen Colonies and foreign markets.

46 P.R.O. London. Customs 3/1–4; Treasury 64/276(B), (385); British Museum Add. MSS 12,431, f. 139: C. E. Long, *Miscellaneous Papers Relating to Jamaica.*
47 *Martin L. B.*, vol. 6, f. 25: Lre. to Samuel Martin, Jr., 5 Feb. 1775.

Table 2.4

Sugar exports of Barbados
(annual averages in 000 cwt)

Years	To North America	To England	Total	Percent to North America
1745–48	7.1	122.6	129.7	5.5
1749–51	10.5	120.5	131.0	8.0
1763–67	30.2	169.5	199.7	15.1

Source: P.R.O., London. Treasury 64/276(B), (360), (361); George Frere, *A Short History of Barbadoes* (London, 1767), p. 114; Noel Deerr, *The History of Sugar* (London, 1949–50), vol. 1, p. 193.

Table 2.5

Sugar exports of Jamaica
(annual averages in 000 cwt)

Years	To North America	To England	Total	Percent to North America
1745–48	9.9	288.9	298.8	3.3
1749–51	16.3	393.8	410.1	4.0
1768	15.3	798.0	813.3	1.9
1773	31.2	1,017.1	1,048.3	3.0

Source: P.R.O., London. Treasury 64/274; 64/276(B), (360), (361); David MacPherson, *Annals of Commerce* (Edinburgh, 1805), vol. 3, p. 485; Noel Deerr, *The History of Sugar* (London, 1949–50), vol. 1, p. 193; Sir William Young, *The West-India Common-Place Book* (London, 1807), p. 15.

'Sugar, The Inseparable Companion of Tea'

Tropical and semi-tropical commodities made a significant impact on the social and economic life of the metropolis. Changing consumption patterns were related to the growth of wealth and income both as cause and effect. Most mercantile writers condemned the diversion of wealth to the consumption of sugar and tea. Edmund Burke, on the other hand, asserted that the luxury of his time, 'by being well balanced and diffused, is only decency and convenience, [and] has perhaps as many, or more, good than evil consequences attending it. It certainly excites industry, nourishes emulation, and inspires some sense of personal value into all ranks of people'.[48] Thomas Robert Malthus noted that in contrast to homely products, the accessibility of exotics provided people with incentives for additional expenditure of effort. 'The peasant, who might be induced to labour an additional number of hours for tea and tobacco, might prefer indolence to a new coat...'.[49] Similarly, John Kennedy, the cotton manufacturer, observed: 'Among the lower orders it may, I think, be safely affirmed, that industry can only be found, where artificial wants have crept in, and have acquired the character of necessities'.[50] Dr Elizabeth Gilboy has linked the extension and changing nature of demand to the thrust towards industrialism. She maintains that 'the factory could not become typical until demand had been extended and had become sufficiently flexible throughout the entire population to consume the products of large-scale industry. In other words, the Industrial Revolution presupposes a concomitant development and extension of consumption'.[51] But no such extension of consumption applied to the black slaves who produced the exotics that were consumed by Europeans.

---

48 Edmund Burke, *The Present State of the Nation* (1769), in *The Works of Edmund Burke*, ed. E. B. Willis (London, 1925), vol. 1, p. 357.
49 Thomas R. Malthus, *Principles of Political Economy*, 2nd ed. (London, 1951), p. 354.
50 John Kennedy in *Trans. Manchester Lit. and Phil. Soc.*, vol. 3, pp. 118–19. Quoted by H. L. Beales in *The Industrial Revolution 1750–1850 An Introductory Essay* (London, 1958), pp. 21–2.
51 Elizabeth B. Gilboy, 'Demand as a Factor in the Industrial Revolution', in *Facts and Factors in Economic History Articles by Former Students of Edwin Francis Gay* (Cambridge, Mass., 1932), p. 621.

CHAPTER THREE

The Hated Navigation Acts, 1650-1700

In former daies we were under the pleasing sound of Privileges and Immunities, of which a free Trade was one. Though we counted That, a Right and not a Privilege. But without such Encouragements, the Plantations had been still wild Woods. Now these things are vanisht and forgotten: and we hear of nothing but Taxes and Burdens. All the Care now is, to pare us close, and keep us low. We dread to be mention'd in an Act of Parliament; because it is always to do us Mischief.[1]

Edward Littleton, 1689

1 VIEWS ON THE NAVIGATION SYSTEM

Edmund Burke, in comparing the value of England's colonial trade in the years 1704 and 1767, was impressed by the fact that in the former year 'the whole trade of our plantations was but a few thousand pounds more in the export article, and a third less in the import, than that which we now carry on with the single island of Jamaica'. Burke was surprised to find that England's trade with most of the European nations had increased but little in the same period of time. 'This colony intercourse', he said, 'was a new world of commerce in a manner created; it stands upon principles of its own.... In this new system a principle of commerce, of artificial commerce, must predominate. This commerce must be secured by a multitude of restraints very alien from the spirit of liberty; and a powerful authority must reside in the principal state, in order to enforce them'.[2]

While Burke regarded the navigation system and its attendant monopoly of colonial trade as an essential bulwark of England's power and wealth, Adam Smith was of a contrary opinion. Like Burke, Smith called attention to the shifting theatre of overseas trade. 'Since the establishment of the act of navigation . . . the

---

1 Edward Littleton, *The Groans of the Plantations* (London, 1689), pp. 14–15.
2 Edmund Burke, *The Present State of the Nation* (1769), in *The Works of Edmund Burke*, ed. E. B. Willis (London, 1925), vol. 1, pp. 332–4.

The Hated Navigation Acts, 1650–1700

colony trade has been continually increasing, while many other branches of foreign trade, particularly of that to other parts of Europe, have been continually decaying'. But, unlike Burke, he regarded the monopoly of the colonial trade as pernicious. By raising the profit of colonial trade above that of other trades, the monopoly had served to attract an abnormal proportion of British capital to the plantations, at the same time that foreign capital was repulsed from that trade. The net effect, in Smith's view, was to raise 'the ordinary rate of British profit higher than it otherwise would have been both in that and in all other branches of British trade', and to subject Britain 'to an absolute and to a relative disadvantage in every branch of trade of which she has not the monopoly'.[3]

Adam Smith was undoubtedly right in assigning a key role to the Navigation Acts in changing the direction of Britain's overseas trade. Moreover, there is some logic in his argument that the monopoly, by raising profits in the colonial trade *vis-a-vis* other branches of trade, served to draw British capital into colonies producing exportable staples. But it may be doubted if this drain of capital was a persistent feature of colonial production and trade. Admittedly, some British capital was needed to plant the colonies, to tide the settlers over the difficult period when they were searching for staples that would give them a basis for trade with the metropolis. But it is by no means certain that this draft of capital continued much beyond the initial period, or that British capital was of more significance than Dutch capital. Rather, it is the burden of this study that the initial capital was re-invested, that the sugar industry not only came to be self-financing, but also yielded additional wealth to be channelled back to the mother country. If some wealth went out and much more returned in the century or more of West India ascendancy in Britain's overseas trade, it will be necessary to regard the colonial system as a means of wealth acquisition. In other words, it was a forced-draft system of capital imports instead of a drain on the resources of the metropolis.

2 OUSTING THE DUTCH

England's efforts to redirect her overseas trade and tap the new source of tropical wealth was undertaken in the face of formidable obstacles. Spain and Portugal, on the basis of prior discovery, had staked out claims to all the New World and posted warning signs

---

3 Adam Smitn, *An Enquiry into the Nature and Causes of the Wealth of Nations* (New York, 1937), pp. 563–5.

Sugar and Slavery

against interlopers. To be sure, the Iberian nations claimed more than they could possibly defend. By the early years of the 17th century territorial encroachment by rival powers had already commenced. Initially, the newcomers in the New World treasure hunt submerged their differences and formed alliances against the Iberian powers. In time, however, the newcomers began to quarrel among themselves. Thus we see a series of wars for empire, first the northern nations against the Iberian powers, then a sundering of ties and a free fight for the New World.

The 16th century was the age of the Elizabethan sea dogs, of Drake and the capture of a Spanish treasure fleet, of Hawkins and the beginning of the African slave trade, of Raleigh and his unsuccessful efforts to plant a colony in Guyana. The lure of Spanish treasure continued into the next century, as witness the exploits of buccaneers and privateers, of Cromwell's Western Design, described by Professor Gardiner as 'a reversion to the Elizabethan gold hunt, as opposed to the agricultural and commercial settlements of more recent years'.[4] But colonies of settlement and tropical agriculture had already made substantial progress by 1655, the year Jamaica was captured from Spain. In fact, the sugar revolution of the 1640s and 1650s had already brought the Lesser Antilles into the commercial orbit of the metropolitan nations in north-western Europe. Thus the search for precious metals gradually gave way to the belief that colonies would supply commodities which England drew from other countries and in course of time convert adverse trade balances with rival European nations into favourable balances with overseas dependencies.

The Dutch played a paramount role in the Caribbean sugar revolution. Their extraordinary commercial success antagonized the middlemen of rival nations whose jealousy knew no bounds. Especially frustrating was the fact that greater capital resources and superior maritime and commercial facilities enabled Dutch traders to outbid their rivals in the West India trade. But the merchants of England and France were unwilling to wait for long-term adjustments to improve their competitive position. Instead, they appealed to their governments to oust the foreigner. Most vulnerable were the Dutchmen who had made incursions into the carrying trade of rival colonial empires. Lacking the white manpower to settle plantation colonies of their own, they needed access to the colonies of other nations. English and French merchants thus planned to attack the Dutch at their weakest point.

[4] S. R. Gardiner, *History of the Commonwealth and Protectorate* (London, 1903), vol. 3, p. 344.

The Hated Navigation Acts, 1650-1700

The middle years of the 17th century ushered in a period of economic nationalism. This was in large measure a struggle between the middlemen of rival European nations. Middlemen in countries other than Holland justified restrictions on colonial trade by pointing to the advantages that would accrue to their governments and national economies. Generally speaking, governments were easily convinced of the merits of such restrictions, for the sugar trade was one of the new trades of the period. Had similar proposals been made with respect to established trades, vested interests might have charged the middlemen with profiting at their expense, thus inviting the government to step in to mediate the differences. This was hardly the case with the sugar trade because middlemen could virtually promise something for everybody. Home manufacturers might be assured of new markets; shipowners and operators of additional freights; planters of a monopoly of the home market for their sugar products; and middlemen and investors of commissions, profits and interest. Moreover, the expanded merchant marine would provide sailors for the navy, the government would receive revenue from sugar duties, the home refining industry would be stimulated, and, in short, an exclusive trade in colonial products would add to the wealth and prestige of the nation.

Paradoxically, the English middlemen aimed their first blow at their own countrymen in the colonies, and only indirectly at Dutch middlemen. Their opportunity came during the Commonwealth period when the inhabitants of Barbados, Antigua, Bermuda, and Virginia remained loyal to the cause of Charles I, and when Dutchmen dominated the trade of the English colonies. London merchants seized this opportunity to urge the Council of State to put an embargo on the trade of the Caribbean islands and to dispatch warships to defeat the Royalist cause there. Cromwell not only acceded to the merchants' plea on grounds of commercial advantage, but also because he feared that the West Indies might afford a haven of refuge for Prince Rupert and his Royalist privateers. Declaring these colonists to be 'Notorious Robbers and Traytors', Parliament in 1650 forbade and prohibited 'All Ships of Any Foreign Nation whatsoever to come to, or Trade in, or Traffique with any of the English Plantations in America... without Licence first had and obtained from the Parliament or Councel of State....'.[5]

The first missile aimed at the Dutch was thus a blanket prohibition

---

5 J. A. Williamson, *The Caribbee Islands Under the Proprietary Patents* (Oxford, 1926), pp. 131–3; 'An Act Prohibiting Trade with Barbada's, Virginia, Bermuda's and Antego', 3 Oct. 1650. Reprinted in *Caribbeana, Being Miscellaneous Papers Relating to the British West Indies*, ed. Vere L. Oliver (London, 1916), vol. 4, pp. 171–3.

of unlicensed trade which penalized producing and commercial interests both within and without the British Empire. However, subsequent parliamentary measures of the Commonwealth and Restoration governments were intended to encourage English middlemen, shipowners, and manufacturers without ostensibly penalizing colonial producing interests. Commercial monopoly, it is true, continued to be the leading principle of colonial intercourse, but monopoly combined with regulation in an effort to encourage colonial production and trade and placate divergent economic interests.

3 THE MERCANTILE THEORY OF COLONIES

Mercantile theorists believed that national power depended upon national wealth, and that the planting of colonies and the enforcement of an exclusive trade between the mother country and her colonies were essential means to achieve these twin goals of statecraft. The colonial system was designed to link the New World frontier to the metropolis of western Europe. Trade should be established with outlying regions having resource endowments and climates which differed markedly from those of Europe. For reasons already discussed, these links were established more closely with the slave-plantation colonies in tropical and semi-tropical portions of the New World than they were with temperate-zone colonies.

Of what did these linkages consist? Professor Nettels has written that, insofar as there was a general economic theory of colonization, it did not change from the beginning of settlement to the American Revolution.

> In essence it was simple and consistent. The colonists should buy English goods, paying for them with products which England needed. The trade should employ English merchants and vessels, thereby providing freights, profits, and interests. These were the three pillars of colonial policy designed to support the mercantilist edifice of state security and private profit. Each pillar was necessary to the other; all were mutually supplementary; had any one of them been pulled down, the whole structure would have been toppled to the ground.[6]

Furthermore, Nettels maintains that the mercantilists' concern with commodity exports and imports, the balance of trade, and bullion movements has obscured the role played by profits in colonial trade, that is, the invisible items of insurance, freights, commissions, and

---

6 Curtis P. Nettels 'The Place of Markets in the Old Colonial System', *The New England Quarterly*, vol. VI (Sept. 1933), pp. 509–10.

The Hated Navigation Acts, 1650–1700

interest on invested capital. 'These could be obtained more easily if the colonists had to buy and sell only through England, and if all foreign vessels were excluded from colonial trade'.[7]

So far it has been assumed that the colonial system was designed to regulate the reciprocal trade between England and her colonies. But this is to oversimplify the matter. In practice, the West Indies were linked both formally and informally, to North America, Central and South America, and Africa, as well as to the British Isles. Some of the sugar islands, particularly Barbados and Jamaica, were highly regarded as entrepôts for trade with the Spanish and other foreign colonies. Attempts to confine metropolitan trade to a given colony would have jeopardized the entrepôt trade, thus narrowing the markets for English manufactures and African slaves. We shall see that the Navigation Acts were later relaxed in the interest of the entrepôt trade.[8]

4 THE NAVIGATION ACTS

Five different classes of restrictions were imposed by England on trade with her American and West India colonies:
1. Restrictions on the exportation of produce from the colony elsewhere than to the mother country.
2. Restrictions on the importation of goods into the colony from foreign countries.
3. Restrictions on the importation of colonial produce into the mother country from foreign countries or colonies.
4. Restrictions on the carriage of goods to and from the colonies in other shipping than that of the mother country.
5. Restrictions on the manufacture of their own raw produce by the colonists.[9]

We have seen that England first attempted to restrict the trade of her sugar colonies in 1650, when foreign and other unlicensed vessels were prohibited from the colonial trade. More detailed restrictions and regulations were embodied in the famous Navigation Acts of 1651 and 1660, the Tariff of 1661, and the Staple Act of 1663.

The Act of 1651 went only part way to satisfy the five classes of restrictions. As applied to the West India trade, no colonial produce was to be imported into England, Ireland, or other colonies except in

7 Ibid., p. 497.
8 See Chapter 14, pp. 316–19.
9 Herman Merivale, *Lectures on Colonization and Colonies delivered before the University of Oxford in 1839, 1840, and 1841* (London, 1928), p. 193.

ships owned, and for the most part manned, by Englishmen, including colonials. Conversely, no European goods could be imported into the colonies except in English ships, or in ships belonging to the country where the goods were produced or to the port of usual first shipment. Colonial trade was not confined to England, for by this statute it was possible for the colonies to send their produce to the Continent or elsewhere and get manufactures directly from the countries of origin.[10]

The first class of restrictions was imposed by the Navigation Act of 1660, which required the importation of certain plantation commodities into England before they could be re-exported to foreign markets. Commodities which were marketable in Europe and did not compete directly with the productions of the mother country were subject to this regulation. The 'enumerated' commodities consisted of sugar, tobacco, cotton-wool, indigo, ginger, and fustic or dying woods. They had to be shipped to England, Ireland, Wales, Berwick, or other English plantations. Bond security was required from masters of vessels engaged in the plantation trades and the penalty for infraction was loss of both ship and cargo. The channelling of sugar through England was intended to swell the profits of middlemen, encourage home refiners, and increase freight and customs revenues.[11]

Prohibition of colonial imports from foreign countries, the second class of restrictions, was provided for by the Staple Act of 1663. It specified that all colonial imports, except wine and salt from southern Europe and horses and victuals from Ireland and Scotland, had to come from England or her other colonies. The preamble to the Act said that it was intended to make 'this kingdom a staple, not only of the commodities of the plantations, but also of the commodities of other countries and places for the supply of them, it being the usage of other nations to keep their plantation trade to themselves'. Although foreign goods were not barred from the colonies, they had to come by way of England where duties were levied which were in part drawn back on re-export. English manufactures thus received preferential treatment in colonial markets, crown revenues were increased, and the profits of English middlemen and shippers were enhanced.[12]

10 J. E. Farnell, 'The Navigation Act of 1651, The First Dutch War and the London Merchant Community', *The Economic History Review*, 2nd ser., vol. XVI, no. 3 (April 1964), pp. 439–54.
11 Lawrence A. Harper, *The English Navigation Laws* (New York, 1939), pp. 34–62; George L. Beer, *The Old Colonial System 1660–1754* (New York, 1912), vol. 1, p. 72.
12 Beer, *Old Colonial System*, vol. 1, p. 76–9; Harper, *English Navigation Laws*, pp. 59–60.

The Hated Navigation Acts, 1650-1700

A system of preferential duties was the means by which the third class of restrictions on the importation of colonial produce into the mother country from foreign countries or colonies was enforced. Colonial sugar received preferential treatment in English markets by the Tariff of 1661. It provided for a duty of 1s 5d per cwt on raw or muscovado sugar from the colonies, while the foreign product had to pay 3s 10d. Furthermore, colonial clayed sugar paid 4s 9d per cwt, while the foreign product paid 7s 0d. English refiners were afforded protection by a duty of 16s 1d per cwt on the import of foreign refined sugars.[13]

Colonial shipping, the subject of the fourth class of restrictions, was regulated by three Acts of Trade. By the Act of 1650, unlicensed vessels were barred from the colonies. The statute of the following year provided that no European goods could be imported into the colonies, except in English ships, or in such as belonged to the place of production or to the port whence they were usually shipped. The famous Navigation Act of 1660 superseded the previously enacted measures. It required all trade between England and her colonies to be carried in English (or colonial) ships with crews at least three-fourths Englishmen (or colonists). Except for specified emergencies, all foreign vessels were barred from colonial ports.[14]

The fifth class of restrictions on the manufacture of raw produce in the colonies was enforced by laying heavy duties on colonial refined sugar. In addition to encouraging home refiners, this restriction was designed to benefit English shipowners. Contemporaries estimated that raw sugar was reduced in bulk from about one-fourth to one-half in the refining process, which obviously meant a considerable reduction in freight revenue if sugar was refined in the colonies. Writing in 1695, a pamphleteer asserted that 'More than double the number of Ships are required, to Import Sugars Brown, than if Clay's and White'. A few years later Thomas Tryon repeated a favourite maxim of the mercantilists: 'It is the great quantities of Bulksom Commodities, that multiplies Ships and Men, and that pays the King most Customs'.[15]

Restrictions on colonial refining thus benefited home refiners and shippers at the expense of producers and consumers. Raw sugar not only cost proportionately more to bring home than the refined product, but it also wasted on the long voyage to England. Bryan Edwards ventured to fix the loss, 'on the average of good and bad

---

13 Beer, *Old Colonial System*, vol. 1 p. 134.
14 George L. Beer, *The Origins of the British Colonial System 1578-1660* (New York, 1922), p. 385; Beer, *Old Colonial System*, vol. 1, p. 65.
15 Thomas Tryon, *England's Grandeur, and Way to Get Wealth* (London, 1699), p. 22.

sugar, at one-eighth part: in other words, a hogshead of sugar weighing nett 16 cwt when shipped in Jamaica, shall, when sold in London be found to weigh 14 cwt only'.[16]

5 THE PLANTERS' DISCONTENT

While the merchants of the metropolis probably found few reasons to quarrel with the Acts of Trade and Navigation, the planters found them a source of irritation and discontent. Numerous petitions, memorials, and letters were addressed to the home government, complaining of the harmful effects of the Navigation Acts. Planters claimed that free trade with the Dutch had been responsible for their former prosperity. They felt constrained by the strait-jacket of the Navigation Acts which forced them to trade with English merchants who reportedly charged high prices for manufactures and slaves, refused to grant long-term credit, and paid low prices for sugar products. The inhabitants of Antigua, Montserrat, and St Christopher petitioned Governor Willoughby in 1664, 'That he will represent to the King the hard pressure and disadvantages which they suffer, and their humble request for a grant of free trade'. The Governor complied with the request and wrote to the King of 'the heavy and insupportable pressures they groan under by the restraint laid upon them in their trade by the two Acts of Parliament, for the increase of Shipping and Navigation'.[17]

Planters' memorials and petitions apparently made little impression on the English government. Though ostensibly intended to benefit all groups engaged in the sugar industry, the Navigation Acts tended to favour English shippers, middlemen, and refiners whose interests were well represented in the House of Commons. On the other hand, the planters had few spokesmen in the Commonwealth and Restoration governments.[18]

6 THE PLANTERS' RESPONSE

The planters' response to the navigation system was shaped by their appraisal of market opportunities. If the bulk of the colonial sugar

---

16 Bryan Edwards, *The History, Civil and Commercial, of the British Colonies in the West Indies* (London, 1801), vol. 2, pp. 571–2.
17 *Cal. S. P. Col. 1661–68*, p. 234.
18 Lillian M. Penson, *The Colonial Agents of the British West India Islands from their First Appointment to the Close of the Eighteenth Century.* Unpublished Ph.D. dissertation, University of London, 1921, pp. 244–5.

was re-exported to more profitable foreign markets, they might be expected to exploit loopholes and inconsistencies in the regulations and possibly resort to illegal circumvention. Since several European nations held Caribbean islands in close proximity to one another, onerous restrictions could be expected to encourage illicit inter-island intercourse. Such a trade would be preferred to illicit overseas trade because small vessels might run into out of the way harbours under cover of darkness and run little risk of detection. Even if seized for violating the Acts of Trade, the loss of a small vessel would be negligible compared with that of a large ship. Planters might also reduce the risk of detection by bribing colonial governors and customs officials, and by gaining control of colonial assemblies, councils, and courts so that the Acts of Trade would not be enforced.

If, on the other hand, the home market took off the bulk of the colonial commodity at prices higher than those prevailing elsewhere, the planters might seek to obtain maximum profits by supporting measures to enforce the Navigation Acts. Attempts to smuggle foreign sugar into the home market might then be opposed. Furthermore, planters might sponsor parliamentary legislation to expand the market in which their commodities were protected against the competition of foreign sugar and thus attempt to raise the price in the home market.

The interesting thing is that a shift was made from the former to the latter type of market situation. Closely related to the shift were changes in the planters' attitude and response to the Navigation Acts. From 1650 until about the end of the 17th century, between one-half and two-thirds of the sugar imported into England from the colonies was re-exported to foreign markets. The re-export of such a large proportion of the colonial output tended to keep English prices in line with those on the Continent. English planters were thus encouraged to circumvent the Navigation Acts by shipping sugar directly to foreign markets. By this means they were able to save the burdensome costs of landing sugar in England and paying the duties.

The British re-export trade fell off markedly in the early decades of the 18th century. Except for the war years, re-exports continued to decline. Indeed, only about 5 per cent of the colonial imports were re-exported to markets other than Ireland in the period from 1740 to 1775. British demand tended to run ahead of the supply, forcing prices upward at a time when foreign sugar was kept out of the home market by prohibitive duties. Moreover, prices in the mother country appear to have been somewhat higher than those prevailing on the Continent. British planters thus came to prefer the

Sugar and Slavery

home to foreign markets; they had a vested interest in enforcing and expanding the scope of the Navigation Acts.

Planters were tempted to evade the Navigation Acts in order to maximize profits during the second half of the 17th century. Though a few large ships continued to trade between Holland and the Lesser Antilles in the 1650s and 1660s, stricter enforcement brought this trade almost to a standstill by the early 1670s. In the meantime the Dutch had stocked their tiny and strategically located islands of St Eustatius and Saba with slaves and manufactures and had begun their notorious clandestine trade with the English and French planters. Sir Thomas Lynch wrote from Nevis in 1671 that 'most of the produce of that island and Antigua was carried to Statia [St Eustatius] by the Dutch'.[19] Some 1,500 hogsheads of Leeward Island sugar annually went out the 'Back door for *Holland*, under the name of *St Eustace Sugar*,' according to Sir Dalby Thomas. Leeward Islanders were willing to sell sugar to the Dutch at low prices, 'for those people saving all the Duty as well as the 4½ *per cent* there, as the Customs in *England*, and having Goods in Barter for them directly from *Holland,* can afford their Sugar much Cheaper than their Neighbors'.[20]

Planters also encouraged traders from North America, Ireland, and Scotland to circumvent the Navigation Acts by carrying their produce to foreign markets without first landing it in England and paying the duties. Colonial sugars which reached European markets by way of England were loaded with duties, only one-half of the import duty being drawn back on re-export before 1685. Furthermore, the charges of landing and re-shipment placed the law-abiding English merchant at a serious disadvantage as long as planters encouraged Dutch, North American, Irish, and Scottish traders to circumvent the Acts of Trade.[21]

Another way to evade commercial restrictions was to encourage merchants with foreign trading connections to settle in the colonies. Numerous Sephardic Jews settled in Holland and the English and French West Indies after they were driven out of Brazil. The planters and English merchants of Barbados became involved in a controversy over the desirability of giving Jewish merchants freedom to trade under the Navigation Acts. The planters argued that 'the admission of Jews or any other accession of free trade will tend exceedingly to the advantage of the Colonies, and consequently to his Majesty and trade ... the [English] merchants principally aim at appropriating

---

19 *Cal. S. P. Col. 1669–74*, p. 226.
20 Sir Dalby Thomas, *An Historical Account of the Rise and Growth of the West-India Collonies* (London, 1690), p. 44.
21 Harper, *English Navigation Laws*, p. 245.

the whole trade and necessitating the planter to accept any price they think fitt'.[22] Local English merchants and factors who opposed the Jews complained that Governor Willoughby 'has countenanced Jews who have become very numerous and engrossed the greatest part of the trade of the island to the great discouragement of the English merchants, their dealings being principally with those of their own tribe in Holland'.[23]

In 1671, a petition 'of divers merchants against the Jews' was sent to England by Lieutenant-Governor Lynch of Jamaica. In a letter accompanying the petition the Governor wrote that in his opinion, 'his Majesty cannot have more profitable subjects than they and the Hollanders, for they have great stocks and correspondence; are not numerous enough to supplant us, nor is it in their interest to betray us. Cannot find any but Jews that will adventure their goods or persons to get a trade'.[24]

Although governors and other officials were charged with enforcing the navigation code, they often sided with planters and overlooked infractions of the laws. Adhesion to the planter cause was frequently secured by means of supplementary salary grants, ranging from a few hundred to several thousand pounds per annum, which were voted to governors by island assemblies.

Two 17th century Governors General of Barbados, Lord Willoughby and Sir Jonathan Atkins, complained of the harmful effects of the Navigation Acts. Willoughby openly asserted in 1666: 'Free Trade is the life of all Colonies. . . . Whoever he be that advised his Majesty to restrain and tie up his Colonies in points of trade is more a merchant than a good subject, and would have his Majesty's Island be nursed up to work for him and such men'.[25] Governor Atkins was reprimanded by the Lords of Trade in 1675 for 'these dangerous principles which he entertains contrary to the settled laws of the Kingdom and the apparent advantage of it'.[26]

Official correspondence indicates that the Leeward Island governors were particularly negligent in enforcing the Navigation Acts. In September 1668, the Treasury Lords received information 'concerning the Governor of Antigua's admitting the Dutch and French to trade at that Island to the great prejudice of the navigation and trade and custom of this kingdom'. Admonitions apparently had little effect if the following royal letter of 1681 is a fair sample: 'We

---

22 *Cal. S. P. Col. 1661–68*, p. 47.
23 Ibid., p. 295.
24 Ibid., *1669–74*, p. 298.
25 Quoted in H. E. Egerton, *A Short History of British Colonial Policy*, 5th ed. (London, 1918), p. 76.
26 *Cal. S. P. Col. 1675–76, Appendix 1574–1674*, p. 368.

are well informed that the Plantation laws have been worse observed in the islands under your command and especially in Antigua than in any other of our colonies. You are to take more care for the future'.[27]

Governor Parke was one of the Leeward Island governors who maintained that he was diligent in enforcing the Acts of Trade. The planters, however, accused him of engaging in illicit trade on his own account. Parke wrote in February 1709, that he was offered bribes 'to wink at clandestine trade, and that if £5,000 would procure his removal the planters would freely give it'.[28]

7 THE EXPORT DUTY

Besides the Navigation Acts, planters evaded the 4½ per cent duty on the export of all dead commodities from Barbados and the Leeward Islands. The transition from proprietary to crown government was the occasion for this Act. English dependencies in the Lesser Antilles were originally granted to Lord Carlisle, who levied a poll tax on the inhabitants. When Carlisle lost his patent and the islands became crown colonies in 1661, the English government saw a need for a permanent revenue to defray civil and military expenditures. In exchange for abolishing the poll tax and having defective and uncertain land titles guaranteed, the Assembly of Barbados passed the 4½ per cent Duty Act in 1663. A year later similar acts were passed in the four Leeward Islands. The duty was first collected and appropriated by island governments. However, in 1670 the English government farmed the duty for a period of seven years, the revenue then being sent to England where authorized appropriations were made for the colonies.[29]

Planters chafed under the heavy burden of the 4½ per cent duty. Ingenious means were found to defraud the local collectors who were appointed by the farmers. In 1672, the farmers reported that the Barbadian officials had 'shown so great neglect in aiding such farmers that many have been encouraged to defraud them'.[30] Barbadian planters whose estates bordered the sea were reported to have built wharves and landing places to facilitate the shipment of their sugar without paying the duty. Vessels were frequently loaded at obscure bays and harbours. In Antigua, where there were several good

27 *Cal. Treas. Books 1667–68,* vol. II, pp. 439–40; Ibid. *1681–85,* vol. VII, pt. I, p. 67.
28 *Cal. Treas. Papers 1708–14,* p. 97.
29 *Cal. Treas. Books 1669–72,* vol. III, p. 1217; Ibid. *1681–85,* vol. VII, p. 512; Beer, *Old Colonial System,* vol. I, pp. 174–9.
30 Ibid. *1669–72,* vol. III, p. 1217; Ibid. *1676–79,* vol. V, p. 16.

harbours, the collectors complained that large quantities of sugar escaped the duty. The duty was collected on the average weight of a cask of sugar after allowing for the tare. But the planters reportedly increased the size of their casks and refused to allow the collectors to weigh each cask separately. One of the farmers reported that about one-fifth part of the duty on muscovado sugar was lost for want of weighing.[31]

After the disappointing returns of the farmers, the Commissioners of the Customs took over the collection of the 4½ per cent duty in 1684. Though difficult to assess, the extent of fraud under the new system was apparently quite extensive.[32]

Robert Dinwiddie, Surveyor General of Customs, reported in 1743 that the customs collectors of Barbados were guilty of great frauds and neglect. For the period from Christmas 1734 to Christmas 1738, he compared the sugar charged with the export duty in Barbados with that imported legally into England from the same island and found that 'the said imports exceeded said exports by 29,787 hogsheads, this being therefore the quantity that has escaped paying duty in the island. By the like comparison for 12 years the difference amounts to 126,800 hogsheads'. Furthermore, he found that at least half of all the sugar made in Barbados was improved or clayed, but that the 'collectors had accounted to the Crown for only a sixth part thereof as improved or clayed sugar. The fraud on this head in four years amounts to 9,356 *l*'.[33]

8 EFFORTS TO CLOSE THE LOOPHOLES

Planter evasion of the Navigation Acts and the export duty evoked reaction from England. Parliament was moved to pass three laws to close loopholes in the Acts of Trade. First, the Staple Act of 1663 prohibited direct trade from the Continent of Europe to the English colonies. Moreover, it limited Irish exports to the English plantations to servants, horses, and provisions. Second, the Act of 1671 required sugar and other enumerated commodities to be landed in England before they could be re-exported to Ireland. Third, export duties were levied on all enumerated commodities transported from one English colony to another by the Act of 1673. The 'Plantation Duty', which was equal to the duty on colonial sugar imported into England, was intended to prevent North Americans from carrying

---

31 Ibid., *1676–79*, vol. V, pt. I, p. 16; Ibid. *1681–85*, vol. VII, pt. II, p. 1327; Ibid. *1685–89*, vol. VIII, p. 100.
32 Beer, *Old Colonial System*, vol. I, pp. 188–92.
33 *Cal. Treas. Books and Papers 1742–45*, p. 270.

Sugar and Slavery

English plantation sugar to Europe without first landing it in England. About the same time Scottish ships were virtually excluded from colonial trade, and the provisions of the Navigation Act of 1660 with respect to bonds were enforced more strictly.[34]

It may be doubted if these measures proved very effective in confining colonial trade to legal channels. Besides clandestine inter-island trade which was very difficult to curb, the North American traders carried on a ramified trade in disregard of the Navigation Acts. By the last quarter of the 17th century New England had become the focus of a variety of trades. Already in 1676 a group of English merchants objected to the trade,

> whereby all sorts of merchandise of the produce of Europe are imported directly into New England, and thence carried to all of the other of the king's dominions in America, and sold at far cheaper rates than any that can be sent from hence, and that they take in exchange the commodities of the Plantations which are transported to Europe without coming to England, so that New England is become the great mart and staple, by which means the navigation of the kingdom is greatly prejudiced, the king's revenue lessened, trade decreased, and the king's subjects much improverished.[35]

New England was thus coming forward as a rival sub-metropolis to the mother country itself.

9 THE SUGAR DUTIES IN ENGLAND

To the question of trade restrictions and regulations was added that of the duties levied on sugar products imported into England. It was customary for the interests engaged in the sugar industry to join together to oppose higher duties. But when the government had a majority favouring such a measure, producers, shippers, traders, and processors separated into individual or group interests in an effort to shift the duty to one another.

English middlemen wanted to buy cheap and sell dear, regardless of sources of supply and markets. They hoped to exploit their legally sanctioned rights as monopolists and monopsonists in colonial markets. But as profit opportunities in these markets varied, they regarded the formal empire in the West Indies as a base for the expansion of trade to foreign colonies in the region. They might be expected to oppose any increase of import duties on colonial sugar

---

34 Beer, *Old Colonial System*, vol. I, pp. 57–76, 81, 89–90; A. P. Thornton, *West-India Policy Under the Restoration* (Oxford, 1956), pp. 161–6.
35 *Cal. S. P. Col. 1675–76*, p. 337.

and to favour a full drawback of duties to stimulate re-exports. If additional duties could not be defeated, middlemen might be expected to favour laying them on foreign sugar products. Finally, they might find it advantageous to support measures which would enable them to import and re-export the products of foreign colonies at nominal duties through a system of free ports in the colonies and bonded warehouses in the metropolis.

The carriage of bulky raw sugar was said to give maximum freight revenue, so the English shipowner might be expected to throw the whole burden of additional duties on clayed and refined sugars from the colonies and foreign countries. Moreover, he would oppose any attempt to reduce the drawback on the re-export of the raw product as well as proposals to levy prohibitive duties on the import of foreign raw sugar into the mother country.

English refiners hoped to adjust the duties to be assured of a cheap and abundant supply of raw sugar, achieve a monopoly of the home market for their refined product, and acquire easy access to foreign markets. To ensure an abundant supply of raw sugar, refiners would oppose any attempt to increase the duty on colonial and foreign raw sugar. Moreover, they would favour prohibitive duties on the re-export of raw sugar. If unopposed, refiners would probably lay the full additional duty on the import of foreign and colonial refined and clayed sugar, and maximize re-exports by supporting a full drawback of duties on the refined product of the mother country.

If the duty had to be raised, planters argued that it should be imposed on foreign sugar so as to give the colonial product preferential treatment in the home market. Further, they would resist attempts to reduce the drawback of duties on re-exported sugar, especially in its raw state. Since it was generally profitable to refine sugar in the colonies, planters would oppose measures to discriminate against their refined product in the home market.

Obviously, no interest gained all of its objectives. Compromise was the general rule in the hurly-burly of English politics.

The first additional Sugar Duty Bill was introduced into Parliament in 1671, at a time when King Charles's government was approaching a state of insolvency. On 1 May of that year the Gentlemen Planters in London wrote to the Assembly of Barbados that 'the refiners had brought sugar on the stage, thinking by their interest in the House to get the tax so proportioned so as to prevent the planters from making any improvement by sun-drying, claying, etc., and encouraged by the Barbadoes merchants, they dispersed the enclosed papers amongst the members of the House'.[36] The letter

36 Ibid. *1669–74*, p. 213.

Sugar and Slavery

went on to urge the Barbadians to pass a local law making improved sugar acceptable in payment of debts. It was hoped that such a law would enhance the profits of traders who were concerned in the improved product and 'separate the merchants' interest from the refiners', who, united may prove too powerful should Parliament at their next sitting think of laying an imposition upon sugar'. The issue was unresolved, however, for Parliament was prorogued while the Bill was still in debate.[37]

The question of duties did not arise again until 1685, when Parliament laid additional duties on colonial and foreign sugar products. The additional duty of 2s 4d per cwt on colonial muscovado or raw sugar, and 7s 0d per cwt on clayed sugar drew recrimination from the planters. 'You will find', wrote Edward Littleton, the Barbadian planter, 'that as the Old Duties upon Sugar did *fleece us*, so the Addition of the New doth *fley us*'.[38] Planters were partly compensated, however, by other provisions of the Act. Proportionately heavier duties were imposed on imported foreign sugar, and the drawback was increased on the re-export of raw sugar from the colonies. Refiners complained that the drawback had stimulated the re-export trade to the great advantage of Continental refiners. The Act of 1685 benefited English refiners, on the other hand, since it increased the duty on clayed sugar from the colonies.[39]

When Parliament was debating the Bill in 1685, a pamphleteer wrote that the King gave assurance that if the duty 'was found to fall upon the Planters, he would forbear to Collect it; and at the next Meeting of Parliament, exchange it for some other Revenue'.[40] The Barbadians seized this opportunity and issued pamphlet after pamphlet to demonstrate that the duty was borne by the planters rather than by English consumers. Largely as a result of this agitation, the additional duty of 1685 was not continued after 1693, as was the proportionately higher duty on tobacco.[41]

Two additional duties were imposed on muscovado sugar in 1698 and 1705, the former amounting to 1s 5d per cwt and the latter to 6d. When these two duties were added to the tariff of 1661, the total import duty amounted to 3s 4d, of which all but 8d was drawn back on re-export. Even more burdensome to planters were the additional duties on clayed sugar which raised the total levy to 9s 6d in 1698,

---

37 *Cal. S. P. Col. 1669–74*, p. 213.
38 Littleton, *Groans of Plantations*, p. 1.
39 Beer, *Old Colonial System*, vol. 1 pp. 159–69.
40 Anon., *The Case of their Majesties Sugar Plantations* (London, ca. 1695).
41 Beer, *Old Colonial System*, vol. 1. pp. 159–69.

The Hated Navigation Acts, 1650–1700

and to 11s 1d in 1705. Planters had been encouraged to clay their sugar by the tariff of 1661, largely because this Act was interpreted in such a manner that clayed sugar paid the same duty as raw sugar, 1s 5d. This interpretation was changed in the early 1680s, when the clayed product began to pay the same duty as refined sugar, 4s 9d. Planters raised strong objections to this ruling, especially after the additional duties came into effect.[42]

Conflicts of the nature described above probably masked an even more significant aspect of the sugar duty question. Until the late years of the 17th century, the duties were not high enough to prevent the import of foreign sugar into England. However, in 1698 and 1705, foreign rates were increased in proportion to colonial rates so that the foreign product was virtually excluded from the home market during the greater part of the 18th century. Expressed as percentages of the duty on colonial muscovado sugar, the foreign product paid 200 per cent in 1661, 268 in 1698, and 342 in 1705.[43]

10 CONCLUSION

It has been the contention of this chapter that West India planters attempted to obtain maximum profits by evading and violating the Navigation Acts. Foreign markets were generally more profitable than the home market, but for English sugar to compete abroad it had to by-pass the home market so as to avoid duties and handling charges. English sugar was therefore channelled to foreign markets by way of North America, the Dutch West Indies, and to a lesser extent Ireland and Scotland. While the home government passed laws to close loopholes and enforce the Acts of Trade and Navigation, planters adopted a cavalier attitude toward these measures. As a consequence, considerable quantities of sugar reached foreign markets without first being landed in England. On the other hand, rising duties on foreign sugar led to the creation of a protected home market which, given a demand potential greater than the productive capacity of the colonies, promised to reverse the market preference of English sugar planters.

---

42 John Oldmixon, *The British Empire in America* (London, 1708), vol. 2, p. 166.
43 Noel Deerr, *The History of Sugar* (London, 1949–50), vol. 2, pp. 427–30; Frank W. Pitman, *The Development of the British West Indies 1700–1763* (New Haven, 1917), p. 175.

CHAPTER FOUR

Planter Politics, 1701-1775

The colonial system, like every other system of the kind, was constructed with a view to the present gain of particular classes; once established, it has found ingenious advocates to defend it, on the ground of prospective utility.[1]

Herman Merivale, 1840

1 THE CHANGING STRUCTURE OF THE SUGAR MARKET

The early years of the 18th century witnessed alterations in the sugar market which led the British planters to reconsider their attitude toward the Navigation Acts. Masked by short-run fluctuations was the tendency for demand in the home market to run ahead of the supply forthcoming from the colonies. Rising demand in conjunction with prohibitive duties levied on foreign sugar imports gave rise to price differentials in home and foreign markets. Following the Treaty of Utrecht in 1713, sugar production in the French colonies expanded more rapidly than that of the British colonies. On the other hand, per capita consumption in England increased in relation to that of the Continent. This was owing to such factors as rising living standards and the widespread consumption of tea, coffee and punch. These forces were rather slow to take effect, however, and for a time British sugar prices declined. Re-exports to foreign markets fell off markedly owing to foreign sugars being sold in Europe much cheaper than the British colonial product. In view of these changing circumstances, British planters were encouraged to send the bulk of their output to the home market.

---

[1] Herman Merivale, *Lectures on Colonization and Colonies delivered before the University of Oxford in 1839, 1840 and 1841* (London, 1928), p. 229.

2 THE PLANTERS' MARKET STRATEGY

The above changes brought three major political issues to the forefront. The first arose over the attempt of English middlemen to introduce foreign sugar and rum into England by way of the British sugar colonies. By the early years of the 18th century English sugar prices were somewhat higher than those on the Continent. This disparity was reflected in the prices of sugar products in the British and foreign colonies. The price of molasses and rum in the West Indies was also influenced by the fact that France prohibited the import of molasses spirits from her colonies so as to protect her wine and brandy trade, while England was beginning to import rum to satisfy the home demand for that spirit. English middlemen took advantage of this situation and ordered their West India factors to exchange English manufactures for the cheaper foreign sugar products. The foreign commodities were then shipped to England or sold to North American traders disguised as commodities of British production.

After Queen Anne's War, substantial quantities of foreign sugar were imported into England by way of the British Caribbean colonies. Writing in 1732, a pamphleteer said that

> Barbadoes used formerly to trade with the French and Dutch, and by taking off their sugars, prevented their seeking out for other Markets. They got by this means the Sugar Trade almost entirely into their own Hands, or at least had made themselves the common channel of that Trade.[2]

The profitable inter-island trade also attracted the merchants and factors of the Leeward Islands which were only a few miles distant from several foreign sugar islands. In April 1722, the Governor of this group of islands described the trade as follows:

> There is a most pernicious and unlawful trade carried on between these Islands and the French Islands, which could not (otherwise) be supplied with provisions, materials for shipbuilding, horses and sugar works.... Our purchasing sugars from the French increases our duties, employs our ships, and has other advantages; but submits whether a present conveniency shall outweigh the strong probability of a future ruin.[3]

The direction of inter-island trade was thus reversed. Whereas European markets had been supplied with British sugar by way of the foreign sugar colonies, now foreign sugar entered England by way of the British sugar colonies. The effect of this trade was to raise the price of manufactures and other plantation supplies to British

---

2 Anon., *The Case of the British Northern Colonies* (London, 1732), p. 1.
3 *Cal. Treas. Papers 1720–28*, p. 125: Gov. Hart to Horatio Walpole, 4 April 1722.

planters, and to depress the price of sugar products in island and home markets.

North American and Irish trade with the foreign sugar colonies gave rise to the second political issue. Until the later years of the 17th century North Americans and Irishmen confined their Caribbean trade almost exclusively to the British sugar colonies. But early in the next century they began to trade with the foreign colonies on an increasing scale. In addition to finding new markets for their plantation supplies, they were able to purchase sugar, rum, and molasses more cheaply. This trade assumed such large dimensions at the close of the War in 1713, that British planters complained that they were compelled to pay abnormally high prices for lumber, horses, and provisions, at the same time being deprived of the profitable North American and Irish markets for their sugar products.[4]

The third political issue arose over the attempts of London sugar buyers, particularly the refiners and grocers, to form combinations for the purpose of depressing wholesale prices in the metropolis. 'Planters were compelled to send their sugars to a glutted and restrained market, under the government of the United Companies of Grocers and Sugar Bakers who must buy all our sugars, while we remain under our present circumstances', wrote John Ashley, the Barbados planter.[5] Buying combinations were a persistent feature of the sugar trade. They became a special object of planter hostility in the 1730s, when shrinking export markets and expanded production in the colonies threatened to glut the home market. One planter wrote to the *Barbados Gazette*, complaining that

> Another great Misfortune (or rather a pernicious Evil) that Attends the Loss of our Exportation Trade, is that for Want of that Evacuation, our most general Market at Home has been overstocked with Sugars, which gives an Opportunity to the Buyers to enter into Combinations to beat down the Price as low as they please. This Practice is now grown too notorious to need Explanation, and is what every Shipper is fully apprized of, by his last Letters from London.[6]

British planters thus had three main problems to solve: to keep foreign sugars from entering the mother country by way of the British sugar colonies; to prohibit North American and Irish merchants from trading with the foreign sugar colonies; and to

---

4 *Cal. S. P. Col. 1730*, pp. 300–1.
5 John Ashley, *Some Observations on a Direct Exportation of Sugar from the British Islands* (London, 1735), pp. 7, 10; Malachy Postlethwayt, *Dictionary of Commerce* (London, 1755), vol. 2, p. 766.
6 Anon., 'On the Sugar Trade', 26 March 1735, in *Caribbeana, Containing Letters and Dissertations... on the West Indies* (London, 1741), vol. 2, p. 36.

combat the English refiners and grocers who formed buying combinations to depress the price of sugar.

3 CURBING THE INTER-ISLAND TRADE

Planters first attacked the problem of introducing foreign sugar into England because it could be dealt with by political action in the colonies. West India politics was in part a struggle between royal officials and the elected representatives of the colonists. While the British Government retained a decisive voice in military and foreign affairs, the colonists gained a substantial measure of self-government by strategic control of the power to tax. Probably no less acrimonious was the conflict between planters and merchants. The latter tended to dominate local politics in the infancy of colonies. Power began to shift to the planters during the sugar revolution. The change from an economy of small farmers to one of substantial planters was accompanied by changes in marketing and finance. As more and more planters took over the marketing of their produce through English commission agents, island merchants and factors declined in number and influence. By the early years of the 18th century well-to-do planters held a majority of the seats in a number of island legislatures. As might be expected, they used their influence to cut off a branch of trade which threatened to undermine their economic and political supremacy.

Barbados took the lead in attacking the inter-island trade. In March 1715, the Legislature passed an Act laying prohibitive duties on foreign sugar and other commodities imported into that island.[7] Antigua followed the lead of Barbados and passed a similar measure in November 1715. Failing its intended purpose, the Act was repealed and in its place was substituted the Act of June 1716, which prohibited the import of French and other foreign sugar, rum, molasses, and cotton. When the Act of 1716 was disallowed by an order-in-council, the Antiguans reacted vigorously. They pushed through the Act of 1721, levying prohibitive duties on imports of foreign sugar, molasses, rum, cotton, and ginger. In 1764, the Assembly of Antigua revived an earlier resolution and declared that every person engaged in such trade 'is an Enemy to his Country . . . and is unworthy to be a Member of civil society'.[8]

---

7 *Acts of the Assembly Passed on the Island of Barbados, from 1648 to 1718* (London, 1721), p. 303.

8 Frank W. Pitman, *The Development of the British West Indies 1700–1763* (New Haven, 1917), pp. 228–33; Lowell J. Ragatz, *The Fall of the Planter Class in the British Caribbean, 1763–1833* (New York, 1928), p. 102.

Sugar and Slavery

The planters of Jamaica had difficulty suppressing trade with the foreign colonies because it was supported by a powerful body of local merchants. In the face of their adversaries, the planters pushed through the Act of 1715 to prevent fraudulent trade with St Domingue. Another Act in 1726 imposed heavy penalties for importing French sugar, indigo, and other commodities and re-shipping them to England. Frustrated by infractions of previous measures, the Jamaicans sought a final remedy in the Act of 1756, which prohibited all imports of foreign sugar products. It provided that any violator should 'be deemed guilty of Felony and suffer Death as a Felon without benefit of Clergy'. When the Act was sent to England to be confirmed, the Privy Council was shocked by its harsh penalties and forthwith disallowed it.[9]

It is difficult to say how effective these measures were in keeping foreign sugar out of British markets. Harsher penalties were in all probability a deterring influence. Moreover, the changing structure of the sugar trade probably helped to reduce the clandestine trade. The growth of the commission system led to the decline of independent island merchants who were notorious for their participation in illicit trade. But by raising the price of sugar products in the British West Indies, these restrictive measures forced North American and Irish merchants to trade more extensively with the foreign sugar colonies.

4 THE PLANTER INTEREST IN THE HOUSE OF COMMONS

Local political influence thus served the planters in their efforts to keep foreign sugar products out of the home market. But political influence was needed in the home government if the planters were to combat the buyers and seek to prevent the American and Irish merchants from trading with the foreign sugar colonies. 'The British Parliament must be our Physician', wrote a Barbadian, 'and, in the meantime, I think that our Legislature is not without the Power of administering some Preparatives towards a Cure'.[10]

Generally speaking, there were three classes of men who looked after the political interests of the planters in England: absentee planters, agents of the various colonial governments, and commission agents or merchants. During the 17th century these groups were not very influential because few planters had amassed enough wealth to become absentees, commission agents were far from numerous, and

---

9 Pitman, *Development of British West Indies*, pp. 233–5; *Acts of the Privy Council, Colonial Series, 1745–66*, pp. 509, 517–20.
10 *Caribbeana*, vol. 1, pp. 135–6.

Planter Politics, 1701—1775

the practice of appointing colonial agents was still in its infancy. Furthermore, the sugar colonies had few interests in common.

During the first half of the 18th century the West India interest gained more influence in the home government. It became a general practice for colonial governments to appoint agents, several of whom were prominent planters or merchants, to look after their affairs in England. The agents were constantly soliciting the government on behalf of the planters, cultivating friendships with prominent politicians, submitting evidence to parliamentary committees and government officials, writing pamphlets, and urging members to vote for planter measures in the House of Commons. Professor Penson, the historian of the West India agents, writes:

> At the time when the greatest successes were won for the West India interest, the agents were aided by the assistance of a powerful body of men, including Beckford, the intimate associate of the Elder Pitt, and a vast number of others whose wealth could command influence in British politics.[11]

Commission merchants also increased in number and influence. By the middle of the 18th century they handled the greater part of the Caribbean produce which was marketed in London. Recruited to a considerable extent from prominent planter families, the merchants were diligent in pleading the case of the planters. Several wealthy commission merchants became prominent in the City of London and the House of Commons. William Beckford, Samuel Pennant, Slingsby Bethell, Richard Oliver, and Samuel Turner held the office of Alderman or Lord Mayor of London. Moreover, there were a number of merchants, including Beckford, Bethell, Oliver, Henry Lascelles, Sir Alexander Grant, Arnold Nesbitt, and Rose Fuller, who were members of Parliament. The close community of interest among planters and commission merchants was borne out by a contemporary who wrote that the English merchants who received consignments from the West Indies 'commonly speak the language of those that employ them'.[12]

Absentee proprietors came to play an active role in English politics during the 18th century. A West Indian estimated in 1732 that there were constantly one hundred gentlemen from Barbados in England. From the late 1730s to the American Revolution numerous proprietors from the Leeward Islands and Jamaica amassed sizeable fortunes and retired to England.

---

11 Lillian M. Penson, *The Colonial Agents of the British West India Islands.* Unpublished Ph.D. dissertation, University of London, 1921, p. 255.
12 *Cal. S. P. Col. 1706—08*, p. 630: 'The Condition of Barbados'.

Sugar and Slavery

'If I am not mis-informed', wrote an anonymous author in the *Gentleman's Magazine* in 1766, 'there are now in Parliament upwards of forty members who are either West Indian planters themselves, descended from such, or have concerns there that entitle them to pre-eminence'.[13] Professor Namier observed that while this statement is probably accurate in gauging the voting strength of that interest, it overstates the number of real West Indians in the House. By 'real' West Indians he means those 'who were born in the West Indies, had spent there part of their lives, had been members of a West Indian Assembly or Council, or had held office in one of the islands'.[14] A close reading of the biographies of members of Parliament in the period from 1730 to 1775 reveals at least thirty who qualify as 'real' West Indians, a larger number than Namier was willing to concede.

Besides these, at least thirty-two members of Parliament were in the 'outer ring' of the West India interest, that is, absentee proprietors who came into possession of sugar estates by inheritance or inter-marriage, West India merchants in London and the outports, and agents of colonial governments. Classification presents problems, partly because some members were absentee proprietors as well as merchants or colonial agents, and partly because some had links with more than one colony. By singling out their dominant affiliation, however, it is clear that of the seventy West Indians in Parliament in the years from 1730 to 1775, twenty were merchants and the other fifty were, with few exceptions, absentee proprietors. If the members are classified according to place of birth, residence, proprietorship, political agency, and trade, it is evident that twenty-seven were linked with Jamaica, eleven with St Christopher, ten with Antigua, ten with Barbados, four with Nevis, three with Montserrat, two with Grenada, and one each with Dominica, St Vincent, and Tobago.

5 THE MEMBERS OF PARLIAMENT

Few of the leading planter families of Jamaica were without representatives in Parliament in the century prior to slave emancipation. Numbered among the 'real' Jamaicans in the period of this study were three Beckfords, three Dawkins, and one representative of the families of Bayly, Foster, French, Fuller, Grant, Heathcote, Morant, Nedham, and Swymmer. In 1754 the independent merchants and

---
13 *The Gentleman's Magazine and Historical Chronicler*, vol. XXXVI (London, 1766), p. 229.
14 Sir Lewis Namier, *England in the Age of the American Revolution*, 2nd ed. (London, 1961), pp. 234–5.

Planter Politics, 1701–1775

traders of London complained to the House of Commons that absentees were able 'to support contests in some of the richest and most populous cities in this country'. That the Jamaicans were uppermost in the minds of the complainants is evident from their reference to the membership of 'three brothers from one of our Sugarislands...'.[15] William Beckford, Alderman and twice Lord Mayor of London, sat for Shaftesbury and London; Richard Beckford for Bristol; and Julines Beckford for Salisbury. These brothers had behind them three generations of Beckfords who had laid acre to acre and stocked numerous plantations with slaves and equipment. Their father, Peter Beckford II, at his death in 1735, left personal property in Jamaica valued at £159,933 sterling, besides an undisclosed amount of real property. His second son William, the Lord Mayor, inherited the greater part of his estate and claimed 22,021 acres in Jamaica in 1754. The eccentric author of *Vathek*, William's eldest son and heir by the same name, was referred to frequently as 'England's wealthiest son'.[16]

If the Beckfords were the kings of Jamaica, there were numerous princely families allied to them by ties of kinship who were represented in the mother parliament. James Dawkins, M.P. for Woodstock, was the father of James Dawkins, M.P. for Hindon, and uncle of Henry Dawkins, M.P. for Southampton and Chippenham. Edward Morant, M.P. for Hindon and Lymington; Richard Pennant, 1st Baron Penrhyn, M.P. for Petersfield and Liverpool; and James Dawkins, the younger, were cousins, while Pennant's mother was a first cousin of William Beckford. Another cousin became the wife of Rose Fuller, M.P. for New Romney, Maidstone, and Rye. By 1761 the Jamaica cousinhood had established its parliamentary strongholds in Hampshire and Wiltshire, and had gained a footing in Southampton.[17]

Three other parliamentarians may be singled out by virtue of substantial personalty and realty in Jamaica. Anthony Langley Swymmer, M.P. for Southampton, owned 8,278 acres in Jamaica in 1754. Nathaniel Bayly, M.P. for Abingdon and Westbury, inherited four sugar plantations from his brother Zachary Bayly, whose personalty in Jamaica was valued at £110,462 sterling in 1771. Representing the Scotsmen who formed such an influential group in the

---

15 Anon., *A Short Account of the Interest and Conduct of the Jamaica Planters in an Address to the Merchants, Traders, and Liverymen of London* (London, 1754), p. 3.
16 Jamaica Public Record Office, Spanish Town. *Inventorys*, vol. 18, ff. 105, 108–13, 187–203; Public Record Office, London. C.O. 142/31; Boyd Alexander, *England's Wealthiest Son, A Study of William Beckford* (London, 1962); Gerrit P. Judd, *Members of Parliament 1734–1832* (New Haven, 1955), pp. 117–18.
17 Namier, *England in Age of American Revolution*, p. 237.

Sugar and Slavery

West Indies was Sir Alexander Grant, 5th Bart., M.P. for the Inverness burghs, and a London-West India merchant. He owned 2,258 acres in Jamaica in 1754, and at his death in 1772 possessed personalty in that island amounting to £72,865 sterling.[18]

Other owners of plantations in Jamaica were Benjamin Allen, M.P. for Bridgewater; William Dickinson, M.P. for Great Marlow, Rye, and Somerset; Thomas Foster, M.P. for Dorchester; Jeffrey French, M.P. for Milborne Port and Tavistock; James Modyford Heywood, M.P. for Fowey; Daniel Moore, M.P. for Great Marlow; Arnold Nesbitt, M.P. for St Michael, Winchelsea, and Cricklade; William Nedham, M.P. for Winchelsea and Pontefract; Anthony Morris Storer, M.P. for Carlisle and Morpeth; and Barlow Trecothick, M.P. for London. Arnold Nesbitt and his father Albert Nesbitt, M.P. for Huntingdon and St Michael, were London-West India merchants, as were also Barlow Trecothick; Samuel Touchet, M.P. for Shaftesbury; and George Heathcote, M.P. for Hindon, Southwark, and London. Lovell Stanhope, M.P. for Winchester, was agent for Jamaica; and Hans Sloane-Stanley, M.P. for Newport, Southampton, Christchurch, and Lostwithiel, was in the outer ring of Jamaicans by virtue of family ties.[19]

St Christopher enjoyed a remarkable period of prosperity in the middle decades of the century which enabled a growing number of proprietors to become absentees. Three of the eleven absentees who became M.P.s were also Governors General of the Leeward Islands and natives of St Christopher. Sir Ralph Payne, later Baron Lavington, M.P. for Shaftesbury, Camelford, Plympton Erle, and Woodstock, was descended from a prominent planter family. He served as Governor General from 1771 to 1775, and again from 1799 to 1807. Sir Ralph's brother-in-law was William Woodley, M.P. for Great Bedwin and Marlborough, and Governor General 1766—71, and 1791—3. He inherited the 'Profit' plantation in St Christopher. From a planter family of Nevis and St Christopher came William Mathew Burt, M.P. for Great Marlow, and Governor General, 1776—80. John St Leger Douglas, M.P. for Hindon and Weobley, was the grandson of Walter Douglas, Governor General of the same group of islands in 1711—14.[20]

Other members of Parliament from St Christopher were John Sharpe, M.P. for Callington, and agent for various West India islands;

18 J. P. R. O. Spanish Town. *Wills*, vol. 32, ff. 95—7; *Inventorys*, vol. 50, ff. 166—83; vol. 54, ff. 32—41: P.R.O. London, C.O. 142/31; Judd, *Members of Parliament*, pp. 116, 210, 349.
19 Judd, *Members of Parliament*, pp. 103, 174, 199, 201, 220, 225, 281, 287, 335, 341, 346, 356, 358.
20 Ibid., pp. 137, 176, 299, 381.

and his son Fane William Sharpe, M.P. for Callington; Crisp Molineux, M.P. for Castle Rising and Lynn, who owned plantations in St Christopher; Samuel Greatheed, M.P. for Coventry, who married a daughter of the 3rd Duke of Ancaster; Sir Patrick Blake, 1st Bart., M.P. for Sudbury, also a plantation owner. Then there was William MacDowall, M.P. for Renfrewshire, a Scotsman who married an heiress of St Christopher and later became a prominent West India merchant in Glasgow. Finally, there was Sir Charles Barrow, 1st Bart., M.P. for Gloucester City, who was born in St Christopher.[21]

Ten parliamentarians were linked to Antigua, the seat of government for the Leeward Islands. Two members of the Tudway family, whose large plantation holdings in Antigua dated from 1679, sat in Parliament. Charles Tudway was M.P. for Wells, and his son Clement Tudway also sat for Wells. Similarly, two Sir William Codringtons, descendants of Governors General of the Leeward Islands and proprietors of numerous sugar estates in Antigua, were House of Commons men. The first baronet represented Minehead; and his son, the second baronet, sat for Beverley and Tewkesbury. Slingsby Bethell, brother-in-law of the first baronet, managed the Codrington plantations in Antigua as a young man and then moved to London to establish a sugar factorage business. He was Lord Mayor of London in 1756, and represented the City in Parliament.[22]

Three other City men had Antigua connections. Richard Oliver, Alderman and M.P. for London, was born in Antigua, and as a young man became a partner in his uncle's West India commission agency in London. He was prominent as a supporter of John Wilkes and the Bill of Rights Society. John Tomlinson, M.P. for Steyning, was the son and grandson of Antigua planters; his father, Colonel John Tomlinson, was referred to as 'one of the best planters... in these parts'.[23] Tomlinson and his partner, Barlow Trecothick, were among the leading American and West India merchants and government contractors of their day. Sir George Colebrooke, 2nd Bart., M.P. for Arundel, was a London banker and chairman of the East India Company. In 1754, he married Mary Gaynor, an Antigua heiress, by whom he came into possession of three sugar estates. Similarly, Sir James Laroche, 1st Bart., M.P. for Bodwin, and a Bristol-West India merchant, married Elizabeth Anne Yeamans, an Antigua heiress. Finally, Antigua-born Samuel Martin, son of Colonel Samuel Martin, a leading planter, was M.P. for Camelford and Hastings, Secretary to

21 Ibid., pp. 114, 123, 212, 265, 278, 332.
22 Ibid., pp. 121, 155, 360.
23 Namier, *England in Age of American Revolution*, pp. 246–7.

Sugar and Slavery

the Treasury Board, and Treasurer to the Princess Dowager of Wales. He gained notoriety when he wounded John Wilkes in a duel.[24]

Four of the ten parliamentarians who were connected with Barbados were members of the powerful Lascelles family. Henry Lascelles amassed one of the great fortunes of his age. Together with his brothers Daniel and Edward, he settled in Barbados as a merchant and planter. He was also Collector of Customs, an office which was also held by his half-brother Edward Lascelles. Subsequently, Henry Lascelles moved to London to establish a West India trading house. He was a director of the East India Company and M.P. for Northallerton, which was his birthplace. Edwin Lascelles, 1st Baron Harewood and M.P. for Scarsborough, Northallerton, and Yorkshire, was the eldest son of Henry Lascelles. He was born in Barbados in 1713. Edward Lascelles, son of Edward Lascelles of Barbados and nephew of Henry Lascelles, was born in Barbados in 1740 and became M.P. for Northallerton. In 1796 he was created Baron Harewood of Harewood, and 1812 Earl Harewood and Viscount Lascelles. Daniel, the fourth member of the Lascelles clan to take a seat in Parliament, was born in Barbados in 1714, the second son of Henry Lascelles. He carried on the family's mercantile business in London and sat for Northallerton.[25]

Other Parliamentarians who had ties with Barbados were Henry Bromley, 1st Baron Montfort, M.P. for Cambridgeshire; Thomas Bromley, 2nd Baron Montfort, M.P. for Cambridge borough; James Edward Colleton, M.P. for Lostwithiel and St Mawes; Sir Jermyn Davers, 4th Bart., M.P. for Bury and Suffolk; Thomas Erle Drax, M.P. for Corfe Castle and Wareham; and Sir John Gibbons, 2nd Bart., M.P. for Stockbridge and Wallingford.[26] J. E. Colleton headed the 'Colleton cousinhood', whose other members were T. E. Drax, Robert Nugent, Edmund Nugent, John Garth, Charles Boone, and John Dodd.[27]

Absentees from Nevis and Montserrat made only a minor contribution to the West India body in Parliament. Two members of the Stapleton family, descendants of a Governor General of the Leeward Islands, owned plantations in Nevis and Montserrat. Sir William Stapleton, 4th Bart., was M.P. for Oxfordshire; his son, Sir Thomas

---

24 Judd, *Members of Parliament*, pp. 156, 250, 272, 292, 356. For further genealogical and biographical data see Vere L. Oliver, *The History of the Island of Antigua* (3 vols., London, 1894–99).
25 Judd, *Members of Parliament*, pp. 156, 170, 178, 204, 250–1; Joseph Foster, *Pedigrees of The County Families of Yorkshire* (London 1874), vol. 1.
26 Judd, *Members of Parliament*, pp. 130–1, 156, 170, 178, 204.
27 Sir Lewis Namier, 'Charles Garth and his Connections', *The English Historical Review*, vol. LIV (1939), pp. 443–70.

Planter Politics, 1701–1775

Stapleton, 5th Bart., sat for Oxford City. Elizabeth Stapleton, daughter of Sir William Stapleton, 1st Bart. and Governor General, married Martin Madan, a leading planter of Nevis. Their eldest son and heir, also Martin Madan, was M.P. for Wooton Bassett. Also from Nevis was John Frederick Pinney, M.P. for Bridport, who became a prominent sugar merchant in Bristol.[28]

From Montserrat came the Webb brothers, Robert and Nathaniel, sons of Nathaniel Webb, Collector of Customs, merchant, and planter. Robert Webb was M.P. for Taunton. Nathaniel Webb, who held plantation interests in Montserrat and Antigua, was M.P. for Taunton and Ilchester. Another parliamentarian with Montserrat connections was Sir William Gage, 7th Bart., M.P. for Seaford, who inherited a plantation in that island.[29]

Five members of Parliament had proprietary interests in the four islands which were ceded to Great Britain by the Treaty of Paris in 1763. Absentees from Grenada were Lauchlin MacLeane, M.P. for Arundel; and Sir George Amyand, 1st Bart., banker and M.P. for Barnstaple. Sir James Cockburn, 8th Bart., M.P. for the Linlithgow burghs, owned extensive properties in Dominica. General Robert Monckton, M.P. for Pontefract and Portsmouth, obtained a grant of 4,000 acres in St Vincent. Sir William Pulteney-Johnstone, 5th Bart., M.P. for Cromartyshire and Shrewsbury, owned sugar plantations in Tobago.[30]

Members of Parliament had close ties with non-members whose interests bound them to the West Indies as planters, merchants, manufacturers, annuitants, patentees, and military officers. Besides London and the outports, the watering places were much frequented by the West Indians who formed a social circle of their own, being bound together by intermarriages, common interests, and lasting friendships.[31]

But more formal organization developed in the leading port cities, and especially in London. Near the Exchange in St Michael's Alley was the Jamaica Coffee House which was established in 1674. Within a short time it became a well-known meeting place for merchants, shipmasters, and others concerned in Jamaica. It was used for more political purposes in the early 18th century, writes Professor Penson, 'and as the number of absentee planters grew it became the common resort for them and for the merchants'.[32] Sometime between 1730

---

28 Judd, *Members of Parliament*, pp. 268, 306, 342.
29 Ibid., pp. 203, 371.
30 Ibid., pp. 104, 154, 243, 267, 279.
31 Jay B. Botsford, *English Society in the Eighteenth Century As Influenced from Oversea* (New York, 1924), pp. 227–30.
32 Penson, *Colonial Agents of British West Indies*, pp. 240–1.

Sugar and Slavery

and 1740 a group of absentees formed an association which became known as the 'Planters' Club'. About the same time the London-West India merchants formed a loose association to discuss matters of common concern. In order to finance their political activities in times of common action, the merchants began to collect about one penny per hogshead on all imports from the West Indies.[33]

Before long the West Indians in Parliament had become the subject of common discourse. It was noted in the *Parliamentary History* of 1744, 'how many were either by themselves or their friends, deeply concerned in one part or other of the sugar trade, and that the cause itself was always popular in the House of Commons'.[34] In many constituencies the price of a parliamentary seat was £3,000 in 1760. In a letter to Lord Mansfield, the Duke of Newcastle expressed fear that such a price would 'fling the boroughs into East Indians, West Indians, citizens and brokers, who are very reputable, and yet very troublesome Members'.[35] In 1767, Lord Chesterfield's offer of £2,500 for a seat in Northampton was contemptuously refused by a borough jobber. The Lord was informed 'that there was no such thing as a borough to be had now, for the rich East and West Indians had secured them all, at the rate of three thousand pounds at the least; but many at four thousand, and two or three that he knew at five thousand'.[36] 'The landed interest is beat out', wrote Lady Sarah Osborn in 1768, 'and merchants, nabobs, and those who have gathered riches from the East and West Indies stand the best chance of governing this country'.[37] Fifty or sixty West India members could 'turn the balance on which side they please', asserted the agent for Massachusetts Bay in 1764.[38]

6 THE PLANTERS' STRATEGY IN THE HOUSE OF COMMONS

While the primary objective was to adapt the Navigation Acts to the realities of the market, the planter interest also concerned itself with political strategies designed to prevent any increase of the sugar duties. In 1743, the Pelham ministry needed money to prosecute the

---

33 P.R.O. London. C.O. 137/32, Bb 13, 14: 'Minutes of Jamaica Council', 18 Dec. 1760; Douglas G. Hall, *A Brief History of the West India Committee* (London, 1971), p. 2.
34 *The Parliamentary History of England*, vol. 13, p. 639.
35 Quoted in Sir Lewis Namier, *The Structure of Politics at the Accession of George III* (London, 1929), vol. 1, p. 260.
36 Earl of Chesterfield's *Letters to his Son* (New York, 1857), 19 Sept. 1767.
37 *Political and Social Letters of a Lady of the Eighteenth Century 1721–1771*, ed. E. F. D. Osborn (London, 1890), p. 178.
38 'Jasper Mauduit Letters', *Mass. Hist. Soc., Coll.*, 1st ser., vol. VI, p. 193.

war on the Continent. Rumours began to spread that the ministry intended to introduce a bill which would add 2s 4d per cwt to the import duty on colonial muscovado sugar. That the West Indians were quick to devise counter-measures is evident from the correspondence of the house of Lascelles and Maxwell.

> There have been for some Weeks past frequent meetings of the Agents, Planters & Factors, interested in the Sugar Collonies, from an apprehension of its being in agitation to bring in a Bill, the present Session of Parliament, to lay on an additional duty upon Sugar, and a Case was drawn up to prove, that such a Tax would be sustained by the Planters & importers of Sugar and not by the Consumers, and would be destructive to the said Colonies, as well as highly detrimental to the Trade of Great Britain. This case was put into the press. . . . We have also agreed to divide into small Parties, and attend every Member, & many of the Members have already been waited on, and all of them will be so, before the Bill can be brought into Parliament. We have a great many friends, not interested in the Colonies, who have interest & influence with Members, and being convinced themselves sollicit for us, by endeavouring to convince them.[39]

The defeat of the bill was assured when Scottish and Irish members agreed to vote against the sugar bill in exchange for West Indian votes in favour of a bill to tax foreign linen. Notwithstanding their influence, the planter interest was unable to defeat subsequent attempts to tax sugar. The duty on muscovado was increased by 1s 6d per cwt in 1747, and by the same amount again in 1759.[40]

The chief problems which the planters hoped to solve by means of parliamentary legislation were said to be the North American and Irish trade with the foreign sugar colonies and the combination of London sugar refiners and grocers. These two problems need to be considered together because the planters understood that the solution of the one would contribute to the solution of the other. In other words, if the planters had a forced market in Ireland and North America, they could channel a greater proportion of their commodities to these markets and thus force English buyers to pay higher prices for the reduced portion shipped to the home market. At the same time, the planters hoped to secure legislation which would confine the trade of North America and Ireland to the British sugar colonies. A pamphleteer for the Northern Colonies said that the planters intended 'to force the Northern Colonies into a Necessity of buying their Sugars, Rum and Molasses, of them at their own Rate, and in Consequence thereof, to confine the Northern Colonies for

---

39 *Lascelles and Maxwell L. B.*, ff. 83–4; Lre. to William Gibbons in Barbados, 7 Jan. 1744.
40 Noel Deerr, *The History of Sugar* (London, 1949–50), vol. 2, p. 430.

Sugar and Slavery

the Vent of the Produce of their Lands and Industry, solely to the Sugar Islands'.[41]

The West India interest gained its first parliamentary victory in 1731 when an act was passed which granted liberty to export rum and other unenumerated commodities directly from the British sugar colonies to Ireland.[42] A more important victory was gained in 1733, when the famous Molasses Act was passed in the face of strong opposition from the North American colonies. By this Act prohibitive duties were levied on foreign sugar, molasses, and rum imported into the American colonies. Moreover, French sugar, molasses, and rum were barred from Ireland; and other foreign and British sugar had to be imported into Ireland from Great Britain in vessels which conformed to the Navigation Acts.[43]

Not content with a forced market for their commodities in Ireland and North America, the planters thought that an act granting liberty to ship plantation sugar directly to foreign markets would serve as an additional weapon against the English sugar buyers. In 1735, a correspondent wrote to the *Barbados Gazette* that two things were needed if the planters were to secure relief from their misfortunes: 'A more free and open Trade, with an easier Access to the Foreign Markets, [and] Some effectual method to prevent all unnatural combinations to depreciate the Commodity'. He argued that the achievement of the first objective would in some measure contribute to the second,

> for whatever Sugars pass by the General Market, will keep that Market so much the thinner, and in some Degree help to break those evil Combinations. For the more the Commodity is dispersed, and the nearer it is laid to the Consumer, the better it will go off, since if the Market is not glutted in any one Place, the Price will be the better in all Places: But if too great a

---

41 Anon., *The Case of the British Northern Colonies* (London, 1732), p. 2.
42 4 Geo. II, c. 15. 'An Act for importing from his Majesty's Plantations in America, directly into Ireland, Goods not enumerated in any Act of Parliament'.
43 The original bill, which was reported 26 March, 1731, called for the prohibition of imports of foreign sugar, molasses, or rum into Great Britain, Ireland, or any British dominion and forbade the export of horses or lumber to any foreign sugar colony. After the first bill was defeated, a compromise measure was passed by the Commons on 21 March, 1733, and the Lords on 17 May, 1733, which is commonly known as the Molasses Act (6 Geo. II, c. 13). Although the Act of 1733 did not prohibit the sale of North American lumber, horses, or provisions in the foreign sugar colonies, return cargoes of foreign sugar, molasses, and rum were subject to prohibitive duties, amounting to 5s. per cwt on foreign sugar and paneles, 9d. per gallon on rum, and 6d. per gallon on molasses. The Act also provided for a drawback of the entire import duty on British sugar that was re-exported from Great Britain for one year to help planters recover the European market, and English refiners were encouraged by an additional bounty of 2s. per cwt on the export of refined sugar. With this addition, the total bounty on refined sugar for export amounted to 6s. per cwt. Pitman, *Development of British West Indies*, pp. 254–64.

Quantity falls the Price at the most general Market, that will influence all the rest, and give Room for Combinations to beat it down still lower.[44]

When a bill for a direct trade was introduced in Parliament in April 1739, complaints were heard from the merchants of Bristol, Liverpool, London, Chester, Lancaster, and Whitehaven. The petitioners contended that such a trade would open the manufacturing countries of northern Europe to colonial shipping and hinder the sale of English manufactures in the colonies. Adverse consequences were also predicted for British shipowners and middlemen. In another petition the sugar refiners of London expressed their fear that, in consequence of such a measure, raw sugar prices would rise with adverse effects on their exports of refined sugar. The possibility of such a price rise was denied by the planters, who asserted that they could produce three times as much sugar as they did. After the contending interests were heard by the Lords and Commons, the bill was passed on 12 June 1739. Accordingly, permission was granted to ship sugar directly from the plantations to any foreign port in Europe.[45]

Why did the planters seek permission to export sugar directly to foreign markets when higher prices were apparently realized from sales in the protected home market? Lacking a cartel agreement, they could not be expected to sacrifice a portion of their sugar in Continental markets when the prices at home were higher. But the threat of such exports might be of some service in their dealings with the grocers and refiners. In fact, use was made of only five of the forty-eight licences which authorized participation in the direct trade. The reason for taking out so many unused licences was explained in a letter from Rose Fuller in Jamaica to James Knight in London.

> The great cause of it [the low price of sugar] is the combination of sugar bakers: they have it in their power to meet and agree what they shall give for our commodities, but all their combinations can never prevail if we can bring it about that sugars may not be quite so plenty in England as they have been of late years ... we propose that every ship that comes from

---

44 'On the Sugar Trade', *Caribbeana*, vol. 2, p. 37.
45 15 Geo. II, c. 33. Though the Act of 1739 granted permission to ship sugar directly from the plantations to any foreign port in Europe, ships bound for northern Europe had to touch at some British port, while those going to points south of Cape Finisterre might sail directly without touching in England. In both cases sugar bound for Europe was relieved of all duties formerly collectable in England. Licences must be purchased and bonds taken out to secure enforcement of the law. All ships engaged in the direct trade must return within eight months to England before sailing again to the colonies. This would secure to England the advantages of the 'Staple Act' of 1663. Pitman, *Development of British West Indies*, pp. 181-3.

Sugar and Slavery

London to load here shall bring a license to carry sugars directly to foreign markets either to those to the southward or to the northward and as this license can be had for fifteen shillings, if they make no use of it, it will be but a small cost to the ship, and if it has no other effect it will att least alarm the bakers and keep them in a state of suspence what sugars will be sent to foreign markets.[46]

If the Direct Export Act accomplished little more than to give the planters a weapon to harass the buyers, the other measures were quite effective in expanding the home market. This was especially the case with Ireland. Prior to 1732, Ireland carried on an extensive trade with France and her sugar colonies. Quantities of French brandy, wine, and sugar were imported into Ireland in exchange for beef, butter, raw hides, and tallow. The planter-sponsored acts of Parliament went far to curb this branch of Irish trade. Although smuggling continued to be a source of aggravation, Ireland's official rum imports increased rapidly after the early 1730s.[47] Moreover, quantities of sugar passed through England on their way to Ireland after 1733. Part of the consumption was supplied by smugglers and by legal traders who imported Portuguese sugars. But it is doubtful if these trades impaired the re-export of British plantation sugar to Ireland. Indeed, the re-exports of the colonial product to Ireland increased from 20,159 cwt annually in 1716–20, to 184,877 in 1772–5, or from 11.2 per cent to 67.6 per cent of total re-exports. If these re-exports are considered as part of the home consumption, between 94 and 96 per cent of the sugar imports of the British Isles were retained for home consumption in the period from 1733 to 1775. Ireland's trade was thus diverted from the sugar colonies of France to those of Great Britain, a change brought about largely by the efforts of the British planters.[48]

In addition to Ireland, we have seen that the planters acquired a protected market for their commodities when the Act of Union brought Scotland within the scope of the Navigation Acts in 1707. Glasgow began a direct trade with the West Indies in the early 1730s, a trade which came to rank second only to the prosperous tobacco trade of that port. By mid-century the east coast ports of Edinburgh, Leith and Dundee had established a direct trade with the West Indies which made them less dependent on the London sugar market.[49]

The fourth forced market was the British North American

---

46 British Museum Add. MSS 18,960, f. 13: Papers of Edward Long.
47 Arthur Dobbs, *An Essay on the Trade and Improvement of Ireland* (1729), in *A Collection of Tracts and Treaties... on Ireland* (Dublin, 1861), vol. 2, pp. 88, 140.
48 See Chapter 2, pp. 31–2.
49 See Chapter 2, pp. 31–2.

colonies. Notwithstanding the large quantities of foreign sugar products which entered these markets through illicit channels, British plantation sugar was by no means excluded. Stricter enforcement of the Navigation Acts and the Sugar Act of 1764 probably helped to force more British plantation sugar into North American markets. 'It is well known that since the late war', wrote Edward Long, the Jamaica planter-historian, in 1774, 'the consumption of sugar in North America has been double what it used to be'.[50]

7 THE SUGAR MONOPOLY

If the evidence is too meagre to warrant firm conclusions concerning the North American market, it cannot be doubted that the British sugar planters gained an enlarged and protected home market which was superior to the foreign market. They also gained room to manoeuvre against their enemies. We have seen that planters repeatedly complained of the buying combinations of London sugar refiners and grocers, and that the Molasses Act and the Direct Export Act were intended to break these combinations.

Changes in trading methods also gave the planters greater power of manipulation. The rise of the agency system of marketing and the decline of London merchants who traded on their own account with the West Indies meant that the greater part of the sugar sold in the West Indies was purchased by the factors and supercargoes of outport and North American merchants. Under these circumstances planters could either sell their sugar in the West Indies, in which event it bypassed the London market, or they could consign it to their London commission agents.

Besides selling part of their produce in the West Indies, planters bypassed the London market by consigning parcels of sugar and rum to commission agents in the English outports, Ireland, Scotland, and North America. In the period from 1741 to 1767, Dr Tullideph of Antigua had agents at Bristol, Liverpool, Lancaster, Glasgow, Leith, Dundee, Cork, Dublin, and several North American ports. On several occasions he noted how the demand from these markets influenced the price of sugar in London. For example, he wrote from London in September 1753, that 'our Sugar Mercatt hath been a little brisker oweing to a demand from Leverpoole, Scotland and Ireland'.[51]

Although London declined in relation to the outports as a sugar importer, she retained her supremacy as the great sugar market of

---
50 Edward Long, *The History of Jamaica* (London, 1774), vol. 1, p. 524.
51 *Tullideph L. B.*, vol. 2: Lre. to William Hare, merchant in Bristol, 20 Sept. 1753.

Sugar and Slavery

Europe. It was here, probably more than any other place, that buyers and sellers came into direct conflict. Refiners and grocers frequently entered into agreements to refrain from buying when prices were high, while planters retaliated by instructing their agents to hold sugar off the market when prices were low. 'The bakers have stop't these 3 weeks past, which hath thrown a damp on the Sales, but they must soon come to mercatt again & then Sugars will be brisker', wrote Tullideph from London in July 1754.[52]

High sugar prices led the buyers to seek parliamentary assistance against their adversaries. In March 1753, the refiners, grocers, and other dealers in sugar of the cities of London and Westminster and the borough of Southwark presented to the House of Commons a petition detailing their grievances against the planters. A similar petition was submitted by the grocers and refiners of Bristol. The petitioners made the following allegations before the Committee of the Whole House which was appointed to hear testimony:

> That the Price of Muscovado Sugar is become excessively high, owing to a deficient Importation from our Sugar Colonies in America. . . .
>
> That ever since Lady-Day 1749, the Sugar Planters have received for their Sugars a much higher Price than what they did for many years before the Commencement of the late War. . . .
>
> That the foreign Markets are supplied with Sugar from the *French* at less than half the Price it is here sold for, exclusive of all Duties paid here; and the Price of Sugars at the British Sugar Colonies is more than double the Price of what it is at the *French* Sugar Colonies.
>
> That the excessive Gain of the British Planters by a deficient Importation (all foreign Sugars being excluded by Duties which amount to a Prohibition) may be a Temptation to them to forbear breaking up more Land for Sugar Plantations, especially in the Island of Jamaica, where your Petitioners are informed large Tracts of Land fit for that Purpose do remain uncultivated.[53]

After making these and other allegations, the petitioners asked the House of Commons 'to make it the Interest of the British Sugar Colonies to produce and send home a larger Quantity of Sugar to Great Britain . . . or to grant any other Relief, as to their great Wisdom shall seem meet'.[54]

Although no remedial measures were taken by the British Government at this time, the charges of the London sugar buyers occasioned no little alarm in planter circles. Richard Oliver, a London sugar

---

52 *Tullideph L. B.*, vol. 2: Lre. to Ephraim Jordan in Antigua, 11 July 1754.
53 Anon., *An Account of the Late Application to Parliament, From the Sugar Refiners, Grocers, etc. of London, Westminster, Southwark, and Bristol* (London, 1754), pp. 3–8, 38.
54 Ibid., pp. 8, 26–7.

factor, wrote to a correspondent in October 1752: 'Our Sugr market hath been by the Combination of the Bakers a little heavy but they now buy tho' with great Complaints & are scheeming for Introduceing Forreign Sugr Even upon the Double Duty'.[55] In April 1754, Dr Tullideph wrote of his fear that the supply of plantation sugar might not be adequate to satisfy the home consumption, 'and if that ever happens to be our case, I fear our Enemies the Bakers & Grocers will make Application for leave to Import French Sugars'.[56]

By this time the planters were afraid that their strategy had become too successful. They were confronted by a growing chorus of critics. Probably the leading critic was Joseph Massie, prolific writer of pamphlets on various economic questions of the day. In a pamphlet entitled *A State of the British Sugar-Colony Trade* (1759), he enumerated the many benefits conferred upon the planters during the past thirty years. They included the liberty to import British colonial rum directly into Ireland; the prohibition of French sugar, rum, and molasses imports into Ireland; the high duties levied on all foreign sugar products imported into the British North American colonies; the liberty to carry sugar from the British plantations to foreign ports in Europe; the privilege of landing rum in Great Britain without 'paying the Duty of Excise until such Rum be sold, or hath been landed Six Months'; and the prohibitory duties levied on foreign sugars imported into Great Britain. After reciting these benefits, Massie estimated that the 'exorbitant Gain which the Sugar-Planters have made, over and above large Profits' amounted to £8 million for the thirty-year period.[57]

Whatever the merits and demerits of the complaints against the planters may have been, it is clear that the period following the publication of Massie's pamphlet saw an increase in colonial output and a decline in prices. In fact, the London price of muscovado sugar declined irregularly from 45s 9d per cwt in 1759, to 34s 0d in 1775.[58] Bryan Edwards, the planter-historian, denied that the monopoly of the home market was detrimental to consumers. He maintained that if allowances were made for the differences in quality and fiscal burdens, muscovado sugar would command approximately the same price in France and England.[59]

55 Lre. to John Tomlinson in Antigua, 31 Oct. 1752, quoted in *Caribbeana*, ed. Vere L. Oliver, vol. 3 (London, 1914), p. 47.
56 *Tullideph L. B.*, vol. 2: Lre. to Dr Walter Sydserfe in Antigua, 5 April 1754.
57 Joseph Massie, *A State of the British Sugar-Colony Trade* (London, 1759), pp. 50–3.
58 See Appendix V.
59 Bryan Edwards, *The History, Civil and Commercial, of the British Colonies in the West Indies* (Dublin, 1793), vol. 2, pp. 415–19; Richard B. Sheridan, 'The Molasses Act and the Market Strategy of the British Sugar Planters', *Jour. Econ. Hist.*, vol. XVII, no. 1 (March 1957), pp. 62–83.

8 CONCLUSION

In conclusion, it appears that while the Molasses Act may be dismissed as a near failure in its application to the North American colonies, it cannot be so regarded with respect to the British Isles. Actually, the Act proved to be quite effective in expanding the protected home market to include Ireland. The success of the planter interest may be attributed to four main developments. First, the consumption of sugar and rum underwent considerable expansion in England as a consequence of population growth, rising living standards, and the widespread consumption of tea, coffee, and punch. Second, the supply of sugar forthcoming from the plantations tended to lag behind the demand. Third, changes in the Navigation Acts allowed sugar products to go to Ireland and Scotland; and, fourth, comparatively little foreign sugar invaded the protected home market. These forces may have conspired at times to force British sugar prices above the level prevailing upon the continent of Europe. The planter interest thus enjoyed a period of profitable activity which continued with little abatement from the late 1730s to the outbreak of the American War of Independence in 1775.

CHAPTER FIVE

The Settlement of the Sugar Colonies

> But it is not a worke for euery one to manage such an affaire, as make a discouery and plant a Colony, it requires all the best parts of art, iudgement, courage, honesty, constancy, diligence, and industry, to doe but neere well; some are more proper for one thing then another, and therein best to be imploied: and nothing breeds more confusion then misplacing and misimploying men in their vndertakings.[1]
>
> Captain John Smith, 1624

1 ENGLAND ON THE EVE OF COLONIZATION

The establishment of colonies in the islands of the Caribbean Sea must be seen against the background of late Elizabethan and Stuart England. However intractable the political, social, and religious questions of the time might appear, Englishmen began to regard the New World as a means of resolving their problems. Ideologically, English society became fractured along religious, political, and economic lines until recourse was had to civil war and regicide. Internationally, England was involved in a struggle with the mercantile powers of Spain, Portugal, France, and the Netherlands. Even if not directly involved herself, England's foreign trade was jeopardized by the almost constant succession of wars in Europe.

Colonies were widely regarded as a remedy for England's social condition. The late years of Elizabeth's reign were characterized by widespread social unrest occasioned by poor harvests, plague, enclosures, and the conversion of arable fields into pasture for sheep grazing. Moreover, it was thought that the population was outstripping employment opportunities. Following the Anglo-Spanish treaty of 1604 came a period of prosperity which was attributed in large measure to the boom in woollen cloth exports. But the onset of

---

1 *Travels and Works of Captain John Smith 1580–1631*, ed. Edward Arber (Edinburgh, 1910), vol. 2, p. 705.

Sugar and Slavery

the Thirty Years' War was marked by severe curtailment of export markets. Acute depression marked the years from 1620 to 1624.[2]

Among the writers who saw in colonies a solution to England's social problem was Richard Eburne, a Somerset parson. He observed in 1624 that as nature 'hath taught the bees when their hive is overfull to part company and by swarming to seek a new habitation elsewhere', so 'it is as lawful for men to remove from one country to another as out of the house wherein they are born or the parish wherein they are bred unto another'.[3]

The first permanent English colonies were established in the New World during the two decades of peace with Spain. It is noteworthy that Virginia and Plymouth plantation were tolerated reluctantly by Spain, whereas English settlements in the West Indies would have threatened the Anglo-Spanish peace. Besides the colonization motive, it was hoped that gold and silver mines might be exploited, that a westward passage to Asia might be discovered, and that profitable trade with the Indians might develop, whereby woollens would be exchanged for furs, naval stores, and other raw materials. New trades and trade routes might thus free England from commercial dependence on her European rivals.

These and other motives for colonization were enumerated by Richard Eburne. In favouring Newfoundland and other temperate-zone colonies over tropical settlements, he observed that 'if the plantation proceed by hundreds, Guiana is best; if by thousands, Newfoundland is best'. Moveover, if the objective was riches from tropical produce, Guyana should be preferred, but if room was needed for the overswarming multitudes of England then the sparsely populated and spacious island of Newfoundland should be settled. Eburne favoured Newfoundland over other possible locations because of its remoteness from Spanish America; absence of hostile Indians; cheap passage for immigrants; favourable conditions of health, climate, and soil; ample land reserves; the possibility of combining agricultural settlements with fishing ventures; and the island's strategic position for re-emigration to mainland areas.[4]

---

[2] Barry Supple, *Commercial Crisis and Change in England 1600–1642* (Cambridge, 1959), pp. 20–9, 52–69.
[3] Richard Eburne, *A Plain Pathway to Plantations* (1624), (Ithaca, 1962), p. 41.
[4] Ibid., pp. 135–8.

2 GUYANA AND THE CARIBBEES

The same year that saw the publication of Eburne's *Plain Pathway to Plantations* also witnessed a rupture in Anglo-Spanish relations. The failure of the proposed marriage alliance of the royal families of England and Spain was followed by the renewal of English privateering raids in the Caribbean Sea. Hostilities were opened by the Dutch West India Company against the Portuguese colony of Brazil in 1624, at a time when Portugal was a province of Spain. While the efforts of Spain were diverted to the defence of Brazil, the nations of northern Europe began to seize on the islands of the Lesser Antilles. In the words of Professor Newton, 'After 1625 swarms of English and French colonists poured like flies upon the rotting carcass of Spain's empire in the Caribbean, and within ten years the West Indian scene was changed for ever'.[5]

If the line between the north and south is drawn at the northern boundary of the tobacco colonies, it is clear that the main direction of early English colonization was towards the south. Even after the close of the great migration of the Puritans to New England, there were, in 1640, more than twice as many settlers in the sugar and tobacco colonies (52,000) as in New England (22,550). The impact of the migration was both direct and indirect, for in subsequent decades Barbadians and New Englanders re-emigrated to such newly-established colonies as Jamaica and Carolina.[6]

It is also clear that the shift to the south was motivated by the discovery and cultivation of tropical and subtropical staples, first by white yeomen and indentured servants, and later under a plantation regime of white capital and coloured labour. In Virginia John Rolfe shipped the first cargo of tobacco to England in 1613, thus laying the basis for the economic development of that colony. The planting of tobacco by Englishmen and Dutchmen sprang up simultaneously in Guyana. When the English settlements in Guyana succumbed to sickness, ill-luck, and Spanish opposition, tobacco seeds were carried to the Lesser Antilles. By contrast with Virginia, which remained essentially a tobacco colony until the eve of the American Revolution, the tropical islands to the south were adapted to a wide range of export staples. Tobacco and cotton, the leading staples of the pioneer period, gave way to a near-monoculture sugar regime, notwithstanding the limited production of cotton, ginger, tobacco, indigo, coffee, and numerous other commodities.

5 A. P. Newton, *The European Nations in the West Indies 1493–1688* (London, 1933), pp. 149–50.
6 Curtis P. Nettles, 'The Place of Markets in the Old Colonial System', *New England Quarterly*, vol. VI, no. 3, (1933), p. 502.

Sugar and Slavery

Colonization of the Caribbean islands was both preceded by and causally linked to English privateering raids in Spanish waters. Raiding and trading brought Drake and Hawkins and their followers to the Caribbean in the Elizabethan age. These forays, some leading to the capture of rich booty, continued under sanction of the Crown until the Anglo-Spanish treaty of 1604. By this treaty James I recognized Spain's claim to all territory effectively occupied, but not to the unoccupied parts of the New World. English ports were closed to Spanish prizes and Englishmen were forbidden to fit out vessels in English harbours for privateering raids to the Spanish Main. But to circumvent this ban certain Englishmen launched privateering voyages from such remote ports as Barnstaple and Dartmouth, or they took out letters of marque from the Prince of Orange and other rulers. Among these merchant-adventurers were Robert Rich, later Earl of Warwick, the Courteen brothers of London and Middleburg, and their partners and associates Ralph Merrifield and Marmaduke Rawden, both merchants of London. Privateering was probably an important source of capital for the infant settlements in the West Indies.[7]

Englishmen were first attracted to Guyana, 'the swampy noman's-land' between Spanish Venezuela and Portuguese Brazil. Sir Walter Raleigh in 1595 and again in 1617 searched up the Orinoco River for the golden city of Manoa without success. He published *The Discoverie of the large and bewtiful Empire of Guiana* (1596) which created much interest in the region. Though gold was his primary objective, Raleigh noted the great quantities of Brazil wood, cotton, balsam gums, and Indian pepper. 'The soile besides is so excellent and so full of riuers, as it will carrie sugar, ginger, and all those other commodities, which the West Indies hath'.[8]

Following in the footsteps of Raleigh were Charles Leigh in 1604 and Robert Harcourt in 1609, who founded short-lived settlements for trade with the Indians. Harcourt returned again to Guyana in 1613, this time to project a true plantation colony of tobacco growers. Harcourt's second colonization venture was a failure, as was that of Captain Roger North who had accompanied Raleigh on his last voyage to Guyana.

Captain North's colony is of interest as a link with the first permanent English settlement in the West Indies. A brother of Lord North and a cousin of the Earl of Warwick, who was one of his financial

---

[7] Charles M. Andrews, *The Colonial Period of American History* (New Haven, 1934), vol. 1, pp. 46-7.
[8] Quoted by Louis B. Wright in *The Colonial Search for a Southern Eden* (Birmingham, Alabama, 1953), p. 15.

backers, Captain North founded the Amazon Company in 1618. In 1620, he sailed secretly from Plymouth with some 120 other adventurers and settled 100 leagues up the Amazon river. After a short stay North returned to England with a cargo of tobacco. Upon arrival he found that the Spanish ambassador had complained to James I of his settlement, whereupon North was committed to the Tower of London. Discouraged by lack of support from home, the planters decided to abandon the colony on the Amazon but to continue the business of planting on one of the unoccupied islands of the Lesser Antilles.[9]

Among those quitting the colony was Thomas Warner, who, upon learning from a companion, one Captain Painton, of the fertility of the island of St Christopher, investigated the island and found it well adapted to an agricultural settlement. Warner then returned to England. He arrived at a propitious time, for the rupture with Spain had been followed by proposals by high government officials to undertake a colonization enterprise in the West Indies, partly with a view to drawing off idle people from the kingdom without cost to the King. Warner thus encountered little difficulty in securing support for his venture. He and his fourteen companions sailed in November 1622, and, after touching at Virginia and Barbados, arrived at St Christopher on 28 January 1623, to begin the first permanent English colony in the West Indies. Other colonizers followed until Englishmen were permanently established on six Caribbean islands by the restoration of Charles II.[10]

A mixture of motives lay behind this folk movement from the cloud-shrouded island in the North Sea to remote islands in the sun. Mention has been made of the fear of over-population and unemployment, made acute by the commercial crisis of 1620–4. Coupled with this was the desire for national self-sufficiency in an age when tropical commodities were making inroads into consumption patterns and international rivalry was a bar to trade on a multilateral basis. Preoccupation with trade balances not only influenced commercial policy in intra-European trades, but also dampened enthusiasm for England's trade with the East Indies. Though the East India Company was defended by powerful men, a considerable body of opinion favoured the establishment of colonies where Englishmen might produce tropical wealth for themselves without draining bullion from the metropolis. Then, too, the early settlements in

---

9 Arber, *Works of Captain John Smith*, vol. 2, pp. 896–8.
10 A. P. Newton, *The Colonizing Activities of the English Puritans* (New Haven, 1914), pp. 28–9; V. T. Harlow (ed.), *Colonising Expeditions to the West Indies and Guiana 1623–1667* (London, 1924), p. xv.

Sugar and Slavery

North America and Guyana were slow to yield financial returns. In the words of Professor Williamson, 'the earlier colonization motives — Manoa, goldmines, the Pacific passage, the collection by barter of trade-goods, the sale of clothes to naked savages — had all fallen into the background at the opening of the third decade of the seventeenth century, and the regular planting of tropical produce was now recognized as the prime incentive of the future'.[11]

3 PROBLEMS, PROJECTS, AND PROJECTORS

Numerous hazards attended the establishment of colonies on tropical islands. Colonizers had to cope with the usual difficulties of pioneer settlement, such as searching out the land, clearing forests, adapting export crops to soil and climate, and meeting the inexorable demands of subsistence. Special risks attended colonizers in the tropics. Even if Europeans escaped the blight of tropical disease, they were deterred from physical labour by the enervating climate. Further uncertainties included the threat of Spanish retaliation, rivalry with other European powers, and the warlike Carib Indians who occupied numerous islands in the Lesser Antilles. To overcome these and other obstacles ample supplies of labour and capital under capable leadership and military protection were required.

It is significant that in the early years of settlement economic and demographic conditions in England favoured emigration, while depressed trade in Europe encouraged some merchants to shift their theatre of action to the colonies. One contemporary who regarded the West India business as 'doubtless the most hopeful and feasible design that can be fallen upon, if it could be followed as it ought to be', cautioned that 'it must constantly be pursued at great expence for some years, without expecting a present profit'.[12]

Who were the merchants who projected, financed, and serviced the infant settlements in the West Indies? In the main they were Englishmen until the Civil War period when Dutchmen made heavy inroads into the colonial trade. Though numerous merchants are mentioned in the literature, the big tasks of recruiting settlers, supplying capital, and enlisting the aid of courtiers were undertaken by a group of wealthy London merchants. These men were often engaged in a variety of legitimate trades as well as privateering ventures; they

---

11 James A. Williamson, *The Caribbee Islands Under the Proprietary Patents* (Oxford, 1926), pp. 9–10.
12 *Cal. S. P. Col. 1574–1660*, p. 257: The Earl of Northumberland to Sir Thomas Roe, 6 Aug. 1637.

The Settlement of the Sugar Colonies

spread their risks widely and could afford to venture into unknown waters. Yet the demands were so heavy and the risks so great that merchants often acted together in syndicates, and even then the losses frequently exceeded the gains.

4 THE COURTEEN BROTHERS AND BARBADOS

Sir William Courteen (1572–1636), an Anglo-Dutch merchant with extensive trading and financial connections, planted the first settlement in Barbados. Courteen's father, a Dutch Protestant who had been persecuted by the Spaniards, escaped to England in 1568 and settled in London as a trader in silks and linen. The family business descended to Sir William, who at an early age was sent to Holland as factor to his father's firm. There he married the daughter of a wealthy Dutch merchant. Returning to London he entered into partnership, in 1606, with his brother Sir Peter Courteen and brother-in-law John Mounsey. By 1631, when the firm was reputed to be worth £150,000, the trade had been extended to Guinea, Portugal, Spain, and the East and West Indies. At the height of their business the Courteen fleet numbered twenty vessels which were manned by nearly 5,000 seamen. Trade was the stepping-stone to landed wealth and finance, for besides the purchase of landed estates, Sir William and an associate lent as much as £200,000 to James I and Charles I. In later life Sir William suffered financial reverses, but as late as 1633 he possessed a capital of approximately £128,000.[13]

In 1624, a ship belonging to Sir William Courteen sailed from Brazil to England, touching at the unoccupied island of Barbados. Upon arrival in England the commander of the ship, one John Powell, reported his discovery to his employer. Courteen then prepared an expedition under Powell's direction to take out a party of colonists, possess the island, and commence the planting of tobacco. The first expedition never reached its destination, being diverted by a privateering venture. Courteen then formed a syndicate which outfitted an expedition of eighty men under the direction of Captain Henry Powell. The party arrived at Barbados on 20 February 1627. After the colonists disembarked, Powell sailed on to the river Essequibo in Guyana, where he 'furnished himself with rootes, plants, fowles, tobacco seeds, sugger canes and other matterialls, togither with thirty two Indians which hee carried to the said Iland for the Planting thereof'.[14]

13 *Dictionary of National Biography* (New York, 1885), vol. 12, pp. 333–5.
14 Trinity College, Dublin MSS G, 14, 15: Henry Powell's Examination.

Sugar and Slavery

Favourable reports from the colonists encouraged Courteen to continue the venture. His factors and servants settled several plantations for tobacco and subsistence crops. Additional colonists were recruited, and by the end of 1628 it was reported that 'English, Indians and others, to the Number of 1850 Men, Women and Children, or there abouts' were on the island.[15] By this time, according to Professor Williamson, 'Barbados was a more lusty infant than any English colony as yet planted. The total expenditure of the syndicate was estimated in 1629 at £10,000, and the time was not far distant when it might look for a handsome return upon its outlay'.[16]

But disaster soon overtook the Courteen syndicate. It came from a rival syndicate of merchants, whose patron was the favourite of Charles I. Acting on behalf of Sir William Courteen, the Earl of Pembroke obtained letters patent to certain of the Caribbee Islands on 25 February 1628. In the previous year Thomas Warner and his merchant backers enlisted the aid of the Earl of Carlisle to secure a patent to another group of islands in the Caribbee chain. In the ensuing dispute it was revealed that both patents included the island of Barbados, although Pembroke argued that the Carlisle patent referred to Barbuda in the Leeward Islands rather than to Barbados. The issue was resolved when the Earl of Carlisle asserted his influence over King Charles to secure this most valuable of the Caribbee Islands. Thus defeated, Courteen and his partners were supplanted by the rival syndicate. In an unsuccessful petition for indemnity, the heirs of Sir William claimed that he had planted 1,850 people in Barbados and that £60,000 and upwards had been sunk in that island.[17]

5 SIR MARMADUKE ROYDEN AND BARBADOS

Heading the rival syndicate was the merchant-adventurer, Marmaduke Rawden (1583–1646), afterwards known as Sir Marmaduke Royden. Born and reared in Yorkshire, at the age of sixteen he was apprenticed to a Bordeaux merchant in London, who sent him as his factor to France. In 1610, Rawden returned to London and soon afterwards was elected a common councilman and presented with the freedom of the Clothworkers' Company, of which he later became Master. His upward climb in the mercantile world was aided by his

---

15 British Museum, Egerton MSS 2395, f. 602.
16 Williamson, *The Caribbee Islands*, p. 38.
17 B. M. Egerton MSS 2395, f. 602.

The Settlement of the Sugar Colonies

marriage to an heiress, who brought him a fortune of £10,000. Besides his West India connection, Rawden traded with New England, Spain, Turkey, and the Canaries. In 1628 he was elected M.P. for Aldborough, and in 1643 he was knighted. In the Civil Wars Rawden fought on the King's side.[18]

Rawden apparently traded with St Christopher before he became a prime mover in the Barbados affair. In the background of this affair were large debts owed by the Earl of Carlisle to Rawden and other London merchants. In April 1628, the Earl of Carlisle granted to Rawden and two other London merchants 10,000 acres of land in Barbados, with a government and governor of their own choosing. Six other London merchants were later added to the syndicate. The syndicate then sent a group of eighty settlers to Barbados under Charles Wolverston, their governor. Upon their arrival in 1628 conflict developed between the Rawden and Courteen colonists. In fact, control of the island changed hands several times before the Rawden group emerged victorious.[19]

Though Rawden is not known to have visited Barbados, one of his sons resided there until 1662, and a great grandson claimed two plantations there in 1752. Rawden incurred heavy losses on his Barbadian venture, reputedly to the amount of £10,000.[20]

The island of Barbados was first intended as an estate to be worked for the benefit of the merchants and the proprietor. In the space of a few years it became a land of yeomen cultivators who were later supplanted in large measure by the sugar planters. Under the Courteen syndicate the first settlers were paid employees rather than land-owning planters. Grants to settlers commenced on 2 June 1627, when sixty-four individuals received 100 acres each. The grants continued to the year 1638, when only one grant of fifty acres was made. By this time it appears that all of the useful land was occupied. Altogether, 771 grants were made for a total of 67,929 acres (not including the 10,000 acres granted to the Rawden syndicate), or an average of 88 acres. That the grantees were men of some substance is evident from the fact that landholders were subject to payment of proprietary dues and one servant was required for every ten acres of land on penalty of forfeiture.[21]

Many of the grants were apparently subdivided into tenant holdings or sold in small parcels. Barbados was reported to have had

---

18 *Dictionary of National Biography*, vol. 49, pp. 373–4.
19 B. M. Egerton MSS 2395, f. 602; Williamson, *The Caribbee Islands*, pp. 48–9.
20 *Dictionary of National Biography*, vol. 49, pp. 373–4; *Caribbeana*, ed. Vere L. Oliver, vol. 5 (London, 1919), pp. 121–5.
21 Anon., *Some Memoirs of the First Settlement of the Island of Barbados* (Barbados, 1741), pp. 8–20, 70–84; Williamson, *The Caribbee Islands*, p. 36.

Sugar and Slavery

18,600 effective men in 1643, of whom 8,500 were proprietors. Another contemporary observed that 'much of Barbados was devided into five, ten, twenty, and thirty-Acre devidends . . .', at a time when only 766 individuals were possessed of ten acres or more.[22]

Settlers were initially occupied with the arduous tasks of clearing land and growing provisions for their subsistence. In the words of Richard Ligon, who lived in Barbados from 1647 to 1650:

> Ships were sent, with men, provisions, and working tools, to cut down the Woods, and clear the ground, so as they might plant provisions to keep them alive, which, till then, they found but straglingly amongst the Woods. But having clear'd some part of it, they planted *Potatoes, Plantines,* and *Mayes,* with some other fruits; which, with the Hogflesh they found, serv'd only to keep life and soul together. And their supplies from *England* coming so slow, and so uncertainly, they were often driven to great extremities: and the Tobacco that grew there, so earthy and worthless, so that for a while they lingered in a lamentable conditions.[23]

Greater certainty of imported supplies and the extension of provision culture provided a base for the cultivation of export staples. By 1631 the cultivation of tobacco, cotton, and ginger had become well established.[24]

6 EARLY SETTLEMENT OF ST CHRISTOPHER

Heading the syndicate which planted the colony of St Christopher under Thomas Warner's leadership was Ralph Merrifield, a London, merchant who was interested in the clandestine trade of the West Indies. Warner, who had gone out with the first group of colonists in January 1623, returned to England the following September. Together with Merrifield, he obtained a royal commission for the planting of the islands of St Christopher, Nevis, Montserrat, and Barbados. The commission was superseded by letters patent dated 2 July 1627, granting to the Earl of Carlisle some twenty-two islands in the Lesser Antilles. From this time until 1647 the Caribbee Islands were under the proprietary government of the Earl of Carlisle and his heirs, and from 1647 to 1660 under Francis, Lord Willoughby of Parham, who was lessee of the Carlisle proprietorship.[25]

22 B. M. Sloane MSS 3662, f. 59: John Scott, *The Description of Barbados;* Noel Deerr, *The History of Sugar* (London, 1949–50), vol. 1, pp. 160–1.
23 Richard Ligon, *A True and Exact History of the Island of Barbadoes* (London, 1673), p. 24.
24 Idem.
25 Williamson, *The Caribbee Islands,* pp. 38–47, 120–34.

The Settlement of the Sugar Colonies

Meanwhile, the English colonists in St Christopher had established a foothold made precarious by incursions of warlike Carib Indians and the threat of Spanish retaliation. Another potential danger came from the colony of Frenchmen who had settled in St Christopher in 1624 or 1625. Realizing their weakness in the face of the common enemy, Englishmen and Frenchmen subordinated their differences, occupied separate portions of the island, and joined forces in military defence. One invading force of Caribs numbered 400 or 500, according to one Englishman: 'We bade them be gone, but they would not; whereupon we and the *French* joyned together, and upon the fifth of November [1625] set upon them and put them to flight'.[26]

Natural disasters also took a heavy toll in the early years of settlement. In 1624 and 1626 severe hurricanes virtually wiped out the settlements. On the former occasion, according to Captain John Smith, the settlers had built a fort and a house, had planted fruits and a crop of tobacco; 'but upon the nineteenth of September came a *Hericano* and blew it away: all this while wee lived upon Cassada bread, Potatoes, Plantines, Pines, Turtels, Guanes [lizards], and fish plentie; for drinke wee had *Nicnobbie*'. The second hurricane was equally disastrous: 'All our provisions thus lost, we were very miserable, living onely on what we could get in the wilde woods'.[27]

Though St Christopher recovered from these disasters, an even greater danger was imminent. By 1629 the colony had grown sufficiently to be regarded as a threat to the Spanish Indies. English settlers had been recruited to the number of nearly 3,000, and guns and ammunition had been sent over. Orders were given to the commander of the outward bound Spanish fleet to Mexico to clear out the English and French colonies. The fleet of about thirty-five sail took the infant settlement at Nevis by surprise on 7 September 1629, and then moved on to the sister island. Several days later the settlers at St Christopher surrendered to the Spaniards. By the terms of surrender the Spaniards allotted shipping to carry some 700 of the colonists to England. But other colonists, variously estimated at from 200 to 400, evaded surrender by taking to the hills and woods. After the Spaniards departed from the island the fugitives returned to their plantations to form the nucleus of a new phase of colonization.[28]

From a precariously based foothold in the Caribbean, the settlement at St Christopher gained in numbers and strength until it became a base for expansion into neighbouring islands. In fact, both nationalities took part in this island-hopping activity; the French, for

---

26 Arber, *Works of Captain John Smith*, p. 901.
27 Ibid., pp. 900–1.
28 Williamson, *The Caribbee Islands*, pp. 74–81.

Sugar and Slavery

example, began to colonize the islands of Martinique and Guadeloupe in 1635. But the outward movement of Englishmen commenced even earlier.

7 THE NEVIS SETTLEMENT

The English settlement at Nevis, a near neighbour of St Christopher, was initiated by Anthony Hilton, the colonizer, and supported by Thomas Littleton, a London merchant. Hilton had been previously employed by certain merchants of Barnstaple in the Virginia tobacco trade and in the discovery of a Northwest Passage. On a voyage to Virginia he touched at St Christopher. There he made the acquaintance of Thomas Warner, who impressed him with the possibilities of the island for tobacco growing. Hilton then secured the backing of certain Irish gentlemen and returned to St Christopher with a few followers to commence the planting of tobacco on the windward side of the island. The Caribs destroyed his first plantation. He then cleared another plantation on the leeward side, raised a crop of tobacco, and carried it to Ireland where it fetched a good price. From Ireland, Hilton sailed for London. There he obtained financial support from Thomas Littleton, and with Littleton's aid a patent from the Earl of Carlisle for the settlement of the islands adjacent to St Christopher. Hilton and his associates arrived at Nevis on 22 July 1628. By the end of the year the pioneer settlers had been joined by nearly 150 planters from St Christopher.[29]

The part played by Thomas Littleton in the settlement of Nevis is clearly revealed by the bill of complaint he submitted to the Court of Chancery in April 1631, reciting that he had furnished three ships with meal, bread, munitions, clothing and other necessaries to the value of £5,000. Part of the goods were consigned to one John Procter, his agent and factor in Nevis, and another part sold directly to Hilton. There follows the names of eighty debtors with the individual amounts still owing. Littleton claimed that he had repeatedly demanded payment from 'Captaine Anthony Hilton and the other persons who refused to pay and intended to defraud your orator who hath made so great an adventure for the settlement of a plantacon in the said Island . . .'.[30] Soon after the bill of complaint was submitted Littleton went to Nevis in an effort to collect his debts. Hilton resigned the government to him and went off to the

---

[29] Williamson, *The Caribbee Islands*, pp. 66–9; Newton, *Colonizing Activities of English Puritans*, pp. 100–4.
[30] *Littleton v. Bullock*, Chancery Proceedings, Charles I, L. 6, No. 10, reprinted in *Caribbeana*, ed. V. L. Oliver, vol. 2, p. 3.

The Settlement of the Sugar Colonies

island of Tortuga. Since he was the leading creditor of the planters, it is doubtful if Littleton made a popular governor. About 1634 he also left Nevis for Tortuga where shortly afterwards he died.[31]

8 MONTSERRAT AND ANTIGUA

Montserrat and Antigua, two islands in the vicinity of St Christopher, were colonized by Englishmen in the second quarter of the 17th century. Though both islands are thought to have been settled in 1632, it was not until 1636 that they became recognized colonies. In that year Captain Anthony Brisket, Governor of Montserrat, was in England. There he recruited more planters and applied for a new commission from the heirs of the Earl of Carlisle. Brisket was an Irishman, and Montserrat was largely an Irish colony. The cultivation of tobacco, cotton, and subsistence crops probably occupied the settlers in the early years of the colony. Not until the Commonwealth period do we find much evidence of trade. In 1649, for example, the Council of State issued a warrant to Samuel Atkins to export twenty geldings to Montserrat for the use of his sugar works there. In the following year a similar warrant was issued to Martin Noell and Robert Wilding, both merchants of London, to trade with the islands of Nevis and Montserrat.[32]

As with Montserrat, little is known of the infant colony of Antigua. The first group of settlers probably came from St Christopher, for the first governor is said to have been Edward Warner, son of Sir Thomas Warner. One account says that the colony consisted of about thirty families in 1640. In that year they were attacked by the Caribs, who killed fifty settlers and carried off the governor's lady, her two children, and three other women. Carib raids must have continued intermittently for some years, for in 1655 Captain Gregory Butler wrote to Oliver Cromwell that the inhabitants were 'much mollested with the Indyens ... there not being on the island above twelve hundred men'.[33]

Prospects appear to have been brighter in the subsequent period. An undated document, probably written in 1656 or 1657, said that 'At present divers are in a hopefull way upon ye designe of sugar, cotton, Indico & other Commodityes & all of them generally well stocked with Cattell that they transport them from thence to the

---

31 Williamson, *The Caribbee Islands* pp. 81–2, 150.
32 Ibid., pp. 94–5; *Cal. S. P. Col. 1574–1660*, pp. 330, 348.
33 Vere L. Oliver, *The History of the Island of Antigua* (London, 1894–99), vol. 1, pp. xix, xxv.

Sugar and Slavery

Barbados & all other English plantations in those parts'.³⁴ The document, goes on to complain of the scarcity of men servants and the engrossment of land by absentee proprietors. Governor Keynell wrote that the island suffered from internecine warfare between Cavaliers and Roundheads and the interruption of trade during the first Anglo-Dutch War. On the positive side Keynell called attention to the healthy climate, 'soil not inferior to any of the Caribee islands, and very productive in tobacco, sugar, indigo and cotton. Great store of saltpetre, natural salt ponds, plenty of fish and fowls, and good stock of cattle'.³⁵

9 MAURICE THOMPSON

Relations between London merchants and the infant settlement of Antigua are poorly documented. Though the evidence is sketchy, there are grounds for believing that Maurice Thompson, the merchant-adventurer, had interests in Antigua. Rowland Thompson was a landed proprietor and probably a governor of Antigua in the 1640s. Edward Thompson, his son and heir, may have been the man by the same name who was Maurice Thompson's brother and master of his ship *Ruth*. As it was customary for London merchants to send out relatives to manage their trade and property interests and undertake the political direction of colonies, it may be conjectured that Rowland Thompson was a kinsman of Maurice Thompson.³⁶

Maurice Thompson stands on a par with the Courteens and Martin Noell as a founder and developer of the Caribbean colonies. Extensive trade with Africa, the East and West Indies, and North America, besides numerous privateering voyages, entitle him to rank as one of the leading merchant-adventurers of his time. We learn of his extensive 'interloping' activities in Canada, of his powerful 'combine' to monopolize the entire tobacco output of Virginia, of the five ships he and his brother sent to the coast of Africa in 1656, of his leadership in the Guinea Company, of Cromwell favouring the Maurice Thompson group in the East India trade, and of Thompson dispatching eleven ships on his own account to India in 1656.³⁷ In 1642, he helped to finance the buccaneering expedition of Captain

---

34 B. M. Egerton MSS 2395, f. 108.
35 Oliver, *History of Antigua*, p. xxvii.
36 Ibid., pp. xvii–xix; *Acts of the Privy Council, Colonial Series, 1613–1680* (London, 1908), vol. 1, p. 295.
37 Harlow, *Colonising Expeditions*, p. 26, n. 1; *A Collection of the State Papers of John Thurloe* (London, 1742), vol. 7, pp. 757–9; Maurice Ashley, *Financial and Commercial Policy under the Cromwellian Protectorate* (2nd ed., London, 1962), p. 114.

The Settlement of the Sugar Colonies

William Jackson, whose forces captured the capital city of Jamaica, held the inhabitants to ransom, and retired only on receiving 7,000 pieces of eight and very large stores of victuals. Again, Thompson took a prominent part in fitting out the Penn and Venables expedition which captured Jamaica from the Spaniards in 1655. During the period of the Long Parliament he was a Commissioner of the Navy and Customs.[38] Finally, a recent study shows that the Navigation Act of 1651 was sponsored by Maurice Thompson and a group of his relatives and friends who had interests in trade and colonies.[39]

In the Caribbee Islands Thompson traded chiefly with St Christopher and Barbados. We hear of him first in 1626 when he and his partner Thomas Combe outfitted three ships which carried Thomas Warner and a group of sixty slaves to St Christopher. On the return voyage 9,500 lb of tobacco were carried to London for the account of Thompson and Combe. The following year he received a grant of 1,000 acres of land in that island. At this time Maurice Thompson and Ralph Merrifield were the chief merchants interested in the Leeward Islands, both closely associated with Sir Thomas Warner and the Earl of Carlisle.[40]

Numerous accounts of Thompson's trade with Barbados and Virginia appear in the state papers. When the Earl of Carlisle leased the Caribbee Islands to Lord Willoughby in 1647, interested merchants and planters petitioned the Committee for Foreign Plantations. Included among the twenty-nine signatures were those of Maurice Thompson, George Pasfield, William Pennoyer, and Martin Noell — all prominent London merchants. The petitioners claimed that Barbados had been planted principally at their own expense. They feared disorder and loss if the government was not settled, and prayed that the tenure of their lands might be settled in free and common socage.[41] As for Thompson's property in Barbados, we find that on 2 May 1649, he and William Pennoyer were issued a licence by the Council of State 'to export 50 cart horses to Barbados, for the service of their sugar works there'. Thompson's propositions concerning the reduction of the Cavalier government of Barbados to the Commonwealth government were heard on 10 September 1650, at a time when an act of Parliament was being drafted for the reduction of Barbados, Antigua, Virginia, and Bermuda. A month later the

---

38 Newton, *Colonizing Activities*, pp. 315–16; Harlow, *Colonising Expeditions*, p. 26; Ashley, *Financial Policy*, p. 51.
39 J. E. Farnell, 'The Navigation Act of 1651, The First Dutch War and the London Merchant Community', *The Economic History Review*, 2nd ser., vol. XVI, no. 3 (April 1964), pp. 439–54.
40 Williamson, *The Caribbee Islands*, p. 31.
41 Ibid., pp. 125–6.

Sugar and Slavery

Committee of the Admiralty received a letter from Thompson, concerning ten or twelve ships to go from Middleburgh and Flushing to Barbados.[42]

10 SIR MARTIN NOELL AND THOMAS POVEY

At a time when Maurice Thompson was among the elder brethren of the London mercantile fraternity, another merchant was coming forward to achieve a position of eminence in trade, finance, and politics. Sir Martin Noell (d. 1665), a scrivener by training, first appears as a merchant in 1650, trading with Nevis and Montserrat. In subsequent years he extended his trade to the other Caribbee islands and Jamaica, as well as to New England, Virginia, and the Levant. Records show that he was financially interested in Scotland, Ireland, and the East India Company. His prominence in salt manufacturing earned him the title of the 'Great Saltmaster of England'. According to Professor Andrews,

> His ships trafficked in a great variety of commodities – iron, hemp, pitch, tar, flax, potashes, cables, fish, cocoa, tobacco, etc., and he became a power in London, his place of business in old Jewry being the resort of merchants, ship captains, and persons desiring to cooperate in his ventures.[43]

Some of these commodities were prize goods taken by Noell's privateers during the wars with Holland and Spain. In fact, the great merchant was one of the commissioners of prize goods.[44]

Politics and public finance came to play an important part in Noell's career. From 1656 to 1660 he was M.P. for Stafford. In 1655, he became a member of the Trade Committee; a year later he was appointed to the Committee for Jamaica. His other affiliations included membership in the Royal Company of Merchants, the African Company, and the Society for the Propagation of the Gospel in New England. He was knighted in 1663. As a man of affairs, Noell's advice was sought by leaders in government. 'The services which he performed for Cromwell in the way of financial administration and lending to the Government far exceeded in number and variety those of any other individual', writes Dr Ashley.[45] Noell

---

42 *Cal. S. P. Col. 1574–1660*, pp. 329, 343, 344.
43 Charles M. Andrews, *British Committees, Commissions, and Councils of Trade and Plantations, 1622–1675* (Baltimore, 1908), pp. 49–50.
44 Idem.
45 Ashley, *Financial Policy*, p. 2.

The Settlement of the Sugar Colonies

turned his political influence to good account, for at one time or other he held the farm of the customs on coal exports along with the farm of the excise on salt, glass, alum, coal, copperas, linen, silk, mercury, and wines. Another perquisite took the form of government contracts to supply military forces and diplomatic representatives who were stationed abroad.[46]

Thomas Povey (c. 1615–88), the civil servant, was an intimate friend and business associate of Sir Martin Noell, especially in matters pertaining to the West Indies. Himself the son of a civil servant, Povey entered Gray's Inn in 1642. He was M.P. for Liskeard 1646–7, and Boissiney 1658–9. In 1657 he became a member of the Council for the Colonies, where he became a conspicuous leader among those interested in plantation affairs.[47] As chairman and secretary of the Council, he exchanged letters with the chief men in all the colonies, 'and particularly with Lord Willoughby of Parham, with whom he stood on terms of intimate friendship and over whose policy he exercised considerable control'.[48]

Povey's trade with the West Indies, which began about 1654, was later supplemented by income which came to him as Receiver General of the rents and revenues of the plantations in Africa and America. Furthermore, he and Noell used their influence to place relatives in colonial governments. Thomas Noell, a brother of Martin Noell, was prominent in Barbados and Surinam. Povey had two brothers in the West Indies; Richard Povey was Commissioner General of Provisions at Jamaica, and William Povey was Provost Marshal at Barbados.[49]

That much of Noell's and Povey's interests centred in Barbados is revealed by Povey's letter-book which is preserved in the British Museum. On 8 January 1657, he wrote to Daniel Searle, Governor of Barbados, of 'it being Mr Noell's earnest attempt and perswasion that I give my self to the asserting and prosecuting the genll affaires of America, and perticularly Barbados . . .'. When Searle's tenure was threatened by factional dispute in the island, Povey wrote to his brother William that the Governor was 'allmost wholly defended and kept upp by Mr Martin Noell's Interest and dexteritie . . .'.[50] Other letters reveal Noell's and Povey's interests in trade and customs farming. On 7 January 1657, Povey wrote to his brother William that a Mr Edward Bradbourne was coming to Barbados as a servant and

46 Ibid., pp. 10–12, 65; Andrews, *British Committees*, p. 50.
47 *Dictionary of National Biography*, vol. 46, pp. 235–6.
48 Andrews, *British Commitees*, pp. 51–2.
49 Ibid., pp. 50–1.
50 B. M. Add. MSS 11,411, f. 124: Thomas Povey, *Register of Letters Relating to the West Indies 1655–1661*.

Sugar and Slavery

factor to Mr Noell. Several months later Povey wrote to Bradbourne that the farm of the customs in Barbados brought in 36,000 pounds of sugar annually, and 'the whole from all the Deputy Marshalls, amounts unto 50,000 weight p. anno. to bee paid quarterly, wch is 14,000 more then my Brothers account'.[51]

11 CONQUEST AND EARLY SETTLEMENT OF JAMAICA

Discovered by Columbus in 1494, Jamaica was a thinly populated and pastoral colony during its century and a half of Spanish rule. Failing in their search for precious metals, the Spaniards were content to use Jamaica as a supply base for their other colonies. Included among the forays by pirates and privateers were the English raids of 1596 and 1643. Then on 10 May 1655, the expedition under Penn and Venables launched a full-scale attack, after an earlier defeat at Hispaniola, which was destined to give Cromwell a base near the centre of the Caribbean Sea for his ambitious Western Design.

Though political and religious considerations played a part in Cromwell's design, the most powerful motive was the economic. The ultimate objective was to break through Spain's monopoly in the West Indies and gain control of Spanish America, thus laying the groundwork for a great mercantile empire. The low estimate of temperate-zone colonies in official circles at this time is evident from Cromwell's scheme to people the colonies taken from Spain with settlers from New England.[52] Military means were devised to achieve these ends, partly formal in periods of warfare against Spain, partly informal through the agency of buccaneers.

But to achieve the goal of military conquest the island of Jamaica must be settled, defended, and made economically viable. To a large extent there was a ready-made answer to the problems of recruiting settlers and providing them with a livelihood. Englishmen who had migrated to the small islands eked out a precarious living growing tobacco, cotton, and other minor staples. Few of them survived the sugar boom and the attendant consolidation of small farms into plantations. The fleet under Penn and Venables called at St Christopher and Barbados and took off as many as 5,000 West Indian settlers and soldiers. Other West Indians were recruited after the capture of Jamaica. In 1656, some 1,500 settlers from Nevis arrived

51 B.M. Add. MSS 11, 411, ff. 130–1, 140.
52 Frank Strong, 'The Causes of Cromwell's West Indian Expedition', *The American Historical Review*, vol. IV, no. 2 (1898–99), pp. 228–45.

The Settlement of the Sugar Colonies

in Jamaica, and in the next decade probably as many more came from Barbados, Bermuda and Surinam.[53]

Besides the settlers, capital was essential for the planting of Jamaica. Some capital was taken from the Spanish inhabitants, while some came with the immigrants from England and the Eastern Caribbean. A substantially greater amount probably came from the activities of Henry Morgan and his motley band of rovers. But the greater part was supplied by certain London merchants who had persuaded Cromwell to undertake his Western Design. The ultimate source of much of this capital was privateering and the profits of trade with the Lesser Antilles. West India policy under the Restoration, writes Professor Thornton, was 'to make a profit in the "Caribees", and to invest for a profit in Jamaica. By their own effort the plantations should maintain themselves'.[54]

Foremost among the London merchants were Maurice Thompson, Martin Noell, Thomas Povey, Andrew Riccard, and Thomas Kendall. Alderman Riccard was a prominent capitalist, while Kendall was a leading West India merchant, 'kin to the Kendalls of Barbados, both an intimate and a cousin of Colonel Thomas Modyford of that Island — yet another of Cromwell's advisers on West India policy . . .'.[55]

We have seen that Thompson, Noell, and Povey were prime movers in the conquest of Jamaica. In 1654, Martin Noell organized a committee in London to finance the Penn and Venables expedition, himself advancing £16,000. In company with Captains Alderne, Watts, and others, he contracted for the supplies of the ships and soldiers, and furnished utensils, clothing, bedding, and provisions for the expedition. Professor Andrews says that Noell was General Venables' personal agent in London and agent for the army in general in Jamaica. He also became a contractor for transporting vagrants, prisoners, and servants to various American plantations.[56]

In part payment for these service, Noell was granted 20,000 acres of land in Jamaica. Private business connected with the settlement of the land grant and other matters are referred to in Povey's letter-book. 'You are to know', wrote Povey to his brother Richard in Jamaica on 8 April 1657, 'that Mr Noell intends to take upp Twenty thousand Acres and to supplye and attend it plentifully. He hath now sent 30 Servants to make provisions for more'. More than a year later Richard Povey was instructed to 'buy upon our account any

---

53 Williamson, *The Caribbee Islands*, pp. 93, 137, 154–63; Clinton V. Black, *History of Jamaica* (London, 1958), pp. 46–57.
54 A. P. Thornton, *West-India Policy Under the Restoration* (Oxford, 1956), p. 64.
55 Ibid., pp. 6–7.
56 Andrews, *British Committees*, p. 50.

Cocoa, or any other good bargaine'. In the same letter Thomas Povey said that 'wee are now contriving to raise a joynt stock of about 20,000*l* for the carrying on some Affaires relating to Jamaica, which will be principally intrusted to you as our Agent there . . .'. With the death of Cromwell in 1658, the joint-stock scheme collapsed and Noell and Povey withdrew from their affairs in the West Indies.[57]

If Jamaica gave promise of wealth from tropical agriculture, the winning of such wealth was no quick and easy matter. The settlers were plagued with famine, pestilence and death before their bridgehead on the frontier of civilization was made fast. A condition of 'extreme want and necessitie' was described by General D'Oyley in 1660, at a time when 'the Plantations yield only present Subsistence to such as are upon them to keepe them alive, whilest their Numbers decrease, noe Servants or Planters being added to them, and those fewe there are spread about 100 miles compass, and soe in noe possibilitie of joyning in an united Defence, upon any considerable Invasion or assault'.[58]

Much of the difficulty was traceable to the prolonged guerilla warfare of the Spaniards, who, from mountain retreats, swept down on English settlements and encampments to kill and plunder. In retaliation, English regiments were established on the more defensible plains region along the south coast where they might have easy access to shipping and where they might turn to planting to provide essential foodstuffs. 'The grand business that the Army is now upon', wrote one observer in 1655, 'is to settle each Regiment in the several Quarters, where they have parcels of land, equally proportioned unto them; which being subdivided amongst the officers according to their respective places, some small share is like to fall unto the Common Soldiers . . .'.[59]

After the Spanish threat subsided, the soldiers and settlers were encouraged to turn to planting. In 1661, the Council of Foreign Plantations recommended to the King that the allotments should vary from 50 acres to each common soldier to 500 acres to each colonel; that 30 acres each be allotted to other settlers; and that the Jamaicans should be exempted for seven years from paying customs on any commodity except sugar, tobacco, cotton and indigo.[60]

The short-term consequences of these measures were far from encouraging. Instead of settling down to agricultural pursuits, the

[57] Povey, *Letters Relating to West Indies*, ff. 32, 69.
[58] B. M. Egerton MSS 2395, f. 242.
[59] Barbados Public Library, Bridgetown, Lucas MSS. *Misc. Notes*, vol. 5, ff. 336–7: 'A brief & perfect journal of . . . the English Army in the West Indies (1655)'.
[60] *Cal. S. P. Col. 1661–68*, p. 37.

The Settlement of the Sugar Colonies

soldiers found more lucrative and adventurous occupations. Some, known as hide hunters, turned to hunting wild cattle and hogs; others felled logwood trees which contained a valuable dye; while others still sought their fortunes in the buccaneering raids which were launched from Port Royal, reputedly the wealthiest and wickedest city on earth. Feeble efforts were made to halt these activities. For example, the Governor and Council of Jamaica ordered 'all hunters to be called in within one month, and no one permitted to hunt, or kill cattle, or keep a gang of dogs, unless he have ten acres of land planted, and has a license'. It is doubtful if this order had much effect, for three years later it was reported: 'The old soldiers for the most part are turned hunters, and it is supposed kill not less than 1,000 cwt. of hog per month, which they sell at from 15s. to 25s. per cwt'.[61]

The real planting of Jamaica is said to have commenced in 1664 with the arrival of Sir Thomas Modyford and some 700 experienced planters from Barbados. But Modyford, as Governor of Jamaica, secretly supported Morgan's buccaneering raids, as did his successor Sir Thomas Lynch. If buccaneering and hide hunting diverted attention from planting, real obstacles included the lack of shipping, difficulty of procuring Negro slaves, and insecurity of life and property. Few planters commanded sufficient resources to launch out on sugar planting prior to the 1670s. The greater number appear to have scratched a tiny fraction of their landholdings with the aid of a few white servants and Negro slaves, cultivating for the most part such minor staples as cocoa, indigo and cotton.[62]

12 CONCLUSION

If it was not a work for every man to discover and plant colonies on the tropical islands of the Caribbean, conditions in England were nevertheless conducive to such exploits in the early 17th century. Economic depression in the decade of the twenties, due partly to economic and social troubles at home and partly to loss of markets on the Continent, created a large class of dispossessed peasants and handicraftsmen, who, like bees, were not averse to swarming outward from the overfull hive. Indeed, the direction and nature of European expansion was influenced in no small measure by England's response to her demographic and social crisis in the early Jacobean age.

61 Ibid., pp. 37, 238.
62 Black, *History of Jamaica*, pp. 60–71.

Sugar and Slavery

But emigration to the wilderness required not only large numbers of men, but also leaders and money. Emigrants must be recruited, outfitted, transported and protected before their pioneer ventures yielded fruit. Again, England was fortunate in having a class of substantial merchants who enlisted the support of courtiers in their colonizing ventures. Wealth and experience had been gained in trading and privateering ventures by men who were adept at shifting from one theatre of action to another as wars and the vicissitudes of the market altered their profit horizon. Though the shift from intra- to extra-European trade was already in evidence, as witness the East India and Virginia trades, the Thirty Years' War on the Continent greatly speeded the movement towards Atlantic colonization and trade. In the vanguard were certain merchant-adventurers of London who had extensive trading connections with the East Indies, Africa, and the North American colonies, besides their support of privateering ventures in the Caribbean Sea. When Anglo-Spanish relations were broken in 1624, the road to the south was laid open.

Yet it is misleading to focus attention on the tropical colonies which survived the initial phase of pioneering and in time emerged as wealthy sugar islands. Actually, more Englishmen failed than succeeded in their search for a southern Eden. Numerous colonial offshoots fell victim to the perils of disease, hostile Indians, rival European powers, and internal dissension.[63] Added to the losses of men and whole colonies of men were the financial losses of the merchant-adventurers who supported them. Indeed, the fruits of these ventures were seldom reaped by the men who launched them but by others who moved in at a later stage of economic development.

---

63 Arber, *Works of Captain John Smith*, p. 705. In the West Indies there were attempted colonies which failed at Grenada, St. Lucia, Trinidad, Tobago, and Santa Cataline, the latter of which a Puritan company renamed Providence and occupied for many years.

CHAPTER SIX

Geographic and Economic Influences

> Before we present you the matters of fact it is fit to offer to your view the Stage whereon they were acted: for as Geography without History seemeth a carkasse without motion; so History without Geography, wandreth as a Vagrant without a certaine habitation.[1]
>
> Captain John Smith, 1624

1 INTRODUCTION

European economic organization in the 17th and 18th centuries centred around the production of food for local consumption, using animate sources of power supplemented by the use of wind and water power. Professor Usher calls this a *food economy*, in contrast with the more recent *fuel economy* which is based on the intensive use of minerals and of mechanical forms of energy derived from such mineral fuels as coal and petroleum. He makes the cogent point that scholars have generalized carelessly about the use of power prior to the Industrial Revolution. 'Thus the use of animal power was given little attention, and the importance of water and wind as sources of power was underestimated'.[2]

Given an economy which was relatively self-sufficient in common foodstuffs and industrial raw materials, it is not surprising that the expansion of Europe was chiefly in the direction of the tropics, that is, to the East and West Indies, the sources of exotic foodstuffs, luxury fabrics, precious jewels, and rare metals. Some of these commodities might be obtained by means of trade with indigenous peoples, as was the case with spices, precious stones, and luxury fabrics; but others, chiefly such tropical and semi-tropical agricultural commodities as sugar and tobacco, entailed the combination of

---

1 *Travels and Works of Captain John Smith, 1580–1631*, ed. Edward Arber, Part II (Edinburgh, 1910), p. 625.
2 Abbott P. Usher, 'Man Molds the World', in *The Challenge of Our Times*, ed. Farrington Daniels and Thomas B. Smith (Minneapolis, 1953), pp. 103–6.

Sugar and Slavery

European capital and managerial skills with forced labour in a plantation system of production.

Numerous writers emphasized the role of tropical plantations in the expansion of European nations. Louis XIV wrote to the Governor of Martinique in 1670: 'The more the colonies differ from the mother country in products, so much more nearly are they perfect, as in the case of the Antilles'.[3] About a century later, Arthur Young, the English agricultural writer, observed:

> The great benefit resulting from colonies is the cultivation of staple commodities different from those of the mother country; that, instead of being obliged to purchase them of foreigners at the expence possibly of treasure, they may be had from settlements in exchange for manufactures.[4]

He observed that while the colonies to the north produced only trifling staples, 'those to the south, on the contrary, are immensely valuable — indeed of such infinite importance to this nation, that *general expressions* of the benefit of our settlements should never be indulged'.[5]

2 CANE SUGAR: ORIGIN AND DISPERSAL

Professor Sauer maintains that the cradle of earliest agriculture was in south-eastern Asia. This was an area of 'high physical and organic diversity, of mild climate with reversed monsoons giving abundant rainy and dry periods, of many waters inviting to fishing, of location at the hub of the Old World for communication by water or by land'.[6] Rather than occupying alluvial river valleys or grassy plains, the first agriculturists were sedentary folk who lived in wooded lands; in the rough clearings they grew plants from cuttings rather than from seeds.

Though folklore suggests that the original home of the wild sugar-cane was in the Polynesian islands of the South Pacific, the vegetative selection and reproduction of the plant is thought to have developed in south-east Asia in Neolithic times. From this centre of what Sauer calls the 'Old Planter Culture', the sugar-cane was

---

3 Quoted in Jose L. Suarez, *Caracter de la Revolution Americana* (Buenos Aires, 1917), pp. 6–7.
4 Arthur Young, *Political Essays Concerning the Present State of the British Empire* (London, 1772), p. 274.
5 Ibid., pp. 326–7.
6 Carl O. Sauer, *Agricultural Origins and Dispersals* (New York, 1952), pp. 20–22.

dispersed to other areas, chiefly to the Middle East and Mediterranean before its migration to the New World. Successive civilizations carried the sugar-cane ever westward, the Moslems eventually planting it on several Mediterranean islands, the Barbary Coast, and Southern Spain.

As islands played a part in the transit of the Mediterranean, so the sugar-cane reached the New World by means of island stepping stones. It was from the Canary Islands, where Spaniards had introduced the plant about 1480, that Columbus obtained sugar-canes and experienced cultivators to carry to Hispaniola in 1493, the seat of the first sugar industry in the New World. In 1425, Prince Henry the Navigator directed that the sugar-cane be carried from Sicily to the Madeira Islands, from whence it was introduced into Brazil about 1520. From Brazil and the coastal region of what is now Guyana and Surinam, the cane was introduced into the Lesser Antilles after 1630.[7]

For a century or more Brazil was the pre-eminent source of cane sugar for the Atlantic and Mediterranean world. More than one European nation played a part in this development, for it is noteworthy that during the Dutch occupation of northern Brazil, 1635–45, the sugar industry received liberal infusions of European capital and African labour. The Dutch, forced to flee Brazil in growing numbers after 1645, and finally driven out by the Portuguese in 1654, turned to the English and French islands in the Lesser Antilles where they are credited with launching the sugar industry.

Meanwhile a motley group of Dutchmen, Frenchmen, and Englishmen had settled in the disputed zone between the Portuguese and Spanish colonies. This region, now comprised in the Guianas, first attracted adventurers like Sir Walter Raleigh who searched for the mythical kingdom of Eldorado where gold was reputed to be found in abundance. After a period of fruitless searching some of the adventurers turned to planting. We have seen that Thomas Warner was one of these adventurers. He is said to have made the acquaintance of Captain Thomas Painton, an experienced seaman, who

> suggested to him how much easier it would be to fix and preserve in good order, a colony in one of the small isles in the *West Indies*, despised and deserted by the *Spaniards*, than in that wide country on the continent, where for want of sufficient authority, all things were fallen into confusion.[8]

---

7 Noel Deerr, *The History of Sugar* (London, 1949–50), vol. 1, pp. 13, 73–97, 105–13, 115–43.

8 John Campbell, *Candid and Impartial Considerations on the Nature of the Sugar Trade* (London, 1763), p. 36.

Sugar and Slavery

Table 6.1

Sugar exports of the American tropical colonies, 1766–70[1] (annual averages in tons)

British (10 colonies)[2]	80,285
French (3 colonies)[3]	77,923
Portuguese (1 colony)[4]	20,400
Dutch (3 colonies)[5]	10,126
Spanish (1 colony)[6]	10,000
Danish (1 colony)[7]	8,230
Total	206,964

Notes:
1. Only the colonies which exported 1,000 tons or more of sugar annually are included in this table.
2. Antigua, Barbados, Jamaica, Dominica, Grenada, St Christopher, Nevis, Montserrat, St Vincent, and Tortola.
3. St Domingue for the years 1767–8, Guadeloupe for 1767, and Martinique for 1766–70.
4. Brazil for 1776.
5. Surinam, Essequibo, and Demerara for 1766–70.
6. Cuba for 1770–8.
7. St Croix for 1770.

Source: Noel Deerr, *The History of Sugar* (London, 1949–50), vol. 1, pp. 112, 129–31, 193–203, 212, 235–40, 245.

In particular, Painton pointed to the island of St Christopher as a likely place for planting.

3 SUGAR PRODUCTION IN THE AMERICAN TROPICS

Statistics of sugar production for the period of this study are by no means as plentiful or as reliable as one could wish. Before 1760 the data are too limited to draw up a table of production for the American tropics. Subject to certain qualifications, it is possible to show the legal exports of the colonies to the metropolitan countries in the period 1766–70. The annual averages for these years have been computed for the ten British colonies and the four foreign colonies of Surinam, Essequibo, Demerara, and Martinique. Owing to gaps in the data, less reliance can be placed on the figures for Brazil,

Geographic and Economic Influences

Table 6.2

*Sugar exports of the ten
leading Caribbean islands, 1766–70
(annual averages in tons)*

	Exports	Area in square miles
St Domingue (French)	61,247[1]	10,200
Jamaica (British)	36,021	4,411
Antigua (British)	10,690	108
Cuba (Spanish)	10,000[2]	44,206
St Christopher (British)	9,701	68
Martinique (French)	8,778	380
St Croix (Danish)	8,230[3]	84
Guadeloupe (French)	7,898[4]	619
Barbados (British)	7,819	166
Grenada (British)	6,552	120
Total	166,936	60,362

Notes: 1 1767–8.   2 1770–8.   3 1770.   4 1767.

Source: Noel Deerr, *The History of Sugar* (London, 1949–50), vol. 1, pp. 112, 128–31, 193–203, 212, 235–40, 245.

St Domingue, Cuba, Guadeloupe, and St Croix which are quoted in Tables 6.1 and 6.2.

Of the six European nations possessing sugar colonies in the New World, Table 6.1 shows that Great Britain and France were the pre-eminent powers. The British colonies accounted for 38.8 per cent of the exports, as compared with 37.7 for the French colonies. The remaining 23.5 per cent was distributed among the colonies of Portugal, Holland, Spain, and Denmark. It is also evident that the islands of the Caribbean Sea accounted for the lion's share of the sugar exported from the American tropics. Only the two mainland regions of the Dutch Guianas and Brazil exported 1,000 tons or more in the period of this study. In the aggregate these mainland colonies accounted for only 14.8 per cent of the exports, contrasted with 85.2 per cent for the Caribbean islands.

Table 6.2 ranks the island colonies according to exports and affords a crude measure of production in relation to land area. The great French colony of St Domingue accounted for 29.6 per cent of

101

Sugar and Slavery

the sugar exported from the American tropics, and Jamaica came second with 17.9 per cent. Cuba ranked a poor third among the large islands and fell below tiny Antigua. The seven leading islands in the Lesser Antilles accounted for 35.7 per cent of the sugar entering Europe from the Caribbean islands. Four British islands produced 58.3 per cent of the small-island total, followed by the two French islands with 27.9 per cent, and Danish St Croix with 13.8. One noteworthy feature of the small islands is the relatively narrow range in the size of exports in view of the considerable range in land area.

4 LOCATION FACTORS

Land and labour are the bare essentials of an economy, but they need to be supplied with other factors to enhance their productivity. Land may attract other factors of production because of its soil and climate, wind and water power, healthfulness, ease of defence, and situation in relation to markets and sources of factor supply. Bringing what Europeans regarded as 'surplus' labour from Africa to the 'surplus' lands of the American tropics was no mean undertaking. It was undertaken because the area of land surplus, once it was worked with imported labour and capital, yielded a greater profit than other possible locations. To make this transfer possible, the means of transport had to be sufficiently abundant, reliable, and economical for the task at hand. Transport costs not only involved the forced labourers but also other productive factors which were brought to the region of surplus lands. Then, too, the produce of these lands had to be transported to distant markets before its value could be realized.

Centres of production, factor supply, and consumption were by no means fixed. Shifts occurred in a variety of directions. The need for intermediate goods, that is, foodstuffs, livestock, and building materials, led to the growth of temperate-zone supply centres in close proximity to the centre of tropical production. New supply centres, in turn, became markets of some consequence. Man transformed his environment in other ways. Economic plants and animals were introduced from abroad to diversify production for export and reduce the need for imported intermediate goods. These and other elements entered into the complex equation of location.

Although sugar-canes may be grown under a variety of conditions in tropical and subtropical latitudes, commercial production is confined to certain localities where physical and economic factors may be combined to yield optimum returns over costs. Ideal natural conditions include an annual average temperature of 75°F. with

Geographic and Economic Influences

considerable sunshine and no freezes; approximately 60 inches of rainfall annually which is well distributed, or its equivalent by irrigation; and a fertile soil which drains rapidly and thoroughly.[9] Despite high mountains, arid plains, and swamplands, a goodly portion of the Caribbean island world approaches these ideal natural conditions.

The islands of the Caribbean probably had a lower incidence of pestilential disease than West Africa or the Caribbean rimland. While it is true that cholera, smallpox, dysentery, and yellow fever occasionally took a heavy toll of Europeans and Africans, the record shows that the islands were relatively free from malaria.[10] Mr G. B. Masefield has observed that some of the most populous settlements were made on islands which were free from malaria.[11]

It is also noteworthy that European-type cattle, given careful management, could be bred to advantage in certain Caribbean and Central American localities, a condition which seldom obtained in other tropical areas.[12]

The African contribution to the Caribbean sugar industry has not always been sufficiently appreciated. Rather than being primitive food gatherers and hunters, the Africans in the old slaving area had a culture containing such elements as settled community life, political organization, art, and religion. The roots of this culture have been traced by Professor Sauer to the 'Old Planter Culture' of south-east Asia. On the other hand, Professor Murdock has suggested that the western Sudan was among those centres in which agriculture was an indigenous invention.[13] Whatever their origins, the agricultural economies of West Africa had such common features as occupational specialization, exchange, a rudimentary money system, markets, and the working of metals. The African was a hoe cultivator and not infrequently a skilled artisan before he was brought to America to continue his traditional form of planting culture under the supervision of the European. Africa supplied labour that was generally superior to both whites and Indians in capacity, endurance, and immunity to disease.[14]

---

9 J. Carlyle Sitterson, *Sugar Country The Cane Sugar Industry in the South* (Lexington, 1953), p. 13.
10 Frank W. Pitman, *The Development of the British West Indies, 1700–1763* (New Haven, 1917), pp. 386–90.
11 G. B. Masefield, *A Short History of Agriculture in the British Colonies* (Oxford, 1950), p. 30.
12 Douglas H. K. Lee, *Climate and Economic Development in the Tropics* (New York, 1957), pp. 73–4.
13 George Peter Murdock, *Africa Its People and Their Culture History* (New York, 1959), pp. 64–76.
14 Melville J. Herskovits, *The Myth of the Negro Past* (Boston, 1958), pp. 54–58.

Sugar and Slavery

Small islands were initially favoured over large islands in the establishment of plantations. From the standpoint of transport and defence, the distance from northern Europe was less, islands to windward were more easily defended than those to leeward, and the high ratio of coastline to land area enabled most plantations to have direct access to sea-going vessels. The north-east trade winds not only carried ships to the islands; they also energized the windmills which crushed the canes, and gave the windswept islands of the Lesser Antilles a less enervating climate than most other areas of low elevation in the tropics. Moreover, slave insurrection and escape were less common on small and densely populated islands than they were on large islands and continental coastal plains.[15] When these and other advantages were subsequently offset by the soil-depleting effects of the near-monoculture sugar regime, the planters developed a system of self-sustained agriculture which called for large herds of livestock to yield manure, and tillage practices which bore down heavily on the field slaves. Furthermore, they improved the quality of their sugar products, increasing the proportion of clayed sugar to muscovado sugar and rum to molasses.

European capital was attracted to colonies which supplied non-competitive commodities, having a fairly high value in proportion to bulk, and which were readily accessible to ocean-going vessels. Mercantile regulations generally required that tropical and semitropical staples be shipped in vessels which were owned and manned by nationals (or colonials) and landed in the mother country before being re-exported to foreign markets. To a considerable extent these 'enumeration clauses' were designed to aid the merchants of the metropolis in collecting debts owed by planter correspondents. Moreover, given adequate military protection, islands afforded security to life and property to a greater extent than continental settlements which were subject to Indian attack and white dispersion into frontier areas.

In modern free market economies capital-intensive agriculture means a high ratio of physical capital to labour, land, and managerial outlays. But in a slave economy the slaves themselves were a form of capital investment, and the term 'slave labour' is unfortunately misleading from an economic standpoint. This means that the capital on a sugar plantation consisted of slaves, livestock, mills, tools and other appurtenances, and even much of the cane land when soil exhaustion was corrected by heavy applications of labour and fertilizer. While it is difficult to measure all these capital items in

---

15 Melville J. Herskovits, *The Myth of the Negro Past* (Boston, 1958), pp. 89–109.

money values, estate inventories for several West India islands in the 18th century made the capital amount to as much as two-thirds of total value.

Professor Usher has reminded us of the importance of animal, wind, and water power in the pre-Industrial Revolution era. He neglects to point out, however, that slaves were regarded by Europeans as power in much the same manner as animals. Professor Hall has written that the labour of slaves was 'not "labour" in the sense in which we use it in respect of "free labourers", but rather "power" in the sense that it is used of the efforts of livestock or the work of machinery. The eighteenth century planters' inventories almost invariably classify slaves with "stock".'[16]

5 THE ROLE OF LIVESTOCK

'A sugar plantation is like a little town: it requires the produce, as well as the industry, of every climate', wrote William Beckford, the Jamaica planter.[17] Not only was the Caribbean sugar industry an offshoot of the old planter culture, it also stemmed from the seed planting and animal husbandry cultures of north-western Europe and the North American seaboard colonies. It was these temperate-zone cultures which supplied management, capital, transport, provisions, livestock, and manufactures.

Of these contributions, that of livestock has received little attention by economic historians. Owing to the slight fertility of tropical soils, poor quality grass, and endemic disease, animal husbandry has had a slow growth in the greater part of the tropical world.[18] For mixed farming to be successful, there must be adequate supplies of farm manure to enable cultivators to practise dry farming on the same soil year after year. By contrast with the tropics where the agricultural system generally functioned as if animals did not exist, the agriculture of north-western Europe was in essence a balanced, mixed farming system with primary emphasis upon animal husbandry.[19]

Few elements of European agriculture were adaptable to a tropical environment. European cereals could not be grown to advantage.

16 Douglas G. Hall, 'Incalculability as a Feature of Sugar Production during the Eighteenth Century', *Social and Economic Studies*, vol. 10, no. 3, (Sept. 1961), p. 348.
17 William Beckford, *A Descriptive Account of the Island of Jamaica* (London, 1790), vol. 1, p. 141.
18 Pierre Gourou, *The Tropical World Its Social and Economic Conditions and Its Future Status* (New York, 1962), pp. 52–5.
19 Sauer, *Agricultural Origins*, p. 99.

Sugar and Slavery

Short-fallow cultivation was not practicable where natural vegetation grew so rapidly. As long as the soil retained its fertility a succession of cane crops was harvested from a single planting. Thus the first generation of sugar planters were under no compulsion to fallow or dung their lands. So costly were the first shipments of livestock from England to the West Indies that they were hardly sufficient to power the sugar mills. Though pack animals or animal-drawn carts were essential for transporting the sugar, little thought was given to dunging and ploughing.

Planters responded to soil exhaustion in several ways. Not a few who had patented large tracts of land practised a form of shifting agriculture. When one field lost its fertility it was abandoned and contiguous areas were cleared and planted. Though this system was practised in the large island of Jamaica for many years, it was hardly feasible in the small islands for any extended period. Under any condition the planter had to consider the added cost of land clearance and cane cartage. Planters also began to breed stock. Again, this proved to be quite successful in Jamaica, though much less so in the smaller islands where canes soon covered every acre that would support them to advantage. Therefore, as livestock proved to be a wasting asset in much of the Caribbean territory, and as animal husbandry in Europe and North America expanded to yield an exportable surplus, these temperate and tropical regions were linked together by means of trade.

In North America the colonists from the seed and animal-husbandry culture of Europe came in contact with the seed culture of the Amerindians. The Indians, though they had no domestic animals except the dog, had developed a maize-bean-squash complex, described by Professor Sauer as a symbiotic complex without equal elsewhere.[20] Moreover, they drew sustenance from the rich fisheries of the north-east coastal waters. The interesting thing is that elements of both cultures were drawn upon to create an agricultural system adapted to the American environment. Abundant land reserves in conjunction with scarce labour and capital led to an extensive system of cultivation without the application of manure to arable land. Neither was much labour and capital needed in the conduct of animal husbandry; grasslands were extensive and virtually costless and livestock might be left to fend for themselves.

Supplies of North American foodstuffs came to the sugar islands in small quantities during the English Civil Wars. The trade continued to grow. It did so to such an extent that after the Treaty of Utrecht,

20 Sauer, *Agricultural Origins*, p. 64.

Geographic and Economic Influences

(1713), the North Americans were able to supply both the British and foreign sugar colonies. In the item of horses alone, some 6,700 head were exported from the northern colonies to the West Indies in 1770.[21]

The Caribbean sugar economy thus represented a unique combination of cultures. Asia was the original home of the sugar-cane; Africa supplied hoe cultivators and certain food crops; other food crops were indigenous to the islands or the rimland of the Caribbean; North America sent fish, cereals, building materials, and livestock; and from Europe came managers, capital, technology, and fabricated goods. Intensive applications of capital and power — human, animal, and wind — to tropical soils and climate constituted a significant revolution in tropical agriculture. Professor Mintz maintains that from the perspective of post-Roman European history, 'the plantation was an absolutely unprecedented social, economic and political institution, and by no means simply an innovation in the organization of agriculture'.[22]

6 GROWING THE CANES

The sugar-cane is a stout, tall perennial grass that grows to best advantage in fertile tropical soils. The size of the canes varies greatly, according to variety, soil, climate, and other circumstances. Prior to the late 18th century there was only one variety of cane known to the Western World, *saccharum officinarum*, indigenous to the South Pacific, and commonly known as 'Creole' cane. Not until after the period of this study were British planters introduced to the improved variety of cane known as 'Bourbon' or 'Otaheite'.

The most usual height of the Creole cane was from four to seven or eight feet. Stalks varied in thickness from one-half to two or three inches, the average diameter being about one inch. Stiff, pointed and narrow leaves grew from the joints and top of the cane, the latter known as the 'flag' and consisting of six or more such leaves. The plant might be grown in a variety of soils with varying degrees of success. According to one contemporary, the cane was produced in greatest perfection 'in light, spongy, deep soils, which lie exposed to the sun during the whole time of his shining; and have just descent

21 Curtis P. Nettles, *The Emergence of a National Economy 1775–1815* (New York, 1962), p. 55.
22 Sidney W. Mintz, Foreword to Ramiro Guerra y Sanchez, *Sugar and Society in the Caribbean An Economic History of Cuban Agriculture* (New Haven, 1964), p. xiv.

enough to carry off the rain water'.[23] During the growing season of from fourteen to eighteen months, it was desirable to have uniform high temperatures, strong sunlight and frequent showers. The cane plant derived its commercial value from the watery, saccharine juice which was extracted from the spongy pith encased in a thin skin or bark and converted into a dry, crystalline substance commonly known as sugar. Not all of the cane juice was reducible to sugar, however, and the uncrystallized residue, or molasses, might serve as a cheap substitute for sugar or be distilled into an alcoholic beverage known as rum.

The sugar revolution was effected within a narrow range of technological possibilities. Crude cane-crushing mills, powered by animals, wind, or water, remained the basic unit of heavy equipment on the plantation. Though steam engines and horse-drawn ploughs were introduced in limited numbers during the later part of the 18th century, mechanical invention made little headway until the 19th century when the sugar industry was revolutionized by such innovations as railways, steamships, and central factories equipped with steam engines, evaporators, vacuum pans and centrifugal separators.[24]

Despite the stable technological environment, the cultivation and manufacture of cane sugar was a relatively complex process. Once a plantation unit was established, the labour force was employed in a succession of tasks which required careful organization and co-ordination if the plantation ledger was to show a profit at the end of the crop season. It was not just a matter of growing the cane, but also of subjecting the harvested crop to a series of manufacturing processes which radically altered the parent material. Since the farm and the factory were, with few exceptions, single units of ownership and operation, agriculture and manufacturing were interdependent and highly co-ordinated operations.

The land planted in sugar-canes was laid out in such a manner as to economize on transport costs, apportion task work, prevent the spread of fire, and facilitate the rotation of crops. The land was generally divided into three to five large cane fields, each of which was subdivided into plots of from five to twenty acres each. Intervals of from twelve to eighteen feet were generally left between each plot to serve as a roadway for the oxcarts which carried the harvested canes to the mill. The roadways, if sufficiently wide, might prevent damaging fires from spreading from one cane piece to another. On

23 Anon, *The Art of Making Sugar* (London, 1752), p. 4.
24 Masefield, *Short History of Agriculture*, p. 48.

Geographic and Economic Influences

intensively cultivated plantations, food crops, such as peas and potatoes, might be planted in the intervals while the canes were growing. Sub-division of cane land was also of advantage in apportioning task work, such as holeing, planting, dunging, and harvesting.

Besides the layout of cane fields, locational factors influenced the erection of sugar works. Sugar mills, or even boiling houses, might be situated at several places on a large plantation to save long hauls from the cane fields. In most cases, however, it appears that a centrally located works was the rule. This was due primarily to the difficulty of moving stills and cisterns which contained cane juice and molasses from one part of the plantation to another.[25]

Compared with the size and layout of plantations, the annual production routine was relatively stereotyped. Year after year and decade after decade the system of cultivation and manufacture remained essentially unchanged in broad outline. The sequence of operations consisted of preparing the soil, planting, weeding, harvesting, crushing, boiling, curing, and distilling. No sooner was one task completed, or partially completed, than another demanded the attention of the planter and his labour force. The tempo hardly abated during occasional slack seasons in the sugar routine, for subsidiary operations, such as provision culture and the maintenance and repair of buildings and equipment, occupied the workers.

Rainfall distribution, more than any other factor, influenced the annual production routine. The rainy season, which began in May or June and ended in December or January, was occupied with such agricultural operations as holeing, dunging, planting, weeding, provision culture, and maintenance work. On the other hand, the dry season from January to May or June was taken up with harvesting canes and processing the sugar and rum. During this period the canes were cut and ground at the mill, after which the cane juice was boiled and clarified until it crystallized into sugar, while the molasses was generally conveyed to the still house to be made into rum.

Trenching and holeing were the two methods employed in planting the cuttings from the tops of canes. Trenching, as the name implies, consisted of digging long trenches and laying therein a double row of cane cuttings, after which they were covered with earth. By this way of planting, wrote John Oldmixon, 'the Root is secur'd, and the Produce encreas'd. They will come up in a little while after they are planted, in about 12 Weeks they will be 2 Foot high'.[26] The other system, which appears to have become more

---

25 Richard Pares, *A West India Fortune* (London, 1950), p. 103–4.
26 John Oldmixon, *The British Empire in America* (London, 1708), vol. 2, pp. 137–8.

Holeing a cane-piece (Weatherell's Estate, Antigua)

Planting the sugar-cane (Bodkin's Estate, Antigua)

common by the early 18th century and was essentially a method of conserving top soil, called for the excavation of holes that were five or six inches deep and about five feet square. An able Negro normally dug from sixty to eighty holes in a ten-hour day. The labour was so exhausting that planters sometimes saved their own blacks by hiring others for this work at a rate of £4 to £6 per acre.[27] One or two cane tops were laid longitudinally (or in some cases crosswise) in the centre of each hole and covered with about two inches of mould from the excavation. Then as the plant sprouted and grew taller the excavation was filled with mould, and in some cases a compost of manure mixed with chopped trash, until eventually the cane field was made level.

Hoe culture might appear incongruous in an age when progressive farmers were following the practices outlined in Jethro Tull's *The Horse-hoeing Husbandry*. Critics of slavery argued that the lot of the black might be lightened by substituting ploughs for the system of hand hoeing without any burden, and a probable net gain, to the slave owner. Planters who responded to these charges by experimenting with ploughs were generally disappointed. In part, it was found that local cattle were unequal to the task of drawing ploughs in heavy soil or on hilly fields. Ploughs were also considered inferior to hoe culture in preparing the seed bed, spreading fertilizer evenly over the cane land, and checking soil erosion. While it was probably feasible from a technical standpoint to use horsedrawn ploughs, actually such a move would have unbalanced the labour force. If the plough was permitted to displace field hands, not enough workers would remain for the harvesting and processing operations. Planters therefore owned enough slaves to perform peak load tasks. They considered it uneconomical, and even dangerous to public order, to leave idle a large proportion of their labour force at other seasons of the year.[28]

When first planted in the West Indies, canes were harvested for as many as ten or fifteen years before it became necessary to grub up the roots and plant new cuttings. In time, however, the soil lost some of its fertility and the cut-over canes, or ratoons, yielded less sugar. To prevent such an occurence canes were planted more frequently. Moreover, fertilizer was added to replace organic matter and plant nutrients.

27 David Watts, 'Origins of Barbadian Cane Hole Agriculture', *Journal of the Barbados Museum and Historical Society*, vol. XXXII, no. 3 (May 1968), pp. 143–51; Bryan Edwards, *The History, Civil and Commercial, of the British Colonies in the West Indies* (Dublin, 1793), vol. 2, pp. 206–8.
28 Deerr, *History of Sugar*, vol. 2, pp. 353–5.

Sugar and Slavery

The labour force and the sugar works could be utilized to greater advantage if the cane pieces were not all planted or harvested at one time. Annual harvests might be more nearly equalized by staggered planting of cane pieces. In some cases no ratoon crops were harvested, in which event about one-half of the cane land would be dunged and planted annually. In other cases, where land was more plentiful, a three- or four-year crop sequence might be followed. The land would be divided into thirds or fourths, so that each year new canes and ratoons might be harvested from part of the land, while the remainder would be divided among growing canes, provision crops, and fallow. If large reserve tracts were available, exhausted fields might be abandoned as new fields were opened and brought into cultivation. Thus, the agricultural system was materially affected by the frequency of planting and dunging.[29]

During the early months of the growing season the canes were weeded, thinned, hoe-ploughed and replanted. At irregular intervals new plants were inserted to fill the gaps left by plants that failed to mature. These operations were repeated at proper intervals until the canes were large enough to keep down the weeds. Then at the age of five or six months the canes were weeded again for the last time.

The period between planting and harvesting was occupied with other tasks. Corn, potatoes, peas, beans and other provision crops were planted, harvested, and stored for future use. Fences and buildings often required extensive repairs, especially in hurricane years. Much of the work involved preparation for the cane harvest and sugar-making operations. Coopers were kept busy assembling barrels to receive the finished products. Mechanics and other artisans attended to repairs of mill machinery, wagons, and miscellaneous equipment. Overseers directed gangs of slaves in the collection of supplies, the gathering of fuel, and the cleaning of utensils. Careful preparation was necessary, for cane harvesting set in motion a chain of operations that required five or six months to complete.[30]

7 THE ART OF MAKING SUGAR

Christmas was a joyous and festive season for all ranks of society despite apprehensions of the arduous labour ahead. Before the first

---

29 Samuel Martin, *An Essay Upon Plantership*, in *Three Tracts on West-Indian Agriculture* (Jamaica, 1802), pp. 53–4; Elsa V. Goveia, *Slave Society in the British Leeward Islands at the End of the Eighteenth Century* (New Haven and London, 1965), pp. 127–42.
30 Edward Long, *The History of Jamaica* (London, 1774), vol. 1, p. 448.

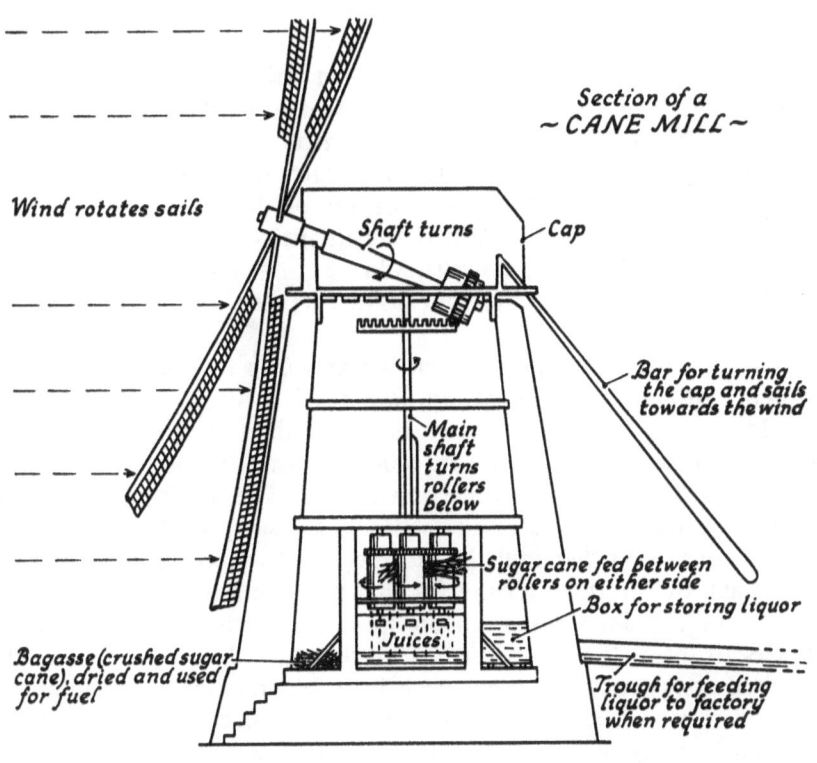
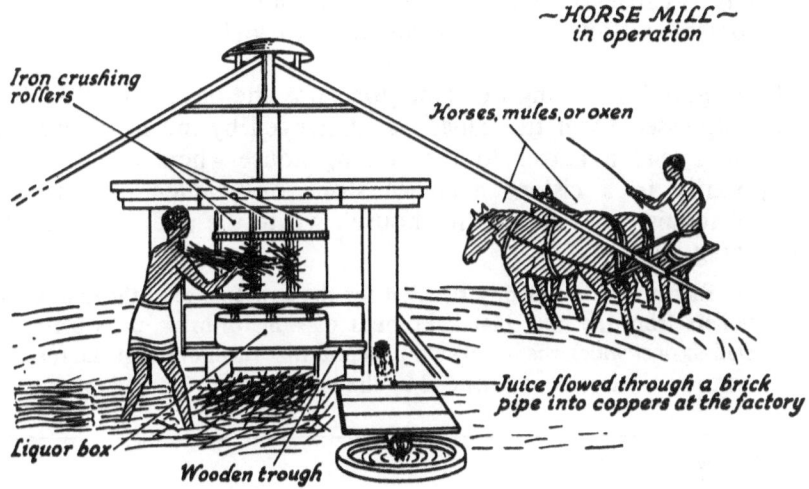

Sugar and Slavery

week of the new year had passed the slaves were usually in the harvest field. Armed with long heavy 'bills'. 'machettes', or 'cutlasses', they proceeded to cut the ripened canes. One at a time the canes were cut close to the root and stripped of leaves and then cut into shorter pieces three or four feet in length. The canes thus cut were bundled up in faggots, tied with cane tops, and carried to the mill by slaves, pack animals, or in carts drawn by draft animals. Owing to rapid fermentation and drying of the saccharine juice, the capacity of the mill determined the quantity of canes harvested at any one time. 'No more canes should be cut at one time, than can be used in the space of twenty four hours', wrote the author of *The Art of Making Sugar*.[31]

The main apparatus of a sugar works was a three-roller cane mill which, with slight modification, was used in Europe and the New World for more than three centuries after its invention by a Sicilian in 1449. The rollers, which were made of iron (or wood covered with iron), stood upright and turned on pivots. 'The middlemost roller is moved by the wind, water or cattle; by the same kind of mechanism as the corn and other mills in Europe; the two others are turned by this, each of the three having for that purpose a cog and teeth at the upper end'.[32] Two slaves fed the mill, one stationed in front of the rollers to insert the newly-cut canes, the other behind to receive the crushed stalks and pass them back in order to extract the remainder of the juice. The mills were small and inefficient by modern standards. Only about 50 to 60 per cent of the juice was expressed from the canes as compared with the present day yields of 90 to 98 per cent. A cattle- or mule-mill on the old model performed very well if it passed sufficient canes in an hour to yield from 300 to 350 gallons of juice.[33]

Boiling and clarifying the cane juice was the next operation. The juice expressed from the canes was conveyed by means of pipes of lead or a leaden gutter to the boiling house where it was stored temporarily in a cistern made of stone or wooden planks. 'The general requisites of the boiling-house', wrote the author of *The Art of Making Sugar*,

> are that it be conveniently situated for the conveyance of the juice to the boilers from the mill; that it be built of stone or brick, particularly the wall against which the boilers are to stand; that the mouths of the furnaces are to be to leeward, or defended by the building from the trade winds; and

---

31 *Art of Making Sugar*, p. 8.
32 Ibid., p. 10.
33 Edwards, *History of British West Indies*, vol. 2, p. 218.

that the room itself be high, airy, well lighted, and have good vents for carrying off the steam which arises in great abundance.[34]

Three or more copper boilers were fitted in the stone furnace at the narrow end of the boiling house. The first boiler, or clarifying copper, was considerably larger than the others, being generally four feet in diameter and three feet in depth. The others were progressively smaller until the last, called the 'teach', or 'tatch', measured only twenty inches in diameter and eighteen in depth.

Fuel requirements were particularly heavy, for day and often night the fires must be tended under the boilers until all of the sugar was made. Native timber, although probably adequate in the large and heavily wooded island of Jamaica, was soon exhausted in the smaller islands. Some fuel was obtained from timber growing in unoccupied neighbouring islands, but this was also a temporary source of supply. Coal was sometimes brought out 'freight free' from England in vessels that needed ballast on the light voyage to the West Indies. Although inferior to wood and coal, the main fuel consisted of crushed canes, or 'trash', which were taken from the mill and dried in the sun.

In the boiling process the raw cane juice was first conveyed from the cistern into a strainer consisting of a basket lined with hair cloth. It then went to the clarifying copper where it was boiled and stirred until the gross, unctuous matter rose to the surface and was removed by a slave who operated a long handled skimmer. Lime water, or 'temper', was added to the boiling liquid to speed the separation of the gross matter from the saccharine part of the liquor. The liquor was then taken out of the first copper and strained through a woollen blanket placed in a wooden box full of holes. Oldmixon said it was then

> carry'd into the second, and so into a third, fourth, fifth, sixth and seventh [copper]. The least is call'd the *Tach*, where it boyls longest. 'Tis continually kept stirring and boyling, till it comes to a Consistency; and yet all this Boyling would reduce it only to a thick clammy Substance, without kerning or turning it to a Grain, were it not for the *Temper* that is thrown into it.[35]

The slave who superintended these operations was appropriately named the 'boiler'. More than any one else, his skill and judgement meant the difference between a profit or loss on the plantation ledger. He judged the quality of the cane juice and varied the amount of temper accordingly; he determined how long the liquor should

---

34 *Art of Making Sugar*, p. 10.
35 Oldmixon, *British Empire in America*, vol. 2, pp. 141–2.

Interior of a boiling house (Delap's Estate, Antigua)

Interior of a distillery (Delap's Estate, Antigua)

boil in each of the coppers; he superintended the boiling operations and cautioned his helpers to keep liquor in the coppers at all times to prevent the intense heat from melting the metal. Probably his most important task was to determine when the viscous mass should be removed from the fire as the crystallization or 'strike' occurred.

From the last boiler the liquid sugar was emptied into wooden troughs or coolers and allowed to stand until the surface was covered with a saccharine crust. The crust was then broken and stirred in with the more fluid part. This operation was repeated until the mass was cool. The next step was to shovel the soft brown mass into earthernward moulds — sometimes directly into wooden hogsheads — where it was again stirred several times. The hole at the bottom of each mould was plugged when the liquid sugar was first poured in. After standing for thirteen or fourteen hours the sugar concreted into one mass. The plug was then removed to permit the molasses to drain off.[36]

Since the steam from the coppers fouled the sugar, a separate building was needed for the curing process. The curing house was a long narrow building — sometimes two storeys high — where the moulds were set upon earthen pans, or 'dripps', to receive the remainder of the molasses that drained from the sugar. Muscovado sugar, which was the brownest sort, remained in the curing house for about one month. The moulds were then taken to the 'knocking room' where they were turned upside down and the sugar removed. Three different colours and qualities of sugar were found in each mould: a brown top layer, a black bottom layer, and a middle layer described by Oldmixon as 'white, dry, and good; and this is generally three Quarters of the Whole'. The top and bottom layers required further refining, while the middle was 'carry'd to the Store-house, as fit for the Market'. [37]

Some planters went a step further and made a semi-refined grade known as clayed sugar. For this operation it was necessary to have a whitish clay somewhat like tobacco pipe clay. Water was added until it was about the consistency of pancake batter. Only the white sugar, or middle two-thirds of the mould, was used in this process. It was reduced to powder and poured back into moulds. About an inch of clay batter was then poured on top of the sugar. 'Clay has a wonderful Power over the Sugar, to purge the grosser, flatulent, or treacly Part downward, and to cause the Pot of Sugar, which generally contains about half an hundred of Brown-sugar, to become less in

---

36 Martin, *Essay Upon Plantership*, pp. 69–77.
37 Oldmixon, *British Empire in America*, vol. 2, p. 144.

Sugar and Slavery

Quantity, and of several Colours and Goodness', wrote Oldmixon. The several sorts were divided into 'Firsts', 'Seconds', 'Thirds', and 'Fourths', each of which was packed in separate casks and sold at different prices. Besides clayed sugar, a few planters made refined sugar for local and North American consumption.[38]

Except for rum distilling, which will be treated in Chapter Fifteen, the final sugar-making operations consisted of drying and packing. Drying took place in a tightly sealed annex to the curing house which accommodated six or seven hundred moulds at a time. The apartment was heated continuously by means of an iron stove for about eight days and nights until the sugar was perfectly dry. Finally, the dried sugar was removed from the moulds, pounded in large troughs, passed through a sieve, and packed into hogsheads for shipment.[39]

Several conclusions emerge from this discussion of the plantation routine. First, ownership units generally combined the cultivation of canes with the manufacture of raw sugar. This was owing chiefly to the fact that canes fermented rapidly once they were cut, and in an age of animal-drawn vehicles it was necessary to have the sugar works in close proximity to the cane fields. Exceptions to this generalization were found in parts of Surinam and Brazil, where navigable rivers permitted canes to be transported by boat to central factories. Second, the economic benefits resulting from specialization and division of labour were limited by the need to combine so many operations under a single owner-manager. Third, plantation labour requirements were such that agricultural innovations were discouraged. The plough is a case in point. Fourth, the risks were great since all of the steps in the annual production routine 'must necessarily go hand in hand together and not be neglected . . .'.[40]

8 STAGES IN THE GROWTH OF THE SUGAR ECONOMY

Varying the proportions of productive factors over time was another aspect of tropical agriculture. Conceived theoretically, the problem of the planter was to maximize profit by combining the factors of production in such a manner as to minimize the cost of production. In pursuing this goal he tended to adhere to the economic principle that the cheaper a factor of production was, the more generously it should be used; and contrariwise, the dearer the factor of production

38 Oldmixon, *British Empire in America*, vol. 2, p. 145.
39 *Art of Making Sugar*, p. 26.
40 Ibid., pp. 26–9.

was, the more sparingly it should be used. Although this principle considers all factors as variables, actually the supply of land was less variable than that of labour and capital.

Four fairly distinct stages of production can be detected in the period of this study. First came a pioneer or subsistence stage which was characterized by hunting, land clearance, and cultivation of food crops. This was followed by the diversified production of food crops, livestock, and export staples. When the comparative advantage of cane sugar became apparent, there was a movement from diversified production to a modified form of monoculture best described as 'extensive monoculture'. Finally, the small islands and parts of Jamaica approached a one-crop system which will be termed 'intensive monoculture'.

The colonists who first arrived in the West Indies were generally possessed of little capital. At the outset they were confronted with the problems of felling trees and preparing land for the cultivation of food crops. Early colonists were the trail-blazers, the frontiersmen, the pioneers. They annihilated hostile Indians, cleared small tracts of land of trees and undergrowth, built crude cabins, hunted or raised their own food, and experimented with crops that might be marketed in Europe. Lacking knowledge of the country and having few resources to develop it, they practised a subsistence economy that was supplemented at intervals by the exchange of crude tropical commodities for supplies brought from Europe.

Generally speaking, the subsistence stage was short lived, for settlers quickly learned that cash crops could be grown at a profit. European merchants were encouraged by this discovery to grant trade credit, thus enabling settlers to obtain capital and labour for the production of export staples. In the shift to commercial agriculture small staples, such as tobacco, indigo, cotton, cocoa, and ginger, generally took precedence over cane sugar. This was owing to the low labour and capital requirements and the adaptability of these crops to small units of cultivation. Mercantile credit and re-invested profits enabled some settlers to expand the production of small staples. At the same time the uncertainty of trade and commerce made it necessary to grow provisions and livestock to supply the needs of local consumers. For a time, then, the island economies were characterized by the diversified production of exportable staples, provisions, and livestock.

During the diversified stage a few planters accumulated or borrowed sufficient capital to shift from minor staples to the more profitable cane sugar. However, it was not economical to produce sugar on small farms because a considerable amount of fixed capital was needed for a sugar work. Large plantations thus enjoyed economies of scale that were not accessible to small farms. Moreover, relatively more labourers were needed to operate a sugar plantation. While white servants supplied part of the labour requirements, Negro slaves were imported in increasing numbers to perform the unskilled but arduous and monotonous field work.

Most of the planters who formed sugar estates during the diversified stage became heavily indebted to merchants for supplies of capital and labour. Since merchants generally charged high interest and cut off credit when debts went unpaid, few planters were able to obtain enough slaves and equipment to devote much of their land to sugar cultivation. As a consequence, the typical plantation was understocked. Considerable land remained for food crops and pasture. Rather than add to his heavy debt burden by importing costly provisions and livestock, the typical sugar planter kept his working capital needs to a minimum by making his plantation as self-sufficient as possible.

Diversified production of provisions, livestock, sugar, and minor staples continued for a time. The situation was far from static, however, and planters with profits to re-invest or access to trade credit or loans were encouraged to devote more resources to sugar production. Land was not only added to the plantation, but a greater proportion of the land was also planted in canes. Since fewer acres thus remained for pasturing livestock and growing provisions, part of these necessities were purchased from local farmers or imported from abroad. This stage of production, best described as extensive monoculture, was characterized by one-crop specialization and the application of more units of capital and labour to each acre of land. It was economical to farm extensively because land was relatively cheap and the soil had lost little of its original fertility. The chief differences between the diversified and extensive monoculture stages were the more rapid consolidation of small farms into sugar plantations, diminished production of minor staples and provisions, and increased dependence on imported supplies of intermediate goods, that is, provisions and livestock.

Land was obviously the least expansible factor of production. As long as the islands were in process of settlement, it was the prospect of acquiring cheap land that attracted Europeans to the tropics. They came in such numbers that the tiny Caribbean islands were reputedly the most densely populated areas in the world. Capital in the underdeveloped colonies was extremely scarce and subsistence and diversified agriculture was the rule for a time. Then with the introduction of sugar, a commodity requiring considerable tracts of land for economical production, small farms were consolidated into plantations. Many of the small cultivators who were wormed out of their holdings migrated to other colonies. Diminishing supplies of white labour induced planters to resort to the forced labour of Africans. In the early stages of sugar production land was still cheap in comparison with other factors of production. Under these conditions planters tended to appropriate more land than they could cultivate with existing supplies of capital and labour.

However, as the movement towards monoculture gained momentum the supply of good cane land approached exhaustion. Land prices rose to such heights that a fundamental change occurred in the relative value of the factors of production. Land now became scarce in relation to capital and labour. One-crop specialization and intensive cultivation became the characteristic feature of West India agriculture.

During the intensive-monoculture stage high land values made it unprofitable to grow provisions or pasture livestock on land that was in any way suitable for sugar-canes. As a consequence, planters became dependent upon imported supplies of intermediate goods. Complete dependence was seldom if ever achieved, however. In all of the islands there was some land that was unsuitable for cane cultivation, but capable of growing provisions or pasturing livestock. Planters might also grow provisions between the rows of young cane plants. Moreover, cattle might be fed on cane tops to reduce the expense of imported supplies. Nevertheless, livestock imports increased as the need for power and fertilizer mounted.

Another effect of high land values was to encourage planters to keep their land under almost constant cultivation. Repeated cropping of the land with canes tended to exhaust the soil. It thus became necessary to apply fertilizer and cultivate the canes more intensively. Canes had to be planted every year where formerly a single cane plant sent up shoots for several years after its first cutting. Another consequence of intensive cultivation was to reduce the quality of raw sugar and make its sale in European or island markets less profitable. Planters were therefore encouraged to install more equipment and employ additional workers to improve the quality of sugar by such processes as claying, sun drying, and refining. Moreover, distilleries were constructed to convert the molasses by-product into high-proof rum.

Finally, it should be observed that one stage of production shaded imperceptibly into another and different stages coexisted at a given place and time. Furthermore, progression from a lower to a higher stage was dependent on favourable cost-price ratios. Conceivably,

Sugar and Slavery

final product prices might decline in relation to production costs, so that the planter would be encouraged to shift some of his resources into the production of intermediate goods. Indeed, the dynamics of the sugar industry were such that instead of moving into a more intensive pattern of production, the planter might find it necessary to alter his mix of resources in a backward-moving direction.

9 THE GEOGRAPHIC BASE OF PRODUCTION

The fairly stable geographic base is one element which lends unity to this study. Not only was sugar production concentrated on tropical islands rather than coastal plains, but the greater part of the sugar came from a limited number of islands. We have seen that Englishmen first settled on several small islands in the Eastern Caribbean before a military expedition was sent to capture Jamaica. During the century or more prior to 1761, sugar production was confined largely to six islands. Five of these islands — Barbados, St Christopher (or St Kitts), Nevis, Antigua, and Montserrat — had such common features as limited land area (only 7.5 per cent of the aggregate area of the sugar colonies), early settlement, and membership in the chain of islands known as the Lesser Antilles. Barbados, however, stood apart from the other islands. The other four islands in the Lesser Antilles were known collectively as the Leeward Islands, being in close proximity to one another as well as to islands held by foreign powers. Jamaica, comprising four-fifths of the land area of the British sugar colonies, lies some one thousand miles to the west and north of Barbados. British sovereignty also extended to several small islands in the Caribbean which produced little or no sugar in the period of this study. In the Leeward group they consisted of Tortola, Barbuda, Anguilla, Spanish Town and the Virgin Islands. Three other islands, the Caymans, lie to the northwest of Jamaica and south of Cuba.

The islands capable of producing sugar thus remained virtually unchanged until 1761. The only exceptions were Surinam, the English colony in South America which was given up to the Netherlands in 1674 in exchange for New York, and the island of St Kitts which was divided almost equally between France and Great Britain before the latter came into full possession in 1713.

British military victories during the Seven Years' War led to expansion of the Empire in both hemispheres. Besides Canada and India, nearly every French and neutral island in the Caribbean was

Geographic and Economic Influences

Table 6.3

*The British sugar colonies:
method of acquisition, land area, and population*

Colony	How acquired	Year	Area in square miles	Estimated population, 1771–78	
				White	Slave
St Kitts	settled	1623	68	1,900	23,462
Barbados	settled	1627	166	18,532	68,548
Nevis	settled	1628	36	1,000	10,000
Antigua	settled	1632	108	2,590	37,808
Montserrat	settled	1632	39	1,314	9,834
Jamaica	conquered	1655	4,411	18,420	205,261
Dominica	conquered	1761	305	3,850	18,753
Grenada	conquered	1762	120	1,661	26,211
St Vincent	conquered	1762	133	1,450	11,853
Tobago	conquered	1762	116	391	8,643
Total			5,502	51,108	420,373

Source: John Macpherson, *Caribbean Lands, a geography of the West Indies* (London, 1963), pp. 31, 66–88, 93–110; Noel Deerr, *The History of Sugar* (London, 1949–50), vol. 2, pp. 278–9; George W. Roberts, *The Population of Jamaica* (Cambridge, 1957), pp. 33, 36.

taken by British forces. Although Guadeloupe and Martinique were restored to France by the Treaty of Paris in 1763, Britain retained possession of four other sugar islands. Known collectively as the Ceded Islands, the new acquisitions consisted of Dominica, Grenada, St Vincent, and Tobago, all in the Lesser Antilles. Taken together, the Ceded Islands comprised 12.3 per cent of the land area of the sugar colonies. Discussion of the settlement and development of the Ceded Islands will be taken up in the final chapter of this study. The chapters immediately following will be concerned with the growth of the sugar industry in the six islands that were settled in the 17th century, starting with Barbados and then proceeding to the Leeward Islands and Jamaica. As a prelimary 'map' of the sugar islands, Table 6.3 affords an opportunity to compare the colonies as to the method and year of acquisition, land area, and estimated population in the final years of this study.

CHAPTER SEVEN

Barbados, The Brightest Jewel in Our Crown of Trade

> This Island is one of the Riches Spotes of ground in the wordell and fully inhabited. But ware the pepell Sutabell to the Illand it ware not to be compared: it is a most rich soile, all wayes Grone and baring fruit, and the Chefest commoditie is sugar, and some. Indieco, and Cotaine, and Tobaccoe; but the chefest commodiete they now plant is Shuger and Cottaine.[1]
>
> Henry Whistler, 1654

1 AN ISLAND OF 'FIRSTS'

Except for priority of settlement, Barbados may be regarded as an island of 'firsts' in the tropical expansion of the English people. It was the first island to attract English settlers in considerable numbers, the first to introduce the sugar-cane and successfully market its raw sugar in international markets, the first to transform its society from a smallholder, semi-subsistence base to a slave-plantation, near-monoculture regime which was dominated by a class of wealthy sugar planters. The sugar revolution was so disruptive that thousands of smallholders and indentured servants were forced to seek their fortunes elsewhere. Barbados became the mother colony, the centre to which newly-formed colonies looked for labour, experienced planters, capital, and leadership in matters of imperial politics and trade. In view of this heritage of 'firsts', it is not surprising that Barbados is the 'little England' of the Caribbean, the island which is both colony and regional metropolis, both tropical export economy and centre of leadership in culture, politics, and trade.

---

1 'Extracts from Henry Whistler's Journal of the West India Expedition', in *The Narrative of General Venables... and the Conquest of Jamaica*, ed. C. H. Firth (London, 1900), p. 145.

Barbados, The Brightest Jewel in Our Crown of Trade

2 THE PHYSICAL SETTING

Though it presented formidable difficulties to pioneer settlers, the physical environment of Barbados was generally favourable to its development as a sugar colony. Environmental factors consisted of soil and climate, energy sources, health and physical comfort, access to markets and factor supplies, military defence, and the physical control of black slaves.

Barbados was especially favoured by its isolated situation, lying ninety-seven miles to the east of St Vincent, the nearest island. The island was remote from Spanish possessions in the New World and south of the main track of the galleons which plied between Spain and her colonies. As the trade winds in this latitude, 13° 4' north, blow from the north-east with a force of from ten to twenty miles per hour, vessels based at Barbados could run downwind to attack other islands. Conversely, ships based to leeward had difficulty beating upwind to attack Barbados. Largely as a consequence of this factor, Barbados has never suffered incursions from hostile Amerindians or rival European powers since its first settlement. Winds and currents also favoured peaceable traders, for it was customary for transient vessels from Europe and North America to call at Barbados before proceeding to other islands. Then, too, the island was the first port of call for slave ships from Africa. For these and other reasons Barbados enjoyed a profitable entrepôt trade with other islands and the Spanish Main.

Besides laying the track of incoming vessels, trade winds powered the mills and contributed to the health and well-being of the inhabitants. As the island is relatively flat, the highest point being 1,100 feet above sea level, the trade winds sweep the greater part of the island. This made it feasible to install windmills to crush the canes. Moreover, the comparative flatness of the island made it easy to transport canes to the mill and raw sugar to the shipping places. Owing largely to the trade winds, the island's climate is quite pleasant and healthy. The mean temperature in the port city of Bridgetown ranges from 76° F in January to 80° F in the month of August. Today Barbados has a reputation as a health resort for residents of neighbouring islands and the coastal region of South America.

However salubrious the climate may be today, Barbados was not always regarded as a health resort. Scattered references to epidemic disease and chronic tropical disorders point to a high general level of mortality in the 17th century, although it may be conjectured that Barbados was healthier than the other sugar islands. According to

Major John Scott, chronicler of the island's early history, the great yellow fever plague of 1647 'Raged Violently' and 'swept away abundance of People...'. John Winthrop said that this plague carried off 6,000 inhabitants of Barbados and nearly as many in St Christopher.[2] Another 'terrible contagion' attacked the islanders in 1692 and 'raged like a pestilence', continuing with some abatement for several years. Père Labat, the French priest who visited Barbados in 1700, observed that 'every one looked very well and had a good complexion.... It is true that *le mal de Siam* [yellow fever] carries off many people, but this pest is equally common among the Dutch, Portuguese, French and other Europeans who live in the Islands'. If yellow fever, smallpox, and cholera took a heavy toll from time to time, Barbados was apparently free of malaria, the scourge of so many tropical lands.[3]

Conditions of health and longevity improved in the 18th century, if the reports of contemporary writers can be credited. Rev. Griffith Hughes, Rector of St Lucy's parish in Barbados, disputed the view of Aristotle that the torrid zone was uninhabitable. 'Regularity of the Trade-Winds and Weather, and the quick Return of Night, with its moist Vapours' not only made the island habitable, but pleasant, he wrote. Because the inhabitants were not liable to sudden changes of temperature, 'they not only enjoy a great share of Health, but likewise live to an advanced old Age'.[4] George Frere, a leading planter, believed that the destruction of the woods had rendered the country more healthful. On the other hand, Hughes and Frere said little about the health of the Negro slaves except to enumerate and describe the diseases they contracted.[5]

In our age of big business it is not easy to comprehend the advantages which once lay with small economic units, as witness the city states of medieval Italy. By the same token, there were advantages which accrued to small islands in the age of mercantilism. 'A small territory, and even a few People, may by Situation, Trade, and Policy, be made equivalent to a greater', wrote Sir William Petty, 'and that convenience for Shipping, and Water-carriage, do most eminently and fundamentally conduce thereunto'.[6] Petty was

---

2 British Museum, Sloane MSS 3662, f. 58: John Scott, 'The Description of Barbados'; James K. Hosmer, *Winthrop's Journal of New England 1630–1649* (New York, 1908), vol. 2, p. 329.

3 *The Memoirs of Père Labat 1693–1705*, trans. John Eaden (London, 1931), pp. 120–1; G. B. Masefield, *A Short History of Agriculture in the British Colonies* (Oxford, 1950), p. 30.

4 Rev. Griffith Hughes, *The Natural History of Barbados* (London, 1750), pp. 24–39.

5 George Frere, *A Short History of Barbados* (London, 1767), pp. 119–20.

6 *The Economic Writings of Sir William Petty*, ed. Charles H. Hull (Cambridge, 1899), vol. 1, p. 268.

referring to the Dutch Republic, but similar views were expressed concerning colonial dependencies. In the words of Ferdinando Gorges, himself an absentee planter and agent of Barbados, 'Plantations on the continent of America or large islands which swallow up great numbers of people, and are able to produce both food and raiment for their livelihood, are doubtless rather injurious than profitable to this kingdom. But with Barbadoes and the Caribbee Islands it is otherwise'.[7]

Military defence, water transport, and control of servile labour were three of the most conspicuous advantages which accrued to Barbados and other small islands in the lesser Antilles. John Campbell noted that the 'extent of coast in proportion to that of territory ... is also very favourable to commerce ... It is no less apparent, that such islands for the very same reason, that makes them easier settled, are also easier defended, which is another point of very high consequence to the colony and to the mother country'.[8]

Though frequent reports of Negro conspiracies appear in the annals of Barbados, no slave insurrection of any moment occurred until the 'Emancipation riot' of 1816, and then only one European was killed. Forty-two Negroes were executed in 1675 for plotting to massacre all the white population. In 1687 a similar conspiracy was discovered and about twenty of the ringleaders were put to death. The third great conspiracy followed a few years later in 1692, and again the ringleaders and their accomplices were apprehended in advance of the appointed day, tortured, and executed. The conspiracies failed in each instance because 'loyal' slaves informed on their 'disloyal' brothers.[9] The compactness of the island, the difficulty that runaway slaves encountered in finding hide-outs after the land was cleared and densely populated, and the ability to marshal armed white men in the event of a slave-uprising — all these factors made it possible for the whites to maintain the upper hand despite their being far outnumbered by the blacks.

To such advantages as strategic location, limited health hazards, and compact size were added favourable conditions of climate and soil for sugar-cane culture. Barbados lies almost out of the track of the hurricanes, though on two occasions during the period of this study — 1675 and 1731 — these storms did great damage. Annual rainfall varies from about 50 to 70 inches, somewhat less than in

---

[7] *Cal. S. P. Col. 1669–74*, p. 565.
[8] John Campbell, *Candid and Impartial Considerations on the Nature of the Sugar Trade* (London, 1763), pp. 212–13.
[9] Noel Deerr, *The History of Sugar* (London, 1949–50), vol. 2, p. 325; Vincent T. Harlow, *A History of Barbados 1625–1685* (Oxord, 1926), pp. 324–7.

Sugar and Slavery

neighbouring islands, and at times insufficient for normal cane growth. About four-fifths of the island's surface is covered with coral limestone, which, by a process of decay, has produced red and black soils which are well drained and capable of growing canes to advantage. The remaining one-fifth of the island, known as the Scotland District, has less fertile soils which grow foodstuffs, minor staples, and some sugar-canes. Practically the whole island of 166 square miles (or 106,000 acres) is suited to agricultural production owing to slight differences in soil, elevation, and climate. Despite occasional hurricanes, drought, pests, and plant disease, Barbados in the 17th and 18th centuries had the reputation of being the 'Garden of the Caribbean', where hardly an inch of ground was lost 'that can produce one Ounce of any thing more than it does'. In fact, after three hundred years of cane cultivation Barbados today has as much as seven-eighths of its cultivated land, or approximately 59,000 acres, in sugar-canes.[10]

3 THE SUGAR REVOLUTION

Taking all of these natural features into account, it is not surprising that Barbados was the first English colony in the Caribbean to launch a successful sugar industry. From an island of yeomen farmers and small planters, Barbados in the course of two or three decades became an island of numerous sugar plantations, each of substantial acreage, capital, and slave labour force, and supplying sugar to Europeans on a scale sufficient to affect the level of world sugar prices. While it is true that some of the essential preconditions had been established, the coming of the sugar industry awaited the impact of exogenous forces. First there was the sharp decline in tobacco prices which encouraged the inhabitants to search for new staples. Second, there was the coming of the Dutch, whose expulsion from Brazil occurred at a time when the energies of Englishmen were diverted by the trammels of civil war.

Sugar-canes were brought from Brazil to Barbados at a time when tobacco markets were glutted and prices depressed. According to John Scott's version of the story,

---

10 Daniel Defoe, *A Plan of the English Commerce* (1728), in *Defoe's Writings* (London, 1938), vol. 14, p. 231; F. A. Hoyos, *Barbados Our Island Home* (London, 1960), pp. 1–12; John Macpherson, *Caribbean Lands: A Geography of the West Indies* (London, 1963), pp. 70–9.

Barbados, The Brightest Jewel in Our Crown of Trade

> The Sugar Cane was brought thither first by one Peeter Brower of North Holland from Brazile anno 1637, but came to noe Considerable p[er]fection till the year 1645, and soe forward to ye yeare 1652 at wch time the Dutch who had by their Great Credit they gave the Planters, brought the Island to its almost p[er]fection, whereby an Act of Parliament excluded that Trade; during the time I was in Command upon this island.[11]

Richard Ligon, contemporary historian and sugar planter of Barbados, seems to confirm Scott's version of the infant industry:

> At the time we landed on this Island, which was in the beginning of September, 1647, we were informed, partly by those Planters we found there, and partly by our own observations, that the great work of Sugar-making, was but newly practised by the inhabitants from there. Some of the most industrious men, having gotten Plants from *Fernambock* [Pernambuco], a place in *Brasil*, and made tryal of them at *Barbadoes*; and finding them to grow, they planted more and more, as they grew and multiplyed on the place, till they had such a considerable number, as they were worth the while to set up a very small Ingenio [works], and so make tryal what Sugar could be made upon that soyl.[12]

Actually, there is good reason for believing that the sugar-cane had been introduced into Barbados from Surinam by Captain Henry Powell as early as 1627. Though no sugar on a commercial scale was apparently made until the 1640s, the inhabitants may have grown canes to supply juice for sweetening their food and in a fermented form to make rum.

Cane growing was quite simple, but it was no easy matter to link together the processes of cultivation and sugar-making and amass the necessary supplies of land, labour, and capital for viable sugar estates. According to Scott's account, Colonel James Holdip was the first to cultivate the cane and make sugar, 'but it came to little untill the great industry, and more thriving Genius of Sr James Drax engaged in that great worke who brought Collonell Holdups essay to soe great perfection, that many were encouraged, to undertake the makeing of Sugar ...'. Drax, who had independent means and became closely associated with the Dutch, is said to have brought the model of a sugar mill and some coppers from Holland.[13] 'The manner of Planting, the Time of Gathering, and the right placing of their

---

11 Scott, 'Description of Barbados', f. 54.
12 Richard Ligon, *A True and Exact History of the Island of Barbadoes* (London, 1657), p. 85.
13 Scott, 'Description of Barbados', f. 60; Anon., *Some Memoirs of the first Settlement of Barbados* (Barbados, 1741), Appendix, p. 1.

Sugar and Slavery

Coppers in their Furnaces', were three of the difficulties cited by Richard Ligon.

> But they finding their errours by their daily practice, began a little to mend; and by new directions from *Brasil*, sometimes by strangers, and now and then by their own people, [who] were content sometimes to make such a voyage thither, to improve their knowledge in a thing they so much desired.

The first sugars, which were 'so moist, and full of molosses, and so ill-cur'd, as they were hardly worth the bringing home for *England*', were 'much better'd' when Ligon left Barbados in 1650.[14]

At a time when English merchants were distracted by the Civil War at home, Dutchmen not only supplied the Barbadians with Negro slaves and materials for making sugar; they also dominated the carrying trade of Barbados and other plantation colonies. 'Negroes, Coppers, Stills, and all other things Appertaining to the Ingenions for making of Sugar and that were any way necessary for their Comfortable Subsistence', were supplied to the Barbadians by Dutchmen.[15]

Though Dutchmen contributed to the 'comfortable subsistence' of the Barbadians, it cannot be said that the islanders enjoyed political tranquillity. Islanders who supported the King's cause during the Civil Wars were joined by Cavaliers who came from England and gained the upper hand over the local Roundhead faction in the period before 1652. Adherence to the Cavalier cause was motivated in part by the islanders' desire to maintain their favourable trading connection with the Dutch, at the same time escaping their debt obligations to English merchants. Moreover, only a thin line divided political warfare from economic warfare. In fact, a number of sugar estates changed hands when members of the defeated Roundhead faction were imprisoned, exiled, or forced to pay confiscatory fines.[16]

But Barbados did not long remain a refuge for Cavaliers and an unimpeded field of commercial enterprise for the merchants of Holland. On 11 January 1652, the Cavalier government of Barbados surrendered to Commonwealth forces sent out from England under the command of Sir George Ayscue. The terms of surrender called for the restoration of all Roundhead estates on the island. The Barbadian Cavaliers received back their properties in Great Britain

---

14 Ligon, *History of Barbadoes*, p. 85.
15 Scott, 'Description of Barbados', ff. 59–60.
16 Nicholas Foster, *A Briefe Relation of the late Horrid Rebellion Acted in the Island of Barbadas* (London, 1650), p. 64; N. Darnell Davis, *The Cavaliers and Roundheads of Barbados, 1650–1652* (Georgetown, British Guiana, 1887), pp. 145–97; Harlow, *History of Barbados*, pp. 25–82.

and were pardoned for all acts of hostility. Meanwhile, Dutch trade with the English colonies had been prohibited by act of the Commonwealth government in 1650, and a year later the first Navigation Act was placed on the statute book. Subsequently, as we have seen, the Restoration government of Charles II imposed even more stringent controls on colonial trade, much to the disappointment of the Barbadians who for many years afterwards attributed their former prosperity to free trade with the Dutch.[17]

Barbadians chafed under the strait-jacket of the Navigation Acts. Nevertheless, they pressed on with their sugar revolution, re-establishing old ties with English and New England merchants, but not being averse to finding roundabout methods of trade with foreigners. Licensed trade between England and the American colonies commenced in 1649, at which time several London merchants, including Maurice Thompson and Martin Noell, secured licences to send out materials for their newly-established sugar plantations. One export of critical importance was horses to supply power for the cane-crushing mills. Henry Whistler, who accompanied Penn and Venables on the expedition to Jamaica, wrote from Barbados in 1654: 'This Illand may be much improued if they can bring theyer desine of wine mills to perfecktion to grind theyer Shugor, for the mills they now use destroy so many horses that it begors the planters, a good hors for the mill being worth 50 li starling mony'.[18]

Barbados had a numerous population of yeomen farmers at the beginning of the sugar revolution. Since sugar plantations required more land and unfree labour than farms growing minor staples, a process of land consolidation and labour displacement commenced on a large scale. Already, under the small staple regime, indentured servants were employed in considerable numbers along with a few Indian and Negro slaves. The early years of the sugar revolution witnessed an increase in both types of labour, prisoners-of-war augmenting the European component of the plantation labour force, while African slaves were imported in growing numbers. White servants continued to arrive in Barbados, but they declined in number and were eventually displaced by Africans in most plantation occupations. Probably the most spectacular aspect of this tropical enclosure movement was the re-emigration of thousands of Barbadians to other colonies in the West Indies and North America.

Although population statistics leave much to be desired, it would appear that the white population reached a peak in the decade of the

---

17 Harlow, *History of Barbados*, p. 83–5.
18 'Henry Whistler's Journal', in *Narrative of General Venables*, pp. 146–7.

1640s. From 1636 to 1643 the male inhabitants increased from about 6,000 to 18,000, the greater number probably consisting of lower middle-class farmers and artisans of Nonconformist faiths. Men made up about half of the white population in 1645, that is, some 18,300 out of 36,600.[19] English emigration to Barbados was checked in the early years of the Civil War. But after 1646, with the collapse of the Royalist cause, considerable numbers of Cavaliers came to the island. This voluntary emigration became largely involuntary after 1650 when Cromwell began sending prisoners-of-war, together with felons, pirates, and other criminals to Barbados, where they were sold to the planters as indentured servants. One account, probably exaggerated, claimed that at least 12,000 prisoners had arrived on the island before 1655. Both in absolute numbers and in population density, not to mention the great wealth of the sugar industry, Barbados was the leading colony in the Commonwealth period. In fact, one modern authority says that, in 1650, Barbados had approximately 32,000 whites, as compared with 15,000 each in Massachusetts and Virginia. [20]

Land consolidation proceeded ruthlessly as the sugar revolution gained momentum. Between 1645 and 1667, according to John Scott, the number of white men on the island declined from 18,300 to 8,300, and the landed proprietors from 11,200 to 745. Scott cited the example of one Captain Waterman whose sugar plantation, comprising over 800 acres, had at one time been split up into forty smallholdings.[21]

Mortality undoubtedly claimed many of the smallholders, but greater numbers probably re-emigrated to other colonies. In the years prior to 1667, according to one inhabitant, '12,000 good men at least, formerly proprietors, are gone off, and tradesmen wormed out of their small settlements by their more suttle and greedy neighbours...'. The writer goes on to give details of the migration: 1,200 to New England, 1643–7; 600 to Trinidad and Tobago, 1643–7; 2,400 to Virginia and Surinam, 1646–58; 1,600 to Guadeloupe, Martinique, Marie Galante, Grenada, Tobago and Curaçao, 1650–62; 3,300 with Venables' expedition to Hispaniola and Jamaica; and as many as 5,100 who were lost or failed to return from other military engagements in the Caribbean area.[22] Alfred D.

19 Scott, 'Description of Barbados', f. 54; Harlow, *History of Barbados*, pp. 45, 293–6, 338–9; Alfred D. Chandler, 'The Expansion of Barbados', *The Journal of the Barbados Museum and Historical Society*, vol. XIII (May and Nov. 1946), p. 106.
20 N. M. Crouse, 'Causes of the Great Migration', *New England Quarterly*, vol. 5, (Jan. 1932), p. 4.
21 Scott, 'Description of Barbados', ff. 54, 59.
22 *Cal. S. P. Col. 1661–68*, pp. 528–30.

Barbados, The Brightest Jewel in Our Crown of Trade

Chandler, in a modern study of the re-emigration movement, says that some 30,000 people, consisting of planters, freemen, servants, and slaves, left Barbados in the 30 years from 1650 to 1680. Some went to the established colonies in the West Indies and North America, while others migrated to the new colonies of Jamaica, Surinam, and Carolina. Indeed, Chandler maintains that this migration of Barbadians 'was numerically the largest population movement within the colonies during the seventeenth century'.[23]

More than filling the gap left by the departing whites were Negro slaves who were brought to Barbados from Africa. From a reported fifty Africans in 1629, the slave population increased to about 6,000 in 1643, to 20,000 in 1655, and upwards of 50,000 in 1666. Slaves were first imported on a considerable scale by Dutch merchants.[24] From Barbados George Downing (afterwards Sir George) wrote to John Winthrop, Jr in 1645: 'If you go to Barbados, you will see a flourishing Island, many able men. I believe they have bought this year no lesse than a thousand negroes, and the more they buie, the better able they are to buye, for in a yeare and a halfe they will earne (with God's blessing) as much as they cost'.[25] By 1667, according to John Scott, the making of sugar was 'managed Principally by Negroe Slaves, who besides their purchase stood their Masters in little more than a Small Quantity of Land, to Plant Indian Corne, beanes, Potatoes, bonanoes, Plantans, Yams, &c. the Provisions of the Cuntry ...'.[26]

Viewed in the hard light of economic conditions, Barbados was more akin to a human inferno than it was to a tropical paradise in the decades of the sugar revolution. 'This Island', wrote Henry Whistler, 'is inhabited with all sortes: with English, french, Duch, Scotes, Irish, Spaniards ... Ingones and miserabell Negors borne to perpetuall slauery thay and thayer seed'. Describing the island as 'a Dunghill wharone England doth cast forth its rubidg', Whistler said that 'A rodg in England will hardly make a cheater heare: a Baud brought ouer puts one a demuor comportment, a whore if handsume makes a wife for sume rich planter'.[27]

Contrasted with Whistler's pessimistic view was that of the planter elite which regarded the economic and social upheaval as the 'golden age' of Barbados. One inhabitant compared the island in 1643 and 1666, noting that in the former year the buildings were mean, 'with

---

23 Chandler, 'Expansion of Barbados', pp. 106–14.
24 Ibid., p. 110; Harlow, *History of Barbados*, p. 338–9.
25 'Winthrop Papers', *Massachusetts Hist. Soc. Coll.*, 4th ser., vol. VI, p. 536.
26 Scott, 'Description of Barbados', f. 59.
27 'Henry Whistler's Journal', in *Narrative of General Venables*, p. 146.

Sugar and Slavery

things only for necessity', while in the latter year the 'plate, jewels, and household stuffs were estimated at 500,000 *l.*, their buildings very fair and beautiful, and their houses like castles, their sugar houses and negroes' huts show themselves from the sea like so many towns, each defended by its castle'.[28]

4 THE DRIFT TOWARD MONOCULTURE

Despite the great transformation of the Barbadian economy in the Commonwealth and early Restoration period, it is evident that the consolidation of smallholdings into slave-plantations was not at an end. Compared with later decades of the island's leading industry, plantations were fewer in number, occupied fewer acres, and were understocked in terms of servile labour, livestock, and fixed capital structures.

Although we lack information concerning the number of sugar plantations in the early period, some features of the island's economy are revealed by Richard Ligon's illustrated map of 1657. Much of the island was apparently thinly populated, for wild hogs and mounted hunters are observed in several localities. Another horseman is shown firing a gun at two runaway slaves. Cattle are grazing in inland districts, while pack animals and heavily-loaded camels are being driven across the island. On the south-west coast is shown the port, fortress, and capital city of Bridgetown, which is nestled around Carlisle Bay to afford protection to shipping. Four ships are shown hugging the west and south coasts, apparently taking on or depositing cargo which is being shuttled to plantation wharves in lighters. Few plantations are shown at any great distance inland. Out of a total of 259 proprietors whose names are listed on the map, 118 had seaboard sites on the leeward side of the island, while most of the other plantations were in close proximity to the leeward coast.[29] Plantations were generally long and narrow, the narrow side fronting on the sea. 'The reason for this', as Professor Pares has observed, 'was that from the first foundation of the colonies all settlers had to enjoy an equal chance at sea-transportation for their produce, which was the only kind of transportation then in existence'.[30] Improved roads and horse-drawn carts and wagons later permitted the inland migration of plantations.

28 *Cal. S. P. Col. 1661–68*, p. 528–9.
29 Ligon, *History of Barbadoes*. A reproduction of Ligon's map serves as the frontispiece to Harlow's *History of Barbados*.
30 Richard Pares, *Merchants and Planters. Economic History Review Supplement No. 4* (Cambridge, 1960), p. 61, n. 46.

Sugar and Slavery

Besides the illustrated map, Ligon's history supplies information regarding a settled sugar plantation. Ligon's partner, Sir Thomas Modyford, paid £7,000 sterling for a half-interest in a settled plantation which was worth only about £400 before it was equipped to produce sugar. In 1647, this plantation of 500 acres contained a cattle-mill, boiling house, filling room, cisterns, still house, and other buildings and utensils. There were '96 *Negroes*, and three Indian women with their Children; 28 Christians, 45 Cattle for work, 8 Milch Cows, a dozen Horses and Mares, 16 Assinigoes [asses]'. The 500 acres of land was divided as follows:

> There was imployed for sugar some what more than 200 acres; above 80 acres for pasture, 120 for wood, 30 for Tobacco, 5 for Ginger, as many for Cotton wool, and 70 acres for provisions; viz. Corn, Potatoes, Plantines, Cassavie, and Bonavist; some few acres of which for fruit; viz. Pines, Plantines, Milions, Bonanoes, Gnavers, Water Milions, Oranges, Limon Limes, etc., most of these only for the table.[31]

Ligon estimated that in a twenty-month period an acre of canes yielded 3,000lb of muscovado sugar worth 3d per lb at the market in Bridgetown. The gross revenue of 200 acres of canes would thus amount to £7,500 for twenty months, or £4,500 per annum.[32]

Deed records which contain scattered inventories of sugar plantations in the 1650s and 1660s suggest that Ligon's plantation was on the high side. The extant inventories of eight plantations show acreages ranging from 90 to 413 with from 20 to 70 Negro slaves, 3 to 10 horses, and 12 to 36 asses and cattle. One plantation had 61 Negro slaves and 22 white servants, while another had 70 and 5, respectively. No servants are listed in the other inventories. The purchase price of three plantations is expressed in pounds of sugar, three others in sterling money ranging from £1,250 to £2,400, and two others are not valued. One other plantation which approached that of Ligon's contained 403 acres of land, 130 Negro slaves, 9 horses, and 14 asses and cattle. Its purchase price was £4,166 sterling.[33]

Somewhat less spectacular, but nonetheless substantial, was the movement towards land consolidation and sugar-estate formation in the 1670s and 1680s. One measure of consolidation is afforded by the list of 'most eminent' planters of Barbados which was submitted by the President and Council of the island to the Board of Trade in 1673. Acreages held by the seventy-four leading planters are arranged

---

31 Ligon, *History of Barbadoes*, pp. 22, 86.
32 Ibid., pp. 93–6.
33 Barbados Public Library, Nathan Lucas MSS, *Misc. Notes*, vol. 5, ff. 136–341.

Table 7.1
Land held by the most eminent planters of Barbados, 1673

Acres	Number of proprietors	Acres	Number of proprietors
200–299	15	700–799	1
300–399	24	800–899	2
400–499	14	900–999	1
500–599	10	1,000–1,001	1
600–699	6	Total	74

Source: *Cal. S. P. Col. 1669–74*, pp. 495–97.

in a frequency distribution in Table 7.1. John Pierce headed the list with 1,000 acres, and Major Robert Haskett came next with 900. Colonel Henry Drax and Captain John Waterman each held 800 acres, while Sir Peter Colleton, Bart., had 700. Six individuals whose surnames were Sparke, Sharpe, Littleton, Codrington, Davers and Seawell held 600 acres, while in the 500-acre range were the surnames Searle, Farmer, Lambert, Thornhill, Standfast, Bayly, Maycock, Horne, Colleton, and Bulkely. Holding lesser acreages were such prominent families as Yeamans, Morris, Foster, Gibbes, Holder, Frere, Walrond, Willoughby, Middleton, and Kendall.

In the aggregate, the seventy-four most eminent planters held 29,050 acres out of a total of about 92,000 acres of arable land in Barbados. More than two-thirds of the arable land was thus held in units of less than 200 acres.

Further evidence of expansion in the slave-plantation sector of the Barbadian economy is afforded by the censuses of 1680 and 1683. The totals in the former return are as follows: 3,044 landowners, 87,579 acres, 2,317 white servants, and 38,782 Negro slaves.[34] Enumerated in the census of 1683 were 4,056 families and households, 17,187 free persons, 2,381 unfree persons and servants, 46,602 Negro slaves, 6,761 men able to bear arms, 89,306 acres possessed and useful, and 358 sugar works.[35]

---

34 Public Record Office, London: C.O. 1/44, ff. 142–379; Richard S. Dunn, 'The Barbados Census of 1680: Profile of the Richest Colony in English America', *William and Mary Quarterly*, 3rd ser., vol. XXVI, no. 1 (Jan. 1969), pp. 3–30.

35 Sir Richard Dutton to Council of Trade, 1683, Phillipps MSS 8797, printed in Sir Robert H. Schomburgk, *The History of Barbados* (London, 1848), p. 82.

Table 7.2

The large planters share of property, 1680*

	Planters with 60 or more slaves	Per cent	All other landholders	Per cent
Number of planters	175	6.9	2,417	93.1
Acreage	46,775	53.4	40,804	46.6
Servants	1,032	53.9	883	46.1
Slaves	20,289	54.3	17,054	45.7

* The 405 Bridgetown householders, with their 402 servants and 1,439 slaves, have been excluded from this calculation.

Source: P.R.O., London. C.O. 1/44, ff. 142–379. Table reprinted from Richard S. Dunn, 'The Barbados Census of 1680: Profile of the Richest Colony in English America', *William and Mary Quarterly*, 3rd ser., vol. XXVI, no. 1 (January, 1969), p. 17.

The remarkable feature of the census of 1680 is its specific information concerning individual property and office-holding. Accompanying the return is a detailed map of Barbados which has been reproduced in Professor Dunn's article. Though the holdings of the large planters are understated, Professor Dunn is of opinion that the census 'possesses a unique precision by seventeenth-century standards'. There were 1,186 smallholders with less than 10 acres; 1,041 small planters with 10 or more acres and from 0 to 19 slaves; 190 middling planters with from 30 to 100 acres and 20 to 59 slaves; and 175 large planters, all of whom possessed 60 or more slaves and all but seven of whom had 100 or more acres of land.[36] Table 7.2 shows that the large planters, who comprised only 6.9 per cent of all landholders, held a little more than one-half of the total acreage, servants, and slaves.

The considerable range in acreage and slaves held by the 175 large planters is shown in Table 7.3. The median large plantation in 1680 consisted of 220 acres and 100 slaves. Writing a decade later, Sir Dalby Thomas said that 100 acres of land employed in a sugar plantation required 50 black slaves and 7 white servants to manage it.[37] Together with the sugar works, utensils, and livestock, the total cost of such a plantation was estimated at £5,625. If the median large plantation represented a capital outlay of £10,000 then the large plantation sector in 1680 amounted to £1,750,000, and the

36 Dunn, 'Barbados Census of 1680', pp. 11–13.
37 Sir Dalby Thomas, *An Historical Account of the Rise and Growth of the West-India Collonies* (London, 1690), pp. 14–15.

Table 7.3

The large planters, 1680: frequency distribution of holdings of land and slaves

Acres of land	Number of proprietors	Number of slaves	Number of proprietors
Less than 100	7	60–99	86
100–199	62	100–149	45
200–299	43	150–199	26
300–399	38	200–249	10
400–499	11	250–299	5
500–599	6	300–399	2
600–910	8	400–405	1
Total	175		175

Source: P.R.O., London. C.O. 1/44, ff. 142–379. I am indebted to Professor Richard S. Dunn who supplied the data from which this table is derived.

total wealth of Barbados was probably in the neighbourhood of £2,500,000.

Besides statistical data, evidence of estate consolidation and the drift toward monoculture is found in literary sources. By 1675 several absentee planters in London had become so alarmed at the exodus of smallholders that they urged the island government to make a law 'that no man possessed of land in Barbadoes be capable of purchasing any more, which will uphold the number of freeholders'.[38] During the administration of Governors Atkins (1674–80) and Dutton (1680–5), the pressure of population on limited land resources was a matter of concern. Atkins, who was of the opinion that no spot of ground in the universe was better planted or better inhabited, claimed that there was 'not a foot of land in Barbados that is not employed even to the very seaside...'. Similarly, Dutton reported that there was not one piece of unmanured ground large enough 'to draw a regiment of foot on without great damage'.[39] As more and more land was planted in canes, the islanders became increasingly dependent upon outside sources of foodstuffs, building materials, and draft animals. So great was this dependence by 1672 that Governor Willoughby estimated that the

---

38 *Cal. S. P. Col. 1669–74*, p. 141.
39 Ibid., *1675–76*, p. 347; ibid., *1675–76, Appendix 1574–1674*, p. 419; ibid., *1681–5*, p. 109.

Sugar and Slavery

island did not furnish of its own growth 'one quarter Victualls sufficient for its Inhabitants nor any other necessaries for Planting...'.⁴⁰

5 CONSERVING THE SOIL OF BARBADOS

The period subsequent to the sugar revolution was one in which 'high farming' was called for to ensure production on a sustained-yield basis. 'When Sugar was first planted in this Island', wrote John Oldmixon in 1708, 'one Acre of Canes yielded more than now, for four, five, or six, or seven Years together, without any further planting or dunging; the same Root would shoot forth new Branches, and these be fuller of Sap than the Canes are at this time'.⁴¹ Declining soil fertility, of which reports are extant as early as the 1650s, had apparently reached a critical point by the 1680s. This was a decade when inclement weather and low sugar prices compounded the difficulties of Barbadian planters. The groans of the planters found expression in Edward Littleton's pamphlet of 1689. The collection and application of dung was 'a mighty Labour, which in effect is a Charge'. Littleton estimated that thirty cart-loads of dung were needed to fertilize an acre of ground. Terraces were built 'to stop the Mould that washes from our Grounds; which we carry back into Carts or upon *Negroes* Heads. Our *Negroes* work at it like Ants and Bees'.⁴²

Though conditions varied from year to year and from plantation to plantation, there is no mistaking the secular movement toward intensive monoculture. As Oldmixon described it,

> The Planters being limited to a small Proportion of Land, pressed it so often with the same Plant, and never letting it lie still, the Soil is so impoverish'd, that they are now forc'd to dung and plant every Year; insomuch that 100 Acres of Cane require almost double that Number of Hands they did formerly, while the Land retain'd its natural Vigour, which also then did not only bring forth certain Crops, but fewer Weeds too, the Weeds having been encreased by frequent Dunging.⁴³

Added to these difficulties was the increased incidence of plant disease, a condition generally prevalent in one-crop economies.

Cane hole agriculture was one significant innovation which

---

40 B.M. Egerton MSS 2395, f. 477: Lord Willoughby's Proposalls Concerning the West Indies, 8 April 1672.
41 John Oldmixon, *The British Empire in America* (London, 1708), vol. 2, p. 140.
42 Edward Littleton, *The Groans of the Plantations* (London, 1689), p. 16.
43 Oldmixon, *British Empire in America*, vol. 2, pp. 140–1.

probably originated in Barbados during the first decade of the 18th century. To check destructive erosion and soil loss, squares were laid out approximately five feet in size and excavated by the slaves to a depth of five or six inches. Traditional food crops, such as yams, corn, and peas, were planted between the holes and harvested before the canes had grown very tall. By planting in holes, canes were protected from windstorms, a receptacle was provided for manure and other fertilizer, and sheet and gully erosion on sloping land was checked. The cane hole technique was a major development in Barbadian cane growing, writes Dr Watts, 'for it represented the first reasoned and successful attempt to control the catastrophic difficulties of large-scale soil loss, which sugar cane agriculture, associated with the removal of forest cover and the earlier poor planting techniques, had initiated in the island'.[44]

6 THE SLAVE ECONOMY

If one criteria of economic growth was the island's ability to expand its labour force, then it is evident that the expansion continued to the year 1770. While little reliance can be placed on population returns prior to 1748, owing to widespread concealment of slaves to avoid taxes, corrected returns are available for the subsequent period. MacPherson gives corrected returns for the years 1748, 1763, and 1773, and annual corrected returns for the period 1764—88 are recorded in a report submitted by the Assembly of Barbados to the Privy Council. If we accept the uncorrected figure shown in the census of 1683, then the slave population increased from 46,602 in that year to 68,000 in 1748, and to 76,334 in 1770. Declining imports from Africa and the carrying of seasoned slaves to the Ceded Islands reduced the black population to 74,410 in 1775.[45]

Slave imports, while fluctuating widely from year to year, show an upward trend to the year 1769, when the number entered was 6,837. This was probably the high point prior to the prohibition of the slave trade in 1807. Table 7.4, which summarizes the import data for most years in the century prior to 1776, has certain limitations. Smuggled slaves, of which considerable numbers were reported in certain years, were not recorded. Re-exported slaves, for which few statistics are

---

44 David Watts, 'Origin of Barbadian Cane Hole Agriculture', *Jour. Barbados Hist. Soc.*, vol. XXXII, no. 3 (May 1968), pp. 143—51.
45 David Macpherson, *Annals of Commerce* (Edinburgh, 1805), vol. 3, p. 700; *Parliamentary Papers* 1790, vol. XXIX, nos. 697—8.

Table 7.4

Negro slaves imported into Barbados, 1676–1775
(annual averages)

Years	Slave imports	Years	Slave imports
1678–80	1,336	1726–30	3,726
1681–85	1,825	1731–35	2,155
1686–90	1,348	1747–50	1,782
1691–95	1,058	1751–55	4,573
1708–10	1,027	1756–60	2,505
1711–15	3,825	1761–65	3,227
1716–20	4,328	1766–70	5,101
1721–25	2,001	1771–75	1,456

Source: *Parl. Papers*, 1790, vol. XXIX, nos. 697–98; Vincent T. Harlow, *A History of Barbados, 1625–1685* (Oxford, 1926), pp. 316–17; K. G. Davies, *The Royal African Company* (London, 1957), p. 363; Frank W. Pitman, *The Development of The British West Indies, 1700–1763* (New Haven, 1917), p. 72.

extant, would need to be subtracted from imports (both legal and illegal) to arrive at the addition to the island's labour force. Generally speaking, smuggling declined after the Royal African Company lost its monopoly of the slave trade in 1698, and re-exports fell off after the first decade of the 18th century.[46]

Owing to the eroding effects of mortality, only a small portion of the slaves imported into Barbados represented net additions to the labour force. In the period 1701–25, nearly 5 per cent of the slaves on the island had to be replaced annually to maintain the population. The mortality rate declined slowly during the 18th century; the annual replacement rate was approximately 3.7 per cent during the third quarter of the century.[47]

Professor Bennett has discussed the comparative advantage of buying imported slaves or breeding from the Creole population on the Codrington plantation in Barbados. In order to break the vicious circle of high mortality and the need for frequent renewal of the labour force by purchase of imported slaves, the Codrington

---

46 Frank W. Pitman, *The Development of the British West Indies 1700–1763* (New Haven, 1917), pp. 72–3.
47 See Chapter 11, pp. 244, 247.

Barbados, The Brightest Jewel in Our Crown of Trade

managers turned in 1761 to a policy of prolonging the lives of their Negroes and encouraging them to breed by humane treatment.[48]

If, as seems reasonable, it became less profitable to import new workers from Africa than to breed slaves locally, then the ratio of working slaves to total slave population must have declined, at the same time that maintenance charges increased as a percentage of total costs. In part, some of these added maintenance charges, especially foodstuffs, were met by shifting marginal cane lands into the cultivation of provisions.

7 FURTHER ESTATE CONSOLIDATION

Though less spectacular than the great exodus in the period of the sugar revolution, the emigration of whites continued well into the 18th century. From a maximum of approximately 36,000 in 1645, the whites declined to less than 24,000 in 1684, and to between 16,000 and 19,000 in the third quarter of the 18th century. The combination of drought and low sugar prices drove off so many planters and their slaves in the decade of the 1730s that one local official feared that if the emigration continued, 'in a few years this Island will be possessed only by a small number and not have strength enough to manure above a quarter of it'.[49] No such depopulation occurred, however, but in the more prosperous years from 1740 to 1748 about 2,500 Barbadians quitted the island with their families. After 1750 the white population remained fairly stationary at a level that was considerably higher in relation to the servile inhabitants than other British colonies in the West Indies.[50]

Up to the last quarter of the 18th century the sugar sector of the Barbadian economy increased in relation to that of minor staples. Père Labat, the French priest who visited the island in 1700, wrote: 'Formerly much tobacco was grown there. Afterwards, ginger and indigo were cultivated. Cotton was grown in some parts; but the sugar cane is at present almost the sole crop to which they cling'.[51]

48 J. Harry Bennett, Jr., *Bondsmen and Bishops, Slavery and Apprenticeship on the Codrington Plantations of Barbados, 1710–1838* (Berkeley and Los Angeles, 1958), pp. 53–62, 136–40.
49 *Cal. S. P. Col. 1735–36*, pp. 29, 118; Pitman, *Development of British West Indies*, pp. 369–73; Deerr, *History of Sugar*, vol. 2, p. 278.
50 P.R.O. London, C.O. 28/29. Cc 28: Gov. Henry Grenville to Board of Trade, 8 Feb. 1748.
51 Eaden, *Memoirs of Père Labat*, p. 170.

Table 7.5

Estimated wealth of Barbados in 1731

106,000 acres of land at £20 per acre	£2,120,000
65,000 Negroes at £30 per head	1,950,000
Sugar mills, buildings, and equipment	1,110,000
20,000 head of cattle at £10 per head	200,000
6,000 horses at £20 per head	120,000
Total	£5,500,000

Source: John Bennett, *Two Letters and Several Calculations on The Sugar Colonies and Trade* (London, 1738), p. 19.

According to John Bennett's calculation of 1731, annual exports consisted of 25,000 hogshead of sugar, valued at £320,000; 15,000 hogsheads of rum, £80,000; an unascertained quantity of ginger, cotton, and aloes, £20,000; and total exports, £420,000. Sugar and its by-products made up an even greater proportion of total exports in 1772. Arthur Young's estimate for that year gives 20,266 hogsheads of sugar, valued at £303,990; 15,190 hogsheads of rum, £203,992; sundry minor staples, £30,000; and total exports, £537,982.[52]

From the above calculations it is evident that a substantial investment in land, slaves, sugar works, and livestock was needed to yield annual exports valued at upwards of £400,000. Two calculations of the wealth of Barbados are given by John Bennett for the years 1730 and 1731 in the amounts of £5,000,000 and £5,500,000, respectively. The latter calculation 'of the present Value of Barbadoes, considered as a Sugar Colony, drawn as near the Truth as possible, and far from any Exaggeration', is summarized in Table 7.5.

Despite the substantial class of smallholders, the wealth of Barbados probably continued to be concentrated in the hands of fewer proprietors. The detailed map in Rev. Griffith Hughes's *Natural History of Barbados* (1750), shows a total of 536 plantations, 356 windmills, and no cattle-mills. This compares with the census of 1710–12, which returned 1,309 plantations and 485 sugar works, of which 409 were windmills and 76 cattle-mills. Hughes's map gives only the surnames of the proprietors. For this reason Table 7.6 shows the distribution of estates and windmills on a family basis.

[52] John Bennett, *Two Letters and Several Calculations on the Sugar Colonies and Trade* (London, 1738), p. 19; Arthur Young, *Political Essays Concerning the Present State of the British Empire* (London, 1772), p. 287.

Barbados, The Brightest Jewel in Our Crown of Trade

Table 7.6

Family holdings of estates and windmills in Barbados, 1750

Number of families	Number of estates	Total estates	Number of families	Number of windmills	Total windmills
2	12	24	0	12	0
1	9	9	1	9	9
1	8	8	0	8	0
1	7	7	2	7	14
5	6	30	1	6	6
10	5	50	3	5	15
15	4	60	5	4	20
39	3	117	9	3	27
85	2	170	48	2	96
61	1	61	169	1	169
220		536	238		356

Source: Griffith Hughes, *The Natural History of Barbados* (London, 1750), map following table of contents.

From Table 7.6 we learn that less than half of the proprietary families of Barbados were sugar planters, assuming that at least one windmill was needed to produce sugar. Indicative of the concentration of landed estates is the fact that 74 (or one-third) of the families each holding three or more estates, held in the aggregate 305 estates, or 56.9 per cent of the total. Turning to the distribution of windmills, again we find that less than one-third of the families, each with two or more mills, held in the aggregate 187 windmills, or 52.5 per cent of the total. The Holder family had the most estates and windmills, numbering twelve and nine, respectively. Among the other great proprietary families were the Harrisons, Alleynes, Gibbes, Osbornes, Freres, Walkers, and Adams, each with six or more estates and four or more windmills. It seems reasonable to conclude that of the 238 sugar-planting families, upwards of seventy were in an 'elite' category, having sufficient wealth and income to assume positions of political and social leadership in both colony and metropolis.

Certainly a primary technical reason for the movement towards property consolidation was the shift from cattle-mills to windmills. The construction of a windmill involved a considerable outlay of

Sugar and Slavery

capital; at the same time it enabled planters to expand their productive units and take advantage of the economies of large-scale production of sugar and its by-products. The shift in energy sources was well established by 1708 when Oldmixon wrote that 'lately every substantial Planter has one or two Wind-Mills and some three, as at Sir Richard Hacket's, Sir Samuel Husband's, and Col. Drax's Plantations'. In fact, he said that cattle-mills were almost out of use, there being forty windmills to one cattle-mill.[53] From 356 windmills in 1750, the number increased to 423 in 1767, and 432 in 1771. On the other hand, only fourteen cattle-mills were enumerated in 1773.[54]

Windmills were only one source of power for the intensively cultivated plantations. As the fertility of the soil diminished, more slaves and cattle were needed to till and manure the cane lands. 'The Practice now is to dung the Canes', wrote Oldmixon, 'which is done either when they are planted, or when they come up, and are two Foot high, and this is the greatest Trouble and Expence the planter is at; for if it was not for this dunging, a third part of the Negroes would do'. In 1714, the island was said to require the 'utmost art, Industry and Manure, and that too annually'.[55]

George Washington, who, with his brother Lawrence, visited Barbados in 1751–2, was a close observer of the island's sugar industry, particularly the system of manuring cane lands.

> Their dung they are very careful in saving [he wrote], and curious in making, which they do by throughing up large heaps of Earth and a number of Stakes drove there in Sufficient for Sixteen head of Cattle to Stand separately tied too, which they are three months trampling all the trash [dry and green vegetable matter] ... and then its fit to manure the Ground.... The very grass that grows amongst their corn is not Lost but carefully gather'd for provender for their Stock![56]

Besides setting slaves to the task of gathering grass for fodder, planters fed cane tops and the leaves of Indian corn to their cattle so as to avoid the necessity of shifting highly capitalized cane lands into pasture.[57]

From the above discussion it seems evident that by the middle decades of the 18th century the sugar planters of Barbados had

---

53 Oldmixon, *British Empire in America*, vol. 2, pp. 139–40, 151.
54 P.R.O. London, C.O. 28/55, No. 8: Gov. Hay to Lord Dartmouth, 31 Aug. 1774.
55 Ibid., C.O. 28/14, T 44: William Sharp, President of Barbados, to the Council and Assembly, 4 May 1714; Oldmixon, *British Empire in America*, vol. 2, p. 139.
56 *The Diaries of George Washington, 1748–1799*, ed. John C. Fitzpatrick (New York, 1925), vol. 1, pp. 26–8.
57 *American Husbandry Containing an Account of the Agriculture of the British Colonies* (1775), ed. Harry A. Carman (New York, 1939), p. 441.

Barbados, The Brightest Jewel in Our Crown of Trade

arrived at a capital-intensive, power-intensive system of agriculture conducted on a sustained-yield basis. Since the intensity of cultivation varied with economic conditions, it is significant that mild prosperity characterized the island's economy from about 1748 to 1769, followed by hard times beginning in 1770.[58]

8 THE TURNING AWAY FROM INTENSIVE MONOCULTURE

But the forced feeding of the land was not to continue indefinitely, for even the most rational system of management was not sufficient to overcome a major alteration in the cost-price ratio. Not only were the Barbadian planters a small part of an imperial system in which the forces of supply and demand were largely beyond their control, but there were also rival sugar colonies which indirectly influenced their costs and returns. If no single year marks the turning away from intensive monoculture, certainly many of the symptoms were evident by the depression years of the 1730s. In 1747, the Governor called attention to several thousand acres of abandoned cane lands, 'part whereof the Owners of the Sugar Work Plantations Use as Pasture for the large Quantitys of Cattle they are obliged to keep for the Manure even of their best Lands and for carrying their Effects to Markett'.[59]

It was the judgement of Sir Robert Schomburgk, the mid-19th century historian of Barbados, that 'a rational management replaced by artificial means the former fertility'. Indeed, he affirmed that the island had 'not undergone deterioration since Sir Jonathan Atkins' time, when it was considered to have reached its meridian prosperity — a period which has been styled the golden age of Barbados'.[60]

---

58 Bennett, *Bondsmen and Bishops*, pp. 5–6; Hazel M. Hartley, 'Of the Produce of the Plantations', in *Codrington Chronicle An Experiment in Anglican Altruism on a Barbados Plantation, 1710–1834*, ed. Frank J. Klingberg (Berkeley and Los Angeles, 1949), p. 77.
59 P.R.O. London, C.O. 28/57, Bb 57: Gov. Thomas Robinson to Board of Trade, 20 Feb. 1747.
60 Schomburgk, *History of Barbados*, pp. 140–1.

CHAPTER EIGHT

His Majesty's Leeward Islands
Part I. St Christopher, Nevis, Montserrat

> The Natural Produce of these Islands are Sugar, Rum, Molasses, Cotton, Ginger, and a small quantity of Indigo, which when made up for a Market, are the only Manufactures of these Islands.
> These Islands also Produce great Quantities of Indian, and Guinea Corn, Casada, Potatoes, and other Roots and Plants, which serve for Provisions for the Poorer Sort of People and Negroes.[1]
>
> Governor John Hart, 1724

1 THE COLLECTIVE VIEW

Known collectively as the Leeward Islands, St Christopher, Nevis, Montserrat, and Antigua are small islands in the northernmost part of the arc forming the Lesser Antilles. They are lush, green, tropical islands which were settled by Englishmen between 1623 and 1632. Generally speaking, economic development proceeded at a slow and irregular pace until the second decade of the 18th century. Unlike Barbados, which lies almost one hundred miles from its nearest neighbour, the Leeward Islands are in sight of islands which were held by hostile Amerindians and foreign nations. Moreover, St Christopher was divided between the French and English until 1713. On several occasions during the wars of the 17th and early 18th centuries, Frenchmen invaded the English islands and the English portion of St Christopher, burning cane fields and carrying off sugar utensils and slaves. War and the threat of war hindered settlement and investment in plantations. Taxes had to be levied to build fortifications and maintain troops. 'War is very destructive to the planter, who must guard instead of planting', wrote Governor Stapleton.[2]

Less guarding and more planting characterized the period after 1713. After years of intermittent invasion and loss of movable

---

1 Public Record Office, London. C.O. 152/14, R 101, f. 328: Gov. Hart to Board of Trade, 12 July 1724.
2 *Cal. S. P. Col. 1669–74*, p. 392.

wealth, the planter class entered on a long period of economic growth and development. Noteworthy features of the period were land enclosure, emigration of smallholders and white servants, influx of Negro slaves, formation of sugar plantations, and the movement toward monoculture. The change was not abrupt, however, and it will be seen that substantial development occurred in some of the islands prior to 1713.

Occupying about 5 per cent of the area of the British West Indies, the Leeward Islands in the years immediately preceding the American Revolution accounted for one-eighth of the white population, one-fifth of the Negro slaves, one-fourth of the sugar exports, and three-tenths of the value of all exports from the British sugar colonies. Table 8.1 shows that the population of the four islands increased from 18,868 in 1678, when the whites outnumbered the blacks, to 88,908 in 1775, when the ratio of whites to blacks was 1 to 12. It will be seen that the collective contribution of these islands to the Imperial economy was by no means insignificant. Moreover, though in many respects similar, there was sufficient diversity in physical and cultural features to warrant an island-to-island history of the sugar industry in the Leeward Islands.

2 ST CHRISTOPHER: DESCRIPTIVE ACCOUNT

St Christopher, the second largest territory in the Leewards, has an environment which is well adapted to the cultivation of sugar-cane. It is an island of mountains and plains, of tropical rain forest and semi-arid lands covered with cacti, but with a sizeable area — some 25,000 acres, or one-third of the land area — which is relatively level, fertile, and well watered. Three groups of mountains, dominated by Mount Misery which rises to 4,314 feet, form the backbone of the island. In the course of geological time these volcanic peaks have deposited fine ash which has weathered into highly fertile soil on the gently sloping apron of land between the seashore and the base of the mountains. While the rainfall varies from district to district as well as seasonally, most of the sugar plantations receive annually more than 50 inches. Moreover, the average temperature of 79° F, plus the cooling trade winds, provide a comfortable climate for the human occupants. Taken together, these physical features go far to explain St Christopher's superior productiveness as a sugar island. Bryan Edwards spoke of the 'nearly two hogsheads of sixteen cwt per acre for the whole of the lánd in ripe canes' as a 'prodigious return, not equalled I imagine by any other sugar country in any part

Table 8.1

Population of the Leeward Islands
1678–1775*

Years	Antigua	St Christopher	Nevis	Montserrat	Total
1678					
Whites	2,308	1,897	3,521	2,682	10,408
Negroes	2,172	1,436	3,860	992	8,460
1708					
Whites	2,909	1,670	1,104	–	–
Negroes	12,943	3,258	3,676	–	–
1720					
Whites	3,652	2,800	1,343	1,688	9,483
Negroes	19,186	7,321	5,689	3,772	35,968
1745					
Whites	3,538	2,377	857	1,117	7,889
Negroes	27,892	19,174	6,511	5,945	59,522
1756					
Whites	3,435	2,783	1,118	1,430	8,766
Negroes	31,428	21,891	8,380	8,853	70,552
1775					
Whites	2,590	1,900	1,000	1,314	6,804
Negroes	37,808	23,462	11,000	9,834	82,104

*Does not include the nine British Virgin Islands (Tortola, Spanish Town, Jost Van Dyke, Peter's Island, Camains, Scrub Island, Guanna, Beef Island, and Thatch Island), which were inhabited in 1756 by 1,184 whites and 6,121 slaves. Most of the population was concentrated on Tortola (465 whites and 3,864 slaves) and Spanish Town (396 whites and 1,204 slaves). P.R.O., London. C.O. 152/28, Bb 83, 86.

Source: P.R.O., London. C.O. 1/42, f. 98; C.O. 152/13, Q 46; C.O. 152/25, Y 154; C.O. 152/28, Bb 81; Vere L. Oliver (ed.), *Caribbeana*, vol. 3, pp. 137, 173; Noel Deerr, *The History of Sugar* (London, 1949–50), vol. 1, p. 174.

of the globe'. On the other hand, he said that 'the planters of St Christopher's are at a great expence for manure; that they never cut *ratoon* canes; and although there is no want in the country of springs and rivulets for the support of the inhabitants, their plantations suffer much in dry weather, as the substratus does not long retain moisture'.[3]

Despite its natural advantages, St Christopher (hereafter called St Kitts) was plagued by intermittent warfare for many decades. The island was formally partitioned by the treaty of 1627, whereby the English received the middle portion of the island and the French the eastern and western extremities. Furthermore, the treaty called for joint military action against the Spaniards and the Carib Indians. After the threat from the Spaniards and Caribs subsided, local sources of friction were exacerbated by the wars in Europe. The French captured the English portion of the island in 1666, driving off between 5,000 and 8,000 Englishmen who migrated to Virginia, Jamaica, and Nevis. When the Treaty of Breda upheld the *status quo ante bellum,* the Council of Trade and Plantations questioned the wisdom of resettling the English plantations which were 'so ruined and destroyed, and without stock either of negroes and cattle . . .'. Nearly two decades of reconstruction were interrupted by another French invasion in 1689. Again, the English were driven off the island and most of their plantations destroyed. Then, in 1690, the island was retaken by English forces under Colonel Codrington and the French were deported. The English remained in possession thereafter, although in 1706 a French raiding party made off with some 600 Negroes, together with sugar mills and copper basins.[4]

From the Spanish raid in 1629, to the French conquest of 1666, St Kitts attracted numerous settlers whose productions consisted chiefly of minor staples and provisions. In the English portion of the island the population increased from about 3,000 in 1629, to 20,000 in 1643, of whom a considerable number are reported to have been Irish. Despite re-emigration to neighbouring and distant islands, the population probably continued to grow. A Commonwealth officer who toured the Leeward Islands to recruit men for the Jamaica expedition of 1655, reported of St Kitts: 'This island is almost worn out by reason of the multitudes that live upon it'.[5] Though few records are extant, the land was apparently worked in small parcels

---

3 Bryan Edwards, *The History, Civil and Commercial, of the British Colonies in the West Indies* (Dublin, 1793), vol. 1, pp. 412–13; Gordon C. Merrill, *The Historical Geography of St. Kitts and Nevis* (Mexico, 1958), pp. 18–41.
4 *Cal. S. P. Col. 1669–74,* pp. 44–7, 440–1; Ibid. *1706–08,* pp. 83–8.
5 John Thurloe, *A Collection of State Papers* (London, 1742), vol. 3, pp. 754–5.

Sugar and Slavery

by freemen, indentured servants, and a few Negro and Indian slaves. Tobacco was the leading crop for many years; one document shows that St Kitts sent over twice as much tobacco to London than Barbados in the years 1639—40. But declining tobacco prices and soil depletion led to the cultivation of other staples. In 1633—4, Sir Thomas Warner prohibited the cultivation of tobacco and encouraged the settlers to grow cotton instead. A joint decree was signed by Warner and the French governor in 1639, ordering the destruction of all tobacco plants in the Leeward Islands and forbidding planting for a period of eighteen months. Père Labat wrote that sugar was first planted in St Kitts in 1643. While the new crop was apparently successful, it did not overtake tobacco immediately. This is indicated by the seizure of Dutch property in the English portion of the island in 1654, amounting to 89,368 lb of tobacco, 2,444 lb of sugar, 1,286 lb of ginger, and 550 lb of indigo.[6]

Having been virtually stripped bare by French conquest and occupation from 1666 to 1671, the settlers who returned to the island had to start anew. Governor Stapleton reported to the Board of Trade in 1674 that '299 of the old Proprietors of St Christopher's have claimed their estates, of whom 195 are possessed ... and 104 are not possessed ... and 139 of the old Proprietors have not made their claims'.[7] That the bulk of the pre-war inhabitants did not return is evident from the census returns of 1678 and 1708. On the other hand, the labour supply was augmented by importations of slaves by the Royal African Company.

3 CHRISTOPHER JEAFFRESON, ST KITTS PLANTER

Among the proprietors who claimed their estates was Christopher Jeaffreson of Dullingham House, Cambridgeshire, son of Charles Jeaffreson, a prominent supporter of Sir Thomas Warner in the colonization of St Kitts. Upon his arrival in June 1676, Jeaffreson wrote concerning the renter of his plantation: 'I am apt to believe his indigo of late has yielded him but small profit, because it doth now seldom thrive, and I see every body that is able, working upon sugar, which is a certaine gaine'. A few weeks later he wrote to his cousin in London to 'procure me a carpenter and a mason. They would be verry useful to mee, now that I am about to setle my plantation myselfe. For I intende to turne planter, and to set up a sugar worke,

---

[6] British Museum, Egerton MSS 2395, ff. 54—9. Reprinted in *Caribbeana*, ed. Vere L. Oliver (London, 1912), vol. 2, pp. 221, 257.

[7] *Cal. S. P. Col. 1669—74*, p. 547.

which will cost me some pence, but much the lesse if I could have such servants'. Sugar was further emphasized in a letter of 12 May 1677: 'It is now esteemed here a great folly for a man to expose his tyme or goods to the hazard of indigo or tobacco, sugar being now the only thriveing and valuable commodity'.[8]

Jeaffreson's letters underline the troublesome problems of settling a sugar plantation. Confusion and defectiveness of title, accentuated by wartime destruction of deeds, involved him in litigation to drive squatters off his lands. Skilled artisans were needed to build his costly sugar works and perform other vital tasks. But hardly less welcome were 'any sorte of men, and one or two women if they can be found. They are generally wanted in this island; and all my bond-servants are gone free'.[9] Then there were the Negro slaves, costly in their first purchase, requiring great care in the seasoning to check mortality, and involving recurrent charges for food, clothing, and medicine. Jeaffreson was not alone in complaining of the labour shortage; in the English portion of the island there were, in 1678, only 695 men, 539 women, 663 children (total 1,897), and 1,436 slaves. To compound his difficulties, Jeaffreson's hard-won improvements were destroyed by a hurricane in October 1681. He wrote that his house was 'miserably torne, and flat with the ground. My sugar-worke, in like manner, and all my buildings ... It was a deplorable sight to see the spoyle that was done in the canes and provisions, in comparison of which the losse of all our houses and workes is as nothing'. Fortunately, his 'thirty-two Negroes, besides whites', survived to take up the task of rebuilding.[10]

Jeaffreson not only drew money out of England; he also engaged in wholesale and retail trade to finance his costly sugar establishment. Moreover, he rented outlying parts of his estate to men who grew canes and provisions with the aid of white servants and Negro slaves. Lacking capital to construct sugar works of their own, tenants entered into agreements to process their canes at the landlord's mill on a share basis. Concerning the proposal of one such tenant, Jeaffreson advised his manager: 'If you thinke you can grinde Serjeant Waugh's canes, without prejudice or hindrance to your owne, his propositions are not unreasonable; but you know it is neither of our profits to grinde to halves, if we could have canes enough of our own ... You doe well to settle the upper land. You

---

8 John C. Jeaffreson, *A Young Squire of the Seventeenth Century. From the Papers of Christopher Jeaffreson, of Dullingham House, Cambridgeshire* (London, 1878), vol. 1, pp. 184–91, 210–11.
9 Ibid., vol. 1, p. 255.
10 Ibid., vol. 1, pp. 274–80.

must not denye leases to those that will not settle on other termes; but do not exceed seven yeares in any graunt you make'.[11]

After settling and resettling his plantation and training a manager in its operation, Jeaffreson returned to England. From London he wrote to his agent and steward in St Kitts: 'I left Ensign Thorn as manager of my plantation in July, 1682, planted with many acres of young canes of my owne, besides my tenants, and a good quantity of young provisions, forty-six working slaves, a good cattle-mill and sugar worke, with cattle, horses, and all necessary conveniences, as you see by the inventory ...'. Unfortunately, Jeaffreson misjudged the character of Ensign Thorn: 'He has lost 12 or 13 or my slaves, several of my cattle, and almost all my horses, and leaves the plantation in great disorder; few canes in it, no provisions, and the very goods delivered by inventory lost, worn out, and destroyed'.[12] Such were the travails of Christopher Jeaffreson, first a planter-merchant labouring to establish a sugar estate, then an absentee proprietor who was nearly ruined by the carelessness and dishonesty of his manager.

4 ST KITTS IN THE FRENCH WARS

The second French invasion of the English portion of St Kitts in July 1689 was followed by its recapture within the same year by forces under Colonel Christopher Codrington. English property losses, though heavy, were probably more than regained at the reconquest. But of greater importance for the island's future growth as an English sugar colony was the exodus of all, or nearly all, Frenchmen by 1706.

The resettlement of St Kitts was undertaken by Christopher Codrington, newly-appointed Governor General of the Leeward Islands. He regarded the island as 'extremely healthfull' and of great fertility: 'it produces now as well as ye beginning, and the mould being the same a vast depth, it will continue to do so for ever ...'. As Codrington conceived it, the problem was to attract sufficient white men to insure military security without undue sacrifice of the slave-plantation system of production. Accordingly, he proposed to dispose of at least one-fourth of the island, or 15,000 acres, in small

---

11 John C. Jeaffreson, *A Young Squire of the Seventeenth Century. From the Papers of Christopher Jeaffreson, of Dullingham House, Cambridgeshire* (London, 1878), vol. 1, pp. 298–9.
12 Ibid. vol. 2, p. 247.

grants of five, ten, fifteen, and twenty acres, 'so as for each ten acres there may be a fighting man'. The other three-fourths of the island was to be disposed of 'according to the ability of the setlers, with due regard to make no plantation too large, and that they in general run between a 100 and 200 acres, which in these parts is a competent estate, and as much as ye generality of setlers will be in a capacity to improve and manage'. Furthermore, each large landholder would be required to have one militia man for every twenty acres of land. If this plan of settlement was followed, Codrington estimated that there would be a total of 3,700 fighting men.[13]

But Codrington's ambitious resettlement scheme fell far short of fulfilment in the years prior to 1713. Instead of the anticipated 3,700 fighting men, the census of 1708 returned only 1,670 whites (462 men, 462 women, and 746 children), and 3,214 Negro slaves (998 men, 1,237 women, and 979 children). In part, the population remained small because of the French raid of 1706 and general wartime uncertainty. Little effort was apparently made to reserve one-fourth of the island for smallholders, or to keep up the quota of militiamen on large properties. Rather than being encouraged by grants and subsidies, small settlers and indentured servants were virtually driven off the island. The villains, according to Governor Daniel Parke, were the 'merchants in England and Rich Men in Antigua'. Even Colonel Codrington was charged with having 400 Negroes on one plantation and but one white man. 'They breed up their Negroes to all manner of Trades and make Overseers of them; by this means they have drove all the poor from them'.[14]

5 THE SETTLEMENT OF THE FRENCH LANDS

The Treaty of Utrecht (1713), by ceding the French lands in St Kitts to the English, marked the beginning of an era of sugar expansion and prosperity. At the same time the variety of schemes for disposing of the French lands, amounting to about 20,000 acres, involved the inhabitants and interested outsiders in much wrangling. Awaiting formal distribution, provisional grants of the former French grounds were made to English planters by the governors general of the Leeward Islands. Among the land disposal schemes were model plans which sought to check the engrossment of lands by sugar planters

---

13 P.R.O. London. C.O. 152/1, BA Nos. 2 and 3, ff. 16, 20. 12 Sept. 1691.
14 Ibid., C.O. 152/6, K 88, f. 73: Gov. Parke to Board of Trade, 31 Oct. 1706; Oliver, *Caribbeana*, vol. 3, pp. 132–9.

Sugar and Slavery

and the consequent exodus of smallholders. The authors of these plans realized that smallholders were needed to provide military manpower, raise provisions and livestock in an effort to reduce dependence upon imported supplies, and provide a reservoir of labour from which skilled artisans and plantation overseers might be drawn.

Colonel Charles Douglass proposed to make free grants of ten-acre plots to poor people on condition of service in the militia. In all, some 4,000 acres along the seashore were to be parcelled out in this manner so as to provide a military bulwark and to encourage provision culture and stock raising. Another 3,500 acres were to be granted to several French refugees; the 2,500 acres in salt pans were to be held in common; and 1,500 acres were to be reserved for houses, tenements, and forts. The remaining 10,000 acres of 'good land' was to be sold at a nominal price to families who held no land in the English portion of the island, and no person was to have more than 300 acres fit for canes. Moreover, grantees were to have one white servant for every forty acres within six months and one for every twenty acres two years after taking possession.[15]

The principle of sale by auction was decided upon in 1715. Parties interested in purchasing the French lands were instructed to submit sealed bids to the Board of Trade by 24 August 1717. At least fifteen bids were received, some from individual planters and merchants, some from syndicates of English capitalists, and others from groups of London merchants who represented planters of St Kitts and neighbouring sugar islands. Some syndicates, such as the one headed by Colonel Douglass, proposed to purchase the entire ceded area, while others submitted bids for designated tracts of land. The wrangling among interest groups involved different classes and conditions of planters. Some held only provisional grants of French land, some possessed such grants together with property in the English quarter of St Kitts, and others had temporary grants and proprietary interests in two or more sugar islands.

Some evidence of the strength of the provisional grantees is afforded by their numbers and landholdings. In numbers they increased from 97 in 1718 to 137 in 1721. Table 8.2 shows how the grants were distributed in 1721. Contrasted with the nineteen individuals, whose one to nine acre grants amounted to only 1 per cent of the French lands, were fifteen individuals holding from 200 to 523 acres, or 36 per cent of the ceded lands that were taken up by

15 P.R.O. London. C.O. 152/11, O 143, 22 June 1716; David L. Niddrie, 'An Attempt at Planned Settlement in St. Kitts in the Early Eighteenth Century', *Caribbean Studies*, vol. 5, no. 4 (Jan. 1966), pp. 3–11.

Table 8.2

Frequency distribution of possessors of French lands in St Kitts, 1721

Acres	Number of possessors	Total acreage	Percent of total acreage
1–9	19	115	1.0
10–24	21	331	2.8
25–49	23	830	7.1
50–99	26	1,992	16.4
100–149	18	2,243	19.2
150–199	12	2,043	17.5
200–523	15	4,222	36.0
Total	134	11,776	100.0

Source: P.R.O., London. C.O. 152/14, Q 68, ff. 253–4; Q 69, ff. 255–6; List of present possessors of French lands in St Christopher, received with Gov. Hamilton's letter of 12 April 1721.

1721. One-third of the grantees, each holding 100 acres or more, accounted for nearly three-quarters of the land shown in Table 8.2.

The large provisional grantees were most active in bidding for the French lands. Many of them offered through their London merchants £5 to £8 per acre for estates ranging from 100 to 300 acres. In one proposal six London merchants informed the Board of Trade that they were the correspondents of sixteen 'of the most considerable Planters who have settled and Improv'd several quantities of Land on the said late French ground with great Labour, Pains and Industry and who have laid out thereon very great part of their Substance and even stretched their Credit for that purpose....'.[16]

The 'most considerable planters' in the French quarter may be conveniently divided into three groups. According to a report of 1717, there were twenty-three grantees who apparently held no other landed property in the West Indies, eighteen who also possessed estates in the English quarter of St Kitts, and at least seven who possessed estates in the neighbouring sugar islands. The methods of these large planters were described by one inhabitant in a letter to the Board of Trade.

16 P.R.O. London. C.O. 152/12, P 18, f. 16, 23 Aug. 1717.

Sugar and Slavery

> According to the present method of the Possessors (the richest Persons having large Quantities of Ground) they plant as long as the Grounds will bear without Husbandry, then leave them in a poor Condition, and proceed to take up Fresh Grounds, & by being in Favour with the Governours, they frequently got grants of what People of less Substance had made fertile, which in process of Time would not only have made the whole Island unprofitable to the Crown, but depopulate it also by being unfruitfull & barren, and the Tempers of the Suffering People have been so sour'd at the Usage, that above a hundred of them, have already left the Island ... There are few Families can manage above 200 Acres, tho' some at present enjoy above thrice that Quantity; And from thirty Years Experience I have observed; that Grants of large Quantities of Lands to Favorite Families have been the greatest Detriments to the Leeward Islands.[17]

If the above writer meant that French lands were granted to favourite families with proprietorial holdings in the Leeward Islands, his statement is only partly correct. Actually, one-half of the grants of 100 acres or more were made to non-proprietorial families, among whom the Scotsmen were most conspicuous. It is of interest that two governors general in succession, Walter Douglas (1711–15) and Walter Hamilton (1715–20), were Scotsmen, and that the lists of provisional grantees included such names as Cunnyngham, Douglas, Hamilton, MacArthur, MacDowall, and Milliken, who in the aggregate held upwards of 2,000 acres.

Final disposition commenced in 1726, when three commissioners were sent to St Kitts. Upon arrival they cancelled all provisional grants and proceeded to sell the lands in parcels of not over 200 acres to the highest bidders. Several years later a clergyman in a neighbouring island wrote that 'the Commissioners have sold such parcels of the *French* Lands as were fit for little else than Pasture or Provisions at 5, 6, or 7 *l*. Sterling per Acre, such as were better at 8 to 12 *l*., and such as were accounted best at 12 to 17 *l*., and the whole at 20 years Purchase ...'.[18] Another knowledgeable individual said that the poor whites had left the island because of 'the late Sale of the French Lands which has put them into Fewer hands'. The 'Fewer hands' were, with few exceptions, former provisional grantees who financed their purchases through London-West India commission merchants.[19]

17 Ibid., C.O. 152/12, P 42: 'Philo Patria' to the Board of Trade, 23 Aug. 1717.
18 Rev. Robert Robertson, *A Detection of the State and Situation of the Present Sugar Planters* (London, 1732), p. 36.
19 P.R.O. London. C.O. 152/20, V 38: Richard Coope, Agent for St. Kitts, to Board of Trade, 22 May 1734.

6 FURTHER 18TH CENTURY DEVELOPMENTS

'The Improvement of this Island within Twenty Years past is very Extraordinary', wrote Governor Mathew to the Board of Trade in 1734.[20] In that year the white population of St Kitts amounted to 3,881 (1,115 men, 1,118 women, and 1,648 children). While the whites more than doubled from 1708 to 1734, their ranks dwindled to 1,900 in 1775. Negro slaves, on the other hand, far outstripped the whites, increasing from 3,258 in 1708, to 17,355 in 1734, and 23,462 in 1775. The addition of 6,600 slaves from 1722 to 1726 was said to have been a prodigious number imported into so small an island. More slaves meant more sugar. Annual sugar exports to England averaged 16,381 cwt from 1706 to 1710. The next quarter-century witnessed a remarkable expansion, annual average exports rising to 179,808 cwt in 1731–5. Thereafter, annual exports ranged from 79,760 to 236,160 cwt, the average being 182,852 in the 1771–5 period.[21]

Sugar-monoculture had become characteristic of the island's economy by 1734. 'There are Negroes yet wanting', wrote Governor Mathew, 'and the Island wants some Improvements. But this want of Negroes will arise rather from the Lands growing poorer. Consequently, more to be tended and manur'd than from want of Strength to put more of it, than at present, in culture'. The land in sugar plantations, which amounted to nearly 25,000 acres in 1734, did not increase appreciably in subsequent years. But the cane acreage increased at the expense of pasture and provision grounds. According to Rev. James Ramsay, who lived on the island from about 1760 to 1780, '16,000 slaves, all capable of some labour, are employed in the cultivation of about 11,000 acres; for the whole cane-land on the island is about 22,000 acres, and each field gives a crop once in two years'.[22]

Slaves and livestock were not only needed to work the expanded cane acreage; they also tilled and manured the land more diligently. Our system of manuring called for movable pens so that cattle could be shifted from one cane piece to another. The fixed pen, as Ramsay observed,

> is an inclosure, perhaps of sixty by eighty feet, in which, from thirty to fifty cattle and mules are kept and fed. The decayed leaves, and offals of the sugar cane, are from time to time thrown in for litter. Their provender

---

20 Ibid., C.O. 152/20, V 46, ff. 158–9.
21 Noel Deerr, *The History of Sugar* (London, 1949–50), vol. 1, p. 197; vol. 2, p. 279.
22 P.R.O. London. C.O. 152/20, V 46, ff. 158–9; Rev. James Ramsay, *An Essay on the Treatment and Conversion of African Slaves in the British Colonies* (London, 1784), p. 120.

is spread over it, and being mixed with urine, dung, and rain, becomes a fermenting mass, which is emptied once, and in some plantations, twice a year.

In crop time the penned cattle were fed cane tops, but at other seasons they were supplied with grass. Picking grass, especially in periods of severe drought, was 'the greatest hardship that a slave endures, and the most frequent cause of his running away, or absenting himself from his work'.[23]

In proportion to its extent, St Kitts was the richest colony in the British Empire by the eve of the American Revolution. Choice cane lands sold for as much as £100 sterling per acre, and the island's quality sugar yielded premium prices in English markets. The slaves, moderately appraised, were said to exceed £1,300,000, and the realty and personalty on the island came to approximately £4 million. Annual export values in the 1771–5 period averaged about £400,000 sterling, of which £350,000 went to Great Britain and Ireland, and £50,000 to North America. Sugar and rum constituted 97 per cent of the value of all exports from St Kitts to the British Isles, indicating the extent to which monoculture had been pushed.[24]

Marring this picture of planter wealth and affluence were reports of excessive monoculture, slave disaffection, absentee proprietorship, and commercial indebtedness. Ramsay wrote in 1784 that the island was divided among fewer than 120 proprietors who 'could not owe less at this time than 720,000 *l.* sterling'. That a high proportion of these proprietors was absent is evident from the numerous reports of governors that there were insufficient men to staff the island's military and civil establishments. In Ramsay's view, the extensive monoculture 'has lately arisen equally from the demands of extravagance in our absent planters, and of poverty in those on the spot'. Indeed, the peculiar fertility of St Kitts had the most baneful effects. 'It enables the greatest part of its proprietors to live in England; where, insensible of the sufferings of their slaves, they think and dream of nothing but sugar, sugar; to which, in consequence, every spot of land is condemned. Hence ... slaves are more scantily fed, than in the other islands; and the managers are obliged to keep them up to their utmost possible exertion to preserve their employment'.[25]

23 Ramsay, *Essay on African Slaves*, pp. 73–4.
24 These computations are based on data in Deerr, *History of Sugar*, vol. 1, p. 197; John Campbell, *A Political Survey of Britain* (London, 1774), vol. 2, p. 671; and London sugar prices as shown in Appendix V.
25 Ramsay, *Essay on African Slaves*, pp. 57, 80.

7 NEVIS: DESCRIPTIVE ACCOUNT

The small island of Nevis was the birthplace of Alexander Hamilton, the American stateman, and Mrs Nisbet, the widow who married Admiral Lord Nelson. Nevis has an area of 36 square miles, while its near-neighbour St Kitts has 68. The former island is almost circular; the latter is oblong with a tail-like peninsula. Mountainous interiors are characteristic of both islands; the former consisting essentially of a single volcanic cone rising from a platform to 3,596 feet, the latter being ridge-shaped. Writing in 1734, Governor Mathew said that the mountain sloped down gradually on two sides of the island to the sea shore. 'I believe there is near Twenty Thousand acres of Land in Manure, upon this Island, which tho' Prodigiously Rocky and Stony, Yet the Earth between these Stones is Mostly Rich, and does not wear out and grow Barren as the Soil of Antigua or St Christopher's does'.[26] Annual rainfall varies from 40 inches on the lowlands to over 90 inches at heights above 1,200 feet, the average being about 53 inches. Temperatures range between 70° and 85° F during the greater part of the year. Bryan Edwards estimated that the general produce of sugar in 1782 was one hogshead of 16 cwt per acre, and that half of the 8,000 acres in canes was cut annually.[27]

Compared with its sister island, Nevis suffered fewer hostilities from French and Dutch military forces prior to the great raid of 1706. The islanders staved off enemy attacks in the war of 1666–7, but they came near to starvation from their inability to receive supplies from abroad and the added burden of some 1,500 refugees from St Kitts. In May 1673, a Dutch fleet was driven off by shore batteries when it tried to carry off ships anchored in Nevis Road. During King William's War (1689–98), Nevis was the English fortress in the Leeward Islands, from whence expeditions were sent to take neighbouring islands from the French. By contrast, Nevis was less ably defended in Queen Anne's War (1702–13). Its tiny militia was defeated in 1706 by the French commander d'Iberville whose forces also raided St Kitts. The French struck a damaging blow; they burned cane fields and buildings, dismantled and removed mills and coppers, and by their own admission carried off 3,187 Negroes. Losses were so great that the British Parliament was moved to vote £103,003 in debentures to indemnify the sufferers of St Kitts and Nevis.[28]

26 P.R.O. London. C.O. 152/20, V 46, f. 146, 14 Sept. 1734.
27 Edwards, *History of the West Indies*, vol. 1 pp. 416–17.
28 Richard Pares, *A West-India Fortune* (London, 1950), p. 49; *Cal. S. P. Col. 1706–08*, pp. 83–88, 142–7.

Sugar and Slavery

Contemporaries attributed Nevis's relative immunity to attack prior to 1706 to the military prowess of its militia, its population density, and its superior fortifications. The island must have been densely populated in 1656, when some 1,400 men, women, and children re-emigrated with their goods and servants to Jamaica.[29] The first census of 1672 returned 1,411 men able to bear arms and 1,739 Negroes. Six years later the number of men had increased to 1,534, all whites to 3,521, and Negro slaves to 3,849 (1,422 men, 1,321 women, 1,106 children). Nevis was the most considerable of the Leeward Islands in 1671, when Governor Wheler wrote that 'if the King has any interest in the sugar trade, it is owing to the valour and vigilence of its inhabitants which defended themselves against several attempts of the French fleet'.[30]

8 NEVIS MERCHANTS AND THE SUGAR INDUSTRY

Merchants and traders were attracted to Nevis because of its military protection and facilities for trade and shipping. From their warehouses in the port of Charlestown they supplied the inhabitants with slaves and plantation supplies and took off their tropical staples. Moreover, they did an extensive entrepôt trade with the neighbouring islands of St Kitts, Antigua, and Montserrat. For some years after 1673 the Royal African Company conducted its Leeward Island traffic in slaves through its factors in Nevis. More than 6,000 of the Company's slaves were sold there by auction in the fifteen years from 1674 to 1688. Although some of them were re-exported to adjacent islands, the historian of the Company says that 'there is no reason to suppose that Nevis needed more slaves than she was allotted'.[31]

These favouring conditions enabled Nevis to forge ahead of its neighbours in the sugar industry. Tobacco, cotton, and indigo had apparently been overtaken by sugar by 1652, when an Englishman who accompanied Prince Rupert on his West India voyage wrote of Nevis: 'This is esteemed the best island for sugar: it makes little of any other commodities, only some tobacco to windward, which is valued more than any of the English plantations'. Oldmixon wrote in 1708 that little or no tobacco had been planted in Nevis for thirty or forty years, that cotton and ginger had of late been neglected, 'and

29 John Oldmixon, *The British Empire in America* (London, 1708), vol. 2, p. 204.
30 C. S. S. Higham, *The Development of the Leeward Islands Under the Restoration, 1660–1688* (Cambridge, 1921), pp. 145–8; *Cal. S. P. Col. 1669–74*, p. 227.
31 K. G. Davis, *The Royal African Company* (London, 1957), pp. 310–11.

Sugar only taken care of; of which great Quantities have been made, and 50 or 60 Ships loaden in a Year from this Island to Europe'.[32]

The transition to sugar was facilitated by the presence of a mercantile community which was large by comparison with that of neighbouring islands. Not only did the merchants and factors of Nevis supply goods and services to the planters, but they also used their trading profits and principals' effects to acquire plantations of their own. This is borne out by an inspection of early Nevis wills. Captain John Jennings, merchant, directed by his will of 1652 that bequests be made out of his plantation in Nevis 'in which I and one Henry Frame there resident have an equal interest'. In 1662, Henry Gillingham of Southampton, merchant, then resident in Nevis, directed that '15,000lb of sugar out of my estate in this Island' be laid out in Negroes for the use of his children. Before leaving Nevis in 1664, Thomas Ayson, of the city of Bristol, merchant, bequeathed to his kinsmen 50,000lb of muscovado sugar out of his plantation in Nevis. William Mildon of Bristol and Nevis, merchant, referred in his will of 1669 to his 'plantation called the Paull Plantation on the Island of Antigua, lately purchased from the widow Ellinor Paull, with 12 or 13 slaves, etc'. [33]

That all but a handful of the plantations were undermanned is evident from the census of 1678. In that year 301 inhabitants possessed slaves, of which 205 held from 1 to 10; 46, 11 to 20; and 17, 21 to 30. Ten other individuals possessed from 31 to 40 slaves; another ten, 41 to 50; seven, 51 to 75; three, 76 to 100; and three, 101 to 175. John Rodney came to England in 1668, leaving on his plantation in Nevis '33 negroes and Indians, great and small, four white servants, 9 cattle, 2 sugar mills, 7 coppers, with stills, coolers and other necessaries, besides houses and near 100 acres of canes, all fit to make sugar....'.[34] Another plantation belonging to a Mr Wilkins was inventoried in 1681 as follows:

> There is now upon it 70 working Slaves, 35 old and young ones, at p'sent fitt for little, and about 30 horses and Cattle wth two sugar workes, two good mills, 11 Coppers & 3 stills & appurtenances thereto belonging, one very good stone mansion house wth kitchen & other necessary outhouses, etc., also down at towne two good large Store houses consistg of 5 severall tenemts so that ye whole estate may be really worth £8,000.[35]

---

32 E. Warburton, *Memoirs of Prince Rupert* (London, 1849), vol. 3, p. 376; Oldmixon, *British Empire in America*, vol. 2, p. 197.
33 'Abstracts of Nevis Wills in the P.C.C.', in Oliver's *Caribbeana*, vol. 4, pp. 106, 108–9, 111–12.
34 Oliver, *Caribbeana*, vol. 3, pp. 27–35, 70–81; *Cal. S. P. Col. 1669–74*, pp. 429–31.
35 Vere L. Oliver, *The History of the Island of Antigua* (London, 1894–99), vol. 1, p. lxiv.

Sugar and Slavery

Although two inventories are an insufficient basis for generalization, other evidence points to a declining number of proprietors and plantation units.

Scattered census returns show a marked decline in the white inhabitants of Nevis. From a high point of 3,521 in 1678, their numbers fell to 1,104 in 1708, rose to 1,343 (364 men, 444 women, and 535 children) in 1720, and then declined irregularly to about 1,000 in 1775. Heavy losses occurred in 1689 and 1690, when some 1,500 men were carried off by a malignant fever, 'whereby', as Governor Codrington reported, 'the strongest of the Leeward Islands has become the weakest'.[36]

But the most persistent cause of decline was the consolidation of smallholdings into sugar estates. Professor Pares has estimated that there may have been, at most, a hundred sugar plantations in 1719, but hardly more than two or three dozen a century later. The sugar properties required slaves in such numbers that the black population of Nevis trebled from 1708 to 1775, rising from 3,676 to about 11,000. Annual average sugar exports to England in 1771–5 amounted to 50,270 cwt. The London market value of all English imports from Nevis amounted to nearly £100,000 annually in the 1771–5 period, of which more than 90 per cent consisted of sugar products. The only other staple of any consequence was cotton.[37]

9 THE STAPLETON PLANTATIONS IN NEVIS

Colonel William Stapleton was an Irishman, a Cavalier, and a soldier of fortune who had seen service in France, Spain, and Italy. During the war of 1666–7, he joined a regiment in the West Indies, was taken prisoner in the attempt on St Kitts, but released at the armistice. For his services in the peace negotiations he was appointed Deputy Governor of Montserrat, then Governor of the same island, and finally Governor General of the Leeward Islands from 1672 to 1685. He was created a baronet in 1679. He became a typical planter-governor, connected by marriage with the large family of Russell in Nevis, and the Warners and Kaynells in Antigua. At his death in 1686, Sir William was 'seized and possessed of a very great

---

36 Quoted in Pares, *A West-India Fortune*, p. 23.
37 Ibid., p. 24. Computations are based on data in Deerr, *History of Sugar*, vol. 1, p. 194; Campbell, *Political Survey of Britain*, vol. 2, p. 672; and Appendix V.

and considerable Real and Personal Estate in England and in severall different Islands and Places in the West Indies in America . . .'.[38]

Sir William Stapleton's son and heir, Sir James, was succeeded by his brother, Sir William, who died in 1699, leaving two plantations, a dwelling house in Charlestown, and other property in the West Indies and England. A total of 183 Negroes were attached to his two plantations in Nevis — 'Russell's Rest' of 507 acres, and the 'River Plantation' of 287 acres.[39] From Sir William, the third baronet, these plantations descended to Sir William, the fourth baronet, whose manuscript letter-book is preserved in Harvard College Library. The discussion which follows is based on Professor Edwin F. Gay's edited version of the letter-book.[40]

Running from 1723 to 1732, the letters were received by Sir William Stapleton, then living in England, from his plantation manager and attornies in Nevis. The plantation is not clearly identified in the letters, but it is probably the one referred to above as 'Russell's Rest'. An incomplete inventory of 1728 lists 127 Negroes, 16 mules, 24 cattle, 4 mares, 2 colts, and 64 acres of canes planted for the next crop. The letters give an account from time to time of the state and condition of the plantation, including such matters as the weather and its influence on the yield of cane and provision crops, the condition of the slaves and livestock, the conduct of the manager, and many details regarding island business transactions and shipments of incoming supplies and outgoing sugar products.

The letter-book sheds considerable light on the nature of slavery on West India sugar estates. Many Negroes and cattle were said to have died in Nevis for want of provisions and water during the severe drought of 1726, although Stapleton's losses were confined to 'some old Negroes'. Joseph Herbert, the manager, wrote on 24 June 1726, that he had been forced to give the greater part of the plantation rum 'to catch runaway negroes that have plagued everybody this year. Most of their crops have gone this year for herrings and corn'. Fine rains and a large potato crop contributed to the good health of the slaves in 1727, but in December of the following year the manager wrote: 'The negroes are bare of cloaths and pinch'd in their belly

---

[38] Higham, *Development of Leeward Islands*, pp. 212–20; P.R.O. London, Chancery, C11/177/5, Stapleton v. Stapleton, 17 June 1747; J. R. V. Johnston, 'The Stapleton Sugar Plantations in the Leeward Islands', *Bulletin of the John Rylands Library*, vol. 48 (Autumn 1965), pp. 175–206.
[39] P.R.O. London. Chancery C11/177/5, no. 1.
[40] Edwin F. Gay, 'Letters from a Sugar Plantation in Nevis, 1723–1732', *Journal of Economic and Business History*, vol. 1 (Nov. 1928), pp. 149–73.

Sugar and Slavery

haveing lost abundance of potatoes by the great rains in August and Sept'.[41]

Deaths exceeded births for some years until Sir William was moved by the appeals of his manager and attornies to consent to the purchase of new hands. An abstract of a letter from his manager of 15 May 1731, said:

> The six gold coast slaves bought by my attorney's prove well (except one) and the eleven sent from St. Christophers by Capt. Pym are the finest lot of slaves he ever saw. The additional number gives such a spring to the work that notwithstanding the weather he has planted 100 acres for the next crop so that I shall find my expense answer'd if good weather.[42]

Less optimistic was a letter received two months later which reported that two of the slaves bought by Mr Pym had hanged themselves. The suicides prompted a careful inspection by the plantation attornies, one of whom reported:

> There is seldom a weeke but I see your plantation and I do not see any that is better kept and in better order. I cant tell what occasioned your two negroes to hang themselves. I am well assured they [were] well fed and not severely treated and were Mr. Herbert anything inclined to cruelty I am sure there is nothing could give me a greater dislike to him but I am convinced he treats the negroes with a great deal of humanity and good nature.[43]

If the slaves were not severely treated by the manager, other letters reveal that they were not always well fed and adequately clothed. There is reason to suspect that the manager was under constraint to limit feeding costs as illustrated by the memorandum attached by the owner to one letter: '... the beef charg'd for the plantation is excessive as well as flower and Herrings in the Acct. 1729'. Even more severe constraints applied to clothing outlay; the overseer reported that the slaves were badly clothed and 'suffered very much without them and the work that they loose by sickness occasioned from severe colds for the want of cloaths amounts to a greater loss than the price of the cloaths'.[44]

Certainly the plantation returns were more than sufficient to meet these and other recurring charges. Professor Gay writes: 'Most of the current expenses of the plantation, of salary and food of manager and overseer, of maintenance of slaves and livestock, and of usual repairs and building, were met from the provisions grown upon the

41 Ibid., pp. 156–60.
42 Ibid., p. 167.
43 Ibid., p. 171.
44 Ibid., pp. 169, 171.

plantation or were procured by local purchases, plantation sugars being used as commodity money'. By far the greater part of the sugars were shipped to a commission agent in London for the account of the owner, amounting in the whole to 545 hogsheads of 14 cwt each, and yielding annual gross receipts for the seven years, 1725–31, of about £1,250. Although the newly-purchased slaves, a sugar mill, and certain other items were paid for out of the London receipts, Professor Gay concludes that no large deduction, perhaps not more than £100 a year, needs to be made from the gross receipts in order to estimate Sir William Stapleton's net receipts.[45]

10 THE PINNEYS OF NEVIS AND BRISTOL

In his *A West India Fortune*, Professor Pares recounts the business history of the Pinney family of Nevis and Bristol, of their rise from the yeoman class in Dorset to gentry status in the west of England through wealth accumulation in the West Indies. Azariah Pinney, the founder of the fortune, was the youngest son of the Reverend John Pinney, Nonconformist preacher, landowner, and lace maker. Azariah was sentenced to ten years' transportation to the West Indies after participating in Monmouth's Rebellion, arriving in Nevis in 1685 with 'a Bible, six gallons of sack and four of brandy for the voyage, and £15 in his pocket'.[46]

During his early years in Nevis, Azariah acted as factor for his family in the sale of lace, later adding other lines of merchandise to his trade. He gained a reputation as an honest and able businessman and was asked to act as the plantation attorney of absentee proprietors. Intimate knowledge of plantation affairs led him to acquire the mortgages of indebted planters. By the foreclosure route he acquired a sugar plantation of 87 acres and a labour force of six Negro men, nine women, and three children. With this small plantation as a nucleus he added property by purchase and marriage to a sugar heiress until he had one of the great estates on the island at the time of his death in 1720.

Azariah's son and grandson added to the family estate in Nevis. John Frederick Pinney, though not an energetic man of business, acquired a plantation through mortgage foreclosure and left property worth over £20,000, together with substantial debt claims. The grandson, John Pinney, was the second founder of the fortune. Sub-

45 Ibid., pp. 149–53.
46 Pares, *A West-India Fortune*, pp. 3–11.

stantial additions were made during his twenty years' residence in Nevis. He expanded the acreage of the family plantation from 274 to 393½, of which 190 acres consisted of cane land, and increased the Negro labour force from 122 to 181. By these several additions the plantation ran 'from sea to mountain', and thus had some insurance against the fluctuations of weather and the variations of produce between mountain and lowland canes. Under Pinney's expert management the plantation sent away large profits to England every year. When he returned to Bristol in 1784 to establish a sugar factorage business, John Pinney may have been worth about £70,000. According to Professor Pares, 'This sum is made up of £35,650 for the enlarged Lowland plantation, £7,000 for the estimated value of the Gingerland plantation; £16,579 sterling debts owed by planters in Nevis; about £1,500 of other debts in Nevis; and investments in the public funds, of just over £10,000 market value'.[47]

The Stapleton and Pinney sketch histories illustrate some of the main currents of Nevis planter society. The Stapletons were among the Royalists who gained favour at the Restoration and used their military and political influence to advantage in acquiring sugar estates. After a short burst of activity by the founder of the fortune, the plantations descended to heirs who preferred to live in England. By the time of the fourth baronet, if not earlier, absentee proprietorship was the rule. If the quality of management did not deteriorate, as the Stapleton letter-book seems to indicate, there is considerable evidence that the owner was reluctant to lay out money on the plantation for fear that the proceeds would be diverted into the pocket of his manager. Thus the Stapleton plantation, though apparently profitable, underwent very little expansion in the period of the letter-book.

On the other hand, the Pinneys were among the Nonconformist families of yeoman, artisan, and commercial origins who contributed to the mainstream of the Nevis plantocracy. Azariah Pinney's commercial background and religious training fitted him admirably for the opportunities offered by a prosperous and expanding economy. Trading profits and attorney's commissions were invested in plantations at a time when smallholdings were being consolidated into sugar estates and an earlier generation of proprietors were eager to leave their estates in capable hands. But the great West India fortunes were seldom made in one generation, and it remained for John Pinney to expand the base laid by his forebears before moving to that wider stage of activity in a Bristol counting house.

47 Ibid., pp. 32–44, 48–9, 55–6, 83, 87–9, 90–1, 103–6, 320–1.

His Majesty's Leeward Islands

11 JOHN HERBERT AND ADMIRAL LORD NELSON

John Richardson Herbert, the subject of our third sketch, came from a mercantile planter family of Bristol, Montserrat, and Nevis. His great-grandfather was Edward Herbert, of Bristol, merchant, whose will was dated in Montserrat on 5 July 1684. His grandfather and father, both named Thomas, were inhabitants and either merchants or planters of Nevis. John Richardson was born in Nevis in 1732. At the age of twenty he married Elizabeth, daughter of Colonel John Williams of Antigua. Two years later he was appointed to the Council, at which time Governor Thomas wrote to the Board of Trade: 'Mr John Richardson Herbert is a Young Merchant of good Character in the Island of Nevis, but has very little landed Estate there ...'.[48] Herbert served as senior Councillor, or President of Nevis, for twenty-five years and died in 1793. Besides his public service, he became a leading planter, attorney, and financier at a time when absenteeism was rife and planter indebtedness was mounting.[49]

We learn of the great wealth and influence of John Richardson Herbert from the correspondence of Admiral Lord Nelson. As commander of the *Boreas* frigate in the West Indies, Nelson was entertained frequently by the leading planter families. From Nevis he wrote to his uncle on 14 November 1784: 'The lady is a Mrs. Nisbet, widow of a Dr. Nisbet, who died eighteen months after her marriage and has left her with a son ... she has been brought up by her mother's brother, Mr. Herbert, President of Nevis, a gentleman whose fortune and character must be well known to all the West Indian merchants...'. Herbert was described as 'very rich, and very proud'.

> Although his income is immense, yet his expenses must be great, as his house is open to all strangers, and he entertains them most hospitably. I can't give you an idea of his wealth, for I don't believe he knows it himself. Many estates in that Island are mortgaged to him. The stock of Negroes upon his estate and cattle are valued at £60,000 sterling: and he sends to England (average for seven years) 500 casks of sugar. His daughter's fortune must be very large; and as he says, and told me at first, that he looked upon his niece as his child, I can have no reason to suppose that he will not provide handsomely for her. [50]

---

48 P.R.O. London, C.O. 152/29, CC 8, 20 May 1757; Oliver, *History of Antigua*, vol. 1, pp. 70–1.
49 Oliver, *Caribbeana*, vol. 5, pp. 223–9.
50 Robert Johnstone, 'Nelson in the West Indies', *Journal of the Institute of Jamaica*, vol. II (March 1899), pp. 526–8.

Sugar and Slavery

Nelson was married to Mrs Nisbet at Fig Tree Church, Nevis, on 11 March 1787.

12 MONTSERRAT: DESCRIPTIVE ACCOUNT

Lying thirty-five miles to the south-east of Nevis is Montserrat, 'the Emerald Island of the West'. About two-thirds of this tiny island of 39 square miles is barren or mountainous. There are three groups of volcanic mountains, the highest rising to 3,002 feet. The cultivated land, which amounted to about 6,000 acres in the 18th century, is mainly on the western and east-central sides. The climate is quite pleasant and healthful. The mean annual temperature is 78° F, and the annual precipitation ranges from 40 inches on the coast to 70 on the wet, cool uplands. Plymouth, the capital, stands on the south-west coast, and has an open roadstead.

From its first settlement in 1628 to the French conquest in 1666, Montserrat attracted a few Englishmen and numerous Irishmen. Indigo, cotton, and ginger were grown in small quantities, but the chief staple for many years was tobacco. 'In all the early Acts of Montserrat the penalties are expressed in tobacco', writes C. S. S. Higham, 'while the first use of sugar as a fine is in 1668'.[51] Most of the inhabitants are thought to have been freemen and indentured servants who cultivated small tobacco farms. But small staples were not grown to the exclusion of sugar-cane.

Details concerning a tobacco and two sugar plantations are revealed by papers arising out of the trial and execution of one Samuel Waad, an English planter of Dutch extraction. Waad came into possession of plantations in Montserrat through his marriage to the daughter of Governor Anthony Brisket. Brisket was succeeded by his father-in-law, Robert Osborne, also an Irishman, and the guardian of Anthony Brisket, Jr. A quarrel between Samuel Waad and Governor Osborne resulted in Waad's being court-martialled and shot on 1 May 1654. A petition submitted to the Lord Protector by Samuel Waad, father of the man executed, said that Governor Osborne had seized his son's estate to the value of £12,000 and converted it to his own use. The estate consisted of a tobacco plantation 'whereon is a fair house' and two sugar plantations. 'Newarke' was described as 'one of ye Statelyest Sugarworkes in all ye Caribbe Islands, set up by the said Waad'. Waad himself had lived on 'States Castle', 'whereon is a stately built stone house richly furnished with all sorts of ffurniture to a great value being esteemed the fairest of

---

51 Higham, *Development of Leeward Islands*, p. 185.

His Majesty's Leeward Islands

any house in ye Caribbee Islands'. Belonging to the three plantations were 30 Christian servants and 50 slaves, young and old; together with 70 head of cows, bulls and oxen; 500 sheep, 2 horses, 2 colts, and 'hoggs a great number'. Other property consisted of 20,000 [pounds] weight of sugar, a great quantity of tobacco, and 'many debts, amongst the which the said Osborne owed him about 20,000 weight of Sugar and Tobacco'. Witnessing the petition were the late Samuel Waad's two brothers, one a merchant in Topsham, county Devon, the other a London merchant. [52]

Another document which most likely related to one or more of the above plantations was a petition of 1669, submitted by Anthony Brisket, Jr, to the King. Brisket said that at the time of the capture of Montserrat by the French, he was possessed of a plantation there which had since been divided by order of Governor Willoughby into three plantations, the 'Fort House' of 525 acres, the 'Waterwork' of 573 acres, and the 'South Side of the River' of 300 acres.[53]

Montserrat was taken by the French in December 1666, and retaken by the English in June of the following year. Over 600 of the inhabitants arrived in Jamaica in April 1667 'extremely plundered, even to their very shirts...'. About a year later Governor Willoughby wrote that he had visited Montserrat, 'a pretty island with as much plantable land as Nevis, but cruelly destroyed by the French; it is almost an Irish colony'. [54]

The island was reported to be 'well re-settled' on 9 July 1668. In 1672, Governor Stapleton reported 1,171 men and 523 slaves on the island. His detailed census of 1678 returned 2,682 whites (1,148 men, 591 women, 943 children) and 992 Negroes (400 men, 300 women, 292 children). Irishmen made up seven out of every ten whites in 1678 (total 1,869); the remainder consisted of 761 Englishmen and 52 Scotsmen. During the year ending July 1684, Montserrat shipped to England about 200,000lb of sugar and 48,000lb of tobacco.[55]

Montserrat was again invaded and despoiled during Queen Anne's War. An address to the Queen from Governor Douglas and the President, Council, and Assembly of Montserrat said that the island had been invaded by the French on three occasions from 28 January 1710, to 8 July 1712. Most damaging was the third raid by 3,500 Frenchmen who over-ran a great part of the island,

---

52 Rev. Aubrey Gwynn, 'Documents Relating to the Irish in the West Indies', *The Irish Manuscript Commission* (Dublin, 1932), pp. 219-26.
53 *Cal. S. P. Col. 1669-74*, p. 29.
54 Ibid. *1661-68*, pp. 359, 443, 474, 540, 556.
55 Ibid. *1661-68*, pp. 586-7; P.R.O. London. C.O. 390/6, f. 117.

Sugar and Slavery

burnt our towns, destroyed our houses in the country, sugar works and plantations, carried away sundry of our slaves, killed and took with them most of our horses, cattle and small stock, broke, burnt and carried with them our household stuff, cloathing and merchandizes, insomuch that they left many destitute of the very necessaries of subsistence, food and raiment ...[56]

Another report by Governor Douglas said that the French carried off about 1,200 of the 5,000 Negroes on the island. Recovery from the raid was slow: in fact, the census return for 1719 showed 386 whites and 4,192 slaves; for 1720, 1,593 and 3,772; and for 1724, 1,000 and 4,400, respectively.[57]

13 THE POLITICAL ANATOMY OF MONTSERRAT

By contrast with the fragmentary statistics of earlier years, a most comprehensive census, known as the 'Political Anatomy of Montserrat' was submitted to the Board of Trade by Governor Mathew for the year 1729. It names each householder, his occupation and dependants, both free and slave; total acres and acres in canes and other crops; sugar mills; and livestock, both large and small. No reason is given for undertaking such a detailed survey, nor is there any explanation of the procedures that were followed. Although there is little reason to question the general accuracy of the census, acreage figures appear to have been rounded, several errors in addition have been discovered, and other data reveals that some of the individuals who are listed as proprietors in the census were actually renters. Altogether, 245 individuals are named in the census as heads of households.

The high degree of real and personal property concentration in Montserrat in 1729 is revealed by Table 8.3, comparing the different species of property on the thirty leading sugar plantations with the island totals. The thirty plantations accounted for 78.2 per cent of the total land occupied in 1729, 88.5 of the land planted in canes, 59.3 of the Negro slaves, and 75.6 of the sugar mills. On these same plantations were 87.1 per cent of the mules, 40.0 of the horses, 55.2 of the oxen or cows, 77.1 of the sheep, 27.5 of the hogs, and 21.7 of the goats. While the thirty plantations had only one-fourth of the white men and one-fifth of the white women on the island, they accounted for one-half of the men servants and about one-third of

---

56 *Cal. S. P. Col. 1714–15*, p. 2.
57 Ibid. *1712–14*, p. 27; Frank W. Pitman, *The Development of the British West Indies, 1700–1763* (New Haven, 1917), p. 382.

Table 8.3

Survey of Montserrat, 1729: Comparison of the thirty leading sugar plantations and the Island totals

	Island totals	Total on 30 sugar plantations	Average on 30 sugar plantations	Percentage on 30 sugar plantations
Europeans	1,143	255	8.5	22.3
Men	294	77	2.6	26.2
Men servants	70	35	1.2	50.0
Women	284	54	1.8	19.0
Women servants	20	7	0.2	35.0
Children	475	82	2.7	17.3
Negroes	5,855	3,461	115.4	59.3
Men	2,106	1,293	43.1	61.4
Women	1,963	1,110	37.0	56.5
Boys under 14	1,001	596	19.9	59.5
Girls under 13	785	462	15.4	58.9
Acres of Land	11,888	9,291	309.7	78.2
Uncultivated	6,030	4,385	146.2	72.7
Cultivated	*5,858*	*4,906*	*163.5*	*83.7*
Sugar	5,294	4,686	156.2	88.5
Cotton	53	–	–	–
Indigo	36	–	–	–
Other	475	220	7.3	46.3
Sugar Mills	78	59	2.0	75.6
Cattle-mills	52	35	1.2	67.3
Windmills	23	22	0.7	95.7
Water-mills	3	2	0.1	66.7
Livestock	3,538	1,974	65.5	55.8
Horses	472	189	6.3	40.0
Mules	459	400	13.3	87.1
Oxen or cows	1,320	729	24.3	55.2
Sheep	650	501	16.5	77.1
Hogs	291	80	2.6	27.5
Goats	346	75	2.5	21.7

Source: P.R.O., London. C.O. 152/18 T 63, ff. 46–9. 'The Political Anatomy of Montserrat', Referred to in Gov. Mathew's letter of 28 May 1730.

Sugar and Slavery

the women servants. In the island as a whole adults outnumbered children by a ratio of 1.4 to 1, compared with 2.1 to 1 on the thirty plantations. These age, sex, and freemen-servant ratios indicated that it was a difficult matter to maintain the white population on the leading sugar plantations.

Most critical from the standpoint of military security and civic order was the ratio of white men to Negro slaves. For the island as a whole the ratio was 1 to 20; for the leading sugar plantations 1 to 30. Although Montserrat probably had fewer slave revolts than the neighbouring sugar islands, an insurrection was planned to take place on St Patrick's Day, 1768, when the population, mostly Irish, would have been deep in their cups. The plot was foiled by the disclosure of a female slave.[58]

Roughly six-tenths of the slaves in Montserrat were attached to the leading plantations. Males only slightly exceeded females in the island as a whole and on the leading plantations. Bryan Edwards said it was a well-known fact that only one-third of the slaves imported from Africa were females.[59] If Edwards' 'well known fact' applied to Montserrat, it is evident that the mortality of males was much higher than that of females. The need for imported slaves to maintain the labour force is made clear by the fact that adult slaves outnumbered slave children by a ratio of 2.3 to 1.

In the leading sector, 115 slaves were attached to the average plantation unit of 310 acres. Probably the greater part of the 146 acres of uncultivated land consisted of pasture and timber, although some of it may have been taken up by slaves for provision grounds. Thirty sugar plantations occupied nearly three-quarters of the uncultivated land, more than four-fifths of the cultivated land, and nearly nine-tenths of the cane land that was reported in 1729. Looked at another way, 95 per cent of the cultivated acres in the leading sector consisted of cane land. Even if these land-use statistics are only rough approximations, it is remarkable how far sugar-monoculture had progressed in Montserrat by 1729.

Further estate consolidation and an expanded labour force did not add materially to sugar production in subsequent decades. While the white population increased slightly from 1,143 in 1729 to 1,314 in 1775, Negroes increased from 5,855 to 9,834. Sugar entering England through legal channels from Montserrat increased from an annual average of 39,960 cwt in 1726–30 to 44,100 in 1771–5. Annual export values in the 1771–5 period averaged about £101,500

[58] Thomas Southey, *Chronological History of the West Indies* (London, 1827) vol. 2, p. 396.
[59] Edwards, *History of the West Indies*, vol. 2, p. 106.

His Majesty's Leeward Islands

Table 8.4

*Survey of Montserrat, 1729:
census of the thirty leading sugar plantations*

Proprietor's surname	Total acres	Culti-vated acres	Acres of canes	Negroes	White men	Other whites	Sugar mills	Horses and mules	Oxen or cattle
1. Wyke	700	300	300	223	10	9	3	8	40
2. Farrill	340	300	300	155	8	8	2	16	12
3. Trant	350	250	250	225	6	1	2	34	25
4. White	300	200	200	163	4	7	3	15	40
5. Roach	370	220	200	159	3	5	3	47	9
6. Dongan	300	200	200	155	3	10	3	17	25
7. Liddell	450	200	200	145	3	5	3	26	60
8. Hodges	300	200	200	140	1	4	3	18	30
9. Darcy	250	200	200	123	2	–	2	29	32
10. Irish	250	200	200	120	1	–	2	28	12
11. Meade	220	200	200	107	3	4	2	24	9
12. Farrill	191	186	186	111	4	7	1	42	40
13. Brambley	550	200	150	148	4	8	3	16	36
14. Lee	190	150	150	119	2	5	2	18	30
15. Molineux	300	150	150	96	4	3	2	11	50
16. Hussey	180	150	150	90	9	3	2	15	6
17. Skerrett	380	180	150	89	2	5	1	13	25
18. Dyer	250	150	150	75	3	7	3	22	11
19. Daniell	175	175	140	112	3	10	1	19	13
20. Roynan	150	100	100	129	5	7	1	27	24
21. Parson	320	120	100	119	2	6	2	19	30
22. Daly	200	100	100	115	9	2	2	30	–
23. Frye	140	100	100	100	3	5	2	6	60
24. Cooke	300	100	100	85	4	–	2	9	20
25. Lee	130	100	100	57	2	3	2	10	4
26. Gallwey	1,320	120	100	62	5	1	1	20	31
27. Bramley	200	100	90	95	3	–	2	14	12
28. Bevrone	300	100	80	53	2	3	1	22	33
29. Fox	80	80	80	30	–	4	–	2	5
30. Fiz Denis	105	75	60	61	2	11	1	12	5
	9291	4906	4686	3461	112	143	59	589	729

Source: As Table 8.3.

sterling, of which £88,900 went to Great Britain and Ireland, and £12,600 to North America. Sugar and rum accounted for 98.1 per cent of all exports from Montserrat to England; the other 1.9 per cent consisting chiefly of cotton.[60]

[60] Calculated from data in Deerr, *History of Sugar*, vol. 1, p. 196; Campbell, *Political Survey of Britain*, vol. 2, p. 674; and Appendix V.

Sugar and Slavery

Turning from the island-wide survey of the census of the thirty sugar plantations shown in Table 8.4, we find units of widely ranging area, labour force, and livestock population. Plantation acreages ranged from as little as 80 to as much as 1,320, the majority, however, extending from 200 to 400 acres. While most of the plantations had from 50 to 200 acres of uncultivated land, two had none, one had only five acres, another had 20 acres, and three, 30 acres. At the other extreme was David Gallwey's plantation with 1,200 acres of uncultivated land. Cultivated lands ranged from 75 to 300 acres, all but six of the plantations having from 100 to 200 acres in this category.

Similarly, slaveholdings correlate quite closely with cane acreages. One index of intensity of cultivation is the ratio of Negro slaves to cane acreage. The index ranged from a low of one slave to 2.7 acres, to a high of one slave for 0.8 acres. Eight plantations had one slave for 1.7 or more acres, eight for 1.1 or fewer acres, and fourteen fell in the middle range of from 1.2 to 1.6 acres per slave. The index is probably understated by an unknown quantity since large planters commonly rented slaves from outside the plantation sector during periods of peak labour requirements.

The sugar mills, which were powered by animals, wind, and water, represented a sizeable investment of capital. In the island as a whole there were 52 cattle-mills, 23 windmills, and 3 water-mills. Windmills and water-mills were costlier than cattle-mills by a ratio of about three to one. It is therefore understandable that all but two of the more expensive mills were owned by the leading planters who also owned 35 cattle-mills. George Wyke, the leading planter, had two windmills and one water-mill; James Farrill, second largest planter, two windmills; and Dominick Trant, third largest planter, two cattle-mills. The next five plantations each had two cattle-mills and one windmill. Of the remainder those with two mills generally had one of each type, and the one-mill estates used cattle with only two exceptions. Elizabeth Fox's plantation had no mill and presumably ground its cane at an adjoining estate.

Livestock holdings varied so widely from plantation to plantation that few generalizations seem warranted. Leading planters in the aggregate held over one-half of the livestock, but for different categories their holdings ranged from one-fifth to seven-eighths. It seems reasonable that smallholders should have had the greater part of the hogs and goats (not shown in Table 8.4), but not so evident why they should have had 60 per cent of the horses when the leading planters held 87 per cent of the mules. One possible explantation is that mules were regarded as superior to horses for plantation labour.

His Majesty's Leeward Islands

14 CAREER PROFILES OF MONTSERRAT PLANTERS

Characteristics of the Montserrat planter elite not revealed by the census of 1729 are land tenure arrangements, blood relationships, political activity, absenteeism, and other sources of wealth and income.

Genealogical and other records reveal that several of the plantations were not held in fee simple by the individuals named in the census. Most exceptional was the number one plantation on the island. An indenture of 1737 said that Sir William Stapleton's 'Water Work' plantation of 600 acres 'now is or lately was in the tenure of George Wyke his undertenant...'. By his will of 14 March 1739, Nathaniel Webb, merchant in Montserrat, bequeathed to his son Nathaniel his plantation which was under lease to John Dyer (probably No. 18 in Table 8.4). In 1745, Thomas Lord Gage of Ireland mortgaged his plantation of 200 acres in Montserrat (probably No. 11) to Thomas Meade who then held it on lease. William Frye's 'Old Road' plantation (No. 23) was under lease in 1736.[61] If most of the plantations were owned by the individuals named in the census, these four exceptions point to the existence of a plantocracy which was not entirely independent of absentee owners and rentiers.

Each generation witnessed the rise of new men and at times the establishment of new family dynasties alongside the stagnation and decline of planters whose indebtedness and absenteeism made their estates ripe for the plucking. Though the historical record is patchy, the career profiles of Thomas Meade and Nathaniel Webb may perhaps serve to illustrate the rise of new men.

Thomas Meade rose from the lessee of an absentee's plantation to ownership of three plantations and 340 slaves in his own right. Part of his success may have been owing to his marriage tie with another family which came up rapidly during his lifetime. He was married in 1724 to Mary, daughter of Peter Hussey, merchant and owner of plantation No. 16 in the above table. According to the above mentioned indenture of 1745, Meade, as lessee of the Gage plantation, had 'erected a new stone windmill and is entitled to an allowance for it agreed at £1,200 currency and Thomas Meade placed several negroes [on the plantation which] Thomas Lord Gage has agreed to purchase for £1,363 currency'. Gage mortgaged the plantation to Meade for £4,263 at 8 per cent interest. Meade then conveyed the plantation to two trustees, Peter Hussey, Meade's father-in-law, and Nicholas Tuite. Both of the trustees had been planters and merchants

---

61 P.R.O. London. Chancery C11/177/5; Oliver, *History of Antigua*, vol. 3, p. 214; Oliver, *Caribbeana*, vol. 5, pp. 283–7.

Sugar and Slavery

in Montserrat before they moved to London to establish West India commission agencies.

Either before or after Gage's mortgage was discharged, Meade purchased three plantations in Montserrat: the 'Water Work' of 250 acres (probably No. 15); 'Windward' of 200 acres; and the 'New Windward' of 140 acres. On these estates he had 340 slaves in 1753. Thomas Meade, who died in 1763, was succeeded by his son Thomas who added the Hussey plantation to the family estate. It may be presumed that the elder Meade's success was owing to his skill as a planter and businessman and his influential connections in Montserrat and London.[62]

The plantation wealth of the Webb family of Montserrat and Antigua was based on trade, office-holding, and the law. Nathaniel Webb went to Montserrat from his birthplace in Taunton, Somerset. It is very likely that he went at the invitation of his uncle, for the family genealogy shows that Robert Webb of Taunton, father of our subject, married Bethick, daught of William Gerrish who was the foremost merchant of Montserrat prior to 1720. At any event, Nathaniel Webb was in Montserrat by 1720. In that year he ranked third among thirty-seven merchants who paid a poll tax on the value of their trade in the island. He was assessed at £24 and William Gerrish at £50. Records of slave imports from 1721 to 1729 show that Webb was consigned nine out of a total of nineteen cargoes, and 1,268 out of a total of 3,210 slaves who were brought to Montserrat from Africa.[63]

Webb gained possession of a small sugar plantation at a time when he was both merchant and customs collector. The census of 1729 designates him as 'Collector' and lists his holdings as follows: one cattle-mill; 34 slaves (19 men, 6 women, 9 children); 50 acres of cultivated land, of which 40 was cane land; 2 horses; 20 mules; 2 oxen; and 4 hogs. As a sugar proprietor and prominent merchant, Webb gained political preferment. He was appointed to the Governor's Council in 1729 and continued in that office until he left for England in 1736.

Nathaniel Webb died at his home near Taunton in February 1741. An obituary notice referred to him as 'Collector of the Customs at Montserrat, in which Island he had a very good Estate'. By his will of 14 March 1739, he instructed his executors, one of whom was Thomas Meade, to grant a lease to his wife Jane 'of all my negroes on my plantation in St. Anthony's [parish] called "Carrolls" '. Robert,

62 Oliver, *Caribbeana*, vol. 5, pp. 114, 286.
63 Oliver, *History of Antigua*, vol. 3, pp. 214–15; P.R.O. London, C.O. 152/13, Q 34, ff. 103–4; C.O. 152/18, T 67, ff. 75–6.

his eldest son, was bequeathed all his estate in Somerset; Nathaniel, his second son, inherited 'Northward' plantation in Montserrat 'now under lease to John Dyer', together with his house and lands in St Kitts; and John, his third son, inherited 500 acres near the town of Seabrook in the New England colony of Connecticut. Further, Webb left instructions that all sums owing to him in Montserrat and St Kitts should be sent to his uncle William Gerrish in London. Gerrish was described at his death in 1741 as 'an eminent West India Merchant, who never suffer'd his Name to be seen on the Debtor's side of Trademen's Books'.

In the next generation the scene shifts to plantations and officeholding in Antigua, the Inns of Court, and the House of Commons. Robert Webb was closely associated with his cousin, Harry Webb, in legal practice in the Inner Temple, while Robert and Nathaniel at different times represented Taunton in the House of Commons. In 1754, Harry Webb was appointed Attorney General of the Leeward Islands. During his residence in Antigua, and later after returning to the Inner Temple, he lent money to planters and acquired a plantation in partnership with his cousin Nathaniel. By an indenture of 28 January 1777, Harry and Nathaniel Webb sold their 'Rockhill' plantation of 321 acres in Antigua to John Halliday for the sum of £13,000 sterling. This was not the end of the Antigua venture, for Harry's will of 1783 lists numerous debts owed by planters in that island.[64]

While there are no grounds for asserting that for every success there was a failure, not a few of the latter are recorded in the archives of Montserrat and England. That not all failures can be attributed to absenteeism is revealed by a letter concerning William Irish, whose father's plantation ranked tenth in the 1729 census. His stepfather, Colonel Samuel Martin of Antigua, could not understand how he contrived to be always much in debt, 'for I have been told, that when he had not Company, he lived like a Beggar to Windward; but he kept house for his Cousins at Wyke's, which was the Sluice of all ye produce of both his Estates'.[65] The itch to get rich led others to stretch their resources to the breaking point. James Hussey, the younger, grandson of Peter Hussey (No. 16), mortgaged in 1768 'Hammonds', 'Dyers', and 'Germans Bay' plantations and died abroad insolvent before 1800.[66] Michael White, who inherited plantation No. 4 was among several planters of Montserrat who speculated in the Ceded Islands with disastrous results. He was said to

64 Oliver, *History of Antigua*, vol. 3, pp. 214–16.
65 *Martin L.B.*, vol. 2, f. 282: Lre. to Samuel Martin, Jr., 22 Sept. 1767.
66 Oliver, *Caribbeana*, vol. 5, pp. 104–6.

Sugar and Slavery

have 'bought one Brancard's estate at Domenica for £15,000 and Dorsel's of Montserrat for £4,000, and can't pay for them — allows all his family but £400 a year at Lille [France]'. Another purchase consisted of 3,000 acres in North Carolina. Having been a student of the Inner Temple and President of Montserrat for twenty years, Michael White died ignominiously in debtor's prison in 1785.[67]

If the plantocracy was far from homogeneous from the standpoint of its members' abilities and achievements, it was nevertheless a cohesive body to the extent that its members intermarried and dominated the island's political and social life. Montserrat was much like the other sugar islands in having its Legislative Assembly and Council dominated by leading planter families. Fifteen of the thirty leading planters served on the Council between 1720 and 1737, and upwards of two-thirds were assemblymen at one time or another. But wealth did not lead to political preferment for the Irish Catholics. Governor Hart wrote in 1724 that two-thirds of the 400 white men in Montserrat were Catholics 'who are justly excluded by the Law from having any share in the Government'.[68]

It would be easy to conclude that an Anglo-Saxon Protestant minority ruled a disfranchised Irish Catholic majority of the white inhabitants. In the main this was true, but not all Irishmen were Catholics. One influential group of the Anglo-Irish Protestants came from Galway, among whom were the Skerretts and Dalys. The ancestors of William Frye (No. 23 in Table 8.4) are said to have gone from Devon to Ireland and thence to the West Indies. On the other hand, some of the leading planters with such obviously Irish names as Farrill, Roach, and Dongan were not members of the Council, and presumably Catholics.[69]

The Governors General of the Leeward Islands were confined to a very narrow choice in recommending qualified persons to the Council of Montserrat. Their problem was complicated by the blood-ties of the plantocracy which gave the Council the character of an extended family club. Upon suspending William Frye from sitting on the Council in 1724, Governor Hart explained to the Board of Trade

> That a majority of them were his very near relations by blood or alliance, Mr. Wyke being Mr. Fry's own nephew, Mr. Irish married his neice, and is also his relation in blood, Mr. Cook and Mr. Hodges are his cozin Germans;

---

67 Philip C. Yorke (ed.), *The Diary of John Baker* (London, 1931), pp. 148, 284; Oliver, *Caribbeana*, vol. 6, pp. 148–51.
68 *Cal. S. P. Col. 1724–25*, p. 65.
69 Oliver, *History of Antigua*, vol. 1, pp. 278–87.

which if I shou'd have openly mention'd wou'd have been accusing them of partiallity: and wou'd have had a very ill effect.[70]

15 THE SMALL PLANTERS OF MONTSERRAT

Leading sugar planters depended on the other sectors of the island's economy. The non-leading sector in 1729 comprised 888 whites, 2,394 Negro slaves, 2,597 acres of land, 19 sugar mills, and 1,564 head of livestock. There were 215 households, 138 landholders, 184 slaveholders, 29 sugar planters, 24 indigo and cotton planters, and 77 non-landholders.

Dominating the non-leading sector were 29 small sugar planters. In the aggregate they held one water-mill, 16 cattle-mills, 734 slaves, 124 horses, 51 mules, 222 oxen or cows, 178 head of small stock, and 1,859 acres, of which 871 were cultivated. Cane acres amounted to 608, indigo, 13, and cotton, 6. The smallest plantation, which belonged to Margaret Long, had 4 slaves, 22 acres, of which only one was cane land, no livestock, and no sugar mill. At the other extreme was Catherine Lynch's plantation of 300 acres, of which 50 was cane land, 46 slaves, 2 horses, 20 mules, 2 oxen or cows, 8 sheep, 4 goats, and one cattle-mill. Although slaveholdings were generally proportional to cane acreages, Elizabeth Thomson had 73 slaves and 22 cane acres, John Chilcot 39 slaves and 10 acres, and Redmond Heige 31 slaves and 12 acres. Seven individuals had from 1 to 9 acres of cane land; eight, 10 to 19; five, 20 to 29; three, 30 to 39; four, 40 to 49; and two had 50 acres each. Six individuals had from 1 to 9 slaves; six, 10 to 19; five, 20 to 29; seven, 30 to 39; four, 40 to 49; and one had 73 slaves.

Actually, the division between large and small sugar planters is quite arbitrary. Though none of the small planters had as many cane acres as the leading planters, nine of the former had more slaves than the smallest of the latter. By virtue of other sources of wealth, some of the so-called small planters overshadowed their brethren in the leading sector. We have seen that Nathaniel Webb, whose plantation was in the former group, accumulated one of the great fortunes in the island. Nicholas Tuite was another planter-merchant who amassed a great fortune in the Danish island of St Croix. If large and small plantations are combined, the sugar sector of the Montserrat economy in 1729 comprised 93.9 per cent of total acres, 98.6 of

---

70 *Cal. S. P. Col. 1724–25*, p. 65.

Sugar and Slavery

cultivated acres, 71.6 of slaves, and 76.2 of livestock apart from small stock. Monoculture was prevalent even among the small sugar planters. All but three had cane land only. Indigo acres amounted to 13, and cotton to 6.[71]

The minor staple sector of the Montserrat economy was a very small affair indeed. Twenty-five individuals in the 1729 census are named as holders of indigo and cotton lands exclusively. In the aggregate they held 212 slaves, 20 horses, 70 oxen or cows, 111 head of small stock, and 450 acres of land, of which 141 were cultivated. Only 23 acres were planted in indigo and 47 in cotton. Provision culture presumably occupied the remaining 71 acres. Several of these individuals apparently needed supplementary incomes, for numbered among them are three coopers, two carpenters, two labourers, and one tide-waiter.

Other inhabitants of Montserrat held slaves, livestock, and land, but had no land designated for staple cultivation. In this category there were forty-nine individuals, holding in the aggregate 607 slaves, 223 head of horses and oxen, 130 head of small stock, and 318 acres of land. Of the two-thirds of this group for whom occupational designations are given, nineteen were planters who probably raised livestock and provisions to sell to great planters and townspeople. In the non-planting category were merchants, carpenters, masons, coopers, fishermen, labourers, and one doctor. Individuals with numerous slaves and few acres of land may have rented their surplus slaves. This was probably the case with the merchant who had forty-one slaves and five acres, and the doctor who had thirty-four slaves and one acre.

Slaves were not only held by landholders, but also by such non-landholders as merchants, mariners, tavern-keepers, clergymen, spinsters, carpenters, and masons. In the latter category there were seventy-seven individuals who in the aggregate held 681 slaves, 191 head of horses, mules, and oxen, and 217 head of small stock. Apart from household service, slaves were held for a variety of purposes. Artisans purchased blacks to serve as apprentices in their trades, while merchants and mariners used slaves to load and unload ships and to serve as seamen on small craft engaged in coastal and inter-island trade. Slaves were also purchased by non-landholders as an investment. Owing to the scarcity of coin and limited investment opportunities, many inhabitants found it convenient to hold their savings in the form of human chattels. Besides their negotiability, slaves were considered a good investment because they could be

---

71 Yorke, *Diary of John Baker*, pp. 62–3.

hired out and return an income that was high in relation to the risks of sickness, accidents, and death.[72]

16 CONCLUSION

The Montserrat census of 1729 is the only one of its kind in the records of the sugar colonies. It underlines the concentrated character of property holdings and the near-monoculture sugar economy. Impersonal economic forces probably go far to explain these characteristics. Yet, the movement towards bigness was no doubt accelerated by the planter-dominated government, which, according to one lieutenant-governor, 'never minded to make any laws or acts that might be beneficial to the poor and encourage their coming to settle there'. He went on to say that the richer people acted with such a high hand over the others that the latter 'were oblig'd to quit and dispose of their small habitations for one quarter of their value'.[73]

---

72 P.R.O. London. C.O. 152/18, T 63, ff. 46–9: 'The Political Anatomy of Montserrat', referred to in Gov. Mathew's letter of 28 May 1730.
73 *Cal. S. P. Col. 1724–25*, pp. 138–9: Lieut.-Gov. George to Duke of Newcastle, 10 July 1724.

CHAPTER NINE

His Majesty's Leeward Islands
Part II. *Antigua*

Antigua, as 'tis much the largest, so it is the most beautifull and best Inhabited of these Islands; of a fruitfull Soil, but to be wrought with a good deal of labour; contains a great number of safe and commodious Harbours, which are well defended by Forts and Batteries erected on them for their Security: The Island is very healthy, and were it not for the excessive heat of the Sun, it would be in all things agreable to life.[1]

Governor John Hart, 1722

1 INTRODUCTION

Antigua developed slowly until near the end of the 17th century when it moved ahead of the other Leeward Islands and later outstripped Barbados to become Britain's leading sugar island in the Lesser Antilles. This island of 108 square miles is oval-shaped and indented by numerous bays and several harbours. It lies to windward of its sister islands and has a relatively low elevation which gives most parts of the island access to the north-east trade winds. The climate of Antigua is drier than that of the other Leeward Islands and Barbados. The mean annual rainfall is between 43 and 45 inches. Rains are uncertain, and long periods of drought are not uncommon. As there are no rivers of any consequence and few springs, water was stored in ponds and cisterns for household and industrial use.[2]

As with rainfall, variations are observed with respect to geology and relief. There are the rugged volcanic uplands rising to 1,330 feet in the south and south-west region of Antigua, the gently undulating central plains which is the best region for cane growing, and the rolling limestone uplands to the north and north-east. Bryan Edwards estimated that 34,000 of the 70,000 acres in the island were

[1] Public Record Office, London. C.O. 152/14, R 43, f. 158: Gov. Hart to Board of Trade, 11 July 1722.
[2] John Macpherson, *Caribbean Lands a geography of the West Indies* (London, 1963), pp. 99–104.

'appropriated to the growth of sugar, and pasturage annexed'. The average yield was about one hogshead of 16 cwt of sugar for each acre that was cut.[3]

Despite certain physical handicaps, Antigua became the political, commercial, and social centre of the Leeward Islands. Its excellent harbours and position to windward gave it advantages over the other islands in communication and defence. In 1696 it was selected as the seat of Government of the Leeward Islands, and in 1725 construction began on the naval dockyard at English Harbour which has recently been restored and renamed Nelson's Dockyard. Antigua was also unique in having the satellite island of Barbuda, some twenty-five miles to the north. This island of 62 square miles was held on lease from the Crown for nearly two centuries by the Codrington family, which paid an annual rental of a peppercorn. Lacking the physical characteristics for cane cultivation, Barbuda was developed as a stud farm to supply livestock and slaves to the planters of Antigua and to stock the Codrington family's extensive sugar estates.[4]

Antigua developed slowly during the three and a half decades following its first settlement in 1632. The rather obscure records of the period tell of attacks by Carib Indians; internecine conflict between Cavaliers and Roundheads; interrupted trade during the first Anglo-Dutch War; land engrossment; limited immigration of Englishmen, both free and indentured; and few slaves imported from Africa. Antigua had only 1,000 to 1,200 inhabitants in 1655 and about 2,000 a decade later. The early colonists came from neighbouring islands, chiefly St Kitts. After 1640, Antigua was designated by the Earl of Carlisle to receive the overflow from Barbados, from whence came time-expired servants and a number of wealthier men.[5]

With the possible exception of Montserrat, Antigua was more backward than its sister islands in launching the sugar industry. Tobacco was the island's leading staple well into the Restoration period, supplemented by limited quantities of cotton, ginger, indigo, and sugar. The English prize commissioners, who in 1654 took possession of the storehouses of Dutch merchants in the Leeward Islands, found more tobacco in Antigua than the other islands.[6] The year of the Dutch seizures also witnessed the construction of a public

---

[3] Bryan Edwards, *The History, Civil and Commercial, of the British Colonies in the West Indies* (Dublin, 1793), vol. 1, pp. 428–9.

[4] Macpherson, *Caribbean Lands*, p. 104.

[5] John Thurloe, *A Collection of State Papers* (London, 1742), vol. 3, pp. 754–5; *Cal. S. P. Col. 1661–68*, p. 436; James A. Williamson, *The Caribbee Islands Under the Proprietary Patents* (Oxford, 1926), pp. 158–9.

[6] *Cal. S. P. Col. 1669–74*, p. 134; *Caribbeana*, ed. Vere L. Oliver (London, 1912), vol. 2, p. 265; Noel Deerr, *The History of Sugar* (London, 1949–50), vol. 1, p. 172.

Sugar and Slavery

warehouse in Antigua and the issuance of tobacco certificates to serve as substitutes for specie. After collapsing during the French War, the system was restarted in 1669,

> For the propagation of Trade, Ease of the Marchts, and ready payment of the Planters, Who Haveing His Storehouse Notes can Passe them in all places of the Island like ready money, as well to buy what Hee wants, as discharge His just Debts and Ingagements.

The public storehouse was abolished in 1675, in response to complaints by merchants and traders of abuse and ill usage.[7]

2 SAMUEL WINTHROP, EARLY PLANTER AND GOVERNOR

Prominent among the early sugar planters of Antigua was Samuel Winthrop, youngest son of John Winthrop, Puritan leader and first Governor of Massachusetts. Samuel was born at Groton, Suffolk, England, in 1627, and came to America with his mother when he was four. He was a student at Harvard until his father's financial reverses induced him to give up his studies and seek his fortune abroad. Before his twenty-first birthday his trading activities had taken him to Rotterdam, the Azores, Canary Islands, Barbados, and St Kitts. Writing from St Kitts on 30 August 1647, he told his father that he had arrived on the island from Barbados with a parcel of wine which sold well and that he would soon depart for London or Holland: 'I must not lie still and begge'.[8] In 1648 he married a Dutch lady at Rotterdam. Returning to the West Indies after 1650, he alternated between Antigua and St Kitts for several years, where he traded on his own account and did a factorage business for his relatives and friends in New England.

'I have taken much paines out of nothing to gett an estate ... lying in landes & plantacons ...'. wrote Samuel Winthrop from St Kitts in 1660. In the same letter he anticipated difficulty with the new Royalist governor because of his former Roundhead sympathies. Three years later Samuel wrote from Antigua, where he had taken up permanent residence, that Lord Willoughby was expected there in six weeks. Again, he expressed fear for those that held lands from Cromwell's governors, amongst whom he was numbered. His fears were unfounded, however, for he wrote to his brother on 12 July 1664:

---

[7] C. S. S. Higham, *The Development of the Leeward Islands Under the Restoration, 1660–88* (Cambridge, 1921), pp. 193–4.

[8] 'Letters of Samuel Winthrop', *Coll. of the Massachusetts Hist. Soc.* (Boston, 1882), 5th ser., vol. VIII, pp. 234–7.

'My Lord Willoughby hath been here & confirmed O[u]r lands, & setled a custom of 4½ p C[ent]. of all goods of ye growth of ye country yt shal be exported. I haue recd fauors from him more than I did expect'.[9]

Samuel Winthrop acquired a landed estate in Antigua from the profits of trade. He wrote much of collecting debts owing to his correspondents in New England, one of whom was begged to send a ship 'about June next, for wee make sugr only in ye spring & sumer; after July none'. The hazards of trade in wartime were underlined in a letter to his brother in New London, Connecticut, in September 1664:

> I haue last yeare & this lost a considerable businesse; last yeare by miscarryage of ye Antigua Marchant, where Capt. Clarke had here 30 thousand pounds of sugr and this yeare De Rutter his fleet tooke Capt Brookes, in wch I had an adventure, & Mr Wharton also, for I shipt for him 7587 lb in yt ship to pay moneyes for my Newphew Waitstill in London. Here is now a fleet of seuen sayle of Dutchmen wayting vpon us yt wee cannot stirre.

In the same letter he enquired of his sons who were in school in New England; 'I thinke by this time they may be fitt for ye Colledge...'.[10]

French forces numbering 1,500 invaded Antigua at Five Island Harbour on 25 October 1667. After putting up feeble resistance, the English forces retreated to the interior of the island. A shallop belonging to the London merchants' plantation called at Winthrop's landing place and carried his wife and children to Nevis in advance of the enemy. Finding themselves unable to resist the French who were aided by 'ye cruell Indian who lay burning & massacaring', the English agreed to treaty negotiations. Winthrop, who was one of the negotiators, said that inhabitants who took an oath of fealty to the French remained in possession of their estates. Those who refused such an oath had either to sell or leave their estates to agents and leave the island. The English agreed to pay 200,000 lb of sugar to the French in six months, 'for wch ye islanders to be freed from guarding, building fortes, or taking up armes against their country men'. The French then left the island on 4 November threatening to return if the treaty was broken.[11]

Antigua was invaded a second time on 23 November 1667. The French army marched through the country to Winthrop's estate, took over his house as command headquarters, and encamped round

9 Ibid., pp. 238-52.
10 Ibid., pp. 253-4.
11 Ibid., pp. 255-7.

Sugar and Slavery

about it. The commander of the forces was Monsieur de Clodoré, Governor of Martinique.

> He possest himself of 24 of my slaues (ye rest escaped), & of most of ye slaues in ye island, destroyed most of my stock, his soldiers plundering ye country round about. My coppers and sugr worke he medled not wth, nor fired any houses more in ye island, except of those yt runne off ye island.[12]

Having encamped on Winthrop's estate for seven days, the French forces sailed for Guadeloupe with their booty on 1 December. After 1667, though at times cut off from access to overseas markets by enemy privateers and warships, Antigua escaped the devastation of raiding parties and conquerors.

'Great designs are on foot for ye resetlemt of this island', declared Winthrop in a letter of 27 September 1668. In the same letter he wrote of shipping 21 hogsheads of sugar to Richard Wharton to pay his sons' debts in New England. 'It is now all I have left besides my land & 12 workeing negros...'.[13] Winthrop added to his plantation in the years subsequent to the French invasion. In 1669, he purchased 200 acres of land for 66,000 lb of sugar, and in the same year received a government grant of 237 acres. In the previous year he had been granted one-fourth part of the island of Barbuda.[14]

As with his father and brother in New England, Samuel Winthrop became a leader in the Government of Antigua. He was the island's Register from 1667 to 1671, and Deputy Governor from 1668 to 1671. A man of deep religious feeling, he became a Quaker under the influence of George Fox, during the latter's visit to the West Indies. 'I have been much comforted to hear & read of thy tendernesse to persecuted Friends in New England', he wrote to his brother Fitz-John Winthrop in 1671.[15] Samuel Winthrop died in Antigua in 1674. His 'Groton Hall' plantation descended to his three sons, and, after the male line of the family died out, to Colonel Henry Lyons of Antigua, who married Sarah Winthrop, granddaughter of the Deputy Governor. Besides the Lyons, the Winthrops were related by marriage to the Thomases, Fryes, Williamses, and Byams — all prominent planter families of Antigua.[16]

---

12 'Letters of Samuel Winthrop', *Coll. of the Massachusetts Hist. Soc.* (Boston, 1882), 5th ser., vol. VIII, pp. 257–8.
13 Ibid., p. 259.
14 Vere L. Oliver, *The History of the Island of Antigua* (London, 1894–99), vol. 3, pp. 250–3.
15 'Letters of Samuel Winthrop', pp. 260–1.
16 Oliver, *History of Antigua*, vol. 2, pp. 213, 220; vol. 3, pp. 250–3.

3 THE SLOW RECOVERY FROM THE FRENCH INVASION

Contrary to Winthrop's optimistic statement, hope for quick revival from the French invasions was disappointed for some years. Not all of the whites who had fled the island returned, and there was no hope of recovering the movable property taken as booty by the French. Most serious was the loss of slaves, estimated at 1,500 and worth £40,000. These losses were not quickly made up. Governor Byam wrote in 1670 that 'all his Majesty's islands supplied with negroes except poor Antigua, not but that they can have them if they act as some do, the Dutch would supply them, but they dare not embrace it; they languish and decline for want of hands...'. The dearth of slaves was confirmed by the census of 1672, which returned only 570 blacks and 1,052 white men.[17]

Governor Stapleton's detailed census of 1678 reveals that, although the slave population had increased nearly four-fold since 1672, the greater part of the whites possessed no slaves. The white population amounted to 2,308 (1,236 men, 544 women, and 528 children). Englishmen accounted for 1,600 of the whites, followed by 610 Irishmen, and 98 Scotsmen. The 2,172 Negro slaves consisted of 805 men, 868 women, and 499 children. Only 258 of the 563 householders on the island held slaves. Minor staple and provision culture was probably characteristic of the 199 householders who held from one to nine slaves. Of the remaining 59 households, 33 held from 10 to 19 slaves; 6, 20 to 29; 13, 30 to 39; and only 7 had 40 or more slaves. Colonel Philip Warner headed the list with 102 slaves. Three households – Baijer, Willoughby, and Williams – each had from 70 to 79 slaves, two – Winthrop and Watkins – from 60 to 69, and two others – Carlisle and Vernon – from 51 to 59. The number fell to 38 for the households of Pollington and Thorpe, 37 for Thomas, and 36 for Cade, Lee, Hill, and Meyer. Sugar planters, apart from cane growers who possessed no mills, probably did not exceed 25 at the time of the 1678 census.[18]

The problem of attracting white settlers, and indirectly indentured servants and Negro slaves, was aggravated by the engrossment of large tracts of cultivable land by absentee owners. The planters and merchants of Nevis who were interested in Antigua petitioned the King in 1667,

> That the Commandr in Chiefe have power to dispose of ye lands, of such as shall not come or send some Attorney to lay Clayme to their Lands, in

---

17 *Cal. S. P. Col. 1669–74*, p. 205; Higham, *Development of Leeward Islands*, pp. 82, 145.
18 Oliver, *History of Antigua*, vol. 1, pp. lviii–lxi.

> two years, or having laid their Clayme, doe not come and settle some reasonable proportion of Servants upon their Lands in Three years time.

These measures were considered necessary because it was feared that 'some men will never settle their Lands, but keep it till land be growne scarce, that they may make advantage by selling of it . . .'.[19]

After the French invasion three land reform acts were passed in Antigua under the government of Lord Willoughby. The first declared all old titles to land void and lost; the second confirmed the titles to present possessors; and the third put a limit of 600 acres on future grants or sales of land and provided that the lands of absentees should be forfeited unless settled within a specific period of time. The third act of 1668 provided further that 'for every labouring Person brought hither to inhabit and abide in this Island there shall be ordered, allowed, and laid out Ten Acres of good land in Free Socage tenure'. Land reserves were thus created to underwrite the immigration of bond servants and slaves.[20]

The land reform measures grew chiefly out of conflict between English merchants and their factors and plantation overseers in Antigua. We have seen that influential London merchants had been closely associated with the Earl of Carlisle in the establishment of the West India colonies. Large tracts of land came into the possession of merchants, partly by grants from Carlisle, and partly through the inability of Carlisle and the settlers to pay for goods and loans advanced by the merchants. Then came the English Civil Wars and trade with the Dutch. During the period of interrupted trade with the mother country, the factors and overseers appropriated the absentees' plantations and trade goods to their own use. Though some English merchants recovered their property after the ousting of the Dutch, others were unable to prove their claims against planter-governments which were recruited to a large extent from former factors and overseers.

The case of Alexander Pollington sheds light on the power struggle between absentee and resident interests. Pollington was a citizen and haberdasher of London who transacted business at the 'Three Bells' on Lombard Street. His extensive property interests in the West Indies and England are revealed by his will of 4 January 1669. It tells of a plantation in Montserrat, and two others in Antigua called 'Fig Tree' and the 'Body', 'all which are to be sold and the proceeds laid out in negros for my other plantation in the

---

19 Oliver, *History of Antigua* vol. 1, pp. xxxviii.
20 *Acts of Assembly, Passed in the Charibbee Leeward Islands from 1690 to 1730* (London, 1734), pp. 25–30.

Leeward Division of Antigua, now in the possession of Master John Frye my overseer...'. English property consisted of two houses and goods in London, and lands and houses in the counties of Surrey, Sussex, and Kent. Furthermore, Pollington claimed debts owing from Virginia, New England, Montserrat, Barbados, Nevis, Antigua, and Ireland.[21]

On 5 May 1685, Pollington's eldest son and heir, also named Alexander, petitioned the government of Antigua for title to the lands he claimed there. The petitioner said that his father, who was one of the most ancient planters of Antigua, had expended there at least £3,000 and lost five sons who had been sent out from England to manage his properties. He claimed that 'wrongful Possessors still unjustly detain the said Lands', and prayed that title should be made out to him before the act of 1668 was sent over to England to be confirmed. Though we find no record of the disposition of the petition, it is of interest that while the family's connection with Antigua disappeared, that of Pollington's overseer survived to become one of the colonial gentry.[22]

4 THE PLANTOCRACY

The plantocracy of Antigua was recruited from a variety of sources. One group of families came from Surinam after that colony was ceded to Holland by the Treaty of Breda in 1667. Most prominent were the Willoughbys, of whom two members were West India governors general. Francis, Lord Willoughby of Parham, lessee of Lord Carlisle's patent to the Caribee Islands, acquired large landholdings in Antigua. In 1679, the Willoughby plantations were purchased by the Tudways and Turneys, both London mercantile families; the Tudways, who later bought out the Turneys, have held lands in Antigua to the present century.[23] The Martins and Byams also came to Antigua from Surinam. William Byam wrote to a friend in 1668: 'I have deserted our unfortunate colony of Surinam, war and pestilence having almost consumed it. As it is to revert to the Dutch, I have with great loss removed to Antigua, where I am hewing a new fortune out of wild woods'.[24]

While these were families of some means, connection, and plantation experience, others would appear to have started in more humble circumstances. In the latter group were small planters and overseers,

21 Oliver, *History of Antigua*, vol. 3, pp. 30–1.
22 Ibid., vol. 3, pp. 31–2.
23 Ibid., vol. 3, pp. 146–53.
24 'Pym Letters', *Historical Manuscripts Commission*, 10th Report, Part VI, p. 96.

retired soldiers and sailors, former shipmasters, government officials, lawyers, doctors, and merchants. Gentry families were recruited from all these occupational groups and possibly others. If it be asked which group was in the vanguard, it appears that locally based merchants, traders, and factors were most strategically placed to transform mercantile wealth into plantation wealth.[25]

The author's study of the sixty-five leading families of Antigua in the period 1730–75,[26] reveals that thirty-three of them were established on the island before 1680. Not only did they survive a century or more of fluctuating fortunes, but a majority also continued to rank among the first families of the island. Using landownership as a criterion, we find in this group eleven of the twenty leading families, each owning more than 1,000 acres. Although considerable land was purchased, it is noteworthy that twenty-nine of the thirty-three families received proprietary or crown land grants. In government these families contributed four governors general, two lieutenant-governors, and one deputy governor in the period before 1776, not to mention other officials, councillors, and assemblymen.

Besides local politics, these families were represented in Parliament by Samuel Martin, Jr, Sir Henry Martin, Clement Tudway, and the younger Richard Oliver. Moreover, the mercantile and financial connections of these families were a major element of strength. These connections were not confined to Antigua, for it was customary for younger sons to take up residence in London to market the family's sugar, purchase plantation supplies, and perform numerous services connected with trade, shipping, and finance.[27]

Substantial growth characterized the sugar economy of Antigua in the years from 1680 to 1706. The white population, which was 2,308 in 1678, increased slightly to 2,892 in 1708 (1,049 men, 805 women, and 1,038 children). A report in 1705 said that the island contained 4,139 black cattle, 12,187 Negroes, 34 windmills, and 136 cattle-mills. A year later taxes were levied on 55,000 acres of land, 13,000 Negroes, and 5,000 cattle.[28] English custom house records show that 44,840 cwt of sugar were imported from Antigua in 1698, and 81,500 in 1699. The annual average for the period 1700–4 was 56,944 cwt. Sugar products far overshadowed other exports which consisted of cotton, ginger, and lignum vitae.[29]

25 *Cal. S. P. Col. 1681–85*, p. 276.
26 R. B. Sheridan, 'The Rise of a Colonial Gentry: A Case Study of Antigua, 1730–1775', *The Economic History Review*, 2nd ser., vol. XIII, no. 3 (April 1961), pp. 342–57.
27 Ibid., pp. 346–9.
28 *Cal. S. P. Col. 1712–14*, p. 33; Oliver, *History of Antigua*, vol. 1, pp. lxxv, lxxviii.
29 John Oldmixon, *The British Empire in America* (London, 1708), vol. 2, p. 180; Deerr, *History of Sugar*, vol. 1, p. 195.

His Majesty's Leeward Islands

Popular legend credits Christopher Codrington II with establishing the sugar industry in Antigua when he arrived there from Barbados in 1674. Actually, the record shows that the industry antedates his arrival, that he did not settle permanently until he became Governor General in 1689, and that his large landholdings were poorly supplied with slaves as late as 1678. Despite these qualifications, the legend is probably not without substance. Oldmixon wrote that Codrington was a planter of great knowledge, experience, and wealth who set an example for the other planters of Antigua. He acquired 'as good an Estate as any Planter had got at Barbados or Jamaica', and during his governorship 'the Isle flourish'd equally at least with the rest, and became wealthy and populous'.[30]

The son of Christopher Codrington I, who had settled in Barbados in 1649, Codrington had a notable career in the West Indies. He was trustee for the sale of St Lucia in 1663, councillor, Colonel of Militia, and Deputy Governor of Barbados in 1669 and 1671. He became Governor General of the Leeward Islands in 1689, and was succeeded in that office in 1699 by his distinguished son and heir, Christopher Codrington III. In the 18th century Sir William Codrington was a Member of Parliament. His brother-in-law, Slingsby Bethell, was a prominent London-West India merchant, Lord Mayor of London, and Member of Parliament.[31]

Christopher Codrington II acquired land in Antigua as early as 1668. In that year the Assembly of Antigua, in passing an act to settle the present inhabitants of that island in their lands, specifically excepted 'the Plantation formerly the Widow Joan Keynell's lying at *Betty Hope*, being granted unto Colonel Christopher Codrington'. This property of 725 acres had belonged to Christopher Keynell, Governor of Antigua in the Commonwealth period. Besides 'Betty's Hope' and the island of Barbuda, Codrington received a grant of 380 acres in 1677. The Codringtons were the leading planter family in Antigua for more than a century. Indeed, the family's five sugar plantations on that island occupied upwards of 1,000 acres of land and contained nearly 800 slaves by the middle years of the 18th century.[32]

Eleven other families made their way into the Antigua gentry after taking up residence on the island from 1680 to 1706. Four families (Browne, Kirwan, Lynch, Skerrett) came from Galway, the

---

30 Oldmixon, *British Empire in America*, vol. 2, p. 181.
31 Sheridan, 'Rise of a Colonial Gentry', p. 349; Vincent T. Harlow, *Christopher Codrington, 1668–1710* (Oxford, 1928).
32 *Acts of the Leeward Islands*, pp. 27–8; Oliver, *History of Antigua*, vol. 1, pp. 43–4, 144–53; Robson Lowe, *The Codrington Correspondence* (London, 1951), pp. 19, 26.

west coast port of Ireland which carried on an extensive trade with the West Indies. From Drumcree came Walter Nugent, of an old Anglo-Irish family. After fighting in the Battle of the Boyne in 1690, he made three successful trading voyages to Antigua and eventually settled in the island as a landed proprietor. Peter Gaynor, also from Ireland, was a merchant and planter in Antigua before his death in 1738. His large fortune of approximately £200,000 was inherited by his son-in-law, Sir George Colebrooke, who was Chairman of the East India Company, Member of Parliament, and a London banker.[33]

Among the English families who came in the middle period, one (Chester) was founded by an agent of the Royal African Company; one (Weatherell) was founded by the commander of a privateer sloop that captured a large and valuable Spanish ship; and another (Pearne) inter-married with the powerful Warner family. Then there was Daniel MacKinnon, a Scottish doctor, whose large plantation was said to have been formerly inhabited by nearly one hundred poor people who had departed the island.[34]

5 ECONOMIC STRUCTURE AND TRENDS, 1700–75

There is little question that the economy of Antigua underwent a remarkable transformation during the first three-quarters of the 18th century. This was the period when the large sugar plantation became the dominant unit of production; when the race to acquire land, slaves, and sugar works sometimes made for conditions approaching a Hobbesian state of nature. The white population increased from approximately 2,300 in 1678 to 5,200 in 1724. From this peak it then declined to 2,590 in 1774, as the process of consolidating small farms and plantations into sugar estates gained momentum. The slave population, on the other hand, experienced an almost continuous growth; it was reported in scattered census returns at 2,172 in 1678, 12,943 in 1708, 27,892 in 1745, and 37,808 in 1774. The ratio of whites to blacks, which was 1 to 4½ in 1708, declined to the very low ratio of 1 to 14 in 1774.[35]

---

33 Oliver, *History of Antigua*, vol. 1, pp. 74–8, 84–6; vol. 2, pp. 9–11, 128–30, 206–9, 212–20, 240–7, 309–15; vol. 3, pp. 87–9, 118–21; Oliver, *Caribbeana*, vol. 2, p. 336.
34 Oliver, *History of Antigua*, vol. 1, pp. 41–4, 126–33, 144–53; vol. 2, pp. 119–22; vol. 3, pp. 16–19, 209–13.
35 Frank W. Pitman, *The Development of the British West Indies 1700–1763* (New Haven, 1917), p. 379; Deerr, *History of Sugar*, vol. 1, p. 174; Oliver, *History of Antigua*, vol. 1, pp. lvii, lxi, lxxviii.

Sugar plantations in Antigua probably numbered 150 at the beginning of the 18th century. Writing in 1764, a local pamphleteer said that the island contained more than 300 sugar estates of an average value of approximately £9,000 sterling. On an island-wide basis the sugar works, buildings, utensils, and stock amounted to £900,000; taxes were paid on 60,000 acres of land valued at £900,000; and there were 37,000 Negroes (valued at £1 million), of which at least 25,000 were employed on sugar estates.[36] Sugar mills on the island increased from 170 in 1705, to 239 in 1748, and then fell to 202 in 1789. The substitution of windmills for cattle-mills contributed to the increased size and valuation of sugar estates. English sugar imports from Antigua increased from an annual average of 64,996 cwt in 1706–10, to a high point of 167,760 cwt in 1756–60, and then fell to 158,460 cwt in 1771–75. Based on London prices, the sugar crop amounted to between £280,000 and £320,000 annually in the third quarter of the century, while the total exports of Antigua ranged between £370,000 and £420,000.[37]

Apart from the ceded portion of St Kitts, Antigua held an advantage over its sister islands and Barbados in possessing greater reserves of agricultural land. As already observed, efforts were made to expropriate unsettled lands held by absentees and grant them to inhabitants. Christopher Codrington said in 1691 that 'the Island of Antigua, tho' long since all taken up, is yet near two-thirds in Standing Wood, and not a fifth of the people on it, which it is capable to receive'. Writing in the early years of the following century, Governor Douglas berated the planters for neglecting to maintain their 'due proportion of white servants and their possessing larger tracts of land then they are perfectly capable to improve'.[38]

Except in wartime, planters were more concerned to get slaves than white servants. One measure of encouragement was the Act of the Assembly of Antigua of 3 May 1675, 'for encouraging the Royal Company in England for the supplying the Island with Negroes'. The preamble stated that the Royal African Company's decision to locate their agency for the Leeward Islands at Nevis had been very prejudicial to the inhabitants of Antigua. In an effort to induce the Company to establish a separate agency in Antigua, the Act set up a special court to settle disputes between slave factors and inhabitants.

36 Anon., *Some Observations; Which May Contribute to Afford a Just Idea of the Nature, Importance, and Settlement of Our New West-India Colonies* (London, 1764), pp. 48–50; Pitman, *Development of British West Indies*, p. 379; Deerr, *History of Sugar*, vol. 2, p. 279.
37 Deerr, *History of Sugar*, vol. 1, p. 174. See Appendix V for price data.
38 P.R.O. London. C.O. 152/1, BA No. 3, f. 20: Gov. Codrington to Board of Trade, 12 Sept. 1691; *Cal. S. P. Col. 1712–14*, p. 34.

Sugar and Slavery

A decade later the Company responded by establishing such an agency, but the planters were disappointed by the small number of slaves the Company saw fit to consign there.[39]

Servile labour was supplied more abundantly when the African Company's monopoly was broken in 1698. From 4 June 1698 to 25 December 1707, the separate traders carried to Antigua 4,945 slaves, and the Royal African Company 1,805 (711 per annum all told). Imports increased to an annual average of 1,362 from 1720 to 1729. But drought and low sugar prices had reduced imports markedly by 1734, when Governor Mathew wrote that for want of Negroes only 24,408 acres out of about 50,000 acres of manurable land were actually planted in canes. On the other hand, new heights were reached in the mid-century period when Antigua and St Kitts each received an estimated annual import of 2,000 slaves, compared with 500 each for Nevis and Montserrat.[40] 'The number of Negroes are increased from the great Importation last Year from Africa', wrote Governor Thomas in 1756, 'and the necessity the Planters are under to manure their Lands which are greatly impoverished by long culture'.[41]

As with the other sugar colonies, Antigua faced the problem of maintaining a ratio of whites to blacks which was commensurate with the collective need for military protection and civic order. As the military bastion of the Leeward Islands in the long wars from 1689 to 1713, Antigua attracted refugees from neighbouring islands and military personnel who stayed on to seek their fortunes in some civil capacity. Other freemen and servants were drawn to the relatively underdeveloped colony of Antigua during the period of peacetime expansion and prosperity after 1713.

Acts to encourage the immigration of white servants may have added to the population, at least in the short run. The 'White Servants' Act' of 1716 was one such measure. By its provisions, proprietors of slaves were required to have in their service one white man for every forty slaves, a heavy annual penalty of £53 6s 8d being imposed for each deficient white man. The census of 18 July 1720 shows that the servants were quite numerous. Out of 3,652 white inhabitants enumerated, the servants numbered 698 (471 men, 140 women, 45 boys, 42 girls). Most critical was the ratio of one man servant for every thirty-six slaves in the island. The three other

---

39 *Acts of the Leeward Islands*, pp. 49–50; K. G. Davies, *The Royal African Company* (London, 1957), pp. 311–12, 363.
40 Davies, *Royal African Company*, pp. 143, 363; P.R.O. London. C.O. 152/20, V 46, f. 149.
41 P.R.O. London. C.O. 152/28, Bb 75: Gov. Thomas to Board of Trade, 26 April 1756.

His Majesty's Leeward Islands

islands lagged far behind Antigua in servants. St Kitts had 113; Montserrat 95; and Nevis 68. If the effect of the White Servants' Act was salutary in the short run, as seems probable, it was later rendered futile and ineffective except as a source of revenue for the island government.[42]

6 DR WALTER TULLIDEPH, SCOTTISH PLANTER

Two events, closely associated in time, brought new elements into the Antigua gentry. The first was the Act of Union in 1707, which enabled energetic Scotsmen to make their way to the British colonies. The second was the Treaty of Utrecht in 1713, which ushered in a peacetime period of expansion in the sugar industry. It was in this setting that the tempo of economic life quickened, although by mid-century the rate of growth had considerably abated.

Scotland not only supplied Antigua with a considerable number of servants after the Act of Union, but also with men of education and some capital who came to play a prominent part in the island's trade, government, professions, and agriculture. While the greater number probably came in a peaceable manner, one ship arrived in Antigua with nearly a hundred Scottish prisoners who were transported after the Rebellion of 1715.[43]

The contribution of the Scots was far out of proportion to their numbers. In fact, thirteen Scotsmen established family dynasties of some consequence in the social and political life of Antigua. Numbered among these families were at least ten doctors and nine merchants. Broadly speaking, these young men combined skills and professional attainment with the desire to make their way in the world. In the changing environment of the West Indies they moved with ease from one vocation to another, often combining several vocations in one crowded career.

A brief sketch of Dr Walter Tullideph's career will shed light on the forces which enabled one Scottish family to gain admittance into the Antigua gentry. The son of a minister of the gospel at Dunbarny, Tullideph went to the High School at Edinburgh and in 1718 was apprenticed to a chirurgeon of that city. About 1726 he went to

---

42 Oliver, *Caribbeana* (London, 1919), vol. 6, pp. 140–1; Pitman, *Development of British West Indies*, p. 378.
43 Abbot E. Smith, *Colonists in Bondage: White Servitude and Convict Labor in America 1607–1776* (Chapel Hill, 1947), pp. 198–9.

Sugar and Slavery

Antigua where several friends and relatives were already established as doctors, merchants, and government officials.[44]

With these connections and his professional skill, Tullideph was able to combine several vocations during his early years in the island. As his brother's factor, he sold Scottish linen and other goods to the planters. He also received consignments from other merchants in England and Scotland. As a doctor, he treated both white and Negro inhabitants, but mainly the latter on a contract basis. When he travelled from plantation to plantation to minister to slaves he carried merchandise to sell to the planters. A happy combination of these occupations was his wholesale and retail business in drugs and medicines. Much of his time was taken up in collecting debts, for planters were notoriously slow to pay.[45]

After a time Tullideph began to trade on his own account. He became a correspondent of William Dunbar, an uncle who was a sugar factor in London. This not only made it possible to bypass local middlemen in buying English goods and selling island produce, but it also enabled Tullideph to borrow money on the promise of future consignments. The young doctor then began to make loans to needy planters, sometimes borrowing at 5 per cent in London and lending the funds locally at 8 or 10 per cent. By 1733 he held one planter's mortgage for £620, and numerous smaller debts on the security of personal bonds and judgements.[46]

While numerous merchants and professional men purchased plantations in this period, others found an easier way to become planters. Our young doctor-merchant fell in the latter group, for in 1736 he wrote to his brother that he had 'married an agreable young Widow by whom I have gott Possession of a very fine Estate to which I am making additions & improvements and am likely to have a heir of my Own'.[47]

After taking up residence on the estate, Tullideph retained his medical practice in the neighbourhood and began to devote most of his time to plantation affairs. Since his newly-acquired plantation contained only 127 acres and 63 slaves, his over-riding concern was to make 'additions & improvements'. In a letter of 1739 he referred to the 'purchase of 50 Acres of Land I made of William Yorke two years agone for which I gave him £700 our money'. A further addition of about 110 acres was made in 1743. In August 1747 he

44 *Tullideph L. B.*, vol. 2: Lre. to Andrew Aiton, 16 May 1757; Oliver, *History of Antigua*, vol. 1, pp. 223–5; vol. 3, pp. 128–33, 155–62.
45 *Walter Tullideph's Medical Ledger*, ff. 1–156.
46 *Walter Tullideph's General Ledger*, ff. 1–12.
47 *Tullideph L. B.*, vol. 1: Lre. to Thomas Tullideph, 28 April 1736.

wrote to his brother that he had purchased 'Yorke's' estate of about 200 acres for £8,888 sterling. 'Bear Garden' estate of some 134 acres was purchased from a Mr Stevens for £9,000 Antigua currency in 1748, a purchase he regarded as too dear 'but I could not help it, another was ready to have given it'.[48] All these additions joined together into one large plantation, to which he added newly-purchased slaves from time to time. Moreover, he built a new and centrally located sugar work with windmills to replace the less efficient cattle-mills. By 1757 he had 536 acres and 271 Negro slaves. A conservative estimate places the value of his plantation at £30,000 sterling in 1763.[49]

Tullideph was not alone in purchasing lands and plantations during this period. Dr Walter Sydserfe, his cousin and business associate, added to his plantation until it contained 570 acres. Several other relatives and friends acquired plantations of 500 acres or more. During the war of 1744–8, Tullideph wrote that 'although our Dangers are great yet Estates rise considerably'.[50] Diminished supplies of land suitable for cane growing helps to explain the land hunger. By 1751 Antigua was said to be 'improved to the utmost there being hardly one Acre of Ground, even to the Top of the Mountains, fit for Sugar Canes and other necessary Produce, but what is taken in and cultivated'.[51]

The ownership of a large sugar plantation opened up new opportunities for our subject. After gaining the confidence of his neighbours, Tullideph was asked to write home for Scottish doctors, merchants, and indentured servants; to superintend the estates of absentees; to purchase shares in ships and join with other planters to purchase imported supplies in cargo lots; to engage in privateering ventures; to serve as executor, administrator, guardian or trustee. On the estates of absentees, for whom he acted as attorney, he placed his Scottish friends and relatives as doctors, plantation managers, attornies, and lessees. When estates came up for sale he sometimes helped his friends to finance the purchase.[52]

Political preferment was to be expected for the planter-merchant on the make. Like a number of his colleagues, Tullideph climbed the island's political ladder as his wealth and influence grew. He became,

48 Ibid., vol. 1: Lre. to Charles Goore in Liverpool, 11 May 1743; Ibid., vol. 2: Lre. to Thomas Tullideph, 15 Aug. 1747; Lre. to Dr Walter Sydserfe, 4 June 1749.
49 *Tullideph's General Ledger*, ff. 17, 107, 190, 255.
50 *Tullideph L. B.*, vol. 2: Lre. to Gov. George Thomas in Philadelphia, 8 Aug. 1745; Oliver, *History of Antigua*, vol. 3, p. 129.
51 British Museum, North MSS A6, f. 173.
52 Richard B. Sheridan, 'Letters from a Sugar Plantation in Antigua, 1734–1758', *Agricultural History*, vol. 31 (July 1957), pp. 3–23.

Sugar and Slavery

in order of succession, parish vestryman, justice of the peace, assemblyman, and councillor. These honours made him the social equal of the island's first families.[53]

Lest it be thought that these honours were the touchstone of a successful career, the reader of the letter-books will learn that the young doctor was making enquiries about estates in Fyffeshire as early as 1734. After several short visits to England and Scotland, Tullideph became a semi-permanent absentee in 1757, thereafter making only short business trips to Antigua. Besides his Antigua plantation, he purchased a Scottish estate which cost approximately £10,000; and his two daughters, one of whom married a baronet, each had dowries of £5,000.

This son of a rural minister lived his later years as a Scottish laird, taking great pride in his grandchildren. From planter on the make, via the route of doctor and merchant, we leave him now in Scotland as an absentee, drawing income from his plantation in Antigua.[54]

7 COLONEL SAMUEL MARTIN OF GREENCASTLE ESTATE

Though similar in several respects, the career of Samuel Martin affords points of striking contrast with that of Walter Tullideph.[55] Both men owned plantations of approximately the same size and capitalized value, both had a marked influence upon the social and political life of Antigua, both spent a substantial part of their adult lives away from the island, and both were able to pass on larger estates to their survivors than they inherited. But here the parallel ends. Samuel Martin moved on a wider stage. He and his three sons had political and social connections of some importance in England and North America. Since Martin inherited a large sugar plantation, he was not compelled to purchase land, build sugar works, and procure a fresh supply of labour. While it is true that he added to the capitalized value of his estate, he already had a substantial base upon which to build. Martin's interests were directed chiefly towards plantership and he conformed more closely to the image of a gentleman planter than his friend Walter Tullideph.

The Martins came to Antigua by way of France, England, Ireland,

---

53 Oliver, *History of Antigua*, vol. 3, pp. 155–62.
54 *Tullideph L. B.*, vols. 2 and 3.
55 See my 'Rise of a Colonial Gentry', pp. 352–4; and 'Samuel Martin, Innovating Sugar Planter of Antigua, 1750–1776', *Agricultural History*, vol. 34, no. 3 (July 1960), pp. 126–39.

and Surinam. Members of the family participated in the Norman Conquest, the Elizabethan conquest of Ireland, and, as Royalists, in the Civil Wars. Colonel Samuel Martin of 'Greencastle' estate in Antigua was the eldest son and heir of Major Samuel Martin, a prominent planter who came to that island from Surinam sometime before 1680. He was born in Antigua in 1693, and after a long and eventful life which included many years' residence in England, died in his native island in 1776. After his father's untimely death at the hands of his slaves, Samuel was sent to live with relatives in Ireland. At the age of fifteen he entered Cambridge University. In the last year of his life Martin wrote to a friend: 'I have lost two wives & sixteen children out of one and twenty'. Of the five who survived, four were sons and one a daughter.[56]

Three of Samuel Martin's sons gained positions of some distinction. Samuel, and Henry, who was made a baronet, were members of Parliament, and Josiah was Governor of North Carolina. Other relatives were prominent in Antigua. Josiah Martin, a brother, was President of the Council and proprietor of a sugar plantation. A half-brother and close business associate, William Byam, married Anne, daughter of John Gunthorpe. Both Byam and Gunthorpe were councillors, while Samuel Martin was Speaker of the Assembly and Colonel of Militia.[57]

Martin and his family alternated between Antigua and England and Ireland for many years. He was in Antigua from about 1714 to 1716, and again from 1718 to 1728. A short residence in England occupied the intervening period. Most of the years from 1729 to 1749 were spent in England, during which time his plantation was managed by relatives and friends.

Unlike Walter Tullideph who returned to Scotland after devoting his best years to his Antigua estate, Samuel Martin returned to his native land in his fifty-seventh year to spend most of his remaining years on his plantation. Upon arrival in 1750, he met with a dismal prospect; his gang of Negroes reduced in numbers, his sugar works in a state of disrepair, and the fertility of his soil greatly diminished. In several letters Martin complained of the evils of absenteeism of which he was a sufferer.[58]

---

56 *Martin L. B.*, vol. 6, f. 65: Lre. to Christopher Baldwin in London, 22 Feb. 1776; *Journal of a Lady of Quality*, ed. Evangeline W. Andrews and Charles M. Andrews (New Haven, 1923), pp. 103–6, 259–62; Oliver, *History of Antigua*, vol. 2, pp. 240–8; vol. 3, pp. 297–302.
57 Andrews, *Lady of Quality*, pp. 271–3; Oliver, *History of Antigua*, vol. 1, pp. 31–2, 96–104; vol. 2, pp. 37–40.
58 *Martin L. B.*, vol. 1, ff. 208, 210; Lres. to Samuel Martin, Jr. in London, 14 and 16 June 1758.

Table 9.1

Inventory of Samuel Martin's Greencastle plantation in Antigua, 1768

	£ sterling
605 acres of land at £30 per acre	£18,150
304 Negro slaves	12,340
Sugar works, including two windmills, a boiling house, curing house, rum distillery, and cisterns	8,000
115 head of mules, oxen, cows, calves, bulls and steers	1,973
Plant canes and ratoon canes	1,730
Dwelling house, stables, hospital house, coach house, etc.	1,000
6 wagons and carts	140
Total	43,333

Source: British Museum Add. MSS 41,353, ff. 84–6. Although Martin said that the above valuation was not exaggerated to the best of his knowledge and conscience, he agreed to sell his whole property for £32,000 sterling because he was growing old and wished to retire from the world and 'no one of my children in all probability will reside here'.

An ambitious rebuilding programme was soon under way. In November 1752, Martin wrote: 'I am in debt here, and must still lay out 3 or 4 thousand pounds before my Plantation can be brought into order'. In a five-year period he purchased fifty slaves, most of them young Negroes from twelve to fifteen years of age. Moreover, he rebuilt his sugar works and increased his stock of cattle and mules. These additions and improvements, which were accomplished by 1768 when the inventory shown in Table 9.1 was taken, were financed chiefly out of plantation profits.[59]

A major undertaking was to make his worn-out land more productive. This was not only a matter of applying more animal manure, but also of discovering other types of fertilizer and improved crop techniques. In the bed of a stream he found abundance of topsoil to spread over his cane fields. Marl pits and sand pits were opened in

---

[59] *Martin L. B.*, vol. 1, f. 40: Lre. to Samuel Martin, Jr. in London, 12 Nov. 1752; Ibid., vol. 1, ff. 70–1, 207, 210: Lres. to same, 24 June 1753, and 14 and 16 June 1758.

His Majesty's Leeward Islands

other parts of his estate. Martin became an authority on plantation management, especially after he published *An Essay Upon Plantership* about 1754.[60]

Miss Janet Schaw, a Scottish lady of quality, wrote of her visit to 'Greencastle' in December 1774. She found the venerable proprietor, then in his eightieth year and unable to walk, seated on his piazza to receive her. 'His conversation was pleasant, entertaining and instructive, his manners not merely polite but amiable in a high degree. It was impossible not to love him', she wrote. Martin was described as 'the loved and revered father of Antigua to whom it owes a thousand advantages, and whose age is daily employed to render it more improved and happy'. In a vein of uncritical praise Miss Schaw wrote that Martin's plantation was 'cultivated to the height by a large troop of healthy Negroes, who cheerfully perform the labour imposed on them by a kind and beneficent Master, not a harsh and unreasonable Tyrant'.[61]

8 DESCRIPTIVE ACCOUNTS BY TWO SCOTTISH VISITORS

Miss Schaw toured almost from one end of the island to the other, being delighted by the lush tropical vegetation, charmed by the 'Negroes in joyful troops' on their way to the town market, and pleased by the civility, kindness and hospitality of the planters. From the high elevation of Dr John Dunbar's 'Eleanora' plantation, some two miles from the port of St Johns, she viewed the bay, the shipping, the town, and many rich plantations. 'Indeed it is almost impossible to conceive so much beauty and riches under the eye in one moment. The fields all the way down to the town are divided into cane pieces by hedges of different kinds'. Setting off early one morning to avoid the heat, she had 'a charming ride thro' many rich and noble plantations, several of which belonged to Scotch proprietors, particularly that of the Dillidaffs [sic. Tullideph]'. The sumptious dinner at Mr Halliday's plantation was said to be equal to that 'given by a Lord Mayor, or the first Duke in the kingdom'.[62]

Lord Adam Gordon was another visitor from Scotland who viewed the island through the eyes of the plantocracy. He was on his

---

60 Ibid., vol. 1, ff. 11, 206–8: Lres. to same, 18 Oct. 1750, and 14 June 1758.
61 Andrews, *Lady of Quality*, pp. 103–6.
62 Ibid., pp. 90–1, 95–6, 100, 107.

203

way to Jamaica to join the 66th Regiment of Foot, of which he was Colonel, when he landed in Antigua in May 1764. St Johns, the principal town and seat of government, was said to be 'regularly laid out, and well calculated to receive all the cool Breezes from both the Sea and Land'. The court house, council house, and assembly room were 'grand and contrived', and the magazine well supplied with small arms and cannons. After a tour of the island he observed that

> Almost all the people of fashion live on their Estates in the Country, and are all more or less engaged in making of Sugar and Rum. There are several large properties in the hands of Familys residing in Britain, who let them out to Managers, that pay them a certain agreed annual rent on the Exchange, and these Gentlemen generally make themselves great fortunes.[63]

The lot of the slaves elicited only brief mention by the Lord, who concluded: 'Upon the whole it is a very happy Island, the Society is good, and they have no disputes, but live all well together, in good harmony. I never met with more Civilities, during a Weeks stay, or left a place with more regret'.[64]

Unlike Lord Gordon, Miss Schaw was not convinced that Antigua was an unalloyed Garden of Eden. The 'frank, open, generous, and I dare say brave' character of the men of fashion was blemished by 'their licentious and even unnatural amours, which appears too plainly from the crouds of Mallotoes, which you meet in the streets, houses and indeed every where'. The danger of slave insurrection cast a pall of fear on the whites, especially during the Christmas season when the slaves enjoyed several days' respite from their toils. This was a season of great uneasiness 'when every man on the Island is in arms and patrols go round the different plantations as well as keep guard in the town'.[65]

Miss Schaw saw certain portents of economic malaise. Besides the misfortunes of hurricanes, fire, and drought, she tells of a scheme for raising beef cattle on the high plantations, 'several of which have begun to wear out, from the constant crops of sugar which have been taken from them'. By turning his cane pieces into grass, Colonel Martin was said to have allowed them 'to rest and recover the strength they have lost, by too many crops of sugar, and by this means is able to rear cattle which he has done with great success'.[66]

---

63 Lord Adam Gordon, *Journal of an Officer in the West Indies, 1764–65*, in *Travels in the American Colonies*, ed. Newton D. Mereness (New York, 1916), pp. 375–6.
64 Ibid., p. 376.
65 Andrews, *Lady of Quality*, pp. 108–9, 112.
66 Ibid., pp. 87–8, 91, 96, 105–6.

9 THE NEAR-MONOCULTURE REGIME

Martin was not alone in viewing the near-monoculture regime as a mixed blessing. John Yeamans, Agent for Antigua and Martin's relation by marriage, had written to the Board of Trade in May 1734:

> Land has been at so high a price from the Smallness of the Quantity in said Island that the Settlers of Ten or Twenty Acres who formerly rais'd only provisions have been tempted to sell their Possessions to the Sugar Planters & have thereupon quitted the Island; but I must observe to their Lordships that this Alteration tho' it may have Occasion'd the loss of some Inhabitants, has been in general beneficial to the Trade, Navigation and revenue of Great Britain, all the improvable land being by that Means employ'd in the raising of Sugar, & provisions coming to them now, Chiefly from his Majesties other Dominions in English Bottoms.[67]

Governor General George Thomas, himself a planter and descendant of planters, appealed to the Board of Trade in February 1756 for a strong squadron of warships. Protection of trade was imperative, he said, for the Leeward Islands were 'incapable, consistent with the Cultivation of the Sugar Cane, which renders them so valuable to the Crown and to their Mother Country, of raising Provisions for the support of the Negros which your Lordships will observe are become very Numerous in the several islands'.[68]

10 CONCLUSION

Professor Ragatz maintains that Antigua affords a notable exception to prevailing conditions of economic backwardness, racial friction, and debasement of island society which were characteristic of the sugar colonies after the middle years of the 18th century. Supporting evidence is found in the superior quality of its public institutions, the larger number of West Indian born Negroes on Antiguan estates than elsewhere, and the real interest in agricultural advancement shown by the gentry under the leadership of Colonel Samuel Martin. 'Society in eighteenth and nineteenth century Antigua was in a distinctly healthy state', Ragatz maintains. He explains this 'healthy state' as due chiefly to the far greater number of Antiguan proprietors who were permanent residents.[69] Among other contemporaries, Governor

---

67 P.R.O. London. C.O. 152/20, V 29: John Yeamans to Board of Trade, 27 May 1734.
68 Ibid., C.O. 152/28, Bb 75: Gov. Thomas to Board of Trade, 20 Feb. 1756.
69 Lowell J. Ragatz, 'Absentee Landlordism in the British Caribbean, 1750–1833', *Agricultural History*, vol. V (Jan. 1931), pp. 22–4; Sheridan, 'Rise of a Colonial Gentry', pp. 342–57.

Sugar and Slavery

General Ralph Payne of the Leeward Islands lent credence to this argument when he wrote to the Earl of Dartmouth in October 1773: 'The number of Proprietors in these Colonies, who live in Europe, is ... infinitely superior to the very few who are left. ... Antigua has much the Advantage of other Islands, with Respect to Men of Fortune and Education, and in Point of an independent and respectable Inhabitancy'.[70]

Granted that there is some merit in Ragatz's thesis, it must nevertheless be qualified by saying that if Antigua differed from its sister colonies, the difference was one of degree rather than one of kind. The writer's study of the sixty-five leading planter families of Antigua shows that at least fifty-two of these families had members away from the island for protracted periods in the years from 1730 to 1775. Included among them were twenty London-West India merchants, twelve members of Parliament, one Lord Mayor of London, and nine titled persons. The wills, indentures, and pedigrees recorded in Dr Oliver's *History of Antigua* point to an increase, rather than a decrease, of absenteeism down to 1775. Samuel Martin not only complained of the many services he was asked to perform for absentees, but on two occasions when he went to North America and England for short visits he was perplexed to know what to do with his own estate because of the scarcity of capable plantation attornies.[71]

While there is some evidence that the white population increased slightly in the half century or more following 1775, the same period witnessed a substantial falling off in the number of slaves. During the American Revolution several thousand Negroes died in Antigua as a result of the scarcity of imported provisions, drought, and epidemics. From a peak Negro population of 37,808 in 1774, the figure fell to 30,283 in 1807, the year that the African trade was prohibited, and to 23,350 in 1834, the year of slave emancipation. Similarly, extant statistics of British sugar imports from Antigua show that 1775 was the peak year down to 1834.[72] Despite its superior institutions, Antigua was not spared the economic crisis which struck the sugar colonies on the eve of slave emancipation. Anthony Brown, Agent for Antigua and Montserrat, told a select committee of the House of Commons in 1832: 'I have but too much reason to know that in Antigua and Montserrat, and I believe in the whole of those Islands which were formerly included in the Leeward Island Government,

70 P.R.O. London. C.O. 152/54, 6 Oct. 1773.
71 *Martin L. B.*, vol. 1, ff. 46, 208: Lres. to Samuel Martin, Jr. in London, ? Dec. 1752, and 14 June 1758.
72 Deerr, *History of Sugar*, vol. 1, p. 195; vol. 2, p. 279.

the distress has arrived at its utmost point; I believe it to threaten one general bankruptcy amongst the landed interests, and the dismemberment of their estates, and the incapacity to provide for the common sustenance of the negro population'.[73]

73 *Report from the Select Committee on the Commercial State of the West-India Colonies* (London, 1832), pp. 117–18.

CHAPTER TEN

Jamaica, The Fairest Island

> In what I have been saying, I have had my Thoughts more particularly at *Jamaica*, the most valuable *Plantation* belonging to the Crown, (its Scituation considered) and an Island, if fully settled, that would produce three times the Quantity of *Sugar, Indico, Ginger, Cotton,* &c. it has hitherto done.[1]
>
> William Wood, 1718

1 THE PHYSICAL ENVIRONMENT

Jamaica, the largest of the British West Indian islands, lies about ninety miles south of Cuba and one thousand miles westward of the Leeward Islands. Although nearly four times as large as the combined area of its sister islands, and the third largest Caribbean island (4,411 square miles), much of Jamaica is either too mountainous or arid for tropical agriculture. The island is indented by numerous bays and harbours into which are discharged the waters carried down from the mountains in swift-flowing or meandering streams. Physiographically, Jamaica is much more diverse than the Lesser Antilles, so much so that generalizations on an island-wide basis are misleading. Elevation varies from coastal plains, almost at sea-level, to high mountains, of which Blue Mountain Peak rises to 7,402 feet. Temperatures vary according to elevation and access to trade winds and ocean breezes. Rainfall is heaviest on the north coast and in the Blue Mountain area, ranging from 100 to 200 inches a year, while other parts of the island are cast in rain shadow and average less than 40 inches. Moreover, the rainfall is seasonal, reaching a maximum in September, October, and November and a minimum in February and March. To these variations are added those of geological formation, soil types, and flora and fauna to make Jamaica an island of scenic splendour and beauty.

Sugar production had spread to almost every parish in Jamaica by the third quarter of the 18th century. The favourably endowed localities consisted of lands along the lower basins and deltas of the

---

1 William Wood, *A Survey of Trade* (London, 1718), p. 173.

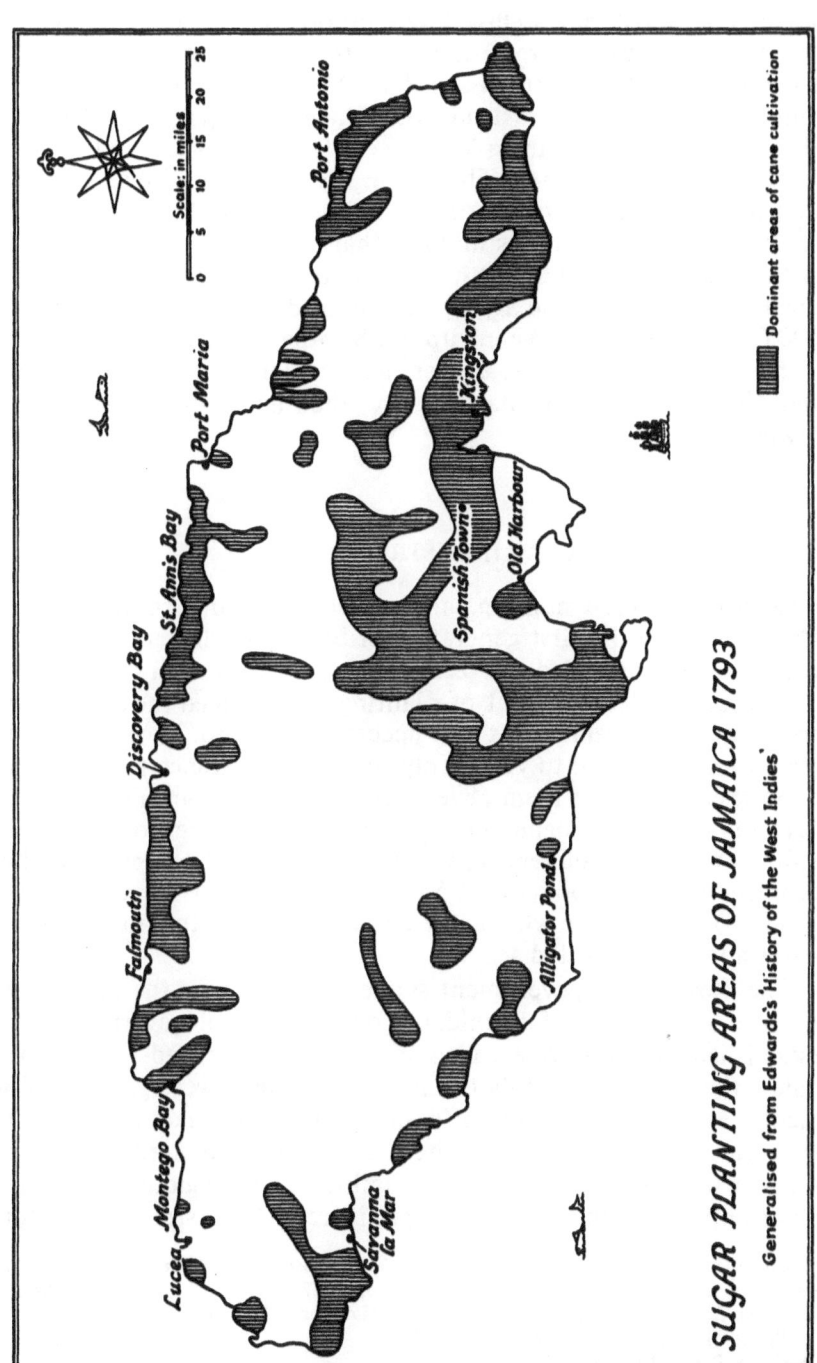

Sugar and Slavery

large rivers, fertile and well-watered interior valleys, and coastal areas of adequate rainfall. Areas of concentrated sugar growing included the Rio Minho Valley, the Black River Valley, St Thomas in the Vale round the town of Linstead, the Queen of Spain's Valley near Montego Bay, the Cabaritta Valley near Savanna-la-Mar, and Plantain Garden River Valley in St Thomas in the East. John Ellis, Agent for Jamaica and resident planter from 1754 to 1773, told a committee of the House of Commons in 1775 that of the nearly 4 million acres in the island, some 160,000 were planted in sugar-canes and that the sugar plantations in the aggregate occupied 500,000 acres. Another 500,000 acres were taken up with other settlements, 'such as piemento, cotton, coffee, ginger, and penland for breeding cattle, and in provision plantations in the neighbourhood of the towns....'.[2]

2 THE EARLY SUGAR INDUSTRY

Buccaneering, hide hunting, and logwood cutting competed with planting during the first generation of English settlement in Jamaica. Little success attended the effort to settle Cromwell's soldiers on plantations. Indeed, neglect of planting had reduced the settlers to a condition of extreme want and necessity by 1660. In that year the plantations were said to yield 'only present Subsistence to such as are upon them to keepe them alive, whilest their Numbers decrease, noe Servants or Planters being added to them ....'.[3] From some 7,000 or 8,000 immigrant soliders and civilians, the white population had been reduced by 1661 to 2,956 (2,458 men, 454 women, and 44 children). Besides the whites, the census of 1661 returned 514 Negro slaves and 2,588 planted acres.[4]

The Restoration government sought to encourage the planting of Jamaica in the face of formidable obstacles. Civil government was established, hunters were called in and not permitted to kill cattle unless they cultivated plots of land, and soldiers were granted allotments according to rank and encouraged to take up planting. Indentured servants were recruited, some coming voluntarily, others transported to Jamaica for civil, military, or religious infractions. Slave imports, both legal and illegal, increased the size of the labour

2 *The Substance of the Evidence of the Petition Presented by the West-India Planters and Merchants, to the House of Commons* (London, 1775), pp. 66–7; John Macpherson, *Caribbean Lands, a geography of the West Indies* (London, 1963), pp. 31–51.
3 British Museum, Egerton MSS 2395, f. 242.
4 *Cal. S. P. Col. 1661–68*, p. 65.

force. By October 1663 the island was 'in a much more prosperous condition than it was some months since, especially as to its plenty of provisions'. However, not more than 200 settlers had arrived, and they probably made no net addition, 'the year being very sickly, and carried away great numbers'.[5]

Lacking sufficient support from the mother country to make much progress in planting, Jamaica turned to its sister islands for experienced planters, white servants, and slaves. From Barbados came Sir Thomas Modyford in 1664 with some 700 planters and their slaves. Less dramatic was the influx of Barbadians and Leeward Islanders in subsequent years. Another group, consisting of 109 planter families and 1,049 slaves, came from Surinam when that colony was ceded to Holland. Governor Vaughan of Jamaica wrote on 20 September 1675, that the sober and wealthy people 'are fully satisfied and everybody bent on planting, which will be much improved by the arrival of these people from Surinam'. Moreover, he expected 'great numbers and some of the best quality from Barbados'.[6] From Africa came Negro slaves in growing numbers, especially after the formation of the Royal African Company in 1672. The Company's deliveries in Jamaica, which averaged 1,000 yearly from 1674 to 1680, rose to an average of 3,674 from 1681 to 1687. Yet the population cannot be said to have grown very rapidly before the 1680s. The census of 1673 returned only 7,768 whites and 9,504 Negroes.[7]

As the leader of the Barbadian immigrants, Sir Thomas Modyford is generally credited with the rise of Jamaica's plantation economy. He was Governor General of Jamaica from 1664 to 1670 and also Agent of the Royal Adventurers Trading to Africa. Part of his influence stemmed from his family connections, for his brother, Sir James Modyford, was Deputy Governor, Chief Judge of the Admiralty Court, and Collector of Customs; and his son Thomas Modyford acted as Major-General of the colony. Charles Modyford, another brother, was a wealthy London merchant and Jamaica's unofficial agent with influential friends at the court of Charles II.[8]

Less well founded is the legend that Modyford quickly transformed Jamaica into an island of great sugar estates. Realizing that few planters had the means to launch out on sugar, he advised them

5 Ibid., p. 164.
6 Ibid. *1675-76, Addenda 1574-1674*, p. 282.
7 K. G. Davies, *The Royal African Company* (London, 1957), p. 363; Bryan Edwards, *The History, Civil and Commercial, of the British Colonies in the West Indies* (Dublin, 1793), vol. 1, p. 232.
8 A. P. Thornton, *West-India Policy Under the Restoration* (Oxford, 1956), pp. 60–6, 149.

Sugar and Slavery

to begin slowly with inexpensive but profitable crops and accumulate capital to construct sugar works and augment their labour force. In particular, he stressed the merits of cacao cultivation, partly because of the growing popularity of the beverage in Europe, partly because the Spaniards had successfully grown cacao trees in Jamaica, and partly because such cultivation entailed a small outlay of capital and labour. Modyford himself had the best cacao walk in the island, and it was not until 1670 that he turned to sugar. While the Jamaicans also grew ginger, indigo, pimento, cotton, and sugar-cane, cacao was the island's leading staple for some years. Sir James Modyford informed a member of the Board of Trade on 21 February 1668, that cacao was 'the best commodity of this island, neither sugars, nor indigo will turn to account nearly so well'. However, the cacao boom was short-lived. In the summer of 1670 a blight set in which rapidly destroyed the trees.[9]

Besides the cacao blight, the decline of buccaneering after 1670 contributed to the rising star of sugar. When Sir Thomas Lynch succeeded Modyford as governor, he was instructed to pardon the buccaneers who submitted to His Majesty, 'and that if they will plant they shall have 35 acres by the head'. It is known, for example, that Henry Morgan invested part of the booty taken at Porto Bello and Panama in plantation property in Jamaica.[10]

Jamaica in the age of Modyford and Lynch was an island of 'many hopeful plantations'. The census of 1670 emumerated '57 sugar works, producing yearly 1,710 thousand weight of sugar; 47 cocoa walks, yielding 188,000 lb. of nuts . . .; 49 indigo works, producing 49,000 weight of indigo per annum, and other walks and works daily adding'.[11] Five years later, when there were seventy sugar works in production and forty more in great forwardness, it was claimed that 'a sugar work with 60 negroes will make more profit than one with 100 in any of the Carribbees, the soil being new, and well shaded with goodly woods'. Peter Beckford, a leading planter, wrote near the end of 1675 that 'no place the King has is more like to thrive, for they increase in planting to a miracle'. He estimated the number of planters to be about 3,000. By this time choice lands had been appropriated and there was 'no plantable land to be taken up near the sea on the south side'.[12]

Among the numerous Englishmen who carved plantations out of the wildwood of Jamaica was Cary Helyar, whose story has been

9 *Cal. S. P. Col. 1661–68*, p. 551; Ibid. *1669–74*, p. 426.
10 Ibid. *1669–74*, pp. 145–6; Clinton V. Black, *History of Jamaica* (London, 1958), p. 65.
11 *Cal. S. P. Col. 1669–74*, p. 104.
12 Ibid. *1675–76, Appendix 1574–1674*, pp. 311, 314; Ibid. *1669–74*, p. 251.

related by Professor Bennett.[13] Helyar was the younger brother of Squire William Helyar of East Coker, Somerset, who encouraged and helped finance Cary's ventures in trade and planting. Cary's first venture in trade with Spain and the Canary Islands proved unrewarding, and in 1664 he took ship for the frontier colony of Jamaica. Probably through the auspices of his brother, Cary found a patron in Sir Thomas Modyford, who set him up in business as a merchant. For several years he was a merchant at Port Royal, dealing in slaves, wines, cacao, sugar, logwood, and elephants' teeth. In the course of two years he sold 258 Negroes, his chief commodity in trade.[14]

Merchants commonly ploughed their profits into plantations, and in this respect Cary Helyar was no exception. In 1669, he began to acquire land, slaves, and equipment with a view to settling a cacao walk. Again, the powerful Governor came to his aid, granting Cary a sizeable tract of land, later given the name of 'Bybrook' plantation, adjacent to Modyford's cacao plantation at Sixteen Mile Walk in St Catherine's parish. By November 1670 Cary had twelve Negroes, one white servant, and about six acres planted in cacao trees. The cost of the undertaking, amounting to £346 5s 6d, was financed in part by Cary's trading profits and a small annuity he had from England. Another part came from Squire William, who, as partner, matched his brother's expenditures and arranged to send out servants and goods needed from England.[15]

When the blight destroyed his cacao trees, Cary turned his efforts to the formidable task of establishing a sugar plantation. He wrote to his brother in April 1671 to send out a cargo of milling equipment, informing him that capital put to sugar-canes would 'make a sweet business ... by the help of God'. Other letters recount the purchase of slaves, most of whom were financed by bills of exchange drawn on the Squire. Early in 1671 brother William began sending servants – mainly tradesmen – to serve four-year terms. 'Bybrook plantation was on the way to becoming East Coker's colony, a trend that the coming years only served to underline'.[16]

Cary Helyar died suddenly on 5 July 1672. Although no sugar had been made by that time, he left the substantial beginnings of a sugar plantation. According to Professor Bennett,

> By June 1672, Cary Helyar had constructed a dwelling house, had begun raising a water mill and sugar works for converting canes into sugar and rum, and had put 24 acres of land in sugar cane, 20 in pasture, and 16 in

---

13 J. Harry Bennett, 'Cary Helyar, Merchant and Planter of Seventeenth-Century Jamaica', *William and Mary Quarterly*, 3rd ser., vol. XXI, no. 1 (Jan. 1964), pp. 53–76.
14 Ibid., pp. 53–8.   15 Ibid., pp. 58–64.   16 Ibid., pp. 65–73.

Sugar and Slavery

provision crops. His labour force at the end of the period consisted of 55 Negroes, 14 white servants, and 5 horses. The Helyar brothers had expended some £1,857 on their venture.

Cary willed his half-interest in Bybrook to William Whaley, godson of Squire William, who had come to Jamaica to serve as book-keeper.[17]

To William Whaley fell the task of making Bybrook into a productive plantation unit. Less patient than his predecessor, Whaley sought at once to have all the buildings, equipment, and labour necessary for a maximum yield. In four years he doubled the slave force, in doing so drawing so heavily on Squire William's pocketbook that he was forbidden to draw any more bills. Though sugar was first made in 1675, more than half of the return went to pay for ten Negroes. Not until the harvest season following Whaley's death in July 1676 did Squire William receive his first small shipment of eight hogsheads of sugar. Notwithstanding the costly and frustrating task of building Bybrook, 'the Squire came in time to have a property, complete with 150 slaves and sugar works, that was capable of producing more than 200 hogsheads of sugar'.[18]

3 THE WAR YEARS, 1689–1713

After three decades of agricultural expansion, only in part interrupted by two Anglo-Dutch wars and buccaneering exploits, Jamaica suffered severe blows in the decade of the 1690s. First, came the violent earthquake of 1692 which killed more than 2,000 people and scarce left a planter's house or sugar works standing all over the island. Port Royal, the stronghold of the buccaneers and trading centre of the island, was overwhelmed by the earthquake and half-plunged into the sea. Next came a man-made disaster. Lying to leeward of the great island of Hispaniola, of which the western part was claimed by France, Jamaica was vulnerable to raids by buccaneers and warships. War broke out between England and France in 1689. Five years later Jamaica was attacked by three warships and twenty-three transports commanded by the French Admiral DuCasse. The forces landed in the easternmost parish and marched inland, burning cane fields, destroying over fifty sugar works, and carrying off about 1,300 slaves. 'The Country has fallen

17 J. Harry Bennett, 'Cary Helyar, Merchant and Planter of Seventeenth-Century Jamaica', *William and Mary Quarterly*, 3rd ser., vol. XXI, no. 1 (Jan. 1964), pp. 73–6; J. Harry Bennett, 'William Whaley, Planter of Seventeenth-Century Jamaica', *Agricultural History*, vol. XL, no. 2 (April 1966), pp. 113–14.
18 Bennett, 'Cary Helyar', p. 76.

in to a very low condition under the calamities of the past four years, by the taxes raised, and the want of trade', wrote Governor Beeston to the Board of Trade in 1695.[19]

By the opening of the 18th century Jamaica had recovered from the hardships of the 1690s. This was the opinion of Admiral Benbow, the English commander in the Caribbean, who wrote of Jamaica at the outbreak of the war with France and Spain in 1702:

> The Government of this Island now is entirely in the hands of Planters who mind nothing but getting Estates and when so to goe off, having no regard to the King's Interest or Subjects... The Inhabitants are grown very rich & value themselves for being Judges & Parties in making & executing their own Laws; they doe whatever the desire of Gain leads them to without any regard to the Laws of our Country.[20]

Although not invaded as in the previous war, the War of Spanish Succession (1702–13) involved Jamaica in shipping losses, interrupted trade, and military expenditures. Moreover, the island suffered from a destructive hurricane in August 1712. Prospects were brighter at the close of the war when Governor Hamilton wrote that 'the State of the Island is generally much improved of late, with respect to the Seasons; there being a very plentiful Crop of Sugars and Plantation-Provisions in most Parts thereof; which I hope may ease the Inhabitants of those Difficulties they lay under lately through the scarcity of both the one and the other'.[21]

For a partial view of Jamaica's plantation economy, we may turn to the *Inventory* series at the Jamaica Public Record Office at Spanish Town. These inventories, which were first recorded in 1674, are thought to have served as the basis for the assessment of a hereditaments tax. At the death of a property holder, two or more of the leading citizens of the deceased's parish inventoried his personal property, recording in some detail the sex, occupations, and appraised value of his Negro slaves, together with data on livestock and other movables. If we assume that the average plantation produced 35 tons of sugar, we find that there were 124 plantations in the 1701–5 period. Thus our sample of thirty plantations is about one-quarter of the total.

The plantations ranged widely in labour force and appraised value. Hannah Boarman's plantation contained 26 slaves, valued at £375; 38 head of livestock, valued at £195; and total personal property amounting to £1,061 15s 4½d. At the other extreme, Captain James

---

19 *Cal. S. P. Col. 1693–96*, p. 575; Black, *History of Jamaica*, pp. 70–7.
20 Public Record Office London. C.O. 137/45: Admiral Benbow to Sec. of State James Vernon, 1 June 1702.
21 Ibid., C.O. 137/10, f. 8: Gov. Archibald Hamilton to Board of Trade, 15 May 1713.

Sugar and Slavery

Banister had 236 slaves, valued at £6,496; 148 head of livestock, at £836; and total personal property of £7,945. Captain Thomas Cox had 198 slaves, valued at £5,259; 263 head of livestock, at £2,007; and a total of £8,337.[22]

The median plantation in terms of inventory valuation was that of John Reid. It contained 86 Negroes (27 men, 30 women, and 29 children), valued at £1,391; 65 head of livestock, at £344; and total inventory value of £2,443 4s 6d. If the value of the land and fixed structures was roughly equal to that of slaves, livestock, and other movables, then John Reid's plantation represented an investment of nearly £5,000. 'The ordinary computation is to lay out about 5,000 *l*. to raise a plantation that may yield 1,000 *l*. per annum, and a thousand acres is a competent proportion of land to accommodate such an estate', wrote Governor Lord Carlisle from Jamaica in 1681.[23]

Twenty-five of the plantations in the sample were individually owned, the other five having co-owners. John Burras, the proprietor of 'Mountain' and 'Withywood' plantations, had a total of 216 slaves and his inventory came to £6,430 16s 6d. Sir Thomas Modyford was the wealthiest proprietor in the group studied, leaving at his death in 1703 three plantations, a town house, and other personalty amounting to £11,327 9s 0d. His 'Prospect' plantation contained 95 Negroes (24 men, 31 women, 40 children), valued at £1,659; 145 head of livestock at £345, and a total of £2,677 1s 0d. On 'Angels' plantation there were 178 Negroes (43 men, 63 women, 72 children), valued at £2,783; 169 head of livestock, at £925; and a total of £3,789. 'Palmers Hut' plantation, valued at £4,325 15s 6d, had 174 Negroes (47 men, 69 women, and 58 children), valued at £3,126; and 87 head of livestock, at £894. Modyford was among the elite planters who maintained an establishment at Spanish Town or St Jago de la Vega, the seat of colonial government. Besides his household furnishings, his great house at St Jago contained six coach horses and one old chariot, six house Negroes, three young pickaninnies, and 'Phyllis'.[24]

4 LAGGARD GROWTH, 1714–39

During the century from 1673 to 1774 the white population of Jamaica increased by a little more than two-fold, slaves by some twenty-fold, livestock by more than nineteen-fold, and sugar

22 Jamaica Public Record Office, Spanish Town. *Inventorys*, vols. 5 and 6.
23 *Cal. S. P. Col. 1681–85*, p. 167.
24 J.P.R.O., Spanish Town, *Inventorys*, vol. 6, ff. 81–8, 151–2.

plantations by nearly fourteen-fold. The whites increased from about 7,800 to 18,000, the black and mulattoes from 9,500 to 197,000, livestock from an estimated 10,000 to 193,000, and sugar plantations from 57 to 775.[25] In 1670, the 57 sugar estates in Jamaica produced 1,710,000lb of sugar (or 763 tons), which yielded approximately £23,000 sterling at the London market. Other staples probably yielded as much as sugar, bringing total exports to about £46,000 sterling. From this small beginning, aggregate exports to the mother country rose to an estimated annual average of £325,000 in 1701–4, £652,000 in 1736–40, £1,025,000 in 1751–5, and £2,400,000 in 1771–5.[26]

The ratio of whites to blacks, which was 1 to 1.1 in 1673, declined to 1 to 6.4 in 1703, and to 1 to 9.9 in 1739, after which it remained nearly steady. Slaves engaged in sugar production and related activities increased until they made up about 80 per cent of the Negro population. The absolute and proportionate increase of the labour force on sugar plantations is reflected in the rising level of production. From an average output of 11.8 tons of sugar per plantation in 1670, the figure rose to 56.6 tons in 1774. Moreover, the uneven growth rate is reflected in the value of the island's exports. Compared with the two-fold increase from 1703 to 1739, there was a 3.7-fold increase in the period 1739–75.[27]

Down to the mid-century period the slow growth of Jamaica was a matter of widespread concern, if not of much remedial action. Grocers and sugar refiners in England contended that sugar prices were abnormally high because the planters of Jamaica entered into collusive agreements to restrict production. Planters, in turn, held the South Sea Company and its factors responsible for manipulating the slave trade to their disadvantage. Merchants, government officials, and smallholders complained that sugar planters dominated the colonial government and used their influence to secure generous land grants and other favours. Amidst the bickering and quarrelling among the whites, a number of slaves ran off to the wild interior and thus may be said to have voted their displeasure with their feet. Wars undoubtedly had some impact, but it is significant that the economy grew slowly during the years of peace from 1713 to 1739, while the subsequent period of surging growth was punctuated by three inter-

25 Noel Deerr, *The History of Sugar* (London, 1949–50), vol. 1, pp. 176–98; Frank W. Pitman, *The Development of the British West Indies 1700–1763* (New Haven, 1917), pp. 373–8; George W. Roberts, *The Population of Jamaica* (Cambridge, 1957), pp. 33–6.
26 P.R.O. London. C.O. 137/19, S 124, ff. 46–9; *Cal. S. P. Col. 1669–74*, p. 104; Deerr, *History of Sugar*, vol. 1, pp. 176–98; Edward Long, *The History of Jamaica* (London, 1774), vol. 1, p. 301; Edwards, *History of British West Indies*, vol. 2, p. 466.
27 Long, *History of Jamaica*, vol. 1, p. 301; Deer, *History of Sugar*, vol. 1, pp. 176–98.

Sugar and Slavery

national conflicts. Rather than war, it was the secular decline of the sugar market that retarded growth and set the stage for inter-group conflict.

The conflict between the South Sea Company and the planters and traders of Jamaica had its origin in the Treaty of Utrecht, by which the Company was awarded the *Asiento* to supply the Spanish colonies with 4,800 slaves annually, together with other trading privileges. Previous to this contract, the port of Kingston had a lively trading community and some twenty-five or thirty sloops which carried slaves and manufactures to the Spanish Main and returned with bullion and tropical goods. Many of the merchants and factors were displaced by the South Sea Company's factors who resided at Kingston and handled the trans-shipment of slaves and manufactures. William Wood, who before 1713 was a resident slave trader as well as the island's Secretary, warned of the dangerous consequences of the South Sea Company to Jamaica, 'by ruining its Trade, and consequently preventing its *encreasing* in People and New Settlements'.[28]

Joining the merchants in complaints against the South Sea Company were the planters, who contended that the greater part of the imported slaves were purchased and resold by the Company's factors to the Spaniards, thus narrowing the market and driving up prices charged to local buyers. 'The Asiento', declared Governor Lawes, 'carries all the able, stout, and Young Negroes ... to the Spaniards and Sell none to the planters but old, Sickly, and decrepid, or what are called Refuse ...'. For choice Negroes the planters had to 'give as much or more than the Spaniards, & that is ready Money ...'.[29] Annual import and re-export statistics show that in eight of the years from 1716 to 1735, more Negroes were re-exported than retained in Jamaica. Expressed in five-year annual averages, the re-exported and retained figures are respectively: 2,850 and 2,065 for 1716–20; 3,302 and 2,889 for 1721–5; 3,329 and 4,978 for 1726–30; and 4,020 and 4,073 for 1731–5.[30] These figures do not necessarily support the planters' case, however, since there is some merit in the South Sea Company's contention that, in the absence of the stimulus it gave to the African trade, the planters would have been less well supplied with servile labour.

Another reason given for laggard growth was the proclivity of the planters to engross lands far in excess of their needs. Whatever their

28 Wood, *Survey of Trade*, p. 285.
29 P.R.O. London. C.O. 137/12, O 178: Sir Nicholas Lawes to Board of Trade, 11 Nov. 1717.
30 Ibid., C.O. 137/38, Hh 3, 4: Stephen Fuller, Agent for Jamaica, to Board of Trade, 30 Jan. 1778.

Table 10.1

Frequency distribution of landholders in Jamaica, 1670 and 1754

Acres	Landholders in 1670	Landholders in 1754
0–99	384	263
100–499	238	566
500–999	55	303
1,000–1,999	34	253
2,000–4,999	11	153
5,000–9,999	2	52
10,000–22,999	0	9
Total	724	1599

Source: *Cal. S. P. Col. 1669–74*, pp. 99–103: Gov. Sir Thomas Modyford to Sec. Lord Arlington, inclosing a *Survey of the Island of Jamaica*, 23 Sept. 1670; P.R.O., London. C.O. 142/31: 'A List of Landholders in the Island of Jamaica together with the number of Acres each Person Possesses, taken from the Quit Rent Books in the Year 1754'. Received with Gov. Knowles letter dated 31 Dec. 1754.

motives, it is clear from Table 10.1 that the greater part of the lands came to be held by a numerous class of large planters.

Table 10.1 shows a tendency for the smallholders who held from 0 to 99 acres to decline in number, while the large proprietors, especially those holding 1,000 acres or more, increased both absolutely and relatively. According to Governor Modyford's survey of 1670, there were 189,020 acres patented by 724 proprietors in the six settled parishes on the south side of Jamaica. Of these, 47 individuals (or 6.5 per cent) possessed 1,000 acres or more, and their holdings in the aggregate amounted to 80,386 (or 42.5 per cent) of the patented acres. By contrast, the Quit Rent Book for 1754 records a total of 1,671,569 acres patented by 1,599 proprietors in nineteen parishes. Of these, 467 individuals (or 29.2 per cent) possessed 1,000 acres or more, and their holdings in the aggregate amounted to 1,299,824 (or 77.8 per cent) of the acreage patented. A considerable number of proprietors thus held acreages sufficient for sugar estates by 1754; one-half held 500 acres or more, and more than one-fourth held 1,000 or more acres.

Sugar and Slavery

Three economic motives would appear to stand uppermost in explaining the tendency for large tracts to be appropriated by the sugar planters. The first was to realize profits from land speculation, the second was to enable proprietors to produce low-cost sugar by employing capital and labour in an extensive manner of production, and the third was to limit the number of planters and their output of sugar with a view toward raising prices in the metropolis. William Wood implored the planters of Jamaica to 'lay aside the false and narrow Notions and Schemes, entertain'd by too many of *them*; such as *that* the *Produce* of their *Plantations* will *sell* the *better*, the *fewer the Settlements*, which induces them to *Engross* great Tracts of *Land*'.[31] In the absence of any collective effort — such as a cartel agreement — to restrict production, it is doubtful if the planters exerted much influence on prices in the short run, although their efforts may have been partly successful in the long run.

On the other hand, considering the ease with which grants were secured and the low cost of holding reserve tracts, freer rein was given to motives of speculation and extensive production. Jamaican overseers, according to Edward Long, considered the number of acres they could annually overspread with cane plants as the surest test of their ability, 'without reflecting, that extraordinary pains, bestowed on half the quantity, would yield an equal crop'. Many planters were said to have worn out their land by incessant cultivation, 'and, after throwing it up, pass on to a new piece, which is destined to be worked to the bone in the same manner; and very few of them understand the method of preparing suitable composts for their land'.[32]

Holding large tracts of uncultivated land, planters might be expected to be self-sufficient in Negro provisions and livestock. Governor Hunter wrote in 1731 that self-sufficiency was both feasible and desirable, 'but the Inhabitants are so Intent upon making of Sugars which it seems turn to better Account, that they Chuse rather to Purchase those Commoditys [flour, bread, corn, beef, pork, butter, salt-fish, rice, staves, lumber, and horses] from their Neighbours than to Employ their own Slaves in that work . . .'.[33]

The dilemma confronting Jamaica was that while a large European population was needed to control the mounting number of slaves and defend the island in wartime, the plantation economy was tending toward monoculture and taking away the livelihood of smallholders and artisans. In an effort to counteract the disadvantages stemming

31 Wood, *Survey of Trade*, p. 172.
32 Long, *History of Jamaica*, vol. 1, pp. 440–1.
33 P.R.O. London. C.O. 137/19, f. 47: Gov. Hunter to Board of Trade, 24 Dec. 1731.

Jamaica, The Fairest Island

from a system of great estates, the island government began, about 1720, to enact legislation designed to encourage white settlers to occupy lands formerly patented but never settled or cultivated. These lands, at least in certain parts of the island, were vested in the Crown and then regranted to immigrants on a headright basis up to a maximum of 300 or 400 acres to a family. At the insistence of the English government the legislature appropriated some £17,300 between 1739 and 1752 to encourage immigration and land settlement. When these schemes failed to achieve any significant results, the legislature sought to revive and strengthen acts compelling planters to maintain a certain ratio of Europeans to Africans on their estates. Numerous 'deficiency laws' levied stiff penalties on planters who failed to maintain a proportionate number of white servants. Planters generally complied with these laws during the Maroon Wars, it is said, but afterwards they preferred to pay the 'penalty of 13 *l*. or at most 26 *l*. for every default ... rather than disburse 40 *l*. or 50 *l*. for the wages and maintenance of every servant'.[34]

Failure to maintain a safe ratio of whites to blacks was both cause and effect of the slave rebellion which plagued the white community from 1730 to 1739, and gave a serious check to the extension of sugar culture. The enemy within were the Maroons, originally freed or runaway Spanish Negro slaves who found refuge in the rugged interior. After the conquest of 1655, the Maroons were joined by slaves who escaped from their English masters in growing numbers. Instead of settling peaceably in the interior, they frequently swept down on frontier plantations to burn, raid, and kill. For a time in the 1730s Jamaica was an armed camp. The local Assembly and Council wrote to the King on 19 March 1737: 'The slaves in rebellion which have cost so many lives and so much expense continue as insolent, troublesome, and we believe as numerous as ever'.[35] British regiments, local militia, Mosquito Coast Indians, and bloodhounds were mobilized to comb the mountain fastnesses and search out the elusive Maroon. Finally, a formal peace was agreed to in 1739 between the English commissioners and Captain Cudjoe, the Maroon leader. The rebels received their freedom, 1,500 acres of land, and limited autonomy within their territory. The real significance of the treaty was that the Maroons agreed to return all runaway slaves, thus effectively sealing off the interior of the island as a refuge for escaped Negroes.[36]

---

34 Long, *History of Jamaica*, vol. 1, pp. 381–2. For a discussion of the colonization schemes which were attempted in Jamaica, see Pitman, *Development of British West Indies*, pp. 108–26.
35 *Cal. S. P. Col. 1737*, p. 79.
36 Black, *History of Jamaica*, pp. 74–5, 83–7.

Sugar and Slavery

5 EXPANSION AND GROWTH, 1740-75

Just as the low state of the sugar market had been the most pervasive factor in Jamaica's slow growth and internal dissension down to about 1740, so it was that the subsequent expansion of the economy came in response to a rising market. Problems which had seemed intractable in the years of adversity now appeared as obstacles of little moment. Measures to encourage immigration met with a positive response, especially by planters from the Lesser Antilles and by young men out of Scotland. As an active land market developed, a growing proportion of the hitherto unsettled lands were either cultivated by patentees or sold to newcomers at a speculative profit. Negro rebellions, such as the insurrection in St Mary's parish in 1760, were less frequent and more quickly suppressed. Slaves were not only imported in greater numbers but a higher proportion were also purchased by Jamaicans. Expressed as five-year annual averages, the number of re-exported slaves ranged from 558 to 1,376 in the period from 1736 to 1775, while the retained slaves ranged from 4,991 to 8,068.[37]

The territorial expansion of the plantations was largely a movement from the eastern and south-central to the western and northern portions of the island. Jamaica in the period of this study was divided into three counties and nineteen parishes. From east to west the counties were Surrey, which contained 383,350 acres; Middlesex, 955,855 acres; and Cornwall, 771,473 acres. The expansion and geographical distribution of the sugar plantations in the period 1739-86 are shown in Table 10.2.

6 LIGUANEA PARISH, 1753

Professor Pitman has analysed the census data of 1753 for St Andrew or Liguanea parish in county Surrey. This parish, which was one of the first to be organized and exploited for its agricultural resources, adjoins the port of Kingston on the south coast and is about fifteen miles broad and twelve miles in depth.

> The total number of estates in the parish in 1753 was 154. They range in size from the little truck garden of Benjamin Israel containing three acres, ten slaves, and two head of cattle, to the broad acres of Philip Pinnock, the

---

37 P.R.O. London. C.O. 137/38, Hh 3, 4: Stephen Fuller to Board of Trade, 30 Jan. 1778. See Appendix IX for slave imports and re-exports.

Table 10.2

Expansion and distribution of sugar plantations, Jamaica, 1739–86

County	1739	1768	1772	1786	Increase 1739–86
Surrey	78	144	178	350	272
Middlesex	198	239	253	323	125
Cornwall	143	265	344	388	245
Total	419	648	775	1,061	642

Source: British Museum Add. MSS 12,431, f. 123; 14,435, ff. 31–2; Noel Deerr, *The History of Sugar* (London, 1949–50), vol. 1, p. 176; Bryan Edwards, *The History of the British West Indies* (5th ed., 1819), vol. 1, pp. 312–14.

show place of Jamaica, containing 2,872 acres, of which 242 were under sugar cane yielding 140 hogsheads a year, and equipped with 16 white servants, 280 slaves, and 326 head of cattle.[38]

Of the 154 estates in Liguanea parish, 128 produced no sugar but were engaged on a moderate scale in raising provisions, coffee, ginger, cotton, and livestock. In total acreage, the 26 sugar plantations ranged from 257 to 2,872; in cane acreage, from 5 to 310; in white servants, from 1 to 16; in Negroes, from 30 to 280; and in cattle, from 0 to 326. Eight sugar estates had no land devoted to provisions and pasture and two reported no cattle. Provision acres ranged from 10 to 250, and pasture or pen from 4 to 1,000. Sixteen estates had woodlands which ranged from 33 to 1,100 acres. Sugar-monoculture was the rule, for only three of the twenty-six estates had small acreages devoted to coffee, ginger, and cotton. If all but the largest of the estates are ranked according to the number of slaves, the median sugar estate in Liguanea parish contained 600 acres, of which 120 were in canes, 200 in provisions, 30 in pasture, and 250 in woodland; together with 3 white servants, 123 Negro slaves, and 65 head of cattle.[39]

---

38 Frank W. Pitman, 'The Settlement and Financing of British West India Plantations in the Eighteenth Century', in *Essays in Colonial History Presented to Charles M. Andrews* (New Haven, 1931), p. 262.
39 Ibid., pp. 261–70.

Sugar and Slavery

7 THE DAWKINS' ESTATES

From reputedly humble circumstances, the Dawkins family rose to affluence and political and social standing, both in Jamaica and England. One knowledgeable Jamaican wrote that the family came from Leicestershire, and that the immigrant, one William Dawkins, 'was an overseer here first'.[40] The land grant records at Spanish Town show that several members of the family were in Jamaica by the 1660s. John Dawkins was granted 28 acres in St Andrew's parish in 1665. Other grants were made to Ann, Henry, and especially William Dawkins, who received 1,775 acres in the years from 1669 to 1682. William held a commission as Lieutenant in the Militia. After he was killed fighting against the French invaders in 1694, his estate descended to his son Richard.[41]

Richard Dawkins added to his father's holdings, became a substantial planter, and served as Colonel of Militia and assemblyman. His election to the Assembly from Clarendon parish in Middlesex county probably enhanced his opportunities to secure land grants. The land patent index shows that he received upwards of 1,300 acres in Clarendon parish. At his death in 1701, Richard Dawkins left personal property valued at £6,659 13s 6d in Jamaica currency, consisting of 143 Negroes 'young and old', valued at £2,784; sugars consigned to merchants in London and Bristol, £1,192 16s 0d; cattle, horses, and mares, £829; ready money in the hands of Mr Jenkins at Port Royal, £704 9s 9d; and miscellaneous items, including plate, furniture, sugar pots, and plantation tools valued at £1,149 7s 9d.[42]

The substantial foothold established by William and Richard was expanded greatly in the third generation by Henry Dawkins (1698–1744), son and heir of Richard Dawkins. By his marriage to Elizabeth, daughter of Edward Pennant, Henry formed an alliance with one of the island's great planter families. He was elected to the Assembly from the parish of Vere in 1728, and called to the Council in 1732. As with his father and grandfather, Henry added much to the family's landholdings. The Quit Rent Book for 1754 shows that Henry's three surviving sons together held 24,927 acres. William, the third son, held 4,874 acres; Henry, the fourth son, 5,761; and James,

---

40 Rev. William May, Rector of Kingston, 'Jamaica: Description of the Principal Persons there', circa 1720. Reprinted in *Caribbeana*, ed. Vere L. Oliver, vol. 3 (London, 1914), p. 6.
41 J.P.R.O. Spanish Town, *Index to Patents*, vols. 2–9; *Burke's Genealogical and Heraldic History of the Landed Gentry*, ed. L. G. Pine, 17th ed. (London, 1952), pp. 629–30.
42 J.P.R.O. Spanish Town, *Index to Patents*, vols. 9–12; *Inventorys*, vol. 5, f. 119; W. A Feurtado, *Official and Other Personages of Jamaica, From 1655 to 1790* (Jamaica, 1896), pp. 26–7.

Jamaica, The Fairest Island

the eldest son and chief heir, 14,294 acres, of which 12,862 were in Clarendon, and 1,432 in the neighbouring parish of Vere.[43]

That Henry Dawkins stocked his lands with great numbers of slaves, livestock, and other movables is evident from the inventory of his estate on 23 January 1745. Altogether, his personal property in Jamaica and produce consigned to England amounted to £116,727 12s 2½d Jamaica currency (approximately £76,200 sterling). Of this sum, £38,728 12s 10d consisted of debts owing to his estate in Jamaica; £9,530 10s 0d for four cattle ranches or pens; £59,503 9s 4½d for eight sugar plantations; and £8,965 for sugar and rum undisposed of at the time of his death. Slaves and livestock made up the greater part of the personalty on his plantations and pens. Indeed, Dawkins and his wife and children owned a total of 1,013 Negro slaves, valued at £40,736; and 1,813 head of livestock, valued at £19,865. If his realty was equal to the inventory value of the personalty invested in sugar properties, then Henry Dawkins' property in Jamaica was in the neighbourhood of £100,000 sterling.[44]

Dawkins must have been sorely taxed to manage such a vast estate, consisting of plantations, pens, and warehouses situated in the three contiguous parishes of Clarendon, Vere, and St Elizabeth. In part, he coped with his management problem by entering into partnership agreements with capable young men of little capital; in part, by leasing estates or parts of estates. The inventory shows that Dawkins held about a three-quarters equity in the eight sugar properties which were valued in Jamaica currency at £62,477 15s 0d. Ranked according to the size of the labour force, 'Windsor' was his smallest plantation with 47 slaves and an inventory value of £3,126 10s 0d. 'Trout Hall' came next with 67 slaves and £5,215, followed by 'One Eye' with 71 slaves and £4,681 10s 0d. 'Leicester Fields' and 'Green River', each with 99 slaves, were valued respectively at £3,422 and £6,009. Then there were three large plantations: 'Friendship' with 221 slaves and a total inventory value of £9,916 5s 0d; 'Parnassus' with 280 slaves and £13,190; and 'Old Plantation' with 371 slaves and £16,887 10s 9d.[45]

Supplementing the Spanish Town papers are the Dawkins manuscripts at the Institute of Jamaica in Kingston. One book entitled 'Jamaica Title Deeds' carries the subtitle 'An Account of all the Lands belonging to or in the Possession of Henry Dawkins Esqr (circa 1764)'. Each parcel of land making up the plantation and pen pro-

43 P.R.O. London. C.O. 142/31: Quit Rent Book for 1754.
44 J.P.R.O. Spanish Town, *Inventorys*, vol. 26, ff. 23–32.
45 Idem.

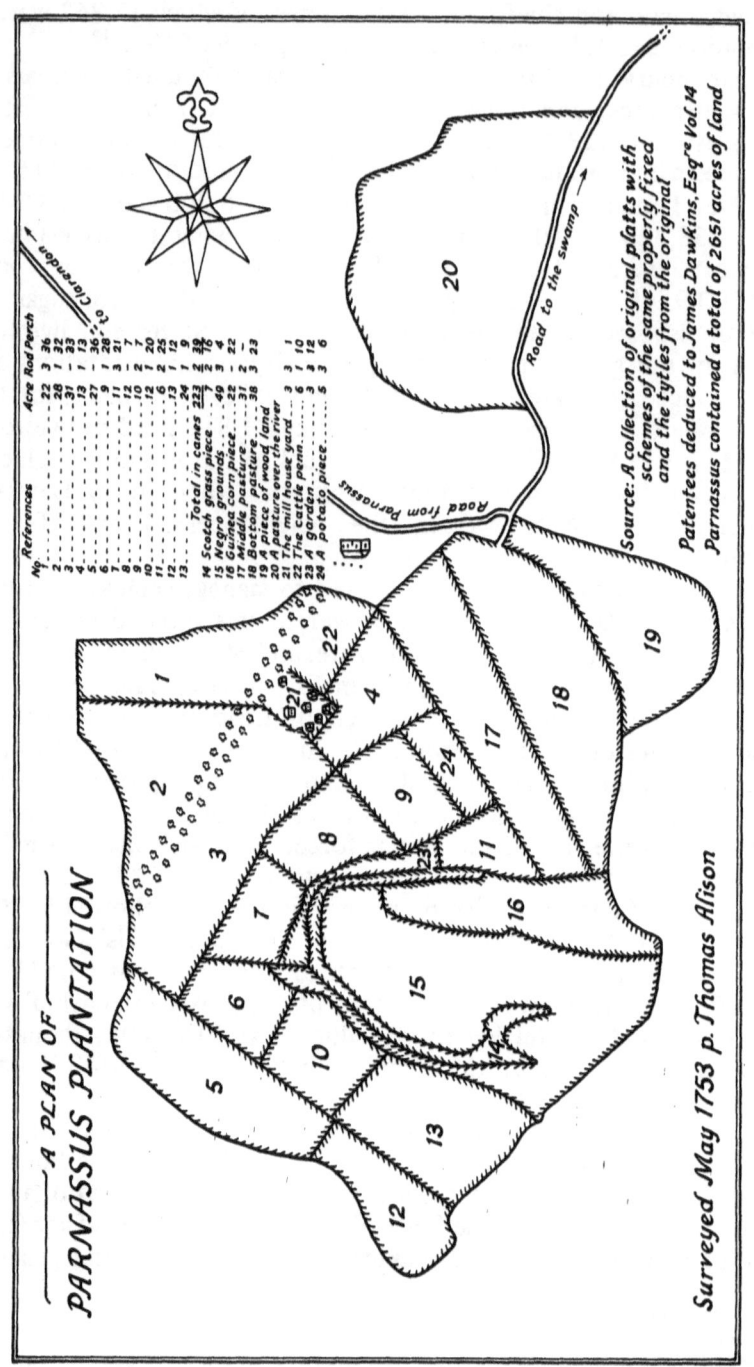

Jamaica, The Fairest Island

perties is listed separately, together with the date of acquisition, the names of former owners or Dawkins' grantees, the acreage patented, and the acreage given in. Though Crown grants to the Dawkins clan were extensive, even more land was acquired from some ninety individuals in tracts ranging from 2 to 2,800 acres. The title deed record gives the patented acreages of the sugar plantations as follows: Tredway, 5,270; Old Plantation, 2,779; Windsor, 2,680; Parnassus, 2,648; Suttons, 2,565; Friendship, 2,366; Pittney, 1,631; and Caymanas, 1,500.[46]

After Henry Dawkins' death in 1744, the scene shifts from Jamaica to England where his sons and grandsons used the family's great income to support contests for seats in Parliament, marriage alliances with aristocratic families, and the acquisition of landed estates. Gross income from the Jamaican properties amounted to upwards of £44,000 sterling in 1775, a better than average year. James Dawkins, eldest son and heir of Henry, was M.P. for Hinden, Wilts., and a great traveller. He discovered the ruins of Palmyra and Baalbec. Henry Dawkins, the fourth son, of Over Norton, Oxfordshire, and Standlynch Park, Wilts., was for many years M.P. for Southampton and Chippenham. In the next generation, three of Henry's grandsons – James, George Hay, and Henry – were parliamentarians. George Hay Dawkins, of Penrhyn Castle, North Wales, succeeded to the estate of his father's cousin Richard Lord Penrhyn in 1808, at which time he added to his own the surname and arms of Pennant.[47]

8 WILLIAM BECKFORD, PLANTER-HISTORIAN

Westmoreland, at the western extremity of Jamaica, was a parish of great sugar estates in the third quarter of the 18th century. William Beckford, the planter-historian and leading proprietor of the parish, wrote of the salubrity of the climate and the fertility of the soil. 'This parish has an advantage over the rest of the Island in its seasons, and in the number of its streams; and is in point of situation as agreeable as any spots in Italy, that have the advantage of a Salvatore Rosa, or a Poussin to perpetuate their beauties'.[48] According to the poll tax roll of 1768, Westmoreland had sixty-nine plantations which

---

46 Institute of Jamaica, Kingston. *Jamaica Title Deeds*, c. 1764.
47 *Burke's Landed Gentry*, pp. 629–30: *Penrhyn Castle, Bangor, Caernarvonshire* (London, Country Life Ltd., 1955), pp. 3–11; J.P.R.O. Spanish Town, *Account Produce*, vol. 6, f. 105; vol. 7, f. 282.
48 *An Unpublished Letter of William Beckford of Hertford*, Edited with an introduction by Thomas B. Brumbaugh, Jamaica Monograph No. 17, p. 6.

produced annually 8,000 hogsheads of sugar and accounted for 11,280 of the 15,196 Negroes in the parish. St Andrew, by comparison, had thirty plantations which produced 2,600 hogsheads and claimed 4,212 of the 9,813 parish Negroes in 1768.[49]

Although their holdings were scattered over eleven of the nineteen parishes in Jamaica, the Beckford brothers – William, the Lord Mayor, Richard, Julines, and Francis – possessed more acres in Westmoreland than in any other parish. In fact, the Quit Rent Book for 1754 shows that of the brothers' holdings in Jamaica of 42,075 acres, 13,516 were situated in Westmoreland parish.[50]

On 19 August 1756, three planters of Westmoreland parish and two other planters of St Catherine parish were instructed by the Governor to inventory and appraise the goods and chattels of Richard Beckford, late of the Kingdom of Great Britain. The *Inventory* records show that Richard Beckford held four sugar plantations in fee simple, one in other leasehold tenure, a cattle pen, a storehouse, a house in Spanish Town, several unattached slaves, and debts on the security of bonds, notes and open account to the aggregate sum of £83,286 12s 4d Jamaica currency. The five sugar plantations, all situated in Westmoreland parish, accounted for nearly one-half of the inventory valuation and 844 of the 910 Negro slaves. Other assets listed in the inventory but not carried to the total because their value could only be estimated were produce shipped to England on consignment, £40,807; and sterling debts due in England, £3,600. Beckford's landholdings were reported in 1754 as 588 acres in St Catherine parish and 6,995 in Westmoreland parish. If we add to the above personal property £40,000 as the estimated value of lands and fixed capital structures, the total of Beckford's estate comes to approximately £168,000 Jamaica currency, or £120,000 sterling.[51]

William Beckford[52] was Richard Beckford's only son and heir. The *Account Produce* records at Spanish Town show that William came into possession of his Jamaican estate upon reaching his majority in 1765. In the following year his three plantations – 'Roaring River', 'Fort William', and 'Williamsfield' – produced 450 hogsheads and one tierce of sugar and 219 puncheons of rum. The

49 British Museum Add. MSS 14,435, ff. 31–2.
50 P.R.O. London. C.O. 142/31: Quit Rent Book for 1754.
51 Richard B. Sheridan, 'Planter and Historian: The Career of William Beckford of Jamaica and England, 1744–1799', *The Jamaican Historical Review*, vol. IV (1964), pp. 37–45.
52 There were three William Beckfords in the period of this study: the Lord Mayor of London and Member of Parliament; his son and heir, the eccentric author of Vathek and builder of Fonthill Abbey; and the subject of this sketch. See Boyd Alexander, *England's Wealthiest Son, A Study of William Beckford* (London, 1962).

Jamaica, The Fairest Island

aggregate value of his account produce in 1766 was £12,727 0s 8d Jamaica currency, of which all but £280 11s 1d was attributed to his three sugar plantations. By this time the produce of his estates had declined to less than a third of their value in 1756. Mismanagement may have accounted for part of this decline, but the greater part was probably owing to the conversion of 'Smithfield and Hatfield' sugar plantation into a cattle pen and the expiration of the lease on 'Shrewsbury' Estate.[53]

William Beckford and his wife came out to Jamaica in 1774 and lived at Hertford Pen for nearly thirteen years. His subsequent career as a planter, historian, and art patron has been chronicled elsewhere. Suffice it to say that he met with misfortunes, including a series of destructive hurricanes, was incarcerated in Fleet prison as a debtor, turned to writing, and died on 5 February 1799. Ironically, Beckford's property stayed in the family, for his principal creditor, to whom his plantations were conveyed as mortgagee, was his cousin Richard Beckford, a London sugar merchant.[54]

9 THE WEALTH OF JAMAICA

Altogether, 502 sugar estate inventories have been extracted from the records at Spanish Town in the period from 1741 to 1775.[55] For the thirty-five year period, the median inventory value is £6,268. This compares with £3,819 in the 1741–5 period, and £9,361 in the 1771–5 period. Median inventories in the terminal periods are summarized in Table 10.3.

It is evident from Table 10.3 that there was a remarkable increase in the movable property on the median Jamaica sugar plantation. Total inventory valuation increased nearly two and a half times, all of which increase is accounted for by the labour force. Negroes not only more than doubled in number, but their average value increased by 76 per cent. A cursory inspection of the inventories reveals wide variation in the sex and age composition of the labour force and the ratio of slaves to livestock, so that it cannot be assumed that these median estates were necessarily typical of other estates of comparable value.

Slaves, livestock, and utensils thus comprised the personal property, but sugar plantations also included land, growing canes,

53 Sheridan, 'Planter and Historian', pp. 45–7.
54 Ibid., pp. 47–59.
55 R. B. Sheridan, 'The Wealth of Jamaica in the Eighteenth Century', *The Economic History Review*, 2nd ser., vol. XVIII, no. 2 (Aug. 1965), pp. 292–301.

Table 10.3

Personal property inventories of median sugar estates, Jamaica, 1741–5 and 1771–5

	Number	Average value*	Total value*
1741–5			
Negro men	32	£29 16s	£953
Negro women	34	20 9s	696
Negro children	33	13 15s	453
Total Negroes	99	21 5s	2,102
Livestock	160	9 8s	1,508
Utensils			209
Inventory total			£3,819
1771–5			
Negro men	73	£48 11s	£3,545
Negro women	71	38 6s	2,721
Negro children	60	22 18s	1,375
Total Negroes	204	37 6s	7,641
Livestock	174	7 19s	1,380
Utensils			340
Inventory total			£9,361

* Jamaica currency values are converted into sterling at the ratio of 1.4 to 1.

Source: Jamaica Public Record Office, Spanish Town, *Inventorys*, vol. 26, ff. 29–31; vol. 50, ff. 177–9.

and fixed structures. Realty must thus be added to personalty to arrive at total estate valuation. Contemporary calculations which bear the mark of authority can be found in Edward Long's *History of Jamaica*. He estimated the cost of settling two plantations, one yielding 100 hogsheads of sugar and 50 puncheons of rum, the other 300 hogsheads and 150 puncheons. Table 10.4 shows the average of these two estimates.

Realty made up 52 per cent and personalty 48 per cent of the value of a representative plantation. Applying these percentages to the data in Table 10.3, we find that the median sugar plantation in

Table 10.4

Estimate of a medium-sized sugar plantation, Jamaica, 1774

	Number	Average value*	Total value*	
Total acres	600	£10 0s	£6,001	
(Acres in canes)	(266)	(16 1s)	(4,273)	
Sugar works, etc.			3,962	
Total realty				£9,963
Negroes	200	35 14s	7,140	
Livestock	95	15 9s	1,495	
Utensils, etc.			429	
Total personalty				9,064
Inventory total				£19,027

* Jamaica currency values are converted into sterling at the ratio of 1.4 to 1.

Source: Edward Long, *The History of Jamaica* (3 vols., London, 1774), vol. 1, pp. 456–63.

the 1741–5 period amounted to £7,956, while that of 1771–5 came to £19,502, a figure which is remarkably close to the one shown in Table 10.4.

Computing the aggregate value of the island's sugar economy is a simple matter of multiplying these median values times the number of plantations, that is, 440 in 1741–5, and 775 in 1771–5. Thus, the plantations, which were valued at £3,500,640 in 1741–5, had increased by more than four-fold to a figure of £15,115,050 in 1771–5.

Though the sugar estates comprised the greater part of Jamaica's wealth, additional wealth took such forms as cattle pens, small staple and provision farms, trading stocks, buildings, and ships. One partial measure of this secondary category of wealth is afforded by the slave population not attached to sugar plantations. The poll tax roll in 1768 listed 67,850 Negroes employed in coffee, cotton, ginger, pimento, and other plantations and establishments, of which 5,799 resided in the port of Kingston. Another 99,062 Negroes were attached to sugar plantations. Thus four out of every ten Negroes were in a

Sugar and Slavery

non-sugar category.[56] If valued at £35 each, the Negroes in this category amounted to £2,374,820. Based on inventory valuation, it is thus apparent that the total wealth of Jamaica in the years prior to the American War of Independence was in the neighbourhood of £18 million sterling.[57]

10 CONCLUSION

Despite some progress in arresting the racial imbalance and augmenting the cultivators of minor staples and provisions, Jamaica remained essentially an island of large sugar plantations and cattle ranches down to the outbreak of the American Revolution. After his short visit in Antigua, Lord Adam Gordon joined his regiment in Jamaica in June 1764. Upon completing an extensive tour of the island, he wrote that the sugar plantations were most frequent in the lands that occupied seven or ten miles of the coast, 'and are extremely rich, altho' the expence of Stock, and of Wear and Tear, is much greater than what attends any other kind of Estate, particularly when Negroes are at a high price'. He found the gentlemen of property residing on the island to be in general 'extremely civil and remarkably hospitable to Strangers', but he also observed that 'the generality of its Inhabitants look upon themselves there as passengers only, for which reason, all their attention is bestowed on their Plantations of Canes, from whence Sugar, Rum and Molasses are produced – these are the Staple Commodities, to this may be added Coffee, Pimento, some Ginger and some Cotton'.[58]

Other observers of longer experience in the island were impressed with the remarkable expansion of the plantation economy. Sir William Trelawney, Governor of Jamaica, reported in 1770 that the county of Cornwall in the western part of the island was so much improved as to make three-sevenths of the whole produce of the island.

> He also represented the prosperity of the north side of the island to be so much advanced by the great number of plantations within ten miles of the sea, and by the increase of commerce at the free ports of Montego bay and Lucea, as to be well worthy of the special protection of government by stationing some ships of war at Port Antonio.... Very large and fruitful pens are now in the neighbourhood, sufficient to supply with vegetables

---

56 B.M. Add. MSS 14,435, ff. 31–2.
57 Sheridan, 'Wealth of Jamaica', pp. 302–11.
58 Lord Adam Gordon, 'Journal of an Officer in the West Indies, 1764–65', in *Travels in the American Colonies,* ed. Newton D. Mereness (New York, 1916), pp. 378–80.

and cattle any number of ships stationed there: and considerable grants of money have been made by the assembly, and expended in making good roads from that port [Montego Bay] to the southern part of the island.[59]

Edward Long drew attention to the Act of 1749, by which £54,000 was appropriated over a nine-year period to encourage settlement. He said that after the Maroon Treaty, settlements began to be formed in those parts where none chose to venture before. 'It was from this period, that, under the encouragement of different acts, but particularly the last mentioned, the parishes of St Mary, St George, St James, Portland, the interior parts of St Thomas in the East, St Anne, Clarendon, Hanover, Westmoreland, and St John, began to be cleared for plantations'.[60]

---

59 David MacPherson, *Annals of Commerce* (Edinburgh, 1805), vol. 3, p. 505.
60 Long, *History of Jamaica*, voL 1, p. 429.

CHAPTER ELEVEN

Slavery and Sugar

> He who writes the history of modern civilization will be culpably negligent if he omit to observe and to describe the black stream of humanity, which has poured into America from the heart of the Soudan. That stream has fertilized half the Western continent. It has affected culture and morality in the Eastern and Western hemispheres, and has been the means of transforming European colonies into a great nationality. Nor can it be denied that the material development of England was aided greatly by means of this same dark stream. By means of Negro labour sugar and tobacco were produced; by means of sugar and tobacco British commerce was increased; by means of increased commerce the arts of culture and refinement were developed.[1]
>
> Edward Blyden, 1887

1 INTRODUCTION

From the standpoint of the supply of labour for the plantations, it is significant that few indigenous peoples occupied the Caribbean islands at the outset of English colonization. Had Englishmen colonized the Lesser Antilles at the beginning of the 16th century instead of more than a century later, it is likely that they would have encountered a numerous population of Amerindians. Spanish historians from the time of Las Casas have recounted the tragic story of the Arawaks who laboured in the gold mines of Española until they were virtually extinct by the third decade of the 16th century. What is not so well known is the story of Spanish efforts to fill the ranks of the Arawaks by means of slave raids on the Carib islands in the Lesser Antilles. With the sanction of the Spanish Crown, Barbados was opened to the taking of slaves in 1511 and quickly depopulated. Raids extended to neighbouring islands, with the effect that the Caribs were reduced while Spanish livestock multiplied and served as a larder for the first English settlers.[2]

Chattel slavery and the near-slavery of indentured servitude had its

---

1 Edward W. Blyden, *Christianity, Islam and the Negro Race* (Edinburgh, 1967), pp. 118–19.
2 Carl O. Sauer, *The Early Spanish Main* (Berkeley and Los Angeles, 1966), pp. 192–4.

Slavery and Sugar

economic origin in the abundance of land in proportion to the population. Free white settlers in the colonies were prone to disperse over the land and practise a semi-subsistence economy which combined such activities as hunting, trapping, and primitive agriculture. On the other hand, the production of staple agricultural commodities required a labour force which was numerous, concentrated, and capable of sustained effort. Since free labour could be obtained on these conditions only by payment of high wages, white masters turned to bonded or enslaved men who could be rigorously disciplined. Writing in 1849, Edward Gibbon Wakefield asserted that 'every colony that has prospered, from the time of Columbus down to this day, has enjoyed in some measure what I have termed combination and constancy of labour. They enjoyed it by means of some kind of slavery'.[3] According to Dr H. J. Nieboer, it is a general rule that 'only among peoples with open resources can slavery and serfdom exist, whereas free labourers dependent on wages are only found among peoples with close resources'.[4]

2 INDIANS AND WHITE SERVANTS

Indians rather than Africans were probably the first slaves to till the soil of Barbados. We have seen that Captain Henry Powell sailed on to the coast of Guiana after leaving the first English settlers in Barbados. While he was collecting plants he met up with a group of Indians. They desired to return to the island with him 'as free people to manure these fruits, and that I should allow them a piece of land, the which I did...'. Unfortunately for the Indians, Powell did not remain long on the island. From England he petitioned the Government of Barbados about 1648 'to set these poor people free, that have been kept thus long in Bondage...'.[5] When Richard Ligon was in Barbados from 1647 to 1650 he found but few Indians, 'and these fetcht from other Countries; some from the neighbouring Islands, some from the Main, which we make slaves'. The Indian women were said to be adept in 'ordering the Cassavie and making bread', while the men were employed in killing fish with bows and arrows and as footmen.[6]

---

3 Edward Gibbon Wakefield, *A View of the Art of Colonization* (Oxford, 1914), p. 175.
4 H. J. Nieboer, *Slavery as an Industrial System* (The Hague, 1900), p. 389.
5 Petition of Capt. Henry Powell to Gov. Daniel Searle of Barbados, c. 1648. Bodleian Library, Oxford, Rawlinson MSS C. 94.
6 Richard Ligon, *A True and Exact History of the Island of Barbadoes* (London, 1673), p. 54.

Sugar and Slavery

As with the Indians, Negroes made up a very small part of the labour force in the early years of West Indian colonization. Slaves were first introduced into St Kitts in 1626, when Maurice Thompson and his partner Thomas Combe equipped three ships which conveyed sixty slaves, who were presumably Africans, to that island.[7] Barbados had a reported fifty Negroes in 1629, but it is not certain that they were slaves. Chattel slavery was given legal sanction in Barbados on 21 July 1636, when the Governor and Council 'resolved that Negroes and Indians, that came here to be sold, should serve for Life, unless a Contract was before made to the contrary'.[8]

In the face of inadequate supplies of Negro and Indian slaves, resort was had to white bonded labour. We have seen that economic and social troubles lay behind the great migration of Englishmen to the colonies in the 1620s and 1630s. With the outbreak of the Civil Wars in 1642, the flow of migrants slowed for a time and then mounted from the mid-1640s to the Restoration in 1660.

Generally speaking, the Civil Wars marked a change in the source and nature of emigration to the West Indies. Voluntary emigration did not cease after 1642, but the emphasis shifted to the forced migration of prisoners-of-war, political prisoners, 'felons condemned to death, sturdy beggars, gipsies, and other incorrigible rogues, poor and idle debauched persons'.[9] Early migrants were chiefly Englishmen of lower middle-class origins. The Civil Wars, on the other hand, threw up a polyglot lot of Englishmen, Scotsmen, and Irishmen, including a few Royalists of distinguished lineage. Scottish and English prisoners were transported to the West Indies after the Royalist armies were defeated at Preston, Dunbar, and Worcester. Irish military prisoners suffered a similar fate after the storming of Drogheda, when Cromwell wrote: 'When they submitted, these officers were knocked on the head, and every tenth man of the soldiers killed, and the rest shipped for Barbados'.[10] Many forced labourers for the plantations came from the defeated armies, although the Barbadians probably exaggerated the numbers involved when they claimed that no less than 12,000 military prisoners had arrived on that island by 1655.[11]

---

7 J. A. Williamson, *The Caribbee Islands Under the Proprietary Patents* (Oxford, 1926), p. 31.
8 Anon., *Some Memoirs of the first Settlement of the Island of Barbados* (Barbados, 1741), p. 19.
9 *Cal. S. P. Col. 1661–68*, p. 229.
10 Vincent T. Harlow, *A History of Barbados 1625–1685* (Oxford, 1926), pp. .294–6; Abbot E. Smith, *Colonists in Bondage White Servitude and Convict Labor in America 1607–1776* (Chapel Hill, 1947), pp. 152–63, 164–70.
11 Harlow, *History of Barbados*, pp. 118–19.

Slavery and Sugar

Though Monmouth's Rebellion and the Jacobite risings in Scotland yielded other military prisoners, increased resort was had to indentured servants who came from the prisons, slums, and workhouses of England in the decades following the Civil Wars. One incident of apparent Puritan zeal was the transportation in 1656 of more than 400 women of loose life from the brothels of London to the island of Barbados, 'in order that by their breeding they should replenish the white population'. In the same year the Council of State voted that 1,000 girls, and as many young men, should be taken from Ireland and sent to Jamaica. A few years later Martin Noell, the merchant prince, told a committee of the House of Commons that he had 'several persons out of Bridewell and other prisons' who had been sent to Barbados as indentured servants.[12] The acute shortage of white labour inspired Christopher Jeaffreson to write from St Kitts to his London merchant on 6 May 1681:

> For if Newgate and Bridewell should spew out their spawne into these islandes, it would meete with no lesse encouragement; for no goale-bird can be so incorrigible, but there is hope of his conformity here, as well as of his preferment, which some have happily experimented.[13]

After Jeaffreson returned to England he negotiated for the transportation of malefactors from Newgate Prison, as well as recruiting skilled servants from outside the prison walls.[14]

Most servants signed articles of indenture which bound them to a period of four or five years' labour and promised certain 'freedom dues' at the end of their service. A committee of the Council for Foreign Plantations reported in 1664 that servants were

> transported at the rate of about 6*l.* per head, are entertained by those to whom they are consigned or are exchanged for commodities ... after certain years they are free to plant for themselves or take wages for their service, and have the value of 10 *l.* to begin planting for themselves.[15]

But by this time it was becoming increasingly difficult to attract voluntary servants to the West Indies; no lands remained for disposal to time-expired servants in Barbados, while the Leeward Islands and Jamaica could offer few attractions by comparison with the mainland colonies in North America.

---

12 Leo F. Stock (ed.), *Proceedings and Debates of The British Parliaments Respecting North America* (Washington, D.C., 1930), vol. 1, p. 248.
13 John C. Jeaffreson, *A Young Squire of the Seventeenth Century* (London, 1878), vol. 1, p. 258.
14 Ibid., vol. 2, pp. 121, 166, 195, 278.
15 *Cal. S. P. Col. 1661–68*, p. 229.

3 AFRO-CARIBBEAN ECONOMIC HISTORY

Adam Smith believed that it was the experience of all ages and nations that the work done by freemen in the end was cheaper than that performed by slaves. Smith's sweeping generalization was qualified by Herman Merivale, the 19th century colonial reformer, who wrote that 'slave labour is dearer than free *whenever abundance of free labour can be procured*'.[16] Since free labour and bonded white labour became less abundant and more costly, planters turned to the cheaper labour of African slaves. They found that although slaves called for a larger original outlay of capital than indentured servants, slaves were perpetual instead of temporary servants, they were usually cheaper to feed and clothe, and they replaced themselves to some extent by natural breeding. It was not that whites were incapable of hard labour on West Indian plantations, but rather that they were too few and too costly.[17] Africa supplied labour — although not without compulsion — that was superior to both whites and Indians in capacity, endurance, and docility. Governor Atkins of Barbados asserted in 1676 that the planters of that island had found by experience that they could 'keepe three Blacks, who work better and cheaper than one White man'.[18]

Perhaps one way to approach the similarities and differences in Afro-Caribbean economic history is to consider the relationship of population to physical resources in a tropical setting.[19] Agriculture in West Africa is thought to have first developed in wooded lands where the inhabitants grew plants from cuttings in rough clearings. Low population density meant that little land was cleared and planted in a given year, although the tribal community claimed cultivation rights to a much larger area for land rotation. Slash and burn agriculture, dependent on the fertilizer of wood ashes, was, in effect, a system of long forest fallow.

Changes in the agricultural system were called for as the pressure of population on the resources of a given area increased. More trees had to be felled and more time and effort devoted to land preparation, planting, weeding, and harvesting. Fire and the digging stick would no longer suffice. Rather, resort must be had to axes, hoes,

---

16 Adam Smith, *The Wealth of Nations* (1776) (New York, 1937), pp. 80–81; Herman Merivale, *Lectures on Colonization and Colonies* (London, 1928), p. 303.
17 Eric Williams, *Capitalism and Slavery* (Chapel Hill, 1944), pp. 19–29.
18 Harlow, *History of Barbados*, p. 309.
19 A primary source for historical and cultural relationships between Negroes in West Africa and the New World is Melville J. Herskovits, *The Myth of The Negro Past* (Boston, Beacon Press, 1958), with a new preface and a supplementary bibliography to the edition of 1941.

spades, and other hand tools, and, conditions permitting, to animal-drawn ploughs. Given a rising man-land ratio, agriculture might be expected to pass through the following stages: long forest fallow, bush fallow, short fallow, and possibly annual cropping or even multi-cropping.[20]

West Africa is divided into three zones, forming a belt-like character, which extend laterally for great distances in an east-west direction. Between the coast and the Sahara Desert there are the successive zones of tropical rain forest, open woodland, and grass and scrub. Professor Forde maintains that there was a general, though by no means complete, dichotomy between the forest and savanna peoples. Before the coming of the Europeans, the former appear to have been chiefly long forest fallow cultivators. They grew a variety of root crops which were supplemented by legumes, fruits, and oil palms. They possessed small livestock — goats, pigs and fowls — but few cattle or horses because of the tsetse fly. Iron tools, particularly hoes, were generally available but often only through trade. Labour was both individual and co-operative, depending on the tasks to be performed. Members of the tribe held general cultivation rights to land, but the right to cultivate a given plot might be lost after the land returned to fallow.

By contrast with the forest peoples, those occupying the savanna zone to the north were predominantly grain cultivators and pastoralists. Their agricultural system was more intensive and their fallow period of shorter duration. Deep hoeing, ridge cultivation, and irrigation were practised by the more advanced Hausa peoples of Northern Nigeria and the Bambara and Mandingka of the French Sudan. Moreover, savanna agriculture supplied greater surpluses to maintain specialists in craft, ritual, and government, and thus supported a higher level of culture than that of the forest peoples to the south.[21]

The anthropologist George Peter Murdock has suggested that the western Sudan was one of the few centres in the world where agriculture was an indigenous invention. Included among the important crops which were probably first domesticated in this region were pearl millet, sorghum, okra, watermelon, sesame, and cotton.[22]

---

20 Ester Boserup, *The Conditions of Agricultural Growth The Economics of Agrarian Change under Population Pressure* (Chicago, 1965), pp. 15–34.
21 Daryll Forde, 'The Cultural Map of West Africa: Successive Adaptations to Tropical Forests and Grasslands', in *Cultures and Societies of Africa*, ed. Simon and Pheobe Ottenberg (New York, 1960), pp. 116–38.
22 George Peter Murdock, *Africa Its Peoples and Their Culture History* (New York, 1959), pp. 64–76.

Sugar and Slavery

The shifting nature of agriculture is alluded to by Olaudah Equiano (*c.* 1745–97), the Ibo slave who was brought from the interior of what is now Eastern Nigeria to the West Indies and later acquired an education and purchased his freedom. 'Our tillage', wrote Equiano in his autobiography, 'is exercised in a large plain or common, some hours walk from our dwellings, and all the neighbours resort thither in a body. They use no beasts of husbandry, and their only instruments are hoes, axes, shovels, and beaks, or pointed iron to dig with'.[23]

West India sugar plantations incorporated certain features of the woodland and savanna cultures of West Africa. Where land reserves were ample, as in Jamaica, canes were grown under a system of bush or long fallow with little or no application of fertilizer. Africans, whether at home or abroad, were hoe cultivators. In both regions they commonly tilled kitchen gardens and kept small livestock in close proximity to their living quarters. As in Africa, provision grounds were cultivated on a shifting basis on the marginal lands of Jamaica. Certain food crops – such as yams, bananas, plantains, and coconuts – were common to Africa and the West Indies; others underwent a sea change as a by-product of the slave trade. Cassava, maize, and sweet potatoes were carried from the West Indies to Africa, while in a reverse direction moved Guinea corn, yellow yams, and kola nuts.

Though certain similarities are evident, the agricultural systems of the two tropical regions differed in most essentials. One was a tradition-directed tribal system geared to self-sufficiency; the other produced staples for overseas markets in response to the profit motive. One was a farm without a factory; the other called for heavy investment in processing equipment, shipping, and marketing. One required few if any livestock inputs; the other employed horses, mules, and oxen for cartage, power, and fertilizer. One was essentially a medium to long fallow system; the other became so intensive in some areas that sugar-canes were interplanted with provision crops.

Altering the pace and timing of agricultural evolution were opportunities for emigration and aggrandizement by means of war and trade. Inter-tribal trade, warfare, and domestic slavery appear to have ancient roots in West Africa. After about A.D. 300 Arab and Berber warriors and traders penetrated the savanna and park lands of West Africa. They introduced the Negroes to Asiatic luxuries and, in

[23] *The interesting Narrative of The Life of Olaudah Equiano, or Gustavus Vassa, The African. Written by Himself.* 4th ed. (Dublin, 1791), p. 15.

Slavery and Sugar

areas not infested with the tsetse fly, to animal husbandry. Their camel caravans returned across the Sahara from Negroland laden with slaves, gold, ivory and a variety of tropical goods. North of the Senegal and Niger rivers great territorial empires were established by Negroes and invaders from North Africa. Then, with the opening of the Age of Discovery in the 15th century, Europeans outflanked the Sahara by sea.[24]

Slavery in the two societies was related functionally to the agricultural systems. Whereas wholesale or gang slavery became a characteristic feature of the Caribbean plantations, retail or domestic slavery was common in West Africa. Apart from the crown plantations worked by gang slaves in 18th-century Dahomey, the African master commonly worked together with his few slaves and regarded them as inferior members of his family. Labour-extensive agriculture appears to have made relatively light demands on domestic slaves. John Newton, the master of a slave vessel who later became an Anglican clergyman and anti-slavery leader, wrote concerning the people of what is now Sierra Leone:

> The state of slavery, among these wild barbarous people, as we esteem them, is much milder than in our colonies. For as, on the one hand, they have no land in high cultivation, like our West Indian plantations, and therefore no call for that excessive, unintermitted labour, which exhausts our slaves; so, on the other hand, no man is permitted to draw blood even from a slave.[25]

Newton's observation finds confirmation in the works of modern anthropologists and historians of West Africa.[26]

4 STAGES IN CARIBBEAN PLANTATION SLAVERY

Though more strenuous than its sister institution in Africa, slavery in the infancy of the sugar industry was considerably milder than it became in the later period of intensive culture. Male and female slaves were imported in about equal proportions, family relationships and breeding were encouraged by planters, land for provision culture was relatively abundant, and slaves were often assigned to lighter tasks than indentured servants. Both Richard Ligon and Richard Blome testified to the planters' policy of buying male and female

---

24 J. D. Fage, *An Introduction to the History of West Africa* (Cambridge, 1961), pp. 1–38.
25 *The Journal of a Slave Trader (John Newton) 1750–1754*, ed. Bernard Martin and Mark Spurrell (London, 1962), pp. 107–8.
26 Fage, *History of West Africa*, pp. 77–9.

Sugar and Slavery

slaves in equal numbers. 'For the increase of the stock of Negroes', wrote Blome in 1672, 'they generally take as many *Men* as *Women*'. Ligon wrote that the slaves in Barbados were 'kept and preserv'd with greater care than the servants, who ... are put to very hard labour, ill lodging, and their dyet very sleight'.[27] Another Barbadian inspected numerous plantations and found that slaves were being trained as tradesmen; he had seen '30 or 40 English, Scotch, and Irish at work in the parching sun, without shirt, shoe, or stocking, and negroes at their trades in good condition'.[28]

West Indian slavery assumed a harsher aspect as the man-land ratio increased and the industrial-type discipline of gang slavery supplanted the extensive cultivation of plantations with a mixed labour force of whites and blacks. Slave imports tended to increase in relation to population growth, for on the one hand there was a rise in mortality and on the other a declining birth-rate. Among the reasons for high mortality were disease, despondency, accidents, malnutrition, and the harsh labour regime. Labour requirements increased under a system of intensive culture which called for the holeing, annual planting, dunging and weeding of cane fields. At times dietary standards were impaired when food imports were delayed or prevented by the exigencies of war and trade. The incidence of disease increased because slave vessels were often overcrowded, unsanitary, and poorly-provisioned, because debilitated slaves were set to heavy field labour before they were properly acclimated, and because contagious diseases were a function of both population density and exposure to European as well as African maladies. The diseases which afflicted the slaves included, dysentery, yaws, smallpox, scurvy, leprosy, lock jaw, dropsy, ulcers, worms, and a variety of fevers.

Rev. Robert Robertson, the Nevis clergyman and planter, revealed some of the reasons for the high mortality and low birth rate when he wrote in 1732:

> The Loss in Slaves (not including those immediately from *Guinea*, of which about two Fifths die in the *Seasoning*) may well, one Year with another, be reckoned at One in Fifteen; in dry Years when Provisions of the Country Growth are scarce, I have known it One in Seven in my Plantations, and the same or worse in Sickly Seasons; and when the Small-Pox ... happens to be imported, it is incredible what Havock it makes among the Blacks.
>
> To this the Births are to be opposed. But, considering how hard the Negroes are generally kept to work, and that *Polygamy* (which ... is

---

27 Richard Blome, *A Description of Jamaica* (London, 1672), p. 86; Ligon, *History of Barbadoes*, p. 43.
28 *Cal. S. P. Col. 1661–68*, p. 530.

Slavery and Sugar

found ... to hinder breeding here) is permitted to them; and allowing for the Numbers of Infants that die, the little Work the Mother can do for three Months before and nine after the Birth, Midwifery, and some other Incidents, and the Maintenance of the Child for six or seven Years at a Penny per *Diem,* the Gain from thence cannot be great.[29]

Contributing to the practice of polygamy was the declining ratio of female to male imports. Of the 2,269 slaves imported into Barbados by the Company of Royal Adventurers between 11 August 1663, and 17 November 1667, 1,051 were men, 1,018 women, 136 boys and 56 girls. On the other hand, the Royal African Company delivered alive approximately 100,000 Negroes in the colonies between 1672 and 1713. An analysis of 60,000 of these slaves reveals that 51 per cent were men, 35 per cent women, 9 per cent boys, and 5 per cent girls. In Jamaica a leading slave dealer imported and sold 10,149 males and 6,145 females between the years 1764 and 1774.[30]

The evils of Barbadian slavery before 1680 were given point by Rev. Morgan Godwyn, resident clergyman and early critic of the peculiar institution. Planters were not very constant 'to that first and so very *agreeable* Principle, of preserving these poor Wretches for Labour (their only end in purchasing of them) by a due *provision* of Food ... and Cloathing ...'. Godwyn was righteously outraged to find that some planters deliberately overworked and underfed their slaves to induce mortality among the superannuated, who, in turn, were replaced by young and vigorous slaves. These cold-blooded practices, which were apparently profitable under the existing circumstances of plentiful and cheap slave imports and costly provisions, were more common among the 'richer' and 'mightier' than among 'the Middle and Meaner sort; who do usually find it less convenient to *buy new,* than (having but a few) to *preserve* their old Negro's'. Great planters contributed indirectly to the re-emigration of whites from Barbados, for an effect of their scant allowance of food to their slaves was 'many *Robberies* and *Thefts* committed by these starved Peoples upon the poorer English'.[31]

Numerous contemporary and modern writers have testified to the inability of the slave population to reproduce itself, with the consequent need for new slaves from Africa. Both Edmund Burke and

---

29 Rev. Robert Robertson, *A Detection of the State and Situation of the Present Sugar Planters* (London, 1732), pp. 42–4.
30 Elizabeth Donnan (ed.), *Documents Illustrative of the History of the Slave Trade to America* (New York, 1965), vol. 1, p. 88; K. G. Davies, *The Royal African Company* (London, 1957), p. 299; *Two Reports from the Committee of the Assembly of Jamaica... on the Slave Trade* (London, 1789), p. 11.
31 Rev. Morgan Godwyn, *The Negro's and Indian's Advocate* (London, 1680), pp. 82–3.

Sugar and Slavery

David Hume called attention to the deplorably high mortality. 'It is computed in the West Indies', wrote Hume, 'that a stock of slaves grow worse five *per cent.* every year, unless new slaves be bought to recruit them. They are not able to keep up their number, even in those warm countries, where cloaths and provisions are so easily got'.[32] Professor Bennett has calculated that fourteen new slaves, or 5.46 per cent of the population of 238 slaves, were needed annually to maintain the labour force on the Codrington plantations in Barbados in the period from 1712 to 1748. A report of a committee of the Assembly of Jamaica said that 'On a very low calculation, and upon a general average, sugar estates in Jamaica require an annual supply of six slaves each, to keep up the health, the strength, and the number of its labourers'. Thus the annual mortality was 3 per cent for the 200 slaves on a median Jamaican estate in the 1770s.[33]

Planter indifference or opposition to breeding was a primary cause of the low birth rate among the slaves in the opinion of contemporary observers. Sir George Younge testified: 'When I was in the West Indies [before 1768], the Planters did not seem desirous to encourage the Breeding of Slaves, but thought it cheaper to purchase'.[34] John Newton was told by a planter in Antigua in 1751 that it was cheaper to work slaves to the utmost, and by 'little relaxation, hard fare, and hard usage, to wear them out before they became useless, and unable to do service; and then to buy new ones, to fill up their places'.[35]

Generally speaking, slavery became somewhat less harsh in the decade or two preceding the American Revolution. Life expectancy appears to have risen because of two main developments. First, there is evidence that the slaves' standard of life underwent some improvement. Nearly every sugar estate had its hospital or 'hot house' for slaves who needed isolation, sick slaves were treated by a physician in residence or one on call, minor wounds and ailments were cared for by old women slaves known as 'doctresses', pregnant women and infants were given better care, and planters had medical supplies sent out from England. Moreover, scattered evidence points to more

---

32 David Hume, 'Of the Populousness of Ancient Nations (1752)', in *David Hume Writings on Economics*, ed. Eugene Rotwein (London, 1955), pp. 118–119; William and Edmund Burke. *An Account of the European Settlements in America* (London, 1777), vol. 2, pp. 124–6.
33 J. Harry Bennett, Jr., *Bondsmen and Bishops, Slavery and Apprenticeship on the Codrington Plantations of Barbados, 1710–1838* (Berkeley and Los Angeles, 1958), p. 61; Bryan Edwards, *The History, Civil and Commercial, of the British Colonies in the West Indies* (Dublin, 1793), vol. 2, p. 467.
34 Public Record Office, London. B.T. 6/10, ff. 588–9: Sir George Younge, testimony, 31 May 1788.
35 Martin and Spurrell, *Journal of a Slave Trader*, p. 112.

ample food and clothing allowances to slaves. After his second visit to the West Indies, Hector M'Neill wrote in 1788: 'The treatment of Slaves in these islands has certainly, within these last twenty years, undergone a wonderful change for the better; but it is still far from being complete'. No one denied, however, that the Negroes in Jamaica were 'in *general* over-worked and under-fed, even on the mildest and best regulated properties'. The improvement was attributed chiefly to the rise in slave prices which had led the proprietors 'to view Negro Property as an object of great concern and consequently to preserve it by every prudent method'.[36]

Another reason for increased life expectancy was the growing proportion of Creole to African slaves. Since the incidence of death was generally lower among slaves born in the islands than it was among imported slaves who had to undergo a difficult period of acclimatization or seasoning, there came a time when the Creole population base so far exceeded annual slave imports that downward pressure was exerted on the death-rate. Moreover, there is some evidence that women outlived men, with a long-run tendency toward a better balance of the sexes and possibly a rise in the birth-rate.[37] According to Governor Seton of St Vincent, the common duration of the slaves' lives in the 1780s was about fifty years. He explained that 'this Calculation is to be confined to the Creole Negroes, or those seasoned to the Climate; for it is very certain that of the Negroes imported from the Coast of Africa, a much greater Proportion of them die under that Age than arrive to it'.[38]

5 THE DIMENSIONS OF THE SLAVE TRADE

Calculations based on statistics of slave imports and slave population support the view of contemporaries who pointed to a rise in the mortality rate during the intensification of agriculture and a decline in the decades preceding the American Revolution. The data needed

36 Hector M'Neill, *Observations on the Treatment of Negroes in the Island of Jamaica* (London, 1788), pp. 2–5, 44; D. W. Thoms, 'Slavery in the Leeward Islands in the Mid-Eighteenth Century: A Reappraisal', *Bulletin of the Institute of Historical Research*, London, vol. XLII (May 1969), pp. 76–85.
37 In 1788, the slaves on 22 plantations in Barbados were enumerated on the basis of age and sex. Of the total of 3,112 slaves, of which all but 429 were Creoles, 597 were girls under the age of 20; 606, boys under 20; 787, women from 20 to 49; 727, men from 20 to 49; 242, women from 50 to 90; and 153, men from 50 to 90. *House of Commons Sessional Papers. Report of the Lords of the Committee of the Council for Trade and Plantations*, 1789, vol. XXVI, no. 646, part 4, Barbados, p. 39 (hereafter called Brit. Parl. Papers).
38 Ibid., Part 3, St Vincent, A. 13.

Sugar and Slavery

for computing the mortality rate are net slave imports, that is, total imports less re-exports, and the slave population at selected intervals of time. Annual imports and re-exports were recorded in Jamaica from 1702 to 1775, and imports in all but a few years from 1676 to 1701. Similarly, except for the decade 1736–46, annual imports into Barbados were recorded during the century from 1676 to 1775. These two series have been adjusted where necessary to show both gross and net imports for quarter-century periods. Given the net slave imports and the slave population at the beginning and end of each quarter-century period, the problem is to compute the annual mortality rate on both the Creole and imported slaves.*

The interesting thing is that while the computed mortality rates for the two islands tend to rise and fall in step with each other, they were consistently lower in Jamaica, as might be expected, than they were in Barbados. Table 11.1 shows the computed rates for Jamaica and Barbados, together with the estimated rates for these two islands before 1676, for the Leeward Islands from 1651 to 1775, and the Ceded Islands from 1761 to 1775.

Based in part on extant statistics, in part on calculations from estimated mortality rates, Table 11.2 shows both the gross and net slave imports of the British West Indies during the period of this study.

Nearly 1,500,000 African slaves were imported into the British West Indies from 1627 to 1775, of whom about four-fifths were retained for labour in the islands. Probably another 1,500,000

---

*The mortality equation adapted to a 25-year period is as follows:

$$M = \frac{I - P}{C \times A + 25 \times P_1} \text{ where}$$

M = slave mortality rate, or annual rate of population decrease.
I = net slave imports during the 25-year period.
P = increase of slave population during the 25-year period.
C = compounding factor, or $1 + 2 + 3 + \ldots 25$, or 325.
A = annual net increase in slave population, or P/25.
P_1 = slave population in year one of the 25-year period.

For Jamaica in the period 1751–75, the solution for M is as follows when I = 177,618, P = 72,000, C = 325, A = 2,880, and P_1 = 121,000:

$$M = \frac{177{,}618 - 72{,}000}{325 \times 2{,}880 + 25 \times 121{,}000} = \frac{105{,}618}{3{,}961{,}000} = 2.7 \text{ per cent}$$

Slavery and Sugar

Table 11.1

Annual percentage decline in slave population

Years	Jamaica	Barbados	Leeward Islands	Ceded Islands
1627–1650		3.5*		
1651–1675	2.8*	3.8*	3.5*	
1676–1700	3.0	4.1	4.0*	
1701–1725	3.6	4.9	4.4*	
1726–1750	3.5	3.6	4.8*	
1751–1775	2.7	3.7	4.4*	4.8*

*Estimated rates

Source: See Table 11.2

Table 11.2

Estimated number of African slaves imported into British West Indies, 1627–1775[1] (thousands)

Years	Jamaica		Barbados		Leeward Islands		Totals	
	Gross	Net	Gross	Net	Gross	Net	Gross	Net
1627–1650			33.5	29.1			33.5	29.1
1651–1675	12.5	11.4	48.0	38.4	11.6	10.2	72.1	60.0
1676–1700	64.8	54.0	58.2	52.4	33.4	29.8	156.4	136.2
1701–1725	145.2	86.1	78.8	70.9	64.7	58.8	288.7	215.8
1726–1750	194.1	132.1	70.6	63.6	94.2	86.6	358.9	282.3
1751–1775	206.2	177.6	84.3	75.8	285.5	184.0	576.0[2]	437.4[2]
Totals	622.8	461.2	373.4	330.2	489.4	369.4	1,485.6	1,160.8

Notes:
1. The procedure here has been to use extant statistics for Jamaica and Barbados. Where such statistics are not available the net imports have been computed from estimated mortality rates and census returns. Estimated re-exports have been added to computed net imports to arrive at gross imports.
2. Included in these totals are the slaves imported into the Ceded Islands, amounting in thousands to 177.3 gross and 85.7 net.

Source: Slave import and population data have been compiled from numerous sources, of which the following are most comprehensive: P.R.O. London, C.O. 1/43, no. 37; Brit. Parl. Papers 1789, vol. XXVI, no. 646a, part III, Jamaica Appendix; Ibid. 1790, vol. XXIX, no. 697; K. G. Davies, *The Royal African Company* (London, 1957), pp. 143, 363; Noel Deerr, *The History of Sugar* (London, 1950), vol. 2, pp. 278–9; Frank W. Pitman, *The Development of the British West Indies* (New Haven, 1917), pp. 71–90, 369–92.

Sugar and Slavery

British-traded slaves were carried to foreign possessions and the Thirteen Colonies without being entered in Caribbean port records. Distributed in time, approximately 18 per cent were imported in the 17th century; 19 per cent in the first quarter of the 18th century; 26 per cent in the second quarter; and 37 per cent in the third quarter. Barbados accounted for the greater part of the imports until the last quarter of the 17th century. Partly in consequence of its re-export trade, Jamaica took off over half of the slaves brought to the British Caribbean in the first half of the 18th century. The same period also witnessed the rapid expansion of the Leeward Islands. The final quarter-century period saw the extension of the slave trade to the Ceded Islands.

Just how many Africans survived the Middle Passage to labour in the mines and on the plantations of the New World is a question that has perplexed demographers and historians for two centuries. The conservative estimate of one modern demographer is 15 million, of whom nearly 90,000 arrived in the 16th century, 2,750,000 in the 17th, 7 million in the 18th, and 4 million in the 19th. Bryan Edwards estimated that 2,130,000 Negro slaves were imported 'into all the British colonies of America and the West Indies' from 1680 to 1786.[39] The West Indies, both British and foreign, accounted for about seven-eighths and the Southern mainland colonies one-eighth of these labourers. Natural increase probably accounted for the greater part of the slave population of the Thirteen Colonies, which was estimated at nearly 460,000 in 1770, by comparison with 420,000 for the ten Caribbean islands.[40]

One of the slaves who survived the Middle Passage and later wrote of his experiences was Olaudah Equiano. He told of the stench of the hold, the galling of the chains, the shrieks of the women and the groans of the dying, and the suicide of two of his wearied countrymen who 'somehow made through the nettings and jumped into the sea'. Arriving at Barbados, many merchants and planters came on board. 'They put us in separate parcels and examined us attentively. They also made us jump, and pointed to the land, signifying we were to go there'. Olaudah and his countrymen were landed the next day and 'conducted immediately to the merchant's yard, where we were all pent up together like so many sheep in a fold without regard to

---

39 Robert R. Kuczynski, *Population Movements* (Oxford, 1936), pp. 6–17; Edwards, *History of British West Indies*, vol. 2, pp. 52–3. Professor Curtin has estimated that 9,556,100 Africans were landed alive in the New World during the four centuries of the slave trade. Philip D. Curtin, *The Atlantic Slave Trade: A Census* (Madison, 1969), p. 286.
40 *Historical Statistics of the United States Colonial Times to 1957* (Washington, D.C., 1960), p. 756.

Slavery and Sugar

sex or age'. The mode of sale by the 'scramble' was described as follows:

> On a signal given, (as the beat of a drum) the buyers rush at once into the yard where the slaves are confined, and make choice of that parcel they like best. The noise and clamour with which this is attended and the eagerness visible in the countenances of the buyers serve not a little to increase the apprehensions of the terrified Africans, who may well be supposed to consider them as the ministers of that destruction to which they think themselves devoted.[41]

It was in this manner, without scruple, that relations and friends were separated, most of them never to see each other again.

6 BRITAIN'S LEADERSHIP IN THE SLAVE TRADE

Britain's leadership in the Atlantic slave trade was not gained quickly or without effort or design. During the second half of the 17th century a foothold was established in West Africa and a flow of slaves to the colonies inaugurated by means of three Anglo-Dutch wars, the chartering of two joint-stock companies in succession, and the preference system under the Navigation Acts.

Charter rights of exclusive trade to Africa were conferred on the Company of Royal Adventurers Trading to Africa in 1660, and to its successor, the Royal African Company, in 1672.[42] In an age of keen international competition, in a trade which required trading posts defensible against hostile Africans and European rivals, it was the African companies, backed by the financial resources of rich merchants, landed aristocrats, and the royal family itself, which supplied the overhead investment in forts and castles, warehouses, and ships. Professor K. G. Davies writes that the Royal African Company had little cause to be ashamed of its building record on the Gold Coast.[43]

Contributing to the growth of the British slave trade in the 18th century were such developments as the opening of the trade to independent traders after 1697, the Neutrality Treaty of 1704, the *Asiento* of 1713, the rise of British seapower, and Britain's growing ability to supply manufactures more cheaply, grant liberal credit, and devise cost-saving innovations in methods of trade, shipping, and

---
41 *The Life of Olaudah Equiano*, pp. 46–57.
42 G. F. Zook, *The Company of Royal Adventurers trading into Africa* (Lancaster, Pa., 1919); Davies, *The Royal African Company*.
43 Davies, *The Royal African Company*, p. 250.

finance. The remarkable rise of the trade at the turn of the century caught the approving eye of William Wood, the mercantile writer. By contrast with the delivery of 5,155 slaves per annum by the Royal African Company from 1680 to 1688, he observed that by 1708 'there were employ'd in this *Trade* above a Hundred Ships capable of Carrying 25,000 *Negroes* a Year into the *Plantations* belonging to the *separate Traders*'.[44]

By the *Asiento* of 1713 with Spain, the South Sea Company of England agreed to furnish the Spanish Americans with 4,800 slaves per annum, and to supply these colonists with English manufactures by means of an annual ship. Loss of the *Asiento* in 1739 and the war with Spain brought only a temporary halt to the expansion of supply centres and markets and the clandestine trade in slaves. During the Seven Years' War the British captured Goree and Senegal, the French West African slave trading posts, and carried large numbers of slaves to such conquered territories as Guadeloupe, Martinique, and Havana.[45]

Professor Polanyi discusses four innovations in the slave trade at Whydah both before and following its conquest by the inland state of Dahomey in 1724. Motivating the conquest was Dahomey's need for safe access to the coast to deliver slaves taken in wars against her enemies for guns and powder. Besides the establishment of the port of trade at Whydah, the innovations consisted of the 'sorting' of several European goods which added up to the rate of trade of a slave; the 'ounce trade', or a fictitious unit of account of a conventional value in the settling of European gold debts with the natives; and the '100 per cent markup', or the payment by Europeans in goods which were marked up an average of 100 per cent on the 'ounces' which they owed. Initiated by Europeans, particularly the British and French, these innovations 'amounted to a one-sided revision of the rate of trade to the advantage of the Europeans'.[46]

These and other innovations facilitated Britain's rise to pre-eminence in the Atlantic slave trade. British slavers forged ahead of the ubiquitous Dutchmen in the early decades of the 18th century, and, though challenged for a time by the French, came in some years to carry more human cargoes than the combined numbers transported by their European rivals. A report of 1753 said that British

---

44 William Wood, *A Survey of Trade* (London, 1718), pp. 185–92.
45 Richard Pares, *War and Trade in the West Indies 1739–1763* (Oxford, 1936), pp. 188–91.
46 Karl Polyanyi, *Dahomey and the Slave Trade An Analysis of an Archaic Economy* (Seattle, 1966), pp. 124, 161, 165–9; R. B. Sheridan, 'The Commercial and Financial Organization of the British Slave Trade, 1750–1806', *Econ. Hist. Rev.*, 2nd ser., vol. XI, no. 2 (Dec. 1958), pp. 249–63.

Slavery and Sugar

Table 11.3

British slave trade in 1771

By Port of Origin			By Source of Slaves		
Port	Ships	Negroes	Country	Ships	Negroes
Liverpool	107	29,250	Bight of Benin	63	23,301
Bristol	23	8,810	Windward Coast	56	11,960
London	58	8,136	Gold Coast	29	7,525
Lancaster	4	950	Senegambia	40	3,310
			Angola	4	1,050
Total	192	47,146	Total	192	47,146

Source: Bryan Edwards, *The History, Civil and Commercial, of The British Colonies in the West Indies* (Dublin, 1793), vol. 2, p. 53.

captains purchased annually 34,250 slaves, of whom 16,000 were supplied to the British colonies and the remainder to the colonies of Spain, France, and Portugal. Another report of 1768 said that European vessels carried off a total of 97,100 natives of Africa. Of this number, British vessels carried 53,100; British American, 6,300; French, 23,500; Dutch, 11,300; Portuguese, 1,700; and Danes, 1,200.[47] Table 11.3 shows in some detail the dimensions and nature of the trade in 1771. Since the annual gross imports of the British sugar islands amounted to about 22,000 in the 1770–2 period, and another 4,000 slaves were carried from Africa directly to the North American colonies, it would appear that some 21,000 slaves were carried directly to foreign colonies in British vessels.

Slave prices varied with the place of origin, physical condition, sex, age, state of the market, credit terms, and bargaining power of the parties to the transaction. Besides the price range at a given time and place, the general level of prices fluctuated widely over time. Buying prices in West Africa were bid up when buyers far outnumbered sellers, or when the bargaining power of buyers was weakened by such exigencies as mortality among seamen and slaves already loaded, lack of water and provisions, and the need to complete a cargo quickly so as to avoid the hurricane season. Conversely, slavers had the bargaining edge when supplies were augmented by means of inter-tribal warfare or famine. Of the many factors which

[47] 'Mr Pownal's Account of the Slave Trade', in Donnan, *Documents on the Slave Trade*, vol. 2, p. 507; David MacPherson, *Annals of Commerce* (Edinburgh, 1805), vol. 3, p. 484.

Table 11.4

Slave prices in Africa and the British West Indies, 1650–1788 (sterling)

Years	Africa[1]	British West Indies
c. 1650	–	£25–£30
1663–1664	–	£14–£23
1676–1679	£3	£15–£17
1679–1688	£3	£13–£16
1698–1707	£8–£12	£10–£14, and £23–£41
1718–1719	–	£12
1723–1725	£10–£18	£15–£22[2]
c. 1738	£9–£12	£20–£30
c. 1750	£12–£16	£28–£40
1752–1762	–	£30[3]
1755	£12	£35 14s 3d[4]
1759	£14	–
1763–1788	£12–£15 £18–£22	£28–£35
1772–1775	–	£34 10s 3½d[5]

Notes:
1. Buying prices in Africa were probably inclusive of the 100 per cent markup in the 18th century.
2. Jamaican sales of the Royal African Company.
3. Average of 71,115 Negroes sold in Jamaica.
4. Men slaves sold in Jamaica.
5. Average of 29 slave cargoes sold in Jamaica.

Source: P.R.O. London, Treas. 70/958–59; Brit. Parl. Papers 1789, vol. XXVI, no. 646a, part IV; Vincent T. Harlow, *A History of Barbados 1625–1685* (Oxford, 1926), pp. 312–13; K. G. Davies, *The Royal African Company* (London, 1957), p. 364; Elizabeth Donnan, *Documents Illustrative of the History of the Slave Trade to America* (New York, 1965), vol. 2, pp. 242, 507; Bryan Edwards, *The History of the British Colonies in the West Indies* (Dublin, 1793), vol. 2, p. 464; David MacPherson, *Annals of Commerce* (Edinburgh, 1805), vol. 3, p. 403.

made for fluctuating slave prices in the West Indies, none exerted a more pervasive influence than the wholesale price of sugar. Except in wartime, sugar and slave prices tended to rise and fall together.

Some indication of price movements can be gained from Table 11.4 which shows prices paid on the Coast of Africa for the purchase

Slavery and Sugar

of Negroes and sales prices in the British West Indies for selected years from 1650 to 1788.

'Thirty pound sterling is a price for the best man Negroe', wrote Richard Ligon, 'and twenty five, twenty six, or twenty seven pound for a Woman; the children are at easier rates'.[48] After Ligon's time, prices declined remarkably, ranging between £13 and £16 from 1679 to 1688. The Privy Council Committee Report, from which the greater part of the data in Table 11.4 is taken, shows a rise in both purchase and sales prices from 1698 to 1707. It may be presumed that prices were high — from £23 to £41 — during the two wars of this period, and that the low sales prices of £10 to £14 apply to the inter-war period from 1698 to 1702.

Prices declined after the War of Spanish Succession, rose in the 1720s, and declined again during the depression of the early 1730s. Prices then rose in the late 1730s and levelled off at about £35 sterling per head during the third quarter of the 18th century. That British prices were considerably lower than those prevailing in the French islands was the opinion of Lord Sheffield who wrote: 'as to the supply of negroes, we have such a decided superiority in the African trade, that it is allowed we have slaves one sixth cheaper'.[49]

7 AFRICA'S ABILITY TO SUPPLY MANPOWER

Africa's ability to supply manpower at the height of the slave trade is a question that has exercised the minds of both contemporary and modern writers. 'Africa', wrote John Hippisley, Governor of Cape Coast Castle on the Gold Coast, 'not only can continue supplying the West Indies in the quantities she has hitherto, but, if necessity required it, could spare thousands, nay, millions more, and go on doing the same to the end of time'.[50] Economist Thomas Robert Malthus concluded from his perusal of the writings on Africa and the slave trade that, notwithstanding the constant emigration, loss of life from incessant wars, and the checks to increase from vice and other causes, the population of Africa was 'continually pressing against the limits of the means of subsistence'.[51]

Modern historians generally support these contemporary views, but admit that the slave trade may have led to depopulation at

48 Ligon, *History of Barbadoes*, p. 46.
49 John Lord Sheffield, *Observations on the Commerce of the American States*, new ed. (London, 1784), p. 160.
50 John Hippisley, *Essays. 1. On the Populousness of Africa* (London, 1764), p. 15.
51 T. R. Malthus, *An Essay on Population* (1803) (Everyman ed., 1958), vol. 1, p. 91.

Sugar and Slavery

certain times and places. Professor Fage estimates that for every African who became acclimatized to plantation slavery in America, at least one other African lost his life through such operations of the slave trade as warfare, the Middle Passage, and the seasoning. Altogether, between twenty and thirty million souls were probably lost to West Africa which had a population that was unlikely more than twenty million at most. However, since the total loss was spread over the more than three centuries of the slave trade, the average annual loss of less than one per cent a year of the total population 'need not necessarily have been a crippling one for a healthy society'. Basil Davidson agrees with Professor Fage that while far-reaching depopulation did not occur, at certain times and places the staggering loss and wastage undoubtedly crippled society. He believes that depopulation was most acute in the intermediate zone between the forest belt and the Niger grasslands where the peoples lacked strong states of their own. Dr Boserup says that slaves were obtained by raids among neighbouring, numerically weaker, tribes living by the system of long fallow.[52]

8 RUNAWAYS AND REBELS

Slaves were not only property but also persons who were possessed of the faculties of activity and will. That they were capable of running away and resisting by passive or violent means the disciplined labour exacted by their white masters is evident from any cursory reading of colonial history. Slaves were prone to run away or resist when they were overworked, underfed, and harshly punished. Imported or 'salt water' slaves were generally more refractory than Creoles. Opportunities to flee and resist were enchanced, among other things, when there was access to wilderness areas affording refuge and sustenance, when the slaves far outnumbered the whites and particularly white men capable of bearing arms, when they retained their tribal identity of warlike resistance, were ably led, and assisted by organized bands of escaped slaves known as Maroons. In the development of a given colony, opportunities for escape and independent sustenance were probably greatest in the infancy of the sugar industry, while violent resistance tended to mount during the

---

52 Fage, *History of West Africa*, pp. 84–5; Basil Davidson, *Black Mother, The Years of the African Slave Trade* (Boston, 1961), pp. 275–7; Boserup, *Conditions of Agricultural Growth*, pp. 73–4.

transition to monoculture. Thereafter, resistance and flight continued, to be sure, but probably at a reduced tempo.

Jamaica was not the only island which had a Maroon problem. A visitor reported from Barbados in 1648 that there were 'many hundreds of Rebell negro slaves in the woods'.[53] St Kitts had a ridge of high and inaccessible mountains which 'encouraged great Numbers of Negroes to run away and resort thereto'. 'In plantations where slaves are ill fed, hard worked, and severely punished', wrote Rev. James Ramsay of the same island, 'it is a circumstance common for a tenth, and even as far as a fourth part of the working slaves, to go off and skulk in the mountains, some for months together'.[54] Runaways became so troublesome in Montserrat that legislative action was required. An act of 31 May 1710 declared that any slave that was absent from his master's service for three months 'and afterwards taken and convicted thereof shall suffer Death as a ffelon', the master to be granted 1,500 pounds of sugar as compensation from the island's treasury.[55]

Numerous reports of slave conspiracies are found in the annals of Caribbean history. As early as 1650 the fear of slave revolt had led the planters of Barbados to take elaborate precautions. 'If any tumult or disorder be in the Island', wrote Ligon, 'the next neighbour to it discharges a musquet, which gives the alarum to the whole Island; for upon the report of that, the next shoots and so the next and next, til it go through the island; upon which warning they make ready'.[56] Other precautions included the policy of stocking plantations with blacks of diverse tribal origins 'whose different tongues and animosities have kept them from insurrection',[57] and rigorously enforced slave codes.[58]

Most of the insurrections and Maroon wars seem to have occurred in the period from 1685 to 1740. Besides the abortive conspiracy of 1675, Barbados had local slave outbreaks in 1685, 1692, and 1702. Antigua had a small revolt in 1685, and a conspiracy which was thwarted in 1736. A small rising took place in Nevis in 1761, followed by an abortive one in Montserrat in 1768. Jamaica had its long and costly Maroon War before 1740, after which the most

---

53 Harlow, *History of Barbados*, pp. 324–5.
54 P.R.O. London, C.O. 152/14, R 42, f. 155: Gov. Hart to Board of Trade 21 June 1722; Rev. James Ramsey, *An Essay on the Treatment and Conversion of African Slaves in the British Sugar Colonies* (London, 1784), pp. 97–8. '
55 P.R.O. London, C.O. 152/13, Q 34, f. 101.
56 Quoted in Harlow, *History of Barbados*, pp. 324–5.
57 *Cal. S. P. Col. 1661–68*, p. 586.
58 Elsa V. Goveia, 'The West Indian Slave Laws of the Eighteenth Century', *Revista de Ciencias Sociales*, vol. IV, no. 1 (March 1960), pp. 75–105.

serious slave outbreak occurred in St Mary's parish in 1760 under the leadership of the Coromantine Negro, Tacky. Some sixty Europeans and free coloured people lost their lives before the rebels were defeated with the aid of the Maroons, who honoured the Treaty of 1739.[59]

The Antigua conspiracy of 1736 occurred in an abnormally dry year when water and provisions were scarce, in the midst of a depression in sugar prices, in an island which had a high proportion of imported to Creole slaves, and at least 24,000 Negroes and not above 3,000 whites. Economic factors, however, go only part way to explain the planned uprising. The plan was to plant gunpowder under a ballroom and blow up the Governor and the principal families during the King's birthday ball on the night of 20 October. This was to be the signal for the slaves, armed with cutlasses, to destroy all the whites on the island. Fortunately for the whites, the plot was discovered before the hour of execution.[60]

Unfortunately for the blacks, the discovery set in motion furious vigilante hunts and a blood bath attended with all the horrors of a medieval torture chamber. Nearly four months after discovery of the plot Dr Walter Tullideph wrote to his brother in London:

> We are in a great deal of trouble in this island; the burning of negroes, hanging them up on gibbets alive, racking them upon the wheel, &c., takes up all our time; that from the 20th of October to this day, there have been destroyed sixty-one intelligent negroes, most of them tradesmen, as carpenters, coopers and masons.[61]

Altogether, six slaves were gibbeted alive, five broken on the wheel, seventy-seven burned, and forty-two banished before the blood bath was halted because no more funds remained in the public treasury to compensate the owners of executed slaves. Of the eighty-eight slaves who were executed, forty-three belonged to twenty-nine leading planter families. Moreover, upwards of fifty were skilled artisans and drivers. The admission of slaves into 'Occupations truly proper only for Freemen' was the underlying cause for insurrection, according to a report of the local justices.[62]

---

59 Noel Deerr, *The History of Sugar* (London, 1949–50), vol. 2, pp. 322–3.
60 *Cal. S. P. Col. 1737*, p. 50.
61 *Tullideph L. B.*, vol. 2: Lre to Thomas Tullideph, 15 Jan. 1736/7.
62 P.R.O. London, C.O. 152/22, W 94: Report of John Vernon and others, Antigua, 30 Dec. 1736, in letter of Gov. Mathew to Board of Trade, 17 Jan. 1736/7. Also see C.O. 152/23, X 7, f. 33, for names, occupations, and owners of executed slaves.

Slavery and Sugar

9 SLAVERY ON ROARING RIVER PLANTATION

Increased security of life and property, together with improved welfare and longevity, probably had a salutary influence on labour productivity after the 1730s. This was especially true of Jamaica where it became safe to settle superior lands in outlying parts of the island. Edward Long observed that after the accommodation with the Maroons, settlements began to be formed in those parts of the country where none chose to venture before. Governor Trelawney wrote to the Board of Trade on 15 August 1752 that 'people may now settle with safety in any part of the Island'.[63]

Newly-settled plantations in Jamaica and the Ceded Islands were generally larger and more heavily capitalized than their counterparts in Barbados and the Leeward Islands. They were better sited and equipped to realize productivity gains stemming from greater specialization and division of labour, investment in slave capital, and technical improvements, such as water-powered sugar mills.

Illustrating the wide range of occupations and skills were the slaves who laboured on Roaring River Estate in Westmoreland parish, Jamaica, in 1756.[64] Of the 258 slaves, 84 were men, 92 women, 43 boys, 36 girls, and three had run away. Working under the white overseers were four drivers — Cromwell, Cabenna, Creole Cudjoe, and Duke — who goaded the field hands in their daily tasks. Cartage service was supplied by three mulemen and three cartmen. Craft work was performed by six carpenters, four coopers, three distillers, two masons, two wheelwrights, one boiler, and one ropemaker.

Planters who formerly depended on white tradesmen found it less costly to train their intelligent slaves as skilled craftsmen. William Beckford, proprietor of Roaring River, wrote that the Negroes, even those imported from Africa, learned the different trades 'with as much facility and perseverance as the white people do in Europe'; his slaves took 'the hoe, the adze, the hammer, or the plane the first time into their hands with as much youthful vanity as a boy at school does his bat; and it is not long before they know how to make an ingenious use of either'.[65]

Working in the cane fields were twenty-eight men and seventy women who holed, planted, weeded, and harvested the canes. 'They

---

63 Edward Long, *The History of Jamaica* (London, 1774), vol. 1, p. 429; P.R.O. London, C.O. 137/25, X 101.
64 Jamaica Public Record Office, Spanish Town, *Inventorys*, vol. 37, ff. 45–54; Richard B. Sheridan, 'Planter and Historian: The Career of William Beckford of Jamaica and England, 1744–1799', *The Jamaican Historical Review*, vol. IV (1964), pp. 36–58.
65 William Beckford, *A Descriptive Account of the Island of Jamaica* (London, 1790), vol. 2, p. 351;——, *Remarks upon the Situation of the Negroes in Jamaica* (London, 1788), p. 52.

Sugar and Slavery

generally turn out at six o'clock in the morning', wrote Beckford, and after breaks for breakfast and dinner, 'seldom continue in the field out of crop after sunset, which is never later than seven: so that, from this hour till six the ensuing morning they may call their own, part of which they consume in broken sleep, the rest in supper, and preparation for breakfast at the matin summons'.[66] Preparing holes for the planting of cane slips was by far the most strenuous labour. Accompanied by rhythmic song, the blacks were said to have raised their gleaming hoes all together, and in as exact time as the performance of a well-conducted orchestra.[67]

A third group of men on Roaring River Estate were in a miscellaneous category. There were eight watchmen, one each who served as cowkeeper, herdsman, hogherd, fisherman, bush chopper, and one who did nothing.

Of the ninety-two women, we have seen that seventy were field workers. The remaining twenty-two were engaged in a variety of occupations. Creole Phibba and Mulato Mary were house wenches, Mulato Dolly and Juran were cooks, and Sue a washer. Ministering to the sick and wounded were the two doctresses, Mulato Molly and Jenny. Flora and Baddow carried water to quench the thirst of the field Negroes, Old Benus took care of the fowl house, and Old Diana was the 'Piquinino driver' who supervised the labour of small children.

Most of the forty-three boys and thirty-six girls on Roaring River were apparently too young to work. The older boys and girls tended carts and cattle, picked grass for livestock, and ran errands for the white overseers and manager.[68]

Beckford and other planters were not unaware of the tribal origins and common characteristics of their slaves. They distinguished the Mandingoes, the Koromantyns, the Whydahs, the Pawpaws and Nagoes, the Eboes and Mocoes, and the slaves from Congo and Angola. One writer noted that the Gold Coast (Koromantyn), Pawpaw, and Whydah Negroes were born in a part of Africa that was very barren. They were in great demand, he said, because of their strong, robust constitutions and ability to perform hard field labour and live upon the sort of food the planters allowed them. On the other hand, Negroes in Gambia, Calabar, Bonny, and Angola were said to have had the necessities of life in great plenty. 'On that account, the men never work, but lead an indolent life . . . for the necessary

66 Beckford, *Negroes in Jamaica*, p. 44.
67 Elsa V. Goveia, *Slave Society in the British Leeward Islands at the End of the Eighteenth Century* (New Haven and London, 1965), pp. 130–51.
68 J.P.R.O. Spanish Town, *Inventorys*, vol. 37, ff. 45–54.

Slavery and Sugar

work among them is done by the women ...'. When these people were carried to the sugar islands they were 'obliged to be nursed, to be taken great care of, and brought to work by degrees'. Being unfit for hard labour in the cane fields, they served as household servants, raised provisions, tended cattle, and were brought up to trades.[69]

10 THE PROFITABILITY OF SLAVERY

According to Max Weber, slave labour has been profitable in a business sense where it has been possible to maintain slaves very cheaply; where there has been an opportunity for regular recruitment through a well-supplied slave market; and in agricultural production on a large scale of the plantation type; or in very simple industrial processes.[70] We have seen that plantation units tended to increase in acreage, labour force, and capitalized value, and that workers were regularly recruited through a well-supplied slave market.

Slave maintenance costs consisted chiefly of food, clothing, shelter, and medical attendance. Foodstuffs were by far the largest item, but it will be shown that the slaves provisioned themselves to a large extent in some of the colonies, and that relatively cheap foodstuffs and building materials were imported from North America.

Though provisions were grown by slaves in all the islands, the ratio of locally-grown to imported foodstuffs varied widely, being generally greater in Jamaica than the small islands. In an absolute sense, and possibly in terms of comparative advantage, slave-grown provisions were generally cheaper than the imported variety in Jamaica. Cost saving, however, was not the only consideration since the planter realized that the slave who was given a plot of land for his own use was less likely to run away. As an incentive to grow provisions, the slave was freed of plantation labour for one and a half days a week (including Sunday), he was allowed to plant what he wanted to, and was not supervised. He could specialize in one type of crop or another, raise poultry or swine, or engage in handicrafts. He could even serve as a middleman or 'higgler'. He was allowed to keep any surplus he produced, to market it if he wished, and then to keep the money. Thus the policy of allowing the slave to grow food on his own land without supervision had important ramifications. It not

---

69 'Considerations on the Present Peace, 1763', in Donnan, *Documents on the Slave Trade*, vol. 2, pp. 516–17.
70 Max Weber, *The Theory of Social and Economic Organization*, trans. by A. R. Henderson and Talcott Parsons (London, 1947), pp. 253–4.

Sugar and Slavery

only widened the slave's area of freedom; it also contributed to the rise of a provision economy in addition to the sugar economy. The slaves' provision land was often located a considerable distance from their cabins, and should not be confused with the garden plots adjacent to their dwellings. This distinction is important, because it gave the Negroes interests in land away from their cabins and at the outskirts of the sugar estates, to which they were willing to move after their emancipation. The type of cultivation may very well have been efficient and well-suited to the terrain. Negroes planted things in layers (root-crops, vines like melons or pumpkins, taller vegetables, and plantains) thus saving the soil from erosion, preventing the over-growth of weeds, and sheltering delicate plants from excessive sun, rain, or wind. Since land for provision farming was relatively abundant in Jamaica, slaves commonly burned one section clear, farmed it until it was exhausted, and then moved elsewhere. Thus although the plots usually appeared cluttered to Europeans who were used to neat rows, the type of agriculture practised by the Negroes was quite rational under the circumstances.[71]

When crop value per slave is compared with maintenance cost and factor inputs, it can be demonstrated that slavery was profitable in a business sense despite the relatively short working life of the black hands. Rough calculations show that if a prime field hand in Jamaica laboured for twelve years he returned 6 per cent per annum, while fifteen years of labour yielded 9 per cent, and twenty years nearly 11 per cent.[72] One knowledgeable master of a slave vessel testified before the Committee of the Privy Council in 1789 that much the larger proportion of planters yearly replaced their slaves 'with what they term Healthy new Negroes, rather than breed them, and look forward to from Sixteen to eighteen Years for their full and actual Service'.[73]

11 CONCLUSION

Slavery was not only profitable in a business sense; it also contributed in no small way to the economic growth of the British

---

71 Sidney W. Mintz and Douglas Hall, 'The Origins of the Jamaican Internal Marketing System', *Yale University Publications in Anthropology No. 57* (New Haven, 1960), pp. 3–26.
72 The author's computations are based on Jamaican data for the period 1765–75, and a methodology based on modern capital theory. See Alfred H. Conrad and John R. Meyer, *The Economics of Slavery and Other Studies in Econometric History* (Chicago, 1964), pp. 43–114.
73 Brit. Parl. Papers, 1789, vol. XXVI, no. 646a, part I: Testimony of Capt. T. Wilson.

Slavery and Sugar

Empire. '*The Labour of Negroes* is the principal *Foundation* of our *Riches* from the Plantations', wrote William Wood in 1718.[74] An anonymous Englishman asserted in 1749 that 'the extensive employment of our shipping in, to, and from America, the great Brood of Seamen consequent thereon, and the Daily Bread of the most considerable Part of our British Manufactures, are owing primarily to the Labour of Negroes'. The writer concluded that the Negro trade, 'and the natural consequences resulting from it may justly be esteemed an inexhaustible Fund of Wealth and Naval Power to this Nation'.[75]

74 Wood, *Survey of Trade*, pp. 179–93.
75 Anon., *The National and Private Advantage of the African Trade Considered* (London, 1749).

CHAPTER TWELVE

The English Merchant as Banker

And I cannot but beg Leave to observe and repeat, First, That whilst the British Sugar Planters had fresh good Lands, a Vent for their Produce, and were not burthen'd with Impositions and Taxes, they afforded their Commodities cheap, grew rich, and yet allowed Interest after the Rate of 15 per cent. The Reason of which, in one Word, was plainly this; the Planter then gain'd 20 *l.* per cent. or more, by the Money which he borrowed and employ'd in Planting.[1]

John Bennett, 1738

1 INTRODUCTION

From a mere handful in the 1640s, the number of sugar plantations in the British Caribbean increased to an estimated 1,800 by the eve of the American War of Independence. They increased not only in number but also in acreage and capitalization until the median sugar plantation unit in Jamaica was valued at approximately £19,500 sterling by the 1770s. If the Jamaican unit was typical of all plantations in the sugar colonies, then the aggregate capital investment in the West Indies was in the neighbourhood of £30 million sterling. The total capital of the British cotton industry did not exceed this figure until the third decade of the 19th century.

Considering the large capital investment and the risks attending colonial property, it is not surprising that credit and finance taxed the ingenuity and resources of men on both sides of the Atlantic Ocean. Political, legal, military, and economic policies and programmes were devised to extend and consolidate the area of financial security. Above all, the Navigation Acts channelled commodity trade and financial arrangements into a bilateral system. By requiring colonial goods to be shipped directly to the mother country, the Act of 1660 helped to protect the merchant-creditors who traded with the colonies. The navigation system made it

---

[1] John Bennett, *Two Letters and Several Calculations on the Sugar Trade* (London, 1738), p. xiii.

The English Merchant as Banker

difficult for the colonials to tap alternative sources of capital and credit, chiefly that of Dutch merchants who had dominated colonial trade and finance in the years of the English Civil Wars. Moreover, the colonials were convinced that the navigation system was the instrument of English and local creditors who used their power for extortionate gain. Thus a main theme that runs through any discussion of colonial finance is the struggle between debtors and creditors.

Contrary to accepted opinion, the West Indies came to be a source of capital for the economic development of the mother country. At the outset, however, European capital and credit were needed for the settlement and development of the colonies. At best four or five years were needed to bring a newly-settled sugar plantation into profitable production. Few men were able to bear the heavy charges of such an undertaking without financial assistance.

Capital came from a variety of sources. Besides the Dutch, we have seen that a group of wealthy London merchants — including the Courteen brothers, Marmaduke Rawdon, Maurice Thompson and Sir Martin Noell — were instrumental in establishing the sugar colonies. Following in the wake of the merchant-adventurers came lesser merchants, government officials, military officers, professional men, and even buccaneers and Royalists. Numbered among them were men of some means and connection who hoped to gain fortunes in the great sugar lottery of the Caribbean. Immigrant capital thus played a part in the development process. But as most of the early settlers were unable to encompass a sugar estate from their own resources, merchant-capital played a key role in the initial phases of the sugar industry.

Though financial arrangements varied widely in time and space, it seems possible to accommodate them to two major systems. Broadly speaking, the system which was characteristic of the 17th century was dominated by English merchants who traded on their own account with the West Indies, sometimes engaging in trade as travelling merchants, but more often acting through supercargoes and factors in the colonies. The major features of the merchant system of finance are the concern of the present chapter. In the following chapter attention will be directed to the financial system which emerged under the domination of the sugar planters. But first it will be well to consider the nature of the capital invested in the sugar industry.

Sugar and Slavery

2 PLANTATION CAPITAL REQUIREMENTS

Two basic facts need to be kept in mind in considering the financing of sugar production in the period of slavery. In the first place, the production function was such that capital investment generally led to lower unit costs of production. Second, the high rate of capital depreciation was a heavy charge on the gross revenue of a plantation.

In answering the question why capital investment tended to lower unit costs of production, it is necessary to distinguish between the capital required for cultivating sugar canes, and that required for processing cane juice into raw sugar, molasses and rum. The cultivation of canes required unskilled labourers working with simple hand tools, while the manufacturing process called for a considerable outlay of capital for sugar works and distilleries. With the assistance of a few labourers and implements the planter might grow canes efficiently on a smallholding. But the canes were useless without a works to convert them into sugar. A small planter might build a crude sugar works at a reasonable cost – for example, a Barbadian wrote in 1646 that an outlay of only £200 'might quickly gaine an estate by sugar, which thrives wonderfully'.[2] Unit costs were high under these conditions, however, and an efficient plantation needed a considerable body of slaves and equipment. The governor of St Vincent called attention to the economies of scale when he wrote that 'a small Estate is at greater Expence in proportion to its produce than a large one, because the Buildings, the Stock and White Servants necessary for the one are sufficient for the other with very little additional expence'.[3]

Granted that it was more economical to produce sugar on large plantations, the question arises as to the nature and value of the capital on sugar estates. No specific answer can be given to this question because of wide variation in the size and capitalized value of production units. It may be useful, however, to present summaries of several plantation estimates.

Sir Dalby Thomas (1690) estimated that a planter needed £5,625 to furnish a plantation of 100 acres which yielded 80 hogsheads of sugar per annum. Of this total, 50 slaves amounted to £1,250; 7 white servants and 3 artisans, £150; 5 horses, £125; and 8 bullocks,

---

2 Rev. James Parker to Gov. John Winthrop, 24 April 1646, in *A Collection of Original Papers Relating to the History of the Colony of Massachusetts-Bay*, ed. Thomas Hutchinson (Boston, 1769), pp. 156–7.

3 Public Record Office, London, C.O. 260/8, no. 40: Gov. Seton of St. Vincent to Lord Sidney, 1 July 1788.

£100. The remaining £4,000 was expended for land, houses, mills, tools, and implements.[4]

In 1732, Rev. Robert Robertson calculated that the typical plantation in St Kitts represented an outlay of £11,700 sterling, of which £3,400 was for 200 acres of land, and £3,300 for 150 slaves. The remaining £5,000 was needed for the following buildings, equipment, and livestock:

> A good and substantial Dwelling-House, Boiling-House, Curing-House, and Still-House ... with the Stables, and Out-Housing, cannot be built for 1500 *l.*
>
> The Coppers, Stills, and other Implements and Utensils for the Boiling, Cureing, and Still-Houses, and Cattle-Mill, 1000 *l.*
>
> And if a Wind-Mill should be thought needful (as indeed it is) on a Plantation of 200 Acres, that would cost little less than 1000 *l.*
>
> Then Horses from the *North*-Continent, Mules from *Porto*-rico, *Curacoa*, or the *Spainish Main*, which are sold at 20 to 28 *l.* Sterling per Head, Carts, Cart-Cattle, and other Appendices, too numerous to set down here, 1500 *l.*[5]

Edward Long included three plantation estimates in his *History of Jamaica* (1774). He calculated that £3,515 sterling was needed to settle a small plantation of 300 acres, yielding from 30 to 50 hogsheads of sugar per annum. Land and growing canes were valued at £1,567; sugar works, other equipment and livestock, £877; and 30 Negroes, £1,071. On a plantation of 300 acres, yielding 100 hogsheads of sugar and 50 puncheons of rum, the total valuation was £10,017 sterling. Land and growing canes were valued at £2,970; sugar works and other equipment, £2,463; 60 head of cattle, £1,014; and 100 Negroes, £3,570. The total cost of a fully-equipped plantation of 900 acres, yielding 300 hogsheads of sugar and 150 puncheons of rum annually, was £28,039 sterling. Land and growing canes amounted to £9,032; sugar works and other equipment, £6,319; 130 head of livestock, £1,978; and 300 Negroes, £10,710.[6]

Negro slaves ranged from one-fifth to one-third or more of the total investment in sugar plantations. The percentage was 28.2 in Robertson's estimate. He observed that

> The next Requisite to Sugar-making, and the most momentous as the World goes is the Negro-Slaves, less than 150 of which Young and Old, cannot manure 200 Acres with any tolerable Prospect of Advantage. ...

---

4 Sir Dalby Thomas, *An Historical Account of the Rise and Growth of the West-India Collonies* (London, 1690), p. 18.

5 Rev. Robert Robertson, *A Detection of the State and Situation of the Present Sugar Planters of Barbadoes and the Leeward Islands* (London, 1732), p. 42.

6 Edward Long, *The History of Jamaica* (London, 1774), vol. 1, pp. 448–64.

Sugar and Slavery

> *Boys* and *Girls* have of late cost 14 to 20 *l*. Sterling, *Women* 20 to 28 *l*. and *Men* 24 to 30 *l*. or more. Take them at 22 *l* per Head, and this comes to 3,300 *l*. Sterling.[7]

Antigua was reported to have had more than 300 sugar estates in 1764. On these estates there were some 25,000 slaves, representing an investment of £1 million sterling. The island's 60,000 taxable acres were valued at £90,000 and another £900,000 was invested in buildings, equipment, and livestock on sugar estates. The slaves thus accounted for 35.7 per cent of total valuation.[8] By comparison, the percentages for the three plantation estimates of Edward Long, moving from small to large, were 30.5, 35.6, and 38.2, respectively.

Fixed capital items included the various buildings comprising the sugar works, customarily of masonry construction, amply proportioned, and representing a capital outlay with the mechanical contrivances and equipment of several thousand pounds sterling. In this category is included the sugar mill itself — depending on wind, water or animal power, the boiling house, curing house, and distillery. Altogether, these capital items made up between 20 and 30 per cent of the value of sugar estates. Another 7 to 13 per cent was represented by livestock, consisting chiefly of horned cattle, horses, and mules. Then there was the sizeable investment in land and growing canes, representing 29.1 per cent of Rev. Robertson's estimate, 32.3 of the Antigua calculation of 1764, and 44.6, 29.6, and 32.2 of Edward Long's estimates, moving from small to large plantation units.

3 THE HIGH RATE OF CAPITAL DEPRECIATION

The second basic fact to keep in mind in financing sugar production was said to be the high rate of capital depreciation. These charges ranged over a considerable area and applied to animate and inanimate items which were used in the culture of canes and the processing of sugar products.

The replacement of slaves who died or became superannuated was undoubtedly the heaviest depreciation charge incurred by the planter. We have seen that the annual rate of decrease among the blacks was in the range of 2 to 5 per cent per annum. If the slave

---

[7] Robertson, *Detection of Sugar Planters*, p. 42.
[8] Anon., *Some Observations: Which May Contribute to Afford a Just Idea of Our New West-India Colonies* (London, 1764), p. 50.

trade had not filled the ranks, the population, given a mortality rate of 5 per cent, would have completely disappeared in twenty years.[9]

Capital invested in sugar works, utensils, and implements was subject to rapid depreciation owing to hard usage and the effect of the humid climate. Wood rotted away quickly and had to be replaced. On the Stapleton plantation in Nevis the manager went to the wooden cistern which held the molasses and found that 'the worms had eaten through and lost all'.[10] Timbers had to be replaced and roofs reshingled. Hurricanes took a heavy toll of wooden buildings and made it necessary to lay out large sums for repairs and replacement.

Ferrous metal corroded badly in the tropical climate, contributing to heavy replacement charges for hardware and implements. John Oldmixon said that 'if any Instrument of Steel is never so clean, let it lie one Night expos'd to the Air, it will be rusty next Morning; which, tho' things do not rust so soon now, occasions the Necessity of frequent Supplies of such sort of Goods'. John Campbell observed that implements and other iron work were 'not only exceedingly expensive at the first setting out, but which from their being in continual use, constantly wear out and require fresh supplies'. Utensils necessary in the sugar works included 'coppers, mil cases, ladles, skimmers, mills, stills, and almost numberless other articles, to which may be added nails, locks, hinges, bolts, and lead, employed by the planter in his other buildings, and almost innumerable kinds of iron works'.[11]

Hoes in particular were subjected to hard usage by the slaves. Not being highly-tempered, they wore out quickly and had to be replaced. Dr Tullideph, who sent to England for hoes each year, said they were 'a grand affair in the Consumption of Iron as a dozen of them are sold from 12/ to 16/. On my Estates I usually wear out 20 dozen a year and supposing them to weigh 4 pounds one with another, here is 960 weight, near half a Tonn'.[12]

Numerous charges were usually met out of working capital. To preserve the health and welfare of his blacks the planter paid out considerable sums annually for medical services, provisions, and

---

9 See Chapter 11, pp. 243–4, 247.
10 Edwin F. Gay, 'Letters from a Sugar Plantation in Nevis, 1723–1732', *Journal of Economic and Business History*, vol. 1 (Nov. 1928), p. 157.
11 John Oldmixon, *The British Empire in America* (London, 1708), vol. 2, p. 157; John Campbell, *Candid and Impartial Considerations on the Nature of the Sugar Trade* (London, 1763), p. 23.
12 *Tullideph, L. B.*, vol. 3: Lre. to the Carron Company, dated Dundee, Scotland, 7 Oct. 1763.

clothing. Some of these charges fluctuated from year to year while others were relatively fixed.

The treatment of illness and injury among slaves was a relatively fixed and burdensome charge. Since a large portion of their capital was tied up in slaves, planters commonly laid out considerable sums to preserve their workers in physical vigour. Dr Tullideph's medical ledger contains accounts with nearly a hundred Antigua planters, most of whom called on the doctor to treat specific cases of illness and injury. Tullideph's charges ranged from 3s 6d for extracting a tooth to £5 for treating a Negro boy and 'laying open a Mortification in his leg with dressing and cure with several visits'. Since single visits were often expensive, substantial planters found it economical to have their slaves treated on a contract basis. Tullideph had twenty-two such accounts from 1732 to 1735. Samuel Byam, for example, was charged £37 10s 'To ye care of 125 negroes from January 25, 1734/5 to December 1735/6 is one year at 6/'.[13]

Large plantations generally had hospitals and full-time doctors. On the Pinney plantation in Nevis there was a hospital and a 'lying-in room' for serious cases, immediately under the manager's eye. John Pinney was very particular about keeping the sick Negroes in the hospital and inspecting them there at least once a day. Most planters also had one or two old women slaves, and sometimes the wife of the manager, to serve as midwives and treat minor ailments and injuries.[14]

Negro clothing and provisions were considerable items of expense. Unlike medical services, however, they fluctuated from year to year. Clothing expenses varied because planters frequently postponed purchases in poor crop seasons. Outlays for provisions fluctuated because some food was grown locally and the need for imported supplies depended on local yields. Crude estimates of the annual provision and clothing charges are not uncommon in the literature. Sir Dalby Thomas said that 'the *English* Cloaths and provisions such 10 Whites and 50 Blacks consume is one with another forty shillings a head and amounts to a hundred and twenty pounds'. The clothing and other British manufactures consumed by each slave in Jamaica was reported to cost 20s per annum, or £100,000 for 100,000 slaves.[15]

Negro provision outlays fluctuated greatly from year to year and

---

13 *Walter Tullideph's Medical Ledger.*
14 Richard Pares, *A West India Fortune* (London, 1950), p. 128.
15 Thomas, *Historical Account of West-India Collonies*, p. 18; Samuel Dicker, *A Letter to a Member of Parliament Concerning the Importance of Our Sugar-Colonies to Great Britain* (London, 1745), pp. 21–2.

were often inversely proportional to the income from sugar products. Little revenue might be realized from the sale of sugar and rum in poor crop years, while outlays for imported foodstuffs might be very great indeed. Conversely, near-self-sufficiency was not uncommon in good crop seasons. Dr Tullideph informed Governor George Thomas of Pennsylvania in April 1742: 'We can make no sugar there next year but what we plant now to use as a nursery, to send flower, bread & corn as we expect hard times'. The Governor learned of more favourable conditions in 1746: 'I hope you'l be at no expence in ffeeding this year & will endeavour to prevent that charge yearly excepting Salt kind'.[16]

Working capital was usually needed to pay the wages of white overseers, coopers, blacksmiths, and other artisans who were employed on plantations. The overseer's wage, according to several writers, ranged from £100 to £200 a year, besides a variety of non-monetary perquisites. Absentee proprietors incurred additional charges for commissions paid to plantation attornies, generally 6 or 7 per cent of the produce raised or shipped from estates in the West Indies. Then there were other expenses, such as taxes on land, slaves, and houses and customs duties.

Annual expenses thus amounted to a considerable sum of money on a large and fully settled plantation. One estimate concerns an Antiguan estate of 500 acres and 300 Negroes, yielding 200 hogsheads of sugar and 120 puncheons of rum annually, and valued at £20,000 sterling. Annual average expenditures ran to £1,274, consisting of provisions, £300; other supplies, £290; salaries and wages, £320; colonial and parish taxes, £254; and crown duties and fees, £110. The author fails to include the depreciation charge for slaves, which would have amounted to about £400, and various duties on commodity exports amounting to about £200. Total annual charges thus come to nearly £1,900, out of an annual gross revenue of approximately £3,600. On the basis of these calculations, the net profit was 8.5 per cent per annum.[17]

4 THE IMPORTANCE OF TRADE CREDIT

'I goe on expending money upon my plantation, in hopes it will repaye mee with interest', wrote Christopher Jeaffreson, 'but I must have patience, for it will require tyme, as well as a large expense,

16 *Tullideph L. B.*, vol. 1: Lre. to Gov. George Thomas in Philadelphia, dated Antigua, 10 April 1742; vol. 2: Lre. to same, 22 May 1746.
17 Anon., *Observations of our New West-India Colonies*, pp. 48–9.

before my sugar-worke can be perfected'.[18] Generally speaking, sugar plantations were built up gradually over a period of years and financed to a large extent from reinvested profits. A statement to this effect was made by a Barbadian in 1732:

> The Planters (speaking of Barbadoes) did in the Beginning, and for many Years, pay the Merchants for the Negroes, Provisions and other Necessaries they supply'd them with, in Muscovado Sugars, valued at no more than 10s. per 100 ... yet, at that Price, they were enabled to encounter all the Difficulties attending a new Settlement, clear their Lands, raise their Chargeable Sugar Works, and live at an extravagant Expense. ... And yet from these Beginnings the Profits have been so immensely great, as that Plantations of 1000 and 2000 *l.* per Annum have been raised from them, and many of the Planters have remitted over their Effects, and purchas'd large Estates in England.[19]

It was one thing for the sugar industry to be self-financing once it was established, but quite another to amass the capital to get it started. We have seen that the limited resources of early settlers confined activity for some years to the cultivation of subsistence crops and minor staples. The general method in Jamaica, wrote James Knight, was 'to begin with 15 or 20 Negroes, who are first employed to clear a piece of land, to build themselves houses, and to plant provisions for their subsistence'. The planter then opened more land,

> and plants Ginger, Cotton, or some other commodity that is raised with a few hands; as he thrives, he purchases more Negroes, clears more land; and when he finds himself in a Condition, or able to attempt it by his Credit, and the Assistance of Friends, he then goes upon settling a Sugar Work.[20]

Small planters thus needed supplementary sources of capital if they were to shift rapidly to the more profitable staple.

Some of them hastened the transition with landed or mercantile capital which they possessed before migrating to the colonies. In other cases capital was acquired by military conquest, confiscation, or privateering raids. To cite only two examples, Spanish capital – chiefly livestock – was taken by the English at the conquest of Jamaica, whereas Dutch capital – chiefly mercantile stores – was confiscated by the inhabitants of the Leeward Islands during the Anglo-Dutch wars.

---

18 John C. Jeaffreson, *A Young Squire of the Seventeenth Century* (London, 1878), vol. 1, pp. 210–11.
19 Anon., *The Dispute between the Northern Colonies and the Sugar Islands, set in Clear View* (London, 1732), p. 1.
20 British Museum Add. MSS 12,419: James Knight, MSS History of Jamaica, vol. 2, pt. 8, f. 141.

The English Merchant as Banker

Turning to less warlike means of accumulation, some planters found a solution to their financial problem by entering into partnership or 'mateship' agreements. One partner might be an English capitalist who purchased and sent out goods to his working partner in the colonies. One of these capitalists was Sir Josiah Child, the great London merchant. On 4 November 1672 he entered into an agreement with one Samuel Bache, merchant, of Port Royal, Jamaica. The object of the partnership was to build a sugar works and settle a plantation of 1,330 acres in that island. Child agreed to procure and buy the necessary servants, slaves, and supplies, while Bache undertook the direction of the estate. Expenses and profits were to be shared eqully, and both partners entered into penal bonds in the sum of £10,000.[21]

Relatively few pioneer colonists had the wherewithal to enter into partnership agreements or attract loanable funds from England. On the other hand, greater numbers might purchase plantation supplies on credit and delay payment until their crops were harvested. By this means they could postpone some of their charges without borrowing. In other words, trade credit enabled the planter to meet his charges without a fund of working capital.

The suppliers of trade credit were chiefly European merchants who traded on their own account with the West Indies. Both English and Dutch merchants extended credit in the early years of the sugar industry. Moreover, Anglo-Dutch firms like the Courteen brothers probably supplied capital to the colonists by an indirect channel. The source notwithstanding, there is little doubt that trade credit played a key role in capital formation.

Contemporary accounts indicate that trade credit was normally granted until the planters' crops were harvested. In Jamaica, for example, the normal period was nine months. Circumstances varied, however, and longer credit terms were not uncommon. In 1665, it was said that the Jamaicans 'would take all the negroes of the Royal Company if they would give 18 months as the Dutch did formerly at Barbadoes'. English merchants at times gave long credits, as instanced by the sale of slaves in Barbados in 1719 at 'near two years credit'.[22]

Since merchants who extended credit were out of their money for a lengthy period, they might be expected to insist on compensation greater than their normal trading profit. Contemporary accounts

---

21 Jamaica Public Record Office, Spanish Town, *Deeds*, vol. 5, Anno. 1672, ff. 165–6. Nine founders contracts are printed in Appendix II of Richard Pares, *Merchants and Planters. The Economic History Review Supplement 4* (Cambridge, 1960), pp. 43–4, 52–5.
22 *Cal. S. P. Col. 1661–68*, p. 312; Elizabeth Donnan (ed.), *Documents Illustrative of the History of the Slave Trade to America* (New York, 1965), vol. 1, p. 242.

Sugar and Slavery

indicate that instead of levying a separate interest charge, merchants merely raised the price of their goods to allow for the interest. Planters in the Leeward Islands were reported to have 'taken up Goods of the Trader as they want them, to be paid (which long Custom has made a Rule) as their Crops come on. This the Trader knows how to improve, by laying a proper Price on his Wares'.[23] Identical goods thus sold in the West Indies on a two-price basis; one price for cash payment, a considerably higher price for credit sales.

Wide variation appears in the type and quantity of goods sold on credit. Since small planters were poor credit risks, they were generally limited to supplies needed in cultivating and harvesting their crops. Governor Lawes wrote from Jamaica in 1717; 'Negroes are very dear, from £25 to £40 per head, little or no credit will be given to new settlers, without which the country can never increase in Planters, tho' the present possessors may be in riches'.[24]

To some extent trade credit made it possible for the planter to plough back his profits before they were earned. But as credit was generally granted for one crop season, it was difficult to expand production very rapidly by such means. There was thus a normal desire to postpone debt payment even when the planter was able to pay. On the other hand, crop failure and other contingencies might make payment impossible. The planter's survival might thus depend on the merchant's willingness to tide him over the lean years.

Under what conditions, then, would the creditor be willing to relax the terms of repayment? Ability to grant credit on the one hand, and ability to meet debt obligations on the other, were obviously considerations of some moment. In the infancy of the sugar industry Dutch merchants dominated the scene partly owing to their liberal credit terms. But it is incorrect to think that they granted credit indiscriminately to both large and small planters. According to John Scott, a 17th century historian of Barbados:

> The Hollanders that are great encouragers of Plantations did at the first attempt of making Sugar give great credit to the most sober inhabitants; and upon the unhappy Civil War that break out in England, they managed the whole trade in the Western Colonies, and furnished the islands with Negroes, coppers, stills, and all other things.... This put the Barbadoes into a flourishing condition, but it was attended with the inconvenience in that the more industrious and prudent planters became storehouse keepers for the Dutch, and so by giving credit to their profuse and sometimes necitous neighbours on severe terms, insensibly in few years wormed out

---

23 Robertson, *Detection of Sugar Planters*, p. 54.
24 *Cal. S. P. Col. 1717–18*, p. 103.

The English Merchant as Banker

the greatest part of the small proprietors; for the making of Sugar requires many negroes and considerable quantities of land.[25]

Financial stringency was the rule for some years following Dutch exclusion from the English colonies. Apart from certain Anglo-Dutch firms, English merchants were less able to extend credit to needy planters than their former Dutch rivals. Travelling merchants, themselves trading to a large extent on borrowed capital, needed a quick turnover in the colonial trade if they were to remain solvent. Supercargoes and factors were often reluctant to grant extensions because they ran the risk of being cut off from future consignments if remittances were not made promptly.

Merchants and factors sometimes refused extensions when they were not pressed for money or when their debtors were good credit risks. Creditors might be more concerned to gain possession of the debtor's estate than to collect outstanding debts. Scott suggests that Barbadian planters acted as factors of Dutch merchants with this objective in mind. English merchants were sometimes more concerned to gain possession of their debtors' plantations than to take West India produce in payment of debts. To establish a sugar plantation, said Richard Ligon, it was first necessary to procure supplies by means of successive mercantile ventures to the West Indies.[26]

If some planters secured extensions of trade credit, many more were probably refused. Again, the parties involved in such extension were chiefly creditworthy planters and merchants of reputation and capital. The 'real merchants' of Jamaica, wrote Edward Long, 'are men of worth and actuated by the most generous principles'. The merchant of note might be reluctant to take the benefit of the law 'till things are grown desperate; for it is his Interest (as it was the Royal African Company's) to bear as long as possible with the Planter, and to help him to retrieve himself by new Credits'. Sir Dalby Thomas praised the Royal African Company for being 'wonderfully kinde in the Credit they have given the Plantations'. However, creditors did not grant such indulgences on easy terms. Separate interest payments and the additional security of judgements, bonds, or mortgages were among the terms of acceptance.[27]

---

25 B.M. Sloane MSS 3662, f. 34: John Scott, 'The Description of Barbados'.
26 Richard Ligon, *A True and Exact History of the Island of Barbadoes* (London, 1673), pp. 109–12.
27 Long, *History of Jamaica*, vol. 1, p. 575; Robertson, *Detection of Sugar Planters*, p. 57; Thomas, *Historical Account of West-India Collonies*, p. 38.

5 DEBTOR-CREDITOR CONFLICT

Once a planter was denied an extension of credit, he made it difficult for his creditor to collect outstanding debts. In other words, the planter attempted to freeze trade credit. The debtor's ability to forestall his creditor depended in large measure on the nature of the laws pertaining to debt collection. During the transition from small to large units of production the merchants and factors were dominant in island governments and courts. Since the laws were generally favourable to creditors, planters found it difficult to impede merchants in the collection of their debts.

The rise of the planter class was accompanied by a shift in the balance of political power. As planters came to dominate local governments and courts, the laws were amended and interpreted to favour the debtor class. By the early 1660s the legal machinery of Barbados was being used to discriminate against merchant-creditors. Merchants and traders to that island complained of the 'delay of justice and legal proceedings for recovery of debts'. The President and Council of Barbados had ordered the judges in the several precincts to adjourn, thus denying creditors access to court executions on the property of debtors.[28]

Cases of legal discrimination against the creditors of Antigua planters are too numerous to be dismissed. For example, in 1711 the merchants, factors, and traders of that island complained that the proceedings of law were so dilatory with respect to the recovery of debts that they were unable to make remittances to their principals in England. Governor Parke (1705–11) made many enemies in Antigua when he acknowledged his low opinion of the laws for recovery of debts and justified his taking the law into his own hand on the grounds that this was the only way a creditor could receive justice. It was an avowed maxim in Antigua, he asserted, 'never to give any Cause, how just soever, on the Behalf of a stranger, against an Inhabitant'.[29]

Debt collection was a harassing, time-consuming activity for Dr Tullideph of Antigua. He not only acted as his brother's factor but also received powers of attorney from absentee merchants and planters to collect debts. Tullideph said that it was important to establish the precedence of a debt. On several occasions he wrote that debts were uncollectable because other creditors had put in their claims beforehand and the debtor's estate was too small to meet all

---

28 *Cal. S. P. Col. 1661–68*, p. 137; Ibid., *1669–74*, p. 540.
29 George French, *The History of Col. Parke's Administration of the Leeward Islands* (London, 1717), p. 136.

The English Merchant as Banker

claims. Precedence also depended on the nature of the security; judgements, bonds, and mortgages were superior to book entries. Slow communication gave a decided advantage to local creditors who frequently swallowed up the estate of a deceased debtor before the English creditors could be notified.

Tullideph complained of court delays and laws requiring creditors to have white witnesses to prove debts. Instructions from one London creditor were received 'too late for our Courts which sitts only 5 Courts in ye year & if an action is not begun in the first Court the debt can't be recovered that Year'. Morevoer, it was necessary to 'prove every thing our selves in Court for they will grant nothing but what we can prove'.[30]

The heavy expenses incurred in suing for debts was another bone of contention. The provost marshal, who collected debts on the authority of court executions, was said to have charged exorbitant fees. Although Tullideph was reluctant to turn debts over to the marshal for collection, this was often his last resort. 'That office wants much amendment', he wrote to his brother, 'in short a Creditor had better receive his debt himself with some loss rather than goe thro' a Course of Law, for when it has gott into the Marshall's hands he becomes a fresh Creditor'.[31]

Besides legal obstructions and charges, creditors were injured by the cheap-money measures of planter governments. Merchants who sold goods for cash – that is for legal tender sugar or coin – could protect themselves by raising the price to compensate for any depreciation in money values. But as most goods were sold on credit, currency debasement sometimes made it possible for debtors to pay creditors with money of reduced purchasing power. By an act of September 1667, the Assembly of Barbados 'raised their coin, that is Muscovado, from 10s. per 100 lbs., to pass in pay for 16s'. The governor vetoed the act on the grounds that 'it is found by experience that the consequence thereof tends to the impairing of the credit and trade of this Island'.[32]

Jamaica alternated between metallic currency and island produce, depending upon the state of the Spanish bullion trade. Currency stringency led to the act of 1683 whereby sugar and other island produce, as valued by the church wardens of the parish, were declared legal tender. A similar measure in 1728 was condemned by local merchants on the ground that it fixed the legal tender value of sugar higher than the market value. The governor refused to approve

30 *Tullideph, L. B.*, vol. 1: Lre. to James Durham in London, dated Antigua, 23 May 1736.
31 Ibid., Lre. to David Tullideph in London, 14 Aug. 1738.
32 Robert Chalmers, *A History of Currency in the British Colonies* (London, 1893), p. 47.

the act, giving as his reason the injury which would result to creditors. Acts to raise the value of local coins drew the censure of Edward Long, who observed that

> All augmentations of the numerary value of the current coin, must inevitably injure creditors under permanent contracts, such as bonds and mortgages, and therefore must prove extremely detrimental to many in Jamaica; where so vast an amount of debts is continually resolved into securities of this nature.[33]

Over-valued currency aggravated debtor-creditor relations in the Leeward Islands. Numerous branches of trade suffered from such measures, but none quite so much as the African trade. Slavers were avoiding Antigua in 1719, said one London merchant, because when the planters had 'purchased Negros in exchange for Sugar, agreed to be paid the following Cropp, at twelve Shillings the hundred, they would not pay for them unless at twenty-five, or keep the Sellers out of their money seven years'.[34]

Merchant-creditors were not without weapons of their own in this struggle. As a rule they demanded greater security when debtors were slow to pay. Bonds, judgements, and mortgages were sometimes given as security when debts were first incurred. The usual procedure, however, was to require such securities only when debts were overdue. Edward Long has been quoted to the effect that a vast amount of Jamaican debt was continually resolved into bond and mortgage securities. If the debtor was reluctant to pledge such security, the creditor might threaten to sue. Creditors also defended themselves against the debtors' tendency to freeze trade credit by charging interest on delinquent debts. Thus, interest which was initially hidden in the price of goods became at the termination of the credit period a separate charge on the principal sum.

Debtors and creditors crossed swords on the rate of interest as they did on other issues. Planter governments reduced legal interest rates on several occasions, only to find that creditors retaliated by laying extra fees and charges on frozen trade credit. Though the legal and market rates of interest were consistently higher in the West Indies than in the mother country, a downward trend was observed throughout the British Empire in the period of this study. Jamaica and Barbados reduced their legal rates from 15 per cent to 10 per cent in 1667 and 1668, respectively, and further reduction came later. Barbados, Montserrat, and Jamaica reduced the legal rate to 8

---

33 Long, *History of Jamaica*, vol. 1, p. 564.
34 Donnan, *Documents Illustrative of the Slave Trade*, vol. 2, p. 241: Richard Harris to the Secretary of the Board of Trade, 21 Sept. 1719.

per cent in 1729, 1735, and 1739, respectively.[35] In 1738, the rate in Antigua was reduced from 10 to 6 per cent, the latter rate being established in Barbados and Jamaica in 1752. An eruption of debtor-creditor hostility followed enactment of the Antigua law of 1738. The Assembly took umbrage with a memorial presenting the case of local merchants and factors. Dr Tullideph said that he had signed the memorial, in which there were harsh words which 'gave offence and was voted by ye Assembly to be a Scandalous libell highly reflecting upon their Justice & dignity. We were all sent for to make our acknowledgements, I not being in Town scaped being sent to Gaol'.[36]

When it is considered how large a gap existed between legal and market rates of interest, it is doubtful if the Antigua Assembly achieved more than a paper victory. A land bank was proposed for Barbados in 1661 on the grounds that 'the injuries done to the planters and others by usurious sales and contracts at 30 per Cent interest' would come to an end if the planters might borrow at the bank on landed security at the rate of 6 per cent per annum.[37] A few years later a Barbadian complained of several merchants

> who had by subtlety got the whole means of the poor labourers engaged to them, and yearly heap interest upon interest and gnaw them to the bone, and that such exactors take 30 per 100 pr annum and more. Some in England live rich upon it, and certainly Nemiah is needed to force them to deliver these poor men out of their bondage.[38]

Edward Long wrote more than a century later that the Jamaica planter who was driven to establish his consignments to a factor in Kingston, or take up loans in the island of some rich Jew, paid from 16 to 20 per cent instead of the legal maximum of 6 per cent.[39]

Planters frequently sought permission to postpone debt payments. When their requests were denied they took advantage of the law to freeze trade credit. By this means not a few planters were able to hold on to their estates during lean years. 'This delay', wrote Long, 'gives opportunity for the planter's crop to come round again, and affords him the means of making some payment; by which the sinews of his estate may be redeemed from a levy'.[40]

Slave company records suggest that frozen trade credit was a

---

35 *Cal. S. P. Col. 1677–80*, p. 214; Frank W. Pitman, *The Development of the British West Indies 1700–1763* (New Haven, 1917), pp. 135–6.
36 *Tullideph L. B.*, vol. 1: Lre. to William Dunbar in London, dated Antigua, 8 Aug. 1738.
37 *Cal. S. P. Col. 1661–68*, p. 62.
38 Ibid., *1669–74*, p. 44.
39 Long, *History of Jamaica*, vol. 1, p. 558.
40 Ibid., vol. 1, p. 392.

Sugar and Slavery

major source of capital for the early sugar industry. Already by 1665 the Company of Royal Adventurers Trading to Africa were in financial difficulties, owing some £100,000 to their English creditors. Out of the ashes of the Royal Adventurers rose the Royal African Company, part of whose assets consisted of debts owed by planters to the former company. To these were added new debts, partly a large floating debt owed by planters for slaves sold on four or six months' credit or more, and partly a permanent debt owed by planters who were either unwilling or unable to pay when their debts fell due. The total debt owing to the Royal African Company from the West Indies was put at £120,000 in 1680, £136,000 in 1684, and £170,000 in 1690.[41]

6 THE WEST INDIAN LOAN MARKET

Planters thus reduced their needs for working capital by purchasing supplies on credit. However, they were seldom able to get along without some working capital. If costs could not be financed out of accumulated profits and trade credit, the capital had to be obtained elsewhere. One possible solution was to borrow money. Besides meeting current charges, a loan might be needed to replace worn-out capital or to expand plantation operations.

Short-term loans were in great demand in the West Indies because they freed planters from dependence on high cost trade credit. The planter who secured a loan was usually free to spend the money as he saw fit. He could buy goods for cash and obtain them more cheaply than the planter who depended on trade credit. At the same time, the planter who paid cash for his supplies was free to dispose of his sugar to the highest bidder. The Royal African Company was said to have sold their Negroes 'at 1/3 too dear' because of the 'bad pay they Complain of in the Colonies'. The debt-ridden planter sold his produce cheap, 'not being able thro' Poverty to keep his Commodity by him untill it will yield a saving Price'. He was thus in the unenviable position of buying dear and selling cheap.[42]

The lack of a satisfactory medium of exchange was probably the most serious obstacle to the creation of a West Indian loan market. Money lenders, unlike merchants who sold goods on credit, almost invariably demanded payment in specie. But specie was in almost chronic short supply except for Jamaica in the heyday of her Spanish

41 K. G. Davies, *The Royal African Company* (London, 1957), pp. 316–19.
42 Thomas, *Historical Account of West-India Collonies*, p. 40.

The English Merchant as Banker

bullion trade. Money lenders were further impeded by laws making sugar legal tender at over-valued rates. It is a fact, wrote one Leeward Islander in 1740, 'that if a man demands to be paid sterling money or other gold and silver money he lent conditioned to be paid in the same species it is the option of the debtor as the law now stands to pay in country produce'.[43]

Planters seldom obtained loans from England until they became wealthy enough to employ London commission agents.[44] But they were able on occasion to borrow locally. In each colony there were well-to-do planters, merchants, factors, doctors, lawyers, and public officials who loaned money to needy planters. During his early career as a factor and doctor, Walter Tullideph made numerous short-term loans to planters. His familiarity with local business conditions plus his ability to judge the character of prospective borrowers compensated to a large extent for faulty debtor laws and scarce specie.[45]

Jamaica seems to have had more money lenders in proportion to its population than the other Caribbean colonies. This was due in large measure to the entrepôt trade which brought in Spanish coins and bullion. While much of the coin was remitted to England or exchanged for North American supplies, a substantial portion remained to serve as a medium of exchange and loan fund. However, the inflow and outflow was irregular and in certain periods the circulation of Spanish coin was reduced to a trickle. One such period came after the Seven Years' War when it was said that 'many distressed persons are driven to negotiate loans on paying a premium of 10 *l.* and in some cases of 15 *l.* and 20 *l. per cent.* besides the legal interest ... it is scarcely practicable, in the present situation of things, for a planter to borrow money in Jamaica'.[46]

Such disparity in demand and supply called for other measures. One possibility was a land bank. In 1661, the Chancellor of the Exchequer acted favourably on a proposal for a land bank in Barbados and issued a warrant for a bill to be drafted by the Attorney General. In brief, the bill called for the creation of a bank to lend money on landed security in the colony at the rate of 6 per cent per annum.

Though the land bank bill of 1661 failed of enactment, the project was not forgotten. In 1706, a party of Barbadian planters drew up a bill for such a bank and carried it though the Assembly and Council. Planters were to obtain locally issued bills of credit to the amount of

43 *Calendar of Treasury Books and Papers, 1739–41,* vol. CCCII, no. 3.
44 Thomas, *Historical Account of West-India Collonies,* pp. 47–8.
45 *Walter Tullideph's Medical Ledger.*
46 Long, *History of Jamaica,* vol. 1, pp. 558–9.

one-fourth the value of their estates.[47] Merchants in England and Barbados, particularly the Royal African Company, registered strong opposition to the bank. The bills of credit would depreciate quickly, creditors would be ruined, and prices of imports and island produce would be artificially inflated, they predicted. Nevertheless, the planters went forward with the project and the bank was established. Its life-span was extremely short; the act was disallowed by an order in council on 21 October 1706, only a few months after the bank began operations. The economic consequences were not so summarily dealt with, however. Indeed, Barbados experienced an economic upheaval that lasted several years. In the end the planters agreed to make good all bills which had been forced on to creditors.[48]

Another type of bank for the West Indies was proposed by Sir Dalby Thomas in 1690. Observing that 'the want of a stock of Money in the Plantations is a great hindrance to their Increase', he argued that one effective way to help the colonies was to lodge a sufficient fund of money there, 'to which as to an infallible Bank every Planter might have recourse, for credit, proportionable to the reall value of any he had to give in Security, be it Land, Stock or Goods'. Thomas pointed out that although individual Englishmen could not be expected to risk their money in the colonies,

> if a sufficient Joynt-Stock was United under proper Rules and Privileges, for the Use of all the Plantations, there is no doubt but the bare Encouragement of that Extraordinary Interest would sufficiently invite Money'd men into the Society; when without the least personall Care or possibility of hazzard their Business, must of Necessity be rightly Negotiated by those proper Methods all Companies constantly take for the Common Interest of the Society.

He went on to say that the Bank would meet the chief need of the planters, 'which is to Buy what they want for ready Money, at reasonable Rates, which now all men know the needy Planter can no ways do'.[49] Thomas hoped to secure for his company the exclusive right to market colonial sugar in the metropolis. His plan failed of fulfillment, probably owing to the opposition of certain planters and London merchants who were deeply involved in the commission system of trade and finance.[50]

47 Curtis P. Nettels, *The Money Supply of the American Colonies before 1720* (Madison, 1934), pp. 269–71; *Cal. S. P. Col. 1661–68*, p. 62.
48 Pitman, *Development of British West Indies*, p. 143.
49 Thomas, *Historical Account of West-India Collonies*, pp. 47–8.
50 K. G. Davies, 'The Origins of the Commission System in the West India Trade', *Trans. Royal Historical Society*, 5th ser., vol. 52 (London, 1952), pp. 106–7.

7 CONCLUSION

In conclusion, it appears that the merchant system of finance played a key role in the transition from small to large units of sugar production. The transition was chaotic and wasteful of resources, almost resembling a Hobbesian state of nature. Fortunate planters secured trade credit or loans when crops were abundant and profit margins high. Under these conditions debts might be cleared in a surprisingly short period. The planter could then resort to re-invested profits to expand his estate. Others were saddled with heavy debts at the top of the market or the beginning of a period of poor crops and quickly fell victim to predatory creditors. Others, still, adopted delaying tactics in years of adversity, resorting to practices which were questionable even in a society notoriously lax in its code of business conduct. By far the greater number failed in their bid for scarce resources. They lacked the capital required for carving plantations out of wild wood, or for consolidating numerous tobacco or cotton farms into sugar estates. Yet by a variety of means, a considerable number of individuals gained entry into the colonial gentry. We shall see in the following chapters that in most years of the 18th century the sugar industry not only financed itself, but also supplied capital to trading, agricultural and industrial enterprises in the metropolis.

CHAPTER THIRTEEN

The Planter's Agent as Banker

These Englishmen are strange people, because they can live upon what they call bank notes, without working, they think that all the world can do the same ... But if they have no trees to cut down, they have gold in abundance, they say; for they rake it and scrape it from all parts far and near. I have often heard my grandfather tell how they live there by writing. By writing they send this cargo unto us, that to the West, and the other to the East Indies.[1]

J. Hector St John Crevecoeur, 1782

1 INTRODUCTION

Developing alongside the merchant system and eventually overtaking it was the commission system. While both systems combined finance with trade, shipping, insurance, and miscellaneous services, finance became the primary function of the commission system. Moreover, while both systems co-existed in the major ports of the British Empire by the middle decades of the 18th century, the commission system rose to a position of pre-eminence in the London metropolis where the West India merchants had access to the great markets for money, staples, manufactures and services. Commission agents not only gave financial assistance to planters; they also provided a channel for the flow of West India wealth to the metropolis. Though mere agents in a legal sense, the London-West India merchants came to dominate the commercial and financial life of the colonies. Numbered among them were aldermen, lord mayors, members of Parliament, and baronets. In the main these sugar factors had West Indian antecedents. Ties of kinship, early life in the colonies as merchants and planters, and association with absentee proprietors in the metropolis bound them closely to the planting interest.*

Beginning in the middle years of the 17th century, a few wealthy

---

* Synonymous meaning is attached to the terms 'commission agent', 'sugar factor', and 'West India merchant'.

---

1 J. Hector St John Crevecoeur, *Letters from an American Farmer* (London, 1904), pp. 18–19.

The Planter's Agent as Banker

Barbadians freed themselves from dependence upon merchant-creditors and began to market their sugars through agents in England. In his will of 17 July 1654, Francis Ford of Barbados bequeathed to his wife the proceeds of 'the sugar I have sent home for London consigned to my brother Lieut. Charles Hilliard . . .'. Some two years later Peter Colleton, a Barbados merchant, came to London 'to follow his m'chandizing affaires here'. That his London trade was of a factorage nature may be surmised by the fact that his father, Sir Peter Colleton, was a leading planter of Barbados. In May 1666 the Assembly of Barbados consigned 40 butts of sugar to the London firm of Colleton and Paynter in return for arms and ammunition.[2]

The growth of the commission system in the Restoration period was facilitated by the consolidation of English interests in the West Indies and the focusing of the political and social aspirations of the planters upon England. Political consolidation took such forms as the replacement of proprietary rule by crown government and the creation of effective institutions of government in the colonies. By closing loopholes in the Navigation Acts, the Restoration government probably helped to channel a greater proportion of the colonial trade through the London metropolis. West Indians reacted to these centralizing tendencies by seeking representation at the centre of business. Absentee proprietors joined with colonial agents and London merchants to form the Committee for the Concern of Barbados in 1671. Following the lead of the Barbadians, the Jamaicans began to transact business and politics at the Jamaica Coffee House in St Michael's Alley.[3]

From a long-term perspective it was to be expected that the commission system should assume larger dimensions with the growth of the large estate and the expansion of a class of substantial planters. Writing in 1732, one Englishman noted that the trade of the islands was at first carried on with the capital of English merchants who supplied the planters with all their necessities upon credit and brought home their sugar. As the planters grew rich, however, 'they sent us the Produce of their Plantations upon their own Accounts, and with the Proceeds thereof furnished themselves with what they wanted; so that for many Years that Trade has been for the greatest Part manag'd by themselves, and the Merchants get little by them'.[4]

---

2 Vere L. Oliver (ed.), *Caribbeana, Being Miscellaneous Papers Relating to the . . . British West Indies* (London, 1910–19), vol. 3, pp. 299, 368; *Cal. S. P. Col. 1661–68*, pp. 381–2.
3 K. G. Davies, 'The Origins of the Commission System in the West India Trade', *Trans. Royal Historical Society*, 5th ser., vol. 2 (London, 1952), pp. 89–91.
4 Anon., *The Dispute between the Northern Colonies and the Sugar Islands, set in clear View* (London, 1732), p. 1.

Sugar and Slavery

Trade and credit conditions in the early Restoration period may have hastened the growth of the commission system. Noteworthy developments in this period included the decline in sugar prices, uncertainty of shipping and plantation supplies, and the high cost of trade credit and loans. Governor Atkins of Barbados wrote in 1676 that many planters had been ruined by merchants who charged great rates of interest. Finding that they were working as bondsmen for the merchants, the more prudent began to trade for themselves, which in time obtained an influence, and 'they will in a short tyme pay their debts and will for ever keep them out of that Trap'.[5]

The English commission agent served his planter correspondents in a number of capacities. His mercantile and shipping duties, as will be explained more fully in Chapter Fourteen, consisted of receiving the planters' staples off the ship, paying customs duties, warehousing, and eventually selling the goods consigned to his care. Moreover, he purchased plantation supplies and consumer goods that were ordered out of England, chartered and insured vessels and cargoes, and in time of war petitioned the admiralty for warships to escort the fleets of merchantmen. Miscellaneous services included the recruitment of indentured servants and artisans, supervising the education of children who arrived from the West Indies, and collecting and disseminating commercial and political intelligence of concern to his correspondents.

The English factor was not only the planter's buying and selling agent but also his banker. He granted trade credit by sending out plantation supplies before the planter's staples were received or sold. He accepted bills of exchange which his correspondents drew on him in payment of Negro slaves or other outlays. He granted loans to his correspondents with or without such security as promissory notes, bonds, judgements, or mortgages. If the balance of the sterling running account stood on the side of the correspondent, the factor might acknowledge a request to purchase lottery tickets or invest the balance in the public funds. Factors who operated on small capitals were bankers only in a deposit and transfer capacity, but those with funds of their own or with access to the money market (which included their own correspondents' credit balances) might be tempted by the high interest rates in the colonies to engage in extensive credit and loan transactions. Finally the factors and their correspondents might decide to invest their income from the plantations in English landed estates, mercantile, mining and industrial establishments.

5 Public Record Office, London, C.O. 29/2, ff. 77–8.

The Planter's Agent as Banker

The bill of exchange was the commercial instrument which enabled the planter to pay for slaves and merchandise and to discharge other obligations in England and elsewhere. It involved at least three parties, the drawer (who was generally a planter), the drawee (his agent in England), and the payee (the planter's creditor). Commission agents generally charged one-half of one per cent of the face value for paying and receiving bills of exchange, and a much higher charge on protested bills of exchange which were returned to the drawer. If the agent accepted a bill before produce or other remittances were forthcoming, he debited the drawer's account and charged interest at the rate of 5 or 6 per cent per annum.

2 17TH CENTURY COMMISSION AGENTS

The Royal African Company, rather than the London commission agent, was the leading Engish creditor of the planter from about 1672 to 1698. Planters paid for slaves supplied by the Company in produce, specie, or bills of exchange. From an inspection of the Company's records from 1672 to 1694, Professor K. G. Davies finds that about 1,500 bills of a gross value of nearly £350,000 sterling were drawn by planters and slave traders on their London agents. By far the greater number of these bills were drawn by Barbadians, for it was this colony that accounted for all but a few of the substantial planters of the 17th century.[6]

Seventeenth-century commission agents were bankers chiefly in a deposit and transfer capacity. They appear to have operated on small capitals and were so pressed to pay freight, insurance, and other charges on incoming and outgoing shipments that hardly any funds remained to extend credit or grant loans. Long-dated bills were uncommon; in fact, the majority of the bills drawn in the 1670s were payable 30 to 40 days after sight.[7]

One clue to the sources of capital for the London firms lies in the origins of the commission agents themselves. Some agents were English merchants who formerly traded on their own account with the West Indies. Some had been factors, merchants, and customs collectors in the West Indies before coming to London to act as sugar factors. Others were younger sons, nephews, or brothers-in-law of prominent sugar planters. And others, still, appear to have started agency houses without previous residence, trade, or kinship ties with

---

6 Davies, 'Origins of Commission System', pp. 92–6.
7 Ibid., pp. 97–9.

Sugar and Slavery

the West Indies. Capital was thus accumulated from such diverse sources as trade, planting, office-holding, marriage portions, and inheritance.

After a London agency was established, capital might be obtained from other sources. The agent might re-invest the commissions he earned from the sale of sugar and rum, the purchase of plantation supplies, and the provision of other services, particularly the interest he earned on grants of credit and loans. Then there were the balances on sterling running account which the agent held for his correspondents. Planters normally let some of their profits accumulate with their London agents. These credit balances, in many ways resembling bank deposits, were a potential source of loanable funds, although they had necessarily to be used with caution. Finally, the London money market itself was a potential source of capital.

Professor Davies has investigated the origins of the first generation of new-style West India merchants who operated the commission system. He finds that although the 1,500 bills of exchange were drawn on more than 200 people, only a small number of these men were acting as commission agents. In fact, a group of about 20 out of a total of nearly 60 agents engrossed nearly two-thirds of the business. Of the 122 bills drawn between 1672 and 1680 on the three leading agents, 82 were drawn by 'eminent planters' and 10 others by men who were later to be numbered among the great planters of Barbados.[8]

The diverse origins of these new West India merchants can be illustrated by several of their career profiles.

Sir John Bawden, trading in his own name and as Bawden and Company, was the leading commission agent, being named drawee on 136 bills of exchange. Bawden was first a merchant in Barbados. In 1663 he and his partner John Sparkes drew a bill of exchange on Thomas Parris of London for £1,000 in part payment of a sugar plantation in that island.

Bawden came to London sometime before October 1670. In 1677 he was listed among the English merchants trading to Barbados who had very considerable plantations in that island and returned great quantities of sugar. That he was no specialist is evident from his trading interests in Holland and the Canaries, his occasional slaving voyages, and his part-ownership of a number of ships plying for hire. Two honours came his way in 1687; first, he was elected Alderman of Aldersgate Ward in August; second, he was knighted in October. In his will of 30 June 1688, he left property in England, New

---

8 Davies, 'Origins of Commission System', pp. 101–5.

The Planter's Agent as Banker

England, Barbados, and Nevis. John Oldmixon, his brother-in-law, wrote that Sir John and his partner John Gardiner had 'the largest Commissions from Barbadoes of any Merchants in England, and perhaps the largest that ever were lodg'd in one House in the West-India Trade'.[9]

The Lucies (or Lucys) were among the Dutch families who took out naturalization papers in England. John Lucie was born in Antwerp and later became an English citizen and London merchant. Although the nature of his trade is not known, two of his sons became prominent West India merchants. Lucas Lucie, the second son, was listed in a census of London in 1640 as a 'merchant stranger', or one of the 'third sort of men'. In 1654, he signed the petition of the Portugal merchants of London. Sometime before his death in 1663 he acquired large plantation holdings in Barbados and Antigua. His estate descended to his younger brother Jacob who was Alderman of Dowgate Ward, 1683–5, and Aldgate Ward, 1685–6. One of Jacob's correspondents was Samuel Winthrop who wrote from Antigua on 23 February 1672, that the sugar he had shipped to London 'came safe home to an indifferent market. The moneys I put into Jacob Lucyes hands, an eminent marchant their, vpon whom I drew billes of exca. to pay somme to Wm Bond [in Boston] or his order'. By his will of 21 September 1688, Jacob Lucie bequeathed to his daughter his dwelling house in Fenchurch Street, London, and his sugar plantations in Barbados, Antigua, and Jamaica.[10]

Thomas Tryon was a Londoner who traded on his own account with Barbados before he became a commission agent. He was born in the village of Bibury in Gloucestershire, the son of William and Rebeccah Tryon. 'My Father by Trade being a Tyler and Plaisterer, an honest sober Man of good Reputation; but having many Children, was forc'd to bring them all to work betimes', Tryon wrote in his *Memoirs*. At the age of eight he earned two shillings a week as a spinner of woollen yarn. A few years later he began to herd sheep. At seventeen Thomas went to London and apprenticed himself to 'a Caster-maker at Bridewel-Dock, near Fleet-Street'. In 1659, he took a voyage to Barbados where he remained about a year. He returned to London, made an unsuccessful trading voyage to Holland, and

---

9 Ibid., pp. 104–6; Barbados Public Library, Bridgetown, Nathan Lucas MSS, *Misc. Notes* vol. 5, ff. 211, 214, 222; *Cal. S. P. Col. 1661–68*, p. 352; Ibid. *1669–74*, p. 114; Ibid. *1677–80*, p. 110; Rev. Alfred Beaven, *The Aldermen of The City of London* (London, 1913), vol. 2, p. 113; Oliver, *Caribbeana*, vol. 5, p. 282; John Oldmixon, *The British Empire in America* (London, 1708), vol. 2, pp. 47–8.
10 Vere L. Oliver, *The History of the Island of Antigua* (London, 1894–99), vol. 2, pp. 202–4; vol. 3, pp. 242, 302; Beaven, *Aldermen of London*, vol. 2, p. 110; 'Winthrop Letters', *Massachusetts Hist. Soc. Col.* 5th ser., vol. VIII (Boston, 1882), pp. 262–3.

Sugar and Slavery

after a short stay at home, 'went again for *Barbadoes*, where I continued about Four Years, making Beavers to Success'. Tryon was named drawee on 40 bills drawn by Barbadians in the period from 1672 to 1694. His commission business was carried on by his sons and grandsons whose names appear frequently in West Indian wills and deeds.[11]

3 THE CREDIT ACT OF 1732

The commission system continued to grow in the 18th century as planters of substance increased both absolutely and relatively. From a financial standpoint, West India merchants extended more trade credit, accepted longer-dated bills of exchange, granted more loans, and performed more miscellaneous services for their correspondents. But the funds for these expanded services came chiefly from the profits of the sugar industry. While the London money market was a source of short-term credit, this outflow was more than offset by the capital which flowed into the metropolis from the colonies. Furthermore, the expanded commission system of the 18th century came to be dominated by men with West Indian kinship ties and mercantile and planting experience in the islands.

One legal measure which helped to extend the scope of the commission system was the Parliamentary Act of 1732 (5 Geo. II, c. 7.) 'for the more easy Recovery of Debts in his Majesty's Plantations and Colonies in America'. We have seen in the previous chapter how many obstacles to debt collection were erected by colonial governments. By the early 1730s, at a time of depressed sugar prices, the London merchants and factors had sufficient political influence to bypass the colonial assemblies and take their grievances to the British Government. They petitioned the King on 12 August 1731, stating that they had great sums due to them from the colonies, but that 'as the Laws now stand in some of the Colonies and Plantations in America, his Majesty's Subjects residing in Great Britain are left without any Remedy for the Recovery of their just Debts, or have such Remedy only as is very Partiall and precarious . . .'. The petition was signed by Richard Harris, a slave merchant, Micajah Perry, a tobacco factor, and Humphrey Morice, a sugar factor.[12]

Acting on behalf of the King, the Board of Trade reported in January 1732 that while several colonial laws were unreasonable,

---

11 *Some Memoirs of the Life of Mr Tho. Tryon, Late of London, Merchant* (London, 1705), pp. 7–8; Oliver, *Caribbeana*, vol. 3, pp. 206–8, 280.
12 *Cal. S. P. Col. 1731*, pp. 224–5, 293–5.

they were of long standing, had never been complained of before, and might properly lie for the present. The London merchants then turned to Parliament to redress their grievances. The Credit Act of 1732 provided that thenceforth, in any action or suit in the colonies regarding a debt owed to a resident in Great Britain, the creditor might make an affidavit in writing, upon oath or affirmation, before a magistrate. The affidavit could then be transmitted to the colony under the seal of a city, borough or township and have the same force as though made in open court. Lands, tenements, and Negroes owned by colonial debtors were made payable for debts in the like manner as those properties were liable in England. Slaves, which had previously been annexed to the soil in colonies dependent upon their labour, were now regarded as personal property when used as security for debts.[13]

The Credit Act was followed by colonial measures which were intended to improve debtor-creditor relations. The Assembly of Jamaica passed a comprehensive Act in 1751, 'for making good and wholesome provisions for raising and establishing the credit of this island'. Col. Samuel Martin wrote glowingly of Antigua in 1757: 'not one of the British colonies can boast so good Laws for the speedy and effectual recovery of debts; nor is justice more impartially administered in any part of the Globe'.[14]

But what was regarded as a boon to the English creditor was a bane to the colonial slave. William Knox, Under-Secretary of State for America, said that the Act of 1732 'may truly be called the Palladium of Colony credit, and the English Merchant's grand security'. Bryan Edwards, on the other hand, deplored the cruel hardships to which slaves were frequently liable, 'of being sold by creditors, and made subject in a course of administration by executors, to the payment of all debts both of simple contract and specialty'. He pushed through a bill in Parliament in 1797 to repeal as much of the Credit Act as made Negroes chattels for the payment of debts.[15]

The Credit Act of 1732 probably induced commission agents to be more liberal in grants of trade credit and loans. Planters commonly

13 *Board of Trade Journal* (London, 1732), vol. XI, p. 221; *Statutes at Large* (London, 1734), vol. 6, p. 332; Leo F. Stock (ed.), *Proceedings and Debates of the British Parliament respecting North America* (Washington, D.C., 1937), vol. 4, pp. 128–30, 145, 150.
14 *The Laws of Jamaica* (Jamaica, 1792), vol. 1, pp. 372–9; *Martin L. B.*, vol. 4, f. 26: Lre. to John Browning in Bristol, 26 July 1757.
15 William Knox, *The Interest of the Merchants and Manufacturers of Great Britain, In the Present Contest with the Colonies, Stated and Considered* (London, 1774), pp. 34–8; Bryan Edwards, *The History, Civil and Commercial, of the British Colonies in the West Indies* (Dublin, 1793), vol. 2, pp. 140–2; *The Parliamentary History of England* (London, 1816), vol. 33, pp. 831–4.

Sugar and Slavery

needed supplies out of England in advance of the sugar harvest. Not infrequently they requested their London agents to send out goods on credit, or they ordered out supplies at the same time that they consigned sugar, knowing full well that the supplies amounted to more than the value of their produce. Grants of trade credit were carried as a debit balance on the correspondent's sterling running account and charged with interest at 5 per cent per annum.[16]

Factors not only granted more trade credit but also accepted bills of exchange which were drawn by their correspondents for longer time periods. From the customary thirty-days sight bills of the 17th century, the 'usance of planters' bills' from Jamaica was lengthened to sixty and even ninety days by the 1770s. Edward Long attributed this phenomenon to the more plentifully stocked sugar market which resulted from the increase and improvement of the West India settlements. The sugars consigned to England 'lay longer on the merchants' hands before they could be brought to an advantageous sale; and longer credit was given to the sugar-bakers, and other dealers to induce their becoming buyers'.[17]

4 CHANGING FINANCIAL METHODS

Planters needed loans from time to time to purchase plantations and slaves, to settle existing plantations more fully, to pay absentees' expenses, annuities, legacies, and marriage settlements. If the planter was not already heavily indebted and the loan was not large, the usual procedure was to draw bills of exchange on the agent for the amount of the loan, the debt being carried as a debit balance on the sterling running account at 5 per cent interest.

Commission agents needed to insure payment of interest and principal on loans. They commonly insisted on having the debtor's sugar pass through their hands. From the proceeds of the sugar and rum they deducted interest (and sometimes part of the principal), crediting the correspondent with any balance. The firm of Lascelles and Maxwell did not choose to advance money 'but for our Correspondents that consign to us'. Dr Tullideph of Antigua, in requesting loans, invariably promised to make remittances of sugar and bills of exchange. Agents were reluctant to lend money to correspondents who promised only partial consignments. George Maxwell of the firm of Lascelles and Maxwell informed one

16 Richard Pares, 'A London West India Merchant House 1740-69', in *The Historian's Business and other Essays*, ed. R. A. and Elisabeth Humphreys (Oxford, 1961), pp. 205-6.
17 Edward Long, *The History of Jamaica* (London, 1774), vol. 1, p. 569.

correspondent that Henry Lascelles 'judged yet more meanly of my Conduct, when I told him you intended to Consign half your Crops to us, and the other half to Mr Newport, as he thought it but reasonable to expect your whole Consignments on the Consideration of lending so large a sum of money'.[18]

If the correspondent was a planter of credit, he might borrow substantial sums at 5 per cent without pledging security, or at most a bond or judgement. 'We are in no doubt about your Security,' wrote Maxwell to a Barbadian correspondent, 'and shall duly honour your Drafts for the Sum you mention [£210] over and above the amount of your Sugar'.[19] Dr Tullideph purchased a plantation for about £9,000 in June 1749, at which time he wrote to his cousin, then an absentee in London:

> Sound Mr Dunbar, to see if he could trust me with a Sum not exceeding £3,000 Sterlg... he might depend on being paid by me in three years' time at farthest. If he declines please to trie some other Merchant there, such as Mr Bethell or the Frye's or in short whoever you think will do it, whoever does may expect my favours.

Tullideph went on to say that he would give no other security than a bond since he proposed to pay off the loan so soon.[20]

Agents sometimes found it necessary to demand mortgage security. Such security might be insisted upon for advances of a few hundred pounds. More often the debt was not secured until it reached a higher figure, say £500 to £1,000 or more. Debts often began as small balances due to an agency on account current and in the course of years grew so large that mortgage security was demanded. The senior partner made the key financial decisions, and it was to his private account that debts were often transferred when they were secured by mortgages. Henry Lascelles, for example, charged higher interest when he assumed debts formerly carried by the House. In other words, sterling debts were converted into Barbadian or currency debts which earned higher interest.[21]

That practices varied in time and place is evident from Professor Pares' comparison of the houses of Lascelles and Pinney, the former doing business in London chiefly with Barbadian planters in the middle decades of the 18th century, the latter a Bristol commission house with correspondents in the Leeward Islands after 1782. Planters were much less deeply in debt in the earlier than in the latter

18 *Lascelles and Maxwell L. B.*, ff. 272–3, 304: Lre. to Messrs. Abram and Jacob Valverde, 20 Sept. 1745, and to Henry Slingsby, 4 May 1745.
19 Ibid., f. 16: Lre. to James Bruce, 17 Sept. 1743.
20 *Tullideph L. B.*, vol. 2: Lre. to Dr Walter Sydserfe, 4 June 1749.
21 Pares, 'A London West India Merchant House', pp. 220–1.

Sugar and Slavery

period and the House of Lascelles was content with much less security than the House of Pinney demanded. The former house allowed the debts on account current to run into thousands without asking for bonds or mortgages, and correspondents requested mortgages only infrequently prior to 1763.[22]

During the 'silver age' of the sugar industry, when creditors and debtors could afford to overlook mortgages, London factors were alert for opportunities for investing money in the colonies. This was the case with Henry Lascelles who was owed £85,154 sterling by 23 Barbadian correspondents in 1753. Of this sum, £54,855 was secured by judgements and executions, £17,585 by bonds, and £12,714 by mortgages. The preponderance of Barbadian or currency debts is evident from the fact that £69,235 of the money owed to Lascelles earned 8 per cent, £3,000, 6 per cent, and £12,919, 5 per cent.[23]

Debts owed by planters to London factors grew in volume and mortgage security became more common after the mid-century period. The moderate decline in sugar prices after 1759, together with absentee proprietorship and its heavy demands on plantation income, goes part way to explain the indebtedness of planters. The financial resources of London factors were further taxed to accommodate the planters of the Ceded Islands at a time of growing financial stringency in England.

The financing of merchants, especially slave merchants, in the West Indies added to the debts claimed by London factors. Taking the place of English merchants who consigned goods to factors in the colonies were commission agents who authorized island merchants to draw bills of exchange in payment of manufactures, North American supplies, and African slaves. The House of Lascelles did a large part of its business with merchants, first in Barbados, and later extending to Jamaica. Besides the London factors, mercantile finance was also supplied on occasion by substantial planters. Both Dr Tullideph and Col Martin lent cash or their credit with London factors to certain traders in Antigua.[24]

While some of these traders did a general merchandising business, the dealers in slaves were the big businessmen in the colonies. The slave trade altered considerably in its financial, shipping, and trading organization during the third quarter of the 18th century. Traditionally it consisted chiefly of barter transactions and full or nearly-full cargoes on each leg of the triangle. English manufactures were exchanged for slaves in West Africa, the slaves then being carried to

22 Pares, 'A London West India Merchant House', pp. 219–20.
23 *Henry Lascelles' Account Book*, 1753, ff. 1–9.
24 Pares, 'A London West India Merchant House', p. 221–2.

The Planter's Agent as Banker

the West Indies where they were exchanged for staples to be carried home. The commission system affected this triangular trade in several ways. It reduced the volume or at least the proportion of sugar sold in the West Indies and thus made it difficult for slavers to get return cargoes. Besides the scarcity and high price of sugar products, London factors controlled much of the shipping to and from the islands and expected their correspondents to patronize their vessels. Moreover, English slave merchants wanted their ships home from the West Indies quickly with remittances in the form of bills of exchange, and this was another reason why the slavers often returned in ballast.[25]

The commission system also changed the nature of the slave factorage business in the colonies. Factors who formerly sold slaves on commission contracted with the owner of the slave cargo to sell the slaves at or above a certain limit or price and to return the proceeds by the ship which had brought the slaves. This meant that the factor became in effect a merchant who was the real purchaser of the slaves which he resold to the planters for payment in six, nine, or twelve months. Large sums were thus needed to finance the slave trade, and it was to London that the factor-merchant looked for financial backing. Liverpool and Bristol slave merchants expected the London financier to give a specific security or guarantee, say £10,000, that the merchant in the colonies would comply with the conditions imposed by the owner of the ship.[26]

Henry Lascelles made large loans to slave merchants in Barbados and Jamaica. By the mid-1760s the firm was owed at least £120,000 by merchants who dealt in slaves and merchandise. Numerous other London factors became guarantors of the bills drawn on them by island merchants and made payable to English slave merchants. One slave captain was told by his principal in London that 'Hibberts and Co. Bills are as good as the Bank and will tell well here, which is very Material in our Large Concarn'. The Hibbert family was prominent in the slave trade of Jamaica, the sugar factorage business in London, and the manufacture of cotton goods in Manchester.[27]

London was as deeply implicated in the slave trade as the much-maligned Liverpool. The commission agent handled the sugar and the

---

25 R. B. Sheridan, 'The Commercial and Financial Organization of the British Slave Trade, 1750–1807', *The Economic History Review*, 2nd ser., vol. XI, no. 2 (Dec. 1958), pp. 252–4.
26 Ibid., pp. 261–3; Pares, 'A London West India Merchant House', pp. 222–6.
27 Pares, 'London Merchant House', p. 225; Lre. from John Fletcher to Captain Peleg Clarke, dated London, 30 July 1774, in Elizabeth Donnan (ed.), *Documents Illustrative of the History of the Slave Trade to America* (Washington, D. C., 1931), vol. 3, p. 292; Eric Williams, *Capitalism and Slavery* (Chapel Hill, 1944), pp. 71, 88–9.

Sugar and Slavery

bills remitted in payment of slaves. His function was undoubtedly as important as that of his confederate in Liverpool. Planters needed long credits if they were to purchase slaves, while Liverpool merchants needed quick cash remittances in order to buy cargoes to send to Africa. Acting in the dual capacity of broker and banker, the Londoner reaped lucrative commissions and interest for accommodating the peculiar needs of planters and slave merchants.

5 THE LOAN MARKET IN THE WEST INDIES

The extent to which substantial planters depended on financial assistance from their London agents varied in time and place. Alternative sources of loans included island money markets and relatives and friends both in England and the colonies. Planters so circumstanced might also meet emergencies by selling stock in the public funds or by drawing on their landed estates in England.

Many British planters borrowed, not from merchants in England, but from other planters. Debts contracted by Barbadians to fellow Barbadians are referred to frequently in the Lascelles papers, while the existence of a loan market in Antigua is indicated by the Tullideph and Martin papers. Although the small-islanders turned more and more to the London money market, it is doubtful if the same was true of Jamaicans prior to the American Revolution.

That Jamaica was a community of debtors and creditors is evident from an inspection of the personal property inventories in the Island Record Office. Almost every planter and merchant of substance left debt claims which were recorded in some detail by the appraisers. The estates of the twenty-four largest creditors in the decade 1766–75 had claims aggregating £525,975 sterling. The leading creditor was Aaron Baruh Lousada, Kingston merchant (£69,484), followed by George Paplay, merchant-planter (£67,837), Alexander Harvie, merchant-planter (£52,388), and Zachary Bayly, merchant-planter (c. £42,800). Harvie, together with his brother John Harvie, was a leading slave merchant; at one time the brothers owed the House of Lascelles £80,000 sterling. Bayly was a big planter as well as a partner in two trading houses, one doing business in Jamaica, the other a London commission agency. If some of the money lent by these Jamaicans originated in London, the greater part was probably of local origin. Five Jewish merchants (including Lousada) accounted for £148,498 of the total debt claims. During the same decade (1766–75) the inventory records show that six London merchants claimed debts owing from Jamaica of £77,608 sterling. Only two of these merchants were commission agents and their debt claims aggregated only £38,077.[28]

Some of the planter-to-planter loans were negotiated through London commission agents. The planter's problem was to prevent his sterling debt from reaching the point where it was transferred to the agent's private account, charged with additional interest, and secured by a mortgage. One way to keep a debt from rising beyond the danger point was to borrow from fellow planters. Planters with credit balances on account current might draw bills on their agents and thus transfer their credits to friends who needed aid. Because of close friendships and blood-ties, loans of this type were quite common. They were frequently made for extended time periods, with little or no security, and low rates of interest. Dr Tullideph and his cousin Dr Sydserfe helped each other from time to time and were content with a nominal 4 per cent interest. Moreover, other friends and relatives came to Tullideph's aid, for which favours he was obliged to reciprocate.[29]

6 CAPITAL DRAIN OR CAPITAL INFLOW?

Historians of the British sugar colonies have expressed different opinions regarding the sources of capital for the plantations. One school maintains that the colonies were a drain on the limited resources of the mother country. Among other sources, they point to the funds of emigrants, the trade credit and loans granted by merchants and commission agents, and the outlays of government for the civil and military establishments in the colonies. Commission agents did tap the London money market, at least for short-term advances. Besides their overdrafts at banks, there is evidence that they borrowed from London insurance companies. As Edward Long observed:

> Whilst money could freely be come at, on payment of 4 *l.* per cent., it answered a merchant's purpose extremely well to borrow, in order to supply his West India correspondent, by which he secured the benefit of a consignment, and cleared 1 *l.* per cent. on the article of interest; for he borrowed at 4 *l.* and received payment from his correspondent at 5 *l.*[30]

Countering the 'capital drain' view of colonial finance is that of the 'capital inflow' school of thought. Here it is argued that the sugar

---

28 Jamaica Public Record Office, Spanish Town, *Inventorys*, vol. 47–56.
29 *Tullideph L. B.*, vol. 2: Lre. to Dr Walter Sydserfe, 11 July 1749.
30 Long, *History of Jamaica*, vol. 1, p. 556; A. H. John, 'Insurance Investment and the London Money Market in the 18th Century', *Economica*, vol. 20 (May, 1953), pp. 137–58.

industry was not only self-financing but that the colonies also yielded a surplus for investment in the mother country. It is maintained that credits generally exceeded debits on sterling running accounts, that part of these credits were used to finance the sugar industry, while another — and probably larger — part went to purchase such things as counting houses, banks, ships, manufactories, mines, public securities, lottery tickets, landed estates, and even rotten-borough seats in Parliament.

Considerable evidence can be marshalled in support of the 'capital inflow' view of colonial finance. Case studies of numerous planters and merchants point to such a conclusion, as do the works of contemporary and modern writers of reputation and standing. Though statistical data is limited, quantitative studies are available for selected years. One of these is the author's study of the wealth of Jamaica in the 18th century, which is referred to in later chapters.[31] Another is based on the 'Inventory' series in the Jamaica Record Office. In the period 1741–75, the inventories of thirty-four Jamaicans showed claims against London commission agents and/or money in public funds. The list is incomplete because three of the thirty-six volumes in the series are missing. Balances claimed from London merchants totalled £109,715 sterling, and another £35,776 sterling was claimed in the public funds. Some of the inventories mention claims on London but specify no amount. Then the Inventory series omits the English investments of absentee proprietors. One such investment concerns Isaac Lamego, formerly a Kingston merchant, who left instructions in his will of 16 September 1754, to sell his real estate in Jamaica and invest the proceeds in the English funds. A Chancery case of 1771 shows that this heir held £95,150 in the funds. On the other hand, the Inventory series from 1741 to 1775 lists very few claims of London commission agents against Jamaican debtors. Indeed, there were only six such claims for a total of £53,715 sterling.[32]

Commission agents not only provided a vehicle for the transmission of plantation wealth; they also found an outlet for part of their own income in English investments. Henry Lascelles was among the numerous commission agents who made large investments in England. Since his business career has been discussed in great detail by Professor Pares, only a few highlights will suffice here. Lascelles was born in Northallerton in 1690, of an old Yorkshire family whose

---

31 R. B. Sheridan, 'The Wealth of Jamaica in the Eighteenth Century', *Econ. Hist. Rev.*, 2nd ser., vol. XVIII, no. 2 (Aug. 1965), pp. 293–311.
32 J.P.R.O. Spanish Town, *Inventorys*, vols. 20–33, 35–41, 44–56; Oliver, *Caribbeana*, vol. 2, pp. 367–9.

Table 13.1

Henry Lascelles' assets in 1753

	Sterling		
Cash	£ 959.	14.	3
Bank 3½% annuities	23,326.		
Bank Stock	4,290.		
India Stock	970.		
London Assurance Company for £1,000 capital stock	1,130.		
Bank circulation for a 10% payment	510.	10.	
Shares in 21 ships	15,749.	19.	9
Lascelles & Maxwell for their bond	14,000.		
English estates owned by Henry Lascelles	53,681.	14.	1
Hole plantation in Barbados owned by Lascelles	8,000.		
Personal loans	29,077.	3.	3
Loans on security of land and houses in England	137,055.	10.	4
Loans on security of sugar plantations in Barbados	85,153.	15.	8
Trading ventures on own account	3,939.	4.	
Trustee for marriage settlement of son Edwin	12,418.		
Miscellaneous	2,442.	8.	9
Total	£392,704.	0.	1

Source: Henry Lascelles' Account Book, 1753, ff. 1–9.

connections with Barbados date from the late 17th century. He was in Barbados before 1714, married a Barbadian lady, became a collector of customs, and later a merchant trading on his own account. Apparently he had accumulated a moderate fortune by 1734, for in that year he moved to London to establish a sugar factorage business at Hylords Court, Crutched Friars. The commission business prospered, and in 1743 George Maxwell, a relative, returned from Barbados to become a partner. In 1744, the firm had sixty-eight correspondents, the greater number being Barbadians.[33] Before his death in 1753, Lascelles had shifted a major portion of his wealth to English investments. From his private account book, which is summarized in Table 13.1, we get a picture of the diversified

33 Pares, 'London Merchant House', pp. 198–203; Joseph Foster, *Pedigrees of The County Families of Yorkshire* (London, 1874), vol. 1.

investment portfolio of one of the great merchants of his time.

Henry Lascelles' assets fall under three headings. First, his investments in Barbados and West India trade and shipping amount to £122,904 or 31.3 per cent of total assets. Second, his English assets, including his Harewood estate in Yorkshire, loans, and investments in the funds, amount to £220,453, or 56.1 per cent. Third, a miscellaneous category, including his son's marriage settlement, personal property, and personal loans, amounts to £49,347, or 12.6 per cent. If the items in the third category are pro-rated among the first two, it would appear that the West Indies accounted for 35 per cent and England for 65 per cent of Henry Lascelles' assets.

The late Professor Pares was a close student of the flow of capital in the British Empire. Writing in 1937, he was of the opinion that capital was drawn out of England to finance the sugar colonies; 'the planters themselves seem to have been recipients of capital rather than sources of it'.[34] Subsequently, he continued his studies in the private papers of planters and merchants and became impressed with the considerable wealth accumulated by West Indians. In his last published essay on colonial history Pares came to the contrary conclusion, pointing out that

> The profits of the plantations were the source which fed the indebtedness charged upon the plantations themselves. In this sense Adam Smith was wrong: the wealth of the British West Indies did not all proceed from the mother country; after some initial loans in the earliest period which merely primed the pump, the wealth of the West Indies was created out of the profits of the West Indies themselves, and, with some assistance from the British tax-payer, much of it found a permanent home in Great Britain.[35]

Rather than being millstones around the neck of the mother country, the West India colonies thus became a vital part of the British economy in the 18th century.

7 THE AGENTS CONCERNED WITH JAMAICA

Writing in 1759, Joseph Massie said that of late years the British sugar planters had 'seized upon and exercised the profession of MERCHANT in Conjunction with that of PLANTER...'. The 'REAL British Merchants', on the other hand, were said to have 'dwindled into the diminutive Characters of Agents, Factors, etc.,

---

34 Pares, *The Historian's Business*, p. 61.
35 Richard Pares, *Merchants and Planters. Econ. Hist. Rev. Suppl., No. 4* (Cambridge, 1960), p. 50.

instead of appearing as PRINCIPALS in the TRADE of their OWN COUNTRY'.[36]

Insofar as London is concerned, Massie was right in emphasizing the extent to which substantial planters exercised the profession of merchant. Trade directories, genealogies, and other records reveal that there were approximately 172 individuals who transacted business in London as sugar factors during the thirty-six years from 1740 to 1775. Of this number, 36 were single proprietors; and the other 136 were partners in 56 firms of from two to four partners each, the average partnership firm having 2.4 members. Each of the 92 firms traded actively for two or more years, and had five or more planter correspondents. The number of firms increased from approximately 35 in 1740 to 55 in 1774, when a rough breakdown shows that 37 firms were trading chiefly with the Lesser Antilles and 18 chiefly with Jamaica.

The 25 leading commission firms* were more closely identified with the colonies than all 92 firms. This may be more apparent than real, however, since the extant data is more plentiful for the leading firms than for all firms. Numbered among the 57 partners in the leading firms were 23 individuals who had West-Indian family origins, 20 who married into West-Indian families, 25 who were former residents of the colonies, 12 who were former island merchants, 24 who were proprietors of plantations, 6 who were former assemblymen and councillors, and at least 4 who were former office-holders.

Numerous Jamaicans ascended the plantation ladder until they transferred their business activities to a counting house in London. Leading planter families who established London agencies included the Barclays, Baylys, Beckfords, Bourkes, Briscoes, Campbells, Chambers, Dawkins, Fullers, Grants, Grays, Hibberts, Jacksons, Longs, Pennants, and Vaughans. Four Beckfords were proprietors or partners in as many commission houses, besides Alderman Beckford whose affairs turned more to politics and finance than to trade and

---

* Criteria for determining the following 25 leading firms include the number of planter correspondents and bills of exchange accepted, debts claimed from the colonies, reputed fortunes, and election to such offices as alderman, lord mayor, and member of Parliament: Banister, Hammond & Manning; Beckford & James; Singsby Bethell; Bourryau, Turner & Luard; Rowland & Samuel Frye; Stephen & Rose Fuller; Sir Alexander Grant; Hibbert, Purrier & Horton; Alexander Houston & Co.; Lascelles & Maxwell; Long, Drake & Long; Maitland & Boddingtons; Morse & Smith; Mure, Son & Atkinson; Arnold Nesbitt & Co.; Richard & Richard Oliver; Sir Samuel Pennant; Serocold & Jackson; Samuel Touchet & Co,; Trecothick, Apthorp & Thomlinson; Truman, Douglas & Neave; Nicholas Tuite; Samuel Turner & Son; Warner & Johnson; and William Whitaker.

36 Joseph Massie, *A State of the British Sugar-Colony Trade* (London, 1759), p. 48.

Sugar and Slavery

shipping.[37] Beeston Long, uncle of Edward Long, the historian, was a prominent West India merchant and Director of the Royal Exchange Assurance Company. Beeston Long, Jr succeeded to his father's business and was a Director of the Bank of England, while another son, Charles, became Baron Farnborough.[38] Representing another leading family was Sir Samuel Pennant, who was born in Jamaica. He was an eminent West India merchant, Alderman, and Lord Mayor of London at the time of his death in 1750.[39] Rose Fuller lived some years in Jamaica as a planter and politician before he joined his brother Stephen Fuller in the London agency and also became an active Parliamentarian.[40]

Whereas several generations of planters stood behind most commission agents, John Morse ascended the plantation ladder to a London counting house in the course of a few decades. In the 1750s he was a leading attorney in Jamaica, having the supervision of at least nine plantations. Moreover, Morse was a planter and merchant in his own right; he and his two partners paid the quit rent on 12,134 acres in 1754. In 1761, he vacated his seat in the Assembly and moved to London where he received sugar consignments, first in the partnership firm of Morse and Bayly, and later in that of Morse and Smith. Following his death in 1782, Morse's personal property in Jamaica was inventoried. On his three sugar plantations there was a total of 490 Negro slaves who with other property were valued at £26,994 sterling. Additionally, there were 26 debts due to the firm of Morse and Smith amounting to £143,023 sterling, of which one-half belonged to John Morse. A point of some interest is that Sir Alexander Grant, another London agent and former Jamaican, claimed debts due from Jamaica of £27,183 sterling in 1773.[41]

8 AGENTS CONCERNED WITH THE LESSER ANTILLES

Numerous individuals were planters and merchants in Barbados and the Leeward Islands before they established a factorage business in

---

37 These Beckfords were: Thomas; Julines, M. P.; Richard, M.P. and Alderman; and Richard, the Younger. See Boyd Alexander, *England's Wealthiest Son A Study of William Beckford* (London, 1962), pp. 52–3.
38 *Records and Letters of the Family of the Longs of Longville, Jamaica, and Hampton Lodge, Surrey*, ed. Robert M. Howard (London, 1925), vol. 1, pp. 86, 111.
39 Beaven, *Aldermen of London*, vol. 2, p. 128.
40 For Rose Fuller's political career in Jamaica see George Metcalf, *Royal Government and Political Conflict in Jamaica 1729–1783* (London, 1965).
41 W. A. Feurtado, *Offical and Other Personages of Jamaica from 1655 to 1790* (Kingston, 1896), p. 70; P.R.O. London, C.O. 142/31, ff. 15–16, Jamaica Quit Rent Book, 1754; J.P.R.O. Spanish Town, *Account Produce*, vol. 3, ff. 12–14, 17–18, 23, 48, 203; vol. 6, ff. 43, 52, 194; *Inventorys*, vol. 54, ff. 32–41; vol. 63, ff. 107–166.

The Planter's Agent as Banker

London or the outports. We have seen that the two partners in the Lascelles firm lived some years in Barbados before they removed to London. From Montserrat came William Gerrish, Peter Hussey, and Nicholas Tuite, who was also concerned in trade with St Croix.[42] From the planter families of Nevis came Thomas Butler and sons, John Mills, and Tobias Wall.[43] The story of the Pinneys on their plantations in Nevis and subsequently in their Bristol counting house has been told by Professor Pares in *A West-India Fortune*.[44]

St Kitts contributed a number of commission agents after 1713, when there was a plantation boom in the old French quarter of the island. One success story concerns one Peter Soulegre, island merchant, planter, and London sugar factor, whose daughter Catherine married in 1750 Sir Stephen Theodore Jannsen, Lord Mayor and Chamberlain of London and member of Parliament for the City.[45] Augustus Boyd was a planter in St Kitts before he and his brother became London factors. His son, John Boyd, was created a baronet in 1775, and his grandson, the second baronet, was M.P. for Wareham, 1780–4.[46] Zachariah Bourryau, born in St Kitts, became an eminent London-West India merchant and purchased Blyborough Manor in Lincolnshire several years before his death in 1752. William Manning, who came from a merchant-planter family of St Kitts, was the father of William Manning, M.P. and Director of the Bank of England, and grandfather of Cardinal Manning.[47] Then there were several Scotsmen, among whom were Major James Milliken and Colonel William MacDowall, M.P. After marrying sugar heiresses and acquiring old French lands in St Kitts, they did business in London under the firm of James Milliken and Company, later joining with Alexander Houston in the great West India houses in London and Glasgow.[48]

---

42 Oliver, *Caribbeana*, vol. 3, p. 127; vol. 5, pp. 104–6; vol. 6, pp. 60–3; —, *History of Antigua*, vol. 3, pp. 214–16; *The Diary of John Baker Barrister of the Middle Temple Solicitor-General of the Leeward Islands*, ed. Phillip Yorke (London, 1931), pp. 62, 87, 422.
43 Oliver, *Caribbeana*, vol. 2, pp. 60–3; vol. 4, p. 289; vol. 6, p. 38; ———, *History of Antigua*, vol. 1, p. 286; vol. 3, pp. 256–63, 317. For the Mills family see D. W. Thoms, *West India Merchants and Planters in the Mid-Eighteenth Century with Special Reference to St Kitts*. Unpublished M.A. Thesis, University of Kent at Canterbury, 1967; and 'The Mills Family: London Sugar Merchants of the Eighteenth Century', *Business History*, vol. XI, no. 1 (Jan. 1969), pp. 3–10.
44 Richard Pares, *A West-India Fortune* (London, 1950).
45 Oliver, *History of Antigua*, vol. 1, p. xc; vol. 3, pp. 49, 134, 259, 262; Beaven, *Aldermen of London*, vol. 2, p. 198.
46 Yorke, *Diary of John Baker*, p. 314, n. 5; Gerrit P. Judd, *Members of Parliament 1734–1832* (New Haven, 1955), p. 127.
47 Oliver, *Caribbeana*, vol. 1, pp. 241–5, 293–4; vol. 2, p. 358; vol. 3, pp. 251–4; Judd, *Members of Parliament*, p. 270.
48 Oliver, *Caribbeana*, vol. 5, p. 47; vol. 6, p. 15; Judd, *Members of Parliament*, p. 265.

Sugar and Slavery

Except possibly for Jamaica, Antigua sent more planters and merchants to London in the half-century prior to 1776 than any other island. Antigua was not only larger than its neighbours, but it also had a more highly developed plantation economy and was the centre of trade, shipping, finance, politics, and social life of the Leeward Islands. Numerous individuals capitalized on these advantages to establish businesses in the metropolis. From 1740 to 1775 there were at least 41 of these individuals, comprising 27 London firms. There were 22 individuals with West Indian family origins, 24 who married into planter families, 25 who had been resident in Antigua, 12 who had been island merchants, and 20 who owned plantations. Antigua planter families who were represented in London by their kinsmen were the Banisters, Christians, Codringtons, Douglas, Dunbars, Fryes, Johnsons, Kerbys, Kirwans, Lovells, Lucas, Martins, Olivers, Skerretts, Thomlinsons, Turners, Udneys, Warners, and Watkins. Several career profiles will serve to illustrate the relationships between Antigua and London.

The commission house of Messrs Rowland and Samuel Frye of Mark Lane, London, transacted business for a number of Antiguan planters. Rowland Frye, the eldest son and heir of John Frye, a leading planter, graduated from the University of Leyden in 1717 and established his London agency by 1724. One of his correspondents was Abraham Redwood, Jr, an absentee planter of Antigua who lived in Newport, Rhode Island. The entry of Samuel Frye into the business is recorded in a letter of 15 May 1731, when Redwood was informed: 'I have taken my Brother Samuel (whom I believe you knew at Antigua) to be in partnership with me'. In his will of 9 July 1777, Rowland Frye bequeathed to his brother his manors of Thornbury and Pottlemouth in county Devon, and Banstead, Burstow, Horley, Dunshot and Leigh in county Surrey.[49]

Thomas Kerby was the only son and heir of a doctor-planter of Antigua. As a young man he was the factor of the Royal African Company in Antigua, and also did business with North American merchants, one of whom was William Pepperrell of Piscataqua, Maine. His plantations were called 'Parrys' and 'Weirs'. In 1737, Kerby resigned as Speaker of the Assembly and went to England to establish his commission business in Mincing Lane, London. One Antiguan instructed the executor of his will to have 'one half of my sugar to be shipped to Thos. Kerby, late of Antigua, now of London, Merchant, the other half to Messrs Rowld and Samuel Frye, Merchts.

---

49 Oliver, *History of Antigua*, vol. 1, pp. 278–83; vol. 2, p. 34; *Commerce of Rhode Island, Mass. Hist. Soc. Coll.* (Boston, 1914–15), 7th ser., vol. 9, pp. 4, 18.

The Planter's Agent as Banker

in London'. Kerby left instructions in his will of 7 June 1746, to give ten guinea rings to James Douglas, Henry Lascelles, Thomas Tryon, and Richard Oliver — all London merchants.[50]

William Dunbar, who was a London sugar factor from about 1734 to 1749, was born in Scotland and came to Antigua as a young man. In 1716, he is referred to in Oliver's *History* as 'late Deputy-Treasurer' of Antigua. Two years later he was listed among a group of merchants and traders in Antigua. Dunbar had influential connections in the island. His brother Charles was a member of the Council for all the Leeward Islands, Judge in the Court of Chancery, and Surveyor General of the Customs. His brother-in-law, Sir George Thomas, was Lieutenant-Governor of Pennsylvania and Governor General of the Leeward Islands. Dunbar received consignments from Dr Walter Tullideph, his nephew, from 1734 until his death in 1749. Among his other correspondents were William Byam, Sir George Thomas, Dr Walter Sydserfe, Charles Dunbar, Benjamin King, and John Yeamans. William Dunbar's will of 22 December 1747, indicates that he accumulated a sizeable fortune. He left £600 per annum for life to his wife, £10,000 each to his two daughters, and the remainder of his estate, which included a sugar plantation, to his son.[51]

Slingsby Bethell, of an old Yorkshire family, was the namesake of his great uncle, who was Sheriff of London in 1681. Bethell had close ties with Antigua through his brother-in-law, Sir William Codrington, 1st baronet. Codrington submitted evidence in a Chancery case of 1723 that Bethell was 'Chief Agent and Manager of all his Plantations in Antigua'. Bethell had established his commission business by 1731, for in that year he signed the petition of a group of London merchants trading with Jamaica. His signature and place of business on Tower Hill appear on another petition of 1738. Sir William Codrington provided in his will of 6 December 1738: 'All profits to my brother Slingsby Bethell, Esqr. of London, Merchant'. Among Bethell's other planter correspondents were Sir George Thomas, William Byam, Dr Tullideph, Josiah Martin, Col Samuel Martin, Peter Gaynor, Patrick Cusack, and Duncan Grant. As with his great uncle, Slingsby Bethell achieved the high office of Sheriff of London, but he also went on to become Lord Mayor and M.P. for the City and President of the British Herring Fishery. When he died a

---

50 Oliver, *History of Antigua*, vol. 1, pp. ci, 130; vol. 2, pp. 119–21, 141, 271; Byron Fairchild, *Messrs. William Pepperrell: Merchants at Piscataqua* (Ithaca, 1954); P.R.O. London, Treasury 70/958.
51 Oliver, *History of Antigua*, vol. 1, p. 223–5; P.R.O. London, C.O. 152/12, P 108, H 311, 4 March, 1717/18.

bachelor in 1758, he left several manors in Yorkshire, plantations in Antigua, and bequests of more than £20,000.[52]

Edward Codrington (1732–75), who was the nephew of Slingsby Bethell and younger brother of Sir William Codrington, 2nd baronet, succeeded to his uncle's commission business. By his will of 19 August 1758, Bethell bequeathed £4,000 to Edward Codrington and £200 to John Miller. An indenture of the same year mentions Edward Codrington as the partner of John Miller in a London mercantile house. Among other Antiguans, Col Martin consigned sugar to Messrs Codrington and Miller. These partners thus carried on Bethell's commission business and at the same time continued the tradition of having kinsmen of leading planter families as agents in London.[53]

Much of the sugar arriving in London from about 1745 to 1780 was consigned to the two Richard Olivers, who came from a prominent merchant-planter family of Antigua. Actually, there were five Richard Olivers, the first two being brothers, and linendrapers of Bristol and partners in trade with the plantations. Richard III was born in Bristol in 1664. He was probably the Richard Oliver who was a merchant and planter in Antigua. Richard IV was a merchant and planter in Antigua and a London sugar factor, alderman, and member of Parliament. Richard IV, the founder of the London agency, married Mary, the daughter of Jonas Langford who was a well-to-do Quaker planter of Antigua. Like his father, Richard IV was active in the life of the island, serving as assemblyman and councillor. When a list of the Council was published in February of 1745, Richard Oliver was reported 'absent in England'. Presumably he had established his sugar factorage by that time.[54]

Richard Oliver V was both the nephew and son-in-law of the founder of the commission business. He played a prominent part in City and national politics, serving as Alderman and M.P. for the City, and actively supporting John Wilkes and The Bill of Rights Society. He became a partner in his father-in-law's business in 1761.[55]

When the founder of the business died in 1763, he was succeeded by his son, Thomas Oliver, and when Richard Oliver V retired in 1770 to devote his time to politics, he was succeeded by Michael Lovell, his first cousin who had been a merchant-planter in Antigua.

52 Oliver, *History of Antigua*, vol. 1, pp. 42–43, 152; P.R.O. London, C.O. 137/19, f. 64, 7 July 1731; Chancery C11–703/15, Barnadiston vs. Codrington, 21 Jan. 1723; Anon., *The Miserable Case of the British Sugar Planters* (London, 1738), p. viii.
53 Oliver, *History of Antigua*, vol. 1, p. 43, 280.
54 Ibid., vol. 2, pp. 141, 318–30.
55 Ibid., vol. 2, pp. 318–19, 323; Beaven, *Aldermen of London*, vol. 2, p. 134; Judd, *Members of Parliament*, p. 292.

The Planter's Agent as Banker

Dr Tullideph wrote to Thomas Oliver on 29 August 1763, that he would need £1,000 or £1,500 that year, and he asked if he might depend on his assistance 'in the same manner as I could have done with my very worthy ffriend your ffather for whose Death I am heartily concerned'. Upwards of forty Antiguans and other Leeward Islanders consigned sugar to the Olivers, one of whom was Col. Samuel Martin. Some idea of the fortune acquired by the founder of this agency can be gained from the following extract of a letter written by Martin to another London agent in 1769: 'Consider this O ye rich Merchts, who like old Oliver who died worth a Plumb in little more than 20 years. He might have been a Planter 50 years and not worth a Pear'. In the idiom of the time, the word 'Plumb' represented the sum of £100,000.[56]

9 CONCLUSION

Whereas the 17th century commission agents of London were chiefly bankers in a deposit and transfer capacity, those in the 18th century served the financial needs of planters and island merchants by also granting trade credit and loans. The Credit Act of 1732 goes part way to explain the greater security of debts claimed by Englishmen who had business relations with the colonies and thus the expansion of financial services. The London money market became a source of short-term credit and loans for the colonies. Moreover, planters helped one another financially, especially in Jamaica where conditions were favourable for planter-to-planter loans. But as the sugar industry expanded and more and more planters accumulated credit balances in their sterling running accounts (together with money in the funds), their London agents tapped these funds for grants of credit and loans. Not only did the sugar industry develop until it was self-financing; it also yielded surplus capital for investment in Great Britain. Henry Lascelles was probably the typical commission agent whose business career culminated with his English investments far exceeding the debts he claimed from the colonies. Commission agents were recruited chiefly from leading planter families and island merchants who not infrequently married sugar heiresses. This group of translated planter-merchants became a powerful block in the City of London and the House of Commons. Indeed, the period from 1740 to 1775 saw eighteen of these men holding seats in Parliament, nine serving as aldermen, five as lord mayors, and four as colonial agents.

56 Oliver, *Caribbeana*, vol. 4, p. 33; *Martin L. B.*, vol. 5, f. 101: Lre. to Christopher Baldwin in London, 25 Sept. 1769.

CHAPTER FOURTEEN

A Grand Marine Empire

> The European possessions and interests in the Atlantic and in America lye under various forms, in plantations of sugar, tobacco, rice, and indigo, in farms of tillage and pasture, in fisheries, Indian hunts, forests, naval stores, and mines; each different scite produced some special matter of supply necessary to one part of that food and raiment become requisite to the present state of the world.... The spirit of commerce ... has wrought up these plantations to become objects of trade ... and ... extended the British Dominions through every part of the Atlantic Ocean to the actually forming a *Grand Marine Empire*. ...[1]
>
> Thomas Pownall, 1766

1 THE PLANTATION BASE OF TRADE

'From the perspective of post-Roman European history', writes Professor Sidney W. Mintz, 'the plantation was an absolutely unprecedented social, economic and political institution, and by no means simply an innovation in the organization of agriculture'.[2] The plantation stemmed from the growing demand of Europeans for a wider range of foodstuffs and raw materials, the large scale production of which was only feasible in humid tropical and semi-tropical regions of open resources. The New World plantation represented a combination of African labour, European animal husbandry, and American soil and climate. Root crops were grown alongside tree crops and cereals, animal husbandry was combined with tillage, animate sources of energy, such as plants, domesticated animals, and Negro slaves, were combined with inanimate energy captured by windmills, water wheels, and sailing vessels. The plantation was truly an innovation in the Schumpeterian sense. It established new trade routes and shipping lanes, shifted millions of hoe cultivators from

---

1 Thomas Pownall, *The Administration of the Colonies* (London, 1766), pp. 4–5, and 4th ed. (1768), pp. 8–11.

2 Sidney W. Mintz, Foreword to Ramiro Guerra y Sanchez, *Sugar and Society in the Caribbean An Economic History of Cuban Agriculture* (New Haven, 1964), p. xiv.

A Grand Marine Empire

one side of the Atlantic to the other, determined the movement of capital, induced the growth of temperate-zone colonies to supply intermediate products, produced a class of *nouveaux riche* planters and merchants, and became a prize in the contest for power and plenty among the mercantile nations of Europe.

Since combined and constant labour was needed for plantation production and most North European immigrants settled family-sized farms in the temperate-zone colonies, planters resorted to forced labour. They turned to bonded and enslaved men, chiefly to Negro slaves. The slave component of plantations gave rise to a variety of trades. First and foremost, slaves themselves were imported to maintain a labour force which was prone to attrition as well as to expand productive capacity. Second, slaves were supplied by their masters with clothing, bedding, medicines, and other goods which made up part of the cargoes from the metropolis. Third, a wide variety of foodstuffs, building materials, and miscellaneous items were imported from adjacent temperate-zone colonies and Ireland to feed and house the labour force.

The plantation has been described as a factory in the field. It not only produced such agricultural commodities as tobacco, cocoa, coffee, indigo, cotton, and sugar; it also prepared them and made them fit for transportation. Processing operations consisted of curing, drying, hulling, fermenting, distilling, ginning, and refining to make the staples less perishable, less bulky, or less heavy than the parent materials. Processing was followed by packaging in barrels, tierces, hogsheads, and bags to facilitate transport. Transport, in turn, called for great fleets of merchant vessels to bring out equipment and supplies and to return home with the relatively bulky and low-valued staples. Demand for processing equipment, packaging, building materials, and vessels induced investment in workshops, factories, saw mills, and shipyards, both in the metropolis and the North American colonies.

Plantation colonies expanded the resource base of the metropolis and yielded raw materials and foodstuffs to be manufactured and consumed at home and to generate profitable re-export trades. They provided captive markets for home manufactures, expanded the merchant marine and navy, and opened up overseas frontiers of enterprise and investment. But political regulation was needed if the metropolis was to capture the profits of plantation trade, that is, the invisible items of insurance, freights, commissions, and interest on invested capital. Whereas state monopolies or monopoly companies were employed by European nations in the two-way trade route to the Orient, the multivarious trades of the American and West Indian

Sugar and Slavery

colonies called for national monopolies, as exemplified by the French exclusive system and the English Navigation Acts.

Plantation colonies served not only as bases for expanded and diversified Atlantic empires of a 'formal' variety; they also enabled the metropolis to make inroads into the colonial trades of the less commercially active Iberian nations. In other words, 'formal' empire aided and abetted the growth of 'informal' empire. In part, informal empire was gained by means of 'indirect' trade, that is, French and British merchants traded with Brazil and the Indies through agents in Cadiz and Lisbon. On the other hand, the 'direct' trade was chiefly a clandestine entrepot trade conducted from strategically located islands in the Caribbean Sea. Island colonies, once they were peopled, garrisoned, placed under crown government, and linked by trade with the metropolis, served as powerful bases to launch military conquest or to engage in licit or illicit trade with the Spanish Main.

2 DIMENSIONS OF TRADE

From the time of Cromwell down to that of the Younger Pitt, England's foreign trade emphasis shifted from intra- to extra-European markets and sources of supply. Broadly speaking, the shift was induced by the growing popularity of tropical commodities and the ability to supply them in such quantities that prices tended downwards. Tropical produce created new wants and new employments. Ships were built to meet the requirements of long-distance trades, textiles were adapted to the needs of tropical markets, mercantile and financial institutions facilitated the reciprocal flow of raw materials and finished goods, governments encouraged, regulated, and taxed the productions and trades of distant peoples and climates. In sum, 'wealth was more rapidly to be attained by seizing a great share, a monopoly if possible, of the supply of tropical output, and the profits of disposing of it in the European market'.[3]

Quantitative measurement of the shift in trade presents difficulties because of peculiarities in English Customs House statistics: Goods imported into England were valued on the basis of their estimated cost in the country of origin, and these official values remained unaltered for a long span of years. Similarly, goods exported from England were recorded officially at f.o.b. historical market values which remained virtually unaltered during the period from 1703 to

---

3 James A. Williamson, *The Ocean in English History Being The Ford Lectures* (Oxford, 1941), p. 177.

A Grand Marine Empire

1798. Official trade statistics thus afford a measure of market values only in the initial years of the returns; thereafter they measure quantity changes, not value changes.[4]

The West Indies had risen to first place among England's colonies and dependencies by the opening years of the 18th century. In 1701–5, Customs House records show these island colonies accounting for 45.5 per cent of England's exports to her Atlantic empire, 39.0 per cent of her exports to all colonies and dependencies, and 7.2 per cent of all exports. Imports from the West Indies in the same period were 66.7, 41.5, and 10.1, respectively, and combined exports and imports, 57.7, 40.7, and 12.7, respectively. By comparison, the 1771–5 period saw the West Indies taking off 45.7 per cent of England's exports to her Atlantic empire, 34.9 per cent to all colonies and dependencies, and 13.4 of total exports. Imports from the West Indies had risen to 65.5, 48.0, and 24.4, respectively, and combined exports and imports to 57.9, 43.1, and 19.6, respectively. The overall increase was from one-tenth to between one-sixth and one-fifth of the official value of England's foreign trade. It should be noted that, owing to political interference with their trade, the North American colonies made a poorer showing in 1771–5 than they did in 1766–70.[5]

If we shift our vantage point from England to the West Indies, it is evident that the sugar colonies were at the centre of a ramified trade which yielded direct and indirect returns to the mother country considerably in excess of official Customs House values. Besides direct intercourse with England and Wales, the sugar colonies were linked by ties of trade with Scotland, Ireland, Bermuda, Madeira, North America, West Africa, and the foreign colonies in the Caribbean region.

Since all branches of trade gave rise to income from commissions, freight, insurance, interest, and profits which were repatriated to Great Britain and North America, the true dimensions of the trade are best expressed in c.i.f., rather than f.o.b. market values. Extant statistics of quantities and prices of exports to England are available for the 18th century and for selected years of the 17th century. These can be valued at market prices in London. C.i.f. values of imports from England present greater difficulty, as will be explained presently. Slave imports and prices are sufficiently abundant to compute c.i.f. values in most years. Exports to North America can be valued at Philadelphia prices after 1719 if quantities are available,

4 T. S. Ashton, Introduction to Elizabeth B. Schumpeter, *English Overseas Trade Statistics 1697–1808* (Oxford, 1960), pp. 1–14.
5 Ibid., pp. 15–18.

Table 14.1

Estimated value of British West India trade in selected years, 1682–1774, at c.i.f. sterling values (annual averages in £000)

Year	Commodity exports*	Commodity imports	Combined exports and imports
1682–83	580.3	424.7	1,005.0
1699–1701	892.1	776.5	1,668.6
1726–30	1,594.6	1,023.4	2,618.0
1748–50	2,068.2	1,417.3	3,485.5
1773–74	5,197.1	3,151.6	8,348.7

*Exports are exclusive of Spanish coin and bullion

Source: B.M. Add. MSS 38,714, f. 37, and 8133c, f. 237; Sloane MSS 2,902, ff. 135, 151; P.R.O. London, Customs 3 series; Treas. 64/273 (39); Treas. 64/276b (387); C.O. 137/19, S124, ff. 46–9; C.O. 152/14, R 101, f. 326; C.O. 318/1, 13; C.O. 390/6, 31–2, 87, 117; H. C. Bell, 'West India Trade before the American Revolution', *Amer. Hist. Rev.*, vol. XXII, no. 2 (Jan. 1917), pp. 273–4; Anne Bezanson et al., *Prices in Colonial Pennsylvania* (1935), pp. 422–3, 431; John Campbell, *Political Survey of Britain* (1774), vol. 2, pp. 666–92; K. G. Davies, *Royal African Company* (1957), pp. 143, 363–6; Noel Deerr, *History of Sugar* (1949–50), vol. 1, pp. 193–202; vol. 2, pp. 278–9; John MacGregor, *Commercial Statistics* (1850), vol. 5, pp. 378–82; David MacPherson, *Annals of Commerce* (1805), vol. 3, p. 403; F. W. Pitman, *Development of British West Indies* (1917), pp. 72, 391–4, App. IX; L. J. Ragatz, *Statistics for British Caribbean Economic History* (1927); E. B. Schumpeter, *English Overseas Trade Statistics* (1960); Sir Charles Whitworth, *State of the Trade of Great Britain* (1776).

but for most years resort must be had to contemporary estimates of exports and imports. Moreover, crude estimates of trade with Ireland and Madeira can be gleaned from contemporary accounts. Table 14.1 gives the estimated c.i.f. sterling value of West-Indian exports, imports, and combined exports and imports from all but the foreign West-Indian branch of trade in selected years from 1682 to 1774.

British West Indian commodity exports increased nearly nine-fold, imports nearly seven and one-half-fold, and combined exports and imports more than eight-fold during the nine decades from 1682 to 1774. Exports increased from over half a million to more than five million pounds sterling, imports from over four hundred thousand to more than three million, and combined exports and imports from a million to over eight and one-third million.

A Grand Marine Empire

3 TRADE WITH THE MOTHER COUNTRY AND IRELAND

In the century or more prior to 1776, the commerce of the British West Indies followed four general channels: (1) the trade with the mother country, including Scotland and Ireland; (2) the exchange of goods and money with sister colonies to the north; (3) the African slave trade; and (4) the entrepôt trade with foreign colonies conducted through the ports of the British sugar colonies.

The main channel of trade between the sugar colonies and the mother country consisted chiefly of the exchange of British manufactures and some East Indian and European goods· for tropical agricultural commodities and bullion. The rise of industry and trade in the west and north of England and Scotland meant that the outports gained in relation to London as supply centres for the colonies. Similarly, the outports came to take off a rising percentage of the tropical produce entering the United Kingdom. As the West India trade of London became more and more dominated by the planter's commission agent, as the emphasis of the agent's business shifted from trade to finance and other services, and as absentee proprietorship became more prevalent, the metropolis became, in effect, a great magnet for the direct and indirect sources of income from the sugar industry.

English goods of varying types, qualities, and quantities were sent to the plantations. In April 1631, Thomas Littleton, the London merchant, furnished 'three ships with meal, bread, victualls, municon, apparell and other necessarie furniture' to the value of £5,000 and consigned these goods to his factor in Nevis.[6] John Oldmixon enumerated the English and Irish goods exported to Barbados in the early years of the 18th century. He began with 'Oznibrigs, which is a chief Commodity, vast Quantities being consum'd by the Servants and Slaves, whose Cloathing is made of this sort of Linnen'. Other clothing and footwear items were broadcloth and Kersies, silks and stuff, red caps for slaves, stockings, shoes, gloves and hats. Provisions consisted of beef, pork, peas, beans, oats and biscuits. Barbados was said to be a good market for wine, beer and ale, pickles, candles, butter and cheese, copper and iron ware for mills and sugar works, and all sorts of India goods and toys, coals, pantiles, hearth-stones and hoops.[7]

The value of the West Indies trade with England and Wales is shown in broad outline in Table 14.2. Exports are valued at London market prices for the major staples, sugar and rum, and in some

---

[6] Quoted in Vere L. Oliver (ed.), *Caribbeana*, vol. 2 (London, 1912), p. 3.
[7] John Oldmixon, *The British Empire in America* (London, 1708), vol. 2, pp. 155–7.

311

Table 14.2

Estimated value of British West India trade with England and Wales in selected years, 1682–1774, at c.i.f. sterling values*
(annual averages in £000)

Year	Commodity exports†	Commodity imports	Combined exports and imports
1682–83	495.3	263.2	758.5
1699–1701	742.1	423.8	1,165.9
1726–30	1,385.1	395.9	1,781.0
1748–50	1,736.7	616.9	2,353.6
1773–74	4,271.5	1,652.8	5,924.3

*Includes Scotland after 1754.
†Exports are exclusive of Spanish coin and bullion.

Source: As for Table 14.1

years, especially 1682–3 and 1773–4, for all but a few of the minor staples. Where minor staples prices are not extant it is possible to use estimated ratios of the market value of sugar to that of all staples and thus convert official values into market values. C.i.f. import values are based on the official value of English exports to the West Indies. These are corrected by means of a wholesale price index,[8] and by adding an estimated percentage of the corrected values to cover the cost of freight, insurance, commissions and profits. Imports in 1682–3 are computed on the basis of corrected per capita official imports in 1699–1701.

Table 14.2 shows that commodity exports to England increased more than eight-fold, imports more than six-fold, and combined exports and imports nearly eight-fold during the nine decades from 1682 to 1774. Exports to England and Wales remained fairly steady between 82 and 87 per cent of all exports in the nine-decade period. Imports from England and Wales declined substantially as a per cent of all imports as the West Indies became more dependent on North America and Ireland for intermediate goods and as slave imports from Africa expanded. The percentage decline in imports was from

[8] Elizabeth B. Schumpeter, 'English Prices and Public Finance 1660–1822', *The Review of Economic Statistics*, vol. XX, no. 1 (Feb. 1938), pp. 34–5.

A Grand Marine Empire

62.0 in 1682–3 to 52.4 in 1773–4. Since imports declined by more than exports, in relation to other branches of trade, the balance of trade with the mother country became more favourable to the West Indies. Income from freight, insurance, interest, commissions, and other 'invisible' exports probably absorbed the greater part of the trade surplus which increased from about £232,100 in 1682–3 to £2,618,700 in 1773–4.

Ireland was treated on a par with England by the Navigation Acts until 1663, when direct exports to the colonies were limited to servants, horses and provisions. Four years later Parliament prohibited the importation of Irish cattle into England. Irishmen responded to the Cattle Act by turning their surplus cattle into salt beef, which along with salt pork and butter, rapidly became a leading export to the colonies and to foreign ports. Moreover, after 1705 certain kinds of Irish linen cloth were permitted in the direct trade with the colonies. Most of Ireland's colonial exports went to the West Indies where they complemented the provisions from North America which consisted primarily of corn, flour, and bread rather than meat and butter. In a reverse direction Ireland developed into a substantial market for colonial sugar, rum, indigo, tobacco and flax seed.[9] Irish exports to the West Indies increased from an estimated £35,000 in 1682–3 to £287,900 in 1773–4, while in the same period imports grew from about £30,000 to £180,000.

The economies of Bermuda and other Atlantic islands were transformed in response to the sugar revolution in the Caribbean. Tobacco was the leading staple of Bermuda until about 1658, when the feeding of Barbados became perhaps the island's chief business. Bermuda exported live cattle, salt, beef, pork, fish, and onions to the plantations, and also found there a market for its well-constructed coasting vessels. The tropical goods taken in exchange were peddled up and down the mainland coast.[10]

The Portuguese islands of Madeira and the Azores developed a special relationship with the English colonies in 1663, when an Act of Parliament permitted wines of the growth of those islands to be carried to the colonies in English vessels.[11] Prior to the American Revolution Jamaica alone imported annually about 125,000 gallons of Madeira wine, valued at £30,000 sterling.[12]

---

9 Francis G. James, 'Irish Colonial Trade in the Eighteenth Century', *William and Mary Quarterly*, 3rd ser., vol. XX, no. 4 (Oct. 1963), pp. 574–82.
10 Henry C. Wilkinson, *The Adventurers of Bermuda* (Oxford, 1958), pp. 302–3.
11 15 Car. II, cap. 7.
12 Edward Long, *The History of Jamaica* (London, 1774), vol. 1, p. 501.

4 TRADE WITH NORTH AMERICA

On 19th July 1647, Richard Vines of Barbados wrote to Governor John Winthrop of Massachusetts: 'This gentleman, Mr. John Mainford, merchant, is coming to your porte to trade for provisions for the belly, which at present is very scarce . . . men are so intent upon planting sugar that they had rather buy foode at very deare rates than produce it by labour, soe infinite is the profitt of sugar workes after once accomplished'.[13] It is significant that the sugar revolution occurred at a time of economic crisis in New England. Before its virtual cessation in 1641, the 'great migration' of Puritans to New England had encouraged the inhabitants to produce an agricultural surplus to exchange for the cash and metropolitan wares of the newcomers. The sudden collapse of the immigrant market so threatened the existence of the settlers that their leaders considered relocating the colony in a more congenial environment. Fortunately, an alternative was at hand, for Boston had an active mercantile and shipping community with capital resources to exploit the agricultural surplus. At first, markets for pipe staves, grain, fish, and other products were sought out in Spain and the Atlantic islands.[14] But large-scale trading began in June 1647, when John Winthrop recorded in his diary: 'it pleased the Lord to open to us a trade with Barbados and the other Islands in the West Indies . . .'. Grain, beef, bread, fish, live cattle, and horses were exchanged for sugar, cotton, tobacco, and indigo 'which were a good help to discharge our engagements in England'.[15]

If, at the outset, intercolonial trade was more vital to the New Englanders than it was to their tropical brethren, the dependency relationship was subsequently reversed. Advantage was taken of the unique combination of soil, climate, trade winds, and other location features to expand the cultivation and processing of tropical staples. As cane lands on a given plantation encroached on provision grounds, pasture, and woodland, the proprietor turned more and more to imported supplies. In time, the Caribbean islands and the colonies along the Atlantic seaboard became in a sense 'one great plantation'. England was virtually unique among the European powers in having detached temperate-zone colonies to supply products of the field,

---

13 *A Collection of Original Papers Relating to the History of the Colony of Massachusetts-Bay*, ed. Thomas Hutchinson (Boston, 1769), p. 222.
14 Darrett B. Rutman, 'Governor Winthrop's Garden Crop: The Significance of Agriculture in the Early Commerce of Massachusetts Bay', *William and Mary Quarterly*, 3rd ser., vol. XX, no. 3 (July 1963), pp. 396–415.
15 *Winthrop's Journal, 1630–1649*, ed. James K. Hosmer (New York, 1908), vol. 2, p. 328.

A Grand Marine Empire

Table 14.3

Estimated value of British West India trade with North America in selected years, 1682–1774, at c.i.f. sterling values (annual averages in £000)

Year	Commodity exports	Commodity imports	Combined exports and imports
1682–83	55.0	65.0	120.0
1699–1701	100.0	110.0	210.0
1726–30	139.5	190.0	329.5
1748–50	241.5	313.5	555.0
1773–74	420.0	725.0	1,145.0

Source: As for Table 14.1

forest, and fishery and to absorb such tropical goods as molasses, rum and sugar.

Despite the auspicious beginning of New England's trade with Barbados in 1647, England continued to be the chief source of imported provisions for several decades. Ireland became the great supplier of provisions to the West Indies from about 1670 to 1700, after which time the trade was dominated by the North Americans. Sir William Young was of the opinion that England, by relinquishing the provision trade to the West Indies in favour of the North Americans, fostered the industry and agriculture of its people in those temperate-zone colonies, and at the same time provided for the necessities of its people at home, since the corn grown in England was not at all times equal to the home consumption.[16]

Any effort to quantify the trade between North America and the British West Indies must be undertaken at some peril. It does seem possible, however, to work from benchmark years (e.g. 1682–3, 1726–30, and 1773–4), when fairly complete and accurate statistics are extant and supplement these with contemporary estimates to arrive at crude measures of the sterling value of the trade. These estimates are shown for selected years in Table 14.3.

British West Indian commodity exports to North America increased by some seven and a-half-fold, imports by more than eleven-fold, and combined exports and imports by more than nine and a-half-fold during the nine decades from 1682 to 1774. From

16 Sir William Young, *The West-India Common-Place Book* (London, 1807), pp. 128–9.

Sugar and Slavery

less than 3 per cent of the combined value of the exports and imports in the main channel of trade with England in 1682—3, the North American trade increased to nearly 20 per cent of the sugar colony trade with the mother country on the eve of the American Revolution. That the Revolution was in part caused by the growing imbalance of trade between the sister colonies in the tropical and temperate zones can be surmised from the lag of exports behind imports. Nevertheless, the trade continued to grow down to the outbreak of hostilities. Indeed, the North-South trade of some £1,145,000 sterling engaged 533 vessels with a total of 38,544 tons and manned by 3,339 seamen. Moreover, most of these vessels were of North American build, registry, ownership, and manned by Yankee sailors.[17]

5 TRADE WITH AFRICA AND THE INFORMAL EMPIRE

Since the African slave trade has been discussed in former chapters, it will suffice here to estimate the value of the trade in selected years and then move to a fuller treatment of the sale of slaves and merchandise to the foreign colonies in the Caribbean region. Working from the slave imports (exclusive of re-exports) into the British West Indies and sterling prices in the islands, it is estimated that the Negro slaves amounted to £61,500 in 1682—3, £142,700 in 1699—1701, £277,500 in 1726—30, £271,900 in 1748—50, and £791,000 in 1773—4. But when it is considered that British vessels brought to the New World some 47,000 slaves annually in the early 1770s, and that only about 18,000 of them were purchased by British planters, there is reason to credit the statement of John Campbell, who wrote in 1774, that the annual produce of all slaves amounted to £1,500,000 sterling, and the produce of the other branches of the African trade to £500,000 more.[18]

British expansion in the mercantile era was not confined to colonies of settlement and colonies of exploitation which served as a basis for trade within the 'formal' empire. Commercial treaties were negotiated which gave British traders indirect access to the colonies of other European nations, as witness the Methuen Treaty with Portugal. In the Caribbean the policy was to encourage re-exports of African slaves, British manufactures, and North American provisions and lumber to the foreign colonies, to conduct this entrepôt trade

17 George Chalmers, *Opinions on . . . American Independence* (London, 1784), pp. 130—4.
18 John Campbell, *A Political Survey of Britain* (London, 1774), vol. 2, p. 633, note m.

A Grand Marine Empire

largely in a clandestine manner so as not to antagonize other colonial powers, and to take in exchange commodities produced by Spanish and French colonials which did not compete with the produce of the British West Indies.[19]

The American Treaty of 1670 created a favourable setting for launching the entrepôt trade, particularly from the island of Jamaica. By this treaty Spain acknowledged England's right to the possession of colonies in her effective occupation, while England gave assurance that buccaneering would be suppressed. Although the treaty prohibited trade between English and Spanish colonists, both countries saw fit to close their eyes to such trade. The English government encouraged the Royal African Company to use Jamaica as a base for running slaves into the Spanish colonies, while the Spanish government allowed the governors at Havana, Porto Bello, and Cartagena to send to Jamaica for slaves. Professor Nettels, who has documented this lucrative but troublesome trade from 1680 to 1715, shows how it led to a partial suspension of the Navigation Acts and the ending of the monopoly of the Royal African Company, how it encouraged rival French slave traders and the awarding of the *Asiento* to a French company, how it helped to cause the War of Spanish Succession, and how it served as a precedent for the much-prized *Asiento* which England gained at the Peace of Utrecht.[20]

The awarding of the *Asiento* to the South Sea Company did not end the clandestine trade in slaves and manufactures to the Spanish Main. In part, the trade was conducted by the resident merchants of Jamaica and other colonies who had long carried on a 'sloop trade' with the foreign colonies; in part, officials of the South Sea Company created a system whereby the legal business in Negroes was used as a screen for running contraband into the Spanish possessions. Professor Nelson has shown how a small group of determined officials made fortunes for themselves rather than for the general stockholders of the Company. The upshot of the clandestine trade was growing bitterness between the governments of Spain and England, retaliatory naval incidents, and finally the outbreak of the War of Jenkins' Ear in 1739.[21]

No doubt clandestine trade continued, but it probably ran a poor second to privateering during the War of Jenkins' Ear and the Anglo-French War from 1744 to 1748. Again, privateering became promi-

19 Frances Armytage, *The Free Port System in the British West Indies* (London, 1953), p. 27.
20 Curtis Nettels, 'England and the Spanish-American Trade, 1680–1715', *The Journal of Modern History*, vol. III, no. 1 (March 1931), pp. 1–32.
21 George H. Nelson, 'Contraband Trade under the Asiento, 1730–1739', *The American Historical Review*, vol. LI, no. 1 (Oct. 1945), pp. 55–67.

Sugar and Slavery

nent in the Seven Years' War (1756—63), but the British conquests of Guadeloupe, Martinique, and Havana opened up new markets for slaves and British manufactures to legal traders. The return of the conquered colonies at the Peace of Paris, together with stricter enforcement of the Navigation Acts, helps to explain the decline of the entrepôt trade of Jamaica in the years of peace after 1763. Overall, however, there is reason to believe that Britain's informal empire trade increased, rather than declined, owing to the rise of new entrepôts in the Ceded Islands and East Florida, and the establishment of free ports in Jamaica and Dominica.[22]

Estimates of the value of Britain's informal empire trade in the Caribbean vary widely in time and place. Most of the estimates apply to Jamaica which was almost as much a trading colony as a plantation colony before 1740. The Governor of Jamaica reported in 1678 that there were eighty vessels employed in coastal traffic and trade with the Spaniards, and that the latter had been carried on to the value of £20,000 in the last sixteen months.[23] From this small beginning the trade had increased by the beginning of the 18th century to between £150,000 and £200,000 in Spanish gold, pieces of eight, and bullion brought from Jamaica to England.[24] William Wood, himself a slave dealer in Jamaica, wrote in 1718 that from £250,000 to £300,000 in gold and silver had been brought into his majesty's dominions in return for Negroes, manufactures, flour and other goods.[25] The secret books of the inner clique of South Sea Company directors show that some £6 million worth of goods and slaves were traded clandestinely from 1730 to 1739. James Knight, a leading slave factor in Jamaica, believed that upwards of £500,000 in specie was remitted annually from that island for some years prior to the War of Jenkins' Ear.[26] Appendix XI shows the bullion imported and brought to the Bank of England from Jamaica and the other West India islands from 1748 to 1765. It should be noted that gold and silver imports were not entered in the English Customs House ledgers.

We have seen that the number of slaves carried in British vessels in 1771 was more than double the estimated requirements of the British plantations.[27] Since legal re-exports subject to duty pay-

22 Allan Christelow, 'Contraband Trade between Jamaica and the Spanish Main, and the Freeport Act of 1766', *The Hispanic American Historical Review*, vol. XXII, no. 2 (May 1942), pp. 309—43.
23 *Cal. S. P. Col. 1677—1680*, p. 344.
24 Nettels, 'England and the Spanish-American Trade', p. 8.
25 William Wood, *A Survey of Trade* (London, 1718), p. 285.
26 Nelson, 'Contraband Trade under the Asiento', pp. 62—4; British Museum Add. MSS 12,411, ff. 25—6: Edward Long's Collection for the History of Jamaica.
27 See Chapter 11, pp. 250—1.

A Grand Marine Empire

ments account for only a small part of the difference, the greater number must have been re-exported in a clandestine manner or shipped directly from Africa to the foreign colonies. When Charles III mounted the Spanish throne in 1759, he ordered an enquiry to be made into the economic life of the empire. One section of the report submitted to him in 1761 attributed many of the disorders in the Spanish colonies to the clandestine trade carried on chiefly from Jamaica. Though probably exaggerated, the report alleged that this was the most considerable branch of trade which the English had in America; 'It reaches at least 6 million pesos [approximately £1,350,000 sterling] each year...'.[28] Besides the Spanish trade, Negroes were smuggled into the French colony of St Domingue from the north coast of Jamaica. Abbé Raynal wrote that the planters of the French island received four or five thousand slaves annually from the English, paying for them with cotton and indigo.[29]

The extent to which the North Americans shared in the informal empire trade is revealed by the report of one British official in the colonies. In 1740, the Board of Trade received 'A Computation of the Value and Trade of the British Empire in America', from Robert Dinwiddie, Surveyor General of Customs for the Southern District of America. He calculated that 'the Amount of Cash, Dye Woods, Druggs, Cocoa, &c: imported to the British Plantations, being the consequence of a Trade carried on to the Spanish and French Dominions in America' amounted yearly to £425,000. Of this sum, the New England colonies received £100,000, New York £25,000, Bermuda £10,000, Barbados £20,000, the Leeward Islands £20,000, and Jamaica £250,000.[30] Spanish coins and bullion provided a circulating medium for the colonies, they were remitted to England to help settle adverse trade balances, and they enabled the East India Company to purchase Oriental wares.

6 TRADING METHODS

The trading methods employed in the several branches of West India commerce may be conveniently considered under the four following heads: (1) travelling merchants, (2) supercargoes, (3) colonial-based factors, and (4) commission agents resident in the metropolis.

28 Quoted in Christelow, 'Trade between Jamaica and the Spanish Main', p. 313.
29. Abbé Raynal, *A Philosophical and Political History of the Settlements and Trade of the Europeans in the East and West Indies*, trans. J. O. Justamond (London, 1788), vol. 6, p. 179.
30 Report of Robert Dinwiddie to the Lords of Trade, 29 April 1740, printed in *The Archives of The State of New Jersey*, ed. William A. Whitehead, 1st ser., vol. 6, p. 88.

Sugar and Slavery

Seventeenth-century European merchants undertook dangerous voyages to the infant settlements in the West Indies. Customarily they accompanied their goods and transacted business in person. Upon arrival the merchant might open a shop in the leading port town or travel through the country selling his wares. At the same time he would study the needs and creditworthiness of the inhabitants, the nature of their commodities, and general business conditions. He might encourage the planters to experiment with new crops which would meet with a ready sale in the home market. Being short of capital, the colonists could seldom buy European goods except on credit. Credit sales were thus the rule. Moreover, as specie was in short supply, bookkeeping barter transactions were common.

Upon returning home the merchant superintended the unloading of his goods and paid out sums for lighterage, drayage, storage and customs. He inspected, sorted, repackaged, and if necessary processed and fabricated his goods to make them saleable to wholesalers or retailers. Some expense might be incurred to develop new tastes and marketing channels for the disposal of his goods.

After disposing of his cargo the merchant might find his profit too meagre to justify another trading voyage. If, on the other hand, he believed that his pioneering activity would eventually bear fruit, he might launch a second venture. The second or third trading voyage would confirm or deny his expectations. If his profit remained substantial he might decide to conduct a regular trade with the colony.

The merchant who accompanied his cargo to the colony was limited in the volume of business he could transact. Obviously, much of his time was taken up in travel. Establishing business relationships at each port of call was a further time-consuming experience. Given the promise of a profitable shuttle trade, the merchant might be expected to engage a reliable young man to travel and act as his agent. The merchant could then stay at home to dispose of colonial wares and assemble cargoes to send abroad, while his employee or supercargo accompanied his goods and transacted his business abroad. As an agent, the supercargo carried out the orders of his employer in selling, purchasing, granting credit, collecting debts, and protecting the goods entrusted to his care. He might perform these functions for one or more sedentary merchants; not infrequently he acted in the capacity of master of the cargo vessel as well. Besides his commission or salary, the supercargo was generally permitted to carry a parcel of goods to sell on his own account.

Travelling merchants and supercargoes commonly remained in the colony until their cargoes were sold and payment was received in kind. Payment for goods sold on credit was generally postponed until

A Grand Marine Empire

harvest time. Further delays might result from debtor delinquency or inability to secure shipping space. Thus the supercargo remained in the colony for an indefinite period, during which time the letters from his European principal became increasingly querulous and insistent.

Resident middlemen came to be established in colonies which produced staples in quantities sufficient to support regular trading relations with the metropolis. Few middlemen possessed sufficient capital to purchase cargoes directly from travelling merchants and supercargoes. On the contrary, the greater number were men of small capital who served as agents or factors of European merchants. Professor Westerfield has defined a factor as a 'merchant's agent, residing abroad, constituted by letter of attorney, to transact the business of purchasing, selling, transporting, and exchanging, that shall be committed to his care by his principal'.[31]

The factor type of trading organization was particularly advantageous in dealing with a slow turnover, as was characteristic of colonies producing agricultural staples. The factor, by confining his activity to a colonial port and its hinterland, was in a position to make arrangements for the receipt and shipment of goods, reduce the turnaround time of ships, and thus handle more incoming and outgoing cargoes in a given period than could the travelling merchant or supercargo. Moreover, the factor was in a position to further his employer's business by expanding his clientele and dealing with planters of superior creditworthiness. He kept his principal informed of the state of the local market, the types of goods that would meet with a ready sale, and the best seasons to receive cargoes from home. Probably his most complex task was to make the most advantageous remittance. Remittances consisted of a variety of tropical staples, bills of exchange, and specie. The choice of remittance was influenced by crop prospects in local and rival production centres, price intelligence from home, specie movements, and exchange fluctuations.

Despite certain limitations, the travelling merchant, supercargo, and factor types of trading methods were adapted to colonies of small agricultural units and diversified production of exportable staples. Since smallholders had little security to pledge, limited quantities of plantation supplies could be purchased on credit in a given year. Incoming cargoes generally consisted of assorted goods which were sold in small quantities to individual purchasers. Furthermore, the colonial produce taken in exchange were in small and

31 Ray B. Westerfield, *Middlemen in English Business, 1660–1760* (New Haven, 1915), pp. 351–4.

Sugar and Slavery

diverse units. They had to be valued, graded, and packaged for shipment. The merchant and his agent therefore performed very useful functions.

When there was a tendency for small-scale, diversified production to give way to the large-scale production of a standardized commodity, the planter generally dispensed with the services of local middlemen and began to trade for himself. In other words, he no longer depended on local middlemen for all his needs, since he had his own factor or commission agent in the European market to sell his produce, buy plantation supplies, grant credit, charter vessels, insure cargoes and provide other services. The planter might employ an agent who was a long-time merchant and resident of the market city. More often, as we have seen, his business was entrusted to a merchant whose kinship ties and former residence in the colony gave promise of an intimate planter-merchant relationship.

Commission agents might be expected to locate in metropolitan centres where great quantities of tropical staples were consumed, where trans-shipment facilities were available, where a wide variety of plantation supplies could be purchased, and where shipping, insurance, banking, and other services were amply provided. Conversely, few if any specialist agents might be expected to locate in small ports where the advantage lay with merchants who disposed of a wide range of tropical goods in both a wholesale and retail capacity.

7 THE MERCHANT SYSTEM

Probably the most striking contrast in trading methods was the persistence, on the one hand, of travelling merchants, supercargoes, and factors in the North American Branch of the Caribbean trade, and the rapid rise of the commission system in the London branch on the other hand. Falling in between were the English outports and Scotland where only a few specialized sugar dealers managed to gain a foothold before 1776. In a special category was the African trade which not only combined elements of the systems already described but also had unique features of its own.

Trading organization and methods in the North American branch of West Indies trade were influenced by the nature of markets and sources of supply. Here the European population was spread unevenly along the narrow seaboard from Georgia to Newfoundland, with some degree of concentration in fertile river valleys and harbours. Settlements were generally too small and widely dispersed to permit of specialization in the marketing of sugar products. Merchants therefore imported a variety of commodities from the West Indies to sell in limited quantities to local inhabitants. Even the sizeable markets of Boston, Philadelphia, and New York were permitted little specialization. Before 1776 the separation of New York merchants into wholesalers and retailers was not complete. Moreover, there was little specialization in any particular line of goods. Though some merchants dealt principally with the West Indies, the typical merchant 'called himself a "general importer" and his warehouse resembled a miniature department store or the inclusive emporium of the country village'.[32]

Northern markets for West India produce were scattered along a coastline some 1,500 miles in length. But even more dispersed were the lumber, provisions, and other supplies sent to the sugar islands. Every continental colony produced some commodities of value to the West Indies, but certain groups of colonies were dominant in the export of particular articles. Professor Bell has described this regional specialization as follows:

> Pennsylvania and New York, with some assistance from Maryland and Virginia, offered virtually the whole amount of flour and bread; New England ... stood responsible for most of the fish and oil, though large quantities of both reached the islands through the markets of Pennsylvania, Maryland and New York. Pennsylvania again led in supplying beef, pork, hams and tongues, but her exports were heavily supplemented by those of Virgina and North Carolina. Corn and peas came from the same colonies with the addition of Maryland, while South Carolina and Georgia made their principal contribution in rice.[33]

Moreover, the continental colonies supplied the island plantations with such forest products as planks, boards and scantling, shingles, staves, headings and hoops; horses and other livestock; minor foodstuffs, such as butter, cheese, potatoes, and fruit; and manufactures in the shape of soap, lamp oil, pottery, chintzes, and shoes.

The North American trade was dominated by independent merchants who dispatched small vessels with assorted cargoes to exchange for tropical produce, bills of exchange and specie. Vessels ranged from about 10 to 300 tons, few exceeding 100 tons. Averaging about 40 tons, the smaller vessels were provided with a single deck on which much of the cargo was placed. Larger vessels of

---

32 Virginia D. Harrington, *The New York Merchants on the Eve of the Revolution* (New York, 1935), pp. 58–63. For the trade between the two colonial regions, see Richard Pares, *Yankees and Creoles, The trade between North America and the West Indies before the American Revolution* (Cambridge, Mass., 1956).
33 Herbert C. Bell, 'The West India Trade before the American Revolution', *Amer. Hist. Rev.*, vol. XXII, no. 2 (Jan. 1917), pp. 272–3.

from 100 to 300 tons were usually double-decked craft which traded with the West Indies and Europe. Occasionally they carried lumber and provisions to the West Indies, there to load sugar and rum for the long voyage to England. Ships themselves were articles of trade. 'As the "out" cargoes south and east bound were much more bulky than the return ladings either from the West Indies or from Europe, and as shipbuilding was in general cheaper in North America than in Europe, these vessels were often sold in British and West Indian ports'.[34]

The typical vessel was the property of several individuals. Ships were held in partnership by merchants, shipmasters, professional people, and even an occasional widow and orphan. 'Most New York merchants', writes Professor Harrington, 'owned shares in ships, usually eighths'.[35] Joint-ownership on an inter-regional basis was not infrequent. In other words, shares in a given vessel were held by merchants and factors resident in North American and West Indian ports.

At times the cargo was the property of a single individual. More often a number of people sent small 'ventures' to the sugar colonies on their own account. Edward Long said that 'these American Cargoes are often the property of a great many of American Settlers, whose several little ventures go in to make a cargo'.[36]

Because of the prevailing winds and currents the captain with orders to search out the best market generally went first to the Windward Islands — chiefly Barbados, then to the Leewards, and finally Jamaica. On his way to and from the islands he frequently stopped at continental ports to secure the desired assortment of trade goods.[37] Evidence which casts doubt on the pervasiveness of multilateral trade has been presented by Professor Walton; he maintains that shuttle voyages were dominant in the Yankee-Creole trade.[38]

Trading organization in the English outports and Scotland was shaped by the nature of the sugar market and the supplies sent to the West Indies. Outport markets were small by comparison with London but considerably larger than those of North America. Bristol and Liverpool, it is true, became considerable markets in their own right, yet it appears that local consumption accounted for a small

---

34 Herbert C. Bell, 'The West India Trade before the American Revolution', *Amer. Hist. Rev.*, vol. XXII, no. 2 (Jan. 1917), pp. 278.
35 Harrington, *New York Merchants*, p. 65; Bell, 'West India Trade', p. 279.
36 Long, *History of Jamaica*, vol. 1, p. 422.
37 Harrington, *New York Merchants*, p. 63; Bell, 'West India Trade', p. 276.
38 Gary M. Walton, 'New Evidence on Colonial Commerce', *The Journal of Economic History*, vol. XXVIII, no. 3 (Sept. 1968), p. 383.

part of the sugar imports. Probably the greater part went to inland, coastal, and foreign markets. Although some of the coastal trade of the major outports was lost when Lancaster, Whitehaven, and Glasgow began a direct trade with the West Indies, the re-export trade to Ireland and the growing inland trade more than compensated for the loss of the coastal traffic.

Bristol, Liverpool, and Glasgow thus became important entrepôts where middlemen were engaged in importing, grading, processing, packaging, and trans-shipping sugar products. Bristol merchants are said to have dominated nearly all phases of the sugar trade in the 17th and early decades of the 18th century; they 'owned ships, imported the raw materials, built the sugar houses, provided the equipment, paid the labour and sold the refined products to small grocers living along the banks of the Severn, the coasts of Western England, Wales and Ireland'.[39] The merchant in the outport, observed an anonymous Englishman in 1749, 'when he hath gotten his goods Home, after a dangerous risk at Sea, is forced to run a second Adventure in sending them to a foreign Market, or else to wait for the slow Returns of a Country Sale, wherein he must not expect his Payments so regularly made as in the Metropolis'.[40]

Relatively few outport merchants appear to have been sugar specialists. As compared with London, incoming cargoes from the West Indies contained a wider assortment of tropical produce, particularly industrial raw materials. Raw cotton, for example, was imported in growing quantities to supply the infant Lancashire industry. Besides West India produce, the merchants of Glasgow. Liverpool, and Bristol traded largely in Virginia tobacco. The chief cause of the wonderful development of Liverpool was said to have been 'the African slave-trade and the West-Indian and Virginia trade – for the first half of the period [1716–93] chiefly in tobacco, for the second half chiefly in sugar, rum, coffee, and cotton'.[41]

With expanding inland and Irish markets to supply with West India produce, outport merchants were encouraged to search out goods that were saleable in the sugar islands. They opened new markets for the textile and metallurgical industries of the Midlands and North Country. Irish and English provisions also found a ready sale in the plantations and helped to fill cargo space in the small vessels that ventured on the West India trade.

39 I. V. Hall, 'Whitson Court Sugar House, Bristol, 1665–1824', *Trans. of Bristol and Gloucestershire Archaeological Society for 1944*, vol. 65 (March 1946), p. 90.
40 Anon., *An Essay on the Increase and Decline of Trade, in London and the Out-Ports* (London, 1749), p. 5.
41 H. R. Fox Bourne, *English Merchants: Memoirs in Illustration of the Progress of British Commerce* (London, 1866), vol. 2, p. 58.

Sugar and Slavery

Numerous individuals supplied cargoes and held shares in vessels. Ships were owned by groups of shareholders, often six or more in number, whose holdings were bought and sold like shares in a joint-stock company. Although most of the shares were held by merchants, shopkeepers and dealers of all kinds also took up shares. The shipmaster was frequently a shareholder in the vessel he sailed. Besides venturing a few goods on his own account, he often acted as supercargo for the ventures of other owners and non-owners. Later the establishment of shuttle trades made it feasible to transfer the business to factors resident in the colonies.

Certain facets of the outport trade are revealed by the autobiography of William Stout, grocer and ironmonger of Lancaster and member of the Society of Friends.[42] As with other outport merchants and tradesmen, Stout held shares in vessels. On these and other vessels he sent small ventures to the West Indies and North America. His returns generally consisted of assorted tropical produce; there is no evidence that he specialized in any one commodity. Neither did he confine his trade to one colony. Goods were dispatched to Barbados, Jamaica, and Virginia when he saw an opportunity to make a profit. Some ventures were consigned to shipmasters, others to factors in the West Indies and Virginia.

After returning from Virginia with tobacco in May 1699, the ship *Employment*, of which Stout was one-sixth owner, was fitted out for a voyage to Barbados. Stout's share of the cargo of 'sundry dry goods' and provisions which were taken in at Dublin 'to make up her load' was £110. The cargo was consigned to William Heysham, a factor in Barbados. The first venture to Barbados was a disappointment. 'I had returned in goods £132, freight and duty £30', he wrote, 'so that I had in return only the value I sent; so that the profit remained there, in debts outstanding and goods unsold about £23, to be accounted for the next voyage thither'.[43]

In September of the following year the *Employment* was fitted out for a second voyage to Barbados 'and was mostly freighted by her owners'. Stout consigned butter, cheese, tallow, candles, and Irish beef valued at £161 to the same factor. His returns on this voyage consisted of sugar, cotton-wool, and ginger valued at £172 in Barbadian currency. An additional £32 remained behind in debts and goods unsold.

After a short voyage to Bergen, Norway, for tar and fir deals, the

---

42 *Autobiography of William Stout of Lancaster, Wholesale and Retail Grocer and Ironmonger, A Member of the Society of Friends, A. D. 1665–1752*, ed. J. Harland, The Lancashire and Cheshire Historical Society (London and Manchester, 1851).
43 Ibid., pp. 54–5.

A Grand Marine Empire

ship *Employment* was again sent to Barbados in the summer of 1701. Stout consigned goods to the value of £150 to 'John Grove in Barbadoes, being not satisfied with William Heysham's management, who always sent short of returns'. The ship was captured by the French on the return voyage; after it was ransomed it ran aground and most of the cargo was lost.[44]

At the end of the war in 1715 Stout consigned goods of an unspecified value to a supercargo on a Barbados-bound vessel. Again he met with disappointment, for the returns in sugar and cotton-wool yielded 'not above £10 the £100 for profit for money laid out for a year, a (profit for the) risk which I thought was too little to encourage adventure any further . . .'.[45]

Stout's poor profit record would appear to have been atypical. He himself wrote in 1692 that 'if a merchant here made an adventure in three ships, if but one came in safe he was no loser, and if two came safe a good gainer, and if all much more; and in the main it could not be computed that above one in five miscarried'.[46]

It was the profits of these small ventures which enabled Bristol and Liverpool merchants to engage in the more profitable but highly capitalized slave trade. Profits from the sale of provisions and Manchester goods in the West Indies and North America were said to have enabled the merchants of Liverpool to participate in the more lucrative slave traffic which tied up their capital for a year or more in triangular voyages to West Africa, the plantations, and home.[47]

When the Royal African Company lost its monopoly of the slave trade in 1698, numerous Bristol merchants had sufficient capital to embark on the African trade. From the years 1701 to 1709 no less than 57 ships left Bristol annually for the coast of Africa. By 1725 the number had increased to 63, each with room for 150 to 450 slaves, or 16,950 in all. London, on the other hand, had 104 vessels engaged in the Guinea trade in 1702. The number declined to 72 in 1703, 50 in 1704, and 30 in 1707. By the middle years of the 18th century the London branch of the African trade had declined markedly to from 3 to 14 vessels annually. The trade revived, however, and in 1771 London sent 58 ships to Africa as compared with 107 from Liverpool, 23 from Bristol, and 4 from Lancaster.[48]

The proximity of Liverpool to Manchester and other growing

---

44 Ibid., pp. 55–6, 60.
45 Ibid., pp. 89–90.
46 Ibid., p. 45.
47 Gomer Williams, *History of the Liverpool Privateers and Letters of Marque with an Account of the Liverpool Slave Trade* (London and Liverpool, 1897), p. 467.
48 Ibid., p. 467; Frank W. Pitman, *The Development of the British West Indies 1700–1763* (New Haven, 1917), p. 67.

Sugar and Slavery

industrial centres enabled the port to overtake Bristol in the Guinea trade. Woollens, fustians, linen, firearms, powder, bullets, cutlery, ironmongery, and other wares were bartered for African slaves. Gomer Williams says that the number of vessels dispatched from Liverpool to Africa increased from 15 in 1730, to 33 in 1737. By 1752, Liverpool possessed no less than 87 slavers which had a capacity for conveying about 25,000 Negroes. This compares with the 29,250 Negroes carried by 107 Liverpool vessels in 1771.[49]

8 THE LONDON COMMISSION SYSTEM

From the standpoint of trade and shipping, the London commission system grew out of the troubled conditions of the Commonwealth and early Restoration periods. The ousting of Dutch traders from the colonies and the enactment and progressive enforcement of the Navigation Acts worked a real hardship on the colonial planter. Greater quantities of sugar were forced into England, and particularly the London market, by the enumeration clause of the Act of 1660. Burdened by duties and trans-shipment costs, English sugar merchants found themselves at a disadvantage in supplying foreign markets. The consequence was an irregular but substantial price decline from the early 1660s to the mid-1680s.

In the face of these conditions the London merchants were reluctant to send goods to the colonies in exchange for tropical produce. 'Sugar is at so low a rate that the merchants send no goods to Barbadoes', complained the President and Council of Barbados in July 1661.[50] Many years later a Barbadian explained how the commission system grew out of this period of adversity:

> The very first Declension of our Exportation-Trade was attended with ill Consequences to the Sugar-Colonies; it lowered the Price of Sugar so much at Home, and discouraged the Merchants from sending to purchase Sugar here. This obliged the Sugar-Planters to turn Merchant-Adventurers in a declining Trade, and to Ship their Sugars upon their own Account and Risk. This put a stop to that Currency of Cash which before was brought over Yearly to purchase Sugars, and laid the whole Burthen of Freight, Duty and Commissions upon the Plantations, that were formerly paid by the British Merchants.[51]

---

49 Williams, *History of Liverpool*, pp. 472–3; Pitman, *Development of British West Indies*, p. 67.
50 *Cal. S. P. Col. 1661–68*, p. 45.
51 'On the Sugar-Trade', *Barbados Gazette*, 26 March 1735, reprinted in *Caribbeana, Containing Letters and Dissertations*... (London, 1741), vol. 2, p. 36.

A Grand Marine Empire

London merchants who traded on their own account with the West Indies were not immediately ousted by the commission agents. For some years they continued to service the smallholders and small planters in the sugar colonies. Because of the more diversified production of Jamaica and its entrepôt trade with the Spanish colonies, the independent merchants traded with that island after they had been largely supplanted by commission agents elsewhere. But only a handful of Gentile merchants remained by 1736, when it was reported that the Jews of London were 'almost the only Persons that send any dry, fine Goods to Jamaica, at their own Risque, and on their own Account....'.[52]

While on the one hand the commission system developed in response to the needs of substantial planters, on the other hand it owed much of its strength to the facilities afforded by the metropolis. London in the period of this study was becoming a great metropolis. Here, as one Englishman observed in 1749, was a 'prodigious' consumption and 'the best and largest Market for all Commodities, which the Merchant can at any Time turn into ready Money'. London was also the '*grand Ware-House* from whence all the British Merchants must receive several of the Commodities that they export into foreign countries'. As a financial, exchange, and insurance centre, London was winning its independence from Amsterdam and moving forward to the position of world banker. Here the planters and commission agents of credit might be supplied with loans on short notice. 'In London, Bills are negotiated, and Insurances made with more Ease to the Merchant, and a less Expense than in any other Port of Britain'.[53]

The growth of large estates in conjunction with expansion of the metropolis made for differentiation in trading organization and methods. Very likely the differentiation had become marked by 1749, when the above quoted Englishman observed that

> only a small Number of London Merchants trade upon their own Account to the American Colonies; but the greater part act by *Commission*, as Factors or Agents to the Planters, selling their Commodities, and sending them in return *East-India* Goods, and *British* and other *European* Manufactures. But the Merchants in the Out-Ports are almost wholly excluded from that lucrative Commerce, and trade chiefly on *their own Account;* employing Factors in our Colonies there to purchase *American* Commodities, in return for such Goods as they consign to them from *Europe*.[54]

---

52 Public Record Office, London. C.O. 137/22, p. vii.
53 Anon., *Essay on the Increase and Decline of Trade*, pp. 5–6, 33.
54 Ibid., pp. 31–2.

Sugar and Slavery

The marketing of sugar was the primary trading function of the London agent and to this task he devoted much time and energy. Acting by himself, the agent could give only limited attention to the sale of his correspondents' sugar. For this reason he commonly found a reliable partner and engaged brokers, clerks, and others to provide a specialist marketing service.

The letter-book of Lascelles and Maxwell indicates that the division of labour was substantial by 1743. In that year George Maxwell, who had recently arrived from Barbados, supervised the marketing of sugar and the purchase of plantation supplies. Moreover, he wrote most of the letters to correspondents. He described his activities as follows:

> Hitherto I have studied nothing so much as the art to know how to sell Sugars, & to buy Goods in the best manner, and though I am yet but a Novice in the business, no application shall be wanting to make me a Compleat master of it, wch I must be in time unless my dulness is superior to my inclination, but besides, I find there is still more to be learned, and that is, to form a right judgement of the times & Seasons when to sell and when to keep.[55]

As the marketing specialist, Maxwell supervised the work of the cooper, broker, and several clerks. One clerk took care of the water-side business, recording incoming shipments and 'casting up the several imposts in the Custom house manner, & making deductions again for prompt payment, besides the business to be done in the Excise Office'.[56] Sugar was sold by sample to grocers and refiners. The cooper opened the casks and sent samples to the commission house at Hylord's Court, Crutched Friars. The buyers generally called at the counting house to inspect the samples. When sales were slow, however, the broker carried samples around to the houses of the buyers. One Barbadian correspondent was informed that 'our Broker carries a sample in his pocket in order to Shew & sell them to fine folks'.[57]

Unlike the general traders of North America and the English outports, London commission agents were sugar specialists. In that capacity they were familiar with the different grades of sugar purchased by different classes of buyers. They instructed planter correspondents how to improve the quality of their sugar, how to pack it for shipment, and what seasons to send it to market. Most of the correspondents of Lascelles and Maxwell were Barbadians who

---

55 *Lascelles and Maxwell L. B.*, f. 69: Lre. to Benjamin Charnock in Barbados, 16 Nov. 1743.
56 Ibid., f. 101: Lre. to James Bruce in Barbados, 17 Jan. 1744.
57 Ibid., f. 16: Lre. to same, 16 Sept. 1743.

clayed a goodly portion of their sugar. The firm's letters usually comment on the quality of sugar received, sometimes adding instructions for its improvement. Absentee planters frequently came to the counting house to enquire about the state of the sugar market and to seek advice about quality improvement. This information was then passed on to their attorneys and managers in the West Indies.

Obtaining the best price for his correspondents' sugar was a matter of concern to the agent. George Maxwell said that this was largely a matter of forming 'a right judgement of the times & Seasons when to sell and when to keep'. The problem of the agent was to avoid selling when the price was temporarily depressed by the arrival of large shipments from the West Indies. The sugar harvest varied from island to island, generally falling in the months from January to June. Barbados was exceptional because many planters clayed their product and this process delayed shipments until late summer and early fall. Although some planters delayed shipment until the temporary glut had passed, the greater number found it necessary to ship during the harvest season if they were to get shipping space. For this reason most of the sugar arrived in the space of three or four months.

Sugar was sold upon arrival when it was too poor in quality to keep, or when the consignor was indebted to his London agent. On the other hand, planters who improved their sugar and were not heavily encumbered with debt often instructed their agents to store their sugar for a better market. Dr Tullideph and Samuel Martin, among others, frequently instructed their agents to speculate on a market rise. Tullideph sometimes went further and made such requests when he had a sizeable debit on his account current. 'If my affairs would permitt it', he wrote to Richard Oliver on 29 June 1751, 'I am inclined to think they [20 hogsheads of sugar] would answear to be kept as last year, especially if Jamaica hath really failed, but that I leave intirely to your direction & descretion'.[58]

The second trading function of the agent was to purchase from London tradesmen all types of metal wares, dry goods, groceries, and luxury goods and consign them to their correspondents in the West Indies. London long held its advantage as a supply centre, but its competitive position was weakened after about 1750 when the manufacturers of Manchester, Birmingham, and Sheffield began to supply the planters by way of Bristol and Liverpool. In part, these outport advantages were counterbalanced by the liberal credit

---

58 *Tullideph L. B.*, vol. 2.

supplied to correspondents by their London agents and the low freight rates on outbound ships from London.[59]

9 SHIPS AND SHIPPING

The problem of the shipowner in the London-West India trade was to insure a full loading of sugar on the return voyage. So much more shipping space was required for the return cargo of sugar and rum than the outward cargo of plantation supplies, that freight earnings were limited on outward cargoes. Thus failure to return with a full load often meant a loss to the shipowner. The chief disadvantage of the independent London merchant was that he seldom knew how many vessels would be required to carry home the sugar. If he travelled with his goods or sent a supercargo he had little or no knowledge of crop prospects and had to run the risk of failing to secure a return cargo. Merchants who employed factors in the colonies were better supplied with such information, but factors were often unreliable in assessing shipping requirements and informing their principals in time to send out ships.

In most years there were either too few or too many ships in relation to crop needs. 'There are now 10 or 12 vessels ready to load, which will not carry one-third of the goods of the island, which makes freight at 14 *l.* per ton, or four times as dear as formerly', wrote Governor Lynch from Jamaica on 4 April 1673.[60] A contrary situation was reported by Governor Atkins of Barbados on 21 May 1680: 'The backwardness of the sugar crop this year has caused some ships to wait here six months for freight, very little sugar being yet ready for them'.[61]

Before shipping could be organized on a systematic basis, planters and commission agents needed to gain control of the craft which plied between England and the colonies. The extent of ownership and control is not known, but the papers of Lascelles and Maxwell, Dr. Tullideph, and Samuel Martin suggest that a large number of the London-West India ships were owned and managed by these interests. For example, Henry Lascelles not only held shares in twenty-one ships in 1753, but thirteen of his planter correspondents

---

59 The marketing and other functions of London commission agents are ably treated in the following works by the late Richard Pares: 'The London Sugar Market, 1740–1769', *The Economic History Review*, 2nd ser., vol. IX, no. 2 (Dec. 1956), pp. 254–70; 'A London West India Merchant House 1740–69', in *The Historian's Business and other Essays*, ed. R. A. and Elisabeth Humphreys (Oxford, 1961), pp. 203–6; *Merchants and Planters. Econ. Hist. Rev. Suppl. 4* (Cambridge, 1960), pp. 33–4.
60 *Cal. S. P. Col. 1669–74*, p. 476.
61 Ibid., *1677–80*, p. 532.

also held shares in the period 1743—5.[62] Dr Tullideph, Samuel Martin, and other planters of Antigua held shares in ships which were also partly owned and managed by their London agents.

Several advantages resulted from the ownership and management of shipping by agents and planters. In the first place, a regular or shuttle service was established with different islands and different harbours in the same island. Planter-owners in the West Indies informed agents and absentees in London of the estimated number of vessels required to bring home the crop. In years of exceptionally large crops, agents and planters chartered ships not normally engaged in the West India trade to bring home their sugar. On the other hand, in years of crop failure the 'stationed' ships might be laid up in the Thames or chartered to merchants engaged in other trades.

A second advantage was that ships owned by agents and planters were generally assured of a full loading on the return voyage. Planter-owners not only encouraged friends and relatives to load their vessels, but it was also common practice for agents to write ahead and request correspondents to load their ships. 'We beg your kindness in the loading of Capt. Blackman's Ship wch will be much needed this bad year', wrote George Maxwell to a Barbadian correspondent in 1744.[63] Dr. Tullideph used his not inconsiderable influence to assist agents in securing cargoes; 'every Vessell in your Interest shall meet with all the Assistance in my power', he assured Richard Oliver.[64] Turn-around time in the colonies was probably reduced by these arrangements.

Planters were not bound to heed these requests unless they had entered into formal agreements to ship their sugar on designated vessels. These agreements were of particular benefit to planters when shipping was in short supply; conversely, they benefited captains and owners in years of crop failure when ships without 'subscribers' returned half loaded. Shipping agreements limited the freedom of the planter to bargain with masters for the cheapest freight. Moreover, ships often came late to market when they had to wait for their subscribers' crops. The advantages probably outweighed the disadvantages, however, for increasingly in the 18th century, writes Professor Davis, 'the ships from London were tied to giving priority to the cargoes of particular planters, from whom the masters in their turn expected preference in loading'.[65]

62 *Henry Lascelles' Account Book*, 1753, f. 1.
63 *Lascelles and Maxwell L. B.*, f. 101: Lre. to Thomas Applewhaite in Barbados, 17 Jan. 1744.
64 *Tullideph L. B.*, vol. 2: Lre. dated Antigua, 24 Feb. 1755.
65 Ralph Davis, *The Rise of the English Shipping Industry in the Seventeenth and Eighteenth Centuries* (London, 1962), pp. 272—3.

Sugar and Slavery

Table 14.4

Shipping between Great Britain and the British West Indies, selected years, 1676–1775 (annual averages)

Inwards or outwards	Years	Ships	Total tons	Average tons
In	1676–77*	153	15,555	101.7
Out	1676–77*	78	11,165	143.1
Out	1690	110	12,840	116.7
In	1721–25	304	30,803	101.3
In	1726–30	364	36,180	99.4
Out	1751–55	289	40,758	141.0
Out	1756–60	376	54,116	143.9
Out	1761–65	389	65,672	168.8
Out	1766–70	438	75,554	172.5
Out	1771–75	459	84,789	184.7
In	1772	679	96,071	141.5

*Port of London only

Source: P.R.O. London, C.O. 324/4, 58–59; C.O. 318/1, ff. 17, 43; Treas. 64/276A (270); George Chalmers, *Opinions on . . . American Independence* (London, 1784), pp. 93–4.

Table 14.5

Vessels entering Jamaica, c. 1773

	Ships	Tons	Average tons	White seamen
From Europe, chiefly ships	272	43,544	160	4,564
North American ships, brigs, etc.	293	20,916	71	2,425
Neighbouring colonies and dependencies, snows, brigs, sloops, & schooners	85	3,789	45	712
Coasting sloops and schooners	16	400	25	80
Total	666	68,649	103	7,781

Source: Edward Long, *The History of Jamaica* (London, 1774), vol. 1, p. 504.

A third advantage of the system of agent-planter ownership and control was that ships could be built to fit the requirements of the sugar trade. The use of large, seaworthy vessels reduced the risk of shipping sugar products. Partly for this reason, and partly because crew requirements were relatively lower on large than on small vessels, the tonnage of ships in the West India trade increased substantially during the 18th century. Table 14.4 points to an upward drift in average tonnage, particularly after 1760. Vessels leaving

A Grand Marine Empire

Great Britain for the West Indies in a given year were less numerous but somewhat larger than those entering because the latter included ships engaged in other branches of trade, particularly the slave ships which were generally smaller than the sugar-carrying craft. London ships were generally larger than those from the outports. Lloyd's Register of Shipping for the year 1775–6 shows that there were a total of 283 entries and clearances at London in the trade with the West Indies. Tonnage ranged from 30 to 480; the median ship in the London trade was 200 tons. For all other ports in Great Britain the entries and clearances in 1775–6 totalled 246, tonnage ranged from 20 to 400, and the median ship was 150 tons.[66]

The number and variety of vessels engaged in the different branches of the Jamaican trade, together with the number of seamen, are shown in Table 14.5.

Planter-agent ownership and control thus made possible the construction of larger and more efficient vessels and went far to ensure a full loading on the return voyage. But a full cargo was needed on the outward voyage from London if shipping was to reach maximum efficiency. The problem was that much cargo space remained after the annual plantation supplies were taken on board. This difficulty was partly overcome by sending out coal, bricks, stone, provisions and earthenware sugar pots. Another method of getting a full loading was to direct the master to call at Ireland for provisions and at Madeira for wine. Planter correspondents sent orders for provisions and wine to Lascelles and Maxwell; the firm then routed their ships by way of Ireland and Madeira to pick up these orders from local factors. The factors drew bills of exchange on the London firm which, in turn, debited the account of its correspondents.

10 COMMISSION SYSTEM AND OTHER BRANCHES OF TRADE

Planter-commission agent domination of trade and shipping between London and the West Indies could hardly be expected to leave unaltered the other branches of the sugar trade. For one thing, planters came to consign the greater part of their sugar products to London agents, thus limiting the market opportunities of merchants who traded on their own account. For example, it was estimated that 15,000 hogsheads out of a total of 23,000 hogsheads were shipped annually from Barbados in the 1730s 'on Gentlemen's own Accounts'.[67] Merchants who came to Barbados expecting to

66 *Lloyd's Register of Shipping for 1775–6* (Republished by the Gregg Press Ltd., London, 1964).
67 'On the Sugar-Trade', *Barbados Gazette*, in *Caribbeana*, vol. 2, p. 36.

purchase a return cargo were likely to find a circumscribed and dear market.

Planters exploited their advantage in the local market in several ways. They offered poor quality sugar to local buyers and marketed the improved variety on their own accounts. Island merchants and factors thus ran the risk of shipping a product which had a low value in proportion to its bulk and which deteriorated on the long voyage to England. Planters also discriminated against merchants and factors by devaluing the currency, obstructing the collection of debts, lowering the legal rate of interest, and forcing creditors to accept sugar at inflated values as legal tender in payment of debts. Governor Parke wrote from Antigua in 1701 that 'the Towne party were the weakest, there being a kind of a warr between the Shopp keepers in towne and the Planters, the Tradesmen complaine the Planters pay them bad Sugar . . . ; the Planters at the same time complaine they sell their goods at expensive rates, both which complaints are too true'.[68] The upshot of this wrangling was the decline of colony merchants and factors except at Bridgetown, Barbados, and Kingston, Jamaica, where trading opportunities remained quite abundant until the 1770s.

Both the English outport and North American trades were altered substantially by the London commission system. Outport slave merchants, who formerly exchanged slaves for sugar products, frequently ordered their ships home in ballast after planters began to consign the bulk of their sugar to London agents. It was not only the scarcity and high prices of West India produce, but also the fact that slavers were not well suited to the carriage of sugar and they could not be relied upon to arrive in crop time.

The fact that slavers frequently returned to the outports in ballast might seem inconsistent with the fact that the outports were gaining on London in imports of West India produce. It may be that the growth of the outport consignment system more than compensated for the sugar which was formerly returned by the Guinea vessels. Some of the more considerable slave merchants are known to have combined the factorage and commission systems. Besides their Guinea vessels, they operated ships between the outports and the West Indies which were specially built to carry the sugar consigned to their business houses.[69]

Planters also consigned sugar to outport merchants who were not directly engaged in the slave trade. Dr Tullideph had agents in Liverpool, Bristol, Lancaster, and Glasgow, while Samuel Martin

68 P.R.O. London. C.O. 152/8, M 96, f. 470.
69 Fox Bourne, *English Merchants*, vol. 2, p. 57.

entered into correspondence with agents in Bristol, Liverpool and Whitehaven. Bristol merchants are reported to have gone to the West Indies in the 18th century 'to learn the trade conditions and return home later in life to conduct a merchant-brokerage business on behalf of the planters'.[70] Though the evidence is sketchy, it appears that outport merchants seldom specialized in sugar until the later decades of the century.

While the outport merchants gained on their London brethren in the merchandise trade, they lagged behind them in the more sophisticated matters of finance, exchange and insurance. In fact, the division of labour had become so obvious by 1749 that one anonymous Englishman observed that London commission agents drew large sums from their correspondents in the outports,

> for negotiating their Bills, receiving and paying their Money, discounting their Tickets and Tallies, purchasing *India* Goods and many other Commodities for them, at the *London* Market, insuring their Ships, and making a great Variety of Bargains and Contracts for them. So that these *London* Agents may well be supposed to receive annually two or three per Cent. out of all the Money that the Merchants in the Out-Ports employ in Trade.[71]

These functions, as we have seen, were almost identical with those performed by the London agents for their correspondents in the West Indies. As the planter's banker, the London agent even received money from the sale of his correspondents' sugar products in the outports and Ireland. Dr Tullideph, for example, almost invariably ordered his outport and Irish factors to make such transfers 'without any commission or expense'.[72]

Besides the outport trade, the London agency system played a part in altering the North American trade. In 1680, the staples of Massachusetts consisted of fish, peltry, horses, provisions, cider, boards, timber, and pipe-staves. These products were exchanged for sugar, rum, indigo, cotton-wool, and tobacco which the merchants were said to 'transport usually in their own vessels to England'.[73]

Little difficulty was experienced in the triangular trade so long as all branches of the sugar trade were in the hands of independent merchants. In time, however, planters and their London agents entered into relationships which included consignments and tied shipping. In order to secure low freights, the planters who remained outside this sphere of influence sometimes invited competition

---

70 Hall, 'Whitson Court Sugar House', p. 74.
71 Anon., *Essay on the Increase and Decline of Trade*, pp. 32–3.
72 *Tullideph L. B.*, vol. 2: Lre. to Ebenezer Hare, Merchant in Bristol, 25 April 1755.
73 *Cal. S. P. Col. 1677–80*, pp. 528–9.

Sugar and Slavery

between North American and London vessels. But the planters who were attracted by the low freights of the 'seekers' came to fear future retaliation by the Londoners when shipping was in short supply. Similar reservations applied to outport vessels. The Barbadian factor of a Bristol firm wrote on 17 May 1723, 'the planters are so ingaged to Londoners who constantly use this trade that it is no easy matter to procure a stranger freight . . .'.[74] A recent study based on West Indian shipping records reveals that after about 1700 very few vessels entered the British West Indies from North America which later cleared with sugar products for Great Britain.[75]

11 CONCLUSION

We have seen that the rise of the sugar plantations was attended by the rise of multivarious channels of trade and shipping which came to constitute an important part of Britain's 'grand marine empire' in the Atlantic basin. The infant colonies in the 17th century drew on the mother country for the greater part of their labour force, provisions, draft animals and manufactures. The rise of auxiliary branches began on a considerable scale during the Civil Wars. Dutchmen introduced slaves and equipment to begin the sugar revolution, while the New Englanders came with provisions, building materials, and draft animals to begin a trade which proved mutually beneficial to colonies in remote climatic zones. The conquest of Jamaica gave England a strategic base from which to launch the important entrepôt trade with foreign colonies. Minor channels of trade were opened with Ireland, Bermuda and Madeira.

Differentiation in the channels of trade was attended by differentiation in trading organization and methods. Initially, yeomen farmers and small planters were serviced by travelling merchants, supercargoes, and factors. The rise of a class of substantial planters, however, led to the rise of the commission system. From their base in London, the agents and absentees came to exercise control over the sugar industry and the main channel of trade, shipping, and finance which developed between the metropolis and the colonies. But the West Indians were unable to subordinate the North Americans to their scheme of imperial hegemony. As we shall see in the following chapter, much of the economic and political conflict in Britain's Atlantic empire revolved around those prosaic articles of consumption and stimulation, molasses and rum.

74 Messrs Crump and Hasell to Isaac Hobhouse and Co., in *The Trade of Bristol in the Eighteenth Century*, ed. W. E. Minchinton (Bristol, 1957), pp. 98–9.
75 Walton, 'New Evidence on Colonial Commerce', p. 371.

CHAPTER FIFTEEN

Rum and Molasses in British Imperial Trade

I know not why we should blush to confess that molasses was an essential ingredient in American independence. Many great events have proceeded from much smaller causes.[1]

John Adams, 1775

1 TECHNOLOGICAL AND ECONOMIC POSSIBILITIES

In the manufacture of sugar, crystals were extracted from the saccharine part of the raw cane juice. The juice also contained a substantial quantity of gross, unctuous matter commonly known as molasses. For purposes of distillation the coarse molasses, scummings of the copper boilers, and 'dunder', which was the residue left in the still from a previous distillation, were diluted and fermented together in stone or wooden cisterns and then conveyed into copper stills where the rum was made. The production of sugar thus meant the production of molasses, but the quantity of molasses by-product varied with the physiographic conditions applying to cane cultivation and the quantity and quality of sugar processed from the cane juice.

It is obvious that the molasses varied with the output of sugar, but this was by no means a fixed ratio. Variations in rainfall, temperature, and soil influenced the ratio of sugar to molasses, and indirectly the ratio of sugar to rum. Canes grown in the fertile and well-watered soil on the north side of Jamaica were said to yield syrup that was 'so viscid, that it often will not boil into sugar; but these estates produce an extraordinary quantity of rum. The South side lands, on the contrary, produce a less proportion of rum, to a larger quantity of sugar'.[2] Furthermore, the quantity of molasses by-product was influenced by the quality of sugar processed from the cane juice. Muscovado or raw sugar was manufactured by the

---

[1] John Adams, *Novangulus, or Political Essays Published in the Years 1774 and 1775* (Boston, 1819), p. 290.
[2] Edward Long, *The History of Jamaica* (London, 1774), vol. 1, pp. 441–2.

Sugar and Slavery

simple process of boiling off the impurities of the cane juice and letting the clarified liquid cool and crystallize in wooden casks or earthenware pots. Relatively little molasses drained from muscovado sugar, the crystals being large in size and yellow in colour. On the other hand, as the quality was improved by such processes as claying and refining, more of the impurities were removed and the quantity of molasses was proportionately greater.[3]

But the range of alternatives was even greater than is outlined above, for the planter might go to the extremes of using his cane juice to make all sugar or all rum. A letter to the *Barbados Gazette* in October 1737 said that 'a Planter may convert his whole crop into Rum if he finds an Advantage in it, and in some Cases, in some Years, it may answer ...'. As a qualification, it was noted that those who claimed to make more rum 'make so much the Less of Sugar, tho' it may be not so much taken notice of or so easily discerned ...'.[4] Similarly, Samuel Martin of Antigua explained:

> The boasters in the art of making much more rum than their neighbours, give room to suspect that they defraud the boilinghouse, and so by diminishing the quantity of sugar may easily increase the quantity of rum which is by no means an equivalent.[5]

These alternatives therefore made it possible for planters to vary the proportion of sugar and rum within very wide limits.

2 17TH CENTURY MARKET LIMITATIONS

From the beginning of sugar production in the West Indies, planters were faced with the problem of disposing of their molasses by-product. They weighed the possible alternatives of throwing it away or finding some use for it. This problem inevitably became larger as the amount of sugar produced, and therefore the amount of molasses produced, increased.

Though the by-products were of little consequence in the early years of the sugar industry, the emergence of large plantation units gave rise to a serious disposal problem. Possible uses of molasses included both human and animal consumption. Slaves and indentured servants might find molasses a cheap and satisfactory

---

3 For descriptions of rum making see Anon., *The Art of Making Sugar* (London, 1752), p. 31; Samuel Martin, *An Essay Upon Plantership*, in *Three Tracts on West-Indian Agriculture* (Jamaica, 1862), pp. 82–95.

4 Anon., *Caribbeana, Containing Letters and Dissertations, etc.* (London, 1741), vol. 2, p. 245.

5 Martin, *Essay Upon Plantership*, p. 83.

substitute for sugar. But if human consumption fell short of supply, molasses might be mixed with grain and fodder to feed livestock. Then, too, planters might be encouraged to supply overseas markets if they saw an opportunity for profit after meeting the heavy charges for packaging and shipping. Given an overseas market for by-products, the planter would need to weigh the comparative advantages of sugar, molasses, and rum. Conceivably, rum might enjoy such a comparative advantage that he would not only distill all of his molasses by-product but also convert his cane juice directly into rum.

The reason for the growing importance of molasses and rum is obviously to be found in the markets for these by-products. Though small quantities were exported to North America, the mid-17th century market was confined chiefly to the West Indies. One reason for this was that output was limited under conditions of small-scale, diversified production. Another was the fact that raw sugar yielded relatively small quantities of molasses. Under these conditions it was hardly worth the trouble of searching out overseas markets. Planters supplied molasses to their slaves and indentured servants, and even fed the scummings to their cattle.

In view of their capacity for imbibing intoxicating beverages, it is not surprising that the early settlers turned to rum distilling. Richard Ligon observed that the planters of Barbados were distilling rum or 'Kill-Devil' as early as 1647. In that year he and his partners bought a settled plantation which contained a still house. In enumerating the casualties of plantership, he noted that 'if the Stills be at fault, the *kill-devil* cannot be made'. The islanders distilled a variety of beverages, one of which was made

> of skimmings of sugar, but not very pleasant in taste; it is common and therefore the less esteemed; the value of it is half a Crown a gallon; the people drink much of it, indeed too much; for it often lays them asleep on the ground, and that is accounted a very unwholesome lodging.[6]

During the later years of the 17th century the by-products found growing market outlets. Most of the demand came from North America, where fishermen, fur traders, lumbermen, shipbuilders, farmers, frontiersmen, and Indians were beginning to consume large quantities of molasses and rum. Massachusetts was said to have imported about 156,000 gallons of molasses from the British West Indies in six months of 1688. In the years prior to 1712 the British sugar islands exported to all of British North America a yearly average of about 325,000 gallons of molasses and 325,000 gallons of

---

6 Richard Ligon, *A True and Exact History of the Island of Barbadoes* (London, 1673), pp. 39, 56.

Sugar and Slavery

rum. By this time rum had become an important commercial factor in the New England colonies.[7]

By contrast with North America, England imported little colonial rum and molasses until the late years of the 17th century. The expense of the long sea voyage, high duties, and low prices generally made ventures in these by-products unprofitable. Although molasses and treacle were consumed in quantities by the poorer classes, the demand was largely satisfied by English sugar refiners. Considerable quantities of molasses also entered England from Holland and France. The foreign imports so alarmed the refiners, absentee planters, and West India merchants that they prevailed upon the Lords of the Treasury to prohibit them.[8]

3 18TH CENTURY MARKETS

Owing mainly to expanding overseas markets, molasses and rum became of real significance to the plantation economy in the 18th century. At the same time the markets in the sugar colonies themselves were of no mean importance. Quantities of rum and molasses were consumed by all sections of West India society. The lordly planter was a connoisseur of rum punch and Madeira wine, while at the lower end of the social scale the Negro slave drank the poor quality product and used molasses to sweeten his food. In between were white servants, sailors, soldiers, and artisans, who consumed these by-products copiously. After the rigours of life at sea, newcomers to Jamaica were said to have swallowed down rum 'with excessive Pleasure, get drunk, expose themselves to noxious Dews, are seized with Fevers, and die'.[9]

Rum and molasses were generally too valuable to be given to slaves except as a reward for extra effort. Slaves commonly grew provisions and bred poultry, pigs and goats. Some of their produce was exchanged for sugar by-products. The slaves in Jamaica were estimated to have consumed 11,860 puncheons out of the total island output of 46,110 puncheons of rum in 1770. Each puncheon contained about 100 gallons.[10]

7 Public Record Office, London: C.O. 390/6; William B. Weeden, *Economic and Social History of New England, 1620–1789* (Boston, 1890), vol. 1, p. 416.
8 *Calendar of Treasury Books, 1685–89*, vol. VIII, part III, p. 1841; Ibid., vol. VIII, part IV, p. 1919.
9 Charles Leslie, *A New and Exact Account of Jamaica* (Edinburgh, 1739), pp. 50–2.
10 Long, *History of Jamaica*, vol. 1, p. 382.

Wars greatly influenced the local demand for rum. Prices shot up on the arrival of troops, convoys and warships. In fact, the demand was so great in some years that little remained for export. Dr Tullideph noted, for example, 'all our Men of Warr are Just returned from a long cruize and want Rum much which keeps it up at 2/9d per Gallon'. Foresighted planters stored rum in anticipation of peak war needs. They also realized that the quality improved with age and that 'old rum' might command premium prices. In Antigua the price of new rum rose from 3s 2d to 7s 0d per gallon from 6 June 1759, to 18 January 1760. On the other hand, old rum, of which Tullideph had a quantity on hand, realized 18s 0d per gallon at the latter date.[11]

Local markets were of considerable importance even in peacetime. Edward Long's computations show that 14,660 hogsheads, or 31.8 per cent of Jamaica's rum production, were consumed by local inhabitants and transients. A similar conclusion emerges from a Barbadian computation of the same period; total production amounted to 22,430 hogsheads of 100 gallons each, local consumption to 7,000 hogsheads.[12]

During the 18th century the important overseas markets for rum and molasses were North America, the Coast of Africa, Great Britain and Ireland. The Spanish colonies, on the other hand, constituted a minor market. Great quantities of these by-products were consumed in North America by local inhabitants and transients. Furthermore, the New England colonies began a lucrative trade to Africa where rum was exchanged for Negro slaves. By the early 1730s, Boston and Newport had established rum distilleries which had a voracious appetite for cheap molasses. 'The Molasses are absolutely necessary for the Northern colonies for their own consumption', said a pamphleteer in 1731, 'and also to make the vast Quantity of Rum that is used in that great Country, as well as by the Indians'.[13]

Cheap rum and brandy enabled Europeans to debauch the 'savage' Indian and secure his furs. As a case in point, David Taitt was sent by Captain John Stuart, Superintendent of Indian Affairs for the

11 *Tullideph L. B.*, vol. 2. Lre. to Joseph Turner in Philadelphia, dated Antigua, 3 March 1744; Lre. to Dr Walter Sydserfe in Antigua, dated Dundee, Scotland, 6 June 1759; Lre. to James Russell in Antigua, Dundee, 18 Jan. 1760; Lre. to Capt. Thomas Tew in Antigua, Dundee, 23 Jan. 1760.
12 Long, *History of Jamaica*, vol. 1, p. 382; George Frere, *A Short History of Barbados* (London, 1768), pp. 113–14.
13 Anon., *The Case of the British Northern Colonies* (London, 1732), p. 3. For the North American rum and molasses trades see William D. Houlette, 'Rum Trading in the American Colonies before 1763', *The Journal of American History*, vol. 27, no. 3 (1934), pp. 129–52; Gilman M. Ostrander, 'The Colonial Molasses Trade', *Agricultural History*, vol. XXX (1956), pp. 77–84.

Sugar and Slavery

Southern District, to promote peaceful relations among the Indians and between the Indians and whites. Taitt reported to his superior in 1772: 'Unless there is a Stop put to sending Rum in such large quantities amongst the Indians no man will be safe amongst them .... Some [traders] indeed will give a Kegg of Rum to every fellow that will sell his Skins to them'.[14]

Likewise, the coast of Africa was the scene of a great traffic in cheap spirits and firearms. One of the truly vicious circles of economic history was the one in which slave-grown sugar yielded molasses, molasses yielded rum, and rum, in turn, served as currency for replenishing the plantations with forced labourers.

Prior to the rise of the New England distillery, one not inconsiderable trade involved the direct exchange of rum for slaves. English and North American vessels called at the sugar islands and exchanged their cargoes for rum. The rum was then carried to Africa and exchanged for slaves for a return voyage to the islands. More commonly, planters and merchants in the West Indies owned small vessels which carried rum to Africa to purchase slaves. Ten sloops, ranging from 30 to 70 tons and all under Antigua registry, carried rum to Africa on eleven voyages from 1704 to 1719. In the same period, the Antigua rum-slave traffic involved a ship from Bristol, a sloop from Philadelphia, and a sloop from Virginia. Also engaged in the direct trade was the Royal African Company which shipped rum from Barbados, Antigua, and Jamaica to its forts and castles on the African coast. In the years from 1700 to 1727 these shipments amounted to 182,347 gallons. Commenting on the profitable nature of the trade, Governor Hart said that rum which originally cost about one shilling per gallon in the Leeward Islands was sold in Africa for five shillings sterling.[15]

4 MARKETS IN THE MOTHER COUNTRY

Ardent spirits became an article of general consumption in Great Britain during the 17th century. By the second quarter of the next century gin drinking had developed into the vice of alcoholism, the horrors of which are so vividly portrayed by 'Gin Lane' and the other prints of William Hogarth. During the 'Gin Age' rum was a subsidiary

---

14 *Travels in the American Colonies*, ed. Newton D. Mereness (New York, 1916), p. 525.
15 P.R.O. London. C.O. 157/1; C.O. 152/14, R 101.

spirit, sometimes consumed alone but more often mixed with other ingredients to make punch.[16]

Fiscal measures went far to change the Englishman's drinking habits from spirits distilled from grape juice to those distilled from grain mash and molasses. Wine and brandy imports fell off drastically when, at the outbreak of King William's War in 1689, the English government prohibited commercial intercourse with France. After that date, despite substantial imports of wine and brandy from Portugal, Spain, and Holland, the English distillers of malt and molasses spirits benefited from legal restrictions on French spirits. Moreover, numerous acts of Parliament gave direct encouragement to English distillers. William Stout, the Lancaster grocer and ironmonger, noted in his autobiography in 1689 that 'abundance of stills were set up for extracting good and strong spirits from malt, molasses, fruit and other materials, instead of French brandy'.[17]

Queen Anne's ministers continued to encourage home distilleries and discriminate against French spirits. The distilling of grain mash was greatly stimulated by the cancellation of the Distilling Company's monopoly in the London area. Hundreds of Londoners took advantage of the new freedom after 1713 to set up gin shops where they dispensed cheap and often poisonous liquors.

Gin shops soon became such a plague that Parliament was moved to action. In 1729, 1736, and 1743 acts were passed in an effort to check the trade. They not only aroused the gin drinking public but also the powerful landed class with its vested interest in the sale of grain to distilleries. Consequently, attempts to enforce the acts met with little success. Gin consumption continued to mount at a dizzy pace, rising from about two million gallons in 1714 to twenty millions in 1742. Not until the drastic Act of 1751 was gin drinking successfully curbed.[18]

The West India interest was inevitably drawn into the controversy over gin drinking. Fearing blanket action against all ardent spirits, the sugar interest launched a campaign to dissociate molasses spirits from malt spirits in the public mind. Paid scribblers were set to work turning out pamphlets which shouted the merits of molasses spirits, while viewing with alarm the harmful effects of malt spirits. One fashionable magazine said that 'great intercession was made in particular for Mr Rum and Mme Punch; it being alleged in their

---

16 For a description of the 'Gin Age' see George M. Trevelyan, *English Social History A Survey of Six Centuries Chaucer to Queen Victoria* (London, 1945), pp. 341–4.
17 *Autobiography of William Stout*, ed. J. Harland (London, 1851), p. 25.
18 Dorothy M. George, *London Life in the XVIIIth Century* (London, 1925), pp. 26–43.

Behalf, that our Sugar Colonies and several other Branches of our Trade depended very much upon them'.[19]

Efforts to influence the drinking habits of Englishmen apparently met with some success. The sharp decline in imports of brandy and other foreign spirits, according to a pamphlet written in 1742, was 'owing to the great Improvement of English Spirits and the prevailing Taste for Rum'. A London sugar merchant observed in 1743 that rum was 'much more drank here in Punch than formerly...'. Served in ornately decorated bowls, punch was widely consumed by ladies and gentlemen of the fashionable set. The merchants of Liverpool, according to Samuel Derrick, had plenteously furnished tables, 'their rum is excellent of which they consume large quantities in punch, made when the West India fleets come in mostly with limes, which are very cooling, and afford a delicious flavour'.[20]

Drunkenness was the vice of the high as well as the low, and punch drinking played no small part in the inebriated condition of men of high station. Boswell, Johnson, Reynolds, Garrick, Sheridan, and Fox were among the men of note who were punch drinkers. In his 'London Journal' of 4 June 1763, James Boswell wrote: 'It was the King's birthnight, and I resolved to be a blackguard and see all that was to be seen... I then went as far as St. Paul's Church-yard, roaring along, and then came to Ashley's Punch-house and drank three threepenny bowls'. James Ashley kept this punch-house on Ludgate Hill for forty-five years. The notice of his death in 1776 said that 'He was the first to introduce the selling of punch in small quantities, by which he not only made a large fortune, but greatly promoted the interest of the British [Sugar] Islands, and the increase of the revenue'.[21]

Rum drinking invaded other areas of English social life. Eighteenth century elections were notorious for their bribery, corruption, and drunkenness. Rum punch was freely supplied to the electors during the stormy election of 1715. Dr Tullideph wrote from London to his plantation attorney in 1754, 'what Rum comes by ye ship Bassnett will come to a good Mercatt on account of the Election'.[22]

Rum was a special favourite with seamen. British sailors in the Caribbean received a daily allowance of rum which was served out

19 *The Country Journal, or The Craftsman*, 5 June 1736.
20 Anon., *An Inquiry into the Revenue, Credit, and Commerce of France* (London, 1743), p. 6; *Lascelles and Maxwell L. B.* Lre. to John Collins in Barbados, 16 Sept. 1743; Thomas Baines, *History of the Commerce and Town of Liverpool* (London, 1852), p. 427.
21 *Boswell's London Journal, 1762–1763*, ed. Frederick A. Pottle (London, 1951), p. 272; *An Eighteenth-Century Journal, Being a Record of the Years 1774–1776*, comp. John Hampden (London, 1940), p. 296.
22 *Tullideph L. B.*, vol. 2. Lre. to James Doig in Antigua, dated London, 4 March 1754.

Rum and Molasses in British Imperial Trade

'neat'. This practice continued until 1740, when Admiral Vernon ordered his sailors' rum to be mixed with water so as to reduce drunkenness and crime. The Admiral, who wore an old grogram coat in wet weather, was nicknamed 'Old Grog'. His sailors soon began to call the diluted spirit 'Grog'. Hot rum, sometimes mixed with eggs and milk, was recommended as an effective remedy for colds and an antidote for the damp English climate. The spread of vice and opulence did not escape the eye of Adam Smith, who observed that rum, sugar, and tobacco had become objects 'of almost universal consumption'.[23]

The West India interest, while it was unable to prevent rum from being included in certain acts to restrict spirit drinking, won a signal victory over the landed interest in the years from 1757 to 1760. These were years of poor harvests when the government prohibited the distilling of grain mash. From London Dr Tullideph reported the good news to his plantation attorneys in Antigua:

> About a month agone Sugars rose very high, owing to a Prohibition to use grain in makeing Spirits for a year to come. This induced the Distillers to buy up at once a large quantity of Course Sugar for their use. I have heard 10,000 hogsheads mentioned.[24]

The evils of gin drinking and a series of harvest failures had thus led the government to discourage the distilling of grain mash and to favour molasses spirits and the import of colonial rum and molasses.

Although the prohibition against distilled grain mash was removed in 1760, English rum consumption continued to rise. One measure of increase is afforded by the Custom House statistics. Imports were at the negligible figure of 207 gallons in 1698. They rose, however, in subsequent years, reaching a high point of more than two million gallons annually in the late 1760s and early 1770s. As little rum was re-exported to countries other than Ireland, it may be assumed that the quantities in Table 15.1 were consumed in the British Isles.

Import statistics understate actual consumption, however, because they fail to include rum distilled from the molasses by-product of English refineries, and because they take no account of smuggling. In 1736, Sir Robert Walpole estimated that in the previous eight years an average of 1,317,062 gallons of spirits had been made in England from molasses, compared with 6,775,500 gallons from corn. Another

---

23 Stephen Dowell, *A History of Taxation and Taxes in England* (London, 1888), vol. 4, p. 198; Adam Smith, *The Wealth of Nations* (1776) (New York, 1937), p. 889.
24 *Tullideph L. B.*, vol. 2. Lre. to Messrs Duncan Grant, Thomas Tew, and James Russell in Antigua, dated Edinburgh, 31 Dec. 1757. For a discussion of the prohibition of the distillery from 1757 to 1760, see Richard Pares, *War and Trade in the West Indies 1739–1763* (Oxford, 1936), pp. 484–6.

Table 15.1

British plantation rum imported into England and Wales, 1700–75 (annual averages in gallons)

1700–04	1,950	1741–45	429,424
1706–10	12,055	1746–50	585,888
1711–15	22,425	1751–55	821,912
1716–20	44,881	1756–60	935,821
1721–25	89,364	1761–65	1,452,028
1726–30	198,359	1766–70	2,354,550
1731–35	336,210	1771–75	2,336,760*
1736–40	310,982		

*Imports into Great Britain

Source: P.R.O., London. Trcas. 64/273 (274); Elizabeth B. Schumpeter, *English Overseas Trade Statistics 1697–1808* (Oxford, 1960), pp. 52–6.

writer estimated that 10,000 hogsheads of molasses were distilled annually in Great Britain in the years prior to 1759.[25] Since very little molasses was imported after 1720, it may be assumed that the above estimates refer to the molasses by-product of English sugar refineries.

Rum was smuggled into the British Isles in considerable quantities. Smuggling was encouraged by the heavy duties and excises on the legally imported product. Much of the illicit traffic centred in the Isle of Man, from whence rum and other products were smuggled into England, Scotland, and Ireland. Action was taken against the smugglers in 1765, when an Act of Parliament made it illegal for rum or other spirits to be 'shipped or laden in any British colony or plantation in America but on condition that the same shall not be carried to or landed in the Isle of Man ...'. Illegal imports also came through the Port of London, where the pilfering of rum and sugar ships gave rise to frequent complaints from West India merchants and planters.[26]

The growth in consumption was accompanied by an upward movement in prices. In London the price of Jamaica rum was 8s 0d per gallon in 1718, 7s 0d from 1728 to 1733, and from 7s 3d to 7s 9d in the period 1734–55. Prices rose sharply during the prohibition on

---

25 *Historical Manuscripts Commission. Earl of Egmont MSS* (London, 1923), vol. 2, p. 257; Joseph Massie, *A State of the British Sugar Colony Trade* (London 1759), p. 25.
26 5 Geo. III, c. 43.

malt distilling from 1757 to 1760: molasses from 10s to 37s per hundredweight, and rum to about 14s 0d per gallon (including the duty and excise). During the period of prohibition Joseph Massie asserted:

> the great Consumption of Rum in this Kingdom, hath not only raised the Price of British Rum to Double or Treble what it was before, but hath raised the Price of British Melasses also, as much greater Quantities are now used for making of Rum.[27]

Though prices declined somewhat after the prohibition was lifted, the general level was higher than in the period before 1757. At Brandsby the price of rum rose from 9s 6d to 12s 0d per gallon between 1762 and 1766; it then remained fairly steady in the years from 1771 to 1775, ranging from 9s 6d to 10s 6d. The price in London was 10s 6d in 1773.[28]

Prices were generally high enough after 1740 to overcome obstacles which formerly discouraged planters from shipping rum to Great Britain. Two obstacles of some consequence were high shipping costs and the perishable nature of the spirit. By distilling rum to a high proof in the West Indies and shipping it in iron-bound casks, planters were able to overcome both obstacles to a large extent. Besides retaining its strength on the long voyage, high-proof rum was more compact than the ordinary product and less costly to ship. Dr Tullideph, who consigned about 325 hogsheads of rum to Great Britain and Ireland between 1736 and 1766, almost invariably wrote that his rum was shipped in iron-bound casks and that it was 'double distilled' and able to 'sink oyl'. Upon arrival in port it was reduced in strength by adding two or three gallons of water to each gallon of rum.[29]

High duties and excises were other obstacles. That these charges had a restraining effect was the judgement of one Barbadian, who wrote in 1713 that they amounted to a prohibition.[30] After about 1740, on the other hand, planters generally found their rum remittances profitable after paying the 4½ per cent export duty and the English import duty and excise which amounted to 4s 9d per gallon in 1747, and 5s 1d in 1770. In 1742, some relief was granted to planters and merchants when Parliament permitted rum to be warehoused in bond, postponing the collection of duties and excises

---

27 Massie, *British Sugar Colony Trade*, p. 25.
28 James E. Thorold Rogers, *A History of Agriculture and Prices in England* (Oxford, 1902), vol. 7, pp. 355–60.
29 *Tullideph L. B.*, vol. 2. Lre. to Thomas Martin in London, dated Antigua, 20 March 1750
30 Anon., *The Present State of the Sugar Plantations Considered* (London, 1713) p. 22.

Sugar and Slavery

until the rum was sold or within six months of its being landed. Colonial rum was also given legal protection against foreign brandy and geneva in the market by a discriminatory duty.[31]

5 THE IRISH RUM MARKET

Besides the markets in Great Britain, Ireland became a rum market of no mean consequence after 1750. The situation with respect to ardent spirits in Ireland before 1733 was much the same as it had been in England before 1689. Ireland imported so much French wine and brandy in 1727 that the value of these imports exceeded the value of all Irish exports to France. Favouring more trade with the British colonies and less trade with France, Arthur Dobbs argued that if Ireland obtained

> rum and sugars at the cheapest hand from the [British] plantations, we should be encouraged to distil spirits from sugar at home, and to make use of rum instead of *French* brandy.... This would increase our demand for sugars and rum, and the colonies would reap great part of the benefit which *France* and the French [West India] islands reap now by our trade.[32]

Realizing the potential of the Irish market, the West India interest pushed through two acts of Parliament which removed restrictions on the colonial trade of Ireland and gave their commodities preferential treatment in that market. An Act of 1731 permitted the direct export of British plantation rum and other unenumerated commodities to Ireland without landing them first in England, as had been the case previously. This was a preliminary to the Molasses Act which, among other things, prohibited the import of French sugar, rum and molasses into Ireland. Largely as a consequence of these acts it was said in 1745 that 'great Quantities of British rum have since been imported and consum'd there, instead of French Brandy'.[33]

The boom in the Irish market began in 1763, when, in consequence of a decision to drawback all duties on re-exported West India rum, it became cheaper for Irish merchants to get their rum from England than to import it directly from the sugar colonies and pay the Irish import duty. This measure went far to shift consumption habits from French brandy to West India rum, for it gave rum a

---

31 Dowell, *History of Taxation*, vol. 4, p. 198–9.
32 Arthur Dobbs, *An Essay on the Trade and Improvement of Ireland* (1729), in *A Collection of Tracts and Treatises... of Ireland* (Dublin, 1761), vol. 2, p. 398.
33 4 Geo. II, c. 15; 6 Geo. II, c. 13; Anon., *The Present State of the British and French Trade to Africa and America Consider'd and Compar'd* (London, 1745), pp. 17, 52.

Table 15.2

Rum imports of Ireland compared with retained imports of England and Wales, 1764–75
(millions of gallons)

Year	Ireland	England and Wales	Total	Year	Ireland	England and Wales*	Total
1764	0.46	0.94	1.40	1770	1.64	1.38	3.02
1765	0.89	1.20	2.09	1771	2.01	1.33	3.34
1766	1.39	0.85	2.24	1772	1.96	1.55	3.51
1767	1.62	0.82	2.44	1773	1.70	1.31	3.01
1768	1.86	1.19	3.05	1774	1.50	1.07	2.57
1769	2.07	1.12	3.19	1775	1.32	1.62	2.94

*Imports into Great Britain from 1771 to 1775.

Source: *Ireland: Exports and Imports for the Ten Years Ending 1773.* MS in The British Library of Economics and Political Science, London; Edward Wakefield, *An Account of Ireland, Statistical and Political* (London, 1812), vol. 2, p. 43; Elizabeth B. Schumpeter, *English Overseas Trade Statistics 1697–1808* (Oxford, 1960), p. 60.

duty preference of 9s 6d over brandy. It was then, said a report of the West India Committee, that 'the Consumption of Rum began to make a Rapid Progress, inasmuch, that the Importation into Ireland rose in the Year 1764 to upwards of 900,000 Gallons ... in 1769 to upwards of 2,100,000 Gallons'.[34] Re-exports from England and Wales, which did not exceed 37,000 gallons before 1763, rose to between 1,000,000 and 1,312,000 gallons from 1765 to 1771. Indeed, Table 15.2 shows that Ireland absorbed more colonial rum than England and Wales in the years from 1766 to 1774.

Letters from the West Indies point to a marked preference for the European market in the boom years of the late 1760s and early 1770s. Samuel Martin wrote from Antigua in May 1768, that 'the price of Rum has risen so high from ye great demand in Ireland' that he regretted having sent a consignment of twenty hogsheads to a merchant in New York.[35] On 9 March 1768, Benjamin Wright of Jamaica wrote to Aaron Lopez, his principal in Newport, Rhode Island: 'the price of produce here is at last broke, and can assure you

34 West India Committee MSS. *Minutes of the West India Merchants, April 1769 to April 1779,* ff. 23–4, 29, 33–4, 52–5.
35 *Martin L. B.,* vol. 5, f. 60: Lre. to Henry White in New York, dated Antigua, ? May 1768.

Sugar and Slavery

my heart is allmost broke with it, Rum at the extravagant price 2/6 per Gallon, Molasses at 12d per Gallon. If it had been in my power to purchase produce at the price it went at last year should have done sumthing worthy your notice . . .'. He wrote again on 10 April 1771: 'I find a much greater quantity of Rum shippd for London market, than has been for many years past'.[36] After 1771 the situation altered somewhat; rum re-exports declined as a consequence of the cancellation of the drawback, but the decline in re-exports made no serious inroads into British and Irish rum imports and consumption.

The above evidence suggests that the demand in Great Britain and Ireland sometimes encouraged planters to convert their cane juice directly into rum. Two periods of such conversion were the early 1730s when sugar prices fell much more rapidly than rum prices, and the 1757–60 period of the ban on malt distilling.[37]

6 ILLICIT TRADE AND MARKETS IN NORTH AMERICA

Another effect of the growing demand in the British Isles was to price British West India molasses and rum out of much of the North American market. So long as planters exported few by-products to the British Isles, the price of these commodities varied little as between the British and foreign sugar colonies. North American traders exchanged temperate-zone supplies for the sugar products of the British Caribbean; their trade with the foreign sugar colonies appears to have been negligible. But when Englishmen and Irishmen became rum imbibers on a large scale, they bid up prices both at home and in the sugar colonies.

The fact that Boston merchants were importing small quantities of molasses from the Dutch colony of Surinam by the late years of the 17th century suggests that there was already a price differential. The differential became much greater when the French sugar islands moved into a high growth phase in the next century. Testifying in the House of Commons in 1731, the veteran North American trader, Fayrer Hall, said that prior to 1714 the Northern Colonies had been supplied with molasses, rum and other spirits 'from Surinam, our own Islands, and with *French* Brandy'. After that time, however, they turned more and more to the French colonies. French planters

---

36 *Commerce of Rhode Island*, vol. 1, 1726–1800, in *Coll. of Massachusetts Hist. Soc.*, 7th ser. (Boston, 1914), vol. IX, pp. 229, 363.
37 For evidence of 'spirit' distilled straight from cane juice see Richard Pares, *Yankees and Creoles The Trade between North America and the West Indies before the American Revolution* (Cambridge, Mass., 1956), p. 125, n. 7.

Rum and Molasses in British Imperial Trade

not only outbid their British counterparts by as much as 50 to 100 per cent for North American provisions, horses, asses, and mules, but they also sold their sugar products more cheaply. Hall stated that while rum was selling in Barbados at 11d to 12d and upwards per gallon in 1714, the Bostonians were then buying French molasses for only 3d and 4d. Prior to the commencement of the trade French planters were said to have 'never esteemed [molasses] more than Dung; for they used to throw it away'. They did so in large measure because rum imports were prohibited in France in order to protect native wines and brandy.[38]

North Americans expanded their trade with the foreign sugar colonies as the price gap between British and foreign rum and molasses grew wider. In Boston alone, the import of foreign molasses increased from about 3,000 hogsheads in 1725, to 20,000 in 1731. 'The consumption of rum in New England is so great', said one knowledgeable observer,

> that there have been 20,000 hogsheads of French molasses manufactured into rum at Boston in one year: and as every gallon of melasses will make a gallon of rum, this will amount to 1,260,000 gallons of rum in one year; so vast is the demand for that liquor by their fishery, and by the Indian trade.[39]

North American vessels returned empty from Jamaica because of the 'high prices of Rum and Molasses there', said a pamphleteer in 1731. 'It is allowed that the finest Rum is made in Jamaica, and therefore is in such Demand to send Home, that the Northern People can seldom afford to purchase, especially when Fleets are upon Sailing'.[40] Jamaica was not the only colony whose rum and molasses were too dear for the North Americans, for Governor Worsley wrote from Barbados in 1730 that molasses at the French island of Martinique was 'about 4d. per Gallon, and here 'tis worth 9d. and 10d., if they could not export their Mellasses, they must fling it away as they formerly did when they had no vent for it'. New York City was reported to have had sixteen distilleries in 1723 'which are wholly supplied with Mollasses from Martinico'.[41]

By the early 1730s British planters had joined in a chorus of complaint against the high prices they were charged for lumber, horses, and provisions, at the same time that their sugar products were said to yield meagre profits. Charles Dunbar, Surveyor General

---

38 P.R.O. London. C.O. 5/4, ff. 6–7 of printed evidence.
39 David MacPherson, *Annals of Commerce* (Edinburgh, 1805), vol. 3, p. 176.
40 P.R.O. London. Treas. 64/42, No. 2; Anon., *The Importance of the British Plantations in America* (London, 1731), p. 95.
41 Ibid., C.O. 20/21, Y 41: Gov. Worsley to the Board of Trade, 7 July 1730.

Sugar and Slavery

of Customs in the Leeward Islands, estimated in 1730 that the Northern trade to the foreign colonies had enhanced the price of lumber, provisions, and horses in the British sugar colonies 'at least 1/3 or 1/4 ... these supplys are the most considerable incidents in the annual expence of their plantations (Negroes excepted), without which they cannot be carried on'. Rum was said to yield 16d per gallon one year with another.

> But if the Northern trade of exporting from the French and Dutch settlements melass[es] (a commodity improvable and distilled into rum in the Northern Colonys) be continued, it would unavoidably reduce the price at least 1/6th or 1/7th to 12d. or 13d. per gall.[42]

In the light of the above evidence it is not surprising that British planters took their grievances to the mother Parliament. After three unsuccessful attempts to restrict or prohibit trade between North America and the foreign colonies, the Molasses Act was pushed through Parliament in 1733. While it permitted the sale of North American lumber, horses, and foodstuffs in markets outside the British Empire, return cargoes of foreign sugar, molasses, and rum were subject to prohibitive import duties amounting to 4s per cwt on sugar and paneles (later raised to 5s), 9d per gallon on rum, and 6d per gallon on molasses.[43]

Despite the high hopes of the planter interest, the Molasses Act failed to alter existing channels of intercolonial trade. Colonies which depended upon cheap molasses for their rum distilleries continued their trade with the foreign sugar colonies. Merchants in the Northern Colonies found ingenious ways and means to circumvent the Molasses Act in the years immediately following its passage. When they discovered that British customs officials were making only half-hearted attempts at enforcement, the law was openly and brazenly violated. Professor Pitman says that by 1748 the prosperity and standard of living of New England and the Middle Colonies were intimately connected with the existence of illicit trade with foreign markets.[44]

Illicit trade continued during the early years of the Seven Years' War. From 1756 to 1759 there was much intercourse through the neutral Caribbean ports of St Eustatius, St Thomas, St Croix, and Monte Cristi. Illicit trade was negligible, however, during the last three years of the war. British annexation of the French islands of

42 *Cal. S. P. Col. 1730*, pp. 300–1.
43 Frank W. Pitman, *The Development of the British West Indies 1700–1763* (New Haven, 1917), pp. 211, 242–70; Pares, *War and Trade*, pp. 81–2.
44 Pitman, *Development of British West Indies*, pp. 295–6.

Guadeloupe and Martinique enabled the North Americans to do openly what they had long done illegally; from these islands came vast quantities of molasses to supply the distilleries of North America.[45]

While the Molasses Act was virtually ignored before 1759, all this was changed in the reorganization of imperial finance at the close of the Seven Years' War. The Sugar Act of 1764, the first measure to implement the new policy, prohibited the import of foreign rum, reduced the duty on foreign molasses from 6d to 3d per gallon, and retained the duty on foreign sugar at the level of the Molasses Act. Although the Sugar Act, like the Molasses Act, sought to hamper the French sugar islands and to benefit the British, a new purpose was to raise a colonial revenue to help defray the cost of the imperial establishment. Edmund Burke said it was 'A revenue not substantiated in place of, but superadded to a monopoly, which monopoly was enforced at the same time with additional strictness, and the execution put into military hands'.[46]

Embitterment followed in the wake of the Sugar Act. 'There was not a man on the continent of America', wrote John Adams, 'who does not consider the Sugar Act, as far as it regards molasses, as a sacrifice made of the northern colonies to the superior interest in Parliament of the West Indians'. Especially onerous was the strict enforcement of the Act by the British Navy and Courts of Vice Admiralty. 'The discontent sprang chiefly from the duty on foreign molasses, which, though cut in two in 1764, was still considered burdensome', writes Professor Beer.[47]

Parliament heard vigorous protests from the legislative bodies of Rhode Island, Massachusetts, Connecticut, New York and Pennsylvania. The Assembly of Rhode Island set forth the strongest case against the Sugar Act in its Remonstrance of 1764. This small colony of about thirty square miles and 48,000 inhabitants was said to consume £120,000 sterling of British manufactures annually, to export native products valued at only £5,000, and to meet its adverse commodity balance from the profits of its molasses and rum trade. Approximately 14,000 hogsheads of molasses came into Rhode Island annually, of which only 2,500 were of British Caribbean origin. Upwards of thirty distilleries, 'the main hinge upon which the trade of the colony turns', faced ruin, it was predicted, if the British

---

45 Ibid., pp. 297–333.
46 4 Geo. III, c. 15; Edmund Burke, *Speeches and Letters on American Affairs*, ed. Ernest Rhys (London, 1945), p. 31; Pares, *Yankees and Creoles*, p. 48–65.
47 George L. Beer, *British Colonial Policy, 1754–1765* (New York, 1933), pp. 291–4.

Sugar and Slavery

Table 15.3

Rum exports from the Thirteen Colonies to Nova Scotia, Quebec, and Newfoundland, 1770–73 (gallons)

	1770	1771	1772	1773
West India rum	52,712	36,873	47,736	50,716
North American rum	590,748	550,514	520,525	608,025
Total exports	643,460	587,387	568,261	658,741

Source: David MacPherson, *Annals of Commerce* (Edinburgh, 1805), vol. 3, p. 567.

Government persisted in its disastrous course of taxing foreign molasses.[48]

The protest from Massachusetts revealed an even greater dependence upon foreign molasses which supplied upwards of sixty distilleries. All but 500 of the 15,000 hogsheads imported into that colony came from the foreign colonies in 1763.[49]

The predominance of American distilled rum in the export trade of the Thirteen Colonies is indicated by Table 15.3. Not included in the above table were the exports to the coast of Africa, averaging about 270,000 gallons annually in the years from 1768 to 1770, and commanding in exchange some 2,280 Gold Coast slaves.[50]

Partly in consequence of the protests against the Sugar Act, the duty was lowered in 1766 to one penny a gallon and made uniform on all molasses, whether British or foreign. The prohibition on foreign rum, however, remained unchanged.

From the standpoint of British sugar planters, the Acts of 1764 and 1766 represented a substantial, although partial, victory. They had little to lose from the molasses trade since the greater part of their by-product was converted directly into rum. On the other hand, they gained from the ban on foreign rum. The reason for this was twofold. First, there were two fairly distinct and non-competitive markets in North America – one for cheap rum distilled from foreign molasses, the other for the quality product of the British sugar colonies. Secondly, the planters gained a protected and effectively

---
48 *Records of the Colony of Rhode Island and Providence Plantations,* ed. John R. Bartlett (Providence, 1861), vol. 6, pp. 378–83.
49 *Massachusetts His. Soc. Coll.,* vol. 74 (1918), pp. 204–5.
50 MacPherson, *Annals of Commerce,* vol. 3, pp. 403, 603.

Rum and Molasses in British Imperial Trade

policed market for quality rum instead of the protected but inadequately policed market that existed from 1733 to 1759. This was no inconsequential gain, for the trade statistics show that North American rum imports of British Caribbean origin nearly matched those of Great Britain and Ireland in the years from 1770 to 1773. Expressed in millions of gallons, the annual average for these years was 2.95 for North America and 3.22 for Great Britain and Ireland. On the other hand, foreign molasses practically displaced the British Caribbean product in North American markets.[51]

7 CONTRIBUTORY FACTORS

Contributing to the expanded role of rum and molasses in the British Caribbean economy were several factors of lesser import than the rise of overseas markets. One of these was the growth of the plantation system of production. The distilling of rum, like the claying and refining of sugar, was feasible only on heavily capitalized estates. For example, Edward Long estimated that a Jamaican plantation producing 300 hogsheads of sugar and 150 puncheons of rum, and valued in the aggregate at £28,039 sterling, required one distilling house, four large stills, and other equipment amounting to £1,071 sterling. Each puncheon yielded £7 3s, or a total of £1,071 out of a total gross income of £4,284 sterling per annum.[52]

Another contributory factor was the growth of absentee ownership. Absentees found it difficult to check on the proceeds from the sale of by-products as well as the proportion of rum and sugar that was made. A considerable portion of the by-products was bartered for plantation supplies in the West Indies. Attorneys and managers were thus tempted to increase the proportion of rum to sugar and defraud absentees. They customarily transacted local business through town agents who disposed of the rum and molasses, purchased plantation supplies, and paid local debts and taxes. As one case in point, Sir William Stapleton, a Nevis absentee, suspected that part of his receipts, especially from the sale of rum, were being withheld from him.[53]

Although these contributory factors were of fairly general application, the by-products played a more important economic role in

51 See Table 15.2; George Chalmers, *Opinions on . . . American Independence* (London, 1784), p. 121.
52 Long, *History of Jamaica*, vol. 1, pp. 461–3.
53 Edwin F. Gay, 'Letters from a Sugar Plantation in Nevis, 1723–1732', *Journal of Economic and Business History*, vol. 1 (Nov. 1928), p. 152.

Sugar and Slavery

some islands than they did in others. West India agriculture became highly capitalized under a regime of substantial planters. Whereas planters first extracted raw materials from cane juice in the form of muscovado sugar and molasses, they came in time to engage in the claying and refining of sugar and the distilling of rum.

Rough computations of the ratio of rum to sugar point to substantial variation among the islands. Compared with Jamaica, the small islands produced relatively more improved sugar, and thus had proportionately more molasses to distill into rum. Moreover, the small islands depended more heavily on North American supplies than did the large and more diversified economy of Jamaica. Planters in the small islands probably increased the proportion of rum to sugar in order to pay for plantation necessities.[54]

8 CONCLUSION

In conclusion, it has been shown that the by-products were not always utilized in the mid-17th century period; they found few markets outside the Caribbean colonies. By the late 17th and early 18th centuries the North American market was growing rapidly, while the rum trade to Africa had begun to assume considerable importance. Moreover, the revolution in British spirit drinking was beginning to alter the direction of the by-product trade. By the third quarter of the 18th century Great Britain and Ireland were at times the most profitable markets for colonial rum. The rise in overseas demand encouraged planters to convert more of their molasses into rum; in some years they probably maximized profits by converting cane juice directly into this spirit.

The year 1713 would seem to mark a broad dividing line in the nature of the rum and molasses trade. Before that date planters were able to supply both the British and North American markets with their by-products. On the other hand, their inability to supply both markets after 1713 created serious problems. Great Britain and Ireland, the most profitable markets in certain years, could not supply the planters with provisions and lumber as cheaply as North America. A further complication was the expansion of the foreign sugar colonies. As these colonies had few European outlets for their by-products, they were able to undersell their British counterparts. Then, too, there were the conditions peculiar to North Americans. Given their voracious appetites for rum and molasses and their

---

54 Frere, *Short History of Barbados*, pp. 113–14; MacPherson, *Annals of Commerce*, vol. 3, p. 485.

capacity to supply plantation necessities, it is understandable that they should turn to the foreign sugar islands. Retaliation was not long in coming from the British sugar planters who complained that the unfavourable terms of trade were a threat to their livelihood. Though retaliation first came in the form of the Molasses Act, the British Government refrained from strict enforcement for many years. Subsequent attempts to stop smuggling and increase customs revenue only fired the resentment of the North Americans. The Sugar Act of 1764 thus marks the beginning of a period of strained relations which led to rebellion and war.

CHAPTER SIXTEEN

Planters and Plantership

> When Merchants who settle here [Nevis], or Men of the Learned Professions, of the Law especially, have got a little before hand let them but once get a Footing on a Piece of Land or on a Plantation ever so poorly settled, whether by Marriage, Purchase, or otherwise, and they seldom fail (as their other Business or Practice is daily bringing them in Money) of soon becoming considerable Planters . . .[1]
>
> Rev. Robert Robertson, 1732

1 INTRODUCTION

The substantial sugar planter in the 18th century was a complex personality; at once landlord, slaveowner, farmer, manufacturer, and merchant. He owned the land, slaves, and equipment; he supervised the labourers in the cultivation and processing of the sugar-cane; he purchased plantation supplies and consigned the final products to overseas merchants; he arranged for credit and loans. In short, the planter organized and directed the agents of production in an effort to maximize profits. He and his fellow planters dominated the social and political life of the colony and forged links with the metropolis. His ultimate objective was to build up an income-earning property which would enable him to achieve social and political standing in the mother country. Having climbed the plantation ladder and taken up residence in the metropolis, the proprietor entrusted his estate to the care of managers and attornies, who aspired to ascend the same ladder as their employer.

Probably the leading authority on plantation management was the Antigua planter Colonel Samuel Martin, author of *An Essay Upon Plantership*, which was first published about 1754. Martin defined plantership as 'the art of managing a sugar-plantation to the best advantage, so as to make it produce the most, both in quantity and quality'. He outlined the 'proper qualifications' of a planter, both in his public and private capacities. Public responsibilities included

---

[1] Rev. Robert Robertson, *A Detection of the State and Situation of the Present Sugar Planters of Barbados and the Leeward Islands* (London, 1732), pp. 51–2.

service in the legislative assembly, militia, and magistrate courts. In his private character the planter must be

> an adept in figures, and in all the arts of economy, something of an architect, and well skilled in mechanics, because there is in every plantation a variety of buildings and machinery, upon the right contrivance and use of which, much of the planter's success depends.[2]

If he expected to make the most of his estate, the planter should be an expert sugar-boiler and distiller. He should have a rudimentary knowledge of drugs and medicine to treat his wounded and sick Negroes. In all relations with his dependants he should be just, temperate, patient, forebearing, 'suppress wickedness by suitable punishments, and encourage goodness with generosity...' More particularly, the planter should be 'a very skilful husbandman; because upon the right culture of his soil depends absolutely the QUANTITY, and in a great measure the QUALITY also, of his produce'.[3]

The proper qualifications of a planter might be expected to vary in time and place. At the outset of the sugar revolution the planter faced such problems as acquiring knowledge of sugar production, recruiting and training his labour force, gaining title to enough land to feed his dependants and livestock and grow canes to support his sugar mill, constructing buildings for industrial and domestic purposes, supervising his workers in the many tasks to be accomplished, and keeping a close rein on cash outlays during the long interval between harvests. Plantations typically had reserve areas for growing provisions, pasturing animals, and supplying forest products; cash crops consisted of a mixture of major and minor staples, and the most complicated piece of machinery was the three-roller cattle-mill. Plantations were thus under-capitalized by comparison with those at a later stage of production. Under these conditions the planter was an entrepreneurial jack-of-all-trades. Although aspiring to the status of gentleman farmer, he frequently worked alongside his white servants and black slaves in tasks requiring technical skill and close attendance.

Plantership took on added dimensions during the drive to monoculture. Survival as a business unit was hardly possible without the economies of scale that went with sugar works equipped with windmills or water-wheels, rum distilleries, and facilities to make improved sugar. Larger sugar works, in turn, called for expanded

---

2 Samuel Martin, *An Essay Upon Plantership*, printed in *Three Tracts on West-Indian Agriculture* (Jamaica, 1802), p. x.
3 Ibid., pp. i–xii.

Sugar and Slavery

cane acreage, often at the expense of pasture and provision grounds. As the white servant class declined in relation to that of Negro slaves, and as the labour force on a given plantation expanded, the planter was no longer able to attend to day-to-day training, supervision and correction. More of his time was taken up with planning and co-ordination, buying and selling, and meeting his fellow planters at Government House and the local exchange to get news of the weather, markets, labour conditions and shipping. Wings were added to the great house to accommodate his growing family, staff of servants, and managerial staff. While the planter continued to ride out daily to oversee the workers in the fields and sugar works, a good part of his working day was taken up with more sedentary tasks. He heard reports and issued instructions to his overseer, doctor, and town agent; he roughed out letters to his London commission agent which were copied in triplicate by his writer; he supervised his book-keeper in the keeping of plantation journals and ledgers.

Plantership tended to be more formally structured when the proprietor was an absentee. Short visits abroad need not impair the quality of plantership if a competent manager was left in charge of routine business and relatives and friends of the absentee agreed to inspect the plantation periodically and handle commercial, financial, and other matters that were beyond the competence of the manager. In the event of mismanagement under delegated authority, the proprietor might be expected to return before irreparable damage was done. Permanent absenteeism, on the other hand, presented the undermanagers with opportunities for fraud and mismanagement which might continue indefinitely in the absence of suitable mechanisms of surveillance, reporting and correction. Informal and unpaid supervision by friends and relatives thus tended to be supplanted by the employment of quasi-professional attorneys, who, either on salary or commission, performed, or were expected to perform, the managerial functions normally undertaken by resident proprietors.

One of the paradoxes of West Indian history is the diversity of planter origins and quality of plantership as revealed by contemporary literature, and the narrow, one-sided view of these matters which has been presented by all but a few modern historians of the British Caribbean colonies. The general consensus is that the islands were first peopled by the scum and riff-raff of English society, that social and political conditions deteriorated until the Civil War period when there was a happy conjunction of Royalists fleeing Cromwell's Ironsides, and Dutchmen fleeing northern Brazil. The latter brought knowledge of sugar-cane culture, technology, and commerce, together with capital, credit, and above all Negro slaves; while the former, who came from the rural aristocracy of England, brought not only agricultural experience and love of the land, but also qualities of leadership and character which enabled them to establish order and justice in a hitherto unruly and degenerate society.[4]

The salutary influence of the Royalist planters, it is contended, was short lived. The enervating climate and slave society are thought to have acted as a screen in filtering out potentially desirable immigrants. The plantations, writes Professor Ragatz, 'became the goal of spendthrift bankrupts eager to recoup their wasted fortunes, of penniless younger sons of gentility desirous of amassing means sufficient to become landed proprietors in the homeland, and the dumping-ground for the riff raff of the parent country'.[5] Religion, family life, education, art, music, among other refining influences, were largely absent from a society polarized between a minority of affluent planters and a mass of degraded slaves.

From the above premises it is argued that the quality of plantership underwent marked deterioration. Planters reputedly had an ingrained hostility to innovation and were content to jog along with their primitive and wasteful agrarian system. Easy credit led to gross extravagance and a spirit of speculation without due regard to the actual risk involved. Debts tended to pile up until mortgage holders were forced to foreclose. What kept the system viable and at times very profitable, it is maintained, was the high price of tropical staples, which, in turn, rested upon a monopoly of supplying the home and British-American mainland markets with Caribbean commodities.[6]

Though some contemporary literature supports these consensus views of planter origins, character, and society, one must be sceptical of generalizations which spring from a rather narrow base of primary data, which highlight certain facets of the story and leave other matters obscure, which tend to give a static rather than a dynamic view of Creole society and its principal actors. Actually, the record reveals qualifications and exceptions to every generalization. Royalist refugees and their descendants were not the only individuals who became successful sugar planters; the so-called riff-raff element waxed and waned in response to wars, rebellions, and crop failures in

---

4 C. S. S. Higham, *The Development of the Leeward Islands Under the Restoration 1660–1688* (Cambridge, 1921), pp. 1–23.
5 Lowell J. Ragatz, *The Fall of the Planter Class in the British Caribbean, 1763–1833* (New York, 1928), pp. 1–3; Frank W. Pitman, *The Development of the British West Indies 1700–1763* (New Haven, 1917), pp. 1–41.
6 Ragatz, *Fall of Planter Class*, pp. 4–39.

Sugar and Slavery

Europe, and the structure of economic opportunities in the colonies; Creole economic behaviour was probably influenced more by cultural factors than those of a climatic nature; religion was by no means a negligible influence on economic behaviour; middle-class mercantile and professional men exerted an influence that was disproportionate to their numbers; family life coexisted with bachelorhood; and it was not unusual for families to remain in possession of plantations for many generations.

2 THE NONCONFORMISTS

When Henry Whistler came to Barbados in 1655, he found that the white population consisted of Englishmen, Frenchmen, Dutchmen, Scotsmen, Irishmen and Sephardic Jews. He wrote that the island was a dunghill whereon England had cast forth its rubbish.[7] Whistler was no doubt entitled to his low opinion of the colonists, since his visit coincided with the turbulent aftermath of the English and Barbadian civil wars and booming conditions in the sugar industry.

But apart from the gentlemen planters, not all of the West Indians were godless and penniless rogues, vagabonds, debtors, and prisoners-of-war. Alfred Chandler has found evidence which suggests that lower middle class farmers and artisans made up the bulk of the 12,000 or more English emigrants to Barbados from 1636 to 1643. 'These immigrants', he writes, 'probably were Dissenters similar to those who went to New England, though perhaps, from a somewhat lower economic class'.[8] Further evidence of Dissenter activity is an Act of Barbados of 1647, condemning unorthodox conventicles held by 'divers opinionated and self conceited persons', and calling for the punishment of people who did not conform to the government and discipline of the Church of England.[9]

Less than a decade from enactment of the Conventicle Act, two Quaker ladies, Mary Fisher and Ann Austin, came to Barbados to win converts to their faith. Mary Fisher wrote to her friends in England in 1655: 'Here is many convinced and many desire to know the way'.[10] After a short trip to New England, the ladies returned to

7 Henry Whistler's *Journal*, February 1655, in *Narrative of General Venables*, ed. C. H. Firth (London, 1900), pp. 145–7.
8 Alfred D. Chandler, 'The Expansion of Barbados', *Jour. of Barbados Museum and Hist. Soc.*, vol. XII, nos. 3, 4 (May–Nov, 1946), p. 109.
9 Vincent T. Harlow, *A History of Barbados 1625–1685* (Oxford, 1926), pp. 26–7, 249–50.
10 Quoted in Rufus M. Jones, *The Quakers in the American Colonies* (New York, 1962), pp. 26–8, 42–4.

Planters and Plantership

Barbados and won to their faith two of the island's leading planters, Lieutenant-Colonel Thomas Rous and his son John Rous. Early in 1656 Mary Fisher and two other Quakers visited the island of Nevis and planted the seed there. Other missionaries followed, one of whom wrote from Barbados in 1661 and called that island 'the nursery of truth'.[11]

Further evidence of missionary activity is found in the journal of William Edmundson, the Irish Quaker. Edmundson went to London and joined George Fox, the founder of the Society of Friends, and eleven other Quakers on a missionary expedition to the West Indies and North America. Soon after their landing in Barbados in October 1671, Edmundson wrote that 'we had great service for the Lord and the good of the people, many were convinced and turned to the Lord, and brought into the way of life and peace'.[12] Later he and Colonel Lewis Morris, a leading planter and Quaker convert, went to Antigua, 'where we had great meetings, and many were convinced and turned to the Lord. Several justices of the peace, officers, and chief men came to meetings, and confessed the truth ....'.[13]

From Antigua, Edmundson went to Nevis with Colonel Morris and Samuel Winthrop, the former governor and Quaker convert. There they were met on docking by 'several honest tender Friends' who were joyful at their coming. However, Governor Stapleton prohibited their coming on shore on the grounds that several hundred militiamen had turned Quakers and refused to bear arms. Edmundson and his party returned to Antigua and were received with gladness. A few weeks later he was back in Barbados, where he found George Fox carrying on an active ministry.[14]

Jamaica was the next missionary field to attract Edmundson, who accompanied George Fox and several other Quakers on a ten-day voyage from Bridgetown to Port Royal. 'We travelled much in that island', he wrote, 'and had good service in gathering people to the Lord Jesus Christ, and settling meetings among them'.[15]

Edmundson returned to Ireland after his visit to Jamaica, but he journeyed again to the West Indies and North America in 1675, and again in 1683. On one of his visits in Barbados he was challenged to a theological debate by an Anglican clergyman. The debaters confronted each other in an open-air setting and drew upwards of three

---

11 Ibid., p. 41; Frederick B. Tolles, *Quakers and the Atlantic Culture* (New York, 1960), pp. 1–35.
12 *A Journal of the Life, Travels, Sufferings, and Labour of Love in the Work of the Ministry of William Edmundson* (London, 1829), pp. 53–5.
13 Ibid., p. 55.
14 Ibid., pp. 55–7.
15 Ibid., p. 58.

Sugar and Slavery

thousand spectators, including several justices of the peace and other leading citizens.[16]

Although Barbados was a veritable 'hive' of Quakerism for several decades, and the faith spread to other Caribbean colonies, the movement declined in the 18th century. Scarcely a hundred Friends, including children, were left in Barbados by 1744. Compulsory militia service, the slave system, and the laxity of morals were incompatible with the tenets of the faith. Some of the members migrated to a more congenial environment in Pennsylvania; others stayed on to become Anglicans or they lost their faith.[17] But there is reason to believe that Nonconformity continued to have an influence on economic behaviour in the colonies, even after the movement had lost its organizational dress. One reason for so thinking is that the islands received a stream of English merchants and professional men of Nonconformist leanings. Another is that there was a sizeable influx of Scotsmen who had been reared in the austere atmosphere of John Knox's Calvinism.

3 THE SEPHARDIC JEWS

The Sephardic Jews were a minority group which aided the growth of the British sugar industry without playing a major role in the ownership and management of plantations. Long settled in the Iberian peninsula, the Jews began their forced migration in 1478, when they were persecuted at the establishment of the Spanish Inquisition. For a time they found a more tolerant attitude in neighbouring Portugal. But after a century or more of relative security, the Inquisition harried those who refused to become 'new Christians' out of Portugal. One group migrated to Antwerp and Amsterdam, another to the Portuguese colony of Brazil. In Brazil the Sephardic Jews played a most important part as financiers of the sugar industry, as suppliers of Negro slaves, and as brokers and exporters of sugar. Later they became allies of the Dutch during the latter's conquest of northern Brazil. Then at the Portuguese reconquest in 1654, the Sephardic Jews were forced to migrate to the Guianas, Caribbean islands, North America, Holland and England.

---

16 *A Journal of the Life, Travels, Sufferings, and Labour of Love in the Work of the Ministry of William Edmundson* (London, 1829), pp. 72–9.
17 Jones, *Quakers in American Colonies*, pp. 26–7; William C. Braithwaite, *The Second Period of Quakerism*, 2nd ed., revised by Henry J. Cadbury (Cambridge, 1961), pp. 618, 621.

Meanwhile, numbers of them had settled in the Guianas and Caribbean islands.[18]

Jewish refugees from the mainland became numerous in the English islands beginning in the mid-century period. They concentrated first in Barbados, where their numbers had increased by 1680 to 313, of whom 238 resided in Bridgetown. Another colony was established in Nevis, the trading centre of the Leeward Islands. But most numerous and influential were the Jews of Jamaica. Ten Portuguese Jewish families with 322 slaves are reported to have migrated from Surinam to Jamaica after the Treaty of Breda in 1667. They were joined by other Jews from the Eastern Caribbean and from England and Holland. At the end of the 17th century there were some eighty families in Jamaica; in 1736 a leader of the local Jewish community reported their numbers at 'About Seven or Eight Hundred, Reckoning Men, Women & Children'.[19]

Together with the Dutch, the Sephardic Jews transferred the centre of the New World sugar industry from northern Brazil to the Caribbean islands. They brought knowledge of cane culture and processing, together with cane cuttings, seasoned slaves, mills, utensils, Holland and English wares, and African slaves. More than the Dutch, they were masters of sugar technology and taught the English the art of sugar making.

Numerous Jews stayed on after launching the sugar industry to engage in a variety of activities. Though strongly opposed by local English merchants and subject to discriminatory taxation and other hindrances, they generally had the backing of colonial governors and the Board of Trade and were issued patents of naturalization. The Jews capitalized on their international connections to import luxury and convenience goods, to find outlets for tropical produce, and to become money changers and foreign exchange dealers. They imported light coins and exchanged them for heavy coins and bills of exchange which they remitted to their principals in Europe. Being multilingual and cosmopolitan, they had advantages not possessed by their English rivals in the clandestine entrepôt trade with the foreign colonies. As money lenders and shopkeepers, they dealt extensively with small planters and Negroes who brought their produce to the

---

18 Gordon Merrill, 'The Role of the Sephardic Jews in the British Caribbean Area during the Seventeenth Century', *Caribbean Studies*, vol. 4, no. 3 (Oct. 1964), pp. 32–40; Arnold Wiznitzer, 'The Jews in the Sugar Industry of Colonial Brazil', *Jewish Social Studies*, vol. XVIII, no. 3 (July 1956), pp. 189–98.

19 Merrill, 'Role of the Sephardic Jews', pp. 40–6; Public Record Office, London. C.O. 137/22, V 10, f. 34: Benjamin Bravo's answers to queries of the Board of Trade, 17 Feb. 1736.

Sunday markets.[20] The Jews were described by the English merchants in Port Royal, Jamaica, as a 'kind of joint stock company . . . frequently buy up whole cargoes, undersell petitioners, which they can better because of their own penurious way of living, and at last give the whole measure to the market . . .'.[21]

4 THE SCOTSMEN AND IRISHMEN

As we have seen, Scotsmen played an important part in the planter societies of Antigua and St Kitts, while Irishmen were numerous and quite influential in Montserrat. These two nationalities ranged more broadly over the Caribbean, however, and their coming to the sugar colonies can be explained in part by certain historical events. Before 1660, when there was free trade between Scotland and the plantations, many of the indentured servants were said to have been Scotsmen who made excellent planters and soldiers.[22] Many Scotsmen and Irishmen came as prisoners-of-war during the English Civil Wars. Near the end of the 17th century a shipload of survivors reached Jamaica after the tragic effort to establish a Scottish colony on the isthmus of Darien. Scotsmen gained access to the English colonies by the Act of Union in 1707. Many rebels fled to the West Indies after the failure of the Scottish risings in 1715 and 1745. Finally, Scotsmen found new plantation frontiers to conquer when Britain acquired the four Ceded Islands by the Treaty of Paris in 1763.[23]

While the Act of Union gave access to the colonies, economic and social conditions in the homeland fuelled the outward migration. Population growth, enclosures, and a low level of material well-being co-existed in 18th century Scotland with a high level of primary and secondary education, the flowering of university life, and intellectual and cultural achievements. As Richard Pares has observed, theological Calvinism was losing its hold on the people, and the great mental and moral energies which it generated were transferred to secular studies and secular interests.[24]

20 N. Darnell Davis, 'Notes on the History of the Jews in Barbados', *Pub. of The American Jewish Hist. Soc.*, no. 18 (1909), pp. 129–48.
21 *Cal. S. P. Col. 1669–74*, p. 366: Petition to Gov. Lynch, 2 July 1672.
22 Anon., 'An Account of the English Sugar Plantations', no date, British Museum, Egerton MSS 2395, f. 632.
23 Ian C. C. Graham, *Colonists from Scotland: Emigration to North America* (Ithaca, 1956), pp. 1–22; George Pratt Insh, *The Company of Scotland Trading to Africa and the Indies* (London, 1932).
24 Richard Pares, 'A Quarter of a Millennium of Anglo-Scottish Union', in *The Historian's Business and Other Essays*, ed. R. A. and Elisabeth Humphreys (Oxford, 1961), pp. 84–94.

Planters and Plantership

Many Scotsmen sought a new life in the colonies. The Scottish family system helped to make the migration a continuous one, for one Scotsman was hardly established abroad before he sent for his brothers, cousins, nephews, and fellow townsmen. Politics aided the outward movement, for the Scottish M.P.s at Westminster generally voted in a bloc, and they traded their votes for posts in the colonies which they conferred on their relatives and friends. Another source of strength were the Scotsmen who fought in colonial wars. [25]

Scotsmen of all ranks and conditions of life came to the West Indies after 1707. Included among them were indentured servants, bookkeepers, farmers, artisans, merchants, doctors, lawyers, soldiers, sailors, customs collectors, provost marshals and colonial governors. In the main, however, they were probably of lower middle class origin and possessed of superior education and training. They found many opportunities upon which to exercise their energy and skills as craftsmen, agriculturists, professionals, merchants, soldiers and administrators. We have seen that Scotsmen were the leading developers of the former French lands in St Kitts, and they occupied positions of leadership in the colonial gentry of Antigua.

However, no colony except possibly Virginia offered more opportunities than did Jamaica. One of the pioneer settlers was Colonel John Campbell (1674–1740). Born in Inverary in Argyleshire, he served in several campaigns in Flanders and was a captain of the troops sent to Darien. He came to Jamaica in 1700, married an heiress, acquired a large estate, and was elevated to the island's privy council. The inscription on his tomb said that he was the first Campbell who settled in Jamaica, and through his extreme generosity and assistance many of his fellow clansmen had become possessed of opulent fortunes. Edward Long wrote some years later that he had heard that no fewer than one hundred of the name of Campbell were residents of Jamaica, all claiming alliance with the Argyle family.[26]

If the Campbells led the ranks, numerous other families came from the glens and dales of the north land. 'Jamaica, indeed, is greatly indebted to North-Britain', wrote Long, 'as very near one third of the inhabitants are either natives of that country, or descendants from those who were'.[27] A comparison of the Jamaica Quit Rent Book of 1754 with a work on Scottish surnames reveals that some 485 Scotsmen held a total of 442,700 acres (average 1,150 acres). They constituted nearly one-fourth of all landholders and claimed about

---

25 Ibid., pp. 95–8.
26 W. A. Feurtado, *Official and Other Personages of Jamaica from 1655 to 1790* (Kingston, 1896), p. 18; Edward Long, *The History of Jamaica* (London, 1774), vol. 2, p. 286.
27 Long, *History of Jamaica*, vol. 2, p. 287.

Sugar and Slavery

the same proportion of the taxable land.[28] Another comparative measure is afforded by the personal property inventories which were taken soon after the death of persons claiming movable wealth. For the five-year period, 1771–5, the inventories number 894 and amount to £2,375,343 sterling. To make the comparison manageable, we will exclude all inventories under £1,000, which leaves 363 inventories aggregating £2,207,611. Scots' inventories of £1,000 or more number 77 (or 21.3 per cent) and amount to £891,916 (or 40.4 per cent). If the inventories of the Scots-Irish, Irish, and Jews are added to those of the Scotsmen, it is likely that the non-English personal property in Jamaica amounted to one-half of the total.[29]

Edward Long enumerated the qualities which enabled Scotsmen and Irishmen to get ahead in Jamaica. First, they generally brought sounder constitutions and adapted to the environment much better than the English. Second, they helped one another. New arrivals were often beholden to the benevolence of their patrons, 'who do not suffer them to languish and fall into despondence for want of employment, but ... soon put them into a way of doing something for themselves'. Third, those who came out as artisans, particularly the stone masons and millwrights, were 'remarkably expert, and in general are sober, frugal and civil'. Fourth, the good education, which the poorest of them received, had a salutary influence on their morals and behaviour. Finally, they had their eye on the main chance, were 'so clever and prudent in general, as, by an obliging behaviour, good sense, and zealous services, to gain esteem, and make their way through every obstacle'.[30]

5 THE PROFESSIONALS AND ADMINISTRATORS

'Let those persons be as worthy as they will, yet it must be allowed that the Bulk of them, who come here to prey upon us, are either of the Learned Professions, or are Merchants', wrote a correspondent to *The Barbadoes Gazette* on 7 October 1732. He went on to assert 'that the Lawyers thrive by our Contentions, the Physicians by our Diseases, and the Clergy live by the Sins of the People'.[31] Not a few lawyers, doctors, clergymen, and government officials practised their professions with a view toward accumulating money to purchase

28 P.R.O. London. C.O. 142/31: Jamaica Quit Rent Book, 1754; George F. Black, *The Surnames of Scotland Their Origin, Meaning, and History* (New York, 1946).
29 Jamaica Public Record Office, Spanish Town. *Inventorys*, vols. 51–56.
30 Long, *History of Jamaica*, vol. 2, pp. 286–92.
31 Anon., *Caribbeana, Containing Letters and Dissertations, etc.* (London, 1741), vol. 1, p. 61.

plantations. Accumulation might be speeded if professions were combined with trade, money lending, and the superintendence of absentees' estates. Moreover, ambitious young men might acquire property by marrying rich heiresses and widows. Unattached white males far outnumbered eligible females, partly because the colonies were regarded as a field of adventure for young bachelors, and partly because male intemperance and sensuality made for a disparate incidence of mortality among the sexes. 'We no sooner hear of a rich Widow than we are told of half a Dozen young Gentlemen that have already made or intend to offer their Addresses to her', wrote another correspondent to *The Barbadoes Gazette*.[32]

Legal business was apparently big business in the colonies. An anonymous Jamaican who railed against the high cost of debt collection estimated in 1752 that as much as £57,000 sterling was annually expended in that island for attorneys' fees and other charges.[33] Planters were notorious for their litigious spirit. Barristers and attorneys who came out from England were often appalled at the loose practices they observed in courts presided over by amateur jurists. Attorneys ranged all the way from men who had served an arduous apprenticeship at the Inns of Court to petty bill collectors who received powers of attorney from creditors in England. In a special category were the attorneys who managed the estates of absentees and minors.[34]

The legal profession was probably upgraded during the 18th century. Qualified attorneys came out from England, as did John Baker, who was Solicitor General of the Leeward Islands and a practising barrister in St Kitts, and Robert Richards, Attorney General of Jamaica. Baker's second wife was a West Indian, while Richards married two rich widows in succession, who left him all their possessions amounting to £9,000 a year.[35] Besides the newcomers, not a few Creoles studied at the Inns of Court and were admitted to the bar before they returned home to practise law. During the century from 1675 to 1775, thirty-seven West Indians were admitted to Gray's Inn, all but ten of whom entered after 1740. Of this group, twenty-one came from Antigua, eight from Jamaica, four from Barbados, and two each from St Kitts and Grenada.[36]

32 Ibid., vol. 2, p. 5.
33 Anon., *An Inquiry Concerning the Trade, Commerce, and Policy of Jamaica* (Jamaica, 1757), pp. 27–9.
34 Richard Pares, *A West-India Fortune* (London, 1950), pp. 27–8.
35 *The Diary of John Baker, Barrister of the Middle Temple, Solicitor-General of the Leeward Islands*, ed. Philip C. Yorke (London, 1931), pp. 9–12.
36 Joseph Foster, 'Admissions to Gray's Inn, 1521–1889', in Vere L. Oliver (ed.), *Caribbeana*, vol. 3 (London, 1914), pp. 291–4.

Sugar and Slavery

William Hickey came out to Jamaica in 1775 with the intention of studying law with two eminent attorneys. He found that every attorney's office was overcrowded with articled clerks, and that 'for the benefit of the profession in general' few newcomers were admitted to practise in the courts.[37]

Doctors found a wide field of service and opportunities for personal gain in the sugar colonies. Europeans who encountered strange diseases in the tropics probably expended a larger proportion of their income for medical services than their counterparts at home. This was one source of income for doctors. But as the white population tended to become small in relation to that of the blacks, and the latter represented a large and wasting asset which it was expedient to make some effort to preserve, the medical profession probably came to derive the greater part of its income from the treatment of sick and injured Negroes.

It is difficult to say how many doctors practised in the West Indies and to ascertain their income. In his *History of Antigua,* Dr Oliver lists a total of fifty-three practitioners of physic in that island from 1731 to 1775, of whom twenty-two were active in 1731. One of these doctors was Walter Tullideph, who charged 3s 9d sterling annually for each slave he treated, besides his charges for emergency calls.[38] If we assume that the whites incurred medical charges to double the amount of the slaves, and then apply these rates to the approximately 4,500 whites and 24,000 blacks, we get an annual medical bill of £6,188. The average gross income of the twenty-two doctors in 1731 thus amounts to about £280 sterling. By comparison, twenty-eight deceased doctors in Jamaica had their personal property inventoried in the five-year period 1771–5. These inventories total £46,760 sterling, the average being £1,670.[39]

Scottish doctors far outnumbered those of English origin after the early years of the 18th century. Two-thirds of the doctors in Antigua, that is thirty-five out of fifty-three, were Scotsmen, and it is likely that about the same ratio obtained in the other islands. Probably the greater number were educated at the great medical school at Edinburgh, although others served apprenticeships with chirurgeons as did Dr Tullideph and his cousin Dr Walter Sydserfe.

James Stephen, the barrister and anti-slavery leader, wrote of his own family's medical experiences. Uncle William Stephen had settled in St Kitts where he was very successful in his profession. One of the

37 *Memoirs of William Hickey,* ed. Alfred Spencer (London, 1948), vol. 2, p. 25.
38 Vere L. Oliver, *The History of the Island of Antigua* (London, 1894–99), vol. 1, pp. xcviii–cxxi; *Walter Tullideph's Medical Ledger,* 1733–40.
39 J.P.R.O. Spanish Town, *Inventorys,* vols. 51–56.

ways he made considerable gains was by 'purchasing what are called "refuse negroes" at the Guinea Yard Sales in the Island he lived in, and curing them and then reselling them in their healthy state at prices greatly advanced'.[40] Being a bachelor and wanting a successor, Uncle William sent his nephew to Aberdeen and recommended him to the special care of two of his friends who were eminent physicians and surgeons there. The young man qualified himself for practice in the West Indies, 'where, as in the North of Scotland, Physic, Surgery, Pharmacy, and all the other branches of the healing art are united in the same practitioner...'. Afterwards he went to Edinburgh and took his degree at its University.[41]

Lawyers and doctors were joined by government officials in gaining wealth. Colonial public finance was so arranged that the revenues collected from customs, poll taxes, quit rents, and other taxes were quite inadequate to meet the cost of government, yet the colonies more than paid their way except possibly in wartime. The explanation of this apparent paradox lies largely in the nature of the patentee system which dates from the Commonwealth period. Important offices in the West Indies were granted by letters patent to men who had obligations or duties in England, who had no intention of leaving England, and who performed their colonial duties by deputy. Supported by fees, the offices were expected to earn sums sufficient to support both the deputies who were the functionaries in the colonies and the patentees who were generally absentees. Offices granted by letters patent included the secretary who was in charge of all public records, the provost marshal who was the chief constable, the naval officer who enforced the Navigation Acts, and in Jamaica the lucrative post of Receiver General. Governors who were expected to perform their duties in person received salaries from the Crown which were generally supplemented by grants from colonial assemblies.[42]

Substantial incomes were derived from the West Indies by governors, patentees, and their deputies. Henry Worsley, Governor of Barbados from 1722 to 1731, reputedly made £10,000 a year, of which £2,000 was paid by the Crown, £6,000 by Barbados, and £2,000 from fees in the island.[43] Rents paid by deputies to patentees who held offices in the Leeward Islands amounted annually to about £600 for the office of provost marshal, from £800

---

40 *The Memoirs of James Stephen*, ed. Merle M. Bevington (London, 1954), pp. 41–2.
41 Ibid., pp. 171–3.
42 J. H. Parry, 'The Patent Offices in the British West Indies', *The English Historical Review*, vol. LXIX, no. 271 (April 1954), pp. 200–25.
43 P.R.O. London. C.O. 28/39, ff. 59–60: Memorandum of income of Gov. Worsley, 1722.

Sugar and Slavery

to £1,000 for the secretaryship, and £500 for the naval office.⁴⁴ Bryan Edwards said that, exclusive of certain classes of fees which were not easily ascertained, the Governor of Jamaica received £6,100 sterling annually, and that he could live very honourably for £3,000. On the whole, he computed that not less than £30,000 sterling was remitted annually by the Jamaican deputies to their principals in the mother country.⁴⁵

Not a few governors and deputies invested part of their income in sugar properties. Prominent among them were the deputy provost marshals and their subordinates. Jamaican under-deputies were said to have seized and set up for sale the Negroes and other effects of debtors, pocketing the difference between the forced sale and subsequent resale values of the property. In this way 'an under-officer may acquire in eight years or less, 200 negroes, a sugar-work, a valuable polink, and other possessions, to the value of thirty-thousand pounds', besides £500 per annum clear from the visible profits of his office.⁴⁶

6 THE MERCHANTS

The term merchant will be defined broadly in this chapter to include individuals who traded on their own account, factors who did business on consignment, shopkeepers who bought and sold general merchandise or specialized in one line, and men who lent money and discounted bills of exchange. Merchants often combined two or more of these activities, and many of them were planters and shipowners as well.

Ascertaining the number of resident merchants in the different islands is no easy matter. The number of white inhabitants and houses in the leading ports and interior towns provides a crude measure of mercantile activity. St Johns, Antigua, according to the census of 1753, had 1,668 whites (594 men, 622 women, 222 boys, and 230 girls).⁴⁷ Before the great fire of 1766, Bridgetown, Barbados, consisted of about 1,500 houses and stores which were mostly built of brick or stone. Kingston, Jamaica, in 1774 had 1,665 houses, while three Jamaican outports taken together had 1,000. Spanish Town, the capital, which is sited some seven miles from the

---

44 *Martin L. B.*, vol. 1, f. 130: Lre. to Samuel Martin, Jr. 10 Jan. 1755.
45 Bryan Edwards, *The History, Civil and Commercial, of the British Colonies in the West Indies* (Dublin, 1793), vol. 1, pp. 209–11.
46 Anon., *Inquiry Concerning the Trade of Jamaica*, pp. 29–30.
47 Oliver, *History of Antigua*, vol. 1, pp. cix–cx.

south coast, had 450 houses and was said to be 'the resort of all the chief merchants who have acquired estates sufficient to enable them to live a pleasurable life'.[48]

Substantial merchants left more traces in extant records than their lesser brethren. Montserrat levied a poll tax on its trading community in 1720 to pay the public debt of the island. The tax was paid by fifty-two men and three women on a total of seventy-three houses which were assessed at from £1 to £50. Roughly one-sixth of the men on the island were engaged in trade, of whom the greater number were small operators.[49] In the neighbouring island of Antigua, twenty-seven local merchants signed a petition in 1711. Two years later a petition was signed by forty-one merchants in Jamaica. The big business in slaves was conducted by twenty-seven local firms and thirty individuals in Barbados in the years from 1730 to 1737.[50]

Merchants were second only to the planters in numbers and wealth in the West Indies. One measure of mercantile wealth is afforded by the personal property inventories in the Jamaica Public Record Office. In the 1741–5 period, the inventories of resident merchants numbered 78 and amounted to £248,372 sterling, which was 10.4 and 23.1 per cent, respectively, of all inventories. In the 1771–5 period, merchants' inventories numbered 108 and amounted to £507,293 sterling, which was 12.1 and 21.3 per cent, respectively, of all inventories. The growth of the London commission system may help to explain the slight decline in the value percentage. In the latter period, roughly two-fifths of the mercantile property belonged to residents of English and Welsh extraction, another two-fifths to those of Scottish (together with Scots-Irish and Irish) extraction, and one-fifth to the Sephardic Jews.[51]

Resident factors were strategically placed to transform mercantile wealth into plantation wealth. Before the commission system became highly developed, the factor stood between the local planter and the overseas merchant. Ostensibly, he drew only his rightfully-claimed commissions from the stream of inward and outward trade and finance, but in reality he used the idle balances belonging to his principal to strike out on trade on his own account. He was motivated to become an independent trader as a stepping stone to

---

48 Edwards, *History of West Indies*, vol. 1, p. 341; Long, *History of Jamaica*, vol. 1, p. 532; Anon., *The Modern Part of an Universal History* (London, 1764), vol. 41, pp. 464–5.
49 P.R.O. London. C.O. 152/13, Q 34, ff. 103–4.
50 Oliver, *History of Antigua*, vol. 1, p. lxxxiii; P.R.O. London. C.O. 137/9, f. 79; Elizabeth Donnan (ed.), *Documents Illustrative of the History of the Slave Trade to America* (New York, 1965), vol. 2, pp. 427–31.
51 J.P.R.O. Spanish Town. *Inventorys*, vols. 21–25, 51–56.

plantership by several considerations. Obviously, an able man might gain wealth more rapidly as an independent merchant than as an agent of other merchants. But the planter-dominated governments took a dim view of resident merchants and factors who were subjected to political, social, and economic constraints. Merchants-on-the-make might overcome these disabilities to a great extent by acquiring landed estates which conferred freehold status, or, in other words, the right to vote and seek membership in the elected assembly or the appointed council. A further incentive to acquire a sugar plantation was to have an income-earning property to support its owner if and when he retired to the mother country.

Historians of the West Indies have given undue importance to the Royalists of aristocratic lineage who fled to the West Indies and established planter families of wealth and influence. The trouble with this version of planter origins is that few Royalists came to the colonies with money, and even when they confiscated the estates of Roundheads, they needed working capital to make their plantations pay. Although no impartial witness, Nicholas Foster, the Barbadian Roundhead, probably gave a true version of Royalist origins when he wrote that

> these are a Generation of people called Agents or Factors for their Masters (the *London* Merchants and others) and having out-run the Constables in *England*, and run out their principalls here, resolve to foote it no longer, but now let the *Sugar*-mills stand, and their Masters expect returnes; they will waite on Walrond [the Royalist leader], for he is the man from whom they expect honour and preferment, for by *Banishing* the *Roundheads*, and bidding defiance to the Parliament, they shall procure a Proclamation of Rebellion against them, which will be a notable excuse for their not comming home to give their Masters an account there.[52]

To acquire working capital for their confiscated plantations, these self-styled gentlemen were said to have become factors to the Dutch merchants who dominated the trade of the sugar colonies before 1651.[53]

Compared with the Barbadians, the leading planters of Jamaica seem to have had even fewer claimants to aristocratic lineage. Character sketches of these leaders were recorded by Rev. William May of Jamaica, who wrote about 1720: 'There is not six families who are well descended as gentlemen on the whole Island'.[54]

Probably the greater number of plantations were established by

[52] Nicholas Foster, *A Briefe Relation of the Late Horrid Rebellion Acted in the Island of Barbadas* (London, 1650), pp. 36–7.
[53] John Scott, 'The Description of Barbados', B. M. Sloane MSS 3662, f. 34.
[54] Rev. William May, 'Jamaica: Description of the Principal Persons there', in *Caribbeana*, ed. Vere L. Oliver, vol. 3 (London, 1914), pp. 5–9.

factors and merchants. Factors frequently complained to their principals in England that planters were slow to pay their debts or that ships were not available to carry home the remittances. In the meantime the less scrupulous factors, whose complaints were ingenuous, invested the remittances in lands, slaves, and sugar works. Governor Stapleton wrote to the Lords of Trade in 1682: 'Many considerable adventurers from London and elsewhere have sent their factors there [Antigua], and converted their employers' goods into acquisitions of plantations and slaves, by which means ships went home empty'.[55]

Numerous merchants and planters, among whom were Henry Lascelles and the elder Christopher Codrington, owned sloops and engaged in clandestine trade which reputedly made them wealthy. Christopher Jeaffreson, who inherited a run-down property in St Kitts, did a mercantile business on the side which enabled him to rebuild his plantation. He noted with satisfaction that the goods he had ordered out of London had yielded a good profit which had been 'flung like seede into my plantation . . .'.[56]

It may be concluded that the planting fraternity was recruited from a number of ethnic and occupational groups. Besides the English and Scottish planters, there were merchant-planters, lawyer-planters, doctor-planters, and provost marshal-planters. After ascending the plantation ladder, no man could survive in the trader-dominated environment unless he was a planter-merchant. The writer's study of the Antigua gentry in the period from 1730 to 1775 shows that the 65 families who dominated the island had among them 29 local merchants, 27 government officials, 18 doctors and 14 lawyers.[57] Lord Brougham was no doubt right in the broad essentials when he asserted: 'The trade of planting, though connected with the soil, is yet . . . much more nearly allied to commerce than to agriculture, and promoted by the spirit of mercantile adventure'.[58]

7 THE ART OF PLANTERSHIP

From the previous discussion, it may be enquired how men who were chiefly merchants, professionals, and administrators learned and

---

55 *Cal. S. P. Col. 1681–85*, p. 276.
56 John C. Jeaffreson, *A Young Squire of the Seventeenth Century* (London, 1878), vol. 1, p. 230.
57 R. B. Sheridan, 'The Rise of a Colonial Gentry: A Case Study of Antigua, 1730–1775', *The Economic History Review*, 2nd ser., vol. XIII, no. 3 (April 1961), pp. 342–57.
58 Henry Brougham, *An Inquiry into the Colonial Policy of the European Powers* (Edinburgh, 1803), vol. 2, pp. 159–60.

influenced the art of planting. At the outset of the sugar revolution these men were on a par with other colonists, for the plantation crops were outside the Old World experience of the European settler. All had to acquire knowledge of the arts of planting, cultivating, harvesting, and processing from outsiders; that is, from Arawak Indians, Sephardic Jews, and Dutchmen. Compared with other settlers from the British Isles, the merchants had access to capital and superior knowledge of trade and finance. Once they had learned the rudiments of planting, they were in a position to forge ahead of their less affluent and less knowledgeable fellow-countrymen. Gaining knowledge of plantership was also less difficult in the 17th century, since productive units were relatively small, under-capitalized, and self-sufficient. Then, too, it was possible to enter into 'mateship' agreements, whereby the merchant-partner put up the capital and conducted the external business of the plantation, while his planter-partner superintended the agricultural and processing operations.

Plantation management became more complex and demanding as the near-monoculture stage of production was approached. Viable plantation units required larger acreages, more slaves, and heavier and more complex machinery. Diminished yields called for better tillage and drainage and the application of fertilizer to cane fields. Crude sugar-making processes were replaced by techniques for making the semi-refined product, while the molasses by-product was distilled into high-proof rum. Since no individual could superintend all of these activities and at the same time attend to the external business of the plantation, it became necessary to develop a managerial hierarchy, each level of which attained some degree of specialization. Given an able manager or overseer to superintend the work of the under-managers, artisans, and field hands, it was possible for the proprietor to combine planting with trade and even professional or administrative careers. The proprietor might then reside in the port or capital town of the island where he pursued his career. Frequent visits to his estate would enable him to oversee the larger aspects of plantation life.

That the art of plantership improved during the near-monoculture era is evident from the career of Samuel Martin.[59] Martin was a close student of Jethro Tull's *Horse-hoeing Husbandry* and the works of other English agricultural improvers. By a process of trial and error he developed a rudimentary system of agronomy for the sugar colonies. On his 'Greencastle' estate Martin experimented with a

59 R. B. Sheridan, 'Samuel Martin, Innovating Sugar Planter of Antigua 1750–1776', *Agricultural History*, vol. 34, no. 3 (July 1960), pp. 126–39.

variety of fertilizers and adapted them to different soil types; he improved his lowland fields by better drainage; he spaced his cane rows to take advantage of variations in moisture and soil types. Martin gave particular attention to the dieting, medical care, housing, and supervision of his Negro slaves; management of his cattle; adoption of new implements of husbandry; and quality of his sugar and rum. He likened a plantation to a 'well-constructed machine, compounded of various wheels, turning different ways, and yet all contributing to the great end proposed; but if any one part runs too fast or too slow in proportion to the rest, the main purpose is defeated'.[60] Martin cautioned against waste and extravagance, observing that 'as a sugar plantation is the most expensive kind of estate, so the clear profit of it will be more or less in proportion to the manager's frugality'.[61]

So successful were most of his experiments that Martin's reputation spread to other parts of Antigua. In 1758, he wrote that his common rules of plantership had been generally established in that island by his example and advice.[62]

Planters in neighbouring islands learned of Martin's achievement, especially after he published *An Essay Upon Plantership* about 1754. The third edition, 'much enlarged with new experiments', was published in Antigua in 1756. Four additional editions and several reprints supply ample evidence that the *Essay* was widely read.[63] Dr James Grainger, a resident of St Kitts, wrote in the preface of 'The Sugar-Cane, a Didactic Poem', that Martin's *Essay* was 'an excellent performance, and to it I owe myself indebted'.[64] In the Leeward Islands, and particularly Montserrat, according to John Campbell, the art of planting had been reduced by 1774 'to a regular system, and almost all the Defects of Soil so thoroughly removed by proper Management and Manure, that except from the Failure of Seasons, or the Want of Hands, there is seldom any Fear of a Crop'.[65] Although Campbell may have exaggerated, plantation improvements in the Leeward Islands were in all probability substantial.

Besides his *Essay*, Martin influenced the quality of plantership by means of his apprentices. Dedicated to 'All the Planters of the British Sugar-Colonies', the *Essay* was first written for the instruction of a

---

60 Martin, *Essay Upon Plantership*, pp. 57–8.
61 Ibid., pp. 3–4.
62 *Martin L. B.*, vol. 1, f. 211: Lre. to Samuel Martin, Jr. 16 June 1758.
63 Joseph Sabin, *A Dictionary of Books Relating to America* (New York, 1879), vol. 11, p. 239.
64 Grainger's poem is printed in *Three Tracts on West-Indian Agriculture* (Jamaica, 1802), p. vii.
65 John Campbell, *A Political Survey of Britain* (London, 1774), vol. 2, p. 674.

Sugar and Slavery

young planter. The master of 'Greencastle' provided a haven for young men who came to the West Indies to seek their fortunes. If a lad behaved in an honest, diligent manner, Martin agreed to teach him 'all the arts of plantership & prefer him at the End of his time as is his custom to all good Servts'.[66] Over the years numerous Englishmen and Scotsmen received diplomas from the Martin school of plantership and found a wide field of opportunity for their talents.

The innovations which enabled the planters of Barbados to cope with soil loss and achieve a level of high farming in the tropics have been delineated by Dr Watts. They consisted of the dung farm and intensive use of animal manure, cane hole agriculture as an erosion control feature, and primitive windbreaks. 'These several methods', he writes, 'were undoubtedly initiated through an increasing contemporary awareness of soil loss, and eventually helped in the renaissance of Barbadian agriculture after 1785'.[67]

Edward Long attributed the improvement of Jamaican plantations chiefly to a spirit of experiment which had lately appeared. Formerly Barbados had been regarded as the only nursery for good planters, and managers had been obtained from that island with great eagerness. These men were excellent managers for the dry, worn-out lands on the south side where the seasons were tolerably regular, but they were at a loss in adapting to the diversity of soils and seasons in other parts of Jamaica. Meanwhile, managers and overseers were recruited from other sources. For the most part they were Scottish servants who had passed through a regular course of service in the agriculture of Jamaica. Salaries and working conditions having been upgraded, these men had been encouraged to strike out on continual improvements.[68]

Not a few of the Scottish servants rose to a higher rung of the plantation ladder than that of salaried overseer or manager. John Luffman wrote from Antigua in 1787:

> The negroes are turned out at sunrise, and employed in gangs from twenty to sixty, or upwards, under the inspection of white overseers, generally poor Scotch lads, who, by their assiduity and industry, frequently become masters of the plantations, to which they came out as indentured servants.[69]

Scottish servants who had risen to positions as overseers found even

---

66 *Martin L. B.*, vol. 4, f. 85: Apprenticeship agreement with Mr MacDowall, 2 June 1766.
67 David Watts, 'Relationships between Estate Agriculture and Soil Loss in Barbados, 1625–1785', unpublished paper based on his Ph.D. Dissertation, McGill University, 1963.
68 Long, *History of Jamaica*, vol. 1, pp. 175, 439.
69 John Luffman, *A Brief Account of the Island of Antigua* (London, 1789), reprinted in Oliver, *History of Antigua*, vol. 1, p. 99.

Planters and Plantership

greater opportunities in the more open society of Jamaica. If they were sensible and thrifty, the overseers of Jamaica enjoyed comfortable lives and saved enough of their salaries to buy settlements of their own; 'some of them have even become possessors, in time, of very large properties, and made a very respectable figure here'.[70]

8 PROFIT AND LOSS

Ascertaining the profitability of the sugar industry is no easy matter, since it involves questions of method and the availability and reliability of quantitative data. Even if it were possible to resolve these matters, certain non-quantifiable costs and benefits would remain to complicate any effort to assess the level of profit. Four possible methods, together with combinations of these methods, merit consideration. First, one may try to construct an 'average' plantation based on the records of a number of plantations. Second, one may attempt to estimate the capital stock of an island or group of islands, and then calculate the rate of profit by dividing this figure into the global net income of the island or islands. Third, one may operate with the economic rather than the accounting concept of profit, that is, shift the focus of attention from the plantation to the slave considered as an economic investment. Fourth, one may attempt a retrospective judgement of profits from calculations made at a later point in time.

At least three authors made some effort to base their profit estimates on the experience of an average sugar plantation. George Frere, a leading Barbadian, wrote in 1768 that the plantations in that island yielded less than formerly because of oppressive taxes, mismanagement, and great and necessary expenses. He estimated that the landed interest throughout the island did not clear 4 per cent annually.[71] The anonymous author, whose calculation of a large Antiguan estate has already been summarized,[72] estimated in 1764 that the 'neat proceeds' of the sugar plantations in Antigua 'scarcely amount to 5 per cent on the value of the principal'. For the four islands of Barbados, Antigua, Nevis, and Montserrat, he estimated that 'the planters do not clear by their estates 6 per cent for their principal'.[73] Edward Long calculated that a plantation valued at

70 Long, *History of Jamaica*, vol. 2, p. 287.
71 George Frere, *A Short History of Barbados* (London, 1768), pp. 105–9.
72 See Chapter 12, p. 269.
73 Anon., *Some Observations... of Our New West-India Colonies* (London, 1764), pp. 21, 50.

Sugar and Slavery

£10,000 sterling, if successfully conducted, yielded a net profit of 10 per cent, which 'proves the ability of a planter to bear up under a great debt for a considerable time . . .'.[74]

These estimates need to be corrected if they are to be meaningful in terms of modern accounting theory. While there is no way to calculate the non-monetary income which planters and their families received in the form of foodstuffs and domestic services that were supplied by their slaves, there is reason to question the 6 per cent interest charged on the Antiguan investment in slaves, land, and equipment which was regarded as an operating expense to be deducted from the gross profit. Unless the slaves and other capital items were purchased on credit and the interest paid to someone else, the interest was actually a profit on investment and the profit calculation was understated by about one percentage point. Another conceptual difficulty is that slaves were part of the capital equipment of plantations and slave maintenance and amortization costs were deducted from gross income to arrive at net income. This means that the rate of profit in a slave economy was understated by comparison with a free-labour economy where employers do not capitalize their labour force.

Estimates of the annual income and profit accruing to the British Empire from the ownership of Jamaica are contained in the works of Edward Long and Bryan Edwards. Long's 'Annual Profit of the Jamaica Trade to Great Britain' for the year 1773 has been compared with other sources and corrected where necessary by the writer. Similarly, the annual average 'neat proceeds' of the 775 sugar plantations for the years 1772–5, as shown in the Report of the Jamaica House of Assembly which is printed in Edwards' *History*, has been corrected and combined with Long's adjusted estimates in Table 16.1. Net profits of £1.55 million on a capital stock – including slaves – of about £18 million[75] gives an earning rate of 8.6 per cent, or a somewhat smaller return if allowance is made for the capital of merchants and manufacturers in the mother country. Even if such an allowance is made, the return was probably well above the 4.5 per cent earned on real estate mortgages in England during this period, and much higher than the 3.5 per cent return on Consols, or government bonds.

If we shift the focus of attention from the plantation and the colony to the slave considered as an economic investment, the evidence suggests that slaveholders on the whole gained a moderate rate of profit. In a previous chapter we have seen that the rate of

74 Long, *History of Jamaica*, vol. 1, p. 461.
75 See Chapter 10, pp. 229–31.

Table 16.1

Estimates of annual income and profit accruing to the Empire from the ownership of the Colony of Jamaica, 1773 (sterling values)

Profits on trade		
Freight earnings	£272,000	
Commission and brokerage	260,000	
Profit on manufactures	116,650	
Slave trade	51,670	
Interest on loans	50,000	
Insurance	51,170	
Remittances to other areas	59,565	
Specie remittances	40,000	£901,055
Profits on residentiary industries		
Urban rents, foodstuffs, etc.		111,300
Profits on production for export		
Retained profits	334,700	
Remittances to Great Britain	200,000	534,700
Total profit from Jamaica		**£1,547,055**

Source: Edward Long, *History of Jamaica* (1774), vol. 1, p. 507; Bryan Edwards, *History of the British West Indies* (1793), vol. 2, pp. 463–7. Critical evaluations of the profit estimates of Edward Long may be found in my 'The Wealth of Jamaica in the Eighteenth Century', *Econ. Hist. Rev.*, 2nd ser., vol. XVIII, no. 2 (August 1965); R. P. Thomas, 'The Sugar Colonies of the Old Empire: Profit or Loss for Great Britain?' and my 'Rejoinder' to Thomas's article in *Econ. Hist. Rev.*, 2nd ser., vol. XXI, no. 1 (April 1968), pp. 30–45 and 46–61.

return on slaves in Jamaica ranged from 6 per cent to 11 per cent, depending on their working life expectancy, and that the median return was probably from 7 to 9 per cent.[76]

Retrospective judgements of profits fall into two categories. First, one may take data from slave-plantations for a period later than the one comprised in this study, and speculate about the changes in costs and returns during the intervening period. Second, one may work backward from modern studies of the sugar industry, making similar speculations about trend lines. In the first category is a computation for Jamaica in 1832, the year before slave emancipation when the

76 See Chapter 11, p. 260.

sugar industry was reputedly in a state of crisis. Yet the total domestic plantation output of that year amounted to £2.16 million, of which the planters' gross profit amounted to £1.21 million.[77] In the second category is a modern study of the Leeward and Windward Islands which says that the price of sugar in the period 1770–1840 was near to the present Commonwealth guaranteed price. Since the pound was considerably higher in value and costs of production lower in the early period, it is maintained that in good years the profits of the sugar industry were considerable.[78]

Contemporary opinion differed as to whether long-established families or newcomers were best situated to reap the profits of the sugar industry. Bryan Edwards was of the opinion that the West Indians were not remarkable, with very few exceptions, either for their gigantic opulence or an ostentatious display of it. Fortunes, instead of being the creation of a day, were the fruits of the toil of successive generations. On the other hand, Edmund Burke maintained that there were no parts of the world in which great estates were made in so short a time as in the West Indies.[79]

Actually, evidence may be presented in support of both of these views. In the writer's study of the Antigua gentry, one-half of the families who were active in the period from 1730 to 1775 came to the island before 1680. Newcomers were added in subsequent decades, with the Scots being most prominent after 1707. But families of long standing in the colony frequently intermarried with those who arrived late. When, for example, the daughter of a saturated planter married a young merchant, a planter-merchant bond of mutual benefit might be established.[80]

Compared with Barbados and the Leeward Islands, the ratio of newcomers to Creoles in the colonial gentry was obviously higher in Jamaica and the Ceded Islands. One Jamaican warned against tempting newcomers with exaggerated prospects of immoderate gain. He stressed the need for careful management, pointing out that sugar properties yielded a very comfortable maintenance to the proprietor who acted with 'constant circumspection and economy, and agreeable to the uneering counsel, which his annual state of accounts will present to his view'.[81]

77 Gisela Eisner, *Jamaica, 1830–1930: A Study in Economic Growth* (Manchester, 1961), p. 37.
78 Carleen O'Loughlin, *Economic and Political Change in the Leeward and Windward Islands* (New Haven and London, 1968), p. 125.
79 Edwards, *History of the West Indies*, vol. 2, p. 456; William and Edmund Burke, *An Account of the European Settlements in America* (London, 1777), vol. 2, p. 104.
80 Sheridan, 'Rise of a Colonial Gentry', pp. 342–57.
81 *The Monthly Review or Literary Journal*, vol. IV, art. VII (1776), reprinted in *American Husbandry*, ed. Harry J. Carman (New York, 1939), pp. xvi–xxx.

9 ABSENTEEISM

The ultimate objective of most planters was to retire to Great Britain, leaving behind a well-settled estate which yielded income to amply support the absentee, his family and servants, together with defraying additional costs of management. Dr Tullideph expressed these aspirations in a letter of 29 October 1746, when he informed his brother in Scotland that he had purchased a second plantation:

> You will probably think me unwise in laying out so much money here but it is the surest foundation to lay up money afterwards pretty fast in England, as it brings us in at least ten or 12 pr Ct for our money; when this other Estate is well settled, I can afford a handsome Sallary to a good Manager to take care of both, which may remitt me annually from 1500 to 2000 *l.* Sterlg. These Crops in a few years will enable me to purchase in Great Brittain, where the Center of my wishes is really fixed.[82]

Though many planters aspired to an English gentry plane of living in the colonies, there is much truth in Lord Brougham's assertion that the objective of emigrants to the West Indies 'is not to live, but to gain – not to enjoy, but to save – not to subsist in the colonies, but to prepare for shining in the mother country'.[83] Shining in the mother country thus meant the remittance of income from the plantations and business and professional establishments in the colonies.

Though it dated from the foundation of the sugar colonies, absentee proprietorship became a movement of consequence during the 18th century. Already in 1740, absenteeism was of sufficient scope to induce the legislators of Jamaica to pass a law requiring the agents and attornies of absentees and minors to submit annual reports of staple crops and their disposition to the local government. The 'Account Produce' volume for 1775 shows that 234 of the 775 sugar plantations were the property of absentees and minors. These properties, which belonged to 180 individuals, produced about 40 per cent of the island's sugar and rum.[84] That many more absentees drew income from Jamaica is evident from Long's estimate of 2,000 annuitants and proprietors who were non-residents.[85] Similar reports of growing absenteeism are extant for the British colonies in the Lesser Antilles.[86]

---

82 *Tullideph L. B.*, vol. 2: Lre. to Thomas Tullideph, Principal of St Andrews University, 29 Oct. 1746.
83 Brougham, *Colonial Policy of European Powers*, vol. 1, p. 48.
84 *The Laws of Jamaica*, printed by Alexander Aikman (Jamaica, 1792), vol. 1, pp. 278–9; J.P.R.O. Spanish Town, *Account Produce*, vols. 6–8.
85 Long, *History of Jamaica*, vol. 1, pp. 377–8.
86 Pitman, *Development of British West Indies*, pp. 11–13, 30–52, 104, 115.

Sugar and Slavery

Modern historians of the West Indies have emphasized the baneful effects of absentee proprietorship. It is contended that absenteeism contributed to the growing disproportion between the whites and blacks; it tended to promote a careless, cruel, and extravagant management of plantations; it established conditions that led to slave insurrections; it drained away wealth and income that might otherwise have gone into public and private improvements. Moreover, by depriving the colonies of men of talent, property, and experience, absenteeism reputedly contributed to the impoverishment of political and social life, at the same time that there grew up a West Indian aristocracy of wealth and political power which had a corrupting influence on the mother country.

Absenteeism varied in extent and nature, however, and broad generalizations about its consequences are likely to be indefensible. As Professor Hall points out, the absentees were a heterogeneous lot:

> some were West Indian born, others had made their first appearance elsewhere; some had lived on their estates, others had never done so; some were completely ignorant of the details of sugar-making and the sugar trade, whereas others had practical experience of both; some were genteel, others were not.[87]

In the light of their diverse character, it cannot be argued that absentees were necessarily superior to local inhabitants in matters of government and social leadership, or in managerial ability. Hall contends that 'the colonial elites were deprived of significant membership as much by internal social and demographic factors as by absenteeism'. Moreover, it cannot be contended that absentees were altogether parasitical, since numbers of them invested colonial wealth in West India trading houses, shipping, insurance, and industrial concerns, or represented the interests of the colonies in the mother Parliament. Finally, Hall asserts: 'It is probably true that with or without absentee-ownership, wealth would have been drained from the colonies to Britain. The expectation of such a drain was one of the motives for the acquisition of "tropical plantations".'[88]

As the saturated planters returned to the mother country to enjoy their slave-produced wealth, planters-on-the-make found their opportunities enhanced. From the ranks of trade, public administration, the professions, and plantation management came individuals to seek their fortunes in the sugar industry. Most influential were the attorneys who superintended non-residents' estates. Among other things, these men appointed the overseers or managers, acted as

87 Douglas Hall, 'Absentee-Proprietorship in the British West Indies, To About 1850', *The Jamaican Historical Review*, vol. IV, (1964), p. 19.
88 Ibid., pp. 15–35.

Planters and Plantership

purchasing agents, arranged for shipping the plantation produce, and kept the estate books. Besides their salaries, or, more commonly, their commission of 6 per cent of the annual produce, the attorneys enjoyed numerous perquisites. They were privileged to occupy the great house, enjoy the services of domestic slaves, live off the plantation produce, and pasture their livestock on the property entrusted to their care. Scotsmen, particularly those engaged in trade, made up the greater number of attorneys who were also, at times, physicians, lawyers, and even clergymen. As a class, the attorneys were charged with getting rich at the expense of their employers. No doubt some did so, but the Account Produce Law of Jamaica is indicative of efforts to impose institutional restraints on peculation and fraud.[89] William Beckford, the planter-historian and bankrupt, wrote many harsh things about the attorneys of Jamaica. Nonetheless, he said that he had seen and been personally acquainted with some attorneys who were an honour to their profession.[90]

10 CONCLUSION

The foregoing discussion of planters and plantership compares the views expressed by modern historians of the British sugar colonies with data drawn from a variety of contemporary sources. We have been concerned with the broad questions of the ethnic and socio-economic origins of the planter elite, how this elite changed in composition and character, and how these changes in the social environment interacted with the physical and technological environments to affect the quality of plantation management, or plantership. Evidence has been presented which casts doubt on the widely-accepted views that the planter elite was recruited chiefly from the rural aristocracy of England; that vertical social mobility was largely absent from the colonies; that, with few exceptions, planters were inept businessmen and uninterested in cost-saving innovations; and that, in consequence, the quality of plantership underwent marked deterioration. A more tenable hypothesis is that planters were recruited largely from lower middle ranks of society; that Nonconformist influences were by no means negligible; that one stream of recruits came from the professional, administrative, and especially the mercantile groups in the colonies; while another stream

---

[89] Ragatz, *Fall of the Planter Class*, pp. 54–7; Richard Pares, *Merchants and Planters. Econ. Hist. Rev. Suppl. 4* (Cambridge, 1960), pp. 42–3.
[90] William Beckford, *A Descriptive Account of the Island of Jamaica* (London, 1790), vol. 2, pp. 361–9.

Sugar and Slavery

emerged from subordinate managerial personnel on plantations; that minority ethnic and nationality groups — chiefly the Scotsmen and Sephardic Jews — made notable contributions; and that on economic, if not on humanitarian, grounds the quality of plantation management tended to improve down to the end of our study.

Ironically, some of the forces which contributed to plantation improvement had the effect of undermining the very institution upon which the success of the planter elite depended. Contributing to the improvement of plantations were merchants, professionals, and administrators who were generally superior to the Creoles in education, professional attainment, and experience in the world of affairs. Many of these men were aware of the conflict between the enlightenment values which were spreading among the intelligentsia of Europe and the horrors of the slave society that they experienced in the colonies. We shall see in a later chapter that some of the leading anti-slavery agitators were men who had been active in the colonies as lawyers, doctors, clergymen, and even overseers.

CHAPTER SEVENTEEN

Booms and Slumps in War and Peace, 1623-1713

...but above all I esteem the *African* and *West-India* Trades most profitable to the Nation, as they imploy more people at home, and encourage Navigation abroad, all their Product is our Wealth, and hath been a means to ballance our Losses this War, and yet they might be better improved to our Advantage.[1]

John Cary, 1695

1 INTRODUCTION

The nine decades from 1623 to 1713 witnessed the development of the West Indies into the most valuable colonies in the British Empire. The story begins with pioneer settlers who struggled to gain a foothold in a strange environment, threatened by Carib Indians and rival European nations and their Caribbean colonies. Prior to the Civil Wars large numbers of freeholders and indentured servants came to the islands to grow tobacco, cotton, indigo, and other minor staples. Then came the sugar revolution with its land consolidation, Negro slavery, highly capitalized plantations, and drift toward monoculture. Dutch enterprise was prominent in the revolution which spread from Barbados to the Leeward Islands and Jamaica. Recovery and expansion of the sugar industry involved the Commonwealth government in war against Holland, enactment of the first Navigation Act, and Cromwell's Western Design against the Spanish West Indies. The Restoration government built on foundations established during the Interregnum, adding such innovations as national monopoly companies in the African trade. On both sides of the Atlantic hardly a year passed without war or rumours of war. Yet in a century of recurring European crises, it is noteworthy that the West Indies contributed markedly to the solution of England's social, political, and economic difficulties. Partly in a fit of absence of mind, and

---

1 John Cary, *An Essay on the State of England in Relation to its Trade* (Bristol, 1695), p. 131.

Sugar and Slavery

partly by design, there developed a plantation-based trading area which came to play a major role in England's rise to commercial, financial, and industrial leadership. Dominating the first chapter of the story is the transformation wrought by the Caribbean sugar revolution in an age of international rivalry, war, and economic crisis.

2 FLUCTUATIONS IN THE SUGAR INDUSTRY

The study of fluctuations in the sugar industry should begin with the setting within which movements in output, costs, prices, and other relevant variables took place. The setting was relatively stable from the outset of the sugar revolution to the American Revolution with respect to the nature of the production units, labour force, technology, political regulation, and geographical base. First, sugar estates were owned chiefly by resident proprietors who combined the functions of ownership and management and sought to maximize profits. Absentee proprietorship came in time to separate ownership and management to a considerable extent. Second, the producing unit was the slave-plantation, a highly capitalized, large-scale establishment which combined agriculture with the processing of cane sugar, molasses, and rum. Third, the labourers who cultivated and processed the canes were African slaves who were more or less supplemented by white indentured servants. Fourth, the British sugar industry was regulated by the Navigation Acts in accordance with the mercantilist doctrines of the period.

The sugar industry lends itself to a unified study in other respects. Production was confined chiefly to six Caribbean islands – Barbados, Jamaica, Antigua, St Kitts, Nevis, and Montserrat. These islands, though changing in relative importance, produced over 90 per cent of the sugar products which entered the metropolis through legal channels during the greater part of the century prior to the Seven Years' War. Apart from the acquisition of the French part of St Kitts in 1713, little change occurred in the potential area of supply until the acquisition of the four Ceded Islands in 1763. Moreover, the study is given unity by the fact that few changes occurred in the technology and methods of cultivation, processing, and transportation. Human and animal power were supplemented by wind and water power, and the equipment for sugar making and rum distilling underwent little alteration.

Fluctuations may be broadly distinguished on the basis of duration and amplitude. Some were of short duration owing to such

Booms and Slumps in War and Peace, 1623–1713

factors as weather, pestilence, war, and fiscal measures. Others of longer duration were influenced by population movements, consumer tastes, income trends, capital movements, and changing factor costs. Both types of fluctuations shed light on the performance of the sugar industry.

Probably the best indices of significant trends are the statistics of English sugar imports, re-exports, and prices from 1623 to 1775. Though a continuous series of imports and re-exports is not extant before 1698, sufficient data exists to establish the direction of movement. Three main sources yield wholesale price data for the London market — the Invoice Books of the Royal African Company from 1674 to 1727, the Custom House sales of the King's sugar taken in payment of the 4½ per cent duty for the period 1728–58, and the prices recorded in Bryan Edwards' *History of the West Indies* for the period 1760–75.[2]

Though annual average prices of the most commonly traded grade of sugar are used in this study, attention should be directed to the wide variety of sugar products and their seasonal price movements. London sugar prices fluctuated greatly from season to season, being lowest during the late spring and summer months when fleets arrived from the West Indies, and highest during the late winter and early spring months before the new sugar came to market. Numerous grades of sugar, based on differences in texture and colour, made for a price structure of considerable complexity. 'Nothing can be more fluctuating than the Market for Sugar', wrote George Maxwell of the firm of Lascelles and Maxwell in September 1745:

> The continuance of an easterly wind for a few weeks shall raise it, and a westerly wind with a bare expectation of Ships shall lower it again.... The least shade of Whiteness by which one Cask of Sugar exceeds another makes a difference in value, and yet would not be perceived otherwise than by Comparison of the Samples shewn together on one board; and the more Shades or degrees that appear between the Samples of some and others make still the greater difference between them in Value.[3]

Price differentials were quite common, even for the same grade of sugar. Muscovado sugar from St Kitts and Jamaica generally sold in the London market from three to six shillings per cwt above the same grade from Barbados.[4]

---

2 K. G. Davies, *The Royal African Company* (London, 1957), pp. 365–6; Public Record Office, London. Treasury 276B (383); Bryan Edwards, *The History, Civil and Commercial, of the British Colonies in the West Indies* (Dublin, 1793), vol. 2, pp. 255–6.

3 *Lascelles and Maxwell L. B.*, f. 296: Lre. to Samuel Husbands in Barbados, 24 Sept. 1745.

4 Anon., *Thoughts on the Discontents of the People Last Year Respecting the Sugar Duties* (London, 1781), Appendix, pp. 12, 17, 20.

A reliable long-run trend calls for a continuous series of average-annual prices. Moreover, conditions need to be uniform with respect to the source of supply, place of sale, grade of sugar, and conditions of sale. These requirements are satisfied quite adequately for the London sugar prices shown in Appendix V. For the most part these prices apply to the low grade muscovado sugar from Barbados and the Leeward Islands sold by auction in the London market on short-term credit. These conditions, with slight variation, apply to the sugars sold by the Royal African Company and the King's agents at the Custom House, although somewhat less so to the data compiled by Bryan Edwards.

Appendix V reveals five trend movements in the period 1650–1775: first, a period of generally declining sugar prices from 1650 to 1688; second, the period dominated by war from 1689 to 1713, when prices fluctuated violently but were consistently higher than those of the previous period; third, another period of generally declining prices from 1714 to 1733; fourth, a period of fluctuating but generally rising prices from 1734 to 1758; and fifth, a period of slightly declining prices from 1759 to 1775.

Sugar prices declined in relation to consumer goods prices from 1650 to 1685, a condition which favoured greater per capita consumption. In the war period, 1689–1713, the sugar series moved upwards more steeply, was consistently higher, and fluctuated more violently. From the Treaty of Utrecht (1713) to 1733 the sugar index again declined more sharply than that of consumer goods, after which the consumer index remained fairly level to 1756, while sugar experienced a remarkable, though uneven, rise to 1758. The final period, 1759–75, was one of slightly declining sugar prices while consumer prices rose substantially.[5]

John Stuart Mill regarded the British West Indies, not as trading and exporting countries carrying on an exchange of commodities with other countries, or having a productive capital of their own, but as outlying agricultural establishments belonging to the larger community.

> The West Indies is the place where England finds it convenient to carry on the production of sugar, coffee, and a few other tropical commodities. All the capital employed is English capital; almost all the industry is carried on for English uses; there is little production of anything except the staple commodities and these are sent to England, not to be exchanged for things

---

5 On average, the king's sugar sold for three shillings per cwt less than the planters' sugar. For consumer goods prices see Elizabeth B. Schumpeter, 'English Prices and Public Finance, 1660–1822', *The Review of Economic Statistics*, vol. XX, no. 1 (Feb. 1938), p. 35.

Booms and Slumps in War and Peace, 1623–1713

exported to the colony and consumed by its inhabitants, but to be sold in England for the benefit of the proprietors there. The trade with the West Indies is therefore hardly to be considered an external trade, but more resembles the traffic between town and country, and is amenable to the principles of home trade.[6]

Though Mill was referring to a later period and it is doubtful if English capital was as crucial a factor as he maintained, nevertheless his remarks have considerable relevance to the period of this study. It is true, for example, that the Caribbean dependencies became specialized producing parts of an imperial economy which had its financial, industrial, and managerial centre in Great Britain. Key investment or disinvestment decisions for the West Indies were made in London by men who were cognizant of business conditions in the metropolis and the colonies, who had a broad command of resources, both material and intellectual, and who were thus in a position to choose between a wide range of alternatives.

3 THE ERA OF MINOR STAPLES

Englishmen settled the islands of the Lesser Antilles in the second quarter of the 17th century when Spain's hold on the West Indies was weakened by the declining output of her precious metal mines and the diversion of her military forces to defend Brazil against attacks launched by the Dutch West India Company. English adventurers, notably Thomas Warner, abandoned Guiana and established tropical agricultural settlements on the more defensible islands of the Eastern Caribbean. In this undertaking Warner and his fellow adventurers enlisted the financial support of certain London merchants who engaged in trades ranging from Africa and the East Indies to Virginia and Newfoundland, and whose knowledge of Caribbean waters was enhanced by their extensive privateering ventures and illicit tobacco trade which probably supplied a large part of the capital for their colonization efforts. Prominent among the merchants who planted West Indian settlements were Ralph Merrifield, Sir William Courteen, Sir Marmaduke Rawden, Edward Littleton, Maurice Thompson, and Sir Martin Noell. Not only did these merchants have the financial resources and trading connections

---

6 John Stuart Mill, *Principles of Political Economy*, ed. Sir W. J. Ashley (London, 1936), pp. 685–6.

to undertake risky colonization ventures, but the more successful among them secured royal patronage through courtiers who were favourites of the King.

If adventurers, merchants, and courtiers were necessary to project colonies, numbers of people were needed to clear forests, build forts and settlements, and plant provisions and staples. From the standpoint of the colonies, it was fortunate that England had large numbers of sturdy peasants and artisans who were willing to emigrate to the colonies. Some were recruited from the disaffected political and religious elements of the population, while others were looking for a new life after being dispossessed of their lands and livelihoods by enclosures and sheep grazing. Accentuating these elements of push was the commercial crisis of 1620–4, which launched the 'great migration' to the colonies in the decades prior to the outbreak of the Civil Wars. It was in this setting of recurring crises at home and on the European continent that England began her tropical agricultural settlements in the West Indies.

Profit from the cultivation and export of tobacco was the chief motive inducing Caribbean colonization. The smoking habit was firmly established by 1612, when the English people were expending some £200,000 for tobacco, most of which came from the Spanish West Indies. The arrival of the first cargo of Virginia tobacco in 1613 gave hope of developing an independent colonial source of supply. These hopes were not disappointed. Indeed, the demand for Virginia tobacco outran the supply and the resulting high prices stimulated colonial production and export by some twenty-five-fold from 1619 to 1627.

English colonists first came to the West Indies in the 1620s, at a time of depression at home and a tobacco boom in the colonies. Merchants sent out indentured servants and supplied goods on credit, taking in exchange the planters' tobacco. Despite the incursions of Carib Indians and other hardships, the colonists in St Kitts were exporting substantial cargoes of tobacco to London by 1627. The following year saw the launching of the Rawden syndicate which expected to clear the expenses of its first year in Barbados by raising 60,000 lb of tobacco worth about £10,000. The influx of labour and capital sustained the expansion for some years. But by 1636 the supply of colonial tobacco had so outrun the metropolitan demand that the West Indians were beginning to turn to cotton and other useful commodities. In 1637 and 1638 together the Port of London received 1.1 million lb from the Caribbean colonies and another 3.4 million from Virginia. By this time falling prices, restrictive planting decrees, and declining exports had brought on a tobacco crisis of

Booms and Slumps in War and Peace, 1623–1713

such magnitude that the very survival of the tropical colonies was in jeopardy.[7]

4 THE SUGAR REVOLUTION

The launching of the sugar revolution in the English and French West Indies was chiefly a Dutch effort. Dutchmen not only introduced the sugar cane into Barbados from Brazil, but they also gave credit to the islanders 'for Black Slaves, and all other necessaries for planting, taking as their Crops throve, the Sugar they made: This with light but sure Gains to themselves, they nourisht the Industrious and consequently Improving Planters, both before, and during the Civill War in these Islands'.[8]

What was to become an essential part of the plantation based trading system was initiated in 1647, when New Englanders, 'the Dutchmen of the New World', brought foodstuffs and building materials to Barbados to exchange for tropical wares. The influx of slaves, sugar mills, fish, lumber, and other imported supplies enabled some of the Barbadians and other islanders to assemble the complex of land, servile labour, and processing equipment that made the sugar plantation such a unique and profitable unit of production. Nicholas Foster, a planter in Barbados, wrote in 1650 that the island had 'a very faire correspondency' with England, New England, Holland, Hamburgh and other places, 'there being many Millions of *Sugars* transported from thence yearely, and the number of Ships that come yearely to that Island, not lesse than a hundred Sayle; the commodities (being not onely *Sugar*) but also *Indico, Ginger*, with *Cotton-wools* and some small quantities of *Tobacco*'.[9] George Gardyner wrote in his *Description of the New World* (1651) that Barbados 'flourisheth so much, that it hath more people and Commerce then all the Ilands of the Indies'.[10]

Great fortunes were building up when Richard Ligon lived in Barbados from 1647 to 1650. Colonel James Drax, who came to the island with £300 sterling, said that 'he would not look towards England, with a purpose to remain there, the rest of his life, till he

---

7 J. A. Williamson, *The Caribbee Islands Under the Proprietary Patents* (Oxford, 1926), pp. 54, 137–41, 148–9, 154–6.
8 Sir Dalby Thomas, *An Historical Account of the Rise and Growth of the West-India Collonies* (London, 1690), pp. 36–7.
9 Nicholas Foster, *A Briefe Relation of the Late Horrid Rebellion in the Island Barbadas* (London, 1650), p. 3.
10 George Gardyner, *A Description of the New World. Or, America Islands and Continent* (London, 1651), pp. 77–8.

Sugar and Slavery

were able to purchase an estate of ten thousand pound land yearly; which he hop'd in a few years to accomplish, with what he was then owner of; and all by this plant of Sugar'. Colonel Thomas Modyford told Ligon he would not set his face for England until he had made £100,000 sterling.[11]

5 THE IMPACT OF THE NAVIGATION ACTS

The year 1650 ushered in a period of turbulence and conflict in the West Indies which was both cause and effect of the remarkable growth of the sugar industry. After years of Civil War, the Commonwealth government sought to regain England's hold on the colonies by military action against the Dutch and the Royalists in the colonies, and by such policies of economic nationalism as the Navigation Act of 1651. Further, the base of the sugar colonies was expanded by the conquest of Jamaica.

Instead of marking a radical departure, the Restoration government continued, expanded, and to a degree modified the imperial and commercial policies initiated during the Interregnum. The Navigation Acts of 1660, 1663, and 1673 attempted with some degree of success to close loopholes in the acts of the Commonwealth government. Two joint-stock companies in succession were chartered in the African trade, primarily to supply slaves to the English colonies, and, secondarily, to expand England's informal empire in Spanish America. After some years of buccaneering and hide hunting, Jamaicans settled down to planting and trade. The Anglo-Spanish treaty of 1670 contributed to the rise of the Jamaican entrepôt trade in slaves and English manufactures.

The second Anglo-Dutch war of 1664–7 marked a turning point in the international struggle to dominate the plantation-based trading area. Dr Farnie writes that the war

> broke the Dutch hold on the trade in tobacco and sugar; in wampum and fur; in slaves and cod-fish. Thus was achieved a victory consolidated by the increased permeation of society by commercial values and by the creation of a structure of trade regulation (1673–97) wherein England sought to be as far as possible both monopolist and monopsonist.[12]

Anglo-French rivalry for Caribbean colonies and trade became a dominant theme by the final decade of the 17th century.

11 Richard Ligon, *A True and Exact History of the Island of Barbadoes* (London, 1673), p. 96.
12 D. A. Farnie, 'The Commercial Empire of the Atlantic, 1607–1783', *The Economic History Review*, 2nd ser., vol. XV, no. 2 (Dec. 1962), p. 206.

Booms and Slumps in War and Peace, 1623–1713

The phenomenal fall in the price of sugar gave rise to a burst of interest in the West Indies in the mid-17th century period. Reduced prices most likely diminished profits to producers, but these losses were probably more than offset by such benefits as expanded consumer markets, middlemen's profits, shipping earnings, and customs revenue. From the defeat of the Armada down to the Commonwealth period, muscovado sugar sold at retail for 1s to 1s 6d per lb. It declined sharply from an average of 14.4d per lb in 1643–52, to 7.4 in 1652–62, then rose to 9.0 in 1663–72, and fell to 6.8 in 1683–92. Wholesale prices declined by more than retail prices. Sir Dalby Thomas wrote in 1690 'that before Sugars were produced in our Collonies, it bore three times the Price it doth now ...'. Muscovado sugar, which before the West India colonies were settled, sold in London for £4 or £5 per cwt, declined to about 40s in 1660, and to a low point of 17s 3d in 1682.[13]

English and Continental markets had been supplied to a very great extent with Brazilian sugar prior to 1650. After that time the Brazilian product entering European markets declined irregularly from about 570,000 cwt in 1650, to 336,000 in 1710. English colonial sugar — particularly that of Barbados — was still contending with the Brazilian product for the English market in the early 1660s. However, the situation altered so radically that Sir Josiah Child declared in 1669:

> In my time we have beat their [Portuguese] Muscovado and Paneal sugars quite out of use in Europe, their Whites we have brought down in all these parts of Europe in price from seven to eight pound per [100] lb. to fifty shillings and three pence per [100] lb., whereas formerly their Brazil fleets consisted of 100 to 120 thousand chests of sugar, they are now reduced to about 30 thousand chests, since the great encrease of Barbadoes.[14]

Contributing to the decline of the Brazilian product were such factors as dislocation resulting from the expulsion of Dutchmen and Portuguese Jews, heavy imposts laid on colonial sugar by the King of Portugal, diversion of colonial resources to gold mining, and the rise of rival production centres in the West Indies.

Besides their old rivals in Brazil, English planters had to meet the competition of new rivals in the West Indies. The French and Dutch sugar colonies made some inroads into European markets during the 1670s and 1680s. Measured in cwt, French sugar production increased from about 107,000 in 1674 to 184,000 in 1683, while the Dutch colony of Surinam exported about 49,700 in 1688. Con-

---
13 Thomas, *Historical Account of West-India Collonies*, p. 9; Davies, *Royal African Company*, pp. 365–6.
14 Sir Josiah Child, *A New Discourse of Trade* (London, 1669), p. 220.

Sugar and Slavery

siderably more than the combined exports of these colonies were the 372,000 cwt sent home from the English West Indies in 1682/3.[15]

Imposition of restrictions and duties contributed to the decline in English sugar prices. We have seen that the Navigation Act of 1660, by requiring sugar intended for Europe to be shipped via England, made the staple less competitive in Continental markets and thus depressed prices at home. Planters complained that the Navigation Acts forced them into a cost-price squeeze. Another consequence of the Navigation Acts was to invite retaliation from abroad, especially from the French government which laid heavy duties on English and other foreign sugars in 1664.

It should not be thought that English planters immediately lost the foreign sugar market in consequence of restrictions and duties. On the contrary, the Navigation Acts were rather loosely enforced for a time. While it is true that re-exports had declined to about one-half of the English colonial imports by 1675, much sugar escaped the net of imperial regulation and duties. Dutchmen, Irishmen, and North Americans carried the West Indian staple to foreign markets in such quantities that Parliament was moved to close loopholes by the Navigation Act of 1673. Moreover, competition from foreign producers was not too keen in the 1660s and early 1670s. Expressed in cwt, exports from Barbados to England increased from 139,000 in 1655, to an annual average of 198,400 in 1699–1701. By comparison, the combined sugar imports from the Leeward Islands and Jamaica increased from negligible quantities in 1655 to an annual average of 239,880 cwt in 1699–1701. The Barbadian contribution to total English sugar imports thus declined from upwards of 90 per cent in 1660 to 45.3 per cent in 1699–1701.

6 BARBADOS AND THE RECESSION OF THE 1680s

Growing foreign competition and enforcement of the Navigation Acts accelerated the decline in English sugar prices in the 1680s. Beginning in the 1670s, the governors of the Leeward Islands undertook the prosecution of planters and merchants who sold sugar products to the Dutch. Circumvention of the Navigation Acts by North American traders was checked by the duty on intercolonial shipments of enumerated commodities which was first levied in 1673. Furthermore, the early 1670s witnessed parliamentary

---

15 Charles W. Cole, *Colbert and a Century of French Mercantilism 1683–1700* (New York, 1943), vol. 2, p. 55; Herbert I. Bloom, *The Economic Activities of the Jews of Amsterdam in the 17th and 18th Centuries* (Williamsport, Penna., 1937), p. 157.

enactments which limited the colonial trade of Ireland and Scotland. Across the Channel the French government was taking more forceful action against foreign sugar with unexpected repercussions on the English market. Duties on foreign sugar came to be higher as the French colonies increased in ability to supply the home market. Writing in 1681, one Englishman said that 'By the aforesaid great impositions on fforain Sugers in France, the Sugers of Brasile are as it were prohibited of that Country, and are therefore in greater Quantity brought into England which lessens the Vallue of English Sugers'.[16]

Colonials reacted to the fall in sugar prices by devising new trade channels and marketing institutions. The great proprietors of Barbados had enjoyed a decade of exuberant prosperity in the 1650s. The early 1660s, on the other hand, were years of declining prices and profits and of difficult adjustment to the Navigation Acts. In the face of declining profit margins, several responses were to be expected. Unit costs of production might be reduced by establishing large plantations worked by Negro slaves. Given such units, it then became possible to bypass local middlemen and establish commission agencies in the metropolis. But if the returns from legally traded sugar products were disappointing, planters might be expected to encourage illicit traders. These and other expedients were resorted to in years of adversity.

Underlying these adjustments was a series of natural disasters which visited the planters of Barbados. These included a plague of locusts in 1663, a fire which destroyed Bridgetown in 1667, and in the same year a hurricane of moderate violence. Crops were so reduced by the drought of 1668 that the inhabitants were ready to desert their plantations. After a year of excessive rain in 1669, Barbados was plagued by dry weather and epidemic in 1670, the latter carrying off large numbers of slaves and indentured servants. Added to these shortrun hardships was the decline in soil fertility. In 1668, Governor Willoughby declared that 'Barbados contains one hundred thousand acres and renders not by two-thirds its former production by acres. The land is almost worn out, and the thickets where cotton and corn are planted are so burnt up that the inhabitants are ready to desert their plantations'.[17]

Despite these natural disasters and the strait-jacket of the Navigation Acts, the decade of the 1660s appears to have been one of

---

16 Anon., 'The True State of the Manufacture of Sugars within our Plantations (1681)', quoted in Vere L. Oliver, *The History of the Island of Antigua* (London, 1894–99), vol. 1, p. lxii.
17 *Cal. S. P. Col. 1661–68*, p. 586.

general but somewhat diminished prosperity for the large planters of Barbados. Benjamin Moseley relates that 'Charles II in 1669 created 13 Baronets of Barbadoes; each of whom had in the island not less than a thousand pounds a year, and some ten thousand pounds a year'. Although the accuracy of Moseley's statement has been questioned, there is no reason to doubt other contemporaries who commented on the prosperous state of the island. Sir Robert Hartley wrote from Barbados on 24 December 1663, that 'the island is in soe flourishing a condition that it can hardly be improved'. John Scott, Geographer to Charles II, said that Barbados was forty times as rich in 1667 as she had been in 1645.[18]

The natural disasters of the late 1660s and early 1670s were followed by a hurricane of moderate severity in August 1674, and one of disaster proportions in 1675. Governor Atkins said that '200,000 *l.* will not repay the damage caused by the hurricane of last August, churches, houses and mills being destroyed and the sugar canes twisted and spoiled'. Besides these losses, a Barbadian sugar fleet was captured by the enemy during the Anglo-Dutch War of 1672–4. Conditions improved considerably from 1677 to 1680, however. Cane crops were bountiful and English sugar prices remained fairly steady. The island was in a flourishing condition when Goverrr Dutton arrived in 1680.[19]

The years of peace and uninterrupted trade from 1675 to 1688 witnessed a remarkable expansion of tropical agriculture, both within and without the English colonies. Underlying this expansion was the influx of Negro slaves from Africa, some introduced clandestinely by the Dutch, others entered through legal channels by the Royal African Company. In 1673, the Company delivered 220 slaves in Barbados at an average price in colonial currency of £18. From 1674 to 1678, when Jamaica and Nevis were added to the Company's markets, deliveries ranged between 1,945 and 4,009; the Barbadian quota varied from 940 to 2,392. While deliveries fell to 2,198 in 1679, they shot up afterwards, reaching the high point of 10,815 in 1686–7. The decline in the Company's slave prices was no less significant than the expanded deliveries. In Barbados the price fell from £18 per head in 1673, to £12 10s in 1683; in Jamaica from £22 10s in 1674 to £14 10s in 1687.[20]

18 Benjamin Moseley, *A Treatise on Sugar* (London, 1800), p. 28; *Duke of Portland MSS, Historical Manuscripts Commission*, 14th Report, vol. 3, p. 279; John Scott, 'The Description of Barbados', British Museum, Sloane MSS 3662, f. 54.
19 *Cal. S. P. Col. 1675–76*, pp. 347–9; Otis P. Starkey, *The Economic Geography of Barbados* (New York, 1939), pp. 78–9.
20 Davies, *Royal African Company*, pp. 303–4, 361–4.

Cheaper and more abundant labourers increased production in relation to market demand with a consequent decline in sugar prices. Barbadian muscovado sugar sold in London by the Royal African Company held fairly steady from 1674 to 1681 at prices ranging from 20s 9d to 23s 6d per 100 lb. Subsequent years saw an irregular decline to a low point of 16s 9d in 1686.[21]

If the period from 1660 to 1680 was one of general but somewhat diminished prosperity, the years from 1681 to 1688 brought moderate to severe hardship. Hardships were particularly acute in Barbados where there was a coincidence of high costs, low sugar prices, heavy indebtedness, and in 1685 'the loss of this year's crop through ill weather, and by the mortality among negroes and servants through smallpox'. Another burden was the additional duty of 1685, amounting to 2s 4d per cwt on colonial muscovado sugar imported into England. Company slaves brought to Barbados declined from an annual average of 3,630 in the 1682–5 period, to 1,516 in 1688, and to 1,119 in 1690.[22]

Edward Littleton, a Barbadian planter, recounted the hardships of these years in his *Groans of the Plantations* (1689). He wrote that the ordinary 'midling' price of muscovado sugar was reckoned at 26s per cwt at most, and that it cost the planter ten shillings 'in the making, and ten the transporting'. At the best he estimated the gross profit to be six shillings,

> and then the duties draw Two Shillings out of Six; and are as a Land-Tax of a Noble in the Pound. But if the Sugar yields only Two and Twenty Shillings, the Duty swallows up the whole Profit; if it yields but Twenty, the Planter pays the Duty out of his Pocket, and must live by the less, and there is many a hundred of Sugar sold under Twenty.[23]

Another pamphleteer, who attributed all of the ills of Barbados to the additional duty on sugar, said that 'the Island was miserably depopulated, insomuch that before the Revolution above 40 Sugar-works were laid waste . . .'.[24]

Barbadian planters were the marginal sugar producers of the Caribbean region by the decade of the 1680s. By this time they were meeting with growing competition from other English and foreign sugar colonies. While many small planters lost their property and sought their fortunes elsewhere, large planters who took pains to improve their tillage and processing practices managed to weather the

---

21 Ibid., p. 363.
22 Idem.
23 Edward Littleton, *The Groans of the Plantations* (London, 1689), pp. 3, 10.
24 Anon., *The Present Case of a Barbados Planter, and Reasons against Laying a Further Duty on Sugar* (London, c. 1695), p. 2.

Sugar and Slavery

crisis. This was the opinion of Sir Dalby Thomas, who wrote in 1690: 'It is true, many of the first comers, especially in *Barbados* are got above the danger of Ruine by these and other following mischief, that dayly must, if not prevented, Increase upon all who are not in the like Circumstances for Wealth'.[25]

7 THE LEEWARD ISLANDS AND JAMAICA

Planters in the Leeward Islands and Jamaica enjoyed certain advantages over their counterparts in Barbados. For one thing, production costs were generally lower in consequence of virgin soils, savannas for livestock grazing, and timber lands to supply building materials and fuel. Then, too, their economies were more diversified and thus less vulnerable to fluctuations in the sugar market. Another advantage enjoyed by the Leeward Islanders was proximity to the Dutch island of St Eustatius, an important source of slaves and plantation supplies and the entrepôt through which substantial quantities of English sugar passed on its way to Europe. Counterbalancing these advantages was the diversionary effect of buccaneering in Jamaica, and the Indian raids and wars in the Leeward Islands. Christopher Jeaffreson wrote from St Kitts after the French invasion and occupation of 1666–71: 'The wars here are the more destructive than in any other partes of the world; for twenty yeares' peace will hardly resettle the devastation of one yeares' warre'.[26]

Except for the island of Nevis, where sugar had become the leading staple in the 1650s, small staple and provision culture dominated the economic life of the Leeward Islands well into the Restoration period. On the eve of the French conquest of 1666, St Kitts was said to consist 'mostly of persons who had formerly been servants, whose plantations of 10 or 12 acres were managed generally with English hands, those requiring slaves being very few comparatively...'.[27] Then came the conquering French who burned cane fields, destroyed sugar works, and carried away Negroes, horses, and utensils. The war of 1665–7 was so destructive in its impact that whereas the single island of St Kitts had about 5,000 white men at the commencement of hostilities, only 3,679 armed men, together

25 Thomas, *Historical Account of West-India Collonies*, p. 41.
26 John C. Jeaffreson, *A Young Squire of the Seventeenth Century* (London, 1878), vol. 1, p. 215.
27 *Cal. S. P. Col. 1669–74*, pp. 440–1.

with 3,184 Negro slaves, were reported in the four Leeward Islands in 1671.[28]

Considerable economic growth characterized the Leeward Islands in the years from 1671 to 1689, when peacetime conditions were generally prevalent. Land reform, especially in Antigua, contributed to population growth and capital investment. The pace of white immigration became brisker in consequence of the overflow of Barbados, the loss of Surinam to the Dutch, and the arrival of freemen and indentured servants from the mother country. Substantial profits, together with credit and loans, enabled more planters to purchase Negro slaves and equipment for sugar works. Sugar had become the leading staple by 1680, when the Leeward Islanders were said to have loaded '200 ships yearly, worth 1,000,000 *l.* annually to the nation'.[29]

Nevis, with its active mercantile community and access to Royal African Company slaves, developed more rapidly than its sister islands. It was much like Barbados in having large sugar plantations worked by Negro slaves and a few white servants. Indeed, Nevis possessed nearly two-thirds of the total wealth of the Leeward Islands. According to Governor Stapleton's estimate of 1676, the total wealth of these islands was £584,660 [or £581,160] sterling, made up of Nevis, £384,660; St Kitts, £67,000; Antigua, £67,000; and Montserrat, £62,500.[30]

The economic history of Jamaica from the English conquest of 1655 to the outbreak of war in 1689, is one of guerrilla warfare, disease, and near-starvation for several years after the conquest; buccaneering raids on the Spanish Main launched from the fortress city of Port Royal; extractive industries based on wild cattle and dye woods; and a succession of planting frontiers, of which cocoa was most prominent for a time. Jamaica was an island of bountiful resources by comparison with the small islands in the Lesser Antilles. Exports from Jamaica during the seven years and nine months from 25 June 1671, to 25 March 1679, consisted of 7,637¼ tons of sugar, 44¾ of cacao, 305 of indigo, 177 of ginger, 2,357 of fustic, 5,119 of logwood, 43¾ of tobacco, and 134¼ of pimento. Moreover, there were exported 38,587 hides, and 866 bags of cotton.[31] After years of turbulence and fluctuating fortune, the Jamaicans had begun to develop their agricultural resources on a systematic basis by 1674, when Governor Lynch wrote: 'The island has improved these last

---

28 Oliver, *History of Antigua*, vol. 1, p. li.
29 *Cal. S. P. Col. 1677–80*, p. 642.
30 Ibid. *1675–76, Appendix 1574–1674*, p. 561.
31 Ibid. *1677–80*, p. 344.

Sugar and Slavery

Table 17.1

*English sugar imports, re-exports,
and retained imports, 1690 and 1699–1713
(annual averages in 000 cwt)*

Years	Imports	Re-exports	Retained imports	Percentage retained
1690	257.0	128.5	128.5	50.0
1699–1701	450.8	160.5	290.3	64.5
1702–05	338.5	85.0	253.5	74.8
1706–09	374.7	96.2	278.5	74.1
1710–13	450.3	129.9	320.4	71.2

Source: John MacGregor, *Commercial Statistics* (London, 1850), vol. 5, p. 378.

three years to a marvel, and the people are as contented as English can be'.[32]

8 ECONOMIC FLUCTUATIONS IN WARTIME

The period from 1689 to 1713 was characterized by violent sugar price fluctuations, reflecting the risks and uncertainties of war. Wartime sugar prices were generally higher in spite of increased imports, and a larger percentage of imports was retained for home consumption. Appendix V shows the generally high and erratic prices, while Table 17.1 shows the tendency for imports and home consumption to rise. English sugar imports increased by 75 per cent between 1690 and 1710–13, at a time when the amount retained for home consumption increased about two and a half times. Retained imports increased from about one-half to nearly three-fourths of total imports.

The ability to pay higher prices in a period when home consumption increased about two and a half times indicates a remarkable expansion of market demand. Evidence of the growing capacity to consume sugar products may be found in a variety of sources. Thomas Tryon wrote in 1699 that 'the great Wages and free Circulation of Trade amongst the common people as well as others, hath made England exceed all her Neighbouring Nations in Riches'.

32 *Cal. S. P. Col. 1669–74*, p. 624.

He estimated that England's sugar consumption exceeded the combined consumption of Poland, Denmark, and France.[33]

It is noteworthy that London sugar prices rose in relation to Continental prices. An English pamphleteer wrote about 1695 that the King of France was using 'all imaginary industry to strengthen and fill his Plantations with Inhabitants'. Owing to the absence of customs at the free port of Dunkirk, the markets of Flanders and Holland were 'furnished with French Sugars at 2s. 6d. per hundred cheaper than the English can by reason of the Acts of Trade'.[34]

In part, English sugar prices rose because of added protection and the inclusion of Scotland in the protected home market after 1706. The Tariff of 1661 levied a duty of 4s per cwt on foreign muscovado as compared with 1s 5d on the colonial product. In 1685, the foreign duty was increased by 4s 6d and the colonial by 2s 4d. Since very little foreign sugar was entered through legal channels and the smuggled product was negligible, the home market was supplied almost exclusively by English planters by the turn of the 18th century.

Thus protection, rising demand, and limited productive capacity brought a fundamental transformation in the sugar industry. By the beginning of the 18th century English markets were absorbing a growing proportion of colonial sugar at prices higher than those prevailing abroad. Whereas planters had formerly evaded the Navigation Acts by selling their sugar to Dutchmen and North Americans, they now began to prefer the English market. Because of higher prices in England, merchants in the English sugar colonies were encouraged to import sugar from foreign colonies and ship it to England disguised as the English-grown product. During Queen Anne's War much Martinique sugar was brought to Barbados under pretext of flags of truce and then trans-shipped to England. Moreover, the same period witnessed the beginning of the troublesome trade between North America and the foreign sugar colonies.

Short-term movements from 1689 to 1713 necessarily hinged on the vicissitudes of war and peace. War years far outnumbered those of peace. Indeed, King William's War (1689–97) and Queen Anne's War (1702–13) occupied all but four of the twenty-five years of this period. The outbreak of hostilities disrupted the pattern of peacetime trade and shipping in numerous ways. Merchant vessels were converted into privateers and merchant seamen were impressed

---

[33] Thomas Tryon, *England's Grandeur, and the Way to get Wealth* (London, 1699), pp. 7–8.
[34] Anon., *The Case of Their Majesties Sugar Plantations* (London, *c.* 1695).

into the navy. The risks of enemy capture raised insurance rates and made shipowners reluctant to send their vessels to the West Indies. Wide disparity between the demand for and supply of vessels raised shipping costs and thus made sugar products scarce and costly in European markets. In the West Indies, on the other hand, sugar prices declined because few ships came to carry away the island produce. At the same time, imported plantation supplies became more costly. The first effect of war on the Caribbean economy was thus to increase the prices of imports and lower those of island produce. Under these conditions planters were reluctant to sell their sugars locally or run the risk of shipping it on their own account. Some of them stored their exportable produce in anticipation of more settled times.

Compared with trade and shipping, sugar production was not as immediately affected by the outbreak of war. During the first year of each war sugar was made from canes which had been planted under peacetime conditions. Production costs increased in consequence of dearer imported supplies, but the quantity of sugar produced probably did not diminish appreciably. In time, however, cane output fell off. Planters were burdened with a heavy tax load to defray the cost of strengthening fortifications and purchasing arms and ammunition. Numbers of slaves were set to work building fortifications. Able-bodied white men were occupied with militia duties. In these and other ways the supply of labour for tropical agriculture was diminished.

Wartime insecurity made it difficult to obtain credit, and without credit few planters were able to maintain peacetime levels of production. Credit stringency and costly imported supplies made necessary a regime of self-sufficiency; provisions were grown on lands that normally grew canes. Capital was diverted into privateering and clandestine trade. So attractive were these speculative ventures that they frequently absorbed the planter's nestegg of cash. Resource diversion, the normal accompaniment of war, might be followed by property loss and destruction in the dreaded event of enemy invasion and plunder.

While metropolitan sugar prices generally shot upward at the outbreak of hostilities, a reverse movement generally characterized the late years of warfare. Improved military and naval installations and protection of shipping lanes go far to explain this phenomenon. At the outbreak of war planters and merchants petitioned the home government for regiments to relieve local militia, warships to cruise around the islands and drive off enemy privateers, and convoys to lower shipping costs and insure regular shipments of staples and plantation supplies. As the government responded rather slowly, planters assumed most of the initial burdens of defence. The picture changed measurably once military and naval aid was forthcoming.

Initiation of convoy service between the metropolis and the colony was of key importance in the transformation. By providing convoys at no cost to the shipper, the English government gave planters and merchants the full benefit of savings on freight and insurance which such protection made possible. Economically speaking, the establishment of regular convoy service meant the return to a colonial cost-price structure approaching peacetime conditions. Lower shipping costs not only encouraged planters to ship newly-made sugars but also the quantities stored in years of adversity. Metropolitan prices thus declined as supply ran ahead of demand.

9 KING WILLIAM'S WAR, 1689–97

The striking feature of King William's War was the sharp and almost steady rise in London sugar prices from an index of 92 (1683/4 = 100) in 1687 to that of 267 in 1695. The growth in English sugar consumption goes some way to explain the rise, but much more crucial were heavy shipping losses and the planters' reluctance to ship sugar when they saw little hope of profit.

Dependence upon external markets and supplies made the Barbadians most vulnerable to the disruptive effects of war. The wartime plight of the island was underscored in a representation of the Council and Assembly in July 1696. It affirmed that the land had become so barren that it would not produce sugar-canes 'unless forced by great quantities of dung and other extraordinary husbandry and labour, which requires double the number of negroes, cattle, and horses that were needed when the land was fruitful'. Prices of these and other productive factors had risen to such heights that 'Many of the best plantations, which once made great quantities of sugar, now make little or none, and near fifty other plantations are ruined or discontinued. One-third of the sugar-cane land lies waste and over-run with weeds'.[35]

Besides inflated production costs, Barbadians suffered heavy shipping losses and were burdened with exorbitant rates of freight and insurance. In less than twelve months prior to July 1696, French privateers were said to have taken 'more than fifty sail of laden ships, over and above two hundred vessels trading to and from the Island'. Shipping losses, amounting to some £387,100 in 1695 alone,

35 *Cal. S. P. Col. 1696–97*, p. 61.

> discouraged ships from coming to the Island so much that freight is risen from £5 to £25 per ton, insurance from 3 to 20 guineas *per Cent.*, salt beef and pork from 25 shillings to 70 or 80 shillings per barrel, salt fish from 10 shillings to 25 shillings per quintal, and all other commodities in like proportion; so that though the value of sugar may be much increased yet all is eaten up by the increase of charges.[36]

Planters were more fortunate in other years. Almost everything depended on the luck of the planter in getting his produce to market despite hurricanes, privateers, and enemy warships. High prices in the metropolis encouraged planters to undertake these risky ventures. As Oldmixon viewed it, the Barbadians suffered terrible losses, it is true, 'but their Sugars sold well, from 50s. to 3 *l.* a Hundred'.[37]

Leeward Island planters probably escaped with the least damage in King William's War. Though burdened with defence expenditures and other wartime charges, planters took advantage of fertile soils and extensive methods of cultivation to minimize costs. They were encouraged to expand production because of high sugar prices and the protection afforded shipping. Governor Codrington wrote from Antigua in December 1695:

> There are prospects of a great crop of sugar, and the Islands will want only ships to carry it home securely. St. Christophers is a very flourishing Island and would considerably increase the strength of this Government had I the King's leave to settle it, there being many settlers from the Northern Colonies that daily wait to see when they may have encouragement to remove and settle there.[38]

Merchant shipping was better protected near the end of the war. Codrington wrote home in May 1696 that 'by fitting out three privateers and keeping the [warship] *Hastings* at sea cruising, I have kept the enemy at some distance, whereby our merchant-ships have arrived with greater security than heretofore'.[39]

The wartime balance sheet of Jamaica, though it contained numerous credits, was most likely weighted on the debit side. Overbalancing such plus factors as virgin soil, diversified resources, and low costs of staple production were such negative features as the great earthquake of 1692, the internal threat of Maroon war and slave insurrection, the sparse male population to man defence works, and the scattered bays and coves which invited enemy raids and invasions. The upshot was a damaging blow to the eastern parishes of the island in 1694. The French invaders of that year destroyed fifty

---

36 *Cal. S. P. Col. 1696–97*, p. 62.
37 John Oldmixon, *The British Empire in America* (London, 1708), vol. 2, p. 166.
38 *Cal. S. P. Col. 1693–96*, p. 628.
39 Ibid., p. 680.

Booms and Slumps in War and Peace, 1623—1713

sugar works, burned cane fields, and carried off numerous slaves.[40]

After the fluctuating fortunes of war, prosperity was the dominant theme of the interwar years from 1698 to 1702. Though London sugar prices declined sharply from 1696 to 1698, it is significant that the low point in 1698 was still about 60 index points above the low level of the mid-eighties. Costs of production, particularly in Jamaica and the Leeward Islands, probably declined more rapidly than prices of exportable staples. The Governor of Jamaica reported in March 1701: 'In all likelihood there will be above 1,000 hhds. [of sugar] made more this year than there was last, the country being in perfect health, and all people very sedulous in improving their estates'.[41]

10 QUEEN ANNE'S WAR, 1702—13

The impact of Queen Anne's War on the sugar industry was probably no less severe than the conflict of King William's reign. As in the previous war, London sugar prices rose near the beginning and declined near the end of hostilities. The two wars differed in other respects, however. The falling off in the re-export trade goes far to explain the lower price level in Queen Anne's War. 'The French begin to tred upon our heels in ye sugar trade', exclaimed Governor Codrington in 1701: 'they have better Islands, I assure your Lordships, than wee; and St Domingo will in time be a vast settlement'.[42] With French and other foreign sugar undercutting the English product in Continental markets, it is not surprising that re-exports fell to about one-fourth of imports and that sugar prices in the home market were sluggish.

Table 17.2 summarizes England's sugar imports from her West India colonies from 1699 to 1713, with the exception of the year 1705.

The absolute and relative decline of Barbados was a noteworthy feature of the war period. Sugar imports from that island fell off by 46 per cent between 1699—1701 and 1710—13. Troubles were compounded from 1702 to 1706 by declining sugar prices, high freight and insurance, and shipping losses. Freight was at the excessive rate of £20 and £25 per ton, wrote John Oldmixon, while 'Insurances are so high, thé planters cannot pay the Premio's'.[43] Shipping losses dealt a dreadful blow to the planters and merchants.

---

40 Clinton V. Black, *History of Jamaica* (London, 1958), pp. 74—7.
41 *Cal. S. P. Col. 1701*, p. 203.
42 P.R.O. London, C.O. 152/4, E 51, f. 106.
43 Oldmixon, *British Empire in America*, vol. 2, pp. 165—7.

Sugar and Slavery

Table 17.2

English sugar imports from the Caribbean colonies, 1698–1713 (annual averages in 000 cwt)

Year	Barbados	Jamaica	Leeward Islands	Total
1699–1701	198.4	94.8	145.1	438.3
1702–04	127.7	82.7	132.0	342.4
1706–09	165.6	100.1	88.9	354.6
1710–13	138.1	118.6	184.3	441.0

Source: Noel Deerr, *The History of Sugar* (London, 1949–50), vol. 1, pp. 193–8. Tons are converted into hundredweights at the ratio of 1 to 20.

They have suffer'd more than any other Trade whatsoever. Their Loss by Captures, within the Compass of one Year, being Computed at 380,000 *l.* And in the year 1704 out of a Fleet of 33 Ships, 27 were taken. Out of another 6 Ships 4 were taken: And out of a Fleet of 40 Ships the greatest Number were lost to the French.[44]

'For want of a regiment and regular convoys and cruisers', wrote another contemporary, 'ye inhabitants are exposed to inexpressible trouble, labour and expence in the necessary dutys of the militia, and to great difficulties and hardships for want of regular convoys and supplies...'.[45] Measures to establish a land bank and raise the current coin of the island had led to the general decay of trade and credit.

But not all war years were as disastrous as those portrayed by the above writers. Shipping and insurance costs were reduced in the late war years when regular convoy service was established. Planters were encouraged to expand output by the rise in London sugar prices after 1705. Losses to French privateers in the Lesser Antilles were probably counterbalanced by the prizes taken by Jamaicans. The people of Jamaica were said to be 'intent on nothing so much as encouraging the privateers... not a day passed but prizes were brought in... and the island became richer than it had been since the days of Morgan'.[46]

The growing importance of Jamaica and the Leeward Islands is

---

44 Oldmixon, *British Empire in America*, vol. 2, pp. 165–7.
45 *Cal. S. P. Col. 1706–08*, p. 630.
46 Anon., *A New History of Jamaica* (London, 1740), pp. 272–3.

revealed by the import figures in Table 17.2. Imports from Jamaica increased by 43.4 per cent between 1702—4 and 1710—13, and those from the Leeward Islands by 39.6. Jamaica's share of total imports rose from 24.2 to 26.9 per cent; the Leeward Islands' from 38.5 to 41.8.

Wartime expansion of the Leeward Islands was seriously interrupted by privateering depredations and the French invasions of St Kitts and Nevis in 1706, and Montserrat in 1712. Cane fields and buildings were destroyed and numerous slaves carried off to the French plantations. Antigua alone was spared such devastation, although this island and its neighbours were visited by the destructive force of a hurricane in 1707. Antigua's sugar production expanded during the war despite the hurricane and internal political troubles which culminated in the murder of Governor Daniel Parke. Shortly before his death in 1710, Parke said that the number of windmills had increased from 27 to 74, with Negro slaves roughly in proportion. 'This Island may, unless by Accident, annually produce as much more Sugar, as when I came to my Government [in 1706]', he wrote. Nevis and St Kitts, although destroyed when he took office, 'are now in a very flourishing Condition... the annual Produce of this Government may be twice as much as when I came to it'.[47]

11 CONCLUSION

Booms and slumps in war and peace should not be allowed to obscure the substantial growth of the West Indies and their contribution to the metropolitan economy in the nine decades prior to the Peace of Utrecht. While the planters and merchants almost never ceased in their outpouring of complaints, the less harried mercantile writers were generally enthusiastic about the progress of the sugar colonies and the slave trade which supplied the planters with their labour force. To John Cary, the slave trade was 'the best Traffick the Kingdom hath, as it doth occasionally give so vast an Imployment to our People both by Sea and Land'.

> These are the Hands whereby our Plantations are improved, and 'tis by their Labours such great Quantities of *Sugar, Tobacco, Cotten, Ginger,* and *Indigo,* are raised which being bulky Commodities imploy great Numbers

---

47 George French, *The History of Col. Parke's Administration as Chief Governor of the Leeward Islands* (London, 1717), pp. 196—7.

of our Ships for their transporting hither, and the greater number of Ships imploys the greater number of Handecraft Trades at home, spends more of our Product and Manufactures, and makes more Saylors, who are maintained by the separate Imploy . . . .

Besides the gains from tropical agriculture, Cary called attention to 'another sort of Commerce . . . *Jamaica* being now become a Magazine of Trade to *New-Spain* and the *Terra Firma*, from whence we have yearly vast Quantities of Bullion imported to this Kingdom both for the *Negroes* and Manufactures we send them . . .'.[48]

Barbados was the brightest gem in the crown of trade during the middle decades of the 17th century. Malachy Postlethwayt may not have exaggerated when he wrote that England acquired £2,000,000 by Barbados in the two decades from 1636 to 1656, and another £4,000,000 in the two decades from 1656 to 1676.[49] Some £278,000 was realized from the 139,000 cwt of Barbadian sugar brought to England in 1655, while some £257,000 was yielded by the 190,496 cwt which came to London from the sugar colonies in 1668/9.[50] Joshua Gee estimated that the trade of re-exporting sugar 'Yearly added three or four Hundred Thousand Pounds to the Stock of the Nation, which in thirty Years Time amounted to upwards of ten Million Sterling'.[51] John Oldmixon wrote in 1708 that Barbados had been as good as a mine of silver or gold to England. According to his 'modest computation', the trade with the island 'did not subsist less than 60,000 Persons in England . . .'.[52]

Sugar production more than compensated for the price decline in the two decades or more following the restoration of Charles II. In 1682/3, the English West Indies supplied the mother country with some 372,000 cwt of sugar valued at £378,200 at London wholesale prices. Together with minor staples, the exports of 1682/3 amounted to about £580,300 valued at London prices, of which Barbados and the Leeward Islands accounted for £382,700, and Jamaica for £197,600.[53] At the commencement of King William's War, the trade between England and the West Indies engaged 110 vessels of an aggregate tonnage of 12,848, and manned by 1,171 sailors. Barbados

---

48 Cary, *Essay on the State of England*, pp. 74–7.
49 Malachy Postlethwayt, *The Universal Dictionary of Trade and Commerce* (London, 1774), vol. 2, art. Sugar.
50 *Cal. S. P. Col. 1675–76, Appendix 1574–1674*, p. 434; B.M. Add. MSS 36,785; Davies, *Royal African Company*, pp. 365–6.
51 Joshua Gee, *The Trade and Navigation of Great Britain* (London, 1731), pp. 80–3.
52 Oldmixon, *British Empire in America*, p. 162.
53 B.M. Add. MSS 38,714, f. 37; P.R.O. London, C. O. 390/6, 31–2; Davies, *Royal African Company*, pp. 365–6. See also Chapter 14, p. 310.

accounted for two-thirds of the tonnage, Jamaica for one-fifth, and the Leeward Islands for one-eighth.[54]

If the estimates of John Pollexfen, member of the Board of Trade, are to be believed, the West Indies continued to grow during King William's War and the interval of peace from 1698 to 1702. He wrote in 1700 that the landowners of Barbados received £300,000 annually from their estates, while the Crown secured a revenue from the island of £70,000. Jamaica was far more valuable in his estimation, with annual returns to the merchants, planters, and the Crown of £600,000, of which £200,000 was in bullion. In the same year Governor Sir William Beeston estimated that Jamaica exported yearly to England commodities and bullion worth £531,000.[55]

Although the above estimates exceed the official values recorded in the Customs Ledgers after 1697, it should be remembered that official values diverged from market values and bullion imports from the West Indies and elsewhere were not recorded.

When we turn to the final years of Queen Anne's War, official and market values show considerable divergence. For the period 1711–13, the Customs Ledgers show annual average imports from the West Indies of £665,972, and a reverse movement of English exports and re-exports of £281,568.[56] On the other hand, calculations based on market values in London show that the sugar colonies in the same period exported to England commodities worth about £1,068,000 annually (exclusive of bullion). Moreover, the end of the war saw a marked change in the relative importance of different islands and groups of islands. Taking the lead were the Leeward Islands with exports to England amounting to about £437,000, followed by Jamaica with £322,000, and Barbados with £309,000.[57]

The West Indies played a major role in expanding and restructuring England's foreign trade and in ultimately altering the economic life of its people. The character of England's foreign trade changed in three important respects during the last four decades of the 17th century. First, trade emphasis shifted from intra-European to extra-European markets and sources of supply. Second, enormous growth of imports from the New World and the East Indies gave rise to a re-export trade of no small dimensions. Third, new markets abroad created a demand for a wider range of manufactures and

---

54 P.R.O. London, C.O. 318/1, 17.
55 *Cal. S. P. Col. 1700*, p. 508: John Pollexfen to Board of Trade, 4 Sept. 1700; B.M. Sloane MSS 2902, f. 151: Gov. Beeston's estimate, 20 April 1700.
56 P.R.O. London. Customs 3/3 and 3/4.
57 See Chapter 14, p. 310.

services than the traditional intra-European trades. Professor Davis has calculated that three commodities — tobacco, calico, and sugar — comprised in value two-thirds of the imports to England from outside Europe and almost two-thirds of English re-exports to Europe. These imports and re-exports, in turn, helped to expand colonial markets for English ships, manufactures, and services. Exports of miscellaneous manufactures, such as lightweight textiles, metal goods, and earthenware, far outpaced those of traditional woollens, and it was to the markets of West Africa, America, and the East that these products were chiefly attracted.[58]

England responded to the 17th century crisis by joining together the manpower of West Africa with the tropical climate and soil of the New World to supply exotics to expanding markets in Europe. Thus was constructed that close circle, 'sea-power, commerce, and colonies', which served to expand the Atlantic trading area, the matrix of future commercial and industrial developments as well as divisive political and racial movements.

---

58 Ralph Davis, 'English Foreign Trade, 1660–1700', *Econ. Hist. Rev.*, 2nd ser., vol. VII, no. 2 (Dec. 1954), pp. 150–66.

CHAPTER EIGHTEEN

The Drive to Monoculture, 1714-1755

> Sugar, sugar, is the incessant cry of luxury, and of debt. To increase the quantity of this commodity, gardens of half an acre have been grubbed up; and that little patch, which he had used to till for his own pease, or cassava, has the slave been made to dig for the reception of his master's sugar cane.[1]
>
> Rev. James Ramsay, 1784

1 INTRODUCTION

Amidst wars, politics, economic and demographic fluctuations, the emergence of specialist sugar colonies was the central theme in the economic history of the British Caribbean colonies in the period from the Peace of Utrecht to the outbreak of the Seven Years' War. From Barbados the drive to monoculture extended to the four Leeward Islands and Jamaica at a tempo and pace which varied from island to island.

Arnold Heeren, the German historian, observed that it was in the period from 1700 to 1740 that 'Colonial productions, especially those of the West Indies, met with a sale in Europe that exceeded all expectation'. He said that cultivation increased in an equal degree, and as West Indian commodities made up a considerable portion of general commerce, more than one state regarded their Caribbean possessions as 'the foundation of their commercial, and even of their political, greatness'. European politics was influenced by the growing importance of colonies. 'The mother states ... were willing to connive at the contraband trade which their colonies prosecuted with those of other powers, and necessity compelled them to allow greater liberties with respect to exportation'. Among the mother states, England began to take an 'elevated station' in colonial trade, but her leadership was challenged by the French nation which developed

---

[1] Rev. James Ramsay, *An Essay on the Treatment and Conversion of African Slaves in the British Sugar Colonies* (London, 1784), p. 80.

plantation colonies that outgrew their English counterparts during the second quarter of the century.[2]

Colonial trade was the principal dynamic element in English export trade during all the middle decades of the 18th century, according to Professor Ralph Davis. He has drawn on trade statistics to show that while English manufacturers failed to expand their European market significantly, rapid growth characterized exports to colonial markets. Supplementing the markets in North America and the West Indies were those of Scotland, Ireland, Asia, and Africa. The West African demand for English goods grew rapidly in the 1740s, 'providing a stimulus to the cotton industry in particular; a demand ultimately derived, of course, from the colonial import of slaves for the plantations'. Although the second quarter of the century saw the West Indies lag behind the North American colonies as export markets, the island colonies remained the single most important source of English imports to the end of the century. In the last five years of peace before the Seven Years' War, the three greatest sources of English imports were the West Indies, the East Indies, and the mainland colonies of America, in that order. Moreover, raw sugar was the commodity of greatest value in England's import trade.[3]

The Treaty of Utrecht ushered in a period of expansion in the sugar production of the Caribbean colonies. At the same time the colonies of Holland, Denmark, Great Britain, and France experienced divergent rates of growth. Expressed in thousands of cwt, sugar production in the Dutch colony of Surinam increased from an annual average of 156.6 in 1711–15, to 199.2 in 1726–30, and then declined irregularly to 168.6 in 1751–5. The other Dutch colonies of Essequibo, Demerara, and Berbice produced only about 25.0 in 1746–50, and 17.0 in 1751–5. British West India production, as measured by exports to the mother country, outpaced that of the Dutch; it increased from 484.3 in 1711–15 to 866.8 in 1726–30, declined to 790.1 in 1736–40, and rose to 962.2 in 1751–5. But far outpacing the British were the French West Indies. Incomplete statistics show that Martinique's sugar output increased from 115.4 in 1710 to 410.9 in 1753, Guadeloupe's from 124.6 in 1730 to 158.0 in 1767, and St Domingue's from 138.9 in 1714, to 848.0 in 1742, and to 1,252.8 in 1767. From an estimated total Caribbean produc-

---

2 A. H. L. Hereen, *A Manual of the History of the Political System of Europe and its Colonies* (London, 1873), p. 199.

3 Ralph Davis, 'English Foreign Trade, 1700–1774', *The Economic History Review*, 2nd ser., vol. XV, no. 2 (Dec. 1962), pp. 285–303; Elizabeth B. Schumpeter, *English Overseas Trade Statistics 1697–1808* (Oxford, 1906), pp. 17–18.

The Drive to Monoculture, 1714–1755

tion of 975,200 cwt in 1711–15, sugar output rose to 2,713,000 in 1751–5, or nearly 280 per cent. The increase was 25 per cent for the Dutch colonies, nearly 100 per cent for the British colonies, and approximately 365 per cent for the French colonies.[4]

London sugar prices described an irregular U-shaped curve in the period from Utrecht to the Seven Years' War. In 1714, the low quality muscovado sugar received by the Royal African Company in payment of slaves was sold in London at an average price of 35s 4d per cwt. Two years later the African Company's sugar had declined to 32s 0d. There is a gap in the London data from 1717 to 1720. From 1721 to 1758 we have annual average London prices of the King's muscovado sugar received in payment of the 4½ per cent duty. Prices declined sharply from 32s 0d in 1716 to 22s 0d in 1721, and then recovered to 28s 4d in 1724. From 1725 to 1729 prices ranged between 21s 6d and 24s 10¼d. Then came the serious drop to 16s 11¼d in 1733, the next to lowest price during the two centuries from 1686 to 1884. The price rose to 25s 8½d in 1734, fell back in 1735, and ranged from 19s 5½d to 24s 9d from 1735 to 1738. A somewhat higher plateau was reached during the war with Spain from 1739 to 1743. During the war with France (1744–8) prices shot up to a high of 42s 9½d in 1747, but declined to 31s 7¾d in 1748. Peacetime prices from 1749 to 1755 ranged from 27s 9½d to 38s 7¾d, or some 46 per cent above the average of the seventeen years prior to the War of Jenkins' Ear.[5]

Table 18.1 shows that of all sugar entering England and Wales from 1711 to 1755, not more than 4 per cent came from outside the six islands that comprise this study. Allowance should be made, however, for some foreign sugar which entered the mother country via the British colonies. Total imports into England and Wales nearly doubled during the forty-five-year period, despite the decline in the decade of the 1730s. Barbados fell below the average with an increase of 80 per cent, the four Leeward Islands taken together slightly exceeded the average with a rise of 113 per cent, and Jamaica outpaced her sister islands in the Lesser Antilles with a rise of 238 per cent. Quality improvement in all of the islands, and especially in Barbados where much sugar was clayed, give the figures in Table 18.1 a conservative bias after the decade of the 1720s.

Economic fluctuations during the period from Utrecht to the Seven Years' War may be conveniently considered under six heads.

---

4 Noel Deerr, *The History of Sugar* (London, 1949–50), vol. 1, pp. 112, 131, 203, 212, 235–6; Adam Anderson, *Historical and Chronological Deduction of the Origin of Commerce* (Dublin, 1790), vol. 3, p. 544.
5 See Appendix V.

Sugar and Slavery

Table 18.1
Sugar Imported into England and Wales, 1711–1755
(Annual averages in 000 cwt)

Years	Total	From Barbados	From Leeward Islands	From Jamaica	From other areas
1711–15	484.3	173.7	171.7	123.5	15.4
1716–20	652.9	202.5	251.9	188.5	10.0
1721–25	671.4	165.8	286.4	205.0	14.2
1726–30	866.8	197.8	386.9	272.6	9.5
1731–35	846.5	121.5	415.0	302.6	7.4
1736–40	790.1	125.7	339.9	320.3	4.2
1741–45	820.9	133.3	329.1	311.8	46.7
1746–50	857.3	130.8	352.3	349.5	24.7
1751–55	962.2	139.9	365.5	416.9	39.9

Source: P.R.O., London: Treas. 64/276B, 360, 361, 374; Elizabeth B. Schumpeter, *English Overseas Trade Statistics 1697–1808* (Oxford, 1960), pp. 52–5; Noel Deerr, *The History of Sugar* (London, 1949–50), vol. 1, pp. 193–8.

First came the turbulent aftermath of Queen Anne's War, when, despite widespread piracy and international conflict which culminated in the short war between England and Spain, the plantation economy expanded and yielded substantial profit. The second period comprised the decade of the 1720s, when the output increased at about the same rate as in the previous decade, although lagging behind that of the foreign sugar colonies. Third, the marked decline in sugar prices from 1729 to 1733 ushered in a decade of recession and retrenchment which saw the sugar planters take their grievances to the mother Parliament and secure legislation which antagonized their sister colonists in North America. Fourth, the Caribbean was the theatre of warfare from 1739 to 1748, at a time when the sugar industry was undergoing a secular upturn. This upturn continued into the fifth phase, the years of peace from 1749 to 1755, when the sugar planters were widely criticized for the monopoly profits they reputedly gained at the expense of English consumers. Finally, some of the consequences of monoculture and monopoly will be considered, and chiefly the migration of British planters to the foreign sugar colonies.

The Drive to Monoculture, 1714–1755

2 POSTWAR PROSPERITY, 1714–20

The period following Queen Anne's War was one of turbulence which masked substantial expansion and prosperity in the British sugar industry. From the standpoint of European politics, the turbulence stemmed from uncertainty and dissatisfaction with the peace settlement. Four of the powers – Britain, France, Holland, and the Holy Roman Empire – entered into a defensive alliance for the maintenance of the Treaty of Utrecht. But Spain was bent on upsetting the Utrecht settlement and refused to join the Quadruple Alliance. The upshot was the short war of 1717–20 which ended when Spain agreed to join the Alliance.[6]

The troubles in the West Indies antedated the outbreak of war and were, in part, independent of European politics. Prior to 1688, the European powers had adhered to a policy of 'no peace beyond the line', which meant that European peace was not jeopardized by hostile acts in regions beyond the limits of Europe. However, the West Indians gave little heed to subsequent treaties which said that 'the same relations of peace or war were to prevail both in Europe and the regions outside'.[7] After 1713, it was no easy matter to call in privateersmen and persuade them to take up peacetime trades. Rather, privateersmen of all nations turned to piracy and plundered merchant ships which came to the West Indies in growing numbers. Nearly akin to the pirates in the eyes of Englishmen were the Spanish *guarda costas* which preyed on shipping and at times raided plantations and carried off slaves.

Pirates and *guarda costas* attacked and plundered English shipping throughout the Caribbean, and especially the waters around Jamaica. Jamaica was within easy access of Spanish raiders from Cuba and of some 600 or 700 pirates who made Providence Island in the Bahamas a base from which to attack ships passing through the Straits of Florida. "Tis with great hazard that ships come to us, which has occasioned a great scarcity of all sorts of provisions', wrote the Governor of Jamaica in August 1717.[8] About a month later the Board of Trade received a list of thirty-seven British sloops and vessels taken by the Spaniards since the Peace of 1713 and carried into Spanish ports; they were valued at £76,143 10s 6d, including £600 for twenty-four Negroes taken from a plantation in Jamaica.[9]

6 G. C. Gibbs, 'Parliament and the Treaty of the Quadruple Alliance', in *William III and Louis XIV: Essays 1680–1720 by and for Mark A. Thomson*, ed. Ragnhild Hatton and J. S. Bromley (Toronto, 1968), pp. 287–305.
7 Arthur P. Newton, *The European Nations in the West Indies 1493–1688* (New York, 1967), pp. 335–6.
8 *Cal. S. P. Col. 1717–18*, p. xv.
9 Ibid., p. 26.

Sugar and Slavery

Many of the seafaring men of Port Royal and Kingston, Jamaica, became pirates when they lost their sloop trade to resident factors of the South Sea Company. These vagabonds invited the censure of a group of English merchants, who said that 'under the pretence of a report that there were pirates upon the coasts of America, they fitted out at Jamaica 14 sloops mann'd with about 3,000 men to clear those seas, but the remedy was worse than the disease'. Not only did they seize Spanish ships engaged in lawful trade, but they also went to 'fish upon the wrecks' of Spanish galleons in the Gulf of Florida without drawing any nice distinctions as to whether they had been abandoned by the Spaniards or not.[10]

The years of informal and formal warfare were marked by substantial expansion and prosperity in the sugar industry. Aggregate sugar exports of the six islands increased by over fifty per cent during the seven-year period 1714–20, as compared with the 1707–13 period. Barbados continued to be the leading sugar exporter to the mother country, followed by Jamaica, Antigua, St Kitts, Nevis, and Montserrat, in that order. Crop yields and exports varied widely in consequence of such vicissitudes as the weather, sickness, and interference with trade and shipping. For example, 1717, 1718, 1721, 1724 and 1726 were dry-weather years in most of the Leeward Islands, when it was said that plantations remitted only 20 or 40 hogsheads of sugar which in more favourable years had remitted 60, 80 or 100 hogsheads. In 1719, on the other hand, 'there was a better crop than has been since in most of the Leeward Islands'.[11]

The relationship between final product prices and input costs suggests that the plantations were generally prosperous. London sugar prices, though declining, probably remained high until 1719, when a contemporary said that they fell from the best to the lowest price since the Peace of Utrecht.[12] The cost of imported inputs, on the other hand, presents a mixed picture. While those from England and North America do not appear to have declined significantly, those from Africa declined markedly. Richard Harris, a leading slave merchant, wrote to the Board of Trade on 21 September 1719 that 'for some years past, and particularly the two or three last, Barbados hath been so over supplyed, and the price so low, that very great Numbers of Negros have been carryed from thence, both to

---

10 *Cal. S. P. Col. 1716–17*, pp. xlix, 81.
11 Rev. Robert Robertson, *A Detection of the State and Situation of the Present Sugar Planters* (London, 1732), pp. 42, 50.
12 Ibid., p. 42.

The Drive to Monoculture, 1714–1755

Martinico, Virginia and all the Leeward Islands'. Indeed, the average price of £12 sterling 'and near two years Credit' was slightly below the previously low slave prices of the early 1680s.[13]

Dear sugar and cheap slaves probably meant handsome profits for planters of means and ability. The historian of the Codrington plantations in Barbados has calculated a net profit of over £2,000 sterling in 1715, and concludes that 'profits like this were a product of a boom period in the Barbadian economy which extended from 1713 to 1719'.[14] The Bostonian, Dr William Douglass, visited Barbados in 1717 and found that after the first purchase, the charge of a sugar-plantation Negro was very small, not exceeding forty shillings per annum for food and clothing. 'The rum defrays the ordinary expense of the plantation', he declared.[15] Since sugar was generally produced in Barbados at a higher cost than in the other sugar islands, it is reasonable to suppose that the prosperity of the postwar years was widespread.

That a goodly portion of the profit was remitted to England was the opinion of Henry Martin, one of England's ablest economists. As Inspector General of the Exports and Imports, he discovered that a considerable but unknown value of the imports was purchased every year without any cost paid by England. This applied to the imports that came from many of the people in the plantations who sent annually to England on their own account great quantities of goods which were valued among the public imports.

> All that they send more than serves to pay the freight, the value of the necessaries they receive from hence [England, Ireland, Madeira, and Africa], must be allowed to be purchased by meer [sic.] foreign gains of the planters, and to be no cost at all to England. Almost every planter has a summe of money in the hands of his English correspondent; many of them have estates in the publick funds and lands purchased by them all over the kingdom; and how came they by this money and these estates?

He answered: 'England was at no charge in this matter. The imports that were converted into these estates were purchased every year by mere foreign gains of these planters, and doubtless the imports purchased every year by the mere foreign gains of these people are very great'.[16]

---

13 *Cal. S. P. Col. 1719–20*, pp. 223–4; K. G. Davies, *The Royal African Company* (London, 1960), Appendix III.
14 J. Harry Bennett, Jr, *Bondsmen and Bishops, Slavery and Apprenticeship on the Codrington Plantations of Barbados* (Berkeley and Los Angeles, 1958), p. 4.
15 William Douglass, M.D., *A Summary, Historical and Political, of the ... British Settlements in North America* (London, 1760), vol. 2, pp. 117, 133.
16 Quoted in G. N. Clark, *Guide to the English Commercial Statistics* (London, 1938), pp. 62–4, 90–1.

Sugar and Slavery

3 THE UNEVEN 'TWENTIES

Among the planters who had estates in the public funds and lands in England was Charles Long (1679–1723), grandfather of Edward Long, the historian of Jamaica. Charles was born in Jamaica, the son and heir of Samuel and Elizabeth Long. His first wife was Amy Lawes, and his second was Jane, widow of Sir James Modyford, Bart, and daughter and heiress of Sir William Beeston. As the possessor of a very great income from his Jamaican estates, Charles took up residence in England where he purchased Hurts Hall, Saxmunden, county Suffolk, and was elected Member of Parliament for Dunwich in 1716.

But all but a fraction of Long's great estate was lost in the years of the South Sea Bubble. One of the many companies floated in those years of wild speculation was the Company of Adventurers of all Mines of Gold and Silver in the Island of Jamaica, of which William Wood was Manager, and Charles Long, Treasurer. The historian wrote that his father Samuel Long was left to engage in a 'scene of litigation and distress', and was only able to save the properties he inherited in Jamaica by the good offices and financial support of his brother Beeston Long, the London sugar factor.[17]

Whether or not the collapse of the South Sea Bubble had any material effect on the expansion of the sugar industry is difficult to say. What is certain is that the decade of the 1720s saw the sugar output of the British colonies increase at about the same rate as in the previous decade, while it lagged behind that of the French and Dutch colonies. The slow rate of growth can be explained in terms of a combination of factors, of which special attention will be directed to British imperial policies which tended to favour intensive development of existing colonies in the Lesser Antilles over the extensive development of Jamaica, Anglo-French rivalry in the Caribbean, the failure of the Duke of Montagu's settlements in St Lucia and St Vincent, the concentration of British resources on clandestine trade with the Spanish colonies, and the undeclared war with Spain.

Efforts by the Jamaican government to attract settlers from the Eastern Caribbean were rebuffed by officials at home. After learning that a goodly number of Leeward Islanders had lately migrated to

---

17 *Records and Letters of the Family of the Longs of Longville, Jamaica, and Hampton Lodge, Surrey*, ed. Robert M. Howard (London, 1925), vol. 1, pp. 45–86, 109–10. Prominent among the West India merchants of London was Robert Chester, Director of the South Sea Company and owner of estates in Barbados and Antigua. His brother Edward Chester was the Royal African Company's factor in Antigua. See Vere L. Oliver, *The History of the Island of Antigua* (London, 1894–99), vol. 1, pp. 126–33, and John Carswell, *The South Sea Bubble* (London, 1960), pp. 111 sqq.

The Drive to Monoculture, 1714–1755

Jamaica, the Secretary of State, admonished the Governor of Jamaica not to 'give any countenance or encouragement to the inhabitants of the said Leeward Islands to desert those Colonies'.[18] Numerous poor whites had migrated to the Virgin Islands after being displaced by the sugar revolution in Barbados and the Leeward Islands. The Board of Trade recommended that these people be granted lands in St Kitts where they would be more useful and necessary than at Jamaica.[19]

Difficulties with France in the West Indies centred on the so-called Neutral Islands of St Lucia, St Vincent, and Dominica, to which both nations claimed title. These islands, which were inhabited by Carib Indians and escaped Negro slaves, had been prohibited to European settlers by the treaty of neutrality between Britain and France of 1686. Nevertheless, both nations attempted to plant settlements on the three Neutral Islands, as well as on Tobago which was not included in the treaty of neutrality. The French pushed the settlement of these islands more vigorously than the British until the period of the Seven Years' War. While one British settlement of some magnitude was attempted, its miscarriage probably influenced the imperial authorities to withdraw their support from further colonization schemes.

On 4 May 1722, letters patent were issued to John, Duke of Montagu, granting him the propriety and government of the islands of St Lucia and St Vincent. The Duke proposed to send over at least 500 white people to make a settlement on St Lucia within three years after the date of the grant, and to plant a settlement on St Vincent within the space of ten years. These proposals were included in the patent which also declared that no grants of land were to be made to planters who were already settled in the sugar colonies. Further, no restrictions on planting sugar-canes were inserted in the patent as had been recommended by the Board of Trade.

In the following December the expedition, consisting of two ships and a sloop, with 180 emigrants on board, and escorted by a warship reached St Lucia. However, protests were heard from the French minister at London before the expedition left the Thames, and when his protests were unavailing, the Governor of Martinique was directed to abort the settlement. Accordingly, fifteen sloops with some 1,500 men on board sailed from Martinique to St Lucia in January 1723. They landed and marched through the woods to the English settlement. The English had no choice but to capitulate, agreeing to

18 *Cal. S. P. Col. 1720–21*, p. 401.
19 Ibid., pp. 379–80.

Sugar and Slavery

abandon the island within seven days. The Duke of Montagu was left without any reward for his enterprise; indeed, he lost some £40,000 in the venture.[20]

The suppression of piracy removed one element of risk and uncertainty attending trade and shipping in Caribbean waters. Pirates were either apprehended and hanged or persuaded to engage in lawful activity. Among those hanged were such notorious leaders as Captain Finn, Bartholomew Roberts, Charles Vane, and John Rackham. Rackham and ten other pirates were hanged in Jamaica in November 1720. Also tried there were two spinsters of Providence Island who were proved to have taken an active part in piracy. Being 'quick with child', their sentences were suspended.[21]

But the suppression of piracy seems to have been counterbalanced by continued depredations by *guarda costas*. The Board of Trade received frequent letters from the colonies which complained of the Spaniards who 'let not one vessel escape them which they can make themselves masters of and have carryed them into Spanish ports where they have as constantly been condemned and they received all manner of protection from their Governours'.[22] The *guarda costas*, which were practically pirate craft in a very thin disguise, aroused the ire of the London merchants, whose petition of May 1726 lamented the many Englishmen who had been killed and wounded in defence of their vessels and goods. The damages sustained in this unlawful manner since the Peace of Utrecht were estimated by the merchants at above £300,000.[23]

From the standpoint of Spain, the toll exacted upon English shipping was small recompense for the colonial wealth that was lost to clandestine traders. Much light on the extent, nature, and consequences of the clandestine trade was revealed by two officials of the South Sea Company who sold themselves to the Spanish service in 1729. These informers submitted documents which showed that the Company had from its beginning carried on a large contraband trade, both in its permission-ships and the Negro packet-boats which operated chiefly from the ports of Port Royal and Kingston, Jamaica. Moreover, the Company permitted its employees to trade in their own interest in the Spanish American ports. Warships from the Jamaican station convoyed the vessels carrying contraband goods, and returned with the gold and silver remitted in payment of English

20 The most complete account of the Duke of Montagu's expedition is in Cecil Headlam's preface to *Cal. S. P. Col. 1722–23*, pp. xliii–xlv.
21 *Cal. S. P. Col. 1720–21*, pp. 334–5.
22 Ibid. *1722–23*, p. 107.
23 Ibid., *1726–27*, pp. 74–5.

The Drive to Monoculture, 1714–1755

wares and Negro slaves. In these and other ways the Spanish colonies were kept flooded with goods and legitimate traffic by way of the Spanish galleons suffered heavily.[24]

The conflict between Britain and Spain reached such a pitch that undeclared warfare had commenced by 1727. Spanish privateers seized British ships and cargoes, while the British Government retaliated by ordering Admiral Hosier to cruise off Cartagena and Porto Bello to prevent the Spanish galleons from sailing. For a time martial law was declared in Jamaica when it was rumoured that a Spanish fleet was bent on the conquest of that island. In November 1729 a definitive treaty of peace was signed by the representatives of Britain and Spain at Seville. Yet the peace with Spain was an exceedingly uneasy one, and it by no means ended hostilities in the Caribbean.[25]

The performance of the British sugar industry was no doubt adversely affected by the turbulent international situation. Nevertheless, the year-to-year fluctuations in output were most responsive to market and weather conditions. Muscovado sugar taken in payment of the 4½ per cent duty rose steadily in London from 22s per cwt in 1721 to 28s 4d in 1724, declined to 21s 6d in 1725, and rose to 26s 4d in 1726. After a gap in the data, the three years at the end of the decade saw a decline from 24s 10¼d in 1728 to 21s 8½d in 1730.[26]

Slave prices drifted upwards from the low level of the late 'teens, at a time when imports increased rapidly, especially into the islands where canes were spreading over virgin soils. Average prices received by the Royal African Company from 1723 to 1725 ranged between £16 and £17 sterling in Barbados, and £14 and £22 in Jamaica. In 1726, new slaves sold in the Leeward Islands at £18 sterling.[27] Governor Hart wrote from St Kitts in February 1727 of the 'prodigious' number of slaves imported into that island during the previous five years. He said that there was a full stop put to the trade with St Eustatius: 'For St Christophers has been fully supply'd with Negroes, by the British Traders, from Affrica for three Years past at a Cheaper rate than they can buy them from the Dutch'.[28]

Changes in the relative importance of the islands are revealed by sugar imports into England and Wales. Compared with the previous

---

24 Vera Lee Brown, 'The South Sea Company and Contraband Trade', *The American Historical Review*, vol. XXXI, no. 4 (July 1926), pp. 662–78.
25 *Cal. S. P. Col. 1730*, pp. v–x.
26 See Appendix V.
27 Public Record Office, London: Treasury 70/958–959; ibid., C.O. 152/16, S 27: Gov. Mathew to Board of Trade, 1 Nov. 1727.
28 Ibid., C.O. 152/14, ff. 322–6: Gov. Hart to Board of Trade, 15 Feb. 1726/7.

Sugar and Slavery

decade, the 1720s saw Barbados concede first place to Jamaica, while St Kitts gained on Antigua and moved ahead slightly in the 1726–30 period. Nevis and Montserrat continued to rank in fifth and sixth place, respectively.[29]

Hurricanes, drought, and sickness made for wide variation in sugar production. In the Leeward Islands four years of drought were followed by seasonable weather in 1723, when flourishing conditions were reportedly widespread. Governor Hart was credibly informed that the inhabitants of Nevis had more money in the merchants' hands in London, than any of the inhabitants of the other islands in his government.[30] Crops were short, however, in 1724, owing to the effects of several hurricanes in the previous fall. In 1725, Antigua was said to have lost one-sixth of her inhabitants by malignant fevers. Antiguans imported water at a cost of fifteen shillings a hogshead during the severe drought in 1726, but plentiful rains came later in the year to relieve their necessities. Famine was avoided in drought years only by ample supplies of provisions from North America.[31] Jamaica suffered from a devastating hurricane in 1722 and a less severe one in 1726, while Barbados was visited by unseasonable weather in 1722 and a severe epidemic in 1723. The decade ended on a brighter note, however, since all six islands had better than average crops from 1728 to 1730.[32]

4 RECESSION AND RECOVERY IN THE 'THIRTIES

The decade of the 1730s witnessed the expansion of Britain's trade with the Spanish colonies, at a time when the sugar industry met with adversities that were difficult to overcome. War came late in the decade, and for the most part conditions were favourable for trade and commerce. Piracy which had been so flagrant in the area a few years before had now been suppressed by the governments of Britain and France, but not by that of Spain. Even the Spanish *guarda costas* made fewer seizures than in previous years. Not until the year 1737 did Spanish attacks on British shipping reach alarming proportions.[33]

Trade between Great Britain and Spanish America was at its peak in the early 'thirties. It was chiefly an illicit trade, driven through

29 See Table 18.1.
30 P.R.O. London, C.O. 152/14, R 71: Gov. Hart to Board of Trade, 3 Dec. 1723.
31 *Cal. S. P. Col. 1724–25*, pp. 336–7; ibid. *1726–27*, p. 74.
32 Ibid., *1722–23*, pp. xliii, li–lii, 144–5, 188, 225; ibid., *1726–27*, p. 151.
33 Ibid. *1737*, pp. v–ix.

The Drive to Monoculture, 1714–1755

Jamaica and lesser British entrepôts, and conducted by a small group of South Sea Company officials who were determined to make fortunes for themselves rather than the Company's stockholders. The legal trade in slaves under the *Asiento* Treaty was used by Company officials and their agents as a screen behind which British manufactures were smuggled into the Spanish colonies. Annual slave re-exports from Jamaica, which had exceeded 4,000 in only two years prior to 1730, remained consistently above 5,000 from 1730 to 1733, and then declined during the remainder of the decade. The secret books of the Company directors indicate that over £1,000,000 sterling was obtained through illegal commerce in each of the years 1730 and 1731, around £750,000 in 1732, and over £500,000 annually from 1735 to 1739.[34]

The years of buoyant clandestine trade were also years of recession in the sugar industry. Internationally, it would appear that supply outpaced demand with a consequent decline in price. Forces operating on the demand side of the market are obscure, but it is possible that the agricultural depression in England, which was most acute in the early 1730s, led to diminished sugar consumption per head among agriculturists. On the other hand, good harvests and low prices reduced the cost of living of non-agriculturists, who, if fully employed at steady wages, had more disposable income for such convenience goods as tobacco and sugar.[35] The agricultural depression notwithstanding, the Board of Trade was of the opinion that 'The use of sugar in this Kingdom has augmented very much in the last thirty years, which is undoubtedly owing to the increased consumption of tea and coffee within that period'.[36]

Sugar consumption in England increased during the 'thirties, despite the decline in imports from the colonies. The reason for this was that re-exports declined by more than imports. Retained imports increased from nearly 75 per cent of total imports at the beginning of the century to 87.4 in 1731–5, and 91.1 in 1736–40.[37]

Demand failed to keep pace with the rise in retained imports, with a consequent decline in English sugar prices. London prices of the King's muscovado sugar declined steadily from 24s 10¼d per cwt in

---

34 Annual slave imports and re-exports are appended to a memorial from Stephen Fuller, Agent for Jamaica, to the Board of Trade, London, 1788, P.R.O., C.O. 137/38, Hh 3, 4. For the Spanish trade see George H. Nelson, 'Contraband Trade under the Asiento, 1730–1739', *Amer. Hist. Rev.*, vol. LI, no. 1 (Oct. 1945), pp. 55–67; and Richard Pares, *War and Trade in the West Indies 1739–1763* (Oxford, 1936), Chapters I and II.
35 G. E. Mingay, 'The Agricultural Depression, 1730–1750', *Econ. Hist. Rev.*, 2nd ser., vol. VIII, no. 3 (April 1956), pp. 334–8.
36 *Cal. S. P. Col. 1734–35*, p. 363.
37 See Table 2.1, p. 22.

Sugar and Slavery

1728 to 16s 11¼d in 1733, the lowest annual average of the century. After rising to 25s 8½d in 1734, the price fell back to 18s 9½d in 1735 and 19s 5½d in 1736. The level was subsequently higher, ranging between 21s and 26s from 1737 to 1739, and then shooting up after the declaration of war with Spain to 32s 0½d in 1740. Sugar prices declined in relation to those of English exports to the colonies. Thus, the terms of trade moved in favour of the mother country during the greater part of the decade of the 'thirties.[38]

Barbados, with its high-cost plantation economy, felt the recession most severely. Not only were profit margins squeezed or eliminated by declining sugar prices, but natural disasters took a heavy toll of life and property. On 13 August 1731, came a hurricane 'with the utmost fury, to the Inexpressible terror and immense damage of the Inhabitants'. It destroyed growing crops, windmills, houses, and other buildings at a time when the stock of lumber was not sufficient to repair a 'tenth part of the Buildings damaged by the Tempest'.[39] Two years later came a withering drought. Governor Lord Howe said that the Barbadians could not bear the cost of repairing the fortifications because of 'The Terrible Prospect of having no Crops this Year by the Excessive Drought, the Number of People continually running off and the Miserable Condition and Poverty of the Island in General...'.[40]

Barbadian sugar exports to England and Wales seem to have been influenced by these natural disasters. From the high point of 249,100 cwt in 1730, exports declined to 144,700 in 1731 and 101,600 in 1732. Then, after a rise to 168,200 in 1733, they fell in 1734 to 72,600. Exports ranged from 98,400 to 140,200 cwt during the remainder of the decade.[41]

Drought, excessive rain, crop disease, and a threatened slave revolt plagued the planters of Antigua, but in only one year of the decade was there near crop failure. Jonas Langford gave Abraham Redwood, an absentee proprietor in Rhode Island, a melancholy account of local conditions in March 1731, 'not haveing had one Rain to do us any service for these twelve months past; which has reduc'd your Crop to less than half what I expected, and am affraid will ruin the next years Crop entirely'.[42] By reason of the great want of rain, the

---

38 See Appendix V.
39 P.R.O. London, C.O. 5/4, f. 287: Representation of Barbados to Board of Trade, 27 Aug. 1731.
40 *Cal. S. P. Col. 1734–35*, p. 1.
41 Deerr, *History of Sugar*, vol. 1, p. 193. Tons are converted into hundredweights at a ratio of 1 to 20.
42 'Redwood Letters', in *Commerce of Rhode Island, 1726–1802* (Boston: Mass. Hist. Soc., 7th ser., vol. IX, 1914), vol. I, pp. 12–13.

The Drive to Monoculture, 1714–1755

crop in the spring of 1732 was described as poor. A year later, on the other hand, great rains fell in the harvest season so that the mills could not begin to grind until the month of March. Again, in December 1733, Redwood was informed that the crop was likely to be very backward by reason of the blast.[43] The threatened slave revolt and excessive drought reduced the crop of 1737 by more than two-thirds of the decade average. Not all crops were bad, however. Better than average crops were reported in 1733, 1735, 1736, 1738, and 1739.[44]

Jamaica's sugar exports continued to increase during the first half of the decade, but remained nearly steady during the second half. The island increased its lead over Barbados and drew near to the Leeward Islands in sugar exports to England and Wales. Above-average crops were reported in 1733, 1734, 1738, and 1739. Besides the troubles with the Maroons, a hurricane swept over more than half of the island in September 1734, and there was an 'exceeding great' mortality among the white inhabitants of Kingston in 1737.[45] The Council and Assembly of Jamaica blamed the island's plight on 'the lowness of our produce in Great Brittain, the loss of our trade and the heavy taxes we have been under the necessity of raising to defray the expence of the parties fitted out against the rebellious negroes'.[46]

Numerous smallholders went to the wall in these years of adversity, while small to middling planters found themselves in reduced circumstances. On the other hand, Rev. Robertson of Nevis wrote in 1732 that there were 'several great Estates in *Barbadoes*, three times more, as I apprehend, than in all our *Leeward Islands*, whose yearly Profits exceed their Expences by many Hundreds, or rather some Thousands of Pounds . . .'. That the rich Barbadians were exceptional is indicated by Robertson's assertion that 'a very great Majority, or the Bulk of our Sugar Planters every where are so far from being opulent, that not a few of them are considerably in Debt in England, or to the Traders on the several Islands'.[47]

Zeal to secure passage of the Molasses Act probably led planters to circulate exaggerated accounts of their distress and make it appear that the plight of the marginal planter was typical. One North American pamphleteer who accused the planters of such exaggeration wrote in 1732:

---

43 Ibid., pp. 35–6, 41.
44 Deerr, *History of Sugar*, vol. 1, p. 195.
45 Ibid., p. 198; *Cal. S. P. Col. 1734–35*, p. 190; ibid., *1737*, p. 285.
46 *Cal. S. P. Col. 1734–35*, p. 190.
47 Robertson, *Detection of Present Sugar Planters*, p. 15.

> Their Complaints do not arise from any real Distress, but merely because they don't find their Profits amount to such an extravagance as formerly; but they cannot be said to be brought to any exigence, if they should be reduced from exuberancy to some degree of moderation; and we cannot surely think such people to be in a very deplorable condition, who live like Lords, and ride in a Coach and Six.[48]

During the year 1734, when Jamaica's sugar exports reached the highest level of the decade, William Wood expressed doubts that the planters of that island were in the 'very sad circumstances' which they had represented.[49]

The recession adversely affected both the external and internal economic life of the colonies. Planters became incensed with North Americans and Irishmen who traded to the foreign sugar colonies. On the other hand, the North Americans called attention to the disparate growth rates of the temperate and tropical colonies in the British Empire and felt justified in expanding their trade wherever profits beckoned.[50]

Planters who were in desperate financial straits sometimes took the liberty of drawing bills on their London factors, only to find that their bills were returned under protest. The London firm of Rowland and Samuel Frye informed Abraham Redwood in July 1733 that they had been unable to pay all his drafts on them 'at a time when all the merchants refused to advance anything for their West India correspondents; sugars being then so low and the Islands in so declining a condition'.[51]

A notable internal effect of the recession was heightened racial imbalance and insecurity of life and property. Racial imbalance increased the slave's opportunity to escape or rebel, while the negative incentive to take such action was often the poor fare and harsh labour regime of the recession years. These factors go far to explain why the Jamaican Maroon War was waged with the greatest intensity during the middle years of the 1730s. 'The negroes in many of the British plantations have of late been possessed of a dangerous spirit of liberty', wrote Edward Trelawny to the Duke of Newcastle in June 1737. 'They have actually risen in Antigua and have threatened to do it in the rest of the sugar-plantations'.[52]

Planters and merchants responded to the recession and its consequences in various ways. Slave insurrection and absenteeism were met by military and police action which mirrored the planters' almost

48 Anon., *The Case of the British Northern Colonies* (London, 1732), p. 2.
49 *Cal. S. P. Col. 1734–35*, p. 312.
50 Ibid. *1731*, pp. 258–9.
51 'Redwood Letters', in *Commerce of Rhode Island*, pp. 38–9.
52 *Cal. S. P. Col. 1737*, pp. 191–2.

hysterical fear of general uprising. Proposals were made to correct the racial imbalance. The merchants of London, Bristol, and Liverpool who traded to the island of Jamaica submitted a three-point proposal to the King. First, they proposed that a law be passed whereby all persons should be divested of extensive tracts of uncultivated land, and that such lands be reassumed by the government; second, that recovered lands be granted to smallholders, and that money be appropriated to encourage and subsidize white immigration; and, third, that the deficiency laws requiring slaveholders to maintain a proportionate number of white servants be strengthened, and that the training and employment of Negro tradesmen be prohibited in order to encourage white tradesmen. Although several laws were enacted in accordance with these proposals, they accomplished very little owing to preoccupation with the Maroon War, the low state of the island's treasury, and the reluctance of great planters to surrender uncultivated lands.[53]

Generally speaking, planters lived more frugally and consumed fewer imported wares in recession years. Governor Mathew wrote from Antigua that the discouragements the planters had met with from the low price of sugars had effectually cured them of their former generous ways of living. Moreover, merchants no longer found it expedient to sell goods on long credits. 'These put together have out of Necessity to some, and Discretion to others, brought among us an Oeconomy that Calls for fewer Supplies from Home for our pleasures than heretofore'.[54] Imports of plantation inputs were reduced along with consumer goods. Antigua's slave imports, which amounted to 2,888 in 1729 and 2,228 in 1730, fell to 527 in 1733 and 'almost nothing' in 1734.[55]

So far the recession has been explained chiefly in terms of declining muscovado sugar prices. But the planter class was not committed to a single staple of uniform quality. The quality of sugar might be improved by the process called claying, and as claying yielded proportionately more molasses by-product, it might be feasible to distil more rum. The Jamaicans had improved the quality of their rum to such an extent by 1731 that 'they found it would better answer to send it to England'. The price of the spirit had risen so high that very little of it was reportedly taken from Jamaica by North American traders. Similarly, the Barbadians were said to have

---

53 Ibid. *1735–36*, pp. 92–3.
54 P.R.O. London, C.O. 152/20, V 46, f. 149: Gov. Mathew to Board of Trade, 31 Aug. and 14 Sept. 1734.
55 Ibid., f. 150.

improved their rum to a 'very great degree' within the space of a few years.[56]

Planters varied the proportions of their clayed and muscovado sugars to take advantage of relative price changes. Muscovado prices declined more sharply than those of clayed sugar in the years from 1730 to 1733; in fact, the gap increased from 10s 8d to 14s 2¼d per cwt.[57] From Antigua Josiah Martin wrote to his London factor in March 1732: 'As I understand claying my self and the prices of brown Sugars are so low in England, I intend to ship all clay'd Sugars...'. He estimated that he would gain £1,000 by improving the quality of his products.[58] On the other hand, after a relative decline in the price of clayed sugar, Dr Tullideph wrote in June 1739 that he did not intend to clay any sugars while the price of muscovado remained high.[59] These variations, of which numerous other examples might be cited, should be seen against a background of secular improvement in quality which was most pronounced in Barbados and the Leeward Islands. Moreover, much of the clayed sugar came to England disguised as muscovado to take advantage of the lower duty. English customs commissioners estimated that clayed sugar made up at least half of the sugar imported from Barbados in the years from 1734 to 1738, but that only a sixth part of the total was so reported by the local customs officials.[60]

Probably the most notable secondary effect of the recession was the spate of parliamentary legislation favouring interests connected with the sugar colonies. Not surprisingly, five of the six measures were passed in the years of economic distress, 1731–3. A measure of special interest to merchant-creditors in Great Britain was the Colonial Credit Act of 1732. Ireland was tied more closely to the British colonies by measures which closed that market to French sugar products and permitted direct imports of colonial rum and other unenumerated commodities. The consumption of rum and coffee in England was encouraged by acts which gave these commodities greater preferential duties over imports from foreign sources. The capstone of the legislation of the early 'thirties was the Molasses Act which was designed to aid one group of British colonies at the expense of another. After 1733 the only measure of

56 Anderson, *Origin of Commerce*, vol. 3, p. 17; *Cal. S. P. Col. 1733*, p. 202.
57 See Appendices V and VI.
58 *Martin L. B.*, vol. 8, Pt. 1, f. 65: Josiah Martin to Slingsby Bethell, Merchant in London, 16 March 1732.
59 *Tullideph L. B.*, vol. 1: Lre. to David Tullideph in England, 5 June 1739. For clayed sugar in the London market, see Richard Pares, 'The London Sugar Market, 1740–1769', *Econ. Hist. Rev.*, 2nd ser., vol. IX, no. 2 (Dec. 1956), pp. 259–60.
60 *Calendar of Treasury Books and Papers, 1742–45*, p. 270.

The Drive to Monoculture, 1714-1755

importance was the Act of 1739 which permitted direct exports of colonial sugar to ports in southern Europe. But by this time the protected market in the British Isles had recovered sufficiently to give it a marked preference for the leading staples of the British West Indies.[61]

5 WAR AND TRADE, 1739-48

The War of 1739 has been called the first 'trade war' in English history. Expeditions were launched not for territorial aggrandizement and colonization but to annex or control strategic Spanish-American ports and routes of trade. British warships protected and aided the lowly smugglers who plied between Jamaica and the Spanish Main. Warships and privateers harried the *guarda costas* and searched for galleons carrying precious cargoes. 'We are a trading people', affirmed one Englishman; 'we form no pretensions on their dominions; we do not affect conquests'.[62] The war took on different objectives and strategies and was waged with greater intensity when France joined Spain against Britain from 1744 to 1748. It was, in a sense, a rehearsal for that greater struggle, the Severn Years' War, which will be our concern in the following chapter.

The War of Jenkins' Ear followed upon the breakdown of negotiations over losses sustained by Britain and Spain in carrying out the *Asiento* Treaty. *Guarda costas* had renewed their preying upon the lawful as well as the illicit commerce of the British colonies. West India merchants took their grievances to King, Parliament, and Country. They were joined by Opposition members of Parliament who publicized the legend of Captain Jenkins, the English mariner who declared that the *guarda costas* had boarded his ship and cut off his ear. King Mob forced the hand of Walpole's Government which had sought a peaceful resolution of the controversy. 'It was a sudden and noisy explosion of imperialism', writes Richard Pares, 'a good example of the greedy turbulence which foreign observers attributed to the English nation'.[63]

Anglo-French rivalry in the Caribbean was an underlying motive for going to war. France had dynastic ties with Spain and was Britain's chief rival for the trade of Spanish America. One pamphleteer asserted that so long as the crowns of France, Spain, and the two Sicilys were united, British commerce would 'flourish more under a

---

61 See Chapter 4, pp. 68-71, and Chapter 13, pp. 288-90.
62 Anon., *A Proposal for Humbling Spain* (London, 1740), p. 44.
63 Pares, *War and Trade*, p. 68.

Sugar and Slavery

vigorous and well-managed naval war, than under any peace, which should allow an open intercourse with those two nations'.[64] Postlethwayt, the hack writer on commercial subjects, feared that a peace was far more dangerous than a war, since imperial tax incumbrances 'put it out of our power to support that commercial competition against France and others, that alone can save the nation'.[65] He apparently realized that the French Government subsidized her colonial development and trade. On the other hand, British planters and merchants incurred heavy administrative and defence charges which burdened their staple trades. Thus, production and trade were so circumstanced that colonial commodities could not compete with their subsidized French counterparts in European markets. 'Royal navies are kept by merchants, and must protect the merchants', asserted Lord Carteret, the British Secretary of State.[66]

British objectives in the war with Spain changed over time in response to pressure groups at home and the success or failure of the military forces abroad. In the early part of the war the main issue was between trade and colonization. William Wood was the ablest spokesman of one group of London and Bristol merchants. He wanted to expand the plantations beyond the existing boundaries of the colonies, grow sugar and other staples at low cost, and thus lower prices at home at the same time that European markets were regained and the temperate and tropical colonies of the Empire were brought into better balance. As expected, the independent merchants came into conflict with the West India interest. Although not opposed to all plans of conquest, planter influence was exerted to acquire territories that were not suited to sugar production.[67]

Since the political situation at home demanded large expeditions directed to important objects, and the West India interest influenced the councils determining war strategy, efforts were directed against centres of Spanish trade in the Indies. The first effort was a resounding success, for Admiral Vernon attacked Porto Bello on the Isthmus of Panama and demolished its fortifications. But subsequent expeditions directed at Cartagena, Havana, and other ports foundered on such rocks as the quarrels between commanders of ground and sea forces and tropical disease. Several thousand British troops fell victim to yellow fever and malaria in the unsuccessful effort to take Cartagena.[68]

64 Anon., *Common Sense*, 22 April 1738, quoted in Pares, *War and Trade*, p. 62.
65 Malachy Postlethwayt, *Great Britain's True System* (London, 1757), p. 270, quoted in ibid., p. 63.
66 *Parliamentary History*, vol. 10, p. 1409, quoted in ibid., p. 48.
67 Pares, *War and Trade*, pp. 78–85.
68 Ibid., see Index.

The Drive to Monoculture, 1714–1755

The failure of the great expeditionary force at Cartagena shifted the emphasis of British strategy to the interception of Spanish trade and protection of trade with the enemy. Richard Pares thinks that Spanish trade on the whole was lean prey, and that in spite of one or two extraordinarily rich captures, Britain's gains did not balance her losses before the last years of the war. Evidence in dispute of this view appears in a pamphlet which says that, between July 1739 and July 1741, Britain captured from Spain ships and cargoes to the value of £1,617,400, while her losses of ships and cargoes to Spain during the same period amounted to £612,000.[69] Whatever the merits of these arguments and statistics may be, it is certain that Spanish trade was fatally disorganized. Only one treasure fleet returned to Spain from the West Indies during the nine years of war, while the 'register ships' which supplanted the galleons and *flotas* were frequently taken by the British.[70]

Into the vacuum created by the interruption of Spanish trade moved British and Dutch smugglers who operated chiefly from islands in the Caribbean Sea. Small vessels plied between the British and Spanish colonies, carrying to the enemy slaves and manufactures which were not declared contraband, and returning with drugs, dye woods, and especially bullion. The British Government regarded the trade so highly that it ordered the navy to protect and convoy the smugglers.[71]

Smugglers and privateers reaped a rich harvest of precious metals from the Spanish Main. The firm of Lascelles and Maxwell reported the arrival in London in March 1743 of the Litchfield man-of-war from Jamaica with upwards of 400,000 pieces of eight, valued at nearly £100,000 sterling. Silver had fallen to 5s 2d an ounce on 23 November 1745, when two Spanish prizes of an estimated value of £1,200,000 were daily expected home.[72]

Quite different was the war between Britain and France in the West Indies, which broke out openly in 1744. Though both wars were fought for trade expansion, one was waged between complementary imperial economies which benefited from each other's goods and services; the other was a struggle between competitive empires which had linked tropical plantations to metropolises at advanced stages of mercantilist development. Following in the wake of the sugar recession, the war broke out at a time when both France

---

69 Ibid., pp. 10–11; Gerald B. Hertz, *British Imperialism in the Eighteenth Century* (London, 1908), p. 41.
70 Pares, *War and Trade*, pp. 109–18.
71 Ibid., pp. 119–26.
72 *Lascelles and Maxwell L. B.:* Lres. to Robert Watts and Mathew Miller.

Sugar and Slavery

and Britain were indifferent to the acquisition of sugar islands. Rather, each side hoped to destroy and depopulate the enemy's colonies and thus acquire monopoly power in European sugar markets. Military resources were limited, however, and it became evident that these resources could be employed more advantageously in a strategy of trade interception and defence than in one aimed at the destruction of the enemy's productive capacity.[73]

The sea power, organization, and strategy of the two powers differed in important respects. The French Government assigned fewer naval vessels to the colonial service than did the British Government. Moreover, the French fleets operated from home bases and sailed to the West Indies to take part in particular operations, while the British had permanent squadrons based at Jamaica and Antigua where the dockyards and stores facilitated refitting and victualling. Each system had its advantages and disadvantages, but the balance seems to have been favourable to British forces during the greater part of the war. The Royal Navy was better supplied with victuals and naval stores, better able to make repairs, less prone to mortality from tropical disease, and capable of operating for the greater part of the year and engaging in a wider variety of military duties. On the other hand, the French had more privateers operating from colonial ports which took a heavy toll of shipping, especially the North American provision vessels which generally sailed without convoy protection. In 1745–7, over 170 vessels bound to the Leeward Islands were said to have been taken.[74]

Probably the greatest discrepancy in the two systems was in the protection of trade between the mother countries and the colonies. The powerful West India interest used its influence to secure warships to escort convoys which sailed at fairly regular intervals to and from the British colonies. By contrast, the merchants in the major ports of France wrangled among themselves and frustrated the comprehensive convoy plan which had been designed by the Minister of Marine. The upshot was almost complete breakdown of the French system in the last year of the war; 'her navy was diminished by the loss of two squadrons, and her trade was disorganized and defenceless'.[75]

But not all of the war years were favourable to Great Britain and her colonies. French support of the Stuart pretender to the British throne and the threat of simultaneous invasions from Scotland and France in 1745 brought near panic to the West India interest. On 27

---

73 Pares, *War and Trade*, pp. 182–3.
74 Ibid., pp. 265–311.
75 Ibid., p. 392.

November, when the Scots had advanced into Lancashire, the firm of Lascelles and Maxwell informed a Barbadian correspondent:

> We are sorry to tell you, that the present Rebellion is a vast prejudice to trade, there is no Credit, and money can not be borrowed upon the best private security at 5 P Ct so that we are under the utmost difficulties to support our Credit. We had Bills upon us from Barbados for many thousands, and the fleet with Sugar, on the Credit whereof they were drawn, happened unlucky to put into and be long detained in Ireland, so we accepted and paid the bills before one ounce of sugar came to market.[76]

At the height of the invasion threats in late December, Henry Lascelles could not raise the sum of £3,000 'with all his Credit but at an immense discount. It is impossible to describe the calamities of these times'.[77]

Despite the crises and hardships, the British sugar colonies fared much better in wartime than their French rivals. British shipping was better protected and more regular, freight and insurance rates much lower, and supplies of slaves from Africa and provisions and lumber from North America more dependable. Richard Pares says that the effect of war upon the French West Indies was at once to increase the prices of imports and lower those of island produce. The terms of trade turned so severely against French planters that a pound of sugar or coffee would buy only a quarter, a sixth, or even an eighth of the European goods that it bought before the war.[78]

The British sugar market differed from the European sugar market in several ways. Prices fell less in peace because the market was protected and colonial production was little more than adequate to supply the demand. On the other hand, British sugar prices rose less in war 'because the sugar convoys were protected by the most powerful navy in the world, which was able to intercept the produce of the French colonies on its way to neutral countries'.[79]

London sugar prices rose and fell in both the Spanish and French wars but were generally higher in the latter war. The King's muscovado sugar from Barbados averaged 21s 7¾d per cwt in 1738. It rose to 25s 8¼d in 1739 and to 32s 0½d in 1740, and declined during the next three years to 27s 3½d in 1743. From 1744 to 1747 the price rose from 30s 7d to 42s 9½d, and then fell in the last year of the war to 31s 7¾d. Notwithstanding several natural disasters, the wartime

---

76 *Lascelles and Maxwell L. B.:* Lre. to Jacob Alleyne in Barbados.
77 Ibid., Lre. to Thomas Finlay in Barbados, 15 Jan. 1746.
78 Pares, *War and Trade*, pp. 265–74, 315, 322, 326–9.
79 Ibid., p. 482.

production of the British islands held up much better than that of the French islands.[80]

Richard Pares has calculated very roughly the cost of the War of 1744 to the planters of Barbados. Total costs, consisting of manufactures, slaves, provisions, lumber, freight, insurance, and taxes rose by 15s 9d sterling per cwt of muscovado sugar. Sugar prices, on the other hand, rose by 14s 0d sterling. Thus, it appears that the planters neither gained nor lost much by the war.[81]

But enterprising planters who combined trade and finance with sugar production found opportunities to make exceptional profits in wartime. One of these planter-merchants who benefited from the war was Dr Walter Tullideph of Antigua. From the port of St John's he carried on an active correspondence with merchants in North America and Great Britain. He was the factor of a group of Philadelphia merchants who consigned him a cargo of flour and made him their agent in the sale of prize goods taken by their privateers. On one occasion Tullideph purchased a part interest in a French prize.[82] On 11 June 1744 he ordered a quantity of medicines from London, explaining that he intended to sell them to the warships and privateers that called at Antigua.[83] Two years later he wrote to his brother in Scotland that, although he had lost by the enemy above £500 and had invested about £2,000 in a London cargo under the care of his nephew, he intended to bid for an estate adjoining his own. Negotiations for the purchase were completed by 15 August 1747, when he wrote that the estate would cost about £8,800 sterling.[84] During the last year of the war Tullideph instructed his London factor to lay out £1,288 of his money in Bank of England annuities. At the same time he asked if he could overdraw his account £1,000, to be replaced the following year, 'and I would be unwilling to dispose of what is laid out in the Bank Annuity's, intending that for the use of my Daughters till I can place more there'.[85]

---

80 See Appendix V; Deerr, *History of Sugar*, vol. 1, pp. 194–7; Pares, *War and Trade*, pp. 471, 473.
81 Pares, *War and Trade*, pp. 512–14.
82 *Tullideph L. B.*, vol. 2: Lres. to Messrs Allen and Turner in Philadelphia, 3 March 1744, and William Dunbar, Merchant in London, 11 June 1744.
83 Ibid., Lre. to Alexander Johnston in London, 11 June 1744.
84 Ibid., Lre. to Rev. Thomas Tullideph in Scotland, 29 Oct. 1746.
85 Ibid., Lre. to William Dunbar in London, 16 March 1748.

The Drive to Monoculture, 1714–1755

6 MONOCULTURE AND MONOPOLY, 1749–55

Sugar imported into the mother country from the six islands rose significantly in the last year of the war with France, declined almost steadily during the next five years, and rose to a hitherto unsurpassed level in two of the three years preceding the Seven Years' War. From an annual average of approximately 692,000 cwt in 1744–7, imports rose to nearly 968,000 in 1748, declined to 824,000 in 1752, and fluctuated between 835,000 and 1,041,000 from 1753 to 1755.[86] London prices of the King's muscovado sugars dropped from 42s 9½d in 1747 to 31s 7¾d in 1748, and continued downwards to 27s 9½d in 1750. Then after a rise to 38s 7¾d in 1753, they ranged from 33s 0d to 35s 8¾d in the three last years of the peace.[87]

Interwar quantity and price movements were observed by Dr Tullideph with keen interest. In November 1748 he informed his London factor that the fall of the sugar market would oblige him to alter his plans and induce him to remain in Antigua longer than he could wish. In April of the following year he wrote that 'our Island will make a midling Crope, St Kitts I hear 2/3rds only oweing to dry weather, we likewise hear Barbados hath failed'.[88] Severe dry weather in November and December and much rain and calm weather during harvest greatly injured the crop in 1750, when Tullideph estimated that the four Leeward Islands would fall short 20,000 hogsheads of what was made in a moderate good year.[89] Following another very poor crop in 1751, there was 'a most violent Hurricane, by which this Island in the Article of buildings hath lost £100,000, and in Canes double that Sum in my Mind'.[90] The three neighbouring islands and Jamaica also were damaged by the hurricane, Montserrat reportedly having only two windmills standing. In March 1752, Tullideph estimated that Antigua would not exceed more than 10,000 hogsheads of sugar; Montserrat, 2,000; Nevis and St Kitts less than usual. He was further informed that Barbados had failed, 'and if Jamaica should have suffered much in the Storm, I think there never was a fairer Chance for a good Price for our Sugars all this year, unless we are hurted by forreign Sugars being Imported into Ireland'.[91]

---

86 Deer, *History of Sugar*, vol. 1, pp. 193–9.
87 See Appendix V.
88 *Tullideph L. B.*, vol. 2: Lre. to William Dunbar in London, 23 Nov. 1748; Lre. to Thomas Martin, Merchant in London, 3 April 1749.
89 Ibid., Lre. to Gov. George Thomas, 20 Jan. 1750; Lre. to Thomas Martin, 20 March 1750.
90 Ibid., Lre. to Richard Oliver, Merchant in London, 23 Sept. 1751.
91 Ibid., Lre. to same, 4 March 1752.

The eight shilling rise in the price of muscovado sugar was a mixed blessing, for the benefits which it brought to the planters were probably offset by the adverse publicity circulated by aggrieved sugar refiners, grocers, and merchants. Instead of regarding high prices as a consequence of inclement weather and short crops, the critics focused attention on the planters' failure to expand output. In their petition to Parliament, the sugar refiners and grocers said that while Barbados and the Leeward Islands were fully cultivated, the fact was otherwise and confirmed to be so for Jamaica. They cited a report from the Board of Trade which stated

> that there are upwards of 1,600,000 Acres of Land in that Island; which remain uncultivated, though allowed to be fit for Cultivation; of these, upwards of 600,000 remain unappropriated, 1,500,000 have been granted to Patentees, of which only 500,000 are cultivated, and a Million remain uncultivated, which Million of Acres may belong principally to the Gentlemen who are Owners of the 500,000 which are cultivated, or by their Situation be extremely in the Power of those Gentlemen.[92]

It was not necessary to suppose private combinations, said the petitioners, but it was reasonable to suspect that the Jamaicans had been in some measure insincere in endeavours 'to increase the Number of white Inhabitants, and to enforce the Cultivation of Lands in the Manner which may conduce best to the Security and Defence of that Island . . .'.[93]

The West India interest, led by William Beckford, delayed debate on a bill to encourage the settlement and cultivation of Jamaica's idle land until the parliamentary session was finished. But the attack on the Jamaica planters did not cease. In 1754, there appeared a pamphlet which was written at the behest of independent merchants, traders, and liverymen of the City of London. After detailing the futile efforts of the planter-government to settle Jamaica, the petitioners urged that this matter 'be taken into consideration by the new parliament with a due spirit, to make that island of a more solid advantage to its mother-country than it has hitherto been, and to make it less burthensome, should we hereafter have the misfortune to enter upon a new war with any power whatsoever'.[94] Parliament, however, did not see fit to bring up the matter in the new session.

One of the refiners' grievances which merits brief consideration

---

[92] Anon., *An Account of the Late Application to Parliament, From the Sugar Refiners, Grocers, etc. of the Cities of London and Westminster, The Borough of Southwark, and of the City of Bristol* (London, 1753), p. 29.
[93] Ibid., pp. 32, 33.
[94] Anon., *A Short Account of the Interest and Conduct of the Jamaica Planters in an Address to the Merchants, Traders, and Liverymen of the City of London* (London, 1754), p. 16.

The Drive to Monoculture, 1714-1755

was that they and the public at large suffered from the marked differential in British and Continental sugar prices. The petitioners alleged that foreign markets were supplied with sugar from the French West Indies at less than half the price it was sold for in London, exclusive of all duties.[95] There is reason to doubt the truth of this allegation. French prices were not only depressed by a ring of buyers interested in refining, writes Noel Deerr, but there was also a technical explanation of the differential.

> Much of the French product was clayed sugar. The syrups and molasses draining from this were not wasted or distilled, but were reboiled into a low-grade sugar. French muscovadoes would, then, consist in part of an inferior material and in part of a superior product coming from those factories which did not make clayed sugar. The English muscovado would be wholly of the latter quality.[96]

Bryan Edwards also emphasized the complex relationship between quality and price differentials. Having adopted the practice of claying, most of the French planters were said to 'pay less attention to the manufacture of good *muscovado* than is given to it in our islands. This latter therefore, being generally of inferior quality, may be sold proportionably cheaper than ours; but when it is of equal goodness, the price also is equal, and sometimes higher'.[97]

Ironically, the real and alleged grievances of the processors and traders were in large measure being remedied by the West Indians at the height of the agitation. The year 1753 saw imports from the British sugar colonies increase by nearly 290,000 cwt, while the price of muscovado sugar fell by more than five shillings. Almost every inch of the Leeward Islands was cultivated in 1754, asserted Governor George Thomas.[98] Several years later Samuel Martin of Antigua observed: 'Our sugars are also much improved, by great improvements of our husbandry.... In short without vanity it may be said, that there is not a more industrious, nor improving people in the King's Dominions. Our chief misfortune is, that many of our principal inhabitants are Absent'.[99] Jamaican exports to England and Wales, which had exceeded 400,000 cwt in only one year prior to 1753, were consistently above that figure during the remaining years of the slave regime. Edward Long said that the expansion of plantations into outlying parishes of Jamaica began after the accom-

---

95 Sugar Refiners' Petition of 1753, pp. 4, 26–7.
96 Deerr, *History of Sugar*, vol. 2, pp. 529–31.
97 Bryan Edwards, *The History, Civil and Commercial, of the British Colonies in the West Indies* (Dublin, 1793), vol. 2, pp. 415–19.
98 P.R.O. London, C.O. 152/28, Bb 16: Gov. Thomas to Board of Trade, Antigua, 22 May 1754.
99 *Martin L. B.*, vol. 4, f. 26: Lre. to John Browning, Merchant in Bristol, 26 July 1757.

Sugar and Slavery

modation with the Maroon Negroes in 1739, and that the expansion was speeded by various acts of the island government.[100]

7 THE NEW INFORMAL EMPIRE

British penetration into the Caribbean colonies of rival European nations assumed two forms in the 18th century. First, there was the informal empire of trade, whereby slaves and British manufactures were either smuggled or, as in the case of the *Asiento,* traded legally for the bullion and tropical produce of the Spanish and other foreign colonies. Second, numerous inhabitants of the British sugar colonies migrated to foreign colonies and engaged in planting and trade. They formed such a numerous and influential group that certain colonies, although under a foreign flag, came to be dominated economically by the British inhabitants, who maintained close links with neighbouring British colonies and, either directly or indirectly, remitted a substantial part of their income to Great Britain. The informal empire of trade was thus expanded and strengthened by that of colonization and plantation development.

The new informal empire assumed importance in the second quarter of the 18th century, first with the migration of poor whites from the British colonies in the Lesser Antilles in the depression years of the 1730s, to whom were added a substantial number of middling and even a few great planters and merchants during the prosperous decades of the 1740s and 1750s. The chief cause of the migration was the spread of intensively cultivated sugar plantations which raised levels of productivity, land values, and living costs to such an extent that many smallholders and middling planters were unable or unwilling to remain behind. According to John Yeamans, Agent for Antigua, a planter needed 300 acres of land fit for canes or something near it to bear the great expense of the buildings and utensils necessary for making sugar. While he deplored the loss of white men, which weakened the military strength of the island, he called attention to the compensatory benefits that the near-monoculture regime brought to the great planters and the trade, navigation, and revenue of Great Britain.[101]

The Dutch colonies of Essequibo, Demerara, and Berbice on the mainland of South America attracted a considerable number of

---

100 Edward Long, *The History of Jamaica* (London, 1774), vol. 1, p. 429.
101 P.R.O. London, C.O. 152/20, V 29, f. 91: John Yeamans to Board of Trade, 27 May 1734.

The Drive to Monoculture, 1714–1755

British colonists. Berbice, on the river by the same name, enjoyed a period of prosperity in the mid-18th century before it was virtually destroyed by a series of calamities. In 1756, the white people were attacked by an 'epidemical disorder' which lasted seven years. Greatly reduced in numbers, the whites were unable to control the 2,600 Negro slaves who laboured on 100 or more plantations. The slave revolt which began on 21 February 1763, spread rapidly until the entire colony was at the mercy of the rebels under the command of a Negro, Coffey. Some 200 of the 350 whites lost their lives before the rebels surrendered to Dutch and British military forces in March 1763.[102]

The fluctuating fortunes of Essequibo and Demerara were recorded in vivid detail by Laurens Storm Van's Gravesande, Secretary and Bookkeeper to the Dutch West India Company from 1738 to 1772. After more than a century of settlement, Essequibo in 1762 had sixty-eight plantations belonging to private planters and employing 2,571 slaves, and three plantations belonging to the West India Company. Seven years later there were ninety-two plantations with 3,986 slaves. Much more rapid was the growth of Demerara, which was first organized as a colony in 1746. At the end of 1768 the colony had 'thirty-four plantations more than in 1767', and in 1769 there were 206 plantations with 5,967 slaves.[103]

British planters from Barbados and the Leeward Islands played a prominent role in the development of Essequibo and Demerara. In the former colony there were seven British plantations by 2 October 1744.[104] By 1760, Gravesande reported that the British settlers were in a majority in Demerara. Nine years later they owned fifty-six plantations and managed others for absentee Dutch proprietors. Such plantation names as 'Richmond', 'York', 'Irish Hope', 'Tweedside', 'Dundee', and 'Glasgow' suggest that all parts of the British Isles were represented. In the main, however, the planters came from Barbados, as did also the greater part of the slaves, manufactures, and provisions.[105]

Most prominent among the British planters were the two Gedney Clarkes. The elder Clarke was a customs collector and merchant-planter who came to Barbados from New England. Described as 'a

---

102 Radjnarain M. N. Panday, *Agriculture in Surinam 1650- 1950* (Amsterdam, 1959), pp. 27–30; Abbé Raynal, *A Philosophical and Political History of... the East and West Indies*, trans. J. O. Justamond (London, 1788), vol. 5, pp. 455–6.
103 Storm Van's Gravesande, *The Rise of British Guiana Compiled from his Despatches*, ed. C. A. Harris and J. A. J. De Villiers (London, 1911), vol. 1, pp. 312–14; vol. 2, pp. 399–400. I am indebted to Mr Richard Lobdell for bringing this source to my attention.
104 .Ibid., vol. 1, p. 211.
105 Ibid., vol. 2, pp. 379, 399, n. 1.

man of judgment and of large means', the elder Clarke had commenced, in 1752, 'the construction of a water-mill in Demerara, to be followed by two horsemills, it being his intention to establish three plantations there'. A decade later the father and son owned five plantations in the two colonies, and three other Clarkes were single plantation owners. One of the elder Clarke's plantations was said to have recouped the original investment of £12,000 sterling in a single year. When the Berbice rebellion threatened to engulf Demerara, the elder Clarke, in co-operation with the governor and military commander of Barbados, dispatched five vessels with some 200 British soldiers to save the Dutch colony. After the Berbice revolt Clarke became disenchanted with his eight plantation ventures in the Guianas. 'That gentleman is gradually getting rid of all his possessions, having now only two', wrote Gravesande on 21 February 1769. The two remaining properties had been sold by 15 May 1722.[106] Many of the planters stayed on, however, and lived to see the Union Jack fly over these colonies at the British conquest in 1796.[107]

Denmark was the fourth ranking North European power in the West Indies, holding the small islands of St John, St Thomas, and St Croix. St John and St Thomas each had sixty-nine plantations in 1773, with a combined population of 6,620 slaves and only 446 white men. The somewhat larger island of St Croix was purchased by the Danish West India Company from France in 1733. A period of remarkable growth set in after 1754, when the Danish government purchased the privileges and effects of the Company and opened the colonial trade to all Danish and certain foreign subjects. Between 1753 and 1773 the slave population of St Croix increased from 7,566 to 22,244, while the island's sugar exports rose from about 320 to 8,200 tons.[108]

Lacking experienced planters, Negro slaves, and capital, Denmark made her colonies attractive to European investors and the planters of neighbouring foreign islands. Dutch loans to planters in the Danish West Indies amounted to more than £1,000,000 sterling in 1773, while smaller amounts were claimed by Danes and Englishmen. After the demise of the West India Company Englishmen came to dominate the slave trade to the Danish colonies. Experienced planters came from neighbouring Dutch and French colonies, and

106 Ibid., vol. 1. pp. 286, 390; vol. 2, pp. 399, n. 1, 599, 661.
107 Rawle Farley, 'The Economic Circumstances of the British Annexation of British Guiana, 1795–1815', *Revista de Historia de America*, vol. V, no. 39 (1955), pp. 21–59.
108 Waldemar Westergaard, *The Danish West Indies Under Company Rule* (1671–1754), (New York, 1917), pp. 222–49; Raynal, *History of East and West Indies*, vol. 5, pp. 486–9; Deerr, *History of Sugar*, vol. 1, pp. 244–5.

The Drive to Monoculture, 1714–1755

especially from the British Leeward Islands. Already in 1741 there were said to be about 300 Englishmen in St Croix, 'who were none too amenable to Danish law or Company regulations'.[109]

Prominent among the British colonists of St Croix were Alexander Hamilton and Nicholas Tuite. While Hamilton's career is well documented, that of Tuite's is obscure. Tuite was born in Montserrat in 1705, where he and a majority of the colonists were of Irish extraction. Besides the ownership of a small plantation, he engaged in a variety of trades, including a sloop trade in slaves and Irish provisions to St Croix. By 1766, he owned seven plantations there in his own right, and was part owner of seven others. From St Croix he removed to London and became a West India merchant. Accompanied by John Baker, the barrister and absentee planter, Tuite visited Copenhagen in 1760, where he was granted an audience with the King and Queen and transacted business with the imperial ministers. He was made Chamberlain to the King of Denmark and 'acknowledged the founder of the colony, the sole source of its greatness and the finest character of the realm'. After his death in 1772, a London newspaper said that Tuite had encouraged 700 English families to purchase estates in St Croix. Tuite left £2,000 and £2,000 a year, to his wife; £21,000, and £500 a year, to two daughters; and the remainder of his estate to his son Robert. Nicholas Tuite Selby, a grandson, was a partner in a London banking firm.[110]

8 CONCLUSION

The forty odd years from Utrecht to the outbreak of the Seven Years' War was a period of plantation and trade expansion, of international rivalry, and of colonial policies that sought to preserve and strengthen formal empire ties, at the same time that efforts were made to expand trade with colonies outside the empire. Production of tropical staples, especially sugar, was heavily concentrated in the Caribbean islands. French colonial production outpaced that of the British colonies for a variety of reasons, not the least of which was encouragement and financial aid from the home government. The

---

109 Raynal, *History of East and West Indies*, vol. 5, p. 489; Westergaard, *Danish West Indies*, p. 222.
110 See the biographical sketch and other matters pertaining to Nicholas Tuite in *The Diary of John Baker*, ed. Philip C. Yorke (London, 1931). For Tuite's properties in St Croix, see Waldemar Westergaard, 'A St Croix Map of 1766: With a Note on its Significance in West Indian Plantation Economy', *The Journal of Negro History*, vol. XXIII, no. 2 (April 1938), pp. 216–28.

response to expanded production differed as between France and Britain. French production quickly outstripped consumer demand in the home market, so that more and more tropical produce was re-exported to foreign markets. On the other hand, British consumption tended to keep pace with colonial production, and may have overtaken it in the poor crop years of the early 1750s. British planters were obsessed with fear of over-production which had been a real threat during the years of low sugar prices in the 'thirties. They responded to the threat by seeking parliamentary assistance in curbing North American trade with the foreign colonies and by expanding the protected home market for their produce. To the conflict between the temperate and tropical colonies was added that between the Jamaicans and the sugar refiners of England.

The problem of Britain's Atlantic empire was that supplies of productive factors increased more rapidly than did the capacity of the Caribbean plantations to absorb them. Thus colonial markets outside the empire were sought for British manufactures, African slaves, and North American foodstuffs. Efforts to expand the informal empire of trade met with opposition from rival colonial powers. Spanish efforts to curb the Jamaica smuggling trade, which was much more extensive and profitable than legal trade under the *Asiento,* enflamed the London mob and Walpole's opposition in Parliament. During the war which followed British planters fared better than their French rivals. Following the war came a series of poor crops which delayed expansion of the British sugar industry. Meanwhile, the drive toward monoculture had restricted opportunities for smallholders and middling planters in the Lesser Antilles. The upshot was the creation of a new informal empire of colonization and plantation development for transplanted British colonials in the Dutch and Danish colonies. Despite conflicts and contradictions, the balance sheet of tropical empire was generally favourable to Great Britain in the four decades prior to the Seven Years' War. As Henry Martin expressed it, the 'meer foreign gains' of the colonials were substantial and at times very great.

CHAPTER NINETEEN

The Sugar Colonies and the Industrial Revolution, 1756-1775

> In a commercial country like England, every half century develops some new and vast source of public wealth, which brings into national notice a new and powerful class. A couple of centuries ago, a Turkey Merchant was the great creator of wealth; the West India planter followed him. In the middle of the last century appeared the Nabob. These characters in their zenith in turn merged in the land, and became English aristocrats.[1]
>
> Benjamin Disraeli, 1845

1 INTRODUCTION

Viewed from the standpoint of the British Empire, the expansion of production and trade in tropical and subtropical commodities reached a high point in the years from the outbreak of the Seven Years' War to the beginning of the American Revolution. Tea and spices from India and China; tobacco, rice, and indigo from the southern mainland colonies of North America; and sugar, rum, coffee, cotton, and dyewoods from the West Indies flowed into the mother country to raise standards of material welfare, pay for the reverse flow of British manufactures, employ ships and seamen, and finance the slave trade and the expansion of plantations and trading stations.

That the extra-European trade was mainly in tropical and subtropical wares and British manufactures is suggested by Table 19.1. Total African, Colonial, and Eastern trade amounted to little less than £11,000,000, of which only one and two-thirds millions was with the American colonies north of Maryland. The official value of imports from the British West Indies was 48.0 per cent of all imports from Africa, the Colonies, and East Indies. On the other hand, the West Indies accounted for nearly one-fourth of the English produce and manufactures exported to the African, Eastern, and Colonial

---

1 Benjamin Disraeli, *Sybil or The Two Nations* (1845) (New York, 1927), pp. 87–8.

Table 19.1

Official value of England's African, Eastern, and Colonial trades compared with her total trade, 1766–70
(Annual averages in £000)

	Imports	Exports*	Combined exports and imports
Africa	61	569	630
East Indies	1,854	1,100	2,954
North America	1,195	2,135	3,330
West Indies	2,870	1,174	4,044
Africa, East Indies and Colonies	5,980	4,978	10,958
Other areas	5,938	9,177	15,115
All areas	11,918	14,155	26,073

*Includes the re-exports of foreign and colonial goods

Source: Elizabeth B. Schumpeter, *English Overseas Trade Statistics 1697–1808* (Oxford, 1960), pp. 15–18.

markets. If the colonies of settlement are distinguished from the colonies of exploitation which extended from Tobago on the south to Maryland on the north, it is clear that the latter were the most important part of the British Empire. They produced the most valuable commodities, consumed more British manufactures and employed more shipping than the New England and Middle Atlantic colonies of North America.[2]

2 THE SEVEN YEARS' WAR

The Treaty of Aix-la-Chapelle, which ended the war in 1748, provided for no territorial change in the West Indies. The four

[2] James A. Williamson, *The Ocean in English History Being the Ford Lectures* (Oxford, 1941), pp. 181–6; Richard Pares, 'The Economic Factors in the History of the Empire', in *The Historian's Business and Other Essays*, ed. R. A. and Elisabeth Humphreys (Oxford, 1961), pp. 55–6.

The Sugar Colonies and the Industrial Revolution, 1756-1775

disputed islands of Dominica, St Lucia, St Vincent and Tobago were declared neutral. Although Britain and France agreed to evacuate these islands, little or nothing was done to remove the squatters who were mostly French. The peace settlement was, in effect, a truce which became increasingly difficult to preserve in the face of Anglo-French conflict in North America and the shifting alliances in Europe.

Though a strategy of commerce destruction was common to both wars, the Seven Years' War differed from its predecessor chiefly in the campaigns of territorial conquest in North America, the West Indies, West Africa, and the East Indies. William Pitt, the great War Minister, was cognizant of the failure of the sugar islands to expand in relation to the temperate-zone colonies and the home market. He sought to expand the tropical base of the Empire by means of conquest. Seeking an empire of trade for Great Britain, he realized that commercial supremacy in the West Indies should be the central object of Britain's colonial policy. 'Pitt had a vision of a stream of commerce flowing from the various ends of a vast empire', writes Dr Hotblack. 'Great Britain was to be the brains of this body politic, and the West Indies the heart through which the life-blood flowed'.[3]

The shift from commerce destruction to territorial conquest came in 1758, when Pitt was sure of Cape Breton and the entrance to the St Lawrence. After an unsuccessful attempt to take Martinique, naval and land forces were directed to Guadeloupe which capitulated to British arms in the spring of 1759. No major operations followed until the winter of 1761-2, when Martinique surrendered to British forces. Dominica was captured by a North American force in June 1761. After the fall of Martinique, the islands of St Lucia and St Vincent were taken, while Tobago needed no conquest since it was already a British satellite. The final and most bloody conquest came in August 1762, when Havana, 'the Gibraltar of the Caribbean', fell after a long siege with the loss of over 5,000 British and colonial troops from sickness and wounds. British victories extended to North America, the East Indies, and West Africa, where the French slave trading stations at Goree and Senegal were taken.[4] 'We had got possession of their four trades of the world', exclaimed Horace Walpole. 'Thus had we secured two of those trades, the fisheries and the sugar, all but at St Domingo. . . . Our conquests in Africa gave us

---

3 Kate Hotblack, *Chatham's Colonial Policy A Study in the Fiscal and Economic Implications of the Colonial Policy of the Elder Pitt* (London, 1917), pp. 54, 69-70.
4 Richard Pares, *War and Trade in the West Indies 1739-1763* (Oxford, 1936), see Index; Julian S. Corbett, *England in the Seven Years' War a Study in Combined Strategy* (London, 1907), see Index.

Table 19.2

Sugar imported into England and Wales, 1756–75
(Annual averages in 000 cwt)

Years	Total	From Barbados	From Leeward Islands	From Jamaica	From Ceded Islands	From other areas
1756–60	1,330.6	138.0	430.1	581.9	–	180.6
1761–65	1,450.7	181.4	404.2	620.3	67.7	177.1
1766–70	1,517.3	156.4	505.5	700.4	149.3	5.7
1771–75	1,765.1	112.5	433.4	879.9	289.1	50.2

Source: Elizabeth B. Schumpeter, *English Overseas Trade Statistics 1697–1808* (Oxford, 1960), pp. 52–5; Noel Deerr, *The History of Sugar* (London, 1949–50), vol. 1, pp. 193–8; Lowell J. Ragatz, *Statistics for the Study of British Caribbean Economic History* (London, 1927), p. 19.

the Slave Trade; and those in India the exclusive trade of the Indies'.[5]

Trade between the French sugar islands and the ports of the metropolis became so difficult in the face of British seapower that it was largely given over to neutrals, especially the Dutch. The slave trade of Nantes was almost destroyed, and the West India trade of Bordeaux suffered more disastrously than it had in the previous war. French planters and their slaves actually went hungry when neutral vessels were unwilling or unable to penetrate the British blockade.[6]

Once the foreign colonies were conquered, trade was diverted from the continent of Europe to the British Isles and North America. British planters who opposed the entry of produce from the conquered colonies on the same terms as colonial produce were overruled by the home authorities. In other words, foreign and colonial produce paid the same duties in British markets. After its conquest, Guadeloupe was opened to British traders who found a ready market for their goods and carried off the island's produce. Labourers were in such demand that the British reportedly supplied the inhabitants with 18,721 Negroes during the occupation.[7] Trade with Martinique and Havana, though of shorter duration, was also extensive. Havana

[5] Horace Walpole, *Memoirs of the Reign of King George the Third*, ed. Sir Denis Le Marchant, bart (London, 1845), vol. 1, pp. 227–8.
[6] Pares, *War and Trade*, pp. 293, 360–93, 454–7.
[7] Ibid., p. 482; G. T. F. Raynal, *A Philosphical and Political History of the ... East and West Indies*, trans. J. O. Justamond (London, 1783), vol. 4, p. 182.

The Sugar Colonies and the Industrial Revolution, 1756–1775

took off some 10,700 slaves in 1762 and 1763, and an unascertained number were brought to Martinique. Moreover, British manufactures and North American supplies were eagerly purchased. From 1759 to 1763, British exports to all the conquered islands amounted to £819,355 in official values, while the imports from these colonies were valued at £3,074,907. Besides the commodity imports, the Bank of England received £389,450 in bullion from Havana.[8]

Sugar imports from the conquered islands were of sufficient magnitude to affect prices in the British market. Some idea of the magnitude of these imports can be gathered from the column labelled 'From other areas' in Table 19.2.

Table 19.2 shows annual imports of 180,600 cwt of sugar from other areas (chiefly from the conquered colonies) in 1756–60, and 177,100 in 1761–5. Roughly one-eighth of total imports came from outside the six established colonies during the decade 1756–65. London muscovado sugar, which averaged 33s per cwt in the inter-war period, rose steadily from 34s 3¼d in 1756 to a wartime peak of 45s 9d in 1759. The price declined to 39s 7¾d in 1760, and to 36s 4d in 1761. It then rose to 40s 8d in 1762, and fell to 32s 6d in 1763. Guadeloupe sugar accounted for part of the decline of 9s 5d from 1759 to 1761. Yet there were other factors which affected the market during these war years. These included the poor crops in Barbados and the Leeward Islands in 1759; the additional duty of 1s 6d per cwt of sugar in the same year; and the prohibition of the corn distillery in England from 1757 to 1760. Since repeal of the prohibition of the corn distillery coincided with the influx of non-British sugar, part of the price decline must be attributed to the former action.[9]

Helping to swell the trade with the conquered colonies were such commodities as molasses, rum, coffee, cotton, cacao, and ginger. By official value, these colonies accounted for roughly one-third of all English imports from the West Indies in 1762–3, and they took off about one-fifth of all exports to the West Indies.[10]

Nearly as important as the produce from the conquered colonies were the enemy ships and cargoes taken by British privateers and men-of-war. By official value, imports of prize goods rose from £211,266 in 1756 to £1,052,523 in 1757, and then declined to £160,517 in 1763. The wartime annual average was £438,794. Prize

---

8 Noel Deerr, *The History of Sugar* (London, 1949–50), vol. 1, p. 129; Sir Charles Whitworth, *State of the Trade of Great Britain in its imports and exports, progressively from the year 1697–1773* (London, 1776), pp. 83–9. See Appendix XI for bullion imports.
9 Pares, *War and Trade*, pp. 476–7, 481–6, 510–12.
10 Whitworth, *State of the Trade*, pp. 48–89.

Sugar and Slavery

goods, which came chiefly from the Caribbean area, were allowed to pass through England free of duty, but obliged to pay the duty on foreign produce if sold in England.[11]

Further wartime windfalls took the form of booty. The actual booty taken at Havana was enormous. It consisted of nine Spanish ships of the line, six royal frigates and despatch vessels, nearly a hundred merchantmen, quantities of warlike stores and merchandise, and nearly three-quarters of a million in prize money which was divided equally between the navy and army, with the officers getting the lion's share.[12]

The balance sheet of the Seven Years' War appears to have had many more credits than debits. Arthur Young exclaimed that commerce was carried to an 'amazing and unnatural height . . . being literally erected on the ruins of half our neighbours!' Wartime expenditure by the British Government purchased commerce and conquest, wrote Edmund Burke, while that of the enemy acquired nothing but defeat and bankruptcy.[13]

Rather than retarding economic growth, Professor John finds much evidence that the wars from 1700 to 1763 exerted a beneficial influence on the development of the English economy. While he disclaims any intention of favouring war as a generally beneficial factor in economic growth, he maintains that the wars of this period exhibited 'many common characteristics and consequences from the economic point of view'.[14] Among other things, the wars brought increased demands on the heavy metal industries, shipbuilding, and other capital goods industries; the output of consumer-goods industries increased; levels of employment and earnings were high; and overseas trade generally grew in wartime.[15]

3 THE CEDED ISLANDS

Beginning in 1760, numerous pamphlets were published on the question of whether to keep Canada or Guadeloupe at the peace, should a choice be found necessary. These pamphlets reveal current thought on the structure and performance of the Empire and were

11 Whitworth, *State of the Trade*, p. 81; Pares, *War and Trade*, pp. 477–80.
12 Corbett, *England in Seven Years' War*, vol. 2. pp. 282–3, 321, 354, 369.
13 Arthur Young, *Political Arithmetic* (London, 1774), p. 87; Edmund Burke, *The Present State of the Nation* (1769), in *The Works of Edmund Burke*, ed. E. B. Willis (London, 1925), vol. 1, pp. 242, 246.
14 A. H. John, 'War and the English Economy, 1700–1763', *The Economic History Review*, 2nd ser., vol. VII, no 3 (April 1955), p. 344.
15 Ibid., pp. 329–44; Charles Wilson, *England's Apprenticeship 1603–1763* (London, 1965), pp. 276–87.

The Sugar Colonies and the Industrial Revolution, 1756–1775

intended to influence the shaping of the peace. Pamphleteers who urged the retention of Canada and the return of Guadeloupe maintained that the British sugar colonies were capable of supplying imperial markets by means of internal expansion; that Canada might be improved to a variety of uses; and that the northern colonies, being healthier, were more suited to the development of the white race.[16]

Those on the other side of the debate marshalled a larger battery of arguments. Insisting that the British Empire in North America would be enlarged at the peace even if Canada was not retained, they said that Guadeloupe was necessary to achieve a balanced and self-contained empire. With Guadeloupe added, the North Americans would no longer need to trade with the foreign sugar colonies, they would be less prone to take up manufacturing in rivalry with the mother country, and they would be more likely to continue as loyal subjects of the Crown. Moreover, the taking of Guadeloupe would weaken France's hold on the sugar trade. 'It is our sugar islands that raise the value of North America, and pours in such wealth upon the *mother-country*', wrote William Burke, a kinsman of the great Edmund. 'The more we have of those islands, America becomes from that cause the more important and valuable, and England the richer'. He argued that the nearer the temperate and tropical colonies were proportioned to one another the better off both would be, and the more England would benefit from their trade and wealth.[17]

That the British sugar planters should have favoured Canada over Guadeloupe might seem obvious from the standpoint of economic gain. Although William Beckford and Rose Fuller, the two most important absentees in British politics, favoured such a move, there are grounds for believing that the West India interest as a whole was converted to the annexation of certain new sugar colonies. One reason for so believing is that the planters of Barbados and the Leeward Islands made sizeable contributions of men and materials to the conquests of Guadeloupe and Martinique, and another is that leaders in the colonies spoke up for annexation. Samuel Martin, for example, wrote to his son, the member of Parliament, on 12 February 1762, that 'if our Sugar Colonies are not extended in proportion to our African trade, and the extension of our N. American settlements, the french Colonies will have all ye benefit of

---

16 William L. Grant, 'Canada versus Guadeloupe, An Episode of the Seven Years' War', *The American Historical Review*, vol. XVII, no. 4 (July 1912), pp. 735–43.
17 William Burke, 'A Letter from a Gentleman in Guadeloupe to his Friend in London (London, 1760)', quoted in Frank W. Pitman, *The Development of the British West Indies 1700–1763* (New Haven, 1917), pp. 346–7, n. 34.

Sugar and Slavery

that extension, as it has now, in time of war, the principal benefit of our N. American trade at Hispaniola'.[18] Professor Pares believed that the experience of two wars convinced the planters 'that Martinique and Guadeloupe were too dangerous neighbours, and that rival producers within the Empire were less damaging than the Martinique privateers'.[19]

The pamphlet war does not seem to have had much influence on the British ministers who negotiated the peace with France. By the Treaty of Paris, Great Britain retained Canada, Louisiana, and Florida on the American continent; the Grenadine's, Tobago, St Vincent, and Dominica in the West Indies; and Senegal in Africa. France received the islands of Martinique, Guadeloupe, and St Lucia in the West Indies, and the trading post at Goree in West Africa, while Spain recovered Havana. Without regard to other interests, such as Crown revenues and protection costs, here was a wide field opened for British capital and enterprise.[20]

The islands acquired at the Peace of 1763 were known collectively as the Ceded Islands. The southernmost island in the group is Tobago with an area of 116 square miles. It is separated by a sea passage of only twenty miles from the north-east tip of Trinidad, and is 140 miles south of Barbados. Grenada, which has an area of 120 square miles, lies 180 miles to the south-west of Barbados. Attached to the government of Grenada were more than a hundred small islands called the Grenadines. St Vincent is 120 miles west of Barbados and has an area of 133 square miles. Further north is Dominica with an area of 305 square miles. It is separated by some thirty miles from Guadeloupe on the north and Martinique on the south, and is 180 miles north-west of Barbados. The total area of the Ceded Islands is 674 square miles, while that of Barbados and the Leeward Islands taken together is 410 square miles.[21]

The task of publicizing the Ceded Islands fell to John Campbell, a Scottish lawyer of wide interests and considerable capacity who was a friend of Lord Bute. His books emphasized the advantages of the new islands to the Empire and were written to attract settlers and capitalists who would exploit these advantages.[22] Campbell repeated

18 *Martin L. B.*, vol. 2, f. 122: Samuel Martin to Samuel Martin, Jr, M.P., 12 Feb. 1762.
19 Pares, *War and Trade*, pp. 216–23.
20 Ibid., pp. 223–6.
21 John Macpherson, *Caribbean Lands a geography of the West Indies* (London, 1963), pp. 66–9, 80–9, 93–8.
22 John Campbell, *Description and History of the new sugar islands in the West Indies* (London, 1762); —— , *Candid and impartial considerations on the nature of the sugar trade, the comparative importance of the French islands in the West Indies: with the value and consequence of St Lucia and Grenada truly stated* (London, 1763). For a biography of the author, see D. N. B., vol. 3, pp. 825–7.

The Sugar Colonies and the Industrial Revolution, 1756–1775

the arguments that had been used in the Guadeloupe versus Canada debate and added to them much historical and descriptive material. He was particularly concerned to disarm the critics who said that the smallness of the islands made them economically inconsiderable and insignificant. The competent and candid judge, he said, would find that the soils in these small islands were more fertile, more capable of being manured, and in many respects more easily cultivated than those of the larger islands. The new islands were capable of being 'more easily, more speedily, and more compleatly settled, than if their extent was larger'.[23] In addition to sugar, the cultivation of coffee, cacao, cotton, nutmegs, black pepper and the like would diversify the resources of the Empire and make Britain less dependent on foreign supplies. All these and other advantages might be secured without unduly burdening the mother country for manpower, capital, and military protection.[24]

Other writers were less optimistic concerning the prospects of the new islands. One of these was the proprietor of a large estate in Antigua. Though the new islands possessed numerous advantages over the old, he said, intending settlers should be warned of the difficulties they faced. These included the sickliness and mortality of the country, the wants of comfort and a tolerable society, and the opportunities for slaves to escape. More than offsetting the low land cost would be the costs incurred in acquiring and maintaining a labour force, clearing woodlands, building sugar works, and forgoing income. He predicted that of those who adventured, 'many will fail before the enjoyment; and to the happy few, that providentially succeed, may peace and plenty without envy be their lot, and crown them with felicity'.[25] On the other hand, the profits would be greater, 'the crops more abundant, regular, and adequate to the expectations of the planters'. The new islands would be settled chiefly by persons already in the West Indies, he said, and the sugar plantations would be established by persons of wealth and enterprising dispositions.[26]

One of the West Indians who took a keen interest in the new islands was Samuel Martin, the Antigua planter. In the spring of 1765, he wrote of his intention to visit Dominica and St Vincent and purchase lands in one of these islands. Upon his return, he recounted his experiences and impressions in letters to his eldest son. Dominica

23 Campbell, *Candid and impartial considerations*, p. 212.
24 Ibid., pp. 130–50, 204–28.
25 Anon., *Some Observations; Which May Contribute to Afford a Just Idea of the Nature, Importance, and Settlement of Our New West-India Colonies* (London, 1764), pp. 11–12.
26 Ibid., pp. 10–37.

had but indifferent soil and the face of the country was very rough and mountainous. He was deterred from purchasing there chiefly because he feared French invaders from neighbouring islands in case of war. St Vincent was said to be even more mountainous and rugged than Dominica. Some 3,000 Frenchmen had been driven off by Englishmen who coveted their best settlements, but there remained about 2,500 Black Caribs who possessed one-third or more of the richest and most cultivable land. Though much of the soil was very good, Martin declined to purchase in St Vincent because he feared that neither life nor property would be safe in the presence of the Indians and Black Caribs, who were descended from shipwrecked slaves and indigenous Caribs.[27]

Martin turned next to Tobago. This island in his estimation had good soil, was free of dangerous neighbours, and was in a latitude where there were no hurricanes. He resolved to purchase 500 acres there for about 21 or 22 shillings per acre, payable in instalments over a four-year period. After arranging for an 'honest friend' to select and make the down payment on the land, Martin made a voyage to Tobago with seventy-three Negroes and a Scottish manager who was also a doctor. Returning to Antigua, he wrote of his great disappointment, having found that the land selected for him was 'an aggregate of ridges and steep gullies, two miles within land, over a steep ridge, never to be made cartable, and consequently never capable of being made a Sugar plantation...'. He forthwith gave instructions to sell his land.[28]

Martin was apparently more cautious than most other planters. At the time of his first voyage he said that many people had been authorized from England, some from St Croix, and many who had money or credit in Antigua were resolved to purchase at the first sale in St Vincent.[29] Scotsmen in the West Indies and homeland seem to have formed a vanguard of purchasers. Readers of *The Scots Magazine* kept abreast of the plantation frontier. 'Near thirty vessels arrived with purchasers from the Leeward Islands', wrote a correspondent from St Vincent on 6 June 1765. Lands had sold at a much higher rate than expected; in fact, cleared lands sold from about £15 to £45 sterling per acre, and uncleared about one-fifth as much. Several months later a correspondent in Dominica reported: 'The sales here are just ended. The cleared lands in general sold for about 8 *l.* or 10 *l.* Sterling per acre; the highest lot was 45 *l.* Sterling

27 *Martin L. B.*, vol. 2, ff. 197, 201–2, 205–6: Samuel Martin to Samuel Martin, Jr, M.P., 30 March, 11 June and 5 Aug. 1765.
28 Ibid., ff. 220–2, 228, 253, 255–6: 13 April, 25 June and 9 Dec. 1766, and ? Jan. 1767.
29 Ibid., f. 199: 11 May 1765.

per acre'. Many Antiguans had become tired of 'dry-weather estates' by 1771, and had purchased in the new islands.[30]

Ceded Island lands yielded substantial revenue to the Crown. A total of 20,538 acres were disposed of by Crown auction in St Vincent for the sum of £162,854, and an additional 24,000 acres were granted to two individuals. About half of the island of Dominica, or 96,344 acres were disposed of by the Crown for £312,092.[31] Grenada had 72,141 acres in cultivation in 1776, of which the greater part had been purchased from former French proprietors. Sales in Tobago between 1765 and 1771 amounted to 57,408 acres which sold from £1 to nearly £6 per acre. One of the largest proprietors in the Ceded Islands was Gedney Clarke, Jr, who transferred his operations from the Dutch colonies of Essequibo and Demerara to Tobago, where he held 2,192 acres, as a single proprietor or partner.[32]

The Ceded Islands provided a field of activity for white capitalists and coloured labour, added to the plantation base of the Empire, and yielded a variety of staples which augmented trade and shipping. The timing and pace of these and other developments varied from island to island.

Tobago, the southernmost island, developed more slowly than its sister islands. In 1770, the island had 238 whites, 3,164 slaves, 5,084 acres cleared, and 78 plantations. The next five years saw substantial growth, for in 1775 there were 391 whites, 8,643 slaves, and upwards of 100 plantations, of which those making sugar had 23 windmills, 9 water-mills, and 52 cattle-mills. Sugar was first produced by Gedney Clarke, Jr in 1769. From 1771 to 1775 the number of hogsheads increased from 965 to 4,550, and the puncheons of rum from 411 to 3,247. Minor staples, though of limited importance, included cloves, nutmegs, and cinnamon which excited mercantile writers with the prospect of an industry rivalling that of the Dutch East Indies.[33]

Dominica ranked third among the Ceded Islands in native produce. Extant statistics show that from 1763 to 1773 the whites increased

---

30 *The Scots Magazine*, vol. XXVII (Aug. 1765), pp. 441–2; (Oct. 1765), p. 553; XXXI (April 1769), p. 215; XXXIII (June 1771), p. 317.
31 Bryan Edwards, *The History, Civil and Commercial, of the British Colonies in the West Indies* (Dublin, 1793), vol. 1, pp. 386, 392–3.
32 Daniel Paterson, *A Topographical Description of the Island of Grenada* (London, 1780), p. 13; John Fowler, *A Summary Account of the Present Flourishing State of the Respectable Colony of Tobago in the British West Indies* (London, 1774), pp. 27–30, 64.
33 Public Record Office, London, C.O. 101/14: Statistical table for 1770; C.O. 101/18: Statistical table for 1775; C.O. 285/13: Gov. Sir William Young's Report, 1775; Fowler, *Present State of Tobago*, pp. 25–30, 32–47; David MacPherson, *Annals of Commerce* (Edinburgh, 1805), vol. 3, p. 514.

from 1,718 to 3,850 and the blacks from 5,872 to 18,753, although it may be surmised that the 1773 returns were overstated. Native produce exported to Great Britain in 1770 consisted of 10,380 cwt of coffee, 285 hogsheads of cacao, 307 hogsheads of sugar, and 13 hogsheads of rum, amounting in the aggregate to £46,365 sterling in local prices.[34]

St Vincent not only became a sugar colony of some importance, but also produced quantities of coffee, cacao, and cotton. From the scattered population returns we learn that the whites increased from 695 in 1763 to 1,450 in 1787, while in the same period the blacks increased from 3,430 to 11,853. Exports in 1770 consisted of 4,818 cwt of coffee, 1,000 hogsheads of cacao, 285 bags of cotton, 2,866 hogsheads of sugar, and 346 hogsheads of rum, valued together at £97,126 sterling in local prices. The census of 1779 enumerated 61 sugar plantations, at which time there were 500 acres in coffee, 500 in tobacco, 400 in cotton, 200 in cacao, and 50 in indigo.[35]

Racial conflict disturbed St Vincent in the early 1770s. The Black Caribs who became increasingly restive as settlers encroached on their lands retaliated by committing numerous depredations on the new plantations. Two regiments from North America joined two others in the West Indies to subdue the blacks. By the treaty of 1773, the Caribs recognized British control of the island and accepted a block of land for their exclusive use. One writer referred to the conflict as a 'petty sanguinary war ... which was terminated by an insincere peace in February 1773'.[36]

Grenada was by far the most productive of the new islands. Before 1763 considerable progress in plantation development had been accomplished by the French inhabitants and their slaves. On this base the British erected an island economy which stood second only to that of Jamaica in the British Caribbean and rivalled that of Guadeloupe. In 1772, the island contained 334 plantations which were worked by 26,211 blacks. Sugar estates occupied 32,011 acres; coffee, 12,796; indigo, 742; and cacao, 712. There were 95 water-mills, 18 cattle-mills, and 12 windmills. 'This Island is full of 'large Mountains, forming several fertile Vallies, and producing a great Number of fine Rivulets, which facilitate the Construction of Water Mills for the use of the Sugar Plantations', wrote a contemporary

34 Deerr, *History of Sugar,* vol. 2, p. 279; John Campbell, *A Political Survey of Britain* (London, 1774), vol. 2, p. 684; John Byers (Chief Surveyor), *References to the Plan of the Island of Dominica As Surveyed from the Years 1765 to 1773* (London, 1777).
35 Deerr, *History of Sugar,* vol. 2, p. 279; Campbell, *Political Survey of Britain,* vol. 2, p. 682; MacPherson, *Annals of Commerce,* vol. 3, p. 639.
36 *The Parliamentary History of England* (London, 1813), vol. 17, pp. 625–43; MacPherson, *Annals of Commerce,* vol. 3, p. 639.

The Sugar Colonies and the Industrial Revolution, 1756–1775

inhabitant of Grenada.[37] Taxes were paid on 72,141 acres in 1776. Of the 30,021 slaves in that year, 18,293 were attached to sugar plantations, 8,858 to minor staple estates, and 2,870 were in other occupations. The whites numbered about 1,600 in 1771 and had declined to about 1,300 in 1777. Exports to Great Britain in 1770 amounted to £451,650 sterling in island prices, of which about three-quarters consisted of sugar products and one-quarter of minor staples. That Grenada and other plantation colonies were not developed without straining the financial resources of the Empire is a theme we shall return to after a brief account of the free port system.[38]

4 THE FREE PORT SYSTEM

From the beginning of the sugar colonies it had been difficult to reconcile the ideal of a balanced and self-contained empire with the reality of trade outside the Empire. Structural and functional differences in the Atlantic empires lay at the source of the difficulty. Metropolises differed in their capacity to supply goods and services and absorb colonial wares, while colonies differed in resources, labour force, primary products, and buying power. British merchants, both at home and in the colonies, had taken advantage of these redundancies and scarcities to expand the informal empire of trade. While it is true that efforts had been made to close loopholes in the Navigation Acts, the British Government had found it expedient to pursue a policy of 'salutary neglect'.

The old colonial policy came under attack at the end of the Seven Years' War. The war had greatly increased the public debt, burdening British taxpayers with heavy debt service charges. Moreover, money was needed to protect and govern the new empire. The Grenville ministry sought to expand the revenue base of the Empire by means of stricter enforcement of the Navigation Acts and the imposition of new taxes on the colonists.

Jamaican traders were particularly hard hit by Grenville's policy. 'The commercial concerns of this part of the world were never known so bad', wrote a resident in 1764.

> That part of trade which was the support of this island and its credit at home is entirely subsided by orders from home to suppress all commerce

---

37 P.R.O. London, C.O. 101/18, Part 2, f. 61: Abstract of the State of Grenada, April 1772; Paterson, *Description of Grenada*, pp. 3, 13.
38 MacPherson, *Annals of Commerce*, vol. 3, p. 640; Campbell, *Political Survey of Britain*, vol. 2, p. 689.

459

with the Spaniards who were the only people that brought us money here for our British manufactures, and enabled us to make our remittances to England. Not a Spanish vessel can now come with money to this island, but what is seized by officers either under the admiral or Governor. We have been prevented receiving in this island (since I arrived) near a million dollars....

The Jamaican went on to say that the Spaniards were carrying their money to the French and Dutch islands.[39]

Paradoxically, Grenville's new colonial policy came at a time of limited trade liberalization in the rival Caribbean empires. The French Government gave in to pressure from her colonials and revised her exclusive system to permit North Americans to trade with her sugar colonies. Charles III's government opened the trade of the Spanish islands to every province in Spain, at the same time that renewed efforts were made to suppress illicit trade in Caribbean waters.[40]

Symptomatic of the new spirit of trade was the extension of free ports from the old Dutch islands of St Eustatius and Curacao to the islands of other nations. Beginning in April 1763, the port of Carénage on the French island of St Lucia was given the status of a limited free port. The following year saw the institution of free ports in the Danish islands of St Thomas and St John.[41]

Proposals to establish free ports in the British West Indies gained the support of various interest groups. British merchants, shipowners, and manufacturers saw an opportunity to expand markets and trade, increase bullion imports, draw French colonial produce into British hands, and lure the North Americans away from their direct trade with the foreign sugar colonies. Despite the opposition of certain planters, the West Indian and North American interests in the House of Commons formed a working alliance to push the free port bill, at a time when the Rockingham ministry was seeking to reverse the policies of the Grenville ministry by means of this measure and the repeal of the Stamp Act.

The Free Port Act of 1766 sanctioned a branch of colonial trade which had hitherto been conducted largely in a clandestine manner. The privilege of importing and exporting certain types of goods at certain ports in the British West Indies was accorded to small vessels from neighbouring foreign colonies. This was an elaboration rather

39 *The Gentleman's Magazine*, July 1764, p. 337.
40 Dorothy B. Goebel, 'The "New England Trade" and the French West Indies, 1763–1774: A Study in Trade Policies', *The William and Mary Quarterly*, 3rd ser., vol. XX, no. 3 (July 1963), pp. 351–8.
41 Ibid., p. 348; Lowell J. Ragatz, *The Fall of the Planter Class in the British Caribbean, 1763–1833* (New York, 1928), pp. 137–8.

than a departure from the principles of the Acts of Trade and Navigation, writes Frances Armytage, the historian of the free port system. Imported goods were restricted to those which did not compete with goods produced in Britain or her colonies; exported goods were restricted chiefly to British manufactures, African slaves, and North American supplies; and the carrying trade between the mother country and her colonies remained in British hands.[42]

By the Act of 1766, two quite different systems of trade were authorized. The free ports at Dominica were intended to capture the French trade of the neighbouring islands of Martinique and Guadeloupe, while those at Jamaica should revive the Spanish trade. The two ports in Dominica were Prince Rupert's Bay and Roseau. From these ports could be re-exported all articles of British and colonial origin that had been legally entered except for naval stores, tobacco, and other enumerated commodities. Similarly, slaves entered legally from Africa could be re-exported after paying the import duty of 30s per head. The Dominican ports were authorized to admit and re-export any product of the foreign colonies, including sugar, coffee, pimento, ginger, molasses, and tobacco. No foreign staples could be shipped from Dominica directly to another British colony. Sugar (and rum) of local origin could be sent to Britain and pay the colonial duty if it was certified to have been grown in Dominica.[43]

Regulations of so cumbersome a nature not only impeded trade but also the planting of the newly-opened lands of Dominica. Slaves were reportedly transferred directly from British to foreign vessels to avoid the import duty, and foreign sugar and other staples were sent to Britain and her colonies disguised as products of local growth. However, if the statistics of production are to be believed, by the early 1770s Dominica was producing considerably more sugar than she was importing from the French islands.[44]

Dominica became a trading and planting colony of some importance. The island was in a flourishing situation on the eve of the American Revolution, according to Bryan Edwards, who wrote that the French and Spaniards purchased 'great numbers of Negroes there for the supply of their settlements, together with vast quantities of the merchandize and manufactures of Great Britain; payment for all which was made chiefly in bullion, indigo, and cotton, and completed in mules and cattle; articles of prime necessity

---

42 Frances Armytage, *The Free Port System in the British West Indies A Study in commercial policy, 1766–1822* (London, 1953), pp. 2–12, 22–7, 28–42.
43 Ibid., pp. 42–3; Ragatz, *Fall of Planter Class*, pp. 138–9.
44 Ragatz, *Fall of Planter Class*, pp. 140–1; Armytage, *Free Port System* pp. 43–5.

to the planter'. The official value of English goods imported into Dominica averaged nearly £54,000 annually from 1771 to 1775, while the returns in produce came to £200,000. These figures comprise the trade of the free ports and the domestic economy.[45]

Jamaica's free port regulations differed from those of Dominica chiefly in the safeguards that were made for the planting interest. While the provisions of the Act regarding the re-exports of manufactures and slaves were similar, no products that were grown in Jamaica, such as sugar, molasses, coffee, pimento, and ginger, could be imported in foreign vessels. Foreign manufactures were also banned. The ports opened in Jamaica were Kingston, Savannah-la-Mar, Montego Bay, and Santa Lucea.[46]

Though Jamaica's slave trade revived, most of it seems to have bypassed the free ports until the high import duty was reduced to a nominal sum in 1773. The British ambassador to Spain wrote that Jamaica supplied at least three-quarters of the 2,500 to 3,000 Negroes that were imported annually into Havana from 1769 to 1779.[47] On the other hand, the Naval Office Lists show that the slave exports from the free ports of Jamaica ranged from 22 to 335 from 1767 to 1773, and then shot up to 2,287 in 1774 and 3,054 in 1775. The bullion taken in exchange for slaves and other goods sold to the Spaniards amounted to about £100,000 sterling per annum.[48]

Governor Keith sent home a detailed report of Jamaica's exports for the year 1774, which he valued at £1,508,364 sterling in the prices current of the island. He wrote that these exports were all of the island's growth 'except the Cotton and Indigo, which are mostly foreign; the Tortoise-shell and Sarsaparilla, most of the Logwood, and part of the Mahogany, from the Mosquito-shore and Honduras'. Since the value of all these commodity exports was only £72,854, or 4.8 per cent of total exports, it is clear that the free port trade in tropical goods was a small affair. Indeed, it was chiefly the advantages of the Spanish slave trade which influenced Parliament to renew the Free Port Act for Jamaica in 1773.[49]

---

45 Edwards, *History of British West Indies*, vol. 1, pp. 392–400; Armytage, *Free Port System*, pp. 43–4; MacPherson, *Annals of Commerce*, vol. 3, pp. 519, 533, 550, 564, 583.
46 Armytage, *Free Port System*, p. 42.
47 British Museum, Add. MSS 38,416, ff. 114–15: Liverpool Papers, William Eden to the Marquis of Carmarthen, 10 June 1788.
48 P.R.O. London, C.O. 142/19: Naval Office List for Jamaica, ff. 93–4; C.O. 137/70, f. 89: Gov. Keith to the Earl of Dartmouth, 13 June 1775.
49 Ibid., C.O. 142/19, ff. 90–5; C.O. 137/70, ff. 93–4; Armytage, *Free Port System*, pp. 47–50.

The Sugar Colonies and the Industrial Revolution, 1756—1775

5 THE CREDIT CRISIS OF 1772

By the Treaty of 1763 Great Britain acquired new fields for capital investment as well as vast new lands to govern. From the Ganges to the Mississippi capital was needed to expand trade, shipping, and the production of staples. Even though the profits from the Empire probably exceeded the new investment, gains were increasingly diverted into home investment and conspicuous consumption. Money capital failed to expand in relation to the commercial credit extended to the Empire. Contributing to the money stringency was the decline in specie which entered Britain indirectly from the Spanish and Portuguese colonies.

New colonies, as Adam Smith observed, had an insatiable demand for capital. Scarce capital in conjunction with abundant land resources yielded high returns, generally higher than those on investment in the mother country. The colonists endeavoured to borrow as much as possible from Great Britain, where the capital resources of the Empire were pooled. In explaining the way by which this debt was contracted, Smith said that the colonists seldom borrowed upon bond of the rich people of the mother country, 'but by running as much in arrear to their correspondents, who supply them with goods from Europe, as their correspondents will allow them'.[50]

British capital exports may be considered briefly with respect to three geographical areas: the East Indies, North America, and the West Indies. The British victory over the French in India ushered in for the East India Company a period of turbulence which masked a considerable expansion of trade and capital investment. Proceeds from the sales of the Company's produce increased sharply in 1763—4, and again in 1768—9. Capital exports to India were of sufficient magnitude to induce one modern authority to say that they may possibly explain the fall of the exchanges in Great Britain in 1768—71. Moreover, speculation in the Company's stock at times involved almost the whole credit of the London money market.[51]

The debts owed by North Americans to British creditors on the eve of the American Revolution were estimated at figures ranging from £2,000,000 to £6,000,000 sterling. Notarized claims submitted to the British Government at the conclusion of the war amounted to nearly £3,000,000, exclusive of accrued interest. Most of these claims — nearly £2,500,000 — were made on debtors in the southern

50 Adam Smith, *The Wealth of Nations* (1776) (New York, 1937), pp. 567—8.
51 Lucy S. Sutherland, *The East India Company in Eighteenth-Century Politics* (Oxford, 1952), pp. 32—4; T. S. Ashton, *An Economic History of England: The 18th Century* (London, 1955), p. 193.

colonies. Debtors in Virginia alone accounted for nearly one-half of the claims made by British creditors on their former correspondents in the Thirteen Colonies.[52]

West Indian sterling debts were greater than those owing from North America. Abbé Raynal estimated that the British West Indies owed £16,000,000 sterling to the mother country, but his figure may be too high. British property or stock vested in the West India islands amounted to upwards of £30,000,000 sterling, according to Richard Glover, a planters' spokesman. His statement that £14,000,000 of this sum was 'owned by persons who lived in England' suggests that Raynal's figure included both debts and the property of absentee proprietors.[53]

The expansion of the old sugar colonies led to the accumulation of substantial debt. In the Leeward Islands the debts of St Kitts were estimated at £720,000 in 1773, and at least as much was likely owed by planters in the neighbouring islands. Figures for Barbados are not available, but one of the island's leading capitalists, Gedney Clarke, Jr, went bankrupt in 1774 for £100,000 to £200,000. The remarkable expansion of Jamaica in the interwar years taxed the island's not insubstantial financial resources. Debts owed by Jamaicans to British creditors probably ranged between £2,000,000 and £3,000,000.[54]

But the debts of the Ceded Islands were relatively, if not absolutely, greater than those of the old sugar colonies taken together. Grenada alone had debts of more than £2,000,000. The lure of sugar profits led to a wave of speculation that taxed the resources of the old islands and the sugar merchants in London. One knowledgeable Londoner wrote at the height of the boom in 1771:

> The amazing increase in the value of West-India estates is such, that a few years frequently raise the fee-simple to twenty times its original price. As a proof of this, we are assured, that a plantation was sold about seven years ago, in Dominica, for 500 *l.*; the purchaser in two years after sold it for 5,000 *l.*; the new buyer sold it in three years for 15,000 *l.*; and the present possessor is now preparing to dispose of it for 30,000 *l.*[55]

---

52 Samuel Flagg Bemis, *Jay's Treaty, A Study in Commerce and Diplomacy* (New York, 1923), p. 103. Simple interest at five per cent per annum for fourteen years has been deducted from the 1791 totals which are shown in this book.
53 Raynal, *History of the Two Indies*, vol. 6, pp. 410–11; Richard Glover, *The Substance of the Evidence on the Petition Presented by the West-India Planters and Merchants to the Hon. House of Commons* (London, 1775), pp. 2, 32–3.
54 Rev. James Ramsay, *An Essay on the Treatment and Conversion of African Slaves in the British Sugar Colonies* (London, 1784), p. 57; Richard Pares, *Yankees and Creoles The Trade between North America and the West Indies before the American Revolution* (Cambridge, Mass., 1956), p. 83; Long, *History of Jamaica*, vol. 1, p. 502.
55 *The Scots Magazine*, vol. XXXIII (Aug. 1771), p. 440.

The Sugar Colonies and the Industrial Revolution, 1756–1775

Two financial crises marked the interwar years. First came the crisis of 1763, which brought an end to the credit boom following the Seven Years' War. After originating in Amsterdam, the crisis spread to Hamburg and, to a lesser extent, London. More widespread in its effects was the peacetime crisis of 1772. The years from 1770 to mid-1772 witnessed a remarkable expansion of Britain's foreign and domestic trade, manufacturing, mining, transport, and civic improvements. Accompanying the more tangible evidence of wealth creation was the rapid expansion of credit and banking, leading to a rash of speculation and dubious financial innovation.[56]

From a financial standpoint, at least, the boom and subsequent crisis were most pronounced in Scotland. The years of peace after 1763 were notable for a variety of developments, including the growth of Glasgow in the Chesapeake tobacco trade, expansion of the linen industry, projection of the Forth and Clyde canal, laying out the new town of Edinburgh, agricultural improvement, and West Indian investment. Financial innovations consisted of the notorious practice of drawing and redrawing bills of exchange, or 'swiveling', in an effort to expand credit; and the establishment of a new bank at Ayr with a view toward liberalizing banking policy in Scotland.[57] Some years after the crash an Edinburgh banker recalled 'the extensive speculations which were entered into by some Scotchmen for the purchase and cultivation of lands in the newly acquired West India Islands'.[58]

When its original capital was exhausted, the Ayr bank began to raise money by a chain of bills on London. This source of credit was shut off suddenly on 10 June 1772, when the London correspondent of the Ayr bank closed its doors. A few days later the *Gentleman's Magazine* said that 'no event for 50 years past has been remembered to have given so fatal a blow both to trade and public credit'. Though the expected 'universal bankruptcy' did not materialize, the repercussions of the panic were widespread.[59]

From London the panic spread to other parts of England and Scotland where a number of banks, including the one at Ayr, were forced to suspend payments. A fresh outbreak occurred on the continent of Europe in late 1772 and early 1773, when there was

---

56 Richard B. Sheridan, 'The British Credit Crisis of 1772 and The American Colonies', *The Journal of Economic History*, vol. XX, no. 2 (June 1960), pp. 161–86.
57 Henry Hamilton, 'The Failure of the Ayr Bank, 1772', *Econ. Hist. Rev.*, 2nd ser., vol. VIII, no. 3 (April 1956), pp. 405–17.
58 Sir William Forbes, *Memoirs of a Banking House* (Edinburgh, 1860), p. 39.
59 *The Gentleman's Magazine* (June 1772), MDCCLXXII, p. 293; Sir John Clapham *The Bank of England, A History* (Cambridge, 1944), vol. 1, pp. 157–72, 242–51.

Sugar and Slavery

such 'an extensive crash, that there seemed to be an universal wreck of credit'.[60]

Meanwhile, the crisis had spread to the British colonies and spheres of influence in India. By July 1772 the East India Company was so overwhelmed with debt and burdened with the cost of a disastrous war that it had to confess its inability to carry out its engagements. From Fredericksburg, Virginia, a merchant wrote to his brother in Liverpool: 'The late bankruptcies have made prodigious alterations within these 9 months, the factors for the Scotch merchants in Glasgow are forbid to draw, and a great number of their bills come back protested'.[61]

The West Indies suffered from the financial crisis as well as a severe hurricane which struck on 31 August 1772. Most of the financial distress fell on the Ceded Islands. 'The distressed situation of this island, owing to the failure of credit, the low price of coffee, and the scarcity of money is beyond conception', wrote Governor Leyborne from Grenada in June 1773. The Governor went on to say that many planters, whose estates and Negroes were mortgaged to merchants in London, had withdrawn, with their slaves, from the area which he governed and gone to a neighbouring French island. To check the exodus the Legislature of Grenada had passed a debt moratorium law.[62] An Act of Parliament of 1773 to permit foreigners to lend money on the security of West India estates was a measure of financial assistance to the planters.[63]

Recovery from the crisis of 1772 was rapid, even though some of the repercussions were disturbing. The financial stringency hardly affected the aggregate output of the Caribbean islands; in fact, sugar exports to Great Britain fell only slightly in 1773 and rose to new heights in 1774 and 1775. Higher credit and loan charges, although temporarily a consequence of the crisis, persisted chiefly because alternative investment opportunities at home became more attractive.[64]

---

60 MacPherson, *Annals of Commerce*, vol. 3, pp. 533–4.
61 William Wiatt to Francis Wiatt, 26 June 1773, *William and Mary Quarterly*, 1st ser., (1911–12), vol. XX, p. 235.
62 *Acts of the Privy Council of England, Colonial Series, 'The Unbound Papers'*, ed. James Munro (London, 1912), vol. 6, p. 549.
63 MacPherson, *Annals of Commerce*, vol. 3, pp. 534, 556.
64 Long, *History of Jamaica*, vol. 1, pp. 555–6.

The Sugar Colonies and the Industrial Revolution, 1756–1775

6 THE WEST INDIA BALANCE OF PAYMENTS

'The sugar and rum which the West India merchants purchase in those colonies upon their own account', wrote Adam Smith, 'are not equal in value to the goods which they annually sell there. A balance therefore must necessarily be paid to them in gold and silver, and this balance too is generally found'.[65] Countering Smith's views are those of David MacPherson, the commercial annalist, who maintained that there were

> branches of trade, which would be ruinous, if the imports did not exceed the exports, or, in other words, if the balance were not *unfavourable*. . . . Such is the trade with all our West-India settlements, which have been formed and supported by British capitals, and in a great measure owned by proprietors residing in Great Britain. Therefore the outward cargoes are to be considered as the stock employed in the culture of the plantations; and the homeward cargoes are in fact the proceeds of that culture, the excess of which is not a loss to the nation, but the real amount of the net profits coming into the pockets of the proprietors. . . . In other words, the outward cargoes are the *seed*, and the inward cargoes are the *harvest*. Neither is the balance, stated as due to the islands, remitted to them to increase their stock of circulating money.[66]

Smith erred in asserting that, apart from remittances to absentee proprietors, England had a favourable balance of trade with the West Indies, that West India merchants purchased sugar and rum on their own account, and that a bullion inflow offset the favourable balance of trade. Rather, the trade balance was favourable to the West Indies, West India planters and attorneys consigned all but a fraction of their sugar and rum to English commission agents, and the bullion inflow was independent of the trade balance.

MacPherson, on the other hand, gives too much credit to British capital in the formation and sustenance of the sugar colonies. Moreover, by neglecting the invisible items other than the bills of exchange remitted in payment of slaves, he gives an exaggerated view of the profits accruing to the proprietors. Otherwise, his statement is essentially correct.

Edmund Burke was cognizant of the nature and importance of the Caribbean trades. Unlike the foreign branches of trade, he maintained that the import article was the 'best and indeed the only standard we can have of the value of our West India trade'.

> Our export entry does not comprehend the greatest trade we carry on with any of the West India islands, the sale of negroes; nor does it give any idea

---

65 Smith, *Wealth of Nations*, p. 895.
66 MacPherson, *Annals of Commerce*, vol. 3, pp. 342–3.

Sugar and Slavery

Table 19.3

London prices of West India commodities
(Annual averages)

	1761	1772
Muscovado sugar, per cwt	39s 0d	36s 6d
Rum, per gallon	4s 7d	2s 11d
Pimento, per lb	0s 8d	0s 6½d
Coffee, per cwt	£4 5s 0d	£4 0s 0d
White ginger, per cwt	£2 12s 0d	£2 17½s 0d
Cotton, per lb	0s 11d	0s 8d
Mahogany, per foot	0s 10½d	0s 8½d
Fustic, per ton	£8 2½s 0d	£5 0s 0d
Braziletto wood, per ton	£8 0s 0d	£6 7½s 0d
Logwood, per ton	£7 10s 0d	£4 0s 0d

Source: Edward Long, *The History of Jamaica* (London, 1774), vol. 1, p. 529.

of two other advantages we draw from them; the remittances for money spent here, and the payment of part of the balance of the North American trade. It is therefore quite ridiculous to strike a balance merely on the fact of an excess of imports and exports, in that commerce; though in most foreign branches, it is, on the whole, the best method.

Anticipating the view expressed by John Stuart Mill, Burke maintained that the whole import and export trade of the colonies 'revolves and circulates in this kingdom, and is, so far as it regards our profit, in the nature of a home trade, as much as if the several countries of America and Ireland were all pieced to Cornwall'.[67]

West India produce prices declined appreciably in the years following the Seven Years' War. Muscovado sugar at the London market, which averaged 38s 6d per cwt in the war period, came down to 30s 9d in 1764, and rose to a little more than 38s in 1765 and 1766. From 1767 to 1775 prices ranged from 34s to 37s 2½d, the average from 1771 to 1775 being 35s 8½d.[68] Edward Long's comparison of produce prices in 1761 and 1772 is shown in Table 19.3.

The dimensions of the West India trade have been understated partly because writers have been concerned with one of its branches to the neglect of others, and partly because official values have been used instead of market values. Imports into the mother country were valued on the basis of the estimated cost of the goods in the country

---

67 Burke, *Present State of the Nation*, in *Works*, vol. 1, pp. 241–2, 269–70.
68 See Appendix V.

The Sugar Colonies and the Industrial Revolution, 1756–1775

of origin, and these 'official' or f.o.b. values remained unaltered for a long span of years. In other words, the sugar, rum, and minor staples from the West Indies were recorded in the custom-house books at figures well below their market or c.i.f. values, the difference being represented chiefly by the cost of the freight, insurance, and commissions. Goods exported from Great Britain were recorded officially at historical market values. From the standpoint of the sugar colonies, entry costs were higher than the official values by at least the amount of the freight, insurance, and commissions.[69]

Table 19.4 represents in some detail the value of the West India trade to the British Empire on the eve of the American Revolution. London prices, including those shown in Table 19.3 above, have been used to value the exports from the British West Indies to Great Britain and Ireland, to which has been added the estimated value of the bullion exports. The total c.i.f. value of £4,473,000 sterling compares with the official value of West India produce imported into England and Wales of £3,198,700 and is 40.0 per cent greater.

The difference between the f.o.b. and c.i.f. values represents the 'invisible' earnings of the export trade, of which probably two-thirds consisted of the charges for freight, insurance, and commission, and one-third of remittances to absentee proprietors and other British claimants on income from the sugar colonies. Exports to North America have been added to those going to Great Britain and Ireland to arrive at the total f.o.b. value of West India exports.

Official values of imports from Great Britain have been adjusted with the aid of a wholesale price index, and to this f.o.b. value has been added a markup of 25 per cent to arrive at the c.i.f. value. Irish and North American imports at c.i.f. values have been taken from contemporary estimates, while the net slave imports of about 18,300 per annum have been valued at the average price in the West Indies of £35 sterling. These computed and estimated values suggest that the West Indian trade balance was favourable in the years immediately preceding the American War of Independence.

Invisible earnings afford a true measure of the importance of the sugar colonies. The North American colonies averaged £461,000 annually from their trade with the West Indies from 1768 to 1772.[70] Invisible earnings from the British slave trade, calculated on the difference between buying prices in West Africa and selling prices in

---

69 Phyllis Deane and W. A. Cole, *British Economic Growth 1688–1959: Trends and Structure* (Cambridge, 1962), pp. 318–19.
70 James F. Shepherd and Gary M. Walton, 'Estimates of "Invisible" Earnings in the Balance of Payments of the British North American Colonies, 1768–1772', *Jour. Econ. Hist.*, vol. XXIX, no. 2 (June 1969), pp. 250–6.

Sugar and Slavery

Table 19.4

An estimate of the balance of trade of the British West Indies, 1772–74 (Annual averages in £000 sterling)

EXPORTS				
To	England and Wales,	c.i.f.[1]	£4,058	
	Scotland	c.i.f.[2]	142	
	Ireland	c.i.f.[3]	148	
	Bullion	c.i.f.[4]	125	£4,473
Less freight, insurance, commissions and other 'invisible' exports				1,286
F.o.b. value of exports to British Isles[5]				3,187
F.o.b. value of exports to North America[6]				400
Total f.o.b. value of exports				£3,587
IMPORTS				
From	Great Britain,	c.i.f.[7]	£1,711	
	Ireland	c.i.f.[8]	290	
	Africa	c.i.f.[9]	640	
	North America	c.i.f.[10]	725	3,366
Favourable balance of trade				£ 221

the West Indies, amounted to roughly £330,000 in the 1771–5 period. But the greatest source of income was the two-way trade between the sugar colonies and Great Britain and Ireland which yielded about £1,650,000 annually in invisible earnings.

7 PROFITS AND ABSENTEEISM

Colonies of exploitation not only yielded profits from long-distance trade, but gains also came from informal empire trade as well as from the production of staples and intermediate products. The profits accruing to the Empire from Jamaica c. 1773 have been calculated by the author in the amount of £1,547,000 sterling, of which £901,000 came from trade, £111,300 from residentiary industries, and £534,700 from the production of staples. Jamaica was the source of about 54 per cent of the West India produce

The Sugar Colonies and the Industrial Revolution, 1756–1775

Source:
1. P.R.O., London, Treas. 38/269, ff. 1–4; Treas. 64/273(39); B. M. Add. MSS 8133B, ff. 177–8, Musgrave Papers; B. M. Add. MSS 12,406, f. 129, Long Papers; Edward Long, *The History of Jamaica* (London, 1774), vol. 1, p. 529; Thomas Ellison, *The Cotton Trade of Great Britain* (London, 1886), p. 82; Lord Beveridge, *Prices and Wages in England* (London, 1939), pp. 562, 565. For sugar prices see Appendix V.
2. P.R.O., London, Customs 14/1A, 14/1B.
3. P.R.O., London, Customs 15/76, 15/77, 15/78; John Campbell, *A Political Survey of Britain* (London, 1774), vol. 2, pp. 666–92.
4. B. M. Add. MSS 12,411, ff. 25–6, Long Papers.
5. John MacGregor, *Commercial Statistics* (London, 1850), vol. 5, p. 378.
6. P.R.O., London, B. T. 5/1, ff. 25, 159, 241; Campbell, *Political Survey of Britain*, vol. 2, pp. 666–92.
7. MacGregor, *Commercial Statistics*, vol. 5, p. 378; Elizabeth B. Schumpeter, 'English Prices and Public Finance, 1660–1822', *The Review of Economic Statistics*, vol. XX, No. 1 (Feb. 1938), p. 35.
8. P.R.O., London, Customs 15/76, 15/77, 15/78; C.O. 137/70, ff. 89–90; Long, *History of Jamaica*, vol. 1, p. 501.
9. In the 1771–5 period, annual average slave imports less re-exports amounted to 8,069 for Jamaica, and 1,351 for Barbados. Net slave imports into the other British sugar islands amounted to an estimated 8,866. Total imports of 18,286 times the average price of £35 sterling per slave gives £640,000. See Appendices IX and X.
10. P.R.O., London, B. T. 5/1, ff. 91, 93, 124; Long, *History of Jamaica*, vol. 1, pp. 428, 501–2.

---

marketed in Great Britain and Ireland. But since it is likely that profit rates were somewhat higher in Jamaica than in her sister colonies, it may be well to credit Jamaica with 60 per cent of all profits. On this basis the annual profit from the West Indies as a whole was £2,578,300 or 8.4 per cent on an invested capital of £30,000,000 sterling.[71] That this is a conservative estimate may be surmised from Arthur Young's calculation of 1770 that 'the sugar colonies added about three millions a year to the wealth of Britain; the rice colonies near a million, and the tobacco ones almost as much....'.[72]

It has been contended by Professor Robert P. Thomas that the West Indies yielded substantially less to the Empire than they did to the merchants and planters. In other words, the net profit (or social rate of return) gained by the Empire was what remained after the expenses incurred in the defence of the sugar colonies, in their administration, and in the commercial benefits granted to them had been subtracted from the profits generated in the islands.[73] While it is true that British planters enjoyed a substantial tariff preference in the home market over their foreign rivals, nevertheless it is doubtful

---

71 See Chapter 16, pp. 382–3.
72 Arthur Young, *Annals of Agriculture* (London, 1784), vol. 1, p. 13.
73 R. P. Thomas, 'The Sugar Colonies of the Old Empire: Profit or Loss for Great Britain?' and R. B. Sheridan, 'The Wealth of Jamaica in the Eighteenth Century: A Rejoinder', both in *Econ. Hist. Rev.*, 2nd ser., vol. XXI, no. 1 (April 1968), pp. 30–45 and 46–61.

Sugar and Slavery

if the metropolitan prices of British and French sugars varied widely in the decade prior to 1776.[74]

In the absence of public accounts which show how the cost of colonial government was distributed between the colonies and the mother country, resort must be had to secondary sources. 'Our colonies in the West Indies', wrote Sir John Sinclair, 'are possessions attended with this advantage, that in addition to a very lucrative commerce, they have also in general yielded a revenue, adequate to their civil establishments'.[75] Herman Merivale noted that French policy systematically tended to burden the mother country at the expense of her sugar colonies, that the cost of colonial government was almost wholly defrayed by France, and that 'the advantage of this tribute was not counterbalanced, as in ours, by taxes and restrictions weighing heavily on the colonial producer'.[76]

Defence costs were substantially less in the West Indies than they were in North America.[77] At the close of the Seven Years' War the Grenville ministry planned to station 7,500 troops in North America and 2,500 in the West Indies; in 1775 there were reportedly 8,580 troops in the former and 1,909 in the latter colonies.[78] Although it cost more to maintain a British soldier in the islands than on the mainland, the planter-governments helped to defray the extra cost. When Admiral Rodney came out to take command of the Jamaica station in July 1771, he had five sail of the line and some smaller vessels. This force was gradually reduced and in 1774 there was only a 50-gun ship besides frigates and small craft. Though a larger squadron was stationed at English Harbour in Antigua, it is doubtful if the West India squadrons were as large and costly as those stationed in North American waters. Professor Beer concluded from his study of protection costs in both groups of colonies that 'almost the entire increase in expenditure was due to the necessity of keeping a considerable body of soldiers in North America'.[79]

74 MacPherson, *Annals of Commerce*, vol. 3, p. 583.
75 Sir John Sinclair, *The History of the Public Revenue of the British Empire* (3 vols., London, 1803), vol. 2, p. 101.
76 Herman Merivale, *Lectures on Colonization and Colonies Delivered before the University of Oxford in 1839, 1840, and 1841* (Oxford, 1928), p. 62.
77 For a defence estimate that is grossly overstated, see Thomas, 'Sugar Colonies of Old Empire', p. 38.
78 Shepherd and Walton, 'Payments of British Colonies', pp. 258–61; Jack M. Sosin, *Agents and Merchants British Colonial Policy and the Origins of the American Revolution 1763–1775* (Lincoln, 1965), pp. 36–7; Edward E. Curtis, *The Organization of the British Army in the American Revolution* (New Haven, 1926), pp. 2–3.
79 *The Private Papers of John, Earl of Sandwich First Lord of the Admiralty 1771–1782*, ed. G. R. Barnes and J. H. Owen (Greenwich, The Navy Record Society, 1932, vol. LXIX), vol. 1, pp. 375–6; George Louis Beer, *British Colonial Policy 1754–1765* (New York, 1933), pp. 266–7, 267, n. 1, 2, 268, n. 1.

The Sugar Colonies and the Industrial Revolution, 1756-1775

From the protection costs should be deducted annual Crown revenues of about £50,000 from land sales in the Ceded Islands, and £34,000 from the 4½ per cent export duty. Then, too, part of the customs revenue of about £700,000 annually should be credited to the West Indies. Even if it is conceded that some direct costs were incurred by Britain in the possession of the West Indies, it may be argued that these costs were more than compensated for by the indirect benefits of the sugar colonies to the Empire.[80]

'Our tobacco colonies', wrote Adam Smith, 'send us home no such wealthy planters as we see frequently arrive from our sugar islands'. More and more planters realized their goal of shining in the mother country in the decades prior to the American Revolution. Edward Long wrote of the emigration of many owners of property in Jamaica, 'who of late years have flocked to Britain and N. America, beyond the example of former times, and drained their incomes from the Island...'. He estimated that there were as many as 2,000 'annuitants and proprietors non-resident'.[81]

Many of the emigrants became members of the British landed gentry. Lord Shelburne declared in the House of Commons in November 1778 that 'there were scarcely ten miles together throughout the country where the house and estate of a rich West Indian was not to be seen'.[82] William Beckford thought that the number of people in Great Britain, and particularly Scotland, 'who were dependent upon, and supported by, the colonies, would perhaps startle the calculator and convince the man of reflection, that large portions of land have been cleared, cultivated, and peopled, by the wealth that has been acquired in the Islands; and this fact may be eas ascertained and proved'.[83]

Much has been written of the extravagance, conspicuous display, and dissolute habits of the West Indians who frequented the watering-places, race courses, and gambling casinos. Bath was the favourite watering-place which attracted every upstart of fortune, including planters, Negro-drivers, and hucksters, who were said to have known no criterion of greatness but the ostentation of wealth. Not infrequently the translated colonial was the butt of ridicule as he dissipated his fortune 'at the fountain-head of pleasure, in the land of beauty, of arts, of elegancies'.[84]

80 Long, *History of Jamaica*, vol. 1, p. 417.
81 Smith, *Wealth of Nations*, p. 158; Long, *History of Jamaica*, vol. 1, pp. 377, 386.
82 *Parliamentary History of England*, vol. 19, p. 1316.
83 William Beckford, *A Descriptive Account of the Island of Jamaica* (London, 1790), vol. 2, p. 319.
84 Tobias Smollett, *Humphrey Clinker* (London, 1811), p. 37; Richard Cumberland, *The West Indian* (London, 1771), Act I, Scene II.

Sugar and Slavery

Less well known are the constructive achievements of the ex-colonials. Numbers of West Indians, according to Lord Brougham, used their income in speculations of agriculture, manufacture, or trade. While admitting that these new landowners 'commonly introduce a bad state of manners into the neighbourhood', he contended that 'if their numbers are not very great in any district, they, upon the whole, do more good than harm, by introducing a spirit of active improvement, and a liberality of views, which are not the growth of ancient families, and rural occupations'.[85] 'Nabobs from the *Indies*, planters from *America*, merchants from the exchange', wrote Arthur Young, 'settle in the counties, they farm, garden, plant, improve — they want men, their demand is answered, and was it regular, would around every great house found and support a town'. Generally speaking, the improving landlords of 18th-century England and Scotland derived their wealth from colonial property, mineral rights, and urban rents rather than from the profits of agriculture.[86]

John Baker's *Diary* not only reveals the social life of one group of absentees, but it also details the group's business and professional activity. In July 1757, Baker returned to England from St Kitts, where he had been Solicitor General of the Leeward Islands. His *Diary*, which runs from 1751 to 1778, records his visits to Bath and Tunbridge Wells, travels on the Continent, play-going, attendance at sporting events, and dinners with such notables as David Garrick, Lord North, Edward Gibbon, and Admiral Rodney. But his life was not merely a round of pleasure supported by his plantation in St Croix. As a barrister of the Middle Temple, Baker had an extensive law practice in London and his clients were chiefly absentee proprietors from the Leeward Islands. Many of these absentees were also London sugar merchants, such as Nicholas Tuite, William Manning, Richard Oliver, and John Bannister. Baker's social circle consisted largely of absentee families who were bound together by intermarriage, common interests, and friendships that went back to their early life in the West Indies.[87]

---

[85] Henry Brougham, *An Inquiry into the Colonial Policy of the European Powers* (Edinburgh, 1803), vol. 1, pp. 80, 150–2.
[86] Young, *Political Arithmetic*, p. 62; C. R. Fay, *English Economic History mainly since 1700* (Cambridge, 1948), pp. 83, 97.
[87] *The Diary of John Baker Barrister of the Middle Temple Solicitor-General of the Leeward Islands*. Edited with an Introduction by Philip C. Yorke (London, 1931), pp. 59–60 ff.

The Sugar Colonies and the Industrial Revolution, 1756—1775

8 THE INDUSTRIAL REVOLUTION

It is the contention of this study that the economic growth of Great Britain was chiefly from without inwards, that the Atlantic was the most dynamic trading area, and that, outside the metropolis, the most important element in the growth of this area in the century or more prior to 1776 was the slave-plantation, chiefly of the cane-sugar variety in the islands of the Caribbean Sea. From his survey of the European possessions in the two Indies, Abbé Raynal concluded that the labours of the people settled in the West Indies doubled and perhaps trebled the activity of all Europe. 'They may be considered as the principal cause of the rapid motion which now agitates the universe', he declared.[88]

Britain's eventual failure to accommodate the Thirteen Colonies to her Atlantic empire should not be allowed to obscure the gains which she derived from this trading system. George Walker, agent for Barbados, testified before a committee of the House of Commons in 1775 that the *advantage* of the sugar colonies

> ... is not that the profits all centre here; it is, that it creates, in the course of attaining those profits, a commerce and navigation in which multitudes of your people, and millions of your money are employed; it is that the support which the sugar colonies receive in one shape, they give in another. In proportion to their dependence on North America, and upon Ireland, they enable North America and Ireland to trade with Great Britain. By their dependence upon Great Britain for hands to push the culture of the sugar-cane, they uphold the trade of Great Britain to Africa.... In proportion as the sugar colonies consume, or cause to be consumed, among their neighbours, Asiatic commodities, they increase the trade of the English East India Company.[89]

Walker's testimony is suggestive of what students of the staple theory of economic growth call 'linkages', that is, backward linkages, or the inducement to invest in the production of such plantation inputs and transportation equipment as ships, textiles, hardware, and foodstuffs; forward linkages, or the inducement to invest in sugar refineries and cotton mills which used the output of the export industry; and final demand linkages, or the inducement to invest in metropolitan industries which produced consumer goods for factors in the plantation supply and processing sectors.[90]

---

88 Raynal, *History of the Two Indies*, vol. 6, pp. 412—14. For a modern essay which emphasizes the part played by the Atlantic trading area in Britain's industrial leadership, see K. Berrill, 'International Trade and the Rate of Economic Growth', *Econ. Hist. Rev.*, 2nd ser., vol. XII, no. 3 (April 1960), pp. 351—9.
89 Quoted in *American Archives, Fourth Series, 1774—1776*, ed. Peter Force (Washington, D. C., 1837), vol. 1, pp. 1728—9.
90 Melville H. Watkins, 'A Staple Theory of Economic Growth', *The Canadian Journal of Economics and Political Science*, vol. XXIX, no. 2 (May 1963), pp. 141—54.

Sugar and Slavery

Critics of the Negro and sugar trades maintain that these markets were inferior to those in the temperate-zone colonies, since the non-British inhabitants wore fewer clothes and their low living standards limited per capita consumption of British manufactures. Added to these defects was the limited number of European settlers in the tropics. In fact, however, West Africa and the plantation colonies in America and the West Indies consistently took off more British goods than the colonies north of Maryland. Besides this advantage, the markup on British goods sent to Africa was high. Exports in 1771, which were officially valued at £712,538, were exchanged for 47,146 slaves, the sale of which was reputed to yield 'One Million and a Half Sterling, and the Produce of the other Branches of this Commerce have been computed at Half a Million more, that is, Two Millions in the Whole'.[91]

The tropical trades contributed to changes in the structure of industry. Since slave traders and slaveholders required quantities of standardized textiles, utensils, tools, and heavy equipment, it was easier for manufacturers to substitute machines for handicraftsmen, and to engage in massive production rather than cater to discriminating markets. Moreover, the tropics were an important outlet for such light-weight textiles as linen, fustians, and particularly cottons.

Negro slaves were purchased in Africa by the British merchants with a variety of goods. Birmingham manufacturers took advantage of the opening of the African trade in 1698, and their exports of all sorts increased enormously. Large quantities of cutlery ware, gun barrels and other articles found a market in Africa. The British Linen Company was chartered in 1746 with the principal intention of supplying the merchants trading to Africa and the American plantations 'with the like kinds of linen cloth as they were before obliged to purchase of foreign nations'. The African market was long supplied with East Indian cottons which were re-exported from London. However, by 1769 the home industry had become competitive and nearly one-half of the British exports of cotton piece goods were marketed in Africa.[92]

West coast ports gained in relation to London as the Atlantic trading area expanded. The demand from overseas markets stimulated the growth of a wide range of industries. Navigable rivers extended the industrial hinterlands of these seaports to interior regions. The industrial impact of the African and West Indian trades

---

91 Campbell, *Political Survey of Britain*, vol. 2, p. 633.
92 Henry Hamilton, *The English Brass and Copper Industries to 1800* (London, 1926), pp. 137–8, 291; Adam Anderson, *Historical and Chronological Deduction of the Origin of Commerce* (Dublin, 1790), vol. 3, pp. 531–2; Fay, *English Economic History*, pp. 140–1.

The Sugar Colonies and the Industrial Revolution, 1756–1775

can be traced briefly in the rise of Bristol, Liverpool, Manchester, and Glasgow.

Bristol merchants, who had extensive dealings with Africa and the West Indies, channelled through their port the manufactures from near and far. 'Guns and metal ornaments came from Birmingham', writes Professor Minchinton, 'Indian textiles from London, Manchester cotton goods from Lancashire and woollen fabrics from Somerset for the African trade, to name but one of the branches in which Bristol engaged'. Trade led to capital investment, and by the early 18th century Bristol capital was invested in enterprises in its hinterland. These included mining and metal industries, especially iron, tinplate and copper in South Wales. Sugar refining was an important industry in Bristol, from whence came capital to establish several of the pioneer banks in the city. In fact, most of the Bristol and Liverpool banks contained partners with mercantile interests.[93]

Liverpool became a larger version of Bristol in the tropical trades because of its superior port facilities and industrial hinterland. In 1760, when the town had about 30,000 people, shipbuilding was probably the leading industry. The ships built especially for the African trade carried woollen goods, fustians, cottons and linen; hatchets, cutlasses, knives, fetters, chains, muskets, gunpowder, and metal bars; rum, trinkets, and other wares. It was said that 'almost every man in Liverpool is a merchant, and he who cannot send a bale, will send a bandbox... almost every order of people is interested in a Guinea cargo'.[94] John Woolman, the American Quaker, observed during his visit to England in 1772: 'Great is the trade to Africa for slaves; and for the loading of these ships a great number of people are employed in their factories, among whom are many of our Society'.[95]

Some thirty miles east of Liverpool lay Manchester on the Mersey River which connects these and other towns. It is common knowledge that Manchester became the most important centre for the cotton industry in the world. In the 1771–5 period, the cotton imports of England and Wales averaged 4,232,334 lb annually, of which 63.2 per cent was the growth of the British colonies in the West Indies, and the other 36.8 per cent of foreign growth.[96] Most

---

93 W. E. Minchinton, 'Bristol – Metropolis of the West in the Eighteenth Century', *Transactions of the Royal Historical Society*, 5th ser., vol. 4 (1954), pp. 78, 82–5; L. S. Pressnell, *Country Banking in the Industrial Revolution* (Oxford, 1956), pp. 49–50.
94 *Liverpool and Slavery: An Historical Account of the Liverpool-African Slave Trade. By a Genuine 'Dicky Sam'.* (Liverpool, 1884), p. 112.
95 *The Journal of John Woolman.* With an Introduction by John Greenleaf Whittier (Boston, 1876), p. 257.
96 P.R.O. London, Treas. 64/275 (142), (143).

of the fibre came to Liverpool and was sent by barge to the 'Cottonopolis' to be made into cloth. 'Manchester, Liverpool and London were intermixed in the yarn trade with Ireland and the Continent, in the African trade, and in the West Indian and American trade', write Professors Wadsworth and Mann. 'The trading capitals of the ports and manufacturing centres cross-fertilised, and gave rise not only to sturdier growth but to new branches of capitalist enterprise'.[97]

Two Manchester families had broad-ranging interests that encompassed cotton manufacturing, the slave and sugar trades, and plantation enterprise. From the supply of checks and imitation Indian cottons to the Royal African Company, the Hibbert family came to own the largest slave factorage business in Jamaica, acquired sugar estates in that island, and established a leading West India commission house in London.[98] Samuel Touchet and his brothers had one of the leading check-making firms in Manchester, engaged in the Liverpool slave trade and the London sugar trade, and owned plantations. In 1751, the brothers were concerned in about twenty West India ships. Samuel helped to equip the expedition that captured Senegal in 1758. He was M.P. for Shaftesbury from 1761 to 1768, and left a large fortune at his death in 1773.[99]

While Glasgow's tobacco trade with the Chesapeake region has been ably documented, its relations with the sugar colonies are less well known. During a parliamentary investigation of the linen industry in 1737, a petition of the merchants of Glasgow recited: 'That the American Colonies, particularly the West-India Islands, are the principal Mercat for the Manufactures of this Country; whereby many Thousands of his Majesty's Subjects are employed and maintained'. A report of the Board of Agriculture in 1793 said that Glasgow owed its opulence to its trade in tobacco, sugar, and other goods from America and the West Indies. 'These gave rise to a great demand for articles manufactured in this country, with which the cargoes imported from the colonies were chiefly purchased'.[100]

Outside the leading port cities and their hinterlands certain West Indians made notable contributions to British industry. The Fuller family had iron works and gun foundries in Sussex, plantations in

97 Alfred P. Wadsworth and Julia D. Mann, *The Cotton Trade of Industrial Lancashire 1600–1780* (Manchester, 1931), pp. 212, 227–8.
98 Ibid., p. 231; *Caribbeana*, ed. Vere L. Oliver, vol. 4 (London, 1916), pp. 193–9.
99 Wadsworth and Mann, *The Cotton Trade*, pp. 149, 156–7, 231, 233, 243–7, 447.
100 Jacob M. Price, 'The Rise of Glasgow in the Chesapeake Tobacco Trade, 1707–1775', *The William and Mary Quarterly*, 3rd ser., vol. XI, no. 2 (April 1954), pp. 179–99; *Journal of the House of Commons*, 1737–41, vol. XXIII, p. 95; Col. Fullarton, *General View of the Agriculture and Rural Economy of the County of Ayrshire* (Edinburgh, 1793), pp. 76–9.

The Sugar Colonies and the Industrial Revolution, 1756–1775

Jamaica, and a West India trading firm in London.[101] Another Jamaica family did much to transform the economy of North Wales. Richard Pennant (c. 1737-1808) inherited a large estate in Jamaica. Possession of the great estate of Penrhyn was acquired partly by purchase and partly by his marriage to an heiress. Pennant was the leading agricultural improver in his county, to which activity was added road building and the development of the slate quarries on his property. At the time of his death the Penrhyn quarries employed some 300 men and brought in about £7,000 a year. Pennant devoted his plantation income to the development of his slate quarries, and thus out of the profits of foreign trade brought to North Wales the Industrial Revolution. Besides these activities, Pennant represented Liverpool in the House of Commons and was Chairman of the West India Committee. In 1783 he was created Baron Penrhyn of County Louth in Ireland.[102]

If the Fuller and Pennant families were exceptional, there is considerable evidence pointing to the contribution of the West Indians to agriculture, trade, finance, and the professions. Moreover, the triangle trade in British manufactures, slaves, and sugar did much to stimulate the growth of the leading outports and their industrial hinterlands. Perhaps even more significant in the industrialization process was the change in consumption habits. Work incentives and market demand owed much to the consumption of tobacco, tea, and sugar, those artificial wants that crept in and acquired the character of necessities.

9 SLAVERY AND ITS CRITICS

Numerous cultures streamed into the Caribbean island world from Asia, Africa, Europe, South America, and North America, bringing together economic plants, hoe cultivators, managers, capital, technology, livestock, foodstuffs, clothing, and building materials. These elements were combined in varying proportions with tropical soils and climates to minimize the costs of production, transport, defence, and labour discipline. West India plantations greatly stimulated the British and North American economies, since they were a key component of a market system that was self-generating and con-

---

101 *Caribbeana*, vol. 5 (1919), pp. 140–2; G. E. Mingay, *English Landed Society in the Eighteenth Century* (London, 1963), pp. 102, 106, 199–200.
102 W. A. Feurtado, *Official and Other Personages of Jamaica from 1655 to 1790* (Kingston, 1896), pp. 75–6, 123–4; A. H. Dodd, *The Industrial Revolution in North Wales* (Cardiff, 1933), pp. 37, 91, 125, 204–8, 214.

stantly expanding. Planters responded to the growing overseas demand for their staples by importing productive factors from Europe, Africa, and North America; the resultant income further increased the demand for staples and the required productive agents and services. The plantation-based trading area, born in the crisis-ridden middle decades of the 17th century, thus became a remarkable engine of growth as it drew into its orbit the resources of four continents and scattered islands in the Atlantic basin.

Though production and trade figures continued to mount, the sugar colonies faced difficulties and dangers that cast a pall on their overall prosperity. Internally, there were problems of labour discipline in a situation of growing racial imbalance; of sugar-monoculture with its attendant crop diseases and soil exhaustion; of absenteeism which took off able planters and contributed to the outflow of income. Sugar-monoculture made the islands more vulnerable to external forces and events, as witness the credit crisis of 1772. Moreover, planters feared the consequences of future wars. France and Spain smarted for revenge after their defeats in the Seven Years' War. Equally alarming were the growing troubles between the mother country and her Thirteen Colonies, which threatened to starve the sugar colonies if the vital trade in foodstuffs was cut off. Of less immediate concern to the planters, but nonetheless damaging to their long-term economic well being, was the growth of humanitarian sentiment which directed attention to the anomaly of slavery in an age of middle-class affluence.

Rising material standards for one class of society generally afford its sensitive members the leisure and means to engage in movements of social reform. These individuals, given the advantages of education and travel, develop a sensitivity to evils which have been accepted as necessary or expedient by their forbears. In the British Empire, middle-class reformers might be expected to appear in the colonies as well as the mother country. In an age of growing mobility of persons, ideas, and institutions, reform movements might be expected to assume an international aspect and to converge in the metropolis. Finally, the attack on slavery might be expected to be led by individuals and groups in the colonies who stood apart from the planter oligarchy, and who forged close links with reformers in the metropolis.

Colonial slavery met with only limited criticism prior to the mid-18th century period. For a time in the 17th century it seemed possible that the Quaker and other Nonconformist elements in the sugar colonies might launch a movement of amelioration and conversion of slaves to Christianity. George Fox, the founder of

The Sugar Colonies and the Industrial Revolution, 1756–1775

Quakerism, urged his Barbadian planter converts in 1671 to treat their slaves kindly, to give them religious instruction, and to manumit them after some years of servitude. Morgan Godwyn, the Anglican clergyman, railed against the planters for the cruelty they practised on their slaves.[103] The great planters of Barbados retaliated by taking their case to the Board of Trade, where their absentee spokesmen declared on 8 October 1680:

> that the conversion of their slaves to Christianity would not only destroy their property but endanger the island, inasmuch as converted negroes grow more perverse and intractable than others, and hence of less value for labour or sale. The disproportion of blacks to whites being great, the whites have no greater security than the diversity of the negroes' languages, which would be destroyed by conversion, in that it would be necessary to teach them all English.

The Board of Trade, ever solicitous of the planters' interest, thought it best 'to leave the Governor, Council, and Assembly to find out the best means for converting the negroes without injury or danger to property, which is made an instruction to Sir R. Dutton'.[104]

At least two prominent Englishmen criticized West Indian slavery during the first half of the 18th century. Daniel Defoe complained that the planters of Barbados used their slaves like dogs. More severe was the censure of Edmund Burke, who wrote: 'The negroes in our colonies endure a slavery more compleat, and attended with far worse circumstances, than what any people in their condition suffer in any other part of the world, or have suffered in any other period of time'.[105]

Sugar prosperity in the mid-century period brought certain changes in the slave societies. Rising slave prices seem to have led many planters to give more attention to the provisioning and medical treatment of their blacks. Doctors, lawyers, merchants, clergymen, managers, and artisans came to the colonies in growing numbers to supply needed services. To a considerable extent the new men stood apart from the planter class, bringing not only their knowledge and skills but also a critical attitude towards the slave society. Furthermore, sugar prosperity enabled the more fortunate planters to become absentees. Many slaves accompanied their owners to England and North America, where they acquired insights into the principles

---

103 Thomas Hodgkin, *George Fox* (London, 1896), pp. 228–9; Rev. Morgan Godwyn, *The Negro's and Indian's Advocate, Suing for their Admission into the Church* . . . (London, 1680); pp. 4–6.
104 *Cal. S. P. Col. 1677–80*, pp. 590, 611.
105 Daniel Defoe, *A Review of the State of the British Nation*, 22 May 1712, vol. VIII, no. 182, p. 730; William and Edmund Burke, *An Account of the European Settlements in America* (London, 1777), vol. 2, p. 124.

and effects of liberty, which, upon their return to the colonies, they disseminated among their fellow slaves. Some of the absentee proprietors came under the influence of the humanitarian and evangelical movements which were manifestations of the great reaction to the cold rationalism and materialism of the age.

William Foster and John Foster Barham were absentees who came under the influence of the evangelical movement. In 1754, they invited Moravian missionaries to Jamaica, gave them one of their estates as a base of operations, and encouraged them to work among the slaves on their four other estates.[106]

The Church of the Brethren, or Moravians, began the Christianizing mission among the slaves. From the village of Herrnhut in Saxony the first missionaries came to the Danish West Indies in 1732. The Moravians accepted slavery, owned plantations, and abstained from interference in civil affairs. They came to the West Indies under the impulse of the new evangelistic spirit and worked to achieve a spiritual rather than a social transformation of the slave societies. The response to their efforts varied widely. After considerable success in the Danish islands, they met with serious opposition from the proprietors in Jamaica and their mission in that island met with failure. The Barbadian mission, established in 1765, had a struggle to survive; while that of St Kitts, established in 1774–5, proved a success.[107]

Antigua had the most successful Moravian mission in the British colonies. It was established in 1756, and at the end of two decades the mission claimed 2,000 black converts. Rev. James Ramsay, the Anglican clergyman in St Kitts, wrote of the Moravians:

> The great secret of the missionary's management, besides soliciting the grateful attention of their hearers to our Saviour's sufferings, is to contract an intimacy with them, to enter into their little interests, to hear patiently their doubts and complaints, to condescend to their weakness and ignorance, to lead them on slowly and gently, to exhort them affectionately, to avoid carefully magisterial threatenings and commands.

The consequences of these methods, Ramsay said, was to transmit considerable religious knowledge to the slaves, to lead them into orderly and industrious behaviour, neatness in their persons and clothing, sobriety in their carriage, diligence and faithfulness in their stations, and an attitude of humility and piety.[108]

---

106 Elsa V. Goveia, *Slave Society in the British Leeward Islands at the End of the Eighteenth Century* (New Haven, 1965), p. 271.
107 Ibid., pp. 270–2.
108 Ramsay, *Essay on African Slaves*, p. 162.

The Sugar Colonies and the Industrial Revolution, 1756–1775

The Seven Years' War contributed to the relaxation of rigid race barriers and afforded opportunities to observe the slave systems of foreign colonies. Wartime emergencies brought whites and blacks into closer contact, certain mulattoes and blacks were trusted with arms, and corps of them took part in the conquests of Guadeloupe, Martinique, and Havana. Thousands of British soldiers and sailors came to the West Indies for the first time and later returned home with impressions of slavery. Moreover, the study of comparative slave institutions was probably heightened by the military conquests. Ramsay told of a 'humane intelligent sea officer' who blushed for the barbarous treatment handed out to British slaves. The naval officer told the planters that their slaves escaped to the Spaniards because the latter granted greater privileges and made Christians of their slaves.[109]

In the vanguard of the anti-slavery movement were certain individuals of professional, mercantile, and managerial rank, who, having been exposed to enlightenment principles in Europe, were appalled by the conditions of black servitude they witnessed in the colonies. John Newton, the master of two slave vessels, forsook the sea and became an Anglican minister and anti-slavery leader. James Stephen was a lawyer in St Kitts before he returned to England to write anti-slavery tracts. Zachary Macaulay, father of the great historian, was a book-keeper and plantation manager in Jamaica prior to his active anti-slavery agitation. William Dickson was secretary to the Governor of Barbados before he took up his pen to urge the mitigation of slavery.[110] Rev. James Ramsay, who resided in the West Indies as a doctor and clergyman for about twenty years, left a full account of his ministration to the slaves in an atmosphere of planter hostility. In his judgement there was 'no difference between the intellects of whites and blacks, but such as circumstances and education naturally produce'. Circumstances and education were such, however, that little if any success attended the endeavours of individuals to improve the lot of their slaves.[111]

Experiments in slave amelioration and manumission called for the different circumstances of the Middle Colonies of North America where the peculiar institution was of only marginal utility. Here in the Quaker settlements of Pennsylvania and New Jersey the first assaults on the institution were made. As early as 1696 the Quakers

---

109 Ibid., p. 261.
110 Lowell J. Ragatz, *A Guide for the Study of British Caribbean History 1763–1834, Including the Abolition and Emancipation Movements* (Washington, D.C., 1932), pp. 306, 498, 533, 556.
111 Ibid., pp. 541–2; Ramsay, *Essay on African Slaves*, pp. 89–91, 91–2, 181, 203, 229.

Sugar and Slavery

in the former colony had advised their members against the slave trade and urged them to bring their blacks to meetings and give them religious instruction. The London Yearly Meeting took up the cause and by resolution of 1727 condemned the slave traffic and censured Quakers who participated in it. After 1761 Quakers who persisted in the trade were excluded from the Society. John Woolman, the New Jersey Quaker, published in 1754 his first anti-slavery tract; eight years later Anthony Benezet, the Philadelphia Quaker, published his first propaganda tract against the Atlantic slave trade.[112]

The interesting thing is that three of England's pioneer anti-slavery leaders – Granville Sharp, John Wesley, and Thomas Clarkson – were inspired by Benezet's tract. John Wesley had first-hand experience with slavery in South Carolina. He was also influenced by his Moravian fellow travellers on the voyage to America. His *Thoughts on Slavery* (1774) had an enormous circulation and helped to turn the Methodists as a body against bondage. 'I absolutely deny all Slave-holding to be consistent with any degree of even natural Justice', Wesley wrote. He thought it more desirable that the islands be 'altogether sunk in the depth of the sea, than that they should be cultivated at so high a price as the violation of justice, mercy, and truth; and ... that myriads of innocent men should be murdered, and myriads more dragged into the basest slavery'.[113]

Wesley's teachings influenced two Antiguans almost two decades before the first Methodist missionary arrived on the island. Nathaniel Gilbert, Speaker of the House of Assembly, developed a troubled conscience either by the teaching or by the writings of Wesley. In 1760, he was said to have 'collected a few persons in his own house for exhortation and prayer, and afterwards preached the gospel to his slaves'. He was joined by his brother Francis in the Methodist faith. Despite opposition from fellow planters, the Gilberts had formed a society of nearly 200 slaves by the time of Nathaniel's death in 1774.[114]

Slavery was struck its first legal blow in England rather than the colonies. Since the mid-17th century slaves had accompanied their owners to England, where their bondage had been declared lawful. Granville Sharp, an obscure clerk in the Ordnance Department, took up the cause of the blacks in England the same year (1767) that he

112 Frank J. Klingberg, *The Anti-Slavery Movement in England A Study in English Humanitarianism* (New Haven, 1926), pp. 31–3.
113 David Brion Davis, *The Problem of Slavery in Western Culture* (Ithaca, 1966), p. 489; John Wesley, *Thoughts upon Slavery* (London, 1774), p. 31.
114 Thomas Southey, *Chronological History of the West Indies* (London, 1827), vol. 2, p. 340; Vere L. Oliver, *The History of the Island of Antigua* (London, 1894–99), vol. 2, pp. 12–15; Goveia, *Slave Society in Leeward Islands*, pp. 289–90.

The Sugar Colonies and the Industrial Revolution, 1756–1775

read Benezet's anti-slavery tract. Sharp met defeat in his first effort to free a slave who had been beaten and abandoned by his master who later sued for recovery after Sharp had restored the slave to health. Sharp next turned to the case of James Somerset who, after escaping from his master, was seized as a slave to be taken to Jamaica for sale. After the case was argued at three different terms of the court, Justice Mansfield counselled a settlement out of court. He was reluctant to render a decision, partly owing to the effect of a negative verdict on the slaveholders in England. In 1772, at the time of the trial, between 14,000 and 15,000 blacks, representing property worth £700,000, resided in England. The private agreement failing, Mansfield handed down his famous decision, declaring that slavery was 'so odious that nothing can support it but positive law. Whatever inconvenience, therefore, may follow from the decision, I cannot say this case is allowed or approved by the law of England: and therefore the black must be discharged'.[115]

The Mansfield decision caused consternation among the absentees in England. Samuel Martin, then living in Ashstead, Surrey, wrote to his son in London that the decision influenced the behaviour of his servants: 'You cannot conceive, what a pitch of Insolence they are arrived at: and I fear, the many foolish Writers who are become their Advocates, will put into the heads of our Colony-negroes, to rebel; and occasion at least much blood-shed'.[116] He wrote a small treatise in vindication of slavery in which he encouraged the planters to make the life of their slaves easier and happier. He also returned to Antigua, partly for the purpose of instructing his own slaves in Christian principles. Martin wrote that after the gospel was read to his slaves, he explained to them 'the true and genuine sense of Christianity, after which we have a Hymn of Hallelujahs, and I conclude with a Prayer invoking the Divine Blessing and Protection for the future'. He was delighted with the reformation that came from his efforts.[117]

The attack on slavery came at a time of transition in Western culture. The years which saw the germination of ideas planted by Woolman, Benezet, Wesley, and Sharp also witnessed the cries of 'Wilkes and Liberty', Voltaire's *Candide,* Paine's *Common Sense,* Jefferson's *Declaration of Independence,* and Smith's *Wealth of Nations.* Dr Eric Williams has written:

---

115 T. B. Howell, *A Complete Collection of State Trials* (London, 1814), vol. 20, pp. 79–82; Klingberg, *Anti-Slavery Movement,* pp. 35–41.
116 *Martin L. B.,* vol. 3, f. 153: Lre. to Samuel Martin Jr, M.P., 10 July 1772.
117 Ibid., vol. 6, f. 4: Lre. to Rev. Wharton in Barbados, 21 June 1774; vol. 8, f. 90: Lre. to Mrs Henry Martin, 9 June 1774.

Sugar and Slavery

> The commerical capitalism of the eighteenth century developed the wealth of Europe by means of slavery and monopoly. But in so doing it helped to create the industrial capitalism of the nineteenth century, which turned round and destroyed the power of commercial capitalism, slavery, and all its works.[118]

Chattel slavery lingered on, however, until the late decades of the 19th century when Alfred Marshall, the great economist, was moved to write: 'Silver and sugar seldom came to Europe without a stain of blood'.[119] Indeed, we are reminded of the legacy of slavery by the words Harriet Beecher Stowe put in the mouth of George Harris, the mulatto slave who became a free man and acquired a university education: 'We have *more* than the rights of common men; — we have the claim of an injured race for reparation'.[120]

---

118 Eric Williams, *Capitalism and Slavery* (Chapel Hill, 1944), p. 210.
119 Alfred Marshall, *Industry and Trade* (London, 1919), p. 43, n. 1.
120 Harriet Beecher Stowe, *Uncle Tom's Cabin Or, Life Among the Lowly* (1852) (Cambridge, Mass., 1962), p. 446.

Appendices

I

Sugar imported into England and Wales
(000 cwt)

Year	Total[1]	From Barbados	From Jamaica	From Leeward Islands	Other areas
1700	485.5	238.1	94.2	144.4	8.8
1701	431.7	180.7	87.3	132.4	31.3
1702	358.2	144.9	57.2	126.9	29.2
1703	407.6	158.8	95.6	148.6	4.6
1704	313.8	79.5	57.2	123.0	54.1
1705	n.d.	n.d.	n.d.	n.d.	n.d.
1706	332.3	195.0	82.8	45.5	9.0
1707	386.2	137.9	80.8	132.7	34.8
1708	377.7	162.4	121.5	81.0	12.8
1709	394.7	166.9	118.3	97.2	12.3
1710	504.8	151.0	112.4	226.9	14.5
1711	365.4	168.1	97.8	81.2	18.3
1712	423.5	128.0	134.3	128.4	32.8
1713	503.8	109.2	131.1	249.4	14.1
1714	511.9	203.9	126.7	175.0	6.3
1715	616.6	259.4	127.7	224.8	4.7
1716	684.5	211.9	166.4	295.5	10.7
1717	762.9	252.0	210.0	288.4	12.5
1718	567.3	227.7	205.3	122.9	11.4
1719	544.4	114.6	151.0	270.6	8.2
1720	705.3	206.1	209.6	268.4	21.2
1721	498.0	73.7	245.2	176.3	2.8
1722	617.3	98.3	231.9	277.5	9.6
1723	660.8	168.8	121.7	354.3	16.0
1724	729.1	248.8	187.2	286.2	6.9
1725	851.9	240.2	238.8	367.4	5.5
1726	678.3	177.6	242.0	256.6	2.1
1727	645.2	164.0	176.2	300.4	4.6

Sugar and Slavery

Year	Total[1]	From Barbados	From Jamaica	From Leeward Islands	Other areas
1728	972.2	238.7	271.6	453.8	8.1
1729	994.8	159.8	354.7	472.0	8.3
1730	1,053.5	250.1	319.5	449.6	34.3
1731	818.3	142.7	309.5	359.7	6.4
1732	822.8	102.6	289.1	424.1	7.0
1733	1,001.9	165.3	338.3	496.6	1.7
1734	687.4	72.3	300.0	310.1	5.0
1735	901.8	124.6	276.3	484.4	16.5
1736	877.6	146.4	309.4	413.3	8.5
1737	550.8	98.7	270.1	174.4	7.6
1738	864.3	123.9	349.9	388.8	1.7
1739	951.1	119.3	392.8	437.5	1.5
1740	706.9	140.2	279.5	285.4	1.8
1741	886.1	194.4	338.2	349.4	4.1
1742	731.5	140.4	341.0	248.8	1.3
1743	895.2	168.4	347.9	374.7	4.2
1744	803.0	53.9	326.6	342.0	80.5
1745	688.5	109.5	205.0	330.2	43.8
1746	790.4	140.9	239.7	365.6	44.2
1747	604.8	86.8	322.0	189.2	6.8
1748	1,034.5	153.0	381.2	443.5	56.8
1749	941.4	135.9	387.2	406.9	11.4
1750	915.5	137.5	409.7	356.4	11.9
1751	826.0	88.0	384.5	350.7	2.8
1752	837.2	141.7	371.5	311.2	12.8
1753	1,117.9	177.8	425.5	437.8	76.8
1754	851.9	118.6	467.9	249.0	16.4
1755	1,178.1	173.1	435.1	479.0	90.9
1756	1,083.2	144.9	439.9	444.3	54.1
1757	1,453.1	141.4	497.5	548.0	266.2
1758	1,200.4	144.2	478.1	485.8	92.3
1759	1,311.4	109.9	709.0	294.8	197.7
1760	1,605.0	149.5	785.0	377.8	292.7

Appendices

Year	Total[1]	From Barbados	From Jamaica	From Leeward Islands	From Ceded Islands	Other areas
1761	1,535.1	168.9	561.4	493.3	–	311.5
1762	1,342.7	188.9	488.7	386.1	176.0	103.0
1763	1,751.1	165.3	679.6	349.3	71.6	485.3
1764	1,425.3	188.9	650.9	465.2	67.0	53.3
1765	1,199.3	189.7	561.9	317.9	64.5	65.3
1766	1,492.7	173.3	647.7	560.3	89.3	22.1
1767	1,529.4	124.9	711.6	520.9	102.9	69.1
1768	1,601.7	156.7	698.1	500.6	157.3	89.0
1769	1,525.1	154.3	725.7	375.4	147.9	121.8
1770	1,818.2	172.7	718.9	570.4	249.0	107.2
1771	1,437.7	100.9	684.9	386.2	217.0	48.7
1772	1,766.7	140.9	833.7	441.5	272.1	78.5
1773	1,733.9	110.9	1,017.1	248.5	297.8	59.6
1774	1,964.9	139.6	909.7	552.3	326.5	36.8
1775	1,940.1	70.2	953.8	538.8	332.6	44.7

Note: [1] Dr Schumpeter's total import figure for 1702 has been increased by 100,000 to cover the totals of individual colonies and leave a small remainder for other areas.

Source: Elizabeth B. Schumpeter, *English Overseas Trade Statistics 1697–1808* (Oxford, 1960), pp. 52–6; Noel Deerr, *The History of Sugar* (London, 1949–50), vol. 1, pp. 193–202; Lowell J. Ragatz, *Statistics for the Study of British Caribbean Economic History, 1763–1833* (London, 1927). p. 19.

II
Sugar imported into England and Wales from the Leeward Islands
(000 cwt)

Year	Total	From Antigua	From St Kitts	From Nevis[1]	From Montserrat
1700	144.4	52.8	—	61.9	29.7
1701	132.4	51.0	—	59.9	21.5
1702	126.9	58.2	—	48.1	20.6
1703	148.6	77.8	—	56.7	14.1
1704	123.0	44.9	2.6	59.3	16.2
1705	n.d.	n.d.	n.d.	n.d.	n.d.
1706	45.5	17.4	8.2	11.1	8.8
1707	132.7	90.6	16.0	13.4	12.7
1708	81.0	44.6	13.4	15.7	7.3
1709	97.2	64.8	12.9	10.1	9.4
1710	226.9	112.5	30.2	67.1	17.1
1711	81.2	28.3	18.9	21.9	12.1
1712	128.4	60.5	20.0	30.2	17.7
1713	249.4	118.2	38.6	71.4	21.2
1714	175.0	87.4	34.8	43.4	9.4
1715	224.8	109.5	37.8	58.1	19.4
1716	295.5	121.7	81.8	65.2	26.8
1717	288.4	135.7	80.3	51.5	20.9
1718	122.9	39.6	43.1	18.6	21.6
1719	270.6	114.1	80.5	49.0	27.0
1720	268.4	113.2	91.9	36.7	26.6
1721	176.3	42.9	62.6	48.7	22.1
1722	277.5	79.1	113.0	56.5	28.9
1723	354.3	149.4	121.1	52.9	30.9
1724	286.2	119.4	95.5	52.9	18.4
1725	367.4	149.4	128.7	59.4	29.9
1726	256.6	77.6	127.2	25.8	26.0
1727	300.4	96.1	141.4	30.2	32.7
1728	453.8	187.3	165.6	50.3	50.6
1729	472.0	205.5	158.7	71.5	36.3
1730	449.6	182.3	162.4	60.1	44.8

Appendices

Year	Total	From Antigua	From St Kitts	From Nevis[1]	From Montserrat
1731	359.7	124.4	174.5	27.6	33.2
1732	424.1	130.7	191.7	54.7	47.0
1733	496.6	188.3	197.9	63.4	47.0
1734	310.1	86.6	154.3	34.0	35.2
1735	484.4	185.1	190.5	45.8	63.0
1736	413.3	149.1	177.3	38.7	48.2
1737	174.4	34.7	97.2	12.8	29.7
1738	388.8	146.4	146.0	43.4	53.0
1739	437.5	193.7	170.6	47.1	26.1
1740	285.4	107.5	105.7	25.0	47.2
1741	349.4	133.7	139.4	38.9	37.4
1742	248.8	92.2	113.0	14.7	28.9
1743	374.7	146.1	149.0	38.0	41.6
1744	342.0	127.8	141.0	34.5	38.7
1745	330.2	123.2	140.5	33.6	32.9
1746	365.6	143.8	152.1	36.1	33.6
1747	189.2	62.1	90.4	16.1	20.6
1748	443.5	178.0	175.8	40.2	49.5
1749	406.9	175.1	158.2	22.3	51.3
1750	356.4	136.5	164.4	21.7	33.8
1751	350.7	131.3	157.6	25.1	36.7
1752	311.2	118.0	139.5	30.5	23.2
1753	437.8	249.2	79.8	55.7	53.1
1754	249.0	63.2	118.9	31.7	35.2
1755	479.0	212.9	165.8	49.3	51.0
1756	444.3	176.8	164.0	57.6	45.9
1757	548.0	224.8	218.6	58.4	46.2
1758	485.8	227.5	162.0	47.9	48.4
1759	294.8	102.9	133.7	25.7	32.5
1760	377.8	106.9	181.7	37.8	51.4
1761	493.3	194.0	198.5	46.6	54.2
1762	386.1	167.7	151.2	28.2	39.0
1763	349.3	128.0	150.0	30.6	40.7
1764	465.2	193.0	176.6	40.1	55.5
1765	317.9	91.7	149.9	36.2	40.1

Sugar and Slavery

Year	Total	From Antigua	From St Kitts	From Nevis[1]	From Montserrat
1766	560.3	259.0	203.2	52.1	46.0
1767	520.9	250.3	190.6	43.2	36.8
1768	500.6	208.0	200.0	50.1	42.5
1769	375.4	145.2	150.4	28.6	51.2
1770	570.4	226.5	220.2	68.3	55.4
1771	386.2	112.2	184.4	47.7	41.9
1772	441.5	114.2	210.1	59.2	58.0
1773	248.5	80.9	106.4	27.4	33.8
1774	552.3	233.4	204.7	66.6	47.6
1775	538.8	251.6	197.4	50.5	39.3

Note: [1] Imports from Nevis and St Kitts, 1700–3.

Source: As for Appendix I.

III

Sugar imported into England and Wales from the Ceded Islands (000 cwt)

Year	Total	From Grenada	From St Vincent	From Dominica	From Tobago
1762	176.0	176.0			
1763	71.6	71.6			
1764	67.0	65.7		1.3	
1765	64.5	64.5			
1766	89.3	85.5	0.7	3.1	
1767	102.9	92.8	1.3	8.8	
1768	157.3	145.5	10.3	1.5	
1769	147.9	125.2	21.2	1.5	
1770	249.0	196.1	38.4	12.8	1.7
1771	217.0	157.8	44.4	10.3	4.5
1772	272.1	194.5	53.6	10.4	13.6
1773	297.8	198.2	58.7	26.7	14.2
1774	326.5	179.4	62.6	53.5	31.0
1775	332.6	189.9	51.6	40.7	50.4

Source: As for Appendix I.

Appendices

IV
English sugar imports, re-exports, and home consumption, 1699–1775
(000 cwt)

Year	Imports[1]	Re-exports[2]	Home consumption
1699	427.6	196.6	231.0
1700	489.3	183.0	306.3
1701	435.5	137.4	298.1
1702	259.1	47.9	211.2
1703	408.9	84.6	324.3
1704	315.9	135.1	180.8
1705	370.2	72.5	297.7
1706	335.9	109.1	226.8
1707	388.3	134.0	254.3
1708	377.1	66.5	310.6
1709	397.6	75.3	322.3
1710	507.7	119.2	388.5
1711	366.4	83.9	282.5
1712	423.5	128.1	295.4
1713	503.5	188.1	315.4
1714	512.2	162.5	349.7
1715	617.4	147.8	469.6
1716	684.8	166.5	518.3
1717	763.2	300.2	463.0
1718	566.9	137.6	429.3
1719	544.6	171.3	373.3
1720	706.4	124.9	581.5
1721	497.6	70.5	427.1
1722	616.9	88.9	528.0
1723	660.8	68.4	592.4
1724	729.1	115.3	613.8
1725	852.0	153.7	698.3
1726	668.3	155.3	513.0
1727	645.2	123.8	521.4

Sugar and Slavery

Year	Imports[1]	Re-exports[2]	Home consumption
1728	972.2	239.5	732.7
1729	994.8	172.4	822.4
1730	1,024.1	182.5	841.6
1731	818.3	116.9	701.4
1732	822.8	138.4	684.4
1733	1,001.8	129.3	872.5
1734	695.7	58.2	637.5
1735	903.6	91.0	812.6
1736	877.6	78.3	799.3
1737	550.9	52.1	498.8
1738	864.2	58.6	805.6
1739	951.1	79.0	872.1
1740	706.9	82.2	624.7
1741	886.1	87.9	798.2
1742	731.4	62.8	668.6
1743	895.1	177.8	717.3
1744	724.4	75.9	648.5
1745	655.2	96.0	559.2
1746	753.5	106.4	647.1
1747	806.5	62.0	744.5
1748	982.6	126.5	856.1
1749	933.3	158.8	774.5
1750	915.3	129.8	785.5
1751	825.9	66.1	759.8
1752	825.1	49.2	775.9
1753	1,114.1	66.9	1,047.2
1754	859.1	55.1	804.0
1755	1,202.7	125.2	1,077.5
1756	1,051.3	236.4	814.9
1757	1,230.8	87.4	1,143.4
1758	1,745.6	283.6	1,462.0
1759	1,199.7	281.9	917.8
1760	1,374.7	202.3	1,172.4

Appendices

Year	Imports[1]	Re-exports[2]	Home consumption
1761	1,491.3	502.2	989.1
1762	1,444.6	409.3	1,035.3
1763	1,732.1	515.7	1,216.4
1764	1,488.1	373.9	1,114.2
1765	1,227.2	264.0	963.2
1766	1,522.7	156.8	1,365.9
1767	1,538.8	245.5	1,293.3
1768	1,651.5	266.5	1,385.0
1769	1,525.1	250.4	1,274.7
1770	1,818.2	243.3	1,574.9
1771	1,492.1	251.1	1,241.0
1772	1,786.0	205.0	1.581.0
1773	1,762.4	216.2	1,546.2
1774	2,015.9	257.3	1,758.6
1775	2,002.2	414.8	1,587.4

Notes: [1] Imports into England and Wales between 5 January 1699 and 5 January 1755, and thereafter into Great Britain.
[2] Re-exports of both raw and refined sugars.

Source: John MacGregor, *Commercial Statistics, etc.* (London, 1850), vol. 5, p. 382. These statistics are taken from the accounts made up by the Inspector-General of the Customs and differ somewhat from those compiled by Dr Elizabeth B. Schumpeter and displayed in Appendix I.

V

Annual average price of muscovado sugar in London, 1674–1775

Year	Price per cwt		Year	Price per cwt	
	s	d		s	d
1674	23	6	1702	42	9
1675	20	6	1703	45	3
			1704	41	6
1676	23	0	1705	27	3
1677	20	9			
1678	23	3	1706	29	6
1679	21	3	1707	32	9
1680	22	3	1708	33	3
			1709	45	0
1681	21	6	1710	n.d.	
1682	17	3			
1683	21	9	1711	n.d.	
1684	19	0	1712	n.d.	
1685	20	3	1713	30	3
			1714	35	4
1686	16	9	1715	34	9
1687	18	0			
1688	25	0	1716	32	0
1689	27	6	1717	n.d.	
1690	32	6	1718	n.d.	
			1719	n.d.	
1691	34	6	1720	n.d.	
1692	29	3			
1693	37	0	1721	22	0
1694	43	0	1722	23	0
1695	52	0	1723	25	0
			1724	28	4
1696	54	9	1725	21	6
1697	31	0			
1698	25	3	1726	26	4
1699	34	9	1727	n.d.	
1700	38	9	1728	24	10¼
			1729	24	5½
1701	48	0	1730	21	8½

Appendices

Year	Price per cwt		Year	Price per cwt	
	s	d		s	d
1731	19	8¼	1754	35	8¾
1732	17	10	1755	35	8¾
1733	16	11¼			
1734	25	8½	1756	34	3¼
1735	18	9½	1757	37	1
			1758	42	5¾
1736	19	5½	1759	45	9
1737	24	9	1760	39	7¾
1738	21	7¾			
1739	25	8¼	1761	36	4
1740	32	0½	1762	40	8
			1763	32	6
1741	30	5	1764	30	9
1742	29	1	1765	38	1
1743	27	3½			
1744	30	7	1766	38	3¼
1745	39	11	1767	35	11
			1768	34	8
1746	39	5	1769	37	2½
1747	42	9½	1770	36	0
1748	31	7¾			
1749	28	11¾	1771	36	10¾
1750	27	9½	1772	36	0
			1773	36	6
1751	30	6	1774	35	7
1752	38	7¾	1775	34	0
1753	33	0			

Source: From 1674 to 1726. Prices of Barbados sugar from The Invoice Books Homeward of the Royal African Company. P.R.O., London: Treasury 70/66–96. See K. G. Davies, *The Royal African Company* (London, 1957), pp. 365–6.

From 1728 to 1758. 'An Account of the Several Prices his Majestys Muscovado Sugar from Barbadoes and the Leeward Islands Sold for at each Sale, on an average in every year at the Custom House London from Christmas 1727 to Christmas 1758'. P.R.O., London: Treas. 64/276B (387).

From 1769 to 1775. Bryan Edwards, *The History, Civil and Commercial, of the British Colonies in the West Indies* (London, 1793), vol. 2, p. 267; British Museum Add. MSS 8133c, ff. 224–6; 'The Average Price of Antigua Sugars at the British Market since 1769, taken from the Books of a mercantile House in London', *British Sessional Papers, House of Commons, Accounts and Papers*, vol. XXVI, 1789, No. 646a, part 5. Antigua.

VI

Annual average prices of clayed sugar in London, 1728–58

Year	Price per cwt		Year	Price per cwt	
	s	d		s	d
1728	37	2½	1744	42	0
1729	39	3	1755	50	0¾
1730	32	4½			
			1746	51	1
1731	31	11¼	1747	55	7
1732	31	0	1748	50	1¼
1733	31	1½	1749	42	8
1734	32	9¾	1750	39	6
1735	31	4			
			1751	40	5¾
1736	29	9¾	1752	48	4¾
1737	33	0¾	1753	48	5¼
1738	34	5¼	1754	50	3½
1739	37	6	1755	49	8¼
1740	38	6¾			
			1756	48	10½
1741	38	7¼	1757	48	6
1742	41	1¾	1758	51	2¾
1743	35	0¾			

Source: P.R.O., London. Treas. 64/276B (382), (386): 'An Account of what his Majestys Clayed Sugars Imported from the British Sugar Colonies have been sold for at each Sale on an Average in every Year at the Custom House London from Christmas 1727 to Christmas 1758'.

Appendices

VII

Official and London market values of brown sugar imported into England and Wales
(five-years annual averages)

Years	Quantities imported (000 cwt)	Official value (£000)	Market value (£000)
1700–04	379.3	525.0	821.9
1706–10	419.1	551.2	735.3
1711–15	499.4	691.7	834.5
1716–20	615.6	903.4	882.3
1721–25	671.4	932.4	805.7
1726–30	866.8	1,200.0	1,054.6
1731–35	846.5	1,175.8	832.3
1736–40	790.1	1,097.1	977.8
1741–45	820.9	1,139.0	1,286.0
1746–50	857.3	1,232.6	1,464.6
1751–55	962.2	1,334.7	1,656.8
1756–60	1,330.6	1,508.3	2,650.1
1761–65	1,450.7	2,035.0	2,587.1
1766–70	1,517.3	2,163.8	2,762.8
1771–75	1,768.3	2,347.5	3,154.1

Source: Elizabeth B. Schumpeter, *English Overseas Trade Statistics 1697–1808* (Oxford, 1960), pp. 48–56. For London market prices see Appendix V above.

VIII

*Offical value of imports and exports,
England and her sugar colonies, 1697–1775*[1]
(£000 Sterling)

Year	Imports	Exports	Year	Imports	Exports
			1726	1,126.4	393.7
1697	326.5	143.4	1727	1,049.8	374.0
1698	629.7	310.3	1728	1,509.1	530.7
1699	586.3	342.6	1729	1,523.9	572.7
1700	824.2	334.2	1730	1,580.5	495.9
1701	738.6	340.3	1731	1,317.1	369.9
1702	476.2	255.7	1732	1,321.7	360.7
1703	626.5	285.0	1733	1,602.0	356.3
1704	492.5	307.2	1734	1,190.3	380.9
1705	706.6	337.7	1735	1,466.0	435.1
1706	537.6	300.9	1736	1,436.0	493.3
1707	605.1	306.7	1737	953.6	456.9
1708	593.8	345.9	1738	1,477.5	404.0
1709	647.7	418.4	1739	1,568.9	452.0
1710	785.7	239.4	1740	1,190.5	663.2
1711	558.8	266.1	1741	1,403.9	870.6
1712	686.6	334.6	1742	1,213.8	994.4
1713	796.7	468.3	1743	1,407.2	796.1
1714	847.4	489.0	1744	1,157.8	503.7
1715	1,004.8	409.0	1745	1,038.3	473.4
1716	1,108.4	505.7	1746	1,149.7	852.4
1717	1,210.6	432.0	1747	949.9	730.2
1718	909.4	573.0	1748	1,619.5	790.5
1719	887.8	341.6	1749	1,484.2	734.9
1720	1,118.6	302.9	1750	1,516.5	569.7
1721	870.7	344.2	1751	1,469.8	631.0
1722	1,022.2	412.0	1752	1,453.8	703.9
1723	1,090.5	454.3	1753	1,863.1	832.7
1724	1,190.9	543.2	1754	1,487.6	685.8
1725	1,360.3	603.4	1755	1,894.3	694.7

Appendices

Year	Imports	Exports	Year	Imports	Exports
1756	1,695.2	733.5	1766	2,821.1	1,047.8
1757	1,914.2	777.3	1767	2,706.7	1,069.1
1758	1,866.4	878.3	1768	2,958.7	1,192.8
1759	1,914.4	978.0	1769	2,706.7	1,283.1
1760	2,294.0	1,418.8	1770	3,127.0	1,280.9
1761	2,454.3	1,006.5	1771	2,702.2	1,113.7
1762	2,599.0	1,419.1	1772	3,263.8	1,387.2
1763	3,274.4	1,161.4	1773	2,707.1	1,275.2
1764	2,453.6	960.7	1774	3,445.8	1,360.4
1765	2,286.2	1,047.6	1775	3,501.2	1,626.8

Note: [1]Includes imports and exports of the established colonies plus those of the conquered colonies. Not included are the colonial imports and exports of Scotland.

Source: Sir Charles Whitworth, *State of the Trade of Great Britain in its imports and exports, progressively from the year 1697–1773* (London, 1776); David MacPherson, *Annals of Commerce* (Edinburgh, 1805), vol. 3, pp. 564, 585; Elizabeth B. Schumpeter, *English Overseas Trade Statistics 1697–1808* (Oxford, 1960), pp. 17–18.

IX

Negroes imported into and exported from Jamaica, 1702–75[1]

Year	Slave ships	Number imported	Number exported	Number retained
1702	5	843	327	516
1703	14	2,740	481	2,259
1704	16	4,120	221	3,899
1705	16	3,503	1,669	1,834
1706	14	3,804	1,086	2,718
1707	15	3,358	897	2,461
1708	23	6,627	1,379	5,248
1709	10	2,234	1,275	959
1710	15	3,662	1,191	2,471
1711	26	6,724	1,532	5,192
1712	15	4,128	1,903	2,225
1713	19	4,378	2,712	1,666
1714	24	5,789	3,507	2,282
1715	10	2,372	1,089	1,283
1716	24	6,361	2,872	3,489
1717	29	7,551	3,153	4,398
1718	25	6,253	2,247	4,006
1719	27	5,120	3,161	1,959
1720	23	5,064	2,815	2,249
1721	17	3,715	1,637	2,078
1722	41	8,469	3,263	5,206
1723	20	6,824	4,647	2,177
1724	25	6,852	3,569	3,283
1725	41	10,297	3,368	6,929
Total	494	120,788	50,001	70,787

Appendices

Year	Slave ships	Number imported	Number exported	Number retained
1726	50	11,703	4,112	7,591
1727	17	3,876	1,555	2,321
1728	30	5,350	986	4,364
1729	40	10,499	4,820	5,679
1730	43	10,104	5,222	4,882
1731	45	10,079	5,708	4,371
1732	57	13,552	5,288	8,264
1733	37	7,413	5,176	2,237
1734	20	4,570	1,666	2,904
1735	20	4,851	2,260	2,591
1736	15	3,913	1,647	2,266
1737	35	8,995	2,240	6,755
1738	32	7,695	2,070	5,625
1739	29	6,787	598	6,189
1740	27	5,362	495	4,867
1741	19	4,255	562	3,693
1742	22	5,067	792	4,275
1743	38	8,926	1,368	7,558
1744	38	8,755	1,331	7,424
1745	18	3,843	1,344	2,499
1746	16	4,703	1,502	3,201
1747	33	10,898	3,378	7,520
1748	39	10,430	2,426	8,004
1749	25	6,858	2,128	4,730
1750	16	3,587	721	2,866
Total	761	182,071	59,395	122,676

Sugar and Slavery

Year	Slave ships	Number imported	Number exported	Number retained
1751	21	4,840	713	4,127
1752	27	6,117	1,038	5,079
1753	39	7,661	902	6,759
1754	47	9,551	1,592	7,959
1755	64	12,723	598	12,125
1756	46	11,166	1,902	9,264
1757	32	7,935	943	6,992
1758	11	3,405	411	2,994
1759	18	5,212	681	4,531
1760	23	7,573	2,368	5,205
1761	29	6,480	642	5,838
1762	24	6,279	232	6,047
1763	33	10,079	1,582	8,497
1764	41	10,213	2,639	7,574
1765	41	8,951	2,006	6,945
1766	43	10,208	672	9,536
1767	19	3,248	375	2,873
1768	27	5,950	485	5,465
1769	19	3,575	420	3,155
1770	25	6,824	836	5,988
1771	17	4,183	671	3,512
1772	22	5,278	923	4,355
1773	49	9,676	800	8,876
1774	79	18,448	2,511	15,937
1775	39	9,292	1,629	7,663
Total	835	194,867	27,571	167,296
Grand total	2,090	497,726	136,967	360,759

Note: [1]These records were kept to assess the duties levied on slaves imported into and exported from Jamaica. Numerous slaves were reportedly smuggled into and out of Jamaica in order to avoid the duties.

Source: P.R.O., London, C.O. 137/38, Hh 3, 4: Appendix to a memorial from Stephen Fuller, Agent for Jamaica, to the Board of Trade, 30 Jan. 1778. Two other copies of this report, with some variance in the numbers imported and exported, can be found in the Long Papers in the British Museum. See B. M. Add. MSS 12,435, ff. 27–30.

Appendices

X

Negroes imported into Barbados, 1708–75

Year	Number	Year	Number
		1747	1,802
1708	1,227	1748	1,182
1709	683	1749	1,044
1710	1,170	1750	3,100
1711	1,075	1751	4,908
1712	3,031	1752	3,761
1713	6,467	1753	3,815
1714	5,107	1754	6,139
1715	5,546	1755	4,244
1716	4,084	1756	2,579
1717	5,534	1757	2,778
1718	7,126	1758	2,601
1719	3,705	1759	1,177
1720	1,192	1760	3,388
1721	1,253	1761	642
1722	818	1762	3,069
1723	2,064	1763	4,092
1724	3,251	1764	5,104
1725	2,670	1765	3,228
1726	3,914	1766	4,061
1727	3,007	1767	4,154
1728	4,141	1768	4,628
1729	4,661	1769	6,837
1730	2,908	1770	5,825
1731	3,832	1771	2,728
1732	3,081	1772	2,117
1733	1,532	1773	1,269
1734	953	1774	289
1735	1,375	1775	879

1736–1746 wanting

Source: For the periods 1708–35, and 1747–66, see Frank W. Pitman, *The Development of the British West Indies 1700–1763* (New Haven, 1917), p. 72; for the period 1764–88, see *British Sessional Papers 1731–1800, House of Commons Accounts and Papers*, vol. XXIX, 1790, No. 697, p. 2:

Sugar and Slavery

Report of a Committee of the General Assembly of Barbados relative to the Slave Trade, 18 and 23 February 1788.

XI

An account of bullion imported and brought to the Bank of England from Jamaica and the other West India islands, 1748–65
(£ sterling)

Year	From Jamaica	Other islands	Havana, Cuba	Total
1748	592,944			592,944
1749	300,440			300,440
1750	71,460			71,460
1751	6,200			6,200
1752	121,900		14,720	136,620
1753	27,420		87,000	114,420
1754	122,980			122,980
1755	139,740			139,740
1756	98,590	1,000		99,590
1757	161,760	3,840		165,600
1758	76,900	1,670		78,570
1759	23,400	460		23,860
1760	118,060	1,820		119,880
1761	73,500	5,525		79,025
1762	21,200	3,350		24,550
1763	156,390	2,456	389,450	548,296
1764	138,840	705	20,940	160,485
1765	116,760		47,000	163,760
Totals	2,368,484	20,826	559,110	2,948,420

Source: House of Lords Record Office. *An Account of Bullion imported from Jamaica and the other West India Islands. Delivered at the Bar by Mr Stone from the Bank, 24th February 1766.*

Select Bibliography

A Documentary Authorities

1 Manuscripts in the Public Record Office, London

C.O. 1:	Colonial Office Papers, Class 1.
C.O. 5:	America and West Indies, Original Documents.
C.O. 7:	Antigua, Correspondence with the Secretary of State.
C.O. 8:	Antigua, Acts of the Assembly.
C.O. 28:	Barbados, Original Correspondence with the Board of Trade.
C.O. 29:	Barbados, Entry Books.
C.O. 30:	Barbados, Acts of the Assembly.
C.O. 31:	Barbados, Proceedings of Council and Assembly.
C.O. 33: 16–17	Barbados Naval Office Lists, 1711–1764.
C.O. 137:	Jamaica, Original Correspondence with the Board of Trade.
C.O. 139:	Jamaica, Acts of the Assembly.
C.O. 140:	Jamaica, Proceedings of Council and Assembly.
C.O. 142: 14–17	Jamaica, Naval Office Lists, 1702–1769.
C.O. 142: 31	Jamaica, List of Landholders in 1754.
C.O. 152:	Leeward Islands, Original Correspondence with the Board of Trade.
C.O. 154:	Leeward Islands, Acts of the Assembly.
C.O. 155:	Leeward Islands, Proceedings of the Council and Assembly.
C.O. 157: 1	Leeward Islands, Naval Office Lists, 1704–1715.
C.O. 176:	Montserrat, Acts of the Assembly.
C.O. 185:	Nevis, Acts of the Assembly.
C.O. 187: 1–2	Nevis, Naval Office Lists, 1720–1729.
C.O. 240:	St Kitts, Acts of the Assembly.
C.O. 318:	West Indies, Trade and Miscellaneous Papers.
C.O. 323:	Plantations General, Original Papers.
C.O. 324:	Plantations General, Entry Books and Miscellaneous Papers.
C.O. 388:	Board of Trade, Commercial Series, Papers and Consular Reports on British Foreign Trade.
C.O. 389:	Board of Trade, Commercial Series II, Entry Books.

Sugar and Slavery

C.O. 390:	Board of Trade, Commercial Series, Customs House Accounts.
C.O. 391:	Board of Trade Journal.
Customs 3:	Customs House Accounts, Ledgers of Imports and Exports.
Treas. 38: 253, 256, 258–268, 270, 362–364	
	Revenue Accounts, Miscellaneous, England. Accounts of West-Indian trade and production.
Treas. 64: 273–275 Ibid.	
Treas. 70:	Books and Papers of the Royal African Company.

2 *Printed Calendars of Manuscripts in the Public Record Office*

Acts of the Privy Council, Colonial Series, 1680–1766.
Calendar of State Papers, Colonial Series, America and West Indies, 1661–1737.
Calendar of State Papers, Domestic, 1660–1756.
Calendar of Treasury Books, 1660–1710.
Calendar of Treasury Papers, 1702–1730.
Calendar of Treasury Books and Papers, 1731–1745.
Journal of the Commissioners for Trade and Plantations, 1704–1758.

3 *Manuscripts in the British Museum*

B.M. Egerton MSS 2395.
B.M. Sloane MSS 3662.
B.M. Add. MSS 11,411. Povey's Register of Letters Relating to the West Indies, 1655–1661.
Letter Books of Colonel Samuel Martin of Antigua and England.
B.M. Add. MSS 41,346 (1750–1758), vol. I.
                41,347 (1760–1768), vol. II.
                41,348 (1768–1776), vol. III.
                41,349 (1756–1762), vol. IV.
                41,350 (1765–1770), vol. V.
                41,351 (1774–1776), vol. Vl.
Papers collected by Edward Long of Jamaica and England.
B.M. Add. MSS   12,402 – 12,440.
                18,270 – 18,275.
                18,959 – 18,963.
                21,931 – 22,639.
                22,676 – 22,680.

Select Bibliography

4 *Manuscripts in the West Indies*

Jamaica Public Record Office, Spanish Town. The following series have been used in this study: Inventorys, Account Produce, Wills, Deeds and Patents.

B Other Contemporary Authorities

1 *Manuscript Letters and Account Books*

Letter Book of Messrs Lascelles and Maxwell, London commission agents, vol. 2, Sept. 1743 to Jan. 1745.
Account book of Henry Lascelles, 1753.
  These manuscripts are in the possession of Messrs Wilkinson and Gaviller, 14 Clifford Street, London, W.1.
Letter Books of Dr Walter Tullideph, sugar planter of Antigua.
  Vol. 1. 25 June 1734, to 10 Feb. 1744.
  Vol. 2. 3 March 1744, to 28 March 1759.
  Vol. 3. 2 April 1759, to April 1767.
Plantation and Medical ledgers and journals of Dr Tullideph from 1731 to 1767.
  These manuscripts are in the possession of Sir Herbert Ogilvy, a descendant of Dr Tullideph, at Baldovan Estate, near Dundee, Scotland.
West India Committee, London. Minutes of West India Merchants. April 1769 to April 1779.

2 *Printed Letter Collections, Diaries and Papers*

Andrews, Evangeline and Charles M. (eds.), *Journal of a Lady of Quality* (New Haven, 1921). Contains descriptions of Antigua and St Kitts by a Scots lady.
Caribbeana, Containing Letters and Dissertations ... chiefly wrote by several Hands in the West Indies ... relating to Trade, Government, and Laws in General, but more especially to those of the British Sugar Colonies, and of Barbados in particular. Two vols. London, 1741. This source contains a number of letters which were written by planters and appeared in the *Barbados Gazette* from 1733 to 1737.
Commerce of Rhode Island, 1726–1800. Massachusetts Historical Society Collections, 7th series, vols. IX, X. Boston, 1914–15. Vol. IX contains letters written to Abraham Redwood, an absentee planter of Antigua who resided in Newport, Rhode Island.
Donnan, Elizabeth (ed.), *Documents Illustrative of the History of the*

509

Sugar and Slavery

Slave Trade to America. Four vols. Carnegie Institute of Washington Pub. no. 409. Washington, D.C., 1930–35.

Gay, Edwin F., 'Notes and Documents. Letters from a Sugar Plantation in Nevis, 1723–1732', *Journal of Economic and Business History*, vol. 1, Nov. 1928, pp. 149–73. These letters relate to the sugar plantations of Sir William Stapleton.

Harland, J. (ed.), *Autobiography of William Stout of Lancaster, Wholesale and Retail Grocer and Ironmonger, A Member of the Society of Friends, A.D. 1665–1752.* The Lancashire and Cheshire Historical Society, London and Manchester, 1851.

Howard, Robert Mowbray (ed.), *Records and Letters of the Family of the Longs of Longville, Jamaica, and Hampton Lodge, Surrey.* Two vols. London, 1925.

Jeaffreson, John Cordy, *A Young Squire of the Seventeenth Century, from the Papers (A.D. 1676–1686) of Christopher Jeaffreson of Dullingham House, Cambridgeshire.* Two vols. London, 1878. Contains extracts of letters written by Christopher Jeaffreson who owned plantations and lived for a time in St Kitts.

Martin, Bernard and Mark Spurrel (eds.), *The Journal of a Slave Trader (John Newton) 1750–1754*, London, 1962.

Oliver, Vere Langford (ed.), *Caribbeana. Being Miscellaneous Papers Relating to the History, Genealogy, Topography, and Antiquities of the British West Indies.* Six vols. London, 1909–19. Contains a wealth of material of great value.

Sheridan, Richard B., 'Letters from a Sugar Plantation in Antigua, 1739–1758', *Agricultural History*, vol. 31, no. 3 (July 1957), pp. 3–23. Contains extracts from the letter books of Dr Walter Tullideph.

The Interesting Narrative of The Life of Olaudah Equiano, or Gustavus Vassa, The African. Written by Himself. 4th ed. Dublin, 1791. Paul Edwards has edited an abridged version of this work under the title, *Equiano's Travels*, New York, 1966.

Yorke, Philip C. (ed.), *The Diary of John Baker, Barrister of the Middle Temple, Solicitor-General of the Leeward Islands.* London, 1931. Excellent descriptions of the social life of resident and absentee planters.

C Tracts and Pamphlets

A Short Account of the Interest and Conduct of the Jamaica Planters in an Address to the Merchants, Traders, and Liverymen of the City of London. London, 1754.

Select Bibliography

An Account of the Late Application to Parliament, From the Sugar Refiners, Grocers, etc., of the Cities of London and Westminster, the Borough of Southwark, and of the city of Bristol. London, 1753.

An Essay on the Increase and decline of Trade in London and the Outports, etc. London, 1749.

Ashley, John, *Memoirs and Considerations concerning the Trade and Revenue of the British Colonies in America, etc.* Two parts. London, 1740.

Bennet, John, *Two Letters and Several Calculations on The Sugar Colonies and Trade, etc.* London, 1738.

Campbell, John, *A Political Survey of Britain.* Two vols. London, 1774.

————, *Candid and Impartial Considerations on the Nature of the Sugar Trade, etc.* London, 1763.

Carman, Harry J. (ed.), *American Husbandry*, New York, 1939.

Cary, John, *An Essay on the State of England in Relation to its Trade.* Bristol, 1695.

Child, Sir Josiah, *A New Discourse of Trade.* London, 1718.

Cleland, William, *The Present State of the Sugar Plantations Considered, but more especially that of the Island of Barbadoes.* London, 1713.

Considerations on the State of the Sugar Islands, etc. London, 1773.

[Dicker, Samuel], *A Letter to a Member of Parliament concerning the Importance of the Sugar Colonies to Great Britain, by a Gentleman who resided many years in the Island of Jamaica.* London, 1745.

Foster, Nicholas, *A Briefe Relation of the late Horrid Rebellion Acted in the Island of Barbadas.* London, 1650.

Godwyn, Morgan, *The Negro's and Indians Advocate, Suing for Their Admission into the Church, etc.* London, 1680.

Littleton, Edward, *The Groans of the Plantations: Or, A True Account of Their Grevious and Extreme Sufferings by the Heavy Impositions upon Sugar, And other Hardships Relating more particularly to the Island of Barbados.* London, 1689.

Martin, Samuel, *An Essay on Plantership, etc.* London, 1773.

Massie, Joseph, *A State of the British Sugar Colony Trade, etc.* London, 1759.

M'Neill, Hector, *Observations on the Treatment of Negroes in the Island of Jamaica.* London, 1788.

Ramsay, James, *An Essay on the Treatment and Conversion of African Slaves in the British Sugar Colonies.* London, 1784.

Reasons against laying any further duty upon Sugar. London, 1744.

Sugar and Slavery

Reasons humbly offered against laying a further Imposition upon Sugar. London, c. 1695.

[Robertson, Robert], *A Detection of the State and Situation of the Present Sugar Planters of Barbados and the Leeward Islands, etc.* London, 1732.

Sheffield, John Lord, *Observations on the Commerce of the American States.* London, 1784.

Some Observations: Which May Contribute to Afford a Just Idea . . . of our New West-India Colonies. London, 1764.

The Alarm Bell: or, Considerations on the Present Dangerous State of the Sugar Colonies, etc. London, 1749.

The Art of Making Sugar, etc. London, 1752.

The Case of the British Northern Colonies. London, 1732.

The Case of the British Sugar Colonies. London, 1732.

The Case of the Refiners of Sugar in England. London, 1744.

The Controversy between the Northern Colonies and the Sugar Islands respectively considered, etc. London, 1732.

The Dispute between the Northern Colonies, and the Sugar Islands, set in Clear View. London, 1732.

The Importance of Jamaica to Great Britain Consider'd, With some Account of that Island from its Discovery in 1492 to this Time, etc. London, 1741.

The Importance of the Sugar Colonies to Great Britain Stated, and Some Objections against the Sugar Colony Bill Answer'd, etc. London. 1731.

The Miserable Case of the British Sugar Planters, wherein is contained, some Remarks on the Poverty, Distress, and other difficulties, which they labour under, etc. London, 1738.

The Present Case of the Barbadoes Planter, and Reasons against laying a further Duty on Sugar. London, 1695.

The State of the Case of the Sugar Plantations in America. London, 1695.

Tryon, Thomas, *England's Grandeur and the Way to get Wealth, Or, Promotion of Trade made easy and lands advanced, etc.* London, 1699.

———, *Friendly advice to the Gentlemen Planters of the East and West Indies. In three parts.* London, 1684.

———, *Tryon's Letters, Domestic and Foreign, To several Persons of Quality Occasionally distributed in Subjects, etc.* London, 1700.

Young, Arthur, *Political Essays Concerning the Present State of the British Empire.* London, 1772.

Wood, William, *A Survey of Trade, etc.* London, 1718.

Select Bibliography

D Historical Works of the 17th and 18th Centuries

A New History of Jamaica from the Earliest Accounts of the taking of Porto Bello by Vice Admiral Vernon. London, 1740.

Beckford, William, *A Descriptive Account of the Island of Jamaica, etc.* Two vols. London, 1790.

Blome, Richard, *Description of the Island of Jamaica.* London, 1672.

Browne, Patrick, *Civil and Natural History of Jamaica.* London, 1789.

Burke, William and Edmund, *An Account of the European Settlements in America.* Two vols. London, 1777.

Edwards, Bryan, *The History, Civil and Commercial, of the British Colonies in the West Indies.* Two vols. London and Dublin, 1793.

Frere, George, *A Short History of Barbados, From its First Discovery and Settlement to the End of the Year 1767.* London, 1768.

Hughes, Griffith, *The Natural History of Barbados.* London, 1750.

Labat, Jean B., *Nouveau Voyage aux isles de l'Amerique.* Paris, 1724.

Leslie, Charles, *A New and Exact Account of Jamaica, etc.* Edinburgh, 1739.

Ligon, Richard, *A True and Exact History of the Island of Barbadoes, etc.* London, 1657.

Long, Edward, *The History of Jamaica.* Three vols. London, 1774.

Oldmixon, John, *The British Empire in America, etc.* Two vols. London, 1708.

Raynal, Guillaume T. F., *A Philosophical and Political History of the Settlements and Trade of the Europeans in the East and West Indies.* trans. J. O. Justamond. Eight vols. London, 1788.

Sloane, Sir Hans, *A Voyage to the Islands, Madera, Barbados, Nieves, St. Christophers, and Jamaica, etc.* Two vols. London, 1707.

Smith, Adam, *An Inquiry into the Nature and Causes of the Wealth of Nations.* London, 1776.

Thomas, Sir Dalby, *An Historical Account of the Rise and Growth of the West-India Collonies, And of the Great Advantage they are to England, in respect to Trade.* London, 1690.

E Historical Works of the 19th Century

Anderson, Adam, *An Historical and Chronological Deduction of the Origins of Commerce, etc.* Four vols. London, 1801.

Brougham, Henry, *An Inquiry into the Colonial Policy of the European Powers.* Two vols. Edinburgh, 1803.

Sugar and Slavery

Chalmers, Robert, *A History of Currency in the British Colonies.* London, 1893.

Davis, N. Darnell, *The Cavaliers and Roundheads of Barbados, 1650–1652.* Georgetown, British Guiana, 1887.

Gardiner, W. J., *A History of Jamaica from its First Discovery by Columbus to the Year 1872.* London, 1873.

Heeren, Arnold H. L., *A Manual of the History of the Political System of Europe and its Colonies.* trans. Henry G. Bohn. London, 1873.

List, Friedrich, *The National System of Political Economy*, trans. Sampson P. Lloyd. London, 1885.

MacGregor, John, *Commercial Statistics, etc.* Five vols. London, 1850.

MacPherson, David, *Annals of Commerce, Manufactures, Fisheries, and Navigation, etc.* Four vols. Edinburgh, 1805.

Merivale, Herman, *Lectures on Colonization and Colonies, Delivered before the University of Oxford in 1839, 1840, and 1841.* London 1861.

Moseley, Benjamin, *A Treatise on Sugar with Miscellaneous Observations.* Second edition. London, 1800.

Oliver, Vere Langford, *The History of the Island of Antigua, etc.* Three vols. London, 1894–99.

Schomburgk, Sir Robert H., *The History of Barbadoes Comprising a Geographical and Statistical Description of the Island, etc.* London, 1848.

Southey, Thomas, *Chronological History of the West Indies.* Three vols. London, 1827.

Weeden, William B., *Economic and Social History of New England, 1620–1789.* Two vols. Boston and New York, 1890.

Williams, Gomer, *History of the Liverpool Privateers and Letters of Marque with an Account of the Liverpool Slave Trade.* London, 1897.

Young, Sir William, *The West-India Common-Place Book.* London, 1807.

F Modern Works

1 *Guides to Materials and Bibliographies*

Andrews, Charles M., *Guide to the Materials for American History to 1783 in the Public Record Office of Great Britain.* Two vols. Washington, D.C., 1912, 1914.

Select Bibliography

——— and F. C. Davenport, *Guide to the Manuscript Materials for the History of the United States to 1783, in the British Museum, in Minor London Archives, and in the Libraries of Oxford and Cambridge.* Washington, D.C., 1908.

Baker, E. C., *A Guide to Records in the Leeward Islands.* Oxford, 1965.

Bell, Herbert C. et al., *Guide to British West Indian Archive Materials in London and in the Islands, for the History of the United States.* Washington, D.C., 1926.

Chandler, M. J., *A Guide to Records in Barbados.* Oxford, 1965.

Cundall, Frank, *Bibliographia Jamaicanais, etc.* Kingston, 1902.

———, *Journal of the Institute of Jamaica,* Kingston, 1899.

Meyer, H. H. B., *Select List of References on Sugar Chiefly in its Economic Aspects.* Library of Congress. Washington, D.C., 1910.

Ragatz, Lowell J., *A Guide for the Study of British Caribbean History, 1763–1834, Including the Abolition and Emancipation Movements.* Washington, D.C., 1932.

Roth, H. L., *A Guide to the Literature of Sugar.* London, 1890.

Thompson, Edgar T., *The Plantation: A Bibliography.* Social Science Monograph IV. Pan American Union, Washington, D.C., 1957.

2 *Unpublished Theses*

Hall, I. V., *A History of the Sugar Trade in England with Special Reference to the Sugar Trade of Bristol.* M.A. thesis, University of Bristol, 1925.

Sheridan, Richard B., *The Sugar Trade of the British West Indies from 1660 to 1756 with Special Reference to the Island of Antigua.* Ph.D. thesis, University of London, 1951.

Thoms, David W., *West India Merchants and Planters in The Mid-Eighteenth Century with Special Reference to St. Kitts.* M.A. thesis, University of Kent at Canterbury, 1967.

3 *Other Works*

Alexander, Boyd, *England's Wealthiest Son: A Study of William Beckford.* London, 1962.

Andrews, Charles M., 'Colonial Commerce', *American Historical Review,* vol. XX (1914–15), pp. 43–63.

———, *The Colonial Background of the American Revolution.* Rev. ed. New Haven, 1927.

———, *The Colonial Period of American History.* Four vols. New Haven, 1938.

Armytage, Frances, *The Free port System in the British West Indies.* London, 1953.

Ashley, Maurice, *Financial and Commercial Policy under the Cromwellian Protectorate.* London, 1962.

Ashton, T. S., *An Economic History of England: The 18th Century.* London, 1955.

Augier, F. R., D. G. Hall, S. C. Gordon, and M. Record, *The Making of The West Indies.* London, 1960.

Bailyn, Bernard, *The New England Merchants in the Seventeenth Century.* Cambridge, Mass., 1955.

Beer, George L., *The Origins of the British Colonial System, 1578–1660.* New York, 1908.

———, *The Old Colonial System, 1660–1754.* Two vols. New York, 1912.

———, *British Colonial Policy, 1754–1765.* New York, 1933.

Bell, Herbert C., 'The West-India Trade Before the American Revolution', *Amer. Hist. Rev.* vol. XXII (1917), pp. 272–87.

Bennett, J. Harry, *Bondsmen and Bishops, Slavery and Apprenticeship on the Codrington Plantations of Barbados, 1710–1838.* Berkeley and Los Angeles, 1958.

———, 'Cary Helyar, Merchant and Planter of Seventeenth-Century Jamaica', *William and Mary Quarterly,* 3rd ser., vol. XXI, no. 1 (Jan. 1964), pp. 53–76.

———, 'William Whaley, Planter of Seventeenth-Century Jamaica', *Agricultural History,* vol. XL, no. 2 (April 1966), pp. 113–23.

Black, Clinton V., *History of Jamaica.* London, 1958.

Botsford, Jay B., *English Society in the Eighteenth-Century As Influenced from Oversea.* New York, 1924.

Brown, Vera Lee, 'The South Sea Company and Contraband Trade', *Amer. Hist. Rev.,* vol. XXXI, no. 4 (July 1926), pp. 662–78.

Burns, Sir Alan, *History of the British West Indies.* London, 1954.

Chandler, Aflred D., 'The Expansion of Barbados', *Journal of the Barbados Museum and Historical Society,* vol. XIII, nos. 3 and 4 (1946), pp. 106–30.

Christelow, Allan, 'Contaband Trade between Jamaica and the Spanish Main, and the Freeport Act of 1766', *The Hispanic American Historical Review,* vol. XXII, no. 2 (May 1942), pp. 309–43.

Clark, G. N., *Guide to the English Commercial Statistics, 1696–1782.* London, 1938.

Corbett, Julian S., *England in the Seven Years' War: A Study in Combined Strategy.* London, 1907.

Curtin, Philip, *The Atlantic Slave Trade: A Census.* Madison, 1969.

Select Bibliography

Davies, K. G., *The Royal African Company.* London, 1957.

——, 'The Origins of the Commission System in the West India Trade', *Transactions of the Royal Historical Society,* 5th ser., vol. 52 (1952), pp. 89–107.

Davis, Ralph, *The Rise of the English Shipping Industry in the Seventeenth and Eighteenth Centuries.* London, 1962.

Deane, Phyllis and W. A. Cole, *British Economic Growth 1688–1959, Trends and Structure.* Cambridge, 1962.

Deerr, Noel, *The History of Sugar.* Two vols. London, 1949–50.

Dunn, Richard S., 'The Barbados Census of 1680: Profile of the Richest Colony in English America', *William and Mary Quarterly,* 3rd ser., vol. XXVI, no. 1 (Jan. 1969), pp. 3–30.

Fage, J. D., *An Introduction to the History of West Africa.* Cambridge, 1961.

Farnie, D. A., 'The Commercial Empire of the Atlantic, 1607–1783', *The Economic History Review,* 2nd ser., vol. XV, no. 2 (Dec. 1962), pp. 205–18.

Fay, C. R., *Imperial Economy and its Place in the Formation of Economic Doctrine 1600–1932.* Oxford, 1934.

Fisher, F. J., *Essays in the Economic and Social History of Tudor and Stuart England, in honour of R. H. Tawney.* Cambridge, 1961.

Gipson, Lawrence H., *The British Empire before the American Revolution.* Seven vols. 1936–1949.

Gourou, Pierre, *The Tropical World: Its Social and Economic Conditions and Its Future Status.* New York, 1962.

Goveia, Elsa V., *A Study on the Historiography of the British West Indies to the End of the Nineteenth Century.* Mexico, 1956.

——, *Slave Society in the British Leeward Islands at the End of the Eighteenth Century.* New Haven and London, 1965.

——, 'The West Indian Slave Laws of the Eighteenth Century', *Revista de Ciencias Sociales,* vol. IV, no. 1 (March 1960), pp. 75–105.

Hall, Douglas G., *Free Jamaica 1838–1865: An Economic History.* New Haven, 1959, and London, 1969.

——, 'Incalculability as a Feature of Sugar Production during the Eighteenth Century', *Social and Economic Studies,* vol. 10, no. 3 (Sept. 1961), pp. 340–52.

——, 'Slaves and Slavery in the British West Indies', *Social and Economic Studies,* vol. 11, no. 4 (Dec. 1962), pp. 305–18.

——, 'Absentee-Proprietorship in the British West Indies, To About 1850', *The Jamaican Historical Review,* vol. IV (1964), pp. 15–35.

——, *Ideas and Illustrations in Economic History,* New York, 1964.

Sugar and Slavery

──────, *A Brief History of the West India Committee*. London, 1971.
Hamilton, Henry, *An Economic History of Scotland in the Eighteenth Century*. Oxford, 1963.
Harlow, V. T., *Colonising Expeditions to the West Indies and Guiana 1623–1667*. London, 1924.
──────, *A History of Barbados*. Oxford, 1926.
──────, *Christopher Codrington, 1668–1710*. Oxford, 1928.
Harper, Lawrence A., *The English Navigation Laws*. New York, 1939.
Herskovits, Melville J., *The Myth of the Negro Past*. Boston, 1958.
Hertz, Gerald B., *British Imperialism in the Eighteenth Century*. London, 1908.
Higham, C. S. S., *The Development of the Leeward Islands Under the Restoration, 1660–1688*. Cambridge, 1921.
Hobsbawm, E. J., 'The Crisis of the Seventeenth Century', in *Crisis in Europe 1560–1660*, ed. Trevor Aston, New York, 1965.
Hotblack, Kate, *Chatham's Colonial Policy: A Study in the Fiscal and Economic Implications of the Colonial Policy of the Elder Pitt*. London, 1917.
Innis, Harold A., *The Cod Fisheries: The History of an International Economy*. New Haven, 1940.
John, A. H., 'War and the English Economy, 1700–1763', *Econ. Hist. Rev.*, 2nd ser., vol. VII, no. 3 (April 1955), pp. 329–44.
Judd, Gerrit P., *Members of Parliament 1734–1832*. New Haven, 1955.
Klingberg, Frank J. (ed.), *Codrington Chronicle: An Experiment in Anglican Altruism on a Barbados Plantation, 1710–1834*. Berkeley and Los Angeles, 1949.
Knorr, Klaus E., *British Colonial Theories 1570–1850*. Toronto, 1944.
Macpherson, John, *Caribbean Lands: A Geography of the West Indies*. London, 1963.
Merrill, Gordon C., *The Historical Geography of St. Kitts and Nevis*. Mexico, 1958.
──────, 'The Role of the Sephardic Jews in the British Caribbean Area during the Seventeenth Century', *Caribbean Studies*, vol. 4, no. 3 (Oct. 1964), pp. 32–49.
Metcalf, George, *Royal Government and Political Conflict in Jamaica 1729–1783*. London, 1965.
Minchinton, W. E. (ed.), *The Trade of Bristol in the Eighteenth Century*. Bristol, 1957.
Mintz, Sidney W., Foreword to Ramiro Guerra y Sanchez, *Sugar and*

Select Bibliography

Society in the Caribbean: An Economic History of Cuban Agriculture. New Haven, 1964.

——— and Douglas G. Hall, 'The Origins of the Jamaican Internal Marketing System', *Yale University Publications in Anthropology No. 57.* New Haven, 1960.

Namier, Sir Lewis, *The Structure of Politics at the Accession of George III.* Two vols. London, 1929.

———, *England in the Age of the American Revolution.* London, 1930.

Nelson, George H., 'Contraband Trade under the Asiento, 1730–1739', *Amer. Hist. Rev.,* vol. LI, no. 1 (Oct. 1945), pp. 55–67.

Nettels, Curtis, P., 'England and the Spanish-American Trade, 1680–1715', *The Journal of Modern History,* vol. III, no. 1 (March 1931), pp. 1–32.

———, 'The Place of Markets in the Old Colonial System', *The New England Quarterly,* vol. VI (Sept. 1933), pp. 508–17.

Newton, Arthur P., *The European Nations in the West Indies, 1493–1688.* London, 1933.

Nieboer, H. J., *Slavery as an Industrial System.* The Hague, 1900.

Pares, Richard, *War and Trade in the West Indies, 1739–1763.* Oxford, 1936.

———, *A West India Fortune,* London, 1950.

———, *Yankees and Creoles: The trade between North America and the West Indies before the American Revolution.* Cambridge, Mass., 1956.

———, 'The London Sugar Market, 1740–1769', *Econ. Hist. Rev.,* 2nd ser., vol. IX, no. 2 (Dec. 1956), pp. 254–70.

———, *Merchants and Planters.* Cambridge, 1960.

———, *The Historian's Business and Other Essays.* ed. R. A. and Elisabeth Humphreys. Oxford, 1961.

Parry, J. H. and P. M. Sherlock, *A Short History of the West Indies.* London, 1957.

Penson, Lillian M., 'The London West India Interest in the Eighteenth Century', *The English Historical Review,* vol. 36 (1921), pp. 373–92.

———, *The Colonial Agents of the British West Indies: A Study in Colonial Administration, Mainly in the Eighteenth Century.* London, 1924.

Pitman, Frank W., *The Development of the British West Indies, 1700–1763.* New Haven, 1917.

———, 'Slavery on the British West India Plantations in the

Eighteenth Century', *The Journal of Negro History*, vol. XI, no. 4 (Oct. 1926), pp. 584–660.

———, 'The Settlement and Financing of British West India Plantations in the Eighteenth Century', *Essays in Colonial History Presented to Charles McLean Andrews by his Students.* New Haven, 1931.

Polanyi, Karl, *Dahomey and the Slave Trade: An Analysis of an Archaic Economy.* Seattle, 1966.

Ragatz, Lowell J., *The Fall of the Planter Class in the British Caribbean, 1763–1833.* New York and London, 1928.

———, 'Absentee Landlordism in the British Caribbean, 1750–1833', *Agricultural History*, vol. V, no. 1 (Jan. 1931), pp. 7–26.

———, *Statistics for the Study of British Caribbean Economic History, 1763–1833.* London, 1927.

Roberts, George W., *The Population of Jamaica.* Cambridge, 1957.

Sauer, Carl O., *Agricultural Origins and Dispersals.* New York, 1952.

Schumpeter, Elizabeth B., *English Overseas Trade Statistics 1697–1808. With an Introduction by T. S. Ashton.* Oxford, 1960.

Shephard, C. Y., 'British West Indian Economic History in Imperial Perspective', *Tropical Agriculture*, vol. XVI, nos. 7 and 8 (1939).

Sheridan, Richard B., 'The Molasses Act and the Market Strategy of the British Sugar Planters', *Journal of Economic History*, vol. XVII, no. 1 (March 1957), pp. 62–83.

———, 'The Commercial and Financial Organization of the British Slave Trade, 1750–1807', *Econ. Hist. Rev.*, vol. XI, no. 2 (Dec. 1958), pp. 249–63.

———, 'The British Credit Crisis of 1772 and The American Colonies', *Jour. Econ. Hist.*, vol. XX, no. 2 (June 1960), pp. 161–86.

———, 'Samuel Martin, Innovating Sugar Planter of Antigua 1750–1776', *Agric. Hist.*, vol. 24, no. 3 (July 1960), pp. 126–39.

———, 'The Rise of a Colonial Gentry: A Case Study of Antigua, 1730–1775', *Econ. Hist. Rev.*, vol. XIII, no. 3 (April 1961), pp. 342–57.

———, 'Temperate and Tropical: Aspects of European Penetration into Tropical Regions', *Caribbean Studies*, vol. 3, no. 2 (Aug. 1963), pp. 3–21.

———, 'Planter and Historian: The Career of William Beckford of Jamaica and England, 1744–1799', *The Jamaican Historical Review*, vol. IV (1964), pp. 36–58.

———, 'The Wealth of Jamaica in the Eighteenth Century', *Econ. Hist. Rev.*, 2nd ser., vol. XVIII, no. 2 (Aug. 1965), pp. 292–311.

———, 'The Wealth of Jamaica in the Eighteenth Century: A Rejoinder', *Econ. Hist. Rev.*, 2nd ser., vol. XXI, no. 1 (April 1968), pp. 46–61.

———, 'The Plantation Revolution and The Industrial Revolution, 1625–1775', *Caribbean Studies*, vol. 9, no. 3 (Oct. 1969), pp. 5–25.

———, 'Planters and Merchants: The Oliver Family of Antigua and London 1716–1784', *Business History*, vol. XIII, no. 2 (July 1971), pp. 104–13.

———, 'Africa and the Caribbean in the Atlantic Slave Trade', *The American Historical Review*, vol. 77, no. 1 (Feb. 1972), pp. 15–35.

Starkey, Otis P., *The Economic Geography of Barbados*. New York, 1939.

Strong, Frank, 'The Causes of Cromwell's West Indian Expedition', *Amer. Hist. Rev.*, vol. IV, no. 2 (1898–99), pp. 228–45.

Thomas, R. P., 'The Sugar Colonies of the Old Empire: Profit or Loss for Great Britain?' *Econ. Hist. Rev.*, 2nd ser., vol. XXI, no. 1 (April 1968), pp. 30–45.

Thoms, David W., 'Slavery in the Leeward Islands in the Mid-Eighteenth Century: A Reappraisal', *Bulletin of the Institute of Historical Research*, vol. XLII (May 1969), pp. 76–85.

———, 'The Mills Family: London Sugar Merchants in the Eighteenth Century', *Business History*, vol. XI, no. 1 (Jan. 1969), pp. 3–10.

Thornton, A. P., *West-India Policy under the Restoration*. Oxford, 1956.

Tolles, Frederick B., *Quakers and the Atlantic Culture*. New York, 1960.

Wadsworth, Alfred P. and Julia D. Mann, *The Cotton Trade and Industrial Lancashire, 1600–1780*. Manchester, 1931.

Walton, Gary M., 'New Evidence on Colonial Commerce', *Jour. Econ. Hist.* vol. XXVIII, no. 3 (Sept. 1968), pp. 363–89.

Watts, David, 'Origins of Barbadian Cane Hole Agriculture', *Jour. Barbados Museum and Hist. Soc.*, vol. XXXII, no. 3 (May 1968), pp. 143–51.

West, Robert C. and John P. Augelli, *Middle America: Its Lands and Peoples*. Englewood Cliffs, New Jersey, 1966.

Westerfield, Ray B., *Middlemen in English Business, 1660–1760*. New Haven, 1915.

Williams, Eric, *Capitalism and Slavery*. Chapel Hill, 1944.

———, 'The Golden Age of the Slave System in Britain', *Jour. Negro Hist.*, vol. XXV, no. 1 (Jan. 1940), pp. 60–106.

———, *The Negro in the Caribbean*. Manchester, 1942.

———, *History of The People of Trinidad and Tobago*. Port-of-Spain, 1962.
Williamson, James A., *The Caribbee Islands under the Proprietary Patents*. Oxford, 1925.
———, *The Ocean in English History, Being The Ford Lectures*. Oxford, 1941.
Wilson, Charles, *England's Apprenticeship 1602–1763*. London, 1965.

Index

Throughout the index the following abbreviations are used
W.I.   West Indies or West Indian
B.W.I.   British West Indies or British West Indian.

Absenteeism, 385–7, 470–4
  See also Planters
Acts of Trade, 43, 49
Addison, Joseph, 12
Africa:
  agricultural methods, 103, 238–41
  effects of removal of natives to slavery, 253–4
  slavery in, 241
  trade with B.W.I., 343–4
African Company, 90
Agents, commission (sugar factors), 282–305, 322, 375–6
  in Antigua, 101–5
  and capital for planters, 285–6
  investment of, 292
  in Jamaica, 298–300
  in London, 328–31
  in St Kitts, 301
  services to planters, 284
  and slave trade, 292–4
Amerindians, 234
  See also Carib Indians
Antigua, 184–207, 428
  Commission agents, 301–5
  description, 184
  early settlement of, 87–8, 185–6
  economic development, 194–200
  exports, 195
  French invasions of, 187–8
  planters and plantership, 191–4, 378–9
  population, 189, 192, 194
  representatives in H. of Commons, 63–4
  resettlement after expulsion of French, 189–90
  Scottish settlers in, 197–9
  slave rebellion, 255–6

Antigua, *(Contd)*.
  slaves, 195–6, 206
  sugar exports, 195
  sugar imported into England from, 490–2
  White Servants Act, 196–7
Art of Making Sugar, 114–15
Asiento, 218, 249, 250, 317
Atkins, Gov., 47, 139, 238, 284, 400

Barbados, 124–47, 399–402, 412
  Acts against inter-island trade, 57
  description, 125–8
  Duty Act, 1663, 48
  early settlement of, 81–4
  epidemics in, 125–6
  exports of, 144
  hurricane, 1731, 428
  land bank, 279–80
  migration from, 132–3
  plantations, 133–40, 145
  population, 131–2
  representatives in H. of Commons, 64
  Royalist v. Roundhead in, 130–1
  slave conspiracies, 127
  slave trade, 505
  slaves, 133, 141–3, 243, 400
  sugar cultivation, 128–9, 140–1, 380, 407
  sugar exports, 34, 428
  sugar imported into England from, 487–9
  sugar prices, 401
  trade with French and Dutch, 55
  in wartime, 1698–1713, 409
  wealth, 144
  windmills, 145–6
Barbados Gazette, 28, 68, 340, 370, 371
Barbuda, 185

523

Sugar and Slavery

Bawden, Sir John, commission agent, 286-7
Beckford family, 9, 61, 228-9
Beckford, William, planter-historian, 9, 59, 61, 105, 227-9, 257-8
Beeston, Gov., 215
Bethell, Slingsby, 59, 193, 303
Board of Trade, 23, 156, 157, 205, 288, 423, 424, 427, 481
Brisket, Gov., 87
Bristol, 324-5, 327, 477
Britain:
  drinking habits in, 27-9, 344-50
  effect of colonies on, 7-10, 15-16, 412, 475
  emigrants to B.W.I. from, 236-7
  population growth, 30-1
  and slave trade, 249, 481-6
  sugar consumption, 21-9, 35
  sugar imports from B.W.I. 22, 417-18, 450
  sugar imports from conquered colonies, 451
  trade with B.W.I. 19-20, 311, 412
  trade with colonies, 15, 37, 40
  See also England
British Empire:
  English imports from, 447-8
British West Indies, 122-3, 412-13
  balance of trade, 466-70
  bullion imports into England from, 506
  debts owed to Britain, 463-4
  defence costs, 472-3
  early settlement, 13, 80
  histories of, 2-5
  legislation against foreign traders, 57-8
  population, 13
  trade with England, 309, 312
  trade with Ireland, 313
  trade with North America, 315
  value of imports and exports, 500-1
  See also West Indies
Brown sugar, 20, 29, 32, 499
Bullion, 506
Burke, Edmund, 6, 9, 15, 35, 36, 355, 467, 481
Byam, William, 191, 201, 303

Campbell, Colonel John, 369
Cane-hole agriculture, 111, 141
Capital *see* Finance
Carib Indians, 80, 85, 87, 456
Carlisle, Earl of, 82, 83, 84, 190
Ceded islands, 123, 453-9, 464
  sugar imported into England from, 492

Child, Sir Josiah, 8, 271
Civil Wars (English), 236
Clarke family in Dutch W.I., 444
Clayed sugar, 52, 117, 432, 498
Codrington family, 63, 193, 377
Codrington, Col. Christopher, 151, 154-5, 193, 408-9
Colonial Credit Act, 1732, 432
Colonies:
  effects on Britain of, 7-9, 15-16
  emigration to, 8, 75-6
  reasons for foundation, 75-6
  trade with, 15, 19-20, 37, 40
Commission system, 282-95, 328-9
Commons, House of, *see* House of Commons
Company of Royal Adventurers, 243, 249, 278
Courteen, Sir William, 81-2
Credit Act, 1732, 288-90, 305, 432
Customs House records, 308-9, 347, 391

Danish W.I. colonies, 444-5
Dawkins family, 61, 224-7
Defoe, Daniel, 26-7, 30-1
Direct Export Act, 1739, 24, 69-70
Doctors in B.W.I., 372-3
Dominica, 65, 455, 457, 461
Douglas, Walter, Gov., 158, 171-2
Dunbar, William, sugar factor, 303
Dutch merchants, 14, 38, 272
  Acts restricting, 39
  and Barbados, 130-1
  clandestine trade, 46
Dutch W.I. colonies, 398, 416, 442-3, 460
Duties:
  evasion of, 48-9
  export, 48-9
  import, 50-3
  preferential, 42-3
  rum, 349
  sugar, 43, 46, 50-3, 67, 398
Dutton, Gov., 139, 400
Duty Act, 1663 (Barbados), 48

Eburne, Richard, 76
Edinburgh, 31
Edmundson, William, Quaker, 365
Edwards, Bryan, planter-historian, 10, 43, 73, 149, 151, 161, 248, 289, 374, 382, 391, 441
England:
  import of tropical commodities, 19-20
  imports from British Empire, 447-8
  social problems, 75-6

524

Index

England, *(Contd)*.
   structure of foreign trade, 413–14
   sugar consumption, 25–9, 427, 493–5
   sugar imports, 404, 410, 487–95
   sugar re-exports, 31–2, 67, 70, 493–5
   value of imports and exports, 500–1
Equiano, Olaudah, 240, 248
Europe:
   economic organization, 97–8
   imports from New World, 19

Factors, sugar, *see* Agents, commission
Finance:
   Barbados land bank, 279–80
   bills of exchange, 284–5
   bullion, 506
   capital, 9–10, 37, 263–6, 270, 295
   capital depreciation, 266–9
   capital flow to Britain, 295–8
   capital, working, 269
   commission system, 282–95, 328–9
   credit, 271–8, 290
   Credit Act, 1732, 288–90, 305, 432
   credit crisis, 1772, 463–6
   debt collection, 274–5
   partnership agreements, 271
   rates of interest, 276–7
   slaves as capital, 104, 264–6
   W.I. loan market, 278–80
Fox, George, Quaker, 11, 188, 250, 365, 480–1
France, wars with, 407–11, 435–6, 449–52, 483
Free Port Act, 1766, 460–1
French W.I. colonies, 416–17, 437, 460
   sugar exports, 101
   See also Ceded islands, Guadeloupe, Havana, Martinique
Frye, Rowland and Samuel, commission agents, 302
Fuller, Rose, 59, 69–70

Gin consumption, 344–5
Godwyn, Rev. Morgan, 243
Gordon, Lord Adam, 203–4, 232
Governors and Governors-General:
   Atkins, 47, 139, 238, 284, 332, 400
   Beeston, 215
   Brisket, 87
   Codrington, 151, 154–5, 193, 408–9
   Douglas, 158, 171–2
   Dutton, 139, 400
   Hamilton, 158
   Hart, 55, 180–1, 184, 344, 425
   Hunter, 220

Governers and Governers-General, *(Contd)*.
   Keith, 462
   Keynell, 88
   Lawes, 218, 272
   Littleton, 86–7
   Lynch, 46, 47, 95, 212, 332
   Mathew, 159, 161, 172, 431
   Modyford, 95, 136, 211, 216, 219
   Osborne, 170
   Parke, 47–8, 155, 274, 336, 411
   Payne, 206
   Seton, 245
   Stapleton, 148, 152, 164, 171, 189–90, 365, 377, 403
   Thomas, 169, 205, 441
   Trelawney, 232, 257
   Vaughan, 211
   Wheler, 162
   Willoughby, 44, 47, 139, 171, 186–7, 190, 399
   Winthrop, 186–8, 365
   Worsley, 353, 373
Grenada, 65, 458–9
Guadeloupe, 449, 450, 453
Guarda costas, 419, 424, 433
Guyana, 76–80

Hamilton, Gov., 158
Hart, Gov., 55, 180–1, 184, 344, 425–6
Havana, 449–50
Helyar, Cary, 212–14
Herbert, John R., 169
Hilton, Anthony, 86
House of Commons, 58–69
   absentee planters in, 59–66
   members from:
      Antigua, 63–4
      Barbados, 64
      Jamaica, 61–2
      Montserrat, 65
      Nevis, 64–5
      St Kitts, 62–3
Hughes, Rev. Griffith, 126, 144
Hunter, Gov., 220
Hurricanes, 85, 153, 400, 426, 428, 439

Immigrants from Britain, 236–7, 368–70, 380–1, 394
Industrial Revolution, 7, 16, 35, 476–9
Ireland:
   demand for rum, 350–1
   re-export from England of sugar to, 31–2, 67, 70
   trade with foreign sugar colonies, 67–8
   trade with B.W.I., 313

525

Sugar and Slavery

Jamaica, 208–33, 403–4, 429
  Acts against inter-island trade, 58
  bullion imported into England, 506
  captured from Spain, 92
  commission agents, 298–300
  creditors in, 294
  Dawkins estates, 225–7
  debts to Britain, 464
  description, 208–10
  early colonial history, 210–11
  early English settlement, 92–5
  exports, 217, 403
  free port regulations, 462
  French attack, 1694, 214
  income and profits, 383
  Liguanea Parish Census, 1753, 222–3
  plantations, 212, 215–16, 223
  planters, 218–21
  population, 211, 216–17
  representatives in H. of Commons, 61–2
  slave rebellion, 221
  slave trade, 462, 502–4
  slaves, 218, 220–1
  sugar exports, 34, 217, 403
  sugar imported into England from, 487–9
  sugar industry, 210–12, 217
  in wartime, 1689–98, 408–9
  wealth, 229–32
Jamaica Coffee House, 65–6, 283
Jamaica Public Record Office, Inventories, 215, 228, 296, 375
Jeaffreson, Christopher, 152–4, 237, 269, 377
Jenkins' Ear, War of, 1739, 433
Jews, 366–7
John Baker's *Diary*, 474

Keith, Gov., 462
Kerby, Thomas, sugar factor, 302
Keynell, Gov., 88
King William's War, 161, 345, 405, 407–9

Labour, white, 235–8
Lascelles family, 64
Lascelles, Henry, 59, 291, 292, 296–9
Lascelles & Maxwell, London commission agents, 67, 290, 291–2, 293, 311–30, 435–7
Lawes, Gov., 218, 272
Lawyers in B.W.I., 371–?
Leeward Islands, 148–207, 402–3
  population, 150
  sugar exports, 410–11
  sugar imported into England from, 487–92

Leeward Islands, *(Contd)*.
  in wartime, 1689–98, 408
  wealth, 403
  See also Antigua, Montserrat, Nevis, St Kitts
Ligon, Richard, 84, 129, 130, 134–6, 235, 241–2, 255
Liguanea Parish Census, 1753, 222–3
Littleton, Edward, planter, 52, 140, 401
Littleton, Thomas, Gov., 86–7
Liverpool, 27, 30–1, 33, 325, 327, 477
Livestock, 105–7
London:
  commission agents, 292–3, 329–31
  commission system, 328–31, 336–8
  merchants, 328
  sugar imports, 32
  sugar prices, 405, 407, 417, 427–8, 437, 439, 496–9
Long, Edward, planter-historian, 24, 26, 220, 230, 233, 265, 266, 273, 276, 277, 290, 295, 370, 380, 382, 473
Lucy family, 287
Lynch, Sir Thomas, Gov., 46, 47, 95, 212, 332

MacPherson, David, 466
Malthus, Thomas, 35, 253
Maroons, 221, 254–5
Martin, Col. Samuel, 33, 200–3, 340, 360–1, 378–80, 455–6, 485
Martinique, 449, 453
Massie, Joseph, 30, 73, 298–9, 349
Mathew, Gov., 159, 161, 172, 431
Meade, Thomas, planter, 177–8
Mercantile system, *see* Navigation system
Merchants, 319–21, 374–7
  outport, 336–7
Mill, John Stuart, 392–3
Mills:
  method of working, 114
  on Montserrat, 176
  windmills (Barbados), 144–6
Modyford family, 211–12, 396
Modyford, Sir Thomas, Gov., 95, 136, 211, 216, 219
Molasses, 26, 338–59
  export of, 342–3
  prices, 55
  production, 339
  uses, 340–2
Molasses Act, 1733, 31–2, 68, 74, 350, 354–5
Monoculture, 120–21, 439–42
  in Barbados, 140
  in St Kitts, 160
  See also Plantations

Index

Montagu, John Montagu, 2nd Duke of, 423–4
Montserrat, 170–83
  Census, 1729, 172–6, 183
  description, 170
  early colonial history, 171–2
  early settlement, 87
  exports, 174–75
  French invasions of, 171–2
  plantations, 172–6, 181
  planters, 177–82
  population, 171–2, 174
  representatives in H. of Commons, 65
  slaves, 174, 182–3
  sugar imported into England from, 490–2
Moravians, 482
Morse, John, commission agent, 300
Muscovado sugar:
  duty on, 67
  manufacture of, 117
  prices of, 73, 397, 425, 427–8, 432, 437–8, 451, 496–7

Navigation Acts, 10, 15, 41–53, 262, 396–8
  evasion of, 45–8
  and planters, 44–7
Navigation system, 5–11, 40–1, 262–3
Negroes *see* Slaves
Nelson, Horatio, Viscount Nelson, 169–70
Neutral islands (St Lucia, St Vincent, Dominica, Tobago), 423–4, 449
Nevis, 161–70, 403
  description, 161
  early settlement, 86–7, 161
  exports, 164
  merchants of, 162–3
  population, 162, 163–4
  representatives in H. of Commons, 64–5
  slaves, 165–6
  sugar cultivation on, 162
  sugar imported into England from, 490–2
Noell, Sir Martin, 87, 89–91, 93–4
North, Captain Roger, 78–9
North American colonies:
  illicit rum trade with, 354–6
  trade disagreements with, 67–8
  trade with B.W.I., 33, 46, 50, 56, 71, 106–7, 313–15, 322–4
  trade with foreign sugar colonies, 56

Oldmixon, John, 109, 115, 117–18, 140, 146, 162–3, 409–10

Oliver family, 304–5
Osborne, Gov., 170
Outports, 32–3, 311, 322, 324–6, 336–7

Parke, Daniel, Gov., 47–8, 155, 274, 366, 411
Payne, Gov., 206
Pennant family, 479
Pinney family, 167–8
Piracy, 419–20, 424
Plantations:
  annual expenses, 269
  capital depreciation, 266–9
  capital requirements, 264–6
  development of, 119–22
  on Jamaica, 215–16
  on Montserrat, 173–5, 181
  profits, 269, 381–4, 421
  See also Monoculture
Planters, 360–70, 375–7
  absentee, 13, 59–66, 357, 362, 385–7, 470–4
  in H. of Commons, 59–66
  of Antigua, 190–4
  of Barbados, 137–9
  and commission agents, 284
  on island legislatures, 57, 274
  of Jamaica, 218–21
  loans between, 294–5
  as merchants, 322
  of Montserrat, 177–82
  and Navigation Acts, 44–7
  and recession, 1730s, 429–32
  of St Kitts, 160
  and sugar duties, 52–3
  treatment of slaves, 243–5
Plantership, 360–2, 378–81
Pollington, Alexander, 190–1
Povey, Thomas, 91–2, 93–4
Privateering, 77–8, 317, 435–6

Quakers, 364–6, 480–1, 484
Queen Anne's War (War of the Spanish Succession), 29, 55, 161, 171–2, 215, 405, 409–11

Raleigh, Sir Walter, 78
Ramsay, Rev. James, 159–60
Refined sugar, 43
Refiners, sugar, 51, 440–1
  buying combinations, 56, 67
  petitions against planters, 72–3, 440
Refining industry, 29–30
Roaring River Plantation, 257–9
Robertson, Rev. Robert, planter, 242–3, 265–6, 429

527

Sugar and Slavery

Royal African Company, 152, 195–6, 243, 249, 273, 278, 285, 317, 327, 344, 391, 400–1
Royal Navy, 436
Royalists, 362–3, 376
Royden, Sir Marmaduke, 82–4
Rum, 339–59
    consumption in Britain, 346–8
    consumption in W.I., 342–3
    export, 68, 343–4
    illicit trade, 354–5
    imports into England and Wales, 347–8
    imports into Ireland, 351
    manufacture, 339–40
    prices, 55, 343, 348–9

St Kitts (St Christopher), 149–60, 402–3
    commission agents, 301
    debts to Britain, 464
    description, 149–51
    early settlement, 79, 84–6, 151–2
    exports, 159
    manuring, 159–60
    population, 159
    representative in H. of Commons, 62–3
    resettlement after defeat of French, 154–8
    slaves, 160
    sugar cultivation, 149–51
    sugar imported into England from, 490–2
    wealth, 160
St Lucia, 423–4, 449
St Vincent, 423, 449, 455–6, 458
Schaw, Janet, 203–4
Scotland, 70, 465
Scots in B.W.I., 368–70
    in Antigua, 197–200
    as doctors, 372–3
Scott, John, 128–9, 132, 272
Sephardic Jews, 46–7, 366–8
Seton, Governor, 245
Seven Years' War, 250, 449–52, 483
Sheffield, Lord, 9, 25, 253
Ships and shipping, 323–4
    attacks by Spanish on, 419, 426
    captured by British, 451–2
    cargoes, 324, 332–3
    losses in wartime, 1689–1713, 407–10
    restrictions on, 43
    statistics, 334
Slave trade, 249–54, 292–4, 316, 502–5

Slavery:
    attacks on, 11, 480–6
    history in B.W.I., 241–9
    profitability of, 259–61
Slaves:
    on Antigua, 195–6, 206
    on Barbados, 133, 141–3, 243, 400
    breeding of, 243–4
    cultivation of own crops, 259–60
    diseases and medical treatment of, 242, 268
    imports and exports of, 218, 243, 246–8, 316, 502–5
    Indian, 235
    on Jamaica, 218, 220–1
    on Montserrat, 174, 182–3
    mortality rate, 242, 244–5
    on Nevis, 165–6
    numbers of, 246–8
    prices of, 251–3, 400–1, 425
    profit from, 382–3
    rebellions, 221, 255–6
    runaway, 254–5
    on St Kitts, 160
    'Scramble' sales of, 248–9
    skills of, 257–9
Smith, Adam, 5–6, 9–11, 18, 36–7, 238, 463, 467
Smuggling, 45, 435
Soil exhaustion, 106, 111–12
South Sea Company, 217–18, 250, 317, 318, 424, 427
Spain:
    attacks on British shipping, 419, 426
    ships captured by British, 435
    wars with, 419, 433
Spanish W.I. colonies, 393
Spice trade, 19
Staple Act, 1663, 42, 49
Stapleton family, 64–5, 164–7, 168
Stapleton, Gov., 148, 152, 164, 171, 189–90, 365, 377, 403
Stout, William, merchant, 326–7, 345
Sugar:
    Brazilian, 397
    consumption in Britain, 24–5, 33
    consumption in England, 21–4, 26–9, 493–5
    consumption in Ireland, 31–2
    consumption in Scotland, 31
    direct export to foreign countries, 68–71
    exports from B.W.I., 420
    exports from W.I., 100–1
    imports into England, 404, 410, 418, 427, 439, 450, 487–95

Index

Sugar, *(Contd)*.
    introduction to W.I., 12, 99
    manufacture, 112–18
    natural conditions needed for, 102–3
    prices, 29, 55, 72–3, 390–3, 397, 404–7, 417, 425, 427–8, 437, 496–9
    production in W.I., 416–17
    re-export from Britain, 22–3, 32, 427
    re-export from England, 31–2, 67, 70, 493–5
    and tea drinking, 27–9
    trade, 308–38
    trade monopoly, 71–4
    See also Clayed sugar; Brown sugar; Finance; Monoculture; Refined sugar; Muscovado sugar
Sugar Act, 1764, 355
Sugar-cane:
    cultivation, 107–14
    introduction to W.I., 99
    manufacture of sugar from, 112–18
    origins, 98–9
Sugar Duty Act, 1685, 52
Supercargoes, 320–1

Tariff, 1661, 41, 43, 405
Tea drinking, 27–9
Tea, price of, 28–9
Thomas, Sir Dalby, 19, 26, 46, 138, 264, 268, 273, 280
Thomas, Gov., 169, 205, 441
Thompson, Maurice, 88–90, 93
Tobacco, 394–5
Tobago, 65, 456–7
Trade, 306–38
    clandestine, 317–18, 424
    free port system, 459–62
    inter-island, 55, 57

Trade, *(Contd)*.
    merchant system, 322–8
    methods of, 319–22
    statistics, 309–13
    See also London: Slave trade
Trade winds, 12, 104
Treaty of Breda, 151, 191
Treaty of Paris, 123
Treaty of Utrecht, 155, 218
Trelawney, Gov., 232, 257
Tryon, Thomas, 20–1, 25, 26, 43, 287–8, 404–5
Tuite, Nicholas, 445
Tullideph, Dr Walter, 24, 71, 197–200, 256, 268, 274–5, 277, 290–1, 347, 385, 438–9

Vaughan, Gov., 211

Warner, Thomas, 79, 82, 99, 152
War of Jenkins' Ear, 433
War of the Spanish Succession *see* Queen Anne's War
Webb family, 178–9
West Indies:
    climate, 109
    commodity prices, 468
    economy of, 11–14
    introduction of sugar into, 12, 13
    sugar exports, 100–1, 412–13
    sugar production in, 416–17
    suitability for sugar growing, 102–11
    See also British West Indies
Wheler, Gov., 162
White bonded labour, 236–8
White Servants' Act (Antigua), 196–7
Willoughby, Gov., 44, 47, 139, 171, 186–7, 190, 399
Winthrop, Samuel, Gov., 186–8, 365
Wood, William, 220, 250, 318, 434
Worsley, Henry, Gov., 353, 373

www.ingramcontent.com/pod-product-compliance
Lightning Source LLC
Chambersburg PA
CBHW031700230426
43668CB00006B/55